MY WORLD
MY QUEST

La Búsqueda Final

Delvis Alejandro Fernández Levy

DEDICATION

To My Loving Cousin and Most Valuable Teacher
Para Mi Querida Prima y Más Valiosa Maestra

Guiselda de la Concepción Patriótica Nacional Fernández

ACKNOWLEDGEMENTS

This book is a labor of love thanks to those who nurtured my days with guidance and education that provide images and understanding of our past, present and future journeys on Earth. From ancestors to family members, friends, and acquaintances, I am forever thankful for their inspiration to continue and expand the struggle for a future of peace and justice for all of humanity.

The first person that comes to mind is my mother Sara Levy Rodríguez, a woman who filled me with histories and anecdotes about the *Gran Familia* from her early days in Cuba to the twilight of her life. *Gracias Mami Sara, tu legado vivirá en nuestras almas y corazones como fuente de inspiración para nuestras vidas y futuras generaciones.* Thank you *Mami* Sara, your legacy will live in our hearts and souls as a fountain of inspiration for our lives and future generations.

Norine (Gunn Dix) Fernández, my wife and friendly companion for over sixty years has been a major contributor, not only as the primary editor but as a coauthor of multiple chapter and sections in this book.

I am eternally thankful for the contributions and inspiration given by family and friends in various parts of the world, beginning with my early days in Cuba.

- The *Familia* in Santa Clara led by *Tía* Chicha, Évora Pérez, during difficult times for my parents and sisters, encircled me with love and attention, always taking care of all my daily needs.
- *Maestra* Guiselda Fernández, to whom I dedicate this book, was my guide to overcome barriers and turmoil during times of war and rebellion.
- *Reverendo* Sergio Arce Martínez, a presbyterian minister showed me another side of religion with a God, not seen as a distant iconic figure on a pedestal, but as a person always present among us, giving encouragements to humans struggling for justice, peace, and compassion.
- The *familia* on my mother's side led my *Mamá-Vieja* Felicia Rodríguez Marzall and *Papá-Viejo* Salvador Levy Levy, the most influential family member in my upbringings. His examples as a father and family caretaker remain present in my heart and soul as guiding principles.

I am forever thankful to every family member for their loving care and attention. They filled my life with values that will be passed on to future generations.

Among the many people who had a profound impact on my life, gratitude and acknowledgement goes to: Dr. Myra Yancey - professor and advisor at Westminster College in Salt Lake City, Utah. A person that guided me on my quest for a college degree and served as a new family member.

As a teacher at the first bilingual college in the U.S., I learned and gained deep appreciation from my students at the Elbert Covell College on politics, culture, and life in their home countries.

Students and maintenance workers at Chabot College during the 1960s exposed me to another side of life in America by inviting me to serve as advisor to the first Chicano Student Union at the college. Forever grateful to Professor Rick Moniz who organized educational trips under Faces of Cuba.

In great part my inspiration for writing is due to two dear friends, from separate parts of the world: Dr. Alberto N. Jones for his book *"Mi Vida, mi verdad"* and Professor Joel Hancock who wrote a memoir about his life title "My Blue-Colored World." Also, Rosemarie Skaine through her book "The Cuban Family" - Custom and Change in an Era of Hardship provided me with encouragement and expansion on learning about my own life. *Merci Beaucoup* to Dr. Salim Lamrani who holds a PhD in Iberian and Latin American Studies from Sorbonne-Paris IV University, an excellent academic researcher on issues dealing with the turbulent relations between Cuba and The United States.

My deep appreciation to the Information Technology staffs at California Polytechnic University in San Luis Obispo as well as to the Music Department for help in my last quest - expanding and sharing musical enjoyment.

Forever thankful for their great support to all the people involved with CAAEF - the Cuban American Alliance Education Fund - and other organizations in bringing an end to the blockade of Cuba. Thanks, are also due to ACLIFIM - The Cuban Association for the Physically Impaired – under Ida Hilda Escalona del Toro and Luciana Valle Valdés for their assistance in creating La Familia – our humanitarian assistance group organized by Norine Fernández.

Near the top of the list is the discovery of a human legacy of patriot José Martí through family in the U.S, lined to Eduardo Romero and his daughters Victoria María Romero and Marti Margaret Romero. My deep appreciation to Dr. Armando Hart Dávalos, Professor Jorge Lozano Ros, Dr. Eusebio Leal Spengler, and Roberto Fernández Retamar for their invitations to events in Cuba marking the struggles and achievements of the revered hero of Cuba's Independence.

Table of Contents

Table of Contents

INTRODUCTION
Introducción

Sixty plus years ago, in 1957, I came to the United States, as a penniless seventeen-year-old ready to enter college in Salt Lake City, Utah, while the turmoil in my Cuban homeland offered no opportunity to further my studies. I suffered tremendous cultural shock – arriving in a strange land, without knowledge of English and with marked cultural differences from the vibrant lifestyle, the pulsating rhythms and the vivid, verdant, scenes of my Cuba.

Strived with school assignments as hard as I could, worked on various menial jobs to pay for tuition and earn a Bachelor of Arts college degree with honors and a major in mathematics. By the late 1960s, I was a married man with two sons, embarking on a teaching career in the San Francisco Bay Area of California. Due to my Hispanic last name, I was approached by students of Latino and Mexican backgrounds to help in organizing an association to promote and expand educational opportunities -- I happened to be the only Latino instructor at the time. Through this involvement I had one of the most rewarding learning experiences of my life that enriched my culture with a history and a centuries-old legacy, mostly ignored by historians and educators in American schools. These experiences in combination with my passion for mathematics – as a subject that is at the root of sciences and serves as a language for understanding our universe and human behavior – have served as guide and compass through my life journey, which involved years of teaching, family life, self-improvement through exercise and musical pursuits, and finally devoting my total being to the advocacy of my passion – improving relations between my two Lands: The Republic of Cuba and the United States of America.

From the Canadian Indigenous Leader, Georges Erasmus
"Where common memory is lacking, where people do not share in the same past, there can be no real community. Where community is to be formed, common memory must be created."
This quote recalls divisions existing within our families due to migration and absence of person-to-person contact, resulting in a <u>lack of common memory</u>.

There are at least three distinct periods of my life (1) *LA PRIMERA FAMILIA* **in Cuba; (2) THE NEW FAMILY in the United States**, and (3) **The DREAM FAMILY** that connects distant poles, thus resulting in a legacy of love, peace, and serenity for our future generations.

In this book I reveal testimonials regarding issues of race and ethnic segregation that impacted my *Gran Familia*. There are also revelations about our personal origins through research of facts and anecdotal stories of family, friends, and acquaintances.

The first chapter, "My Human Roots – *Mis Raíces*," provides a general perspective through DNA tests and research about my origins and human roots. Research that also serves to expand on the origins of family, friends, and Cubans in general. The second chapter, "My Dear Family – *Mi Querida Familia*," offers an expansion of my origins that includes details about the ethnic, cultural, and religious backgrounds of my immediate blood related family members, parents, grandparents and their ancestors. Chapter 3, "Santa Clara – *Mi Hogar*- My Family Home (1940-1957)" describes the family home surroundings with descriptions of my parents and the extended family that lived near me and served as caretakers and guides during childhood. Chapter 4, "My Hometown – *Mi Ciudad Natal*," explains the composition of neighborhoods, schools, health, centers, and social clubs. It expands into my experiences as a grade school student and touches on issues of racial and class segregation common in my cultural and social surroundings. Chapter 5, "My Teen Years – *Pupy el Adolescente*," expands on days of trauma, rebellion, and personal growth as a student. It also provides details about disruptions in times of despair incremented by a brutal dictatorship in government. On a personal note, those challenging times in my life offered opportunities to expand my religious awareness and obtain mentoring and guidance for expanding education and hope for surviving the chaos around me. Chapter 6, "Homes of Delight from Childhood," provides descriptions of places of immersion away from Santa Clara with many happy days surrounded by the verdant Cuban nature and loving family. These places of "Delight" also brought awareness of the injustices in society and the human exploitation of native Cubans and others from the nearby Caribbean islands by American foreign companies. Chapter 7, "Life's Hard Choice – Leaving Cuba," ends the first part of my journey with details about my last days in the adored homeland of Cuba, along with the saddest moment in my life travelling all my myself to an unknown faraway place.

Those who cannot remember the past are condemned to repeat it.
George Santayana
Spanish American Philosopher
Life of Reason, Reason in Common Sense, 1906

PART I

My First Life in Cuba

Human Roots and life from birth through times of delight and despair.

1

MY HUMAN ROOTS
Mis Raíces

"Who am I?" is a question searching for answers in our minds and souls. Although a simple answer is not possible, facts abound through stories shared by family and friends that provide images of our past, present, and future journeys in this world.

Our school history lessons are often warped with words implying that our land and national identity originated with the "Columbus discovery" of a continent we now refer to as America. Upon his first arrival in Cuba, in October 1492, he said, "This is the most beautiful land that human eyes have ever seen." Shortly after his arrival, Cuba became a major transit center from Europe to the "New World" for planning dominance of indigenous people and their civilizations.

- Hernán Cortés starting in Trinidad, Cuba, sailed towards Yucatán, Mexico in search of gold and conquest of the Aztec Empire.

- Francisco Pizarro crossed the Panama isthmus and sailed along the Pacific coast towards Peru for dominance of the Inca Empire.

- Ponce de León went in search of an imaginary fountain of youth, landing in Florida in 1513, ending with the decimation of its native Calusa population. (Professor Jerald Milanich, Indian-Country-Today Archives, April 2, 2017).

- Iconic religious figures like Junípero Serra, travelled through Cuba to Mexico and on to California to build Spanish missions and "civilize" native populations while dismissing their family values and cultures.

- The main indigenous people of Cuba at the time of Columbus' arrival were Guanahacabibes, Tainos and Ciboneys; all forming part of a cultural group referred to as Arawak. Although their tribes were decimated, many were assimilated into the new Spanish settlements. A legacy of their language, food, and shelters impacted and established solid roots to the emergent Cuban nation and its culture.

Entering into the population mixture, or as we say the *ajiaco* that makes a *Cubano*, like me, I will venture into the ethnic roots of my neighbors and friends. Although the descendants of native populations were not mentioned, there is ample evidence through facial characteristics and DNA tests that they formed a major part of the Cuban nation. The most noticeable components of the population today are Spanish and Africans. However, many other ethnic groups are vital elements of the Cuban people. Among these I will include persons from my family, friends, and acquaintances.

- There was a wide diversity of people from the Iberian Peninsula, but the most noticeable members in my family-surroundings, were people from the Canary Islands, referred to as **Canarios** or **Isleños**. Folks from many regions of Spain formed part or were close to my family. In particular, I recall uncles and aunts, along with close friends, who had direct ancestors, or had migrated to Cuba from **Galicia, Asturias, Castilla, Catalonia, Viscaya**, and less noticeable people from **Portugal** and **Andalusia** called **Gitanos** or Gypsies. The word **Gallego** or **Gallega** was a commonly misapplied label to any Spaniard living in Cuba. Besides my surnames of "Fernández and Levy," here are other names directly connected to family and close friends: (1) Grandfather **Plácido Moreira** of **Sephardic** origins from **Portugal**; (2) **Tomás Pérez** mistaken for my other grandfather, and the **Casola** farmer family from the **Canary Islands**; (3) Uncle **Patricio Martín de la Parra y de la Fuente Redonda** from Ávila in **Old Castile**; (4) Father of my godfather, **Tomás Orosa**, aunt **Victoria Marcos** and another dear uncle **Pedro Gómez** from Galicia; (5) Friend from the farm **Antonio Cobián** whose family came from Asturias; (6) Great grandmothers **Idelfonsa Marzall** via **Catalonia** - and (7) **Evangelina Izquierdo** via Mindanao in the Phillipines but with roots in the **Basque area** of France and Spain.

- **Jews** were identified as **Turcos** or **Polacos**. The word **Judío** -for Jew - was avoided, since there were still remnants of the Inquisition that gave negative connotations, so instead the word **Hebreo**, meaning Hebrew, was preferred in my provincial surroundings. Persons of Sephardic ancestry, going back to Spain and Portugal, were labeled **Turcos** (from Turkey), or **Moros** – term used to identify those expelled from Spain to northern Africa. The Ashkenazi Jews from other parts of Europe – Germany, Poland, Russia, the Baltic Countries, etc. – were all mislabeled as **Polacos** (from Poland). Among family and friends, I remember my dear aunt *Tía* Raquel Levy, along with cousins, uncles and aunts who lived in the coastal town of Caibarién. *Tía* Raquel revealed to me family stories and Sephardic religious practices during the Passover holiday along with tales of social gatherings, sitting on pillows on the floor singing in the Ladino language. Among other Jewish friends I must include members of my close neighbors, the Behar family that ran a shoe store and exposed me to traditions with a Torah reading in a room singled out for religious rituals in their private home. As far as I knew, there was not temple or synagogue in my town, and Jewish religious practices were kept in family homes or private gatherings. The Behars also let me know about family members who had migrated by way of Cuba to Mexico. Their youngest family member was a boy close to me in age with whom I often played and talked about our education plans - I recall giving him a math book no longer needed since he was a year behind me in secondary school.

- *Árabes* – Mainly people of Lebanese and Syrians ancestry were among some of my close friends and family members. Only a block from home I walked by a social club displaying their national flags. My next-door neighbors, *La Familia Sesín*, led by a loving lady named María of Lebanese origin often took care of me and my sister Sarita. Other people with middle eastern backgrounds were my dear uncle Victor Noemí whose real name was Roque Antonio Noemí Sainz, son of Victoria Sainz Restan, who migrated from Lebanon. The most admired piano teacher of my mother and sister Sarita was Rita Chapú also with the same Lebanese ancestry. A best friend from childhood was Agustín Menéndez Azel, whose mother also had direct Syrian roots.

- **East Asians**, mostly from the Canton Province and Taiwan were present in Cuba since the late 1850s. Some were subject to indentured servitude after the end of slavery, but others managed to settle in Cuba by way of California. I had wonderful daily visits with sweet treats at two grocery stores run by Chinese friends, Julio and Fernando. On my way to primary school, I walked daily by two clubs with opposite political views regarding the leaders Mao Zedong and Chiang Kai-shek. The last young friend I remember from secondary school came directly from China to work at an ice-cream store run by his family near my home.

- *Americanos*, as people from the U.S. were called, were present in the running of sugar mills and nickel mining industry. During my toddler days, my *Papi*, as a road builder in the Oriente Province of Cuba made me stay at the family home of an *Americano* nicknamed *Mister Don* -- the first person I remember from my childhood. There was also a noticeable involvement of people from the U.S. in the expansion of Protestant religions – such as Baptist, Methodist, Presbyterian, Pentecostal and others like Jehovah's Witness and Seventh Day Adventist.

- An **Irish component** was present in Cuba since the 1700s. Within my circle of friends, I dearly remember the O'Farrill family that lived and ran a pharmacy near my home. They had provided medicine and mentoring to my father as a nurse trainee and deliverer of medical supplies. A favorite composer, Ignacio Cervantes Kawanagh, also had Irish ancestry. Another memorable acquaintance during my youth was Aleida March, who became the wife of Ernesto Guevara Lynch -known as *El Che*. Both March and Lynch are names of Scottish and Irish origins.

- There is also a **Swedish** and a **Danish** component in the Cuban population, not necessarily as part of my direct ancestry but certainly close to other family members. The first person that comes to mind is Gustavo Nystrom, a Cuban living in California and with direct roots from Sweden. As a child I visited the town of his family in Eastern Cuba and became aware of the major role they played in expanding cheese and milk production in Camagüey Province. A second person that comes to mind is Eva Magdalena Hiort-Lorenzen, the mother of my brother-in-law – Arturo López-Calleja Hiort-Lorenzen. I had the fortune of meeting her and learn about her Danish father and family of Scandinavian background.

- The town of Cienfuegos, near my hometown of Santa Clara was settled by **French** immigrants, in 1819. Its first settlers came from **Bordeaux** and **Louisiana**. Other people of French and Creole origin settled in eastern Cuba, from nearby **Haiti**.

- I was aware of **Japanese** in Cuba who had been interned in a concentration camp during World War II. It was a sad revelation when I travelled to Cuba with Shizu Izayama to bring assistance to children from Ukraine – children being treated in Cuba after the nuclear accident in Chernobyl. Her husband's relatives were victims of the atomic bombing of Hiroshima. People of Japanese descendancy were present in Cuba since the early 1900s but in 1941 the ruler Fulgencio Batista declared them as "enemy aliens" and thus were imprisoned on the Isle of Pines (now referred as *Isla de la Juventud*). After the war, they were deported from Cuba to the United States.

- It is also worth mentioning people in my midst connected to other areas of the **Caribbean** and **Latin America**: Mexico, Puerto Rico, Haiti, Jamaica, and the Dominican Republic. Two people from Puerto Rico who had a tremendous impact on my life: (1) Doris Valentin, the wife of my mentor and role model Rev. Sergio Arce and (2) a young missionary also from Puerto Rico whose name I do not recall, but who provided assistance to continue my education by helping me to choose a place and filling my application forms for college entrance. Unfortunately, I do not remember the names, but etched in my mind are memories of families in extremely poor living conditions around the *barracones*, sheltered in huts on the cliff of a river near the Nipe Bay of Eastern Cuba; a place that I visited with my oldest cousin Elia Martínez Fernández during summer vacations by the Nipe Bay in Holguín Province of Eastern Cuba.

- **Africa** has infused a legacy in Cuba that goes beyond description. Musical diversity, religious rituals, cuisine, language intonation, family values, and culture in general are the treasures from Africa that form our souls and give foundation to the meaning of being a **Cubano** or **Cubana.** My Santa Clara town adhered to segregation rules in social clubs, medical centers, and places to stroll in its main Central Park – *El Parque Vidal*. Also, the two main catholic private schools only accepted white children, *Las Teresianas* for girls, and *Los Maristas*, for boys. Lucky for me, although there were no black or mulatto children in my neighborhood, my grandmother, *Mamá Ramona* would occasionally take me to meet and play with her godchildren of African ancestry in the *El Condado* neighborhood on the outskirts of town. Several people with strong Afro Cuban roots had tremendous impact on my life: (1)My medical doctor Celestino Hernández saved me as a toddler when I was suffering from severe constipation; (2) *Mi querida* Nicolasa, a proud black woman lived with us as a dear family member, and often took me on walks to meet friends and her brother who was a *Babalao*, a high priest of Yoruba religious traditions; (3) *El Profesor* Alomá, was a highly accomplished black educator who founded and ran the *Colegio Academia Alomá*, the only private school that I attended as a sixth grade student. It was free of charge as a result of a deal worked out by my father, making it possible to bypass junior high and pass the required entrance exam to begin High School during the most turbulent times of my life when I was only 12-years old. *El Instituto de Segunda Enseñanza* was a 5-year public secondary school with a rigid curriculum providing education above a high school equivalence.

Historic Figures Present in My Life

El Cacique **Hatuey** – the Taíno Indigenous Chief – was the first freedom fighter in the Americas, burnt on a cross by Spanish invaders in 1512, came from the Island of Quisqueya - present day Hispaniola, consisting of the Dominican Republic and Haiti. He fought against the Spanish conquistadors in Cuba and Quisqueya. The Spanish landowner priest, Bartolomé de Las Casas quotes that Hatuey showed the Taínos a basket of gold and jewelry, saying: "This is the God the Spaniards worship. This is why they fight and kill; that's why they're after us, and that's why we have to throw them into the sea. They tell us that they worship a god of peace and equality, but they usurp our lands and make us their slaves..."

Mariana Grajales Cuello, was born in Santiago de Cuba and died in Kingston, Jamaica. Her parents came from Quisqueya (Dominican Republic). She was an exemplary mother who gave utmost encouragement to all her children along with the iconic heroic patriot – **Antonio Maceo y Grajales**. Her legacy as a fighter for an independent Cuba free from slavery will live forever.

Carmen Miyares born of Cuban and Puerto Rican parents, a descendant from a Corsican family, was raised in Caracas, Venezuela until the age of 12. She was also a fighter behind the scenes who gave valuable assistance to the revered patriot **José Martí Pérez** in his quest for Cuba's Independence.

Henry Reeve, a U.S. citizen from Brooklyn, New York who died in Matanzas, Cuba. A fighter in The First Cuban War of Independence during the 1860s.

Louis Moreau Gottschalk, born in New Orleans from an English Jewish father and a Creole woman of French and African ancestry, lived in Cuba for extended periods of time. As a pianist composer he helped to expand Puerto Rican and Cuban music to a classical genre around the world.

Julián Fontana, pianist composer, born in Poland of Italian parents, a dear trusted friend of Frederick Chopin who introduced his music to Cuba. Married Camila Dalcour from Matanzas, Cuba. Mentored Nicolás Ruiz Espadero, who played a major role in the expansion of Cuban Classics as a teacher of the admirable pianist and composer **Ignacio Cervantes Kawanagh.**

Origins of Surnames

Fernández

"Son of Fernando" is a pre-5th century German and later of Spanish origin. It derives from Visigoth tribal personal name, composed of the elements "frith," meaning peace and "ninth," meaning daring or brave. The Portuguese version of this surname is Fernandes. The Arabized version is *Ibn Faranda* and it was used by the Mozarabs and Muwallads in Al-Andalus.

Moreira

Was originally a Jewish name. Some of the Jews that were expelled from Spain during the inquisition came to Portugal and adopted names of living things. Moreira, a common surname in Galicia and Portugal, means "mulberry tree." The surname Moreira came to Cuba with immigrants via Brazil, Galicia, and Portugal.

Levy

Also written as "Levi, Levis or Lewis" is a Jewish surname, from Hebrew – transliterated as "לוי"—meaning "joining." According to Jewish tradition, people with the Levi surname are Levites and can claim patrilineal descendance from the Levites of biblical times. A name for my family in Cuba via Turkey, Greece, or France.

Rodríguez

Common name in Spain and Latin America. Rodrigo is the Spanish form of Roderick, meaning "famous power," from the Germanic elements "hrod" (fame) and "ric" (power). It was the name of Roderick, the last Visigoth King before the Muslim conquest. It was known among people of Sephardic ancestry.

Marzall

Surname originating in Catalonia, Spain, the birthplace of my Great grandfather. The origin of the name is not clear, although "Marzal" may be translated as "Marsh" in English. On my grandmother's tomb the name is spelled as Marshall.

Izquierdo

The surname Izquierdo is of nickname origin, being derived from a physical characteristic of the initial bearer. The word "izquierdo" is ultimately of Basque/Celtic origin deriving from a combination of the Basque word "escu" meaning "hand" and the Celtic "kerros" meaning "left." It may be an identification to someone who was left-handed. In family anecdotes, it came with a family immigrant from Mindanao in the Philippine Islands.

García

Most common surname in Spain, probably derived from a Basque adjective "gaztea" or "gaztia" meaning young in English. Most likely, arrived with immigrants from Spain.

Pérez

Two distinct origins: One is a Spanish surname meaning "son of Pedro, or Peter." The other is a Hebrew surname Peretz, derived from Perez (son of Judah) Hebrew cf. Genesis 38:29), meaning to "breach or burst forth." Common name throughout Latin America

Native Surnames

In 1942 Columbus met natives of Cuba and fantasized about arriving in Asia. Within a century, the Arawak indigenous people -- Taino, Guanahatabeyes, and Siboneyes -- came to near extinction due to slavery and disease. Although native surnames do not appear in birth certificates, evidence remains of their blood ancestry among present day Cubans. Words and nicknames of native origin are forever part of the Cuban vocabulary in the names of places and towns.

Surnames from Africa

Between 1650 and 1860 over 10 million enslaved Africans were transported to the Americas – some estimates are as high as 100 million. Although African surnames are not known among Cubans, our vocabulary has been enriched with words of African origin.

DNA Ethnicity Estimates

As a final passage to this chapter, I offer the estimates of my ethnic roots that also reflect on the origins of my *familia* and many *coterráneos* - people from my birthland. The results are listed below in geographical order from Europe, Asia, Africa, and the Americas.

Iberian Peninsula

Spain → 37% to 39%
Portugal → 24 to 45%
Basque region → 0 to 11%

Mediterranean Area

Italy → 0 to 9%; Malta → 0 to 2%; Sardinia → 0 to 3%
Greece & The Balkans (Albania, Greece, Kosovo, Montenegro, North Macedonia) → 0 to 5%

Middle East

Cyprus, Egypt, Iraq, Israel, Jordan, Kuwait, Lebanon, Oman, Saudi Arabia, Syria, United Arab Emirates, Yemen → 0 to 9%

European Jew

Poland, Belarus, Ukraine, Russia, Israel → 0 to 14%

Africa

Senegal Chad, Gambia, Guinea-Bissau → 0 to 3%
Northern Africa (Algeria, Morocco, Tunisia) → 0 to 6%

Indigenous America

Colombia and Venezuela → 0 to 1%
Central America → 0 to 1%
Yucatán Peninsula in México → 0 to 1%
South America from the Andes → 0 to1%

Although many family members and friends seek to place themselves in a single ethnic classification, my DNA estimates are indicatives that my blood-relatives and descendants do not have a unique ethnic classification.

My Ethnic Roots Through Five Continents

Spain → Portugal → Southern Italy → European Jewish → Greece & Albania
Scotland → Cyprus → Senegal
Indigenous Americas
Colombia & Venezuela → Yucatan Peninsula→Andean
Northern Africa → Nigeria
Western Cuba, Canary Islands & Uruguay

Based on DNA tests for
Delvis Alejandro (Moreira) Fernández Levy
Through ancestry.com

2

MY DEAR FAMILY
MI QUERIDA FAMILIA

In this chapter I offer recollections about family bonding including friends and acquaintances that nurtured me during my life journey prior to my departure from the beloved Cuban homeland. Close family members were not always present but their guidance with knowledge of their failures and achievements filled me with hope and strength to face the challenges encountered as I move through a labyrinth of values, cultures, and languages. I envision my whole life as a virtual landscape composed of three distinct periods:

LA PRIMERA FAMILIA beginning with my birth and ending as a teenager with my departure from my unforgettable central hometown of Santa Clara, Cuba.

THE NEW FAMILY, starting in Salt Lake City, Utah, expanding through Florida and ending in California – being totally separated from my Cuban *familia*, coping with acculturation in strange landscapes and social environments.

A DREAM FAMILY of my final quest for reconnection of two distant poles that could bring peace and serenity to my last days on Earth.

MY FAMILY MIX

Mezcla de Familias

Falling in Love

Vive Delvis and *La Mora* Sara

Vive (Delvis Rafael)
when he fell in love with
La Mora Sara
1938.

La Mora
The Moorish Lady
Near time when she first
met my father *Vive* around
1938

Sara Levy Rodríguez and **Delvis Rafael (Moreira) Fernández** at their wedding on October 11, 1939, dressed in black since their relation was opposed by their families. They eloped and went to live in the back room of a pharmacy run by him and his maternal half-sister Évora Pérez Fernández, under approval of his older maternal half-brother, Gaspar Pérez Fernández.

A loving relation and stressful family journey began with my dad's visits to the home of my maternal grandparents - Felicia Rodríguez Marzall and Salvador Levy Levy – when he served as a nurse practitioner and pharmacy messenger bringing medicines and injections for Sara's little toddler brother Benjamin.

On September 18, 1939, soon after falling in love, against the wishes of her parents, my mother Sara eloped with my father Delvis Rafael. Sara had been raised as a princess, sat next to her father during mealtime and even had a nanny to take care of her whimsical girly needs. She was not prepared to cook or wash dishes at a home without running water or bathroom facilities. Her marriage -- to a French Jewish doctor if at all possible -- was to be prearranged by her father Salvador and uncles Victor and Isidoro. As the oldest sibling she was required to set a good example for her sisters; but instead, she rebelled against her family's wishes, ran away with my dad, and ended up living in a small room behind a pharmacy that was being developed by him and his half-sister Évora, later nicknamed *Chicha* by me.

Before my birth, after losing the family home, *Tío* Gaspar travelled to the Canary Islands to recover family inheritance from his father Don Tomás Pérez and managed to move to a dilapidated house next to the old residence. Furthermore, Évora was able to manage a pharmacy with the help of my father - who had received informal training as a pharmacist – a trade he learned as a messenger delivering medications and giving injections to people in need of health care.

The backroom of the pharmacy (on Maceo Street) was the refuge for *Mami* Sara – the place where my father brought her to live. My father had no ownership of anything in the Pérez clan and now he was bringing an outsider, *una Judía*, into a family business. Unfortunately, the pharmacy venture came to an end, and they were welcomed to move to the home of *Tío* Gaspar and his wife, *Tía* Victoria Marcos – a portly woman from Galicia Spain who ran her home with austerity and discipline.

Two nurse practitioners: *Papá Vive* and *Tía Chicha* who ran the Pérez Pharmacy, (c.1938) established thanks to *Tío* Gaspar's inheritance brought from the Canary Islands. A place for my mother Sara's hiding after her affair with my father *Vive* in 1939.

About nine months later, on June 4, 1940, Sara gave birth to her first child – Delvis Alejandro Fernández Levy, born at the *Hospital Militar General Monteagudo* of Santa Clara, Cuba.

Siomara, a younger sister of my mother, who was often confused with my mother Sara for their physical features – both had beautiful eyes, dark hair, and were friendly beauties with flirtatious smiles. *Tía* Siomara was about three years younger than *Mami* Sara and had also shocked her Levy family by leaving home as a young teenager with a military man named Ibrahim Monteagudo. When ready to give birth, Sara took her sister's identity and pretended to be the wife of a military man. She tells the story of how nervous she was on a bed at the Military Hospital, with her newly born baby by her side. She recounts the time when an army officer came to check on her, while trying to pass as Ibrahim's wife, after giving birth. The officer simply held the healthy-looking baby and congratulated her. In fear of being discovered, *Mami* Sara covered half her face with a bed sheet, pretending to be in pain. The birth was safe and free of charges in the best facility in town, and here I am today, eighty-years later to tell the story.

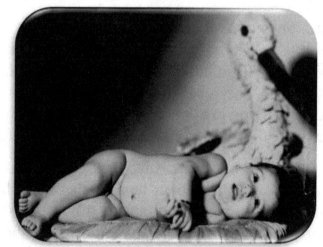

My father was a new addition to the Pérez Clan because of *abuela* Mamá-Ramona's affair with Plácido Moreira, after her landowner and highly admired husband Don Tomás suffered a tragic death. The affair was judged as an "unforgivable sin" that deeply affected family with her children. The *finca* and home inheritance were an ongoing source of dispute in the Pérez family. Whenever *tío* Gaspar came to visit our family home, debates aroused with accusations of dishonesty towards him for not sharing their Spanish inheritance. *Tío* Gaspar as the elder alpha male in the family was entrusted with gathering all of Don Tomás' belongings in Cuba and in the Canary Islands - after his accidental death, due to a fall while guiding an oxen-team next to a steep river cliff. *Tía* Chicha and other siblings felt that Gaspar had misused or kept the money and goods they were supposed to have received. As a result of the family bickering and mismanagement, *Mamá* Ramona and her family lost their prized home inherited from Don Tomás and were forced to move to a smaller dwelling in poor conditions – lacking a bathroom and running water. Even though abrasive remarks appeared to be the order of the day within the clan at *Calle* San Miguel led by *Tía* Chicha with *Abuela* Mamá Ramona and sweet Great-aunt Ana by her side, the *familia* appeared intact as a unit and provided assistance to anyone with dire needs or despair.

When I was a toddler in early childhood, my *Mami* Sara made some attempts to separate from *Papi Vive*. She would drag me to her parents' home and in no uncertain terms would say, "*lo dejo para siempre, no resisto más sus borracheras*" – "I'm leaving him forever, I can't take anymore his drunkenness." But no matter how strong her intentions may have been, my father knew how to regain her trust, asking forgiveness, bringing a singer and guitar player to serenade her, or having his mother Ramona come to her crying and begging Sara to come back to my father. They were seldom able to create a family home environment for me and my sisters. Our stable family home was for the most part with our Half-Aunt *Chicha* (Évora Pérez), my sweetest *Tía* Ana (Anatolia Fernández), and *abuela* Mamá-Ramona. Although the term "Half-Aunt" may be considered offensive, Chicha represents the strength of a family that filled a maternal gap left from family divisions, the unfortunate alcohol addiction of my *Papi* on top of *Mami's* attempt to keep him under control.

Even as a toddler, my mother in desperation would send me out to the street corner bodega bar in search of my *Papá* to bring him home. And then once they were together, she became terribly upset shouting and crying for his lack of attention to the family. The dinner food would be already placed on the table, but *Papá* was nowhere to be seen, or if ever present, he would be swaying almost unable to stand up. His Pérez family - our protectors - would also behave as enablers, treating him with pity, trying to make him comfortable after episodes of heavy drinking and passing out.

During my seventeen years in Cuba, I fantasized about a stable home with my parents, a dream that came close to reality when my little sister nicknamed Puchy was born in 1953. Looking back, since their marriage and through my childhood, they lived in at least ten different places in various parts of Cuba – sometimes under extreme poverty:

(1) In a small room behind a pharmacy; (2) at the home of a brother; (3) in a room near a Sugar Mill; (4) at a country *Bohío* (Taino hut) in Los Haticos of Oriente Province; (5) at a one-room place in the city of Holguín; (6) in a small house part of a four-plex, miles from Santa Clara, without running water, sharing a single outhouse with four families; (7) at the Pérez family home in the *Finca* (farm), with dirt floors in the kitchen and dining area, without a bathroom or outdoor toilet.

Early in 1950 my father, encouraged by his only father figure, his older half-brother who was also my *Tío* Gaspar, was able to get a job in Venezuela, helping to build a highway connecting the Capital city of Caracas with the coastal town of La Guaira. He worked there for about a year and when he returned it appeared that all the money he sent was gone, but my clever *Mamá* Sara– as his financial savior – had so much money in hiding that he was able to buy a Sinclair Garage and Repair Service Station –named *El Relámpago* (The Lighting) - on the Camajuaní highway outside Santa Clara. This was the beginning of what appeared to be a new era for our *familia*. Although addiction was still prevalent in him, he had transitioned from a dysfunctional to a working alcoholic. They rented a little house with two bedrooms, a bathroom, and running water. The house was adjacent to the garage where he and his business partner worked on old clunkers, offered auto mechanical services and parking for wealthier clients, on top of selling oil and gasoline.

At last, in 1952, when I was 12 years old, I thought there was hope for family stability. My mother got pregnant and had her third child, named Guiselda in honor of our admired cousin and family mentor and role model. Baby Guiselda - whom I nicknamed Puchy - was the first daughter under my mother's care and I felt optimistic about our family's future, shopping for groceries, starting a *Bachillerato* (a Cuban type of High School) and taking my little sister to a newly opened Presbyterian Church every Sunday. My *Mami* appeared to be calmed taking care of the new baby, playing piano, sewing, and reading *novelas*. They felt so successful that they ventured into fixing and expanding the old Pérez family home near the center of Santa Clara, with two bathrooms, and their private upstairs residence. My *abuela* Mamá Ramona and *Tía* Chicha (Évora} were willing to share ownership of the home with my parents, while the entire farm was to be divided only among the Pérez siblings – Évora, Celaida, Gaspar, and Juana.

MY MATERNAL GRANDFATHER
Mi Abuelo Materno
Papá Viejo

My Grandfather **Salvador Levy Levy** was the first in his family to make it to Cuba, from Istanbul (Constantinople) to Havana, as a stowaway in 1912, fleeing military conscription near the end of the Ottoman Empire. A year later, he managed to bring family members coming on the Orient Express to Le Havre, France from an area of Turkey in dispute with Greece and Bulgaria. They boarded the ULTONIA Ship on its way to the New World, ending in Havana, Cuba. But sadly, he had to endure family loss with the death of his mother Sara, and the separation of a sister who eloped with a soldier to Bulgaria. There were also early family disagreements in Cuba when his sister Sol Levy left for Havana with a man named José Cohen. My mother filled me with stories about family splits due to their diaspora migrations, and years later, long after my departure from Cuba I was honored and fortunate to meet cousins from the Cohen-Levy side of the *Grand Familia*.

Family sailing from Le Havre, France in the ULTONIA Ship
November 1913

NAME IN FULL Family Name Given Name		Age	Calling Or Occupation	Able to Read Write	Race or People	Last Permanent Residence Country City or Town	
Levy	Salomon	42	workman	yes	Hebrew	Turkey	Gallipoli
Levy	Yoya	40	wife	no	Hebrew	Turkey	Gallipoli
Levy	Rachelle	15	servant	yes	Hebrew	Turkey	Gallipoli
Levy	Alegrina	11	servant	yes	Hebrew	Turkey	Gallipoli
Candiotti	Rachelle	19	servant	no	Hebrew	Turkey	Gallipoli
Levy	Jaak	22	clerk	yes	Hebrew	Turkey	Constantinople

(Excerpts from archives showing a list of travelers in the ULTONIA SHIP)

My maternal *Abuelos'* home was in a middle-class neighborhood of Santa Clara, two blocks from my father's family home. There was a sense of duty and getting things done on time during the daily routine of running the home and tending to the demands of raising a large family. In contrast to most Cuban homes, there were no images of saints or religious symbols on the walls. The first decoration seen on the entry hall was a large tapestry embroidered with a representation of a Turkish marketplace.

The Levy Clan in Kirklisse, Turkey (or Kirklareli, Greece)
Great-grandfather Salomón at the center
Baby Salvador on the left side of the picture. c. 1895

The home was clean, well-organized, had running water, a kitchen, and a full bathroom. There were books, newspapers, bibles, and magazines. It was elongated with an open hall providing light for all the bedrooms as well as an open patio behind the house that faced a large garden with all sorts of vegetable used by a group of Chinese immigrants as a source of revenue. The house ran on the clock. Dinner was always a formal event – at the same time with basically the same choices: *sopa de fideos* (noodle soup), *arroz blanco* (white rice), *frijoles* (beans), and chicken, meat or fish – but never pork. Sometimes when *tía* Raquel and the *familia turca* (Turkish family) came to visit they would prepare a *plato con lentejas* (lentils plate), *bourekas* (puffy pastries), *albóndigas* (matzah balls), or *pipirizas con queso* (stuffed peppers with cheese). Grandfather Salvador Levy Levy was called ***Papá Viejo* - Old Dad -** by his grandchildren.

As I recall during my grade school days, *Papá Viejo* would leave the house carrying a bundle of clothing material on his shoulders early in the morning to catch a bus that would take him to rural areas outside Santa Clara. He seemed to get along with all Cubans regardless of their racial or ethnic origins, and whenever I was near him in public, he would stop conversing and introduce me to his friends with a sense of pride over my school achievements. Daily, I would sit by him after work and tease him about increasing my one-nickel daily allowance, which as I approached my teens he increased to a dime. He provided money during my childhood that I saved for: kites, marbles, yoyos, spinning tops, along with Mother's Day and family birthday presents. My parents never bought me pants or shirts, all my clothing was made and sewn by my mother from material given by my *Papá Viejo.*

Papá Viejo was very sociable around friends and acquaintances. He joked about his foreign accent, which as a child I thought to indicate a lack of education; but later I discovered that he spoke a Judeo-Spanish referred to as Ladino. I recalled friends calling him *Quisite* – pronounced as "Kee-see-teh" – which turned out to be his way of greeting in his accented Ladino/Spanish – like saying *¡Oye,* q*ué hiciste!* - Similar to "Hey, What's Happening!"

Jewish Teachings

In terms of Jewish teachings, his father Salomón was a deeply religious man given the title of Hakham – meaning a wise and educated community leader similar to a Rabbi. *Bisabuelo* (Great grandpa) Salomón endured a tragic emigration to Cuba after the loss of his wife, also named Sara, and the disappearance of a daughter who eloped with a soldier to Bulgaria.

Tomb of Great grandpa Salomón Levy Levy at the Jewish Cemetery of Santa Clara. He died a year before my birthday in 1939 when he was 78 years old.

Papá Viejo seldom tried to influence me on religious beliefs, but when he did, it was with passion and directness unlike the sweetness that he usually portrayed towards me. I recall six events or encounters where he let me know about the family origins and the legacy, they would leave for me and future generations:

• The first dealt with my birth certificate where he was identified as a **Greek citizen.** I asked him about why he was listed as a Greek instead of a person born in Turkey. He appeared upset and in no uncertain terms let me know that he was neither Greek nor Turkish – *¡Soy Hebreo!* **- I am a Hebrew!**

• A second incident relates to my **Levy** last name, which I used to incorrectly spell as **Levis,** as it appears in my birth certificate, perhaps misspelled to match closer to my first name Delvis - often confused with Levis. *Abuelo Papá Viejo* again with directness let me know that "Levy" was the name of a people from Biblical days who endured Diasporas and persecutions in various places of the World -- and perhaps jokingly he mentioned that the Hollywood comedian Jerry Lewis was my cousin.

• The third vivid memory occurred when I was a young teenager who became heavily involved with a newly established Presbyterian Church in Santa Clara. My *Mamá Vieja* had built good relations with the Baptists first, and later helped with the foundation of the Presbyterian Church in Santa Clara. She felt close to Old Testament teachings of Hebrew traditions that provided a way to nurture her children in Jewish related biblical teachings. I became so involved helping to organize the new church, that I was selected as a Sunday School Leader, at a very young age. *El Reverendo* Sergio Arce encouraged me to wait for the Lord's calling to become a minister. I planned on going to a seminary in Costa Rica but waited and waited for the call from the Lord that never came. *Papá Viejo* somehow sensed that I was drifting away from his tribe and again confronted me with a few words of dismay and empty questions: *¿Por qué, te metes en eso?* **– Why are you getting into that?**

• The fourth event that had a profound impact on me was a revelation of secret religious upbringings and a declaration of his wishes for my future life. Upon meeting him at his favorite Café Villaclara, he smiled, put his hands around my shoulders and told me that we were going to a special place. We walked for five or six blocks to a narrow meeting room on a second story floor of a movie house where about ten older men were sitting on two long benches facing each other. A few words of introduction were said in heavily accented Spanish, followed by an incomprehensible foreign tongue, I assumed was *Hebreo*, and then I was introduced to those present, one by one, who recited a prayer or greeting while patting my head. This was the closest I came to what may be called a secretive passage rite into adulthood.

Twenty-two years went by before I returned to Cuba, Papá Viejo was already gone, but I had with me his precious inheritance – his Parker fountain pen brought by *Tío* Benjamín – as a symbol of the love and trust which my dearest *Papá Viejo* left for me, as a completion of a long-forgotten **Bar Mitzvah.**

● A fifth revelation of Jewish life was a prayer session at the private home of *Señor* Behar, a man who was a client and lived near my *Papá's* garage, as well as owned a shoe store. His family offered insights into their secret practice of Jewish worship. I met the family through a boy close to me in age and with whom I played and shared schoolbooks. *Señor* Behar's wife took me to a room in their home converted into a mini synagogue, where they recited prayers and offered stories about their family's Diaspora in the Americas. According to my mother, as a young man, Behar had been suggested to her for marriage before meeting my father.

● A sixth surprise came on a visit arranged by *Papá Viejo* at the home of one of my uncles in the town of Caibarién, on the north coast of Cuba. Most of his Turkish émigré Hebrew *familia* lived there, and still adhered to their Jewish religion and traditions. During a formal meal, on a long table with about ten family members, a book of prayers was brought out and read by each person. Little did I know that I was participating in a Jewish Passover Seder Celebration, with text of the Haggadah but hiding it under the table before and after the readings.

Papá Viejo was the most influential family member in my upbringings. His examples as a father and family caretaker remain present in my heart and soul as guiding principles. He was a mentor, well educated, not through schooling but through enduring life experiences in Turkey, Greece, France, Costa Rica, Venezuela, and Cuba. He provided the means for me to receive a highly valued education with access to a piano, an Encyclopedia, and the 50 dollars for the long journey from Santa Clara by bus to Havana, followed by a short flight to Key West, Florida and finally a five-day Greyhound bus trip to Salt Lake City, Utah.

My Maternal Grandmother
Mamá Vieja

My maternal grandmother ***Mamá-Vieja - Felicia Rodríguez Marzall -*** also known as *La Niña* by family and friends had a mixed ancestral heritage, some Spanish Catalonian and Filipino, plus other obscure ancestry that may be speculated according to her family skin tones and facial features. Cuba is truly a melting pot, mainly Spanish and African, with some indigenous or Taino, French, Haitian, Jamaican, Chinese and others from the Antilles and four corners of the World. She was born in San Juan y Martínez, a village of Pinar del Río Province, notable for growing tobacco in the Cuban Far West. She was a rather quiet person, with strong principles and opinions about social issues and human justice. Her home was clean, well-organized, with a friendly dog, a purring cat, and the sounds of *"¡Buenos Días, Buenos Días!"* greetings screeched by her colorful parrot. *Mamá Vieja,* according to my mother, was raised by an ex-nun who fled from Spain with a Catholic priest. She was a single mother when she met my *Papá Viejo*, but despite strong prejudices, as two peas in a pod, outside mainstream Cuban society, were formally married and raised a vibrant family of nine children: Rubén, the adopted son, followed in age by my mother Sara, and her siblings: Estrella, Siomara, Argelia, Alegrina, Elvira, Hirán, and Benjamín.

Mamá Vieja was a stoic woman, a rebel, with a strong sense of commitment to what she considered fighting for justice and the empowerment of the poor and disenfranchised people in Cuban society. She did not express her views with words but with actions that still linger as a rich legacy with examples for her descendants. For over sixty years Felicia and Salvador formed a grand *familia* fortified with compassion, love and unity through times of war, rebellion, and family tragedies. Although she was not Jewish, she adopted principles and traditions from the Old Testament by nurturing her children through visits to a Baptist Church, and later in life by helping with the foundation of a Presbyterian Church in Santa Clara. Values that were passed on as a legacy of her life, blended with those of her beloved husband Salvador.

Between her mothering duties she managed to write opinion pieces opposing the Franco Government of Spain around the time of my birth in 1940. Later, when I was twelve years old – during my first year in secondary school, she became quite involved in the opening of a Presbyterian Church under difficult settings within a tile factory. I was so impressed with her devotion to this "new" religion, free of saints and idols, housed in a humble place, permitting Bible readings and discussions on how they might encourage changes in society, without waiting for heaven, but doing it here and now. Years later, in the mid-1950s, at the height of the revolutionary struggles in Central Cuba, she got involved collecting money for the Revolution as well as offering refuge to rebels in the city. Three years after leaving Cuba I was surprised to see a photo of *Mamá Vieja*, with a militia uniform, armed with a rifle, and standing guard at the main post office station of Santa Clara.

The parents and siblings of my Grandma *Abuela **Mamá Vieja*** -- Felicia Rodríguez Marzall -- lived in La Palma, Pinar del Río Province at the far west of the Island of Cuba. She was the daughter of Simón Rodríguez and Idelfonsa Marzall. It is difficult to describe my *Mamá Vieja* – she was unique, outside the universe and culture around her. She provided lessons and guidance through her exemplary life as a mother and fighter for a better world. Her legacy will live forever in my life and my descendants who seek a future of justice, with the expansion of educational opportunities, and fair treatment for all humans regardless of gender, class, race, or ethnicity.

My Unknown Paternal Grandfather
The Trauma of *Abuela Mamá-Ramona*

On one memorable occasion, while my aunt *Tía Llalla* was visiting Santa Clara from the The Family Farm - she shouted and reprimanded me for throwing kisses to the picture of my presumed *abuelo* Don Tomás Pérez González (1875 – 1912), the highly admired patriarch of our grand *familia* - a native and prominent landowner from the Canary Islands, Spain.

My aunt Celaida, whom I nicknamed *Tía Llalla,* was morbidly obese, quite melodramatic, always ready to shed tears as she would greet me with hugs and kisses. Now, suddenly for the first time in my life, she showed anger, like I had never seen coming from her, and in no uncertain terms said: *¡Ese NO es tu abuelo!* **- That is NOT your grandfather!** I was about ten years old, felt shocked and rather silly for not having realized earlier in life that my father Delvis Rafael Fernández did not have the Pérez family name – and hence was not a full-member of the Pérez Family Clan -- outside the inheritance benefits and cast status coming from the Pérez Family. However, as the youngest offspring of *Abuela* Mamá-Ramona, my *Papi* was treated with much love and care by his three half-sisters - Juana, Celaida, and Évora as well as by his older half-brother Gaspar who also served as his father figure.

Indirectly, *Tía* Llalla helped me to understand why *abuela* Mamá-Ramona at times received harsh treatments from her daughters Évora and Celaida. Almost daily she left the house to find refuge visiting *ahijados* (godchildren) and friends in the poor neighborhood of *El Condado*. She socialized with town folks through *La Bolita* - a number game based on the Cuban Lottery, where she would collect coins for bets on numbers, or sometimes visit lucky *bolita* winners to give them their cash earnings. As far as I could tell this was not for profits, since I never saw more than a few coins exchanged for betting and prize earnings.

Sometimes she was not well treated by my *Tías*, and I witnessed her leaving the home for her daily jaunts, with words like: *¡Vergüenza, Papá aún estaba tibio en su tumba!* **(Shame, Father was still warm in his grave!)** – words that baffled me as a child but later in life, realizing the emotive suggestion that their father (my presumed *abuelo* Don Tomás) was still warm in his grave when she had a love affair with another man. To add to the trauma, Don Tomás had an accidental death while driving an oxen team in his *Finca*, about two years before my father's birth. It took me quite a bit of time to decipher the messages and discover that her affair was with a man named **Plácido Moreira García**, who turned out to be my true blood-related paternal grandfather; a person I never met since he was already dead long before I was born.

Years later prior to my departure from Cuba, when I was about 15 years old, my *Papá* was quite emotional in revealing the hidden side of his paternal family and took me to the home of his Moreira half-siblings – two sisters and a brother. I remember a loving friendly lady named Aparizada (Parizade) and a highly sociable brother named Bamán (Bahman), who was close in age and had a strong physical resemblance to my Dad. Although I had met Bamán many years before this encounter, I did not realize that he was my uncle, but at the same time I was quite impressed by the family resemblance and warm friendly relation he had with my *Papá*. All of my Dad's siblings in the Moreira family had names based on princes and princesses of the Arabian Nights Tales. Lucky for me, my *abuela* Mamá-Ramona followed that tradition and aimed for Prince Perviz, a Persian name meaning "Fortunate" or "Victorious" that was misspelled as "Delvis," in his birth certificate. Therefore, my *Papi* was spared from the previously chosen name of *Desdichado* (Unfortunate). A name I had heard mentioned in family gatherings in a joking way.

Tales of the Arabian Nights

———

Las Mil y Una Noches

More than 40 years later, while visiting my hometown of Santa Clara, a close family friend, an Afro-Cuban lady named Petronila, showed me a picture of my real grandfather, a handsome man with curly hair, Plácido Moreira García, and revealed details about his life. My unknown *abuelo* Don Moreira also had a well-established family life with a wife, daughters, and a son. Perhaps as a sign of revenge for disloyalty to the family, he was shot and killed while sitting in the dining room of a *Bohío* (an open farm dwelling) by a brother-in-law who fled on a horse. At last, there was closure to the mystery of my father's biological origins and a revelation and understanding about the obvious but unexplainable trauma endured by my *Papi Vive, Abuela Mamá-Ramona,* and our loving Grand *Familia.*

My Paternal Grandmother
Abuela Mamá-Ramona

My *abuela* **Ramona del Carmen Fernández Pérez** (1873-1959), whom I nicknamed *Mamá-Ramona*, had seven children with her Spanish *Terrateniente* – wide-ranging Landowner husband Don Tomás Pérez García. Four of her children survived into adulthood: Juana Ramona de la Asunción, Gaspar Fernando del Carmen, Celaida Felicitas, and Évora Idelfonsa Olvido. The other three offspring met early deaths: Francisco Damián (*Pachín*), Ambrosio Antonio, and Olvido del Consuelo. My aunt Évora, whom I nicknamed *Chicha*, was about ten years older than my father.

Ramona del Carmen Fernández Pérez
(1883-1959)
Abuela Mamá-Ramona, a sweet lady with a spirit of independence, quite competitive while teaching me about gambling and playing card games.

Abuela Mamá-Ramona Fernández was the daughter of Francisco Ramón Fernández Álvarez and Adelaida Pérez Guzmán – as far as I could tell they were both from Cuba or Spain. As a child I recall being taught and having challenging times playing cards and lottery games with her. More than any other family member she made me aware of the life experienced by many people living under extreme poverty when she would take me along to visit and assist families of her *ahijados* (godchildren) in marginal neighborhoods on the outskirts of Santa Clara. In hindsight, I was fortunate to experience a side of Cuba unknown by most of my family members. She also had close connections with Petronila, an Afro Cuban lady who 50 years later showed me pictures of my real *abuelo* Plácido Moreira García and gave me information about the trauma endured by Mamá Ramona, after the untimely death of her husband Don Tomás.

Mamá-Ramona died in 1959, two years after I had left Cuba, but her teachings, love, and motherly care are part of my inner soul as the family legacy left for me and future generations.

3

SANTA CLARA --*Mi Hogar*
My Family Home (1940-1957)

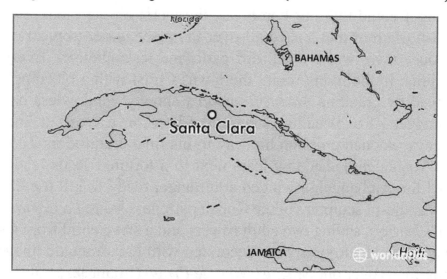

Santa Clara's Central Park - *El Parque Leoncio Vidal*
THE CENTER OF TOWN
Surrounded by social clubs, coffee shops, movie theaters, a secondary
school, the main library and places for music and public gatherings.

Back in the mid 1940s, after my toddler times in Northeastern Cuba, now referred to as Holguín Province, I moved with my parents back to my birthplace of Santa Clara, in the center of the Island to our family home. A home, which along with a large *finca* (farm) miles away, formed part of the inheritance that my *abuela* (grandma) *Mamá-Ramona* received from her husband, Don Tomás Pérez González, long before I was born. On San Miguel Street, five blocks from the city's central park (*El Parque Leoncio Vidal*) we lived in a neighborhood with homes adjacent to each other.

As far as I could tell, our home was the worst on the block, narrow with a broken Spanish tile roof that leaked all over the place under tropical rains. At the end of the house there was a small dirt patio and an outhouse. Every room had pictures of saints: In the living room, there was Christ with a bleeding heart in his hands; followed by grandma *Mamá-Ramona's* spooky windowless dark bedroom filled with images of a bleeding punctured Christ on a cross; a kneeling Jesus carrying a heavy wooden cross on his way to his final crucifixion; *La Dolorosa* (a tearful Mary Magdalene) shedding tears next to a tortured Jesus ready for burial; Saint Michael the Archangel, a winged adult angel ready to kill the devil with his sword; and a candle-lit sculpture of the Cuban patroness saint, *La Caridad del Cobre* (Our Lady of Charity), saving two adult rowers and a slave child from a stormy sea. The second and third bedrooms were decorated with less dramatic images of saints serving as guardians over our beds: *El Niño de Praga* (Infant Jesus of Prague), Saint Teresa of Ávila, the Virgin Mary cradling baby Jesus, *San Lázaro* (Saint Lazarus) a leprous man with open wounds being licked by two dogs, and other images of saints and sculptures that gave the children fear or inspiration for "good behavior."

I do not remember photographs of family members on the walls, except for one picture of the greatly admired family Patriarch Don Tomás Pérez displayed high on a wall near the front door. As far as I knew, he was my *abuelo* (grandpa) and guardian angel – dead but ever-present family protector. Some members of my paternal family, excluding my father, trained me to throw kisses at the photograph of *Abuelo* Don Tomás, shout *adiós,* make the sign of the cross, and ask for blessings as I left home for my daily routines – school or play.

Up to about 1953, our house was one of the smallest on the block, but often the *familia* was the largest, consisting of many relatives of Mamá-Ramona (Grandma on my father's side) and my loving Great Aunt *Tía* Ana. Even though I am not blood-related to the Pérez side of the family, they played a major role in my life and upbringing through childhood. My aunt *Tía* Chicha was a mother figure for me, for my sisters, and other family members. Her home on San Miguel Street in Santa Clara was the center of my life as well as the lives of nieces and nephews.

FAMILY HOME SURROUNDINGS

Évora Idelfonsa Olvido Pérez Fernández (1907-2011) whom I nicknamed *CHICHA*

Chicha (**Aunt Évora**), my father's half-sister oversaw home and family throughout most of her life – a mother figure to all of her nephews and nieces. She never married and became the cornerstone of the entire Pérez-Fernández family, taking care of nieces and nephews until her passing at the age of 104 in the year 2011.

She was born in Taguayabón, Camajuaní Municipality, on January 23, 1907. Her parents were *Doña* Ramona del Carmen Fernández Pérez, a natural of Camajuaní and Don Tomás Pérez González, a natural of Santa Cruz de Tenerife, Canary Islands, Spain. My family environment was in the house on San Miguel Street between the Maceo and Colón Streets, in the central area of the city of Santa Clara. Our home was run by Aunt Evora with the support of my great-aunt Ana and my paternal grandmother Mamá Ramona. As the elders of the family told me, I gave her the nickname Chicha, kept forever since my childhood. In that house Chicha was like a Great Mother to her nephews, erasing distinctions between cousins and brothers, uncles and fathers, grandmothers, and great-aunts.

Tía Chicha filled me with Catholic religious rituals and dogmas that are still present in my memory:

1. Every night Chicha would take me to bed and teach me to recite and memorize prayers to Jesus and the Virgin Mary that were part of a long family tradition in Spanish Catholic culture.

2. The Buenviaje Catholic Church, a few blocks from home, was the place to go every Sunday for Catholic Mass in Latin. No one in the family came with me, and when I would object being sent to church, Chicha responded – *Soy católica a mi manera* – I'm a Catholic in my own way – I don't need to go to church.

3. Catechism and moving iconic religious figures were part of my duties through childhood; as well as confessions or meeting with priests for communion and rituals were part of my obligations prior to taking school exams or dealing with illness and disturbing life experiences.

4. *Espiritismo* (Spiritism) or *Santería* was another type of religious belief with roots in Spain and Africa practiced by family members. I was sent for a *Despojo* – a ritual by a *santería espiritista* (priestess) praying while holding herbs and gently slapping them over my body – as a way to overcome a difficult life experience.

First Communion picture for a Roman Catholic trained *Pupy*

Neither one of my parents, nor the maternal side of the family played a role in these activities, and at times I got the impression that they did not agree with these practices. The surroundings and connections with the Fernández and Pérez sides were by far beyond the contacts I had with my maternal side of the grand *familia*. In Santa Clara and at the nearby farm – *La Finca* – the Pérez family was always present for holidays and family gatherings. During vacation time, almost all of my family visits were with the Fernández side in the coastal towns of Caibarién, north of Santa Clara; or also, in the Preston Sugar Mill -- now called Central Guatemala in the Holguín area of eastern Cuba. Family visits whenever possible were part of my daily routine at my maternal *abuelos'* home with aunts and uncles where I enjoyed meals and playful times with cousins and their pets.

Maternal Aunts and Cousins

Visiting the homes of my maternal aunts in Santa Clara always brought joy and playful times with my little cousins. *Mis queridas Tías* – My Dear Aunts were beautiful, lively, expressive women: Estrella, Alegrina, Argelia, and Elvira, with daughters Mayra, Olguita, Alegrinita, Grisell, and Maruchi (María Elena). My young uncles living nearby: Hirán - nicknamed *Nenín* - and the youngest in the clan. Benjamín were active teenagers that offer me a guide to life and future quests. Nenín was good at telling jokes and was involved in the newly formed Presbyterian Church; he also studied at the *Escuela de Comercio* (Commerce School). Benjamín was the most handsome member of the family, whom I thought would become a successful singer or actor in Havana. My third uncle, *Tío* Rubén, did not live near the home nest but occasionally would come to visit with a friend or his two daughters: Lourdes and Diana who were close to me in age. *Tío* Rubén was the first son of my Grandmother Felicia (*Mamá-Vieja*) before she married my grandfather *Papá-Viejo*. Although I seldom got to see him, *Tío Rubén* was my favorite and most loving uncle. He had been married to a woman nicknamed *Monona Ros* that I never met and lived near the town of Guantánamo in the far eastern province of Oriente. He adopted the Levy name and as far as I could tell he was a bona fide member of the family clan. According to my mother when her father – my *Papá Viejo* - was in San José, Costa Rica running a clothing store, named *La Isla de Cuba* – Rubén was placed in an asylum for orphan children in Havana.

And finally, my last memorable discovery came on my first trip to Havana at the home of my Uncle Carlos Rivero Alonso and Aunt Siomara Levy Rodríguez, plus their adorable new baby Magda and the older daughter Gilda. Tía Siomara also had three children from a previous marriage to a military man named Ibrahim Monteagudo. Their children Jose and Eduardito were delightful playful cousins close to me in age. There was also a cousin named Teresita (Teresa Monteagudo Levy) that I never had a chance to meet.

Family on My Mother's Side
(1940s & 1950s)

Tío Eddie Benjamín – aspiring actor and singer back in the 1950s

Pictures of my cousins Olguita and Mayra in 1951 And their parents: My *Tío* Vitico - Victor Noemí - and *Tía* Estrella on the left side, around 1945

Celebration at the wedding of Tía Alegrina with Luís Felipe Ramos, c. 1945 The picture also shows Tía Chicha (Évora Pérez) and Tía Argelia on the right side.

Tío Rubén the most expressive family member with his daughters Diana and Lourdes and niece Alegrinita on the right side c. 1957

Tía Siomara Levy Rodríguez (1920-1965) in the middle celebrating the Birthday of her 2nd daughter Gilda Rivero Levy (c. 1956), and on the far-right is her oldest daughter Teresa Monteagudo Levy. A 2nd cousin Estercita appears on the far left.

My mother's youngest sister, Elvira Levy Rodríguez (1930-2013) married Justo Núñez and had a precious daughter named María Elena (1951 – 2016)

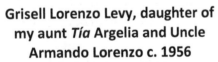

My two male cousins: José Elías in 1941, and the oldest Eduardo Monteagudo Levy in 1954) Sons of *Tía* Siomara and *Tío* Ibrahín

Tío Nenín, Hirán Levy Rodríguez and his wife Carmen Borges (c. 1955). Active member of the Presbyterian Church of Santa Clara

Grisell Lorenzo Levy, daughter of my aunt *Tía* Argelia and Uncle Armando Lorenzo c. 1956

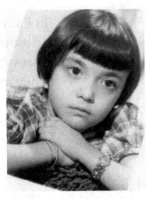

My Second Caretaker

Anatolia Marana Fernández Pérez (c. 1880-1973)
Tía ANA, my favorite aunt, took me to the Sugar
Mill of Preston by the Nipe Bay in the Oriente
Province of Cuba for summer vacations. Preston had
been established by the United Fruit Company of the
United States, but after the Cuban Revolution the
name was changed to Central Guatemala. I was
blessed with wonderful vacation times by the sea
with Ana's oldest daughter and youngest son: **Elia
Martínez Fernández** and **Evis (*Evito*) Fernández**.
Happy memories of love and attention are also
present by Elia's husband, **Pedro Gómez**, and their
children: Raquelita, Sarita, Pepito, Rafaelito, and on
various occasions spending time with our family was
major league baseball star nicknamed Preston
(Pedrito) Gómez. My cousin Evito and his family
also provided me with wonderful meals and playful
times with his daughter Elbita.

　　Ana was perhaps the person I loved the most and took care of me during
childhood. Her husband, Antonio Martínez Recio, had already died when I was
born. He, according to family anecdotes, was always on trips since he was a high-
ranking officer of the Cuban Navy. Of the three children with Ana, only the eldest,
Elia was registered under the Martínez surname; the other two Evis and Guiselda,
like me, only had the maternal surname Fernández.

　　Tía Ana was a caring loving great-aunt, always attentive to my daily needs,
and protective whenever I played on the street outside the home. More than any
other member of the family, Ana expanded my views of the Cuban countryside, by
taking me on memorable tours of the provinces of Camagüey and Oriente in eastern
Cuba. Perhaps in error, for I have no proofs, I always saw her as a person with
indigenous Taíno roots because of her complexion and deep knowledge of our food
and cultural traits, that she would share on long trips by train, bus, and single train
cars (gas-cars). Trips that would require a sleeping quarter from Santa Clara to the
Nipe Bay in *Oriente* (Eastern Cuba.)

The Extended Family: Cousins like Sisters AfroCuban Mother Figure

Cousins, *Inaíta* and *Ileanita*, whose parents, my *Tío* Patricio and *Tía* Llalla, lived out of town and ran the Pérez farm, were like sisters -- caring and spoiling me all through childhood. They had to live away from their parents like me in order to have access to a better future with schools and jobs away from the toils of farming.

Ramona Ignacia Martín Pérez (Born 1933)
***Inaíta, mi prima favorita* (my favorite cousin),**
who secretly, against my father's wishes,
encouraged me to play piano. And even after
my departure would send me Cuban and
classical piano sheet music.

My cousin, Ramona Ignacia, the oldest daughter of Aunt Llalla, whom I affectionately called Inaíta, was like a guardian angel through my childhood. She would take me for walks and give me valuable advice for a lifetime. Even today, she is present in my soul and heart, for almost every day I take out the ragged sheets of Cuban music that she bought for me in the old Dulzaides bookstore in Santa Clara. She encouraged me to learn to play the charming baroque piano of my *Mamá* Sara that we had in the house. She graduated as a Kindergarten Teacher around 1952.

Antonia Ileana Auria Martín Pérez (Born 1936)
***Ileanita* was like a sister, living in the same house**
for most of my life through childhood.
As a spoil brat with temper tantrums, she played
with me, took me out on walks and kept me
company when I began kindergarten in Santa
Clara. Ileanita was the youngest daughter of my
aunt Llalla (Celaida) and uncle Tío Patricio.

Nicolasa or *Nicola* as I called her, although not a blood relative, lived with us as a close family member in our home on San Miguel Street. She worked as a nursing assistant at the *Clínica Médica Quirúrgica* (Surgical Medical Hospital, known as CMQ) of Santa Clara and loved me as if I were her son – taking me for walks and worrying about my health and well-being. Occasionally she would take me to visit her Babalawo brother – a *Santería* priest for immersion in Afro-Cuban culture and religious rituals. Through her I learned and gained appreciation for the roots of Cuban culture beyond the teachings in schools. *Nicola* was the only person, I met who claimed to be of pure African descent in my environment of friends, family, and neighbors. Unfortunately, I do not have pictures but memories of her morals and teachings are etched in my mind.

Thanks to Nicola and my grandmother *Mamá* Ramona, I had access to another side of Santa Clara. As far as I know there were no governmental laws that enforced segregation, but a strong racist and caste discrimination culture was in evidence through Santa Clara:

(1) The central park had divided walking paths for whites and non-whites – not always easy to distinguish.

(2) Social clubs were exclusive and divided for blacks, whites, or mulattoes, people of Spanish descent; and the Catholic schools of *Los Maristas* and *Las Teresianas* were divided exclusively for either white boys or white girls. If a white girl were offered a scholarship without having to pay tuition, she would be required to use a different color uniform and not be allowed to play during recess with other students.

(3) During a Sunday Mass at the *Buenviaje* Catholic Church I was not allowed to sit next to my neighborhood friends, Agustín and Juan Vicente, who were also students at the segregated *Maristas* school for white boys.

On my street block there was only one Afro-Cuban family that were referred to as *Las Mulaticas* – The Little Mulattas. Members of my family would praise a friend who dated or married a person of lighter complexion by saying "*Oye mejoraste la raza*" – "Hey you improved the race." On the opposite side of my living racist experiences, thanks to *Nicola* I was given life assistance by family and friends of African descent that provided me with a road to health and education:

El Doctor Celestino Hernández saved my life when I was about 3 years old.

El Maestro Señor Alomá managed to get me into High School after 6th grade.

La Señora Petronila revealed my paternal family roots along with pictures and anecdotes about my real paternal grandfather.

HIGHLY ADMIRED
FREQUENT VISITORS TO OUR HOME

Guiselda de la Concepción Patriótica Nacional (Martínez) Fernández (1912 - 1991). Cousin *Guiso*, as I called her, was a daughter of my Great-aunt *Tía*

Ana. She had the most unusual name in our family, part of which translates as "National Patriotic Conception." Her father, Antonio Martínez Recio, was a high-ranking Cuban navy officer. She had reached the highest level of education in my family surroundings, becoming the main tutor that assisted me to also reach high levels of education beyond what was available for me in public schools. Her husband, **Raúl Hernández**, was also an exemplary person for his dedication as a family man and manager at *La Plaza* - the main Vegetable and Meat Market Place of Santa Clara. There he gave me advice and taught me to appreciate and enjoy vegetables and delicious fruits of my Homeland. Raúl and Guiselda also raised a niece, named Gladys, who was like a playful friend and cousin to me. **Guiso**, as my best teacher, helped me to bypass Junior High and enter a pre-university public school, *El Instituto de Segunda Enseñanza*, as a 12-year-old nerdy boy. Thus, making it possible to achieve the degree of *Bachiller en Ciencias y Letras*, during one of the most difficult times of my life, when many public secondary schools were closed and over 20,000 people were assassinated during the General Fulgencio Batista Dictatorship, between 1952 and 1958

Celaida Felicitas Pérez Fernández (10 Jul 1901 - Dec 1993)

I used to call her *Llalla (pronounced JAH-JAH)*. She was a very loving and highly emotional *Tía*, who gave hugs and kisses and cried at "the drop of a hat." She along with my dear uncle *Tío* **Patricio** ran the farm inherited from her *terrateniente* (landowner) Father Don Tomás Pérez. I spent many wonderful days at the farm with dirt floor kitchen and dining area, without electricity or running water, as well as lacking bathrooms and outhouses. But lucky for us there was an *arroyo* (little river) nearby for baths and a *platanal* (plantain grove) for pooping and peeing. There was no phone or radio, but nightly entertainment was always present listening to *Llalla*, *Tío* Patricio, and other friendly *guajiros* (farmers) telling ghost stories or singing *Puntos Cubanos* (country Cuban music). *Tío* Patricio was a native of *Castilla la Vieja* (Old Castille) in Spain, where Castilian Spanish originated and, of course, he was proud of his native language and rich vocabulary. His surname was quite unusual, "Martín de La Parra y de La Fuente Redonda," names that also indicate his birthplace near the city of Ávila de los Caballeros in *Castilla la Vieja*. Although he had no formal education, he took pleasure in teaching me pronunciation and nuances of his real *Castellano* language. I enjoyed memorable times with my Aunt Llalla, whom I remember as the best cook of typical Cuban desserts: cut milk candy (*dulce de leche*), rice with milk (*arroz con leche*), sweet flour (*majarete*), and many more. More than any others, they taught me how to survive under dire circumstances, but surrounded by a gorgeous country landscape. There were about 10 families living in huts under extreme poverty who had to pay the Pérez clan with their harvest of fruits, vegetables and hard labor plowing the land.

Juana Ramona de la Asunción Pérez Fernández (15 Aug 1899 – 6 May 1952)

Mi querida Madrina (my dear Godmother), oldest sibling of my *Papi*, whom I nicknamed *Ñaña*, and spoiled me to the max with food and games. She came often to visit and took me to her home to be with her son, **Tomás Orosa Pérez**, who was also my *Padrino Tomasito* (Godfather). There I enjoyed happy times with cousins Serafín and Belarmina, and with their mother named Caridad. Ñaña was the closest person to me during my toddler years and early childhood. Her health deteriorated so much that she did not recognize those around her during the last stages of life. Her death had a tremendous impact on me, especially since I was assigned to go to the homes of friends and relatives to announce her departure.

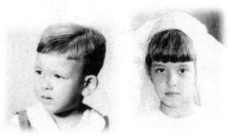

**The cutest 2nd Cousins
Serafín and Belarmina Orosa**

Up to about 1953, our house was one of the smallest on the block, but often the *familia* was the largest, consisting of many relatives of Mamá-Ramona (Grandma on my father's side) and my loving Great Aunt *Tía* Ana. Santa Clara was a place that gave access to schools and work for people from the *finca* and nearby villages. Restaurants or hotels were never visited and in times of need neighbors and friends were ready to serve as babysitters or providers of food to eat. We relied on our nearby Chinese friends and bodega owners, Julio and Manuel, for grocery needs.

Paternal Guidance for *Papá Vive*

Gaspar Fernando del Carmen Pérez Fernández
(16 Jul 1904 – 1971)
My Dad's oldest brother, a stern, hard-working, and father figure for my *Papi*. Provided a job and home for my parents in the late 1930's, as they joined in marriage and began to build a new *familia*.

From my father's stories, I learned that his oldest brother, Gaspar, was like a paternal figure in his life and perhaps a most important guide during his youth for finding work in pharmacy medicine delivery, nursing, road building and finally becoming an outstanding auto mechanic. For me, he was not a loving uncle but certainly I admired him as a person who provided discipline in his job pursuits and dedication to the welfare of his family. *Tío* Gaspar married *Tía* Victoria, a woman from Galicia, Spain; and on various occasions he helped my father by providing opportunities for establishing a pharmacy that also served as the escape route for my mother Sara when she eloped in September 1939.

The Children of Tío Gaspar and Tía Victoria
My oldest male cousin **Tomás Pérez Marcos**
nicknamed *El Nene*, and my cousin **Ángela**
Victoria Pérez Marcos, nicknamed *La Cuqui*.
Pictures from the mid-1940s

42

My father was a pharmacy messenger and nurse practitioner able to give injections to anyone in need. Prior to marriage, my mother met my father at her home when her youngest brother, Benjamin, a toddler, was in need of medical treatments. My Dad would bring medications and provide the necessary injections for a healthy recovery. The Pérez-Fernández Pharmacy was lost before my birth but years later *Tío* Gaspar found the best paying job for my father in Venezuela, helping with the construction of the Caracas-to-La Guaira highway.

At times, the home served as an overnight visitor's place, a temporary home for family or friends from out of town. It was also a place to work for *criadas* (maids or servants), who sometimes were children or young people from the *finca* or poor marginal *barrios* (neighborhoods). In my own case, the house in Santa Clara was the place to be for access to schools, doctors, hospitals, and clinics for medical care. Sometimes we had between ten and twenty people in our home with a single outhouse, using newspaper cuttings as toilet paper, with a single water faucet that functioned for a short time once a day; but years later into my youth we had a cistern that allowed us to save water in small tanks for our daily needs. As we progressed to having a bathroom, we had to fill a *cubo* (bucket) with water and bring it back to flush the toilet. Under our beds, we had a *tibor* and a *palangana* - a chamber urinal pot and a washbowl for night or emergency use.

If a child were to get sick, the first treatment was the reading of prayers with ointments, followed by visits to a *espiritista* or *santero* (a spiritual praying healer or *Santería* priest sometimes associated with African religious cultures, or traditional healing customs common in Cuba like a *pasamanos* healer, i.e., a person notorious for giving hand massages around the abdomen while reciting prayers. If the illness were serious enough – surgeries and broken bones -- we would go to a public hospital, a clinic, or visit a family doctor. Good health facilities were in private hands unavailable to the vast majority of people. I never saw a doctor or a nurse in a rural area outside the city.

SARA LEVY, *Mi Mamá*

Sara Levy Rodríguez
(25 Sept 1918 – 5 Jan 2014)
Mi Mamita **and I as a 3-years old spoiled toddler in 1943, she was my inspiration for playing piano and finding pleasure in music appreciation.**

Mami Sara spent a great deal of time sewing, making the clothing – pants and shirts – I wore in Cuba; also playing piano, worrying about my dad's whereabouts, and hiding money to save the family from bankruptcy. At times she lived in homes in the outskirts of Santa Clara -- or in faraway areas of eastern Cuba. She was born in the village of Cascajal, part of Las Villas Province of Central Cuba. As a child she lived near Havana in Guanabacoa, later in Sagua La Grande on the north central coast, and finally in Santa Clara where she met the love of her life, my *Papá* Delvis Rafael Fernández, nicknamed *Vive*.

Her father, Salvador Levy, as a Sephardic Hebrew immigrant spoke Ladino, a Spanish dialect, and was able to communicate with *campesinos* (farmers) away from major urban areas. Unlike other immigrants from Europe, he quickly assimilated into Cuban culture, making a living as a door-to-door salesman of clothing materials. My grandmother, Felicia Rodríguez Marzall, has unidentified origin records. She had some Catalonian and Filipino ancestors, but the rest of her roots are unknown and can only be speculated. *Mamá-Vieja* (Old Mom) Felicia was born in San Juan y Martínez, a village of Pinar del Río Province, in the Cuban far west.

My mother has no memories of her birthplace, Cascajal, as the family moved soon after her birth. They lived in various towns during her childhood but finally moved to Santa Clara. She remembers that her father was away for long periods of time, in rural areas, as well as on trips to other countries, such as France, Costa Rica, and Venezuela. In 1922, her father Salvador with his brother Victor travelled to France. French culture was greatly admired and there were times when my mother remembers participating in the *ALLIANCE FRANÇAISE*, an association with deep French roots.

Once, while her father was away on a merchant trip outside Cuba, the mayor's family lured little Sara away from her home for a Catholic baptism, which was followed years later by the instruction of catechism for a first communion. According to her, all this was without knowledge or approval of her parents, and certainly against their wishes. In those days, Cuban folklore dictated that for a child not to be baptized in the Catholic faith was a sure passage *al infierno* - to hell, so these well-meaning friends felt compelled to step in on Sara's behalf.

Her greatest gift was the six-year birthday present, when she received a beautiful piano, hand carved in a baroque fashion. This was a rare piece for a Cuban home of that time and place, and a real expression of the love, encouragement, and hopes her father Salvador had for his little "Jewish princess." She was gifted as a piano student, achieving the honor of being able to play for a radio station as a young adult. After several years of marriage, she was finally able to have that piano in her home again and taught a few students. However, as badly as I wanted to take lessons, my dad, in his macho thinking, would not allow me to play, let alone take lessons. Instead, my sister, who hated having to practice, was the one to take lessons. So even though I was not allowed to touch the piano, the sounds of music, through the magic of my mother's fingers, have been a most valuable source for my music appreciation and for my ultimate quest – striving to learn the classics of Bach and Chopin, and of course, delighting in the joy of the Cuban composers, such as, Ignacio Cervantes, Ernesto Lecuona, and others.

As a child, my mother Sara only went as far as sixth grade, mainly because of the difficulty she had doing schoolwork with poor vision. She had always been affected by visual impairments, and in her youth, as a flirtatious beauty, she refused to wear prescription lenses. She used to tell stories about the first time she met my dad. He thought she was so flirtatious at their first dance, because she looked at him with dreamy eyes, he felt they had "fallen in love at first sight." She claimed that, *"No lo miraba con ojos entrecerrados de ensueño."* - "I was not looking at him with enchanted sleepy eyes - but simply squinting my eyes in order to see better."

Despite the lack of a formal education, she learned to play classical piano pieces, and later made my shirts and pants, learned to cook, helped with all the finances, thus saving my dad from near bankruptcy, and ran a home the best she could. To help escape her harsh reality, she listened to the radio *novelas,* (soap opera dramas) kept abreast of current news and was an avid reader of romantic tales.

But those "homemaking" skills did not come easily, as she was raised as a Jewish princess, even playing the role of Queen Esther at a Jewish Purim festival. She had her own maid dedicated to her whimsical desires, and as a young woman, her father and uncles were in search of a wealthy Jewish Frenchman for marriage. She had no training and no preparation for the daily chores that a typical woman of the period would need for marriage. Yet, shortly after meeting my father, they eloped on September 18, of 1939, and she went to live in a tiny single room at the back of the pharmacy where he worked. Much later they moved into the home where several of his family members lived. My father was the result of a tryst my *abuela* Ramona had with a man named Plácido Moreira, shortly after the accidental death of her distinguished landowner husband, Don Tomás Pérez. They toyed with the idea of naming their child, *Desdichado,* (the unfortunate one), but lucky for me, they chose instead the name Parviz from the tale "A Thousand and One Nights." The name was later incorrectly recorded on his birth certificate as Delvis. He had no formal education but was a hardworking man; first as a messenger for a pharmacy which led to becoming a nurse practitioner, then working on road construction, and finally an auto mechanic and garage owner, who could give new life to old clunkers that were ready to be trashed. In spite of a life of alcoholism, he always performed his work duties well, and only caused havoc and pain after hours, which was allowed, in those early years, by caring female family members as well as by my enabling mother during his entire life.

From a well to do and cared for maiden princess, Sara, after her wedding had to transition into a life of poverty. She had moved into a home without her piano, where books were rare, which had no bathrooms or running water. Instead, she was exposed to saints and prayers and candles, a home under the matriarchal care of Évora Pérez, her husband's unmarried half-sister. My aunt Evora, whom I nicknamed *Chicha*, was a wonderful caretaker of all the family children for many years. She cared for the country cousins, so they could attend school, she nurtured myself and later my two sisters and all their children. During my youth, we often had anywhere between ten and twenty people residing in our three-bedroom Santa Clara home, which had just one water faucet, only an outhouse, complete with the newspapers to be used as toilet paper. Sara was now reduced to living under primitive conditions under the female shadows of a domineering sister-in-law. At various times she tried to set up a home with her husband for their children in various parts of Cuba, but my father's severe problems with alcoholism and

OBITUARY The San Luis Obispo Tribune

Sara Levy Rodríguez, 95 a native of Cuba, died peacefully Sunday, Jan 5, 2014, at Bella Vista Transitional Care Center in San Luis Obispo.

She was the first daughter of Salvador Levy Levy and Felicia Rodríguez Marzall.

Her paternal family had a strong Hebrew background as descendants of a Levy clan of Jews expelled from Spain at the time of Columbus and later fleeing Turkey and Greece near the end of the Ottoman Empire in 1912.

Her mother, Felicia and grandfather, Salomon, nurtured Sara in their family religious and cultural traditions.

Sara came to the United States in 1958 from Santa Clara, Cuba. She was talented as a pianist, seamstress and financial adviser to her husband, Delvis Rafael Fernández.

She moved to California upon Delvis' death in 1988 to live with her son, Delvis Alejandro and his wife, Norine Fernández.

Sara is survived by her son; daughter, Guiselda of Cuba; and eight grandchildren; and seven great-grandchildren.

chronic illnesses made that dream impossible. Her family had rejected her due to her choice, and after eloping with Delvis, she was destined to live in his world, where she was also rejected by the domineering women of his family. She could do nothing but endure. With the little time she had to herself, when not consumed with her husband's problems, she retreated into her own world of music, sewing, and the love-life dramatized through her radio *novelas*.

Delvis Rafael (Moreira) Fernández
(5 March 1915 – 13 May 1988)
Mi Papi, nicknamed *Vive* - survived a life of challenges as a nurse practitioner, road builder, auto mechanic, *Bolita Lotería* handler (undercover lottery), and business owner. He had to cope with severe health problems, alcohol addiction and living within a large family without paternal recognition.

• *Papá Vive,* worked in faraway areas from Santa Clara in various parts of Cuba during my childhood, employed by the Cuban Office of Public Roads *(Ministerio de Obras Públicas).* He was always on the move. Then around 1950, for a year he and his brother and paternal mentor Gaspar lived and worked in Venezuela helping to build a highway between the capital city of Caracas and the coastal town of La Guaira in South America. Finally, around 1952 he was able to settle in Santa Clara, running *El Relámpago,* a garage he partially owned and where he worked on servicing and repairing old cars plus selling oil and gasoline.

During my childhood I was quite disturbed by my Papá's behavior -- a hardworking man but often coming home inebriated. My appreciation of his family care came later in life when I was close to finishing my degree at the only public secondary school, beyond high school, in Santa Clara that would permit me to enter a university.

A young worker, with my *Papi* near him, dispatching Sinclair gasoline at *El Relámpago* Garage (c.1955)

It was through our family history and awareness of his sacrifices to provide me with access to doctors, schools, and tutors that I was able to transition into the first *Bachiller* in the family, during times of war, immersed in curfews, strikes, knowledge of tortures and killings among friends and acquaintances. *Papi Vive* lives with me, as a beacon of strength, but indirectly teaching me how to overcome times of war, despair, and painful family separation.

MY SISTERS

Gilda Sara Fernández Levy
1 Sept 1944 - 21 March 1994

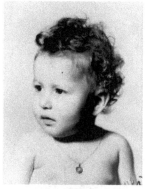

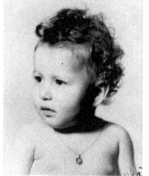

Sarita, as I called her, was the family pride and perhaps the most talented and smartest member of our family. She appeared as a healthy person but died at age 49 as a result of a brain aneurysm. Here she is shown in 1945 at her first birthday and later in her 4th grade at an elementary public school in Santa Clara where she was declared as the first of her class with the honor *El Beso de la Patria* - The Kiss of the Homeland.

For a while I was given the responsibility of making sure that Sarita attended her piano lessons. Although she was not interested, I managed to listen to her teacher, Rita Chapú, and as a result developed a great interest in music and piano playing. Sarita showed strength and independence from an early age. Came to the U.S. during the first year of the Cuban Revolution in 1959 but soon returned to her homeland and became the first woman Mechanical Engineer in Cuba.

Top to Bottom Left
1945 - Baby Sarita as a one-year-old.
1949 - Siblings Pupy and Sarita.
1953 – Top student in grade school.

1957 –Sarita

1960+ - Involvement in literacy campaign and university graduate.

Guiselda Fernández Levy or "Puchita"
Born June 13, 1953

My youngest sister Guiselda, whom I nicknamed Puchy, was born in 1953, at a time when the house went through a major remodeling with the addition of a second-floor apartment, after my father returned from Venezuela. Money hidden and saved by my dear *mamita* Sara made the improvements possible. With the birth of Puchy – Little Guiselda – my parents were finally able to establish a home in Santa Clara.

Brother and sister: **Pupy** with **Puchy** before my lonely departure from Cuba in 1957 at El Relámpago – "The Lightning Flash Garage" -- where our Papá fixed old clunkers. It was a common practice to give nicknames to everyone in the family, even with words that today may be considered offensive. I dropped my Pupy nickname once I left Cuba, since in English it sounds like "POOPY;" a word considered insulting since it is similar to "shitty" or *mierdita* in Spanish.

Puchy brought hope to the family at a time when we finally had a home near grandparents, aunts, uncles, and cousins, with *Papá* in his successful garage job. But soon the world around us became chaotic with bombs going off at night, life threats, school closures, and awareness of killings and tortures of friends. Twenty-two years went by before I could see my beloved family and sisters.

Here is a picture of my sisters Sarita and Puchy near the time of departure from my *Querida Tierra* – Dear Land of Cuba and adored hometown of Santa Clara in 1957.

4

MY HOMETOWN – *Mi Ciudad Natal*

EL VECINDARIO – The Neighborhood

San Miguel and Maceo Streets, showing the *bodega* (grocery store), of *el Chino Manuel* (painted yellow) and the bar-*bodega* of *El Chino Julio*. A view taken from my home in Santa Clara

Santa Clara, my native town was a refuge, filled with friendly neighbors and most of my extended *familia* -- grandparents, aunts, uncles, and cousins who showered me with love, warmth, and attention. The city was often referred to as *La Aldea,* the village, by friends – not because it was a village but due to the fact that we lived within the confines of our neighborhoods, schools, parks, and social clubs and avoided or dismissed those living under extreme poverty in the surrounding *barrios marginados*.

The homes in town were placed adjacent to each other, separated by a wall and a narrow open patio next to a line of bedrooms that permitted conversations between neighbors at any time of day. On our block or nearby, there were families of Lebanese, Irish, Syrian, Turkish, Slavic, Jewish, Chinese, and Spanish ancestry. The majority of our neighbors were *cubanos blancos* -- Cubans referred to as whites, like my own family but without full knowledge of their racial-ethnic origins. Only one family on the block was referred to as *mulatos claros* (light skin within a mixture

50

of African and Spanish roots). Segregation in Cuba was not enforced by laws, as witnessed in the United States, but the divide between *blancos y negros* (whites and blacks) added to a multicast system based on money and family backgrounds that was evident all over town – through schools, private clubs, street beggars, and multiracial slums affected by extreme poverty. In our block several residents had a high level of education, there were at least four physicians with different specialties – Medical Doctors Pino, Fleites, Urbano and Artiles – as well as schoolteachers, skilled workers, and small shop owners. Most families on the block had servants, some of which lived in the house, and did daily shopping, house cleaning, laundry, cooking, and childcare.

On the corners near our house, there were two *bodegas,* small grocery stores, run by friendly immigrants from China: *El Chino Julio* and *El Chino Manuel* -- single men living under tight quarters with relatives or friends who were also Chinese immigrants. The *bodegas* had a single counter, and Julio's place even had a bar section where men would gather at times to drink and socialize. Since our house did not have coolers or refrigerators, we had to purchase food quite frequently, so the store owners and workers interacted with me on a daily basis, more like friends and extended members of our clan. They provided us with credit and *contras*, small gifts added to whatever we bought -- so paying with cash or credit, I always received a free *caramelo prieto,* a dark super sweet sugar candy. At a third corner, a *guajiro,* Cuban farmer, ran a vegetable stand where he sold our basic food staples of *yucas* (cassava roots), *malangas* (similar to taro roots), *plátanos* (plantains from green to almost rotten black), *platanitos manzanos* (small, sweet bananas), and tomatoes varying from green to bright red. Also, in an adjacent one-room building there was a *casilla*, a small counter with live chickens or *guanajos* (Cuban turkeys) on the floor, recently slaughtered pigs, goats, or chunks of fresh cattle meat -- with their inner parts, intestines, hearts, etc. hanging on hooks surrounded by swarming flies.

Three or four doors from my house there was the *Tintoreria* Paramount - a drycleaner - whose owners had three boys close to me in age that I considered playful friends, throughout my preteen years. Next door to us lived a Lebanese descendant family, *Las Sesín* – young Macucha with mother Rosita, Aunt Julia and family head María - that at times took care of me and my sister Sarita. The word babysitter was not in our vocabulary – they were trusted neighbors who watched over me, my sisters, and cousins free of charge whenever needed.

The opposite corner had a small one-room shoe repair shop and a *paradito* bar -- a bar without sitting stools where men also stood joking and telling tales while drinking beer, rum and *aguardiente* – a strong alcoholic drink made from fermented sugar cane - sometimes leaving the joint extremely drunk, swaying from side to side and even falling on the sidewalk. Around the corner there was a small one-counter drug store named O'Farrill, where I would be greeted by shouts "*ahí viene el morito,"* – there comes the Little Moor - followed with hugs as if I were part of the family. Also, nearby, we had the *heladería*, an ice-cream counter where on special occasions I would get my favorite, *coco glacé* – a delicious pure coconut ice-cream served in a coconut shell. In later years, the owner, a Cuban who had lived in the U.S., became my "phony English" teacher at the *Instituto* –High School - during turbulent times of strikes and school closures. I recall meeting only once, a day before the final exam, with pictures on the blackboard of geometric figures identified in English. Around the far corner there was a *quincalla* or small store that sold basic school needs and magazines. Further down on the same block there was a corner bar, where I went at age ten, when I was very upset and tried to run away from home. On the block behind our house there was a *dulceria* that sold delightful pastries like *señoritas*, and *pastelitos de coco, guayaba, y queso* – Cuban pastries resembling turnovers filled with coconut, sugary sweet guava and cream cheese or ground meat. Farther down our street we had the *panadería* where we bought our daily Cuban bread. Our meal servings always came with fresh baguette bread, often with black beans, and white rice *suelto* – preferably loose and not sticky rice.

MEAL CUSTOMS

Our meal customs were partly received from Spanish colonial days with native Cuban and African influence, later modified by large imports of American products. Rice had to be served for lunch and dinner, and the favorite was Arroz Tío Ben (Uncle Ben Rice). Despite the fact that we lived on an island not far from warm ocean waters, we seldom ate fish except for lobster and crabs brought by family from the coastal town of Caibarién; but if fish was served, it would have to be in the form of *Frituras de Bacalao*, Cod Fish Fritters, or *Bacalao a la Viscaína* , Spanish/Basque style Cod Stew -- a rather exotic fish for Cubans since it had to be imported from Canada or waters near Portugal. A favorite type of meat was *tasajo,* if possible, from Uruguay – similar to beef jerky that I stopped eating when I found out that it came from slaughtered horses. For *Nochebuena,* Christmas Eve celebration, we had

the traditional roasted pig (which in *Papá Viejo's* home was substituted with Lamb) with black beans, rice and *tachinos* – smashed fried green plantains – also, called *tostones* in other parts of Cuba. We had to eat fruits and sweets like *higos, dátiles, uvas y turrones* (figs, dates, grapes, and nougat/almond sweets) – all of which had to be imported from Spain.

Street vendors would sell us pears and apples from Washington State, which were considered healthier than our own fresh juicy mangoes and guavas. If ham was to be served, it had to be from Virginia and our favorite yellow cheese was Gouda cheese coming all the way from Holland to mix with our delicious *pasta de guayaba* - guava paste. We almost never bought butter, but if we could, it would have to be some exotic European brand. Olive oil, despite the fact that olives were not grown in the *finca*, was used for special meals as substitutes for pig's lard. Potatoes were not used much, except mashed into a puree with warm milk as medicine for a sick child. *Sambumbia con Leche y con mucha azúcar prieta* - a watery mild coffee with hot milk and lots of unrefined sugar – along with a big chunk of bread was our daily breakfast meal. Lunch and dinner were never completed without *arroz y frijoles* - rice and beans. In the farm the meals were quite different, meat was rare and *harina de maíz* - corn meal - with yucca or *malanga* (taro root) was our daily intake with whatever fruit was ready to eat - guavas, bananas, mangos, tamarinds, guanabanas, and many more.

There was a tradition and culture of discipline when we sat at the table. It was considered rude to start eating without everyone sitting at the table, only one person served the meals, and as we finished eating, it was proper to leave a little food on the plates. The leftovers were turned into *sancocho,* a stew like mixture saved for daily visits by street beggars that included a homeless woman visitor nicknamed **Motoneta** and a friendly donkey we referred to as ***El Burro Perico***. Dogs, cats, chickens, pigs, and any other pet would be fed from the left over *sancocho.* As *cubanos* we were not satisfied with only products from the Island but yearned for connection in a grand style to the wide world around us – sometimes going as far as calling our country: *El Ombligo del Mundo*, The Belly Button of the World. We bragged about our Cuba as *Una Tacita de Oro* - a Little Golden Cup.

***El Burro Perico,* The Super Friendly Donkey, came to our home for daily petting and leftovers from our dinner meals.**

Clínicas y Hospitales - **Medical Care**

Although my *Papi* and *Mami* had nothing to do with the Cuban Army, my mother had to assume her sister Siomara's identity, who was married to a military officer, Ibrahim Monteagudo, in order to give birth to me at the army hospital. Perhaps there are still notes in the hospital giving me the surname Monteagudo instead of Fernández. Four years later she gave birth to my sister Sarita at home with assistance from a *comadrona* – a midwife that was hired for the exchange of favors. That was a memorable occasion since I was rudely awakened and taken out to a neighbor's house while *Mami* Sara shouted in pain of delivery. Luckily, hours later we were all delighted with the beautiful little cutie as an addition to family.

I was a rather sickly boy, suffering from intestinal and throat problems that forced me to miss school for days at a time on a monthly basis. At around age three I remember Doctor Celestino Hernández, a man that my family claims saved my life by extracting all the intestinal blockage stuck inside of me due to severe constipation. It seems like sickness was always around me so *Tía* Chicha would send me to a *pasamanos (*abdomen massager)*, a *curandera* (unschooled trained healer), an *espiritista* (spiritualist), a Catholic priest for confession, or as a last resource a family doctor friend. One time my throat pains were so dangerous that a doctor determined that I needed a tonsillectomy as soon as possible.

When I was in dire need of having a tonsillectomy, I recall running all over town searching for a place to have surgery. My parents lacked money and social status, which made it necessary for *la familia* to get a *palanca* – help from a friend with power - to get me to a good clinic or hospital. Since we had some Spanish ancestry in the family, they tried to get me to *La Clínica de la Colonia Española –* The Clinic for the Spanish Colony - but I was rejected because they could not prove that I was of pure Spanish descent. They could not finagle any deal through favors and family influence with any medical facility, so I ended up in the public *Hospital San Juan de Dios*. That is when I faced one the worse experiences of my childhood, being anesthetized with a cup over my nose, placed in a room filled with screaming children under emergency situations: a hydrocephalic child with a very enlarged head, one suffering from severe burns looking like a mommy entwined with gauze, and at least ten others crying and suffering in pain. That was the closest I have ever been to hell!

ANOTHER SIDE OF SANTA CLARA

Behind the beautiful façade of parks and churches we lived under a system based on race, ethnicity, and social class. Unlike most U.S. towns where the "upper classes" live outside city limits, the opposite was true in Santa Clara. The city was surrounded by poor neighborhoods with shacks and unpaved streets where one encountered bare feet children with potbellied stomachs, living under extreme poverty. *Mi abuela Mamá-Ramona* had several godchildren in those areas, so I became aware and was able to experience and witness their lifestyle, although at the time I was scared to venture into their neighborhoods on my own.

During my preteen years I enjoyed playing all kinds of games with friends. But I particularly remember playing *bolitas* (marbles) for pennies, or kite-fighting -- flying kites with razor blades on their tails to cut the strings of a nearby rival kite fighter. Most friends played outside their homes and were watched by parents and neighbors as part of a grand family. However, there were kids of high privilege who were not allowed to go to the streets without an adult supervisor. My dear friend Juan Vicente was one of those whom I frequently visited. He was raised without rhythmic Cuban music, with pictures of British royalty in his bedroom, and a personal maid and a chauffeur who drove him from a private school to a social club, both for whites only. Although we lived on the same block, he never came to my house, but instead, his nanny would come to fetch me at his beckoning call whenever he wanted to play. No matter how I felt, whenever Juan Vicente's nanny came, I had no choice but to walk with her, holding hands, to his house. He had the latest toys and games of those times – unavailable to most Cuban kids. So, there was excitement as well as bad feelings due to his abrasive behavior as a member of a higher class, shown by his commands to me and his maid. Whenever he got mad or tired of playing, he would say *"vete ya,"* - Go home! – so the maid would take me home right away. That attitude was not considered rude but seemed acceptable by my dad's family, in our home after all I was privileged, as a poor child, to be in a higher-class rich boy's domain. In hindsight I realized the same behavior was repeated in Chicha's home towards *campesino* children from the *finca* that sometimes came to work as servants.

It was not uncommon to see dark-skin boys in town as beggars, *vendedores ambulantes* (street vendors), *limpiabotas* (shoeshining boys), *billeteros* (lottery ticket sellers), conducting menial or non-paying jobs for food and shelter, instead of attending school.

Santa Clara was clearly divided by race, social class, and gender – not through city laws but by remnants of slavery and Spanish colonialism. Black and White formal marriages were uncommon although statistics from Cuba and the U.S. differ with regards to what defines a person of African descent. During my childhood in public schools, it was obvious that Cuba was an *ajiaco* -- a melting pot of races and ethnicities -- most of the Cuban population was mestizo, but as I recall statements by family members, they saw themselves in a cocoon of *blancos solamente* (only whites) and ignored their probable African and native Cuban ancestry.

A light skin person with a black grandmother may be considered "white in Cuba" but "African-American in the U.S.," so the statistical data on that person varies according to where the research has been conducted. Even today a person of my mother's generation would look at a granddaughter and compliment her by saying "*¡Ay qué blanquita saliste!*" – "Wow, you came out so white!" -- or she would remark to someone married to a lighter skin person "*¡Oye, mejoraste la raza!*" – "Hey, you improved the race!" Although many people living under extreme poverty conditions had dark skin, abject poverty was not the exclusive domain of African descendants. Most children in the *Finca*, had an immigrant parent of Iberian origin – from various regions of Spain: Canary Islands, Asturias, Galicia, or Castille. Their families lived under extreme poverty, subjected to daily farm labor, without access to medical care and education beyond early grade school.

It was quite common to know people in our neighborhoods who had formal family relations with concubines or mistresses. Neighborhoods of prostitutes were unnoticed except when we would go out for a night walk through the city. The city was divided by the *Carretera Central,* our main road to Havana, and a small river, the *Río Bélico.* One could marvel at the new Cathedral of Santa Clara de Asís, while on a nearby riverbank-slope, there was the *Bayú Majana,* a building for prostitutes, with a flat roof and many front doors facing a bridge over the river. This was a place for the cheapest, *putas por menos-de-un-peso* – sex-workers for less than a dollar. On weekend evenings, my friends and I would watch from the bridge the lines of men forming by the front doors, following with careful eyes, and speculating about what had taken place during their short visits. Some faces reflected satisfaction while others showed disappointment, perhaps for the loss of a quarter that did not bring positive results. I was also aware of other zones for commercial prostitution, not far from churches, schools, and friends and family homes.

MY OTHER NEIGHBORHOODS
MIS OTROS BARRIOS

My main home was always on San Miguel Street, five blocks from the center of town near aunts, cousins, and grandparents. But at times my mother and father tried to unite our close *familia* in homes in the outskirts of Santa Clara.

Las Cuatro Milpas **-** These were four little homes abutting each other, miles away from town. Our dwelling place had two bedrooms – one for me and my sister Sarita, and the other for my parents. Outside the house there was and a single outhouse with a bench over a hole in the ground that served as a toilet that was shared by four families. There was no running water except for a single *pozo*, a water well, with a hand-pump and a little bucket for the entire group of residents. The name *Cuatro Milpas* comes from a popular Mexican song (translated as the "Four Cornfields") and was used as an identification of the houses along the *Carretera de Camajuaní* – the highway leading to the town of Camajuaní. Next to our home there was also a duplex referred to as *Dos Gardenias*, "Two Gardenias," the title of a Cuban bolero which also served to identify our neighborhood.

Reparto Santa Catalina **-** At last, when I was around 13 years old, my parents with my sisters Sarita and newly born *Puchita* (little Guiselda) moved to a home with a toilet and a water-pump. It was my first experience as a caring brother of my little baby sister. My mother had hidden money sent by my father when he was working in Venezuela, so they were able to partner with a friend to buy a Sinclair Service Station, they named *El Relámpago* **(The Lighting Thunder)**.

**El Relámpago
Garage on the
Camajuaní Road
next to our home
on G Street**

Mami Sara with her little daughter Puchy in front of
their home on G Street next to
Papá's garage in the
Barrio Santa Catalina. 1957

Papi serving gasoline at his
garage on the road to the
town of Camajuaní

El Relámpago. 1957

El Parque Leoncio Vidal

The central park in the city was a beautiful site bringing music and harmony between nature, and surrounding buildings. There I would walk by city offices, bars, *El Instituto* (my High School), Theater *La Caridad, El cine (movie house)* Villaclara, and the corner open cafeteria frequented by my *abuelo Papá Viejo*, plus *El Liceo -- Club the Leones* for white men of distinction who would sit on rocking chairs greeting passers-by. *El Parque Vidal* offered lessons in class and racist division faced on a daily basis by the people of Santa Clara.

Statue of revered Marta Abreu de Estévez at The Leoncio Vidal Park of Santa Clara. Behind the statue is the *Instituto de Segunda Enseñanza* - the secondary (pre-university) school I attended (1952-1957) during tumultuous times of bombs, strikes and killings.

The Park had two circular strolling areas for evening walks. One was for whites only – or those passing for white – around a central *Glorieta,* a rounded open structure with a high floor that served as a platform for musical concerts by the Municipal Band. Nearby was the statue of the venerable benefactress and matron of Santa Clara, Marta Abreu de Estévez. A boundary formed by plants and statues separated the strolling area for *personas de color* (people of color) away from the

59

central *Glorieta*. I recall fights in the park by white thugs who would kick and send a light skin person to the walkway for the *negros* (blacks) based on accusations that someone knew that *"su abuela era de color"* (his grandma was not white, i.e., he was blood related to a person of African descent). Persons accused of being blacks or mulattoes had to walk through a marginal path by the outer perimeter of the park; away from the rhythmic and joyful sounds of the Municipal Band coming from *La Glorieta* at the core center of the park.

Children selling lottery tickets and a shoeshine boy
"La "próspera" Cuba de 1959"
(Ramón Bernal Godoy. mentirasenlamira.wordpress.com)

In front of The *Parque Leoncio Vidal* of Santa Clara there was also a club for Blacks – *La Bella Unión* – not far from the aristocratic Club de Leones for whites. Night and day, we could see poor young children who scurried around the park and near the movie houses and social clubs, some without shoes, poorly dressed, begging for money or trying to clean your *zapatos* (shoes) for a few cents, as well as selling lottery tickets.

Racist rules were also witnessed along the coast by Caibarién, a city in Las Villas Province, north of Santa Clara. The best "public" beaches were for whites only, and beyond the sand, areas into the sea were also divided by ropes to separate whites from blacks or mulattoes.

THE SCHOOLS - *Las Escuelas*

Private Catholic Schools in Santa Clara

COLEGIO TERESIANO DE SANTA CLARA

Las Teresianas was the school that secured success for white girls whose families were able to pay for tuition. One of the most offensive incidents to my mother Sara occurred when my sister Sarita was offered a scholarship for *Las Teresianas*. Sarita was the most distinguished scholastic achiever in our family – our pride and joy. She had received the *Beso de la Patria*, the highest public-school achievement diploma, on more than one occasion. She was so admired that our next-door neighbor managed to get her a scholarship for *Las Teresianas*, but there was a catch: she could attend classes but had to dress in a brown school uniform, different from the white color dresses worn by tuition paying students, and on top of that she was not allowed to play with other girls during recess. Some family members on my father's side were excited about the possibility of Sarita's enrollment in *Las Teresianas* and being able to get the "best education possible," but my *mami Sara* was highly offended, put her foot down, and refused to let her daughter to be exposed to such humiliation.

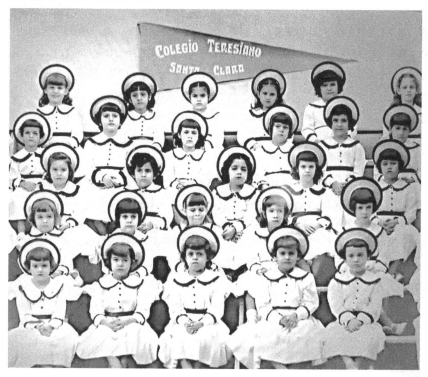

Colegio Teresiano de
Santa Clara
(During the 1950s)
A segregated school
for white girls only
all of them wearing a
white color uniform.

COLEGIO LOS MARISTAS

Los Maristas was a Catholic school for "white boys" from grade school through *Bachillerato* (High School plus one year). Two of my friends went to that school, while others were rejected for being "*de color*" (Black or Mulatto). The school was so successful, that graduating from there was a sign of acceptance to a college or university.

The "Maristas Brothers" trained students well for succeeding at final exams required in Cuba for moving towards graduation. Even in church there was a sitting arrangement that placed the Maristas students into a separate sitting zone. As a child, up to age of 12 years, I attended mass at the Buenviaje Church, across from the Maristas School every Sunday. There I remember being removed from a church pew for sitting next to my friends - standing in the back was my only option during mass.

A third school associated with the Catholic Church was **the Colegio de las Hermanas Oblatas**, exclusively for "*niñas de color*" – Afro-Cuban girls.

My parents were opposed to schools based on ethnic origins or racial segregation. They made sure that we attended integrated public or private schools such as the *Colegio Martí, Colegio Academia Alomá*, or the *Colegio Antolín González del Valle*.

Inspiration for School Achievements

In the lower left-hand corner, my mother Sara is seen at an integrated school during the 1920s in Sagua La Grande. She was ordered by the future town's mayor, *El Señor* Abelardo Martínez into a catholic baptism with the name "Sara María" followed by a communion ritual against the wishes of her parents while her father was in Europe.

As far as I know, art and music were not present for my family and friends during their school days. However, my mother was an exception, since she suffered from severe myopia, she remembered being placed at the back of the classroom. In those days physical impairments, were not properly addressed and students may have been falsely declared mentally deficient as well. As a result of her vision problems, she was unable to go beyond primary grade school. This deficiency turned out to be addressed by her family through the enrollment in music learning. Her grandfather Salomón gave her an old baroque piano, which allowed her to excel as a player, that inspired me in my love for the arts and classical music. In the early 1950s she was able to help our family with her talents as a creative seamstress and piano teacher for kids in the neighborhood and was even invited to play for the local radio station of Santa Clara. Two pieces she often played, etched in my mind, are *"El Currito de la Cruz"* and *"El Minuet de Paderewski."* She made all my pants and shirts plus secretly inspired me to study music.

Two of her sisters, my aunts *Tía* Alegrina and *Tía* Elvira, reached the highest level of education in the family by going to the *Escuela Normal de Maestros*, six years after grade school and graduated as schoolteachers. Hidden music learning was the only extracurricular activity I remember during my grade school days.

MY GRADE SCHOOLS DAYS

Throughout my toddler years up to grade school I was a nerdy brat – spoiled to the max as the only boy in a house surrounded by women: aunts, grandmother, a godmother and two older female cousins, all from my father's side.

I attended my first school for a few days while living in Holguín, where I was exposed to *Mami's* fighting to control *Papi's* drinking. I felt alone and dejected without the *familia* that had given me so much attention and catered to my whimsical desires. In school, I was so distracted that I paid no attention to the teacher or classroom surroundings, and instead I would daydream as I looked at the beautiful *Loma de la Cruz* – a high green mountain with the cross on top and steps for hiking to it. After only a few weeks, my parents decided that it was time to send me back to Santa Clara in Central Cuba to live under the care of Chicha, *Tía* Ana, *Mamá-* Ramona and my cousins, Ileana and Inaita.

I was a spoiled little boy under the doting care of five adoring women. I never had to do any household chores, and I learned to get my way through kisses, hugs, and bratty behavior. Living under poverty but exerting dominance like a royal prince, I had my own plate, my own glass and by own silverware along with a special seat at the dining table. There was always someone to clean any mess I made, to give me showers, and even to help with difficulties going to the bathroom. Pupy was my nickname, which I liked in Cuba but hated once I came to the U.S. because in English it sounded like "poopy." Strangely enough the English pronunciation would have been more fitting as it described my childhood dilemmas, suffering from severe intestinal problems that often made me come home with real "poop" in my pants.

Most kids in my preschool kindergarten days were white from middle to upper middle-class families. The race and gender based private schools for children in my neighborhood went from first grade, past junior high (*Primaria Superior*), and ended with the five years of *bachillerato* (one extra year after High School). So, in kindergarten, the first friendships I developed were with neighborhood kids who later went to exclusive private schools. When I started kindergarten, I felt so insecure that my cousin, Ileana, (four years older) had to take me to school, stay with me throughout the entire class session, then bring me back home. At times she tried to leave, hoping I would walk on to school on my own, but I always got my way by having a terrible tantrum, as I would fall to the ground, screaming and kicking my feet on the sidewalk while people stopped in awe to watch the spectacle of such a crazy kid. I survived kindergarten and finally moved to my first grade at a public school some distance from our home. It was not far from a racially diverse poor area of town, which was a neighborhood that had homes for prostitutes. This was my first encounter with bullies from that part of town, where children were tough and ready to start a fight with any classmate that crossed their way. Through real life experiences and the school of hard knocks, I quickly learned the early lessons of diplomacy by only fighting kids wimpier than myself, avoiding street fights altogether, and in times of utter despair, I would run to the teacher or school principal for protection.

Escuela La Casa Grande (1946-1947) -Pupy In First Grade as 6-year-old

Second grade was more of the same but then by third grade, through *palancas* (family friends with pull), I was moved to a public school closer to a middle-class neighborhood near the *Audiencia* or Santa Clara Court house. But due to problems in city government, within a month or two, the school closed and the *familia* had to appeal to their *palancas* once again which resulted in a move to the best public school in town – *La Escuela Anexa a la Normal de Maestros*. This was a grade school annexed to a teacher's training institution where adult students were given opportunities to practice their teaching skills in various subjects from science to sports and even with artistic projects. Unlike in the U.S., a teaching diploma could be obtained after the four-year past *Primaria Superior,* Junior High. The students in the *Escuela Normal de Maestros*, aspiring to become teachers, had challenging and motivational presentations for the kids that went beyond the general grade school curriculum. Simply getting a teacher's diploma from the *Normal de Maestros* did not secure a teaching job. In order to get a salaried teaching job, after obtaining the diploma, the prospective teacher had to get on an *escalafón*, a priority spot on the list through exam results, but also, many times due to family *palancas* (favors).

Even as a child, based on my own experience living on the farm, I realized that the school system was quite corrupt. At the country school for *campesino* children, which was for first through sixth grade, in a one room, thatched hut, the assigned teacher from town was frequently absent, yet collected a monthly salary from her placement in the *escalafón*. It was my *Tía* Llalla, without a teaching credential and only a partial grade school education, that worked as a "substitute" teacher for all six grades, almost all the time, and for only a fraction of the assigned teacher's pay. Many of the *campesino* children had to walk exceedingly long distance through open fields to get to that school. There were arroyos which they crossed by jumping from rock to rock and even without rain a child would often arrive soaking wet from the rain or falling into the river. All the students would have to dry out after the frequent heavy tropical rains, when the rushing waters had to be carefully crossed on a slippery bridge, made temporarily from a single royal palm trunk.

A most memorable person from the **Escuela Normal de Maestros** was my fifth-grade teacher. Etched in my mind are geography lessons, access to arts, and crafts projects by a strict disciplinarian who demanded full attention in class, gave quizzes and assignments that had to be turned in on time. He was quite inspirational in his classroom presentations where I probably learned more about geography than I ever have, able to identify on maps all the countries and major rivers of the world.

It was during these times that I first considered the possibility of going to the *Instituto de Bachillerato* - a Cuban High School with an extra year for entering a university. I could then pursue a professional career in medicine or engineering with my 'dream' of earning five hundred dollars a month and living in a comfortable home by a *playa* (beach).

This fifth-grade teacher, whose name, I cannot recall, encouraged me to transfer to a private school for sixth grade to ensure access to higher learning, so my father managed to make a deal with the owner of the *Colegio Academia Alomá*. He exchanged servicing the owner's car for my attendance at that school for sixth grade. I was the first member of my family to attend a private school for that one year, not because we could afford it, but because my *Papá* was such a clever negotiator.

The *Colegio Alomá* was an unusual school for Santa Clara in the 1950s. It was integrated, with the students, boys and girls, coming from both middle class and poor families. The owner and principal *El Señor* Alomá, was the first *negro cubano* I had ever seen in such a position, both an educator and school administrator. I remember him well, as not only my teacher, but also a mentor during a critical time of my life. He gave me a much wider view and a new perspective on the Cuban Nation. He opened my eyes to the neighborhood in which I was raised and made me realize how diverse, both good and bad, life was in Cuba in those days. I had always thought we lived in a fairly 'middle class' area, and although our home was probably the poorest of all, I did not think of us as being poor. We had neither bathrooms nor running water, yet there were always people, poorer than us, that served as our maids. We had a woman to clean, a woman to do the laundry, someone to do the shopping and occasionally the cooking, or whatever else was needed. As a child it seemed to me that no one worked to bring in any money, it just seemed to come from other family members or in the form of food from the farm. Businesses were mixed in our neighborhood within the residential homes, and I had upper class friends that lived in my same block. There were sons and daughters of white professionals, a Lebanese/Syrian Club on the corner, and even the mayor's son lived a few doors away. My Cuba was not black or white, or even mulatto; it was a melting pot of humanity, with a unique culture which was just plain *Cubanos* - outside racial, ethnic, or class identification.

On Fridays, the students in my sixth-grade school were encouraged to participate by sharing and showing off their talents. So, for the first time in my life, I was able to express my passion for music by coming out of my shell to sing while dancing and swaying to the rhythmic beat of *Siguaraya:*

En mi cuba nace una mata	In my Cuba grows a plant,
Que sin permiso	without permission
no se pue tumbar	you may not cut it down.
no se pué tumba-e-e-e,	You may not cut it down,
porque son Orichas.	because it is an Oricha.
Esa mata nace en el monte	That plant grows in the forest,
esa mata tiene poder	that plant has power.
¡Esa mata e-e-e-es Siguaraya!	That plant is Siguaraya!

Señor Alomá, with actions more than words, exemplified for me a successful achiever in education who expanded hopes for realizing my dreams. As a mentor he was the first person to encourage me to bypass the *Primaria Superior* (Junior High) and take the national exams required to enter the *Instituto de Bachillerato* (High School with an extra preuniversity year). Such a lofty idea, but how was I to prepare for such a major undertaking?

A member of my *familia*, Guiselda Fernández, a cousin, also raised by a single mother like my dad, was the first in the family to finish secondary school to become a teacher. Because of the lack of *palanca* -- family pull and influence -- she was unable to get a job in town. Guiselda was a charitable soul, a *beata – a* deeply religious Catholic person who attended church early every morning -- and then walked to a bus station to get a ride to her job at a school in the Santo Domingo village far from Santa Clara. She would return home in the afternoon where I would be waiting for her guidance and care to prepare me for the necessary exams to enter the *Instituto* (High School). She was always helpful as a guide, doing math word problems and studying herself to keep one step ahead of what was needed for me to pass the entry exams. She was also always involved in teaching other family members who needed help and guidance in school. Although she did not have children of her own, she and her husband Raúl, were surrogate parents to my sister Sarita and later became the namesake for my younger sister. They also raised as their own daughters, two nieces, Gladys and Elbita, who had been affected by death and divorce.

5

MY TEEN YEARS
Pupy El Adolescente

In Santa Clara, there were many secondary school students still attending and taking classes well into their late teens and even into their twenties, due to the strict adherence to the rules of "graduation." My "high school," *El Institutos de Segunda Enseñanza,* was located across the street from the central plaza known as *El Parque Vidal.* All around the park plaza, near the school, there were cafes, several bars, the main movie theater, *El Teatro de La Caridad*, the library, and various clubs. So, in addition to being a place of learning, for some, *El Instituto* was a grand social gathering place to "chill out" and pass the time with friends and sweethearts at the nearby hangouts. Cuban high schools, or secondary school -- both public and private – had a strict class curriculum. The system in those days was somewhat complicated and offered students different possibilities, although all had to adhere to the exact requirements for completion, which were determined by a national board in Havana. Some students entered schools that were designed for specific career paths that usually took three or four years to complete. For example: (1) The *Escuela Normal de Maestros*, had a four-year program (after Junior High) to become a grade school

teacher; (2) *Escuela de Kindergarten*, required a minimum of three years for becoming a kindergarten teacher; (3) *La Escuela de Comercio*, was similar to a High School but with emphasis on courses for business or accounting; and (4) *El Instituto de Bachillerato*, is referred to as a Pre-University school, a five-year school with a specific set of courses and a curriculum for entering a university. Based on my school experience, only a minority of students entering the *Instituto* managed to complete the *Bachillerato* and were required to pass every single course

Guiselda, my tutor and cousin with her husband, Raúl.

69

before being allowed to receive a *"Título de Bachiller,"* or "certificate of completion" needed for enrollment at one of the two universities far from Santa Clara: The University of Havana or the University in Santiago. For most of the students who managed to acquire a graduation diploma, it took more than five years after *Primaria Superior* (Junior High) to receive the diploma for pursuing a career in just about any field of their choice. This is the path that I followed when I entered *El Bachillerato* at the tender age of twelve in hopes that a university would be open for expanding my education. The summer after primary school was intensely concentrated on studying alone in the back or our home on San Miguel Street. Then later in the afternoon, with the help of my dear cousin, Guiselda, who was an amazing teacher and family guide, I managed to pass the required *bachillerato* (high school plus) entrance exam and qualify near my 12th birthday, completely skipping the *Escuela Primaria Superior* - Junior High School.

My first year were filled with ups and downs, as a preadolescent surrounded by older students, some in their late teens and early twenties. I began classes dressed in my geeky *pantalones bombachos* - knickerbocker pants - and shirts made by my mother with remnants of clothing materials from family and friends. Before the first day of classes, a clique of older students approached me with shouts and scissors, threatening and harassing, calling me all sorts of names. Finally, their pranks ended by giving me a terrible uneven haircut that almost left me bald. I was frightened and in a near panic those first few days, but I soon discovered they meant no real harm and were just following the rituals to be performed on all newcomers to the *Instituto*. Once that had happened there was no further social interaction in high school. There were no clubs, no dances, no outside activities, nor any sport activities associated with my secondary school years. My school was just a place where, on rare occasions, a class was held but more frequently, where students met with teachers for the final exams in hopes of moving on to the next grade. The outcomes of exams, if you passed or failed, were displayed on boards by the school's main entrance -- for everyone to see.

The social involvements with older students came about during the days of revolutionary upheavals, joining in strikes and demonstrations on parades to the central park and by government buildings. These demonstrations taught me firsthand the difficult times experienced in my Cuba with tortures and killings of fellow citizens, as well as the wide support for major changes in government.

During my second year, mental changes came far ahead of puberty, as I enjoyed learning algebra and geometry and became an avid reader of history books at the Santa Clara central library by the *Parque Vidal*. At home I spent hours and hours reading the ten volumes of the UTEHA encyclopedia, given to me by my grandfather *Papá Viejo*.

Inside the Classrooms

The ongoing chaos and social dysfunction outside of school resulted in the same disorder within the classrooms. There were no homework assignments, no quizzes, no course advisors, or any extracurricular activities, and the only exams available to students were the final exams. Some teachers were truly dedicated, but they were faced with great difficulties as they tried to meet course curricula and prepare the students for their final class exams. The curriculum was well delineated, and finals were monitored and standardized by an education department in Havana. This gave rise to cheating in private schools, where students had a chance to practice and train for the exams prior to taking them, so their success rate came close to 100%. On the other hand, at the public high schools at the time of my graduation, we were faced with less than a 2% success rate. I recall many classes where practically every student flunked out.

Classroom pranks and jokes were quite common. I can still see my history teacher the day she broke down in tears in front of all the students and was forced to stop lecturing. She was terribly upset, not only with their mean nonsense, but with her own frustration and lack of control. It was never clear if they simply lacked interest in learning their day-to-day lessons, or perhaps, the fact that living with their own day to day problems was a real history lesson with an urgency that distracted from the history lessons in their books. A favorite prank would be to attach hair pins between cracks in the chairs, out of the teacher's sight, and secretly pluck the pin causing an annoying, vibrating sound during a history lecture. She was so upset, not only because of the high pitch sound, but mainly because she could not identify who was causing the disturbance in class. Cheating during exams was quite common. A favorite for the boys was to make *acordiones,* small pieces of paper strips folded in the form of tiny accordions, which they would hide between their fingers on which they had written possible answers to test questions. The girls often wrote answers on strips of paper they would roll up and attached under their skirts.

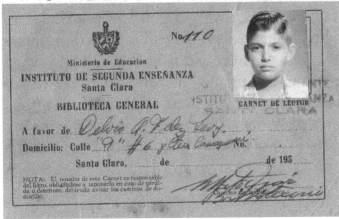

**ID card for
*Instituto de Segunda
Enseñanza, that gave me
access to the public library -
an oasis of peace for study
and meditation in 1952.***

Classroom Disruptions by Teachers

El Viejo Delvis sitting in front of his High School, *El Instituto de Segunda Enseñanza de Santa Clara*, over 60 years *later. c. 2019*

El Instituto de Bachillerato was at the center in the heart of Santa Clara, across from the *Parque Leoncio Vidal*. There was a counter drinking bar right next to the school, a movie theater, and two more bars on each corner. One day we were in class waiting and waiting for our math teacher to come, yet he never came. Some class members finally went out to look for him and there he was - sitting at the bar right next to the school - drinking in front of everyone. But to be fair, certainly not everything was that bad. Some teachers showed great patience and dedication in assisting and encouraging students to learn inside the classroom, as well as outside the classroom. That was the case with my math teacher *el Profesor Más Martín* (not the one found at the bar) whom I could stop anywhere in town to ask questions or engage in conversation regarding my course. He had a reputation for being one of the toughest teachers in town, a disciplinarian, and hard grader, but underneath that image he was a caring soul completely dedicated to the best teaching possible under dire circumstances.

DAYS OF POLITICS

High school students were often harassed by the local police – we were profiled as troublemakers for simply carrying books or walking in groups with other adolescents. I vividly recall three dreadful incidents. The first occurred when I was with a group of students that marched to the *Audiencia* (the Court House Building) calling for the release of students who had been arrested, an end to the killings, and a discontinuation of night curfews. No sooner were we near the building when guards on horseback appeared shooting wildly to disperse the crowd of demonstrators. I ran as fast as I could through a narrow street and was given refuge in a home of absolute strangers. Completely out of breath and trembling, to my disbelief, they pointed to the heel of one of my shoes, which had two large bullet holes.

The second encounter with police happened in *La Plaza* -- the big vegetable and meat market across from the post office near the city center. I was simply walking along with books under my arm when a market employee grabbed me and pushed be into a back room to hide me from the army guards in the area that were patrolling the streets with sticks and guns. Another scary time took place when I was taken into a police station near the Plaza del Carmen – where Santa Clara was founded back in 1689 by families from the town of Remedios fleeing attacks by pirates. The police placed me in a room and began to question me about (1) where was I going? and (2) why I was carrying books so early in the morning. It took me a while to convince them that I was simply going to study with a friend to prepare for a final exam. Lucky for me, the friend's home was within view of the police station, so I was able to point out the address and at last allowed to go. In other words, we were living at a time when the simple act of being a student made you a suspect for being a rebel fighting against the Batista government. Almost daily, students were striking and demonstrating against real oppression attributed to the Batista dictatorship. News of killings and acts of torture were spread all over town.

Tyranny and Rebellion

Since the major invasion of Cuba by American forces back in 1898, and through my years in Cuba, the US presence was all around me: Businesses like Sears, "El Ten Cent" (Woolworth), Gas Stations, Nickle mines, Sugar Mills, and many more controlled the earnings and expenditures the *Cubanos* in the interior of the Island, outside the Capital City of Havana. However, since the 1920s Havana began to develop into Las Vegas of the Caribbean with casinos, night-clubs and bordellos that attracted Americans looking for sins and pleasures during The Times of Prohibition from 1920 to 1933. Control of much of Havana was now in the hands of notorious mafiosi like Meyer Lansky and Lucky Luciano

My awareness of family and friends seeking government changes took place around 1951 when I was only about ten-years old. I listened to radio speeches by Eduardo Chibás, a leader of the Partido *Ortodoxo* - attacking what was seen as a Cuban political system managed by corrupt politicians loyal only to money. His slogan was ¡*Vergüenza contra el Dinero!* - which may translate as "Shame on Money!" – as a way to stop the use of money to control political leaders. Chibás was so passionate in promoting his views that near the end of a speech he pronounced the following words: ¡*Pueblo de Cuba, levántate y anda! ¡Pueblo cubano, despierta! ¡Este es mi último aldabonazo!* **People of Cuba, rise up and move! People of Cuba - Wake up! This is my last knock-call!** Immediately after these words were heard on air, Eduardo Chibás fired a bullet to himself in an attempt to commit suicide - eleven days later he died. His dramatic departure along with his calls for change gave rise to a movement led mostly by young people that gave rise to a call for major changes in government.

Elections planned for June 1ˢᵗ, 1952, had three major parties in line: (1) *Auténtico* led by previous presidents Ramón Grau and Carlos Prío; (2) *Ortodoxo* inspired by Eduardo Chibás; and (3) *Acción Unitaria* led by military General Fulgencio Batista. But the elections never became reality since on March 10ᵗʰ, 1952, General Batista led a Coup-d'état and took power to avoid defeat in the programmed elections where he was the least favorite candidate. Within a few days, on March 27ᵗʰ the United States government recognized the dictatorship under Batista. Prior to the chaotic situation, my *Papá* showed interest in politics when he took me to a demonstration with a large crowd and an *Aplanadora* (Steamroller), moving around as a symbol for changes in government. There were signs of hope for progress through the *Partido Revolucionario Cubano (Auténtico),* which along with the *Ortodoxo*s were the two main parties before the Cuban Revolution.

Revolution in My Surroundings

During the first year of power grabbing by Batista in Havana, Fidel Castro was an unknown figure among my friends and acquaintances. According to historical data, when legislators failed to end Batista's dictatorship, Fidel Castro began to organize a rebel force for an attack on the Military Moncada Barracks of Santiago de Cuba on July 26, 1953. He led about 160 men, most of whom perished in the attack, but Castro survived the attack and was arrested, condemned to 15 years in prison. His passionate defense received wide publicity, and in 1955 Fidel and his brother Raúl received a political amnesty, fleeing to Mexico to continue their efforts to depose the government of Batista. There the rebels organized what came to be called The 26ᵗʰ of July Movement.

On December 2, 1956, a rebel force of 81 men landed on the southeastern coast of Cuba, which was part of the Oriente province, in a rather small yacht named Granma. All of the men were killed or captured except for Fidel Castro and his brother Raúl, Ernesto ("Che") Guevara, and nine more. The survivors fled into the mountainous area of the Sierra Maestra to wage a guerrilla war against the Batista army.

Calls for revolution spread from the Mountains of Oriente Province throughout my area of Las Villas Province and into the Escambray Mountains. Family and friends were getting involved with demonstrations, general strikes, collecting funds to assist the rebel forces and hiding people for fear of torture and death. Awareness of the struggle came to life through my grandmother *Mamá-Vieja* who asked for help in trying to hide a rebel and sell bonuses to help the guerrillas, as well as to distribute copies of a famous self-defense speech by Fidel Castro – ***"La Historia Me Absolverá"*** **("History will Absolve Me")**. My minister, *El Reverendo* Arce, through his sermons also gave me a view of an almighty God, not a distant iconic image in heaven, but as a real mighty person who was present among us. A real creature, nurturing with blessings and encouragements all humans struggling for bringing justice, peace, and compassion in times of war and despair.

The speech given by Castro for his self-defense after the failed attack on the Moncada Barriers on July 26th, 1953, became a cornerstone of the Cuban Revolution. As introduction he highlights quotes by José Martí, the most revered fighter for Cuba's independence from Spain. Then he gives reference to the 700,000 unemployed Cubans, absence of school and health care plus the vast illiteracy in the rural areas with 30% unable to write their own names. He also calls for five laws to be implemented:

1. Bring back **The Cuban Constitution of 1940**.

2. Create a **Major Land Reform** - *La Reforma Agraria.*

3. Provide industrial workers with a 30% share of company profits.

4. Provide sugar workers with 55% of company profits.

5. Take over holdings of people found guilty of frauds. under previous administrative powers.

Although I was not present, by January 1st, 1959, the 800 guerrilla forces defeated the 30,000-men professional army of Fulgencio Batista. Towards the end of 1954, students were motivated to join in the fight, animated by the speech *La Historia Me Absolverá,* that I had secretly seen in Santa Clara during my teen-years. Between 1952 and 1957, the world around me was in turmoil with strikes and awareness of torture and killings of friends and acquaintances. For many of us Fidel was a mythical figure fighting against the Batista tyranny, but his words echoed like signs of hope for my generation and just about everyone around the grand *familia.*

My Cuba in Times of Despair

Quotes from Professor Salim Lamrani

About 60% of the *campesinos* (peasants) lived in *bohíos* (huts) with palm leaves roof and dirt floor devoid of toilets or running water. About 90% had no electricity. About 85% of those huts had one or two parts for the whole family. Only 11% of farmers consumed milk, 4% meat and 2% eggs. 43% were illiterate and 44% had never been to school. The New York Times notes that "the vast majority of them in the rural areas – *guajiros* or peasants – lived in misery, at the subsistence level."

According to the English economist Dudley Seers, the situation in 1958 was "intolerable." What was intolerable was an unemployment rate three times higher than in the United States. On the other hand, in the countryside, social conditions were terrible. About a third of the nation lived in the dirt, eating rice, beans, bananas and vegetables (almost never meat, fish, eggs or milk), living in huts, usually without electricity or latrines, victim of parasite diseases and did not benefit from a health service. They were denied instruction (their children went to school for a maximum of one year). The situation of short-term workers, installed in temporary barracks on collective lands, was particularly difficult. A significant proportion of the urban population was also very miserable."

President John F. Kennedy also said: "I think there is no country in the world, even countries under colonial rule, where economic colonization, humiliation and exploitation were worse than those in Cuba, because of my country's policy, during the Batista regime. We refuse to help Cuba in its desperate need for economic progress. In 1953, the median Cuban family had an income of $6 per week [...] This abysmal level worsened as the population grew. But instead of extending a friendly hand to Cuba's desperate people, almost all of our aid took the form of military assistance – an assistance that simply reinforced Batista's dictatorship, generating the growing feeling that America was indifferent to Cuban aspirations for a decent life."

Salim Lamrani holds a PhD in Iberian and Latin American Studies from Paris Sorbonne-Paris IV University, Salim Lamrani is a full professor at the University of La Reunion and a journalist, a specialist in relations between Cuba and the United States. His latest book is titled **Cuba. Les médias face au défi de l'impartialité**, *Paris, Editions Estrella, 2013, with a prologue by Eduardo Galeano.*

Employment Corruption – *Botellas*

There were problems with teacher accreditation. Some jobs were called *botellas* -- jobs where the "employee" may miss work, or on his/her own initiative could transfer assigned duties to a friend or acquaintance while collecting a government salary without accounting for anything accomplished. Unfortunately, there were also elementary school teachers who qualified through the *escalafón* for a teaching job far from town, and to avoid having to travel, they would hire a substitute, usually not qualified, paying the substitute a fraction of their earnings.

During my third year in *El Instituto*, around 1954, there were so many disruptions, that school was closed most of the time and opened only for a day of lecturing or giving a final exam. Corruption was in front of me when one of my math teachers missed class while having a drink with friends in a bar outside school. I remember my English teacher when he came to class a day before the final exam and drew geometrical figures - lines, circles, triangles, squares, etc. - on the blackboard with the name of each written in English underneath the figures. He then proceeded to explain that for the final exam the following day, he would draw the same figures and ask us to identify them with the proper English term. That same year, I also thought of taking courses to become a land surveyor, so I enrolled in a *dibujo lineal* class (technical drawing). I was excited with the possibility of learning a trade that could guarantee a job and a future career right after high school. The teacher, to my amazement, was a well-known dentist in town who knew practically nothing about drawing and simply showed up to read from a curriculum sheet as to what we were supposed to learn. Classes were often dismissed because of ongoing disruptions and rarely came to a conclusion.

The only opportunity to engage in sports came when there was an announcement that in the sports field belonging to the *Instituto* (not far from my home) the swimming pool had been filled with water. This was very exciting as I had often stood outside the private Tennis Club which had a pool, peeking through a window watching kids, some of them my friends, having fun swimming in a pool that was forbidden for me. I had learned to swim in the *finca* arroyos (streams near the farm), but the pools in town were under control of private clubs that were segregated along the lines of race, class, and ethnic origin. So, the expectation of swimming in a real pool was beyond belief, however, that excitement was quickly dampened with embarrassment and humiliation in the boy's locker room, since I was probably the only naked preadolescent kid putting on a bathing suit. The swimming turned into fiasco since the pool only had about two feet of water, coming up to the knee. Fortunately, they never put water in the pool again and that was the end of my physical education class in secondary school.

When I was in my fifth and final year at the *Instituto*, very few students were concerned with studying for final exams. Schools were practically closed during my last three years of Cuban secondary education, opening only during specific hours for the sole purpose of giving final exams. I was one of a handful of students who strived thanks to the help and guidance of my dear cousin Guiselda, who was also a grade-school teacher. Two private tutors, free of charge, came to my assistance thanks to my father's business dealings: an admirable mathematics teacher, *El Señor* Ocaña and his wife whose name I do not remember but taught me proper grammar and gave me history lessons. These good souls were willing to offer their charity for a promising student, or perhaps receive favors from my *Papá* in his garage. One good friend with whom I manage to conquer the passing of final exams was Inesita San Blas. Another good friend was a Chinese immigrant, I called Mateo. This young man was the first person I met who managed to get excellent grades and worked at his uncle's *Heladeria (Ice-Cream Stand),* where my favorite fruit ice creams were served, during my childhood. We would stand on the school balcony, as two lonely souls, commiserating about what was going on in our troubled world and questioning how we would ever make it to adulthood and cope with life in such a chaotic land.

By the time I received the high school equivalent degree at age 16, I felt cursed by the poor level of formal education I had received – a dentist teaching engineering drawing, an English class and others meeting only one day before the final exam, constant classroom disruptions, and widespread cheatings on exams. It seemed that the entire population was in a state of rebellion; some students had been tortured and killed, others were hiding with town rebels or fled to the mountains with country rebels, some were joining the *Partido Ortodoxo* and meeting in private homes to discuss political philosophies and actions for the Cuban Nation.

It was rare to see women in high administrative positions in either the high schools or at the universities, but I was lucky to meet a wonderful female principal who gave me the green light and total encouragement for plunging into pursuing a university career, at a time when there were no universities for me to attend in Cuba. Sadly, I do not recall her name, but I will be forever grateful for the meeting I had in her office. That meeting encompassed my total graduation experience and the final farewell to the *Instituto de Segunda Enseñanza de Santa Clara*. There, in a very somber yet emotional tone, she warmly congratulated me and told me that I was one of eleven graduates out of a total of six hundred students that had started school back in 1952 with me. I felt so honored, as she gave me her blessing and filled me with encouragement for furthering my education in foreign lands. Again, I faced an incredible challenge and was filled with exhilarating excitement and doubtful concern all at the same time. How could I possibly even consider such a bold move? Even if the University in Cuba had been open, my parents did not have the means to send me there, and even more impossible, would be to be sent outside of Cuba. With my seventeenth birthday just days away in June, I had no family living in the U.S., except Uncle Eddie (Benjamin), who had joined the navy and was off at sea. Even though I had studied English in school, I had always found the spelling and pronunciation extremely difficult and could hardly form a simple sentence, so I could not imagine how I would follow a class lecture nor do my homework, all in that strange tongue. The only positive thing, it seemed to me, was my knowledge of the people and their ways. After all, I had seen almost every American movie that had come to Cuba in those days. In my mind the women had to be blond and beautiful, tall and thin, able to sing and dance to any beat, and with 'pearly whites' behind smiles that made your heart melt, just like Doris Day and Debby Reynolds. The men were tall and rugged, always in charge, and either terribly romantic and sexy like Rock Hudson, or mean and tough like John Wayne. The cities were clean and bustling with excitement and full of opportunities. The homes were large and elegant with huge expansive green lawns, where a white picket fence contained the frisky puppy playing with the two children. My life as a prospective student there, completely baffled me, as I could not recall a single movie depicting the studious life of a college student.

I was blessed by being able to survive those years of chaos. The chaos of politics, as well as family trauma, and social dysfunction all around me. I was fortunate to receive a valuable education that provided strength for survival in times of despair, and the realization of a dear country transforming into a nation that would incorporate the masses of disenfranchised humans and offer fairness and educational opportunities for all its citizens.

Quotes from José Martí help to give meaning to my life.

ONLY LOVE BUILDS, VIRTUES ARE NEEDED MORE THAN TALENTS

SOLO EL AMOR CONSTRUYE
VIRTUDES SE NECESITAN
MAS QUE TALENTOS

My Religious Upbringings - A Rude Awakening

In 1952, I faced a rude awakening with the sudden arrival of social disorder and chaos in my sheltered home and childhood surroundings. *Maestro Alomá,* our school principal, in a somber tone expressing fears and concerns for the students' safety, came to our classroom on the morning of Monday, March 10th, to announce that there had been a sudden take-over of the government in Havana. Everyone was asked to vacate the school as quickly as possible and return home by "moving on sidewalks close to buildings off the streets" to avoid getting hit by armed forces riding on horses, patrolling streets, following orders of a general curfew. An army general by the name of Fulgencio Batista overthrew the government led by the elected president, Carlos Prío Socarrás, while a general presidential election was planned for that same year. When I arrived at home, after walking in fear over deserted streets, I saw a family in disbelief, huddled around the radio with neighbors and friends. They listen intently to learn about the news of what was happening around the country and on their city streets. Facing a world in turmoil, I was filled with desperation and fear about my dreams and plans for an education, a career, and consumed with doubts about the future. Politics, social inequities, and greed for power came to the forefront of my existence - here I was, an innocent eleven-year-old kid preparing for exams to enter the *Instituto*, fantasizing about a beautiful future that was turning into a nightmare of doubts and anxieties. But with the help of my cousin and teacher, Guiselda, I persisted on the path of study and managed to pass the required exams to enroll in a higher secondary school. This exam was the cornerstone for skipping Junior High to enter the *Instituto* in search of a phantasy dream to become a doctor or engineer and live by the sea.

I was aware of the policy at the *Institutos,* devoid of elective courses and the requirement of passing the final exams in single class, and thus forcing students to stay in school for longer than five years repeating failed courses. Students could be in their fifth year attending school and still be taking courses they had failed in previous years. As a preadolescent nerdy kid, the boys around me seem like adults. I was proud of my accomplishments and being able to skip junior high, but at the same time I was filled with fears and anxieties knowing that starting at a tender age would separate me from classmates. I continued to immerse in studies, hoping that my lack of physical development would be overshadowed by a mental edge of knowledge, that could serve to connect with the students around me. Being an odd ball was an asset to my mental development by keeping me busy studying as well as tutoring older students without payment. Long hours were spent checking out facts and historical data in the ten volumes of the UTEHA encyclopedia, a precious gift from my *Abuelo **Papá** Viejo.*

At times I also started questioning the family traditions in which I was immersed through Catholic religious teachings. My *Tía Chicha* and nearby family encircled me with love and attention, always taking care of daily needs, but they also went strongly against the religious traditions on my mother's family side. There was an incident etched in my mind when I spit on the sidewalk and Chicha reprimanded me for acting rude by shouting *"No seas Judío!"* - "Don't act like a Jew!" I was confused and taken aback since my own mother considered herself Jewish – so how else was I supposed to act? Similar comments ignited in me a desire to learn more about the reasons for the Spanish Inquisition and the Diaspora on my maternal family going as far back as the time of the "venerable Columbus."

I was infused with Catholic religious rituals by my *Tía* Chicha. She made sure that I recited prayers every night before bed, that I attended catechism in preparation for first communion, and that I went to confession for blessings and to exonerate my sins before taking exams, after illnesses, before a journey to the *finca* or any other undertaking. At the same time, she would send me to a *espiritista* for a *despojo*, a spiritualist ritual with herbs, prayers and chants that were supposed to promote good energies and blessings from saints or *Orishas*. My *mamá* Sara, called herself *Hebrea*, while my father never went to church and let me know that he did not place value in prayers, saints, or spirits. This all made my aunt's emphasis on Catholic beliefs totally baffling and encouraged my search for other religious beliefs.

Faced with all our family's dysfunction, from an early age, I sometimes had to assume the role of the father figure. I had to take my sister, Sarita, to school or watch her to make sure she went to her piano lessons. Often, I was sent in search of my father, only to find him at a bar or bodega, drunk and hardly able to stand as I stood next to him serving as a walking cane. The maturity that I had developed at a very early age because of the almost daily traumas, was evident as a vivid memory as I knelt in front of my mother begging her not to leave my Papá and find a place where we could all live together. I often dreamed and yearned for a home filled with peace and tranquility with just my *Mami* Sara, my *Papí* Vive, my sister Sarita, and later in life with the newborn Puchy – also given the name Guiselda in honor of our exemplary cousin, teacher, and tutor.

Unlike other members of the family, I attended the Buenviaje Catholic church every Sunday and followed the traditions of communion and confessions, as well as befriended priests and moved small statues of saints from house to house. These actions led to an invitation by a priest to become an altar boy. My family did not give support or encouragement to regular meetings with priests in private settings at the rectory. Although priests were admired by the *familia* for their help with confessions and as holy advisors in times of crisis, at the same time there were deep concerns about accusations of pedophilia or sexual molestation of boys at the Catholic Maristas School attended by my close friends.

The study of Modern History made me aware of wars and struggles in Europe, the development of Protestantism, and the Spanish Jewish Diaspora. This new enlightenment made me wonder about everything: the accepted Roman Catholic dogmas related to repeated prayers and the incomprehensible Latin Mass filled with candles, awe, and mysteries; the support of segregated schools along race, class and gender lines; and the meaningless rituals around images and statues of saints. I questioned why, instead, there was such a negation of spiritual enlightenment through reasoning, scientific discoveries, and just plain Bible readings. Most Cubans called themselves Catholics, but if you were to ask a person, "Are you Catholic?" the response would probably be: *"Sí, soy Católico, pero a mi manera"* – "Yes, I'm Catholic but in my own way." Most people in my neighborhood did not attend church on a weekly basis, except for students enrolled in private Catholic schools. In general, all members of the grand *familia* were expected to be baptized, have a first communion, and attend church for holidays like *Navidad y Semana Santa* - Christmas and Holy Week.

Presbiteriano Mezclado con Hebreo

My maternal grandmother, *Mamá Vieja*, was not keen on Catholic teachings according to my mother since she grew up in a rural setting influenced by a nun who eloped from Spain with a rebellious Catholic priest. Later as a young single mother she found the love of her life: a newly arrived Hebrew Sephardic immigrant, able to communicate in the Spanish language. She adopted some of his religious and cultural traditions and tried to infuse her children with Old Testament teachings, and with a Jesus appreciated for his teachings to humanity and not seen as an all-powerful God. She was associated with the Baptist Church in Santa Clara long before I was born. In her home there were no crosses, no images nor statues of saints, and the Cuban traditional pork was never allowed on her dinner table. With her encouragement, I started to read a version of the Bible that was new to me and was thoroughly inspired by the sermons and speeches of the **Reverend Sergio Arce Martínez**. *El Reverendo Arce* was a newly arrived minister in town, and a recent graduate of the Princeton Theological Seminary of New Jersey. Later during my teenage years of crisis, he became a strong father figure, a mentor, and a school facilitator.

El Señor Arce was married to Doris Valentín, a woman fluent in English and willing to offer me jobs around their home in the outskirts of Santa Clara, with advice on gardening as well as possible careers and professions to pursue. She provided most valuable guidance for my choice of colleges and universities where I could work to achieve higher levels of education. I was impressed with their family bonding and total dedication to building a church, out of practically nothing, within the confines of a tile factory near the city center. It was a dusty place during the workday, but spotlessly clean for evening and Sunday morning services, with folding chairs and a make-do table as an altar decorated with a simple wooden cross. People like me and even my grandmother, *Mamá Vieja,* attended in search of a peaceful existence and a refuge outside the daily strikes, protests and killings affecting our entire community. The work ethics and biblical teachings of this important couple, related to the struggles around us. Issues of fairness and justice were accompanied by a God that related to the here-and-now as a supreme guide and inspiration for fighting the evils on Earth, which to me affected all basic human existence.

The church was born on August 14, 1952, near the time when I was getting ready to enter high school. About a year later, during my days of questioning religion, my *abuela Mamá-Vieja* invited me to attend the newly formed church in a dilapidated tile factory but filled with enthusiasm by those in attendance. I was mesmerized and felt that at last I found a religion with God present "here and now." I became so involved, that I was baptized as a Presbyterian and at an early age, was selected to be Sunday School Superintendent. This was an honor, a sign of trust and the beginnings of a transition into adulthood. *El Reverendo* Arce put on my plate the idea of becoming a minister like himself, if God were to call on me – a call that I took as a literal revelation. I waited for it to come in the form of a dream or of hearing the voice of the Supreme Being; and even investigated the possibility of attending a seminary in Costa Rica. But I prayed and I waited and waited for "God's calling," that it never came.

On the left, in 1957, the ceremony laying the stone for the Presbyterian Church. On the right, church built after I left my loving surroundings.

This commitment away from the Catholic religion created friction and distanced me from my dear family members: Chicha, Guiselda, and other relatives on the paternal side. Even my Jewish grandfather, *Papá Viejo*, who had never advised me on spiritual beliefs, now questioned me about religious direction I was taking. He did not object to my interest in a new church or religious beliefs, but the idea of becoming a minister was more than what he could envision or accept within his family. He reminded me of my ancestry going back to the Hebrews and even joked about my sharing the same last name, Levy, with the American comedian Jerry Lewis. In my birth certificate my last name was written as "LEVIS." Around that time, he took me to a place on a second floor by the *Cine Silva* movie house in Santa Clara, now called "Cine Cubanacán." It was obviously a place for social or religious gatherings, but without outdoor signs for a Jewish meeting place. There I was introduced to the group and had a memorable ritual like I had never seen before with a so-called *Jewish Minyan* - a group of about ten older persons. This was later revealed as a version of my hidden provincial Bar Mitzvah. *Abuelo* introduced me, praised my achievements, made me say a few words of introduction and the older men one-by-one patted my head and uttered words in a language I did not understand – assumed to be Hebrew mixed with Ladino and Yiddish. Not too long after that ritual, he encouraged me to attend a *Pésaj* (Passover) celebration at the home of his brother, Isaac and sister-in-law Raquel in the nearby coastal town of Caibarién. There I experienced a celebration with traditional Sephardic food, and readings, one person at a time from a book brought up and placed underneath their long dinner table. The book referred to as Haggadah tells the story of Passover related to the exodus of Hebrews from Egypt.

Teatro Silva for my Bar-Mitzvah Now *Cine Cubanacán* on Independencia Street *El Boulevard de Santa Clara*

Hopeless about future, I continue to seek peace and calm through religion. I was attracted to a family that lived near my father's garage on the Camajuaní highway. One of their daughters was a beautiful girl, named Inesita, who appear older than me but was working on her *Bachillerato* degree as well. Although I was attracted to her, my main reason for meeting at her home with her mother and sister nearby, was for rigorous studying different subject to prepare for the required final exams leading to a high school certificate. This friendship also impacted my life with the exploration of other religions. Inesita's family was involved with a Pentecostal church near her home, so I was invited by her mother to attend religious services. That gave me a chance to expand my knowledge of religions beyond my Catholic upbringings, my involvement as a Presbyterian, and the private Jewish family practices. Here I am as an usher at the Pentecostal church in the mid-1950s.

The discovery of new parts of Cuba occurred as a result of my involvement with the Presbyterian Church. Reverend Arce and his wife Doris Valentin gave me the opportunity to attend two summer programs at La Progresiva School in the city of Cárdenas. There I had a chance for the first time to be in social gatherings with other young people, and above all discover Varadero, the most famous beach town of Cuba.

The Social Clubs
Race and Ethnic Divisions

Santa Clara also had a noticeable population of immigrants from China, Eastern Europe and the Middle East. Within a block from my home, I walked by the Arab Club displaying flags from Syria, Cuba, and Lebanon with its cedar tree image. Also, on my way to school I passed by two Chinese clubs: one supporting Mao Zedong and the other Chiang Kai-Check. I do not recall any display of Jewish symbols or meeting places for social events; these took place only in private homes - but near my departure from Cuba I discovered a meeting place above a movie house in a shopping district of Santa Clara where Papá Viejo took me for the closest thing to a Bar-Mitzvah, when I was a young teenager. Also, with family in the town of Caibarién I was able to enjoy a Passover Seder in the homes of Jewish family and relatives who also migrated to Cuba from Turkey.

In general Cubans were quite loose and "politically incorrect" in their use of terms to identify nationalities and ethnicities. My mother's sisters were referred to as *Las Moras*, the Moorish Ladies, due to the fact that their father – my grandpa - was a Jew of distant Spanish background but with Greek/Turkish nationality. In general, the word *Judío*- Jewish had a negative connotation in Spanish, so instead of calling himself Jewish, my *Papá Viejo* (grandfather) would be identified as *Hebreo* (Hebrew). Those from Eastern Europe – no matter their country of origin were called "*Polacos*," Polish. Spaniards in general were singled out as *Gallegos,* but those from the Canary Islands were identified *isleños* (islanders). My *Tío* Patricio, a proud native of *Castilla la Vieja*, Old Castille, did not like to be called *Gallego* but there was nothing he could do. Ethnicity or appearance could be turned into a word of endearment like "*mi negra, mi china, morito, galleguita.* Cubans of African descent were called *negro, mulato, jabao, mulato ruso* and other words that identified them in terms of skin color, color of eyes, *pasitas,* hair curliness, and hair color. Some of my friends, neighbors and extended families were of Syrian and Lebanese origin but were seldom identified as Arabs.

Nicknames were common and often reflected a facial or body appearance. For example, a thin girl might be given the nickname *Flaca* (skinny), while someone who was overweight could be called *Gorda* or *Gordita* – "Fatty Girl." As a child, my two front teeth seemed rather large and had quite a space between them so for a while my nickname was D*ientes-de-Hacha* (*A*x-Teeth), along with my nickname PUPY – which I reject since it sounds like POOPY. People around my dad did not know his name until he was registered for first grade, instead he was known as *Vive,* with a meaning similar to "Lively" or "He Lives," perhaps due to his humble origins, his highly social attitudes, or to offset his unwanted arrival to the family. Usually, these nicknames were not perceived as offensive, and perhaps judged as terms of endearment. Although with the tone of voice, a nickname could be considered insulting or endearing.

Clubs in Memory

Unión Libanesa de Santa Clara was around the corner from my home displaying the flags of Lebanon and Syria. Every day I walked by the club and was warmly greeted by members who sat by the sidewalk.

Jewish Association Meeting Place was discovered above my favorite movie house, *El Teatro Silva*, when I was a teenager; a place where my *abuelo Papá-Viejo* (Salvador Levy) took me for a ceremonial of introduction to over 10 members of the community and prayers recited in what I assumed was Hebrew.

La Sociedad Bella Unión was a private club only for *negros* or dark skin Afro-Cubans. It was a small club with one room for social gatherings located near the center of town in front of the Parque Vidal, next to the *Teatro La Caridad*.

El Gran Maceo was a gathering place for mulattoes, Afro-Cubans of lighter skin. Unlike other private clubs, the two clubs for Mulattoes and Afro-Cubans did not have amenities like swimming pools and sports venues common in the clubs for whites.

El Club de la Colonia Española - The Spanish Colony Club was the largest association, located outside the city limits of Santa Clara. It had a large swimming pool placed within the confines of a river creek. I managed to attend some events, but membership was limited to people of direct Spanish ancestry.

The Tennis Club was located a few blocks from my home. It was the most appealing meeting place for young people and those in search of friends and mates for dances and sports – with an Olympic size swimming pool, a big dance floor area, and several tennis courts. My two best friends, Agustín and Juan Vicente went there on a regular basis for fun and entertainment. Juan Vicente as the mayor's son, had a maid to attend his daily needs and a chauffeur to drive him from his house to school, and to the Tennis Club after class.

El Liceo -- Club the Leones for white men of distinction who would sit on rocking chairs greeting passers-by right in front of the Parque Vidal.

6

HOMES OF DELIGHT FROM CHILDHOOD

My first childhood memories come from towns visited in eastern Cuba, throughout the 1940s, in a region near the Nipe Bay of Holguín Province. As a toddler, I remember running around **El Central Preston** – now renamed **Central Guatemala** -- a sugar mill village enclave, claimed and operated by the United Fruit Company of the United States.

The first place that pops into my head as a toddler is the home of a Cuban lady and her American friend, whom I called *Doña Jovita* and *Míster Don*. It was a very unusual home for Cuba, a cottage on stilts, surrounded by a green lawn and garden with trimmed bushes and trees. The front of the house had steps leading to a porch with a large swing strung by four cables from the ceiling, connecting corners of a

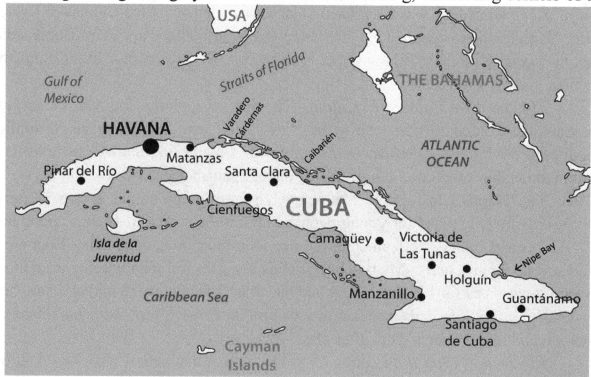

mattress that served as a place for my afternoon naps and playful times with family and the friendly *Americano*, *Míster* Don.

The Nipe Bay is the largest Cuban bay, surrounded by towns, beaches and villages: Antilla, Mayarí, Nikaro; and other towns close to the bay like Birán, La Güira, Banes, and the major city of Holguín.

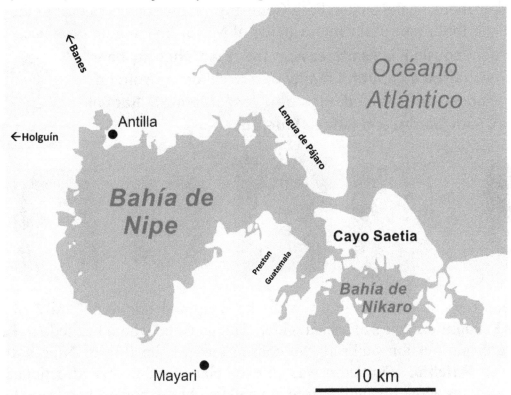

These places recall important events in Cuban History:

- Back in 1942 Christopher Columbus landed in Bariay Bay, not far from the Nipe Bay, and declared Cuba as the "Most beautiful land that human eyes had ever seen."
- In early 17th century, on Nipe Bay, according to Catholic tradition, the patroness saint of Cuba – Our Lady of Charity - appeared for the first time and saved two Cuban natives and a 10-year-old slave boy struggling for their life on a rowboat in a stormy sea.
- The Battle of Nipe Bay was a major naval engagement that occurred in 1898 during the Spanish-American War.

Lengua de Pájaro (Bird's tongue) is a narrow peninsula that borders the north coast of this idyllic Bay, and there, my *Papi (*Daddy) worked for the American Nickel Company as well as building roads.

El Central Preston – The Sugar Mill Town of Preston

El Central Preston (now called Guatemala) was part of a U.S. enterprise owned and operated by the United Fruit Company, on the southern coast of the Nipe Bay. Today it forms part of the municipality of Mayarí in Holguín Province.

My dear cousin Elia Martínez Fernández with her husband Pedro Gómez raised a beautiful family of five children (from left to right): Pedrito (nicknamed Preston), José (Pepito), Raquel (Raquelita), Sara (Sarita) and Rafael (Rafelito)

There I spent pleasant times with the dear and admired family of **Elia Martínez Fernández,** Ana's oldest daughter. Her husband whom I called *Tío* **Pedro Gómez,** took me out for walks in the coastal area of the Bay of Nipe with his youngest son **Rafelito.** *Tío* Pedro was an exemplary figure; very affectionate, he told me anecdotes about his family in Spain and taught me how to fish from the top of a large pier by the bay. There I also enjoyed careful attention and walks with other cousins, sons of Elia and Pedro: **Pepito**, **Raquelita,** and their youngest daughter **Sarita.** Sometimes he enjoyed gifts brought to us by **Pedrito,** the oldest son from the United States. Pedrito was perhaps the most famous family member, a successful player and manager of major baseball league teams in the United States. He was drafted from Cuba, played as short stop for the former Washington Senators team, he even became a manager of The San Diego Padres team of California.

Among other members of Ana's close family were her son **Evis Fernández** with his daughter **Elbita**, with whom we enjoyed playful times and rich meals, since he ran a grocery store in town.

During many summer vacations, I travelled with my sweet aunt *Tía* Ana, from my hometown of Santa Clara, in central Cuba, to Preston. This was a long day's journey, switching from a train with a sleeping compartment, to a railroad *Gas Car*, passing through the towns of Alto Cedro, and Cueto to Mayarí, also riding in a *Guagua* (Cuban bus) and finally taking a taxi from Mayarí to The *Batey,* Town of Central Preston.

Tía Ana and I were welcomed by a loving family: my dear uncle, *Tío* Pedro, his wife, my *Tía* Elia and the rest of cousins and family. There I enjoyed my best vacation by the sea with family surrounded by the gorgeous Eastern Cuban Landscape.

Entering Preston for me was like arriving in a foreign land – a small village on a grid lay out, organized by Americans who adhered to strict racial and ethnic segregation. The town had two churches, schools, two hospitals, and four neighborhoods.

There was an American neighborhood with a guard at every entrance, large homes surrounded by green lawns in an area with easy access to a beach only for *Americano* residents. A second neighborhood for white Cubans, referred to as "New York," had southern style cottage homes, a central park, surrounded by a protestant, a catholic church, and a movie house with separate seating sections for *cubanos* and *americanos*; nearby there was also a hospital. The *Americanos* were free to come into the Cuban neighborhood, but the *Cubanos* were stopped by a guard if they tried to enter the *Americanos* neighborhood and beach areas. "Brooklyn" was the name given to another section where mostly Jamaican and Haitian immigrants as well as Afro-Cuban workers lived in crowded one room huts in a swampy area. There was a place where a large population lived - the *barracones* - on the side of a river. This was a neighborhood composed of single huts with no doors, no bathrooms, no running water, and hammocks for sleeping. Haitians, Jamaicans, and Afro-Cubans, for the most part worked as sugar cane cutters, and were restricted to life on the outskirts of town. I was fortunate to meet loving families in these extremely poor neighborhoods, as my dear Aunt Elia would bring me along when she took gifts to families and her *ahijado*s (godchildren) who lived there.

Segregation was more evident and more strictly enforced here than in the Cuban towns that I had visited. These rulings came from the control exerted by the United Fruit Company in their areas of operation, which was different from the racial, cultural, and cast segregation experienced in Cuba, most prominently observed in private clubs, schools, parks, clinics and hospitals. Although both systems were cruel and demeaning to the majority of *Cubanos* or immigrants from nearby islands: Jamaica, Haiti and others from the Antilles; as a child I became aware of the unjust treatment of human beings in Preston - pervasive but accepted by mostly white Cuban residents in the *Batey* or main Sugar Mill village.

LOS HATICOS DEL PURIAL

The next place in memory was the village of Los Haticos, near the city of Holguín. My *Papi* would drive me to Holguín to attend a school when I was still under 5-years old. I remember a classroom with a window facing the impressive *Loma de la Cruz;* and as a shy and spoiled brat, who did not know any kid in town, I often cried on my way to the classroom – but calmed down in admiration of the beautiful hill with a cross on top. Our home was quite primitive – only one room, without water or an outhouse - but embedded in a gorgeous landscape.

My *Papi* worked building roads with *Obras Públicas* (Cuban Government Public Works) – travelling around Holguín and Los Haticos. He, as a highly sociable person, mixed labor with an uncontrollable zest for good Cuban Rum and *cerveza* (beer), up to the point of being unable to walk home after a hard day of labor. Upon his arrival, my *mami,* Sara, would scream and beg him to stop drinking, so at times he would come home late at night with a group of musicians, waking her with their sad serenade. The musicians were just a singer and a guitar player, but one time, he surprised us by bringing a man with an out-of-tune piano on an old, ragged pickup truck, singing boleros, thus expressing his love and passion for *La Mora* - The Moorish lady – which was my mother's nickname.

She often sent me out into the dark of night to find my *Papi* at the bodega bar to bring him home. His swaying body weighing heavily on my small frame as he staggered along, and I remember well a rainy night when I struggled and strained to steady him, while desperately trying to gather the potatoes he had bought as they rolled down the street from the soggy broken paper bag he was carrying. I fought to hold back tears as they streamed down my face and mixed with the hard pounding Cuban rain.

Description of the life I witnessed during visits to Eastern Cuba in areas controlled by the United Fruit Company

by Dr. Alberto N. Jones

Life in a Cuba under U.S. Control

I was born on a hot and humid day of August 1938 in La Güira, Banes, Cuba, a community of transplanted emigrants, mainly from the English-speaking Caribbean Islands and Haiti, lured to Cuba to what was billed as the "Promised Land" by the United Fruit Company, Manatí Sugar Company, and others.

In this community on the "other" side of the tracks, I learned early on that the only homes we were allowed to build were the shack-type homes with thatched roofs that defined our living quarters. Sewer, running water, electricity, schools, jobs, hospital, or medical services were limited to people living on the "other" side of town.

What we did have was a pervasive infant mortality due primarily to preventable diseases that touched the lives of every family. There were rampant pre- and post-partum deaths; hunger and malnutrition seen predominantly in children with their disproportionate heads and distended abdomens, overflowing with such a variety of intestinal parasites sufficient to produce our own Atlas of Parasitology. Another common landmark was the infamous gully with its putrid drainage winding through our neighborhood.

The only schools in our community of approximately 8-10,000 people, were two or three mock-classrooms of 10-20 children in the living room of some slightly more enlightened members of our community. Two churches had what could be qualified as small schools, with approximately 40 children each. Because of our teachers' own limited education, the level of training by those who were able to stay through the entire school program (3-4 years) was the equivalent of a low third grade.

But this vicious cycle gets even worse if we add that living in Cuba, a Spanish speaking country, the teaching was in English and everything that was taught to us, was either pertaining to England, Ireland, or Jamaica! We learned about Admiral Nelson but nothing about Martí, we learned about Pound, Shilling and Pence, but nothing about *Peso, Peseta y Centavos*. We learned about the Thames River but nothing our own *Rio* Cauto!

Unbelievable as it may sound today, most of the kids could not stay in school, either because their parents could not afford it, or their helping hands were already required on the plantation. As a direct result of this horrendous environment, our community, and tens of similar ones dispersed through what was then the provinces of Camagüey and Oriente did not produce in 60 years a single person who had achieved a mid-level or higher education. An exception was a lady who was able to complete nursing school, only because her parents had the vision and could afford to send her back to Jamaica.

The only jobs available was in the *zafra*, the 4 to 5 months' sugar harvest, which was virtually slave labor, because it was not only the lowest paying job, but it also kept the people in perennial debts: whatever income you made last year would be credited to debts incurred this year. This practice was so pervasive that thousands of workers never saw or received money, they would only receive promissory notes -*VALES*- from the landowners, who were often the owners of the stores. That is why, 10-12-year-old boys went off to work in the fields, while girls in the same age group became maids.

I will be eternally grateful to my grandfather, George Jones. Pappi Georgy, as he was known, was a dignified man of enormous fortitude, respect, and deep religious beliefs, who kept our family together in spite of the most difficult circumstances by instilling in us honesty and moral values. My grandfather was among the fortunate few, because, as an orderly in the United Fruit Company's hospital, he had a year-round job paying 50 cents per day.

There were always people sitting in my backyard, waiting for Georgy to get off his job. Some suffered from diarrhea, vomiting, fever or any sort of injuries. He would cleanse their wounds or give them medication he stored in a coffin-like cabinet he kept in his bedroom. As I pieced these events together, I concluded that this honorable man, who preached values to us, was forced by the brutal society in which he lived, to steal from his workplace, in order to serve those who were deprived of the most basic means of survival.

What can we say about the psychological trauma endured by unfortunate mothers, trapped in abusive relations, domestic violence, and occasional life-threatening situations without anywhere to go, forced to live this hazardous existence as the only means of feeding their hungry children?

LA FINCA - My Childhood Farm

The childhood memories of my visits to the family farm or *finca* - in Spanish - which at the time seemed far from my home in Santa Clara, Cuba, are among the earliest I have and some of the most precious. The *finca* was owned by my *abuela* (grandmother) *Doña* Ramona Fernández de Pérez, whom I nicknamed, *Mamá Ramona*. She inherited the land from her husband, *Don* Tomás Pérez, a native of the Canary Islands in Spain – whom I assumed was my grandfather. All the children in the family considered, *Don* Tomás, their illustrious, most admired, wealthy Grandfather; although no one knew him in person, since he had died before my siblings and cousins were born. The trips to *abuela's finca* were always filled with excitement: a rickety train ride followed by treks into the *manigua* (Cuban wild forest) with idyllic surroundings of royal palms, mysterious *ceiba* trees, rolling sugar cane fields, large expanses of green tobacco, and many water ponds and streams to sooth our tired feet along the journey. The *bohíos* (thatched roof huts for homes) in the distance provided harmony and a sense of human life beyond nature's realm. However, as I approached these homes, a site far from paradise revealed entire families with shoeless, undernourished children with inflated bellies living in a one-room dwelling with dirt floor, which lacked toilets and running water.

I spent wonderful times in the *finca*, run by my dear uncle *Tío* Patricio - a native of Navalperal de la Sierra, a village of Castilla la Vieja in Spain near Ávila de los Caballeros. My Cuban Aunt, *Tía Llalla*, as I called her - pronounced *YahYah* – was Tío Patricio's loving wife and mother of my dear cousins Ileanita and Inaita. Lalla's true name was Celaida Felicitas, but I always gave nicknames to all my close relatives. Her warm, yet heavy obese frame was a testimony of her marvelous cooking ability in spite of the lack of ingredients and stores to buy food – everything came from their natural surroundings. *Tía* Llalla was a sweet loving aunt, who filled my heart and belly with extra-sweet Cuban desserts I still enjoy and yearn for: *casquitos de guayaba, dulce de leche cortada sobre hojas de almendra, arroz con leche, pudin de coco*, and many more - guava shells, sweet, curdled milk served over almond leaves, sweet rice with milk, coconut pudding.

Tío Patricio was from *Castilla la Vieja*, the Spanish province where original Castilian Spanish originated; and although he was illiterate, his Spanish sounded flawless and perfectly pronounced. He would take great pride in correcting my grammar and word pronunciation whenever we were together. As we were walking to the pasture fields shepherding cows helped by his scroungy dogs to the milking corral, he always gave me instructions on farming, milking and Spanish pronunciation. *Tío* Patricio would squeeze the skinny, drooping cow utters to extract every possible drop of milk, then would give me a chance to press and extract the fresh milk into my little *jícara* (a coconut shell). The milk was brought to the *bohío* home with sufficient pieces of wood for a cooking fire to prepare a sugary *café con leche*. This fresh milk was supposed to have magical power for mental development, but later discovered that it was associated with causing polio. There was always work, depending on our "survival" needs for that day, or rather what we would eat. On a regular basis our adventure was a trip to the nearby arroyo with containers on a *rastra* (a V-shaped pair of logs dragged by an oxen pair) to fetch the water. On the trek going there, I was filled with anticipation for getting in the water, as I had learned to swim in the ponds formed by the arroyos nearby. The long trip home was also enjoyable, as we would climb mango and tamarind trees, picking their fruits, as well as gathering plantains, almonds, *yucca, Malanga,* and sugar cane. I still vividly remember the fruit's sweet aroma and taste – up to the point of ecstatic pleasure, mixed with excruciating pain, from the over consumption of those delightful tree-ripened fruits. At times, that indulgence forced me to run into the woods in search of the only natural toilet available – a hidden place in the *platanal* (the plantain grove) with a tender corn cob for clean-up in my back pocket. When I returned, we would sit under a royal palm, and *Tío* would tell me stories, filled with emotion and nostalgia, about his native land of Spain.

AS I REMEMBER
Family Home
In *La Finca*

***Bohío* built with remnants of royal palms – hammocks for beds and neither toilets nor outhouses.**

Once home again, there was always *maiz* (corn) to grind, and wild rice to clean, if it was available. The grinding mill consisted of two cylindrical stones, allowing the placement of kernels between them while rotating the upper stone to grind these kernels into the rough corn flour. If we had rice, they would work for hours preparing if for the dinner table. First picking it from the field, then separate the grains from the branches and smashing it in a large wooden container to separate the rice from the grain enclosures. Finally, giving it to *Tía Llalla* for the long tedious job of carefully separating the good grains from the bad - a boring job for a child like me. Luckily, the children of the *campesinos*, with their heads bent and their eyes always looking down were anxious to do such work, as *Tía* would then reward them with a glass of milk or perhaps something sweet to eat.

The best home in the *finca* with dirt floors in the kitchen and dining room, dry wood for cooking, no toilets or bathrooms, roof made out of palm leaves, and walls made from royal palm trunks.

The humble home where *Tío* Patricio and *Tía* Llalla lived was the largest in the finca. There were about ten campesino families, *arrendatarios* (tenants), that depended entirely on my family's "generosity" to allow them to live and farm there, under conditions equal to that of indentured servitude. Yet even my aunt and uncle, who managed the farm, lived under miserable conditions, which as a child, I hardly noticed, after all, it was all they knew. Meat was seldom available and day-in and day-out, *Tía* spent most of her time in the kitchen with her daily routine of making *harina de maiz* (cornmeal). It was a daily staple of Cuban country cooking enhanced with pieces of pig fat, very ripe plantains, or eggs. Occasionally, root vegetables typical of the area - such as yuca (manioc or cassava root) and malanga (taro root) – was added to the meal. On rare occasions, they would kill a turkey or chicken and for very special events, such as *Nochebuena* (Christmas Eve) a pig would be slaughtered to make *puerco asado*. It was always served with black beans and rice, *tostones* (fried plantains), *yuca con mojo* (garlic flavored manioc), and *frituras de malanga* (taro fritters). To this day, our Christmas Eve dinner consists of these wonderfully memorable flavors.

The cooking stove, on a dirt floor, was a bed-sized rectangular frame area used with pieces of wood or carbon, which when ignited filled the air with heavy thick smoke, making it nearly impossible to stand nearby. The dining area also had a dirt floor and no doors, which allowed flies and all sorts of insects to fly about pestering us. There was no electricity - light at night was provided by *chismosas* (small cans filled with oil and a lighted rag). The living room and two bedrooms were in the main part of the residence, which did have a cement floor, but there was no toilet, nor paper or water for personal hygiene. Yet, despite the apparent miserable living conditions, there was life, joy and entertainment. Groups would gather to play dominoes and dramatically tell frightful stories of ghostly spirits, and eerie diabolic creatures that scared the children, and often the adults, to death. On special days, friends with Cuban guitars would engage in singing *décimas criollas* - a form of free-spirited poetic singing, arguing, or relating to current events. At least once a year, the *campesinos* on our *finca*, would ride many miles on their horses to bring vegetables, chickens, or pigs to my *abuela, Doña* Ramona, and to our family in Santa Clara.

Other families -- deprived of land to farm and subjected to extreme poverty -- lived by the *Camino Real*, a road outside the *finca*. All the homes in the countryside had dirt floors, no running water and the beds consisted of hammocks or *catres* - one-person canvass beds supported by a flimsy wooden frame. For the first time a school opened not far from the *finca*, but the assigned teacher was often absent and *Tía Llalla* had to serve as a substitute since she was the only one in the area able to read and write, even though she had no training as a teacher and only a primary school education. Children had to walk very long distances to school, often crossing dangerous overflowing arroyos over a primitive bridge made from a single palm trunk.

Life in the *finca* had its ups-and-downs. We were in gorgeous natural surroundings and yet far from all of the conveniences of civilization. There were no doctors, no clinics, no pharmacies, no medicines, no electricity, no refrigeration, no bathrooms, nor any running water. If someone became ill or was ready to have a baby, they depended on a *curandera* (a person assumed to know about herbal remedies), or a *espiritista* (a spiritual healer who prayed by your side). There was no apparent work schedule outside the tasks required for finding and putting food on the table. *Lalla* and *Tío* Patricio began the day with a *cafecito sambumbia* (watered down coffee) discussing concerns regarding what they were going to eat. As of routine, the first task was to dress, then next to deal with the natural and animal environment around them. *Tío* would mosey along, then sit on a *taburete* (a simple Cuban country stool) as he slowly laced his boots and *polainas* (leather leggings), smiling, arguing, joking, and teasing *Llalla* all the time. She would often explode in a melodrama of tears or laughter. Once he was finally ready, we would set off for that day's chores and that day's lessons.

While living in the *finca, Tío* Patricio was more than an uncle. He was a father

figure, filling my soul and memory with teachings of fairness, and how to live and survive during difficult times. Although of humble Spanish origin, he was proud with the pronunciation of his royal sounding name, "Patricio Martín de la Parra y de la Fuente Redonda" in his true Castilian accented Spanish. His nostalgic tales of his native *Navalperal de la Sierra* with the beauty of the land he had left behind, and his stories of family separation are forever present in my memory and have shaped many actions in my life.

Despite primitive living conditions, their home was a refuge for the city family folks during difficult financial times. *Tía* and *Tío* had two daughters, Ileana and Ramona Ignacia (*Inaita*) who came to live with us in our Santa Clara home, giving them access to schools and careers. We were all *familia* and that dear cousin, *Inaita*, secretly encouraged me to develop my love for music. Even after my coming to the U.S., she sent sheet music of classical Cuban composures: *Habanera Tú, La Comparsa, La Bella Cubana, A la Antigua*, and other pieces I hope to master as my ultimate quest in life.

7

LIFE'S HARD CHOICE
LEAVING CUBA

DECISION TIME

In 1956 I finished the four-year high school equivalence at the *Instituto* despite the fact that this school was closed almost the entire year. I was 16 years old, too young, and afraid to leave the family, filled with anxiety about what was happening around us: friends who disappeared, horrible cases of torture and killings, no schools for continuing my education, threats to my life, a family near bankruptcy and no apparent end to the fight against Batista.

Doris Valentin and a Puerto Rican missionary who was working in the Santa Clara Presbyterian Church provided me with a list of colleges for possible attendance in the United States. Some friends had already left to study in the U.S., but they were endowed with sufficient money to pay tuition and return to Cuba for holidays or family visits. I knew full well that once I left, it would be extremely difficult to return. My only choice would be a long time off, after years and years of saving enough money for the return trip. My fantasy plan was to be in the U.S. for four years, become an engineer and return for a well-paying job of at least $500 a month. One of my friends from the Maristas Catholic school was in North Carolina, others were closer to home Cuba in places like Florida, Georgia, and Alabama. Perhaps for silly reasons I did not want to be near them and be embarrassed by not being able to return home with them at least once a year. So, I checked the UTEHA encyclopedia for places in the U.S. as far as possible from Cuba, so as to make it nearly impossible for the school to send me back home - due to my lack of money for paying school tuition and knowledge of the English language as well as any other they might have.

Randomly I searched in all the encyclopedia books from volume 1 to volume 10, and to my amazement I read a description of the Mormon journey, pulling carts or riding on rickety wagons from the East to the West of the U.S. in search for the promised land of Zion. With all my biblical readings, I was inspired by such undertaking and right then and there I decided to apply to a college in the western part of the United States, looking for colleges in Kansas, Missouri, Colorado, and Utah. *La Señora* Doris Valentín and a missionary friend helped me to compose the letters of application – I would write them in Spanish and then they would edit and translate them into English. The colleges' admission departments were not aware that I, the applicant, did not know sufficient English to pass any course offered in the U.S. colleges and universities of those days. During the spring of 1957, to my surprise, I received acceptance letters from several colleges but, without any doubt, my choice was Westminster College, not because I knew anything about the school, but simply because it was the farthest away from Cuba and it was in the land of Zion. I knew nothing about the Mormon Church, unlike other American based churches, it had no missionaries in Cuba. Until 1978 the Mormon Church had discriminatory policies against Afro-descendants which made them less desirable for attracting into the Mormon religion. However, people from other races, such as Native Americans, were accepted for conversions, under the assumption that they were descendants of a lost tribe of Israel. So, even though Cuba had a vibrant Protestant community, due to our "undeterminable African mix" the Mormon missionaries bypassed us for other countries in Latin-America.

The family came together after announcing my decision like I had never seen before. My father and my grandfather *Papá Viejo* joined for the first time as a family for a farewell excursion to enjoy the beautiful sights of my native Las Villas Province: The water falls of *Salto del Hanabanilla*, the Escambray Mountains with *Topes de Collantes*, and the impressive city of Cienfuegos with its Moorish palace and the best place to eat *Paella Valenciana* overlooking the blue Caribbean Sea.

Salto del Hanabanilla, waterfall located between the cities of Cienfuegos and Santa Clara

Moorish architecture in Cienfuegos, city founded by Louis D'Clouet via Louisiana in the USA

Days later my *Papá* took me to meet the unknown side of his real father Plácido Moreira. Everyone in the family had names inspired by the "Arabian Nights Tales": Parviz, my Dad's given name, brother Bamán, sister Parizada, and another sister whose name escapes my mind. They cried, hugged, and kissed me as if I were a long lost-and-found family treasure. For me it was an incredible closure to me and my Dad's family, and to learn about who I am. It was unbelievable that I walked by their home daily when I attended the *Escuela Anexa* from 3rd to 5th grade.

Everything for the major and unimaginable trip was moving according to plans. I had chosen a college, I had been accepted, and was close to completing my five years, one year beyond the U.S. high schools. But how was I to travel on a five-hour trip from Santa Clara to Havana then fly to the U.S., plus get all the way to Salt Lake City in the far away and unknown state of Utah. Living in Cuba I had no clear idea about the size and expansion of the United States – I had never been to Havana, and my trips to the sea or eastern Cuba never lasted more than a single day. The next step was to get the proper paperwork for permission to come to the U.S. and sufficient money to pay for the trip. I definitely did not have money to pay for tuition, so I had to find ways to fake how I was to cover my living expenses on top of paying for books and general education costs. The first journey of the trip was to get to the U.S. Embassy in Havana for the required student visa and permission to travel to Westminster College in Utah.

MAKING FINAL PREPARATIONS IN HAVANA

The family, on both sides, came together to help as much as possible, devising ways to pay for the expenses of getting me on the road out of Santa Clara. So, a decision was made to raffle an old photo camera – the only picture equipment we had for the family. This attempt was a total failure since we could hardly sell raffle tickets for such an old camera, and the few tickets that we were able to sell we did not get more than $20. Here, the family savior, my *Papá Viejo* (whose name Salvador translates as Savior) came to the rescue with $50 for the entire journey. I was able to collect a few more dollars from family members that amounted to about $75 altogether. So early in the summer of 1957 I went to Havana for the first time and stayed with my uncle Carlos Rivero and my aunt Siomara Levy in their nice Havana home, enjoying visits with my cousins, newborn Magda and her older sister Gilda.

Dear cousins
Gilda and her adorable
sister Magda
Daughters of
Uncle Carlos Rivero and
Aunt Siomara Levy
near my time of
departure from Cuba.

My Havana *familia, Tío Carlos and Tía Siomara,* did everything they could to keep me well fed, comfortable and ready for my last *adiós* to the *familia*. He would take me with cousins José and Eduardito on trips to the Havana Zoo and I even got to see some sleezy Cuban nightclubs with gorgeous women dancers. I also visited the private all exclusive nun school of Gilda and watched over the adorable baby Magda.

Tío Carlos came from a prominent family of Spanish nobility that owned *El Diario de la Marina;* a large newspaper founded by *Conde Don Nicolás Rivero* during Spain's colonial period in Cuba. It opposed the Independence Movements

Newspaper *Diario de La Marina* Building in Havana

led by Antonio Maceo and José Martí during the second half of the 19th century and later supported Francisco Franco in the Spanish Civil War of the 1930s. However, my uncle Carlos Rivero was one-of-a-kind in his family, a sort of rebel in the Rivero Clan, when he married by Aunt Siomara Levy a woman of Jewish ancestry. His duties as director of the social pages were to keep abreast of news about the Cuban social elite. The paper and his office were housed in an impressive edifice very near to the Capitol building of Havana.

In his little Volkswagen car, we ran all over Havana to deal with the necessary paperwork: buying tickets for a half-hour plane ride in *Aerovías Q* from Havana to Key West, followed by a Greyhound bus ticket for a ride from Key West, Florida to Salt Lake City, Utah, changing pesos to dollars, and of course dealing with the U.S. embassy in Havana. The visa and all the paperwork at the Embassy were successful in part due to a letter with high recommendations from the *Reverendo* Arce, plus his stated commitment to find ways to pay for my college if I were unable to pay for them. We got the tickets for the one-way plane ride, which was only $11, and the one-way bus ride was around $50, which we were able to buy directly back in those days. So, from my original $75, I barely had enough money left for food, certainly no money for lodging expenses, and definitely nothing for tuition and living expenses once I got to Salt Lake.

My secret plan – in total naiveté – was to pay for my education by getting a job, but doing what? I didn't have the foggiest idea since I had neither work skills of any kind, nor any experience earning money and managing my own life. My dad had tried to teach me about servicing automobiles by forcing me to stand next to him and watch as he jiggled spark plugs or changed the oil, but my mind would drift to another space of existence, far from that daily grind of greasy hands and dirty clothing; absorbing nothing of what he was trying to teach.

SAYING MY FINAL GOOD-BYES

My *Mami* Sara and little Sister Puchita were the only family members during my time of departure from Cuba at the Havana Airport. c. September 11, 1957

Late in July I returned to Santa Clara to say my last goodbye to my loving family, after a few days with them, my *Mami* Sara and my adorable, barely 4-year-old sister Puchy boarded a bus to take me to the airport in Havana - *para un último adiós*. All the members of my family were in shock and disbelief about my departure, as was I, but it was only my *Mami* Sara who felt strong enough to be with me during the final departure as we waited in the Havana airport. Once the order was announced to "board the plane," we embraced and kissed goodbye. Sweet little Puchy did not really seem to realize what was happening, and *Mami* seemed stoic and somewhat detached. I started down the walkway toward the stairs of the plane when I suddenly turned around and ran back to hug Mami and Puchy one more time. I was crying uncontrollably and begged and pleaded with her not to let me go. But my mother with a strong, steady voice and in total control of her emotions said,

"Te quiero con toda mi alma.
Sigue adelante, es tu futuro, es por tu propio bien."
"I love you with all my soul.
Go forward, it's your future and it's for your own good."

PART II

My Second Life in the U.S.

**Journey from the homeland to the
Land of Zion
A time for work, study, and search
for a new family.**

8

HARD JOURNEY IN 1957
Viaje Difícil en 1957

ON THE AIRPLANE -- *EN EL AVIÓN*

Finally, I entered the small plane that would take me from Havana to Key West, Florida. This was my first airplane ride, so I was rather scared with the roar of a noisy engine, on top of feeling lonely and confused about what to expect for the next leg of the trip. After the plane lifted off the ground, tears streamed down my cheeks, as I stared at the majestic Cuban scenery below. It was an incredible sight, seeing the Morro Castle and the Malecón seaway between a broad avenue with the tallest buildings I had ever seen, and the rumbling ocean waves, fading in the distance, but soon revealing one last view of my lush green land with its sugarcane plantations and tobacco fields dotted with clusters of royal palm trees. Almost as soon as the Cuban land disappeared from sight, the Florida Keys and mainland appeared. It was exciting, disconcerting, and surreal because the land seemed so well organized, with property boundaries well delineated, giving the impression that I was moving, not to another earthly zone but to another planet, with country mansions and flat landscapes I had never seen. It was a very short trip, only about a half-hour and I could not believe how completely different the sights below looked, and how very far away this new land seemed. The trip became etched in my memory, like no other experience I have had. The emotions of solitude and despair would rush back like a crashing wave and fill my soul with melancholy long after the trip had ended, and even until this day. Yet, as the plane smoothly landed, I hoped it was the sign of a smooth transition to a new life, but my heart felt differently and was heavy with the sadness of leaving my dear family, my home, my friends, and my beloved homeland.

The tears continued to flow as I blindly stumbled down the plane's stairway and headed toward a stark, dark square building where everyone seemed to be headed. I managed to retrieve my battered old suitcase, then entered the swinging door with a large sign above – "CUSTOMS – Welcome to the United States." The uniformed customs official quickly examined my few belongings in my only worn suitcase, and seeing nothing of any interest or value, motioned that I was to proceed to the immigration officer. At this next step, I was met by a very tall, hefty man with a badge, who seemed very serious and rather unfriendly. He asked several questions in English which I did not and could not answer. After I showed him my passport and visa documents, he switched to his very poor Spanish and asked a series of questions again. As best as I could understand he seemed concerned and was asking about my young age, my lack of money, my solo arrival without family or friend, and my plans in the U.S. Then he put a paper in front of me and asked me to sign it. I had not the slightest idea as to what I was signing, and after scribbling my name at the bottom of the paper, he asked me to sign again with clearer not such elaborate handwriting, closer to a printed name I assumed. That was followed by a quick lesson on how I was to pronounce my name – DELvis ~~Alejandro~~ Fernández ~~Levy~~ – with a strong American accent. The immigration officer finally threatened to send me back to Cuba because I was underage, did not have the proper permits, nor the means to pay for my trip to Utah. He said in poor Spanish:

"Como pagar escuela? No poder trabajar en America. Eres niña. Tener regresar Cuba. Espera avion por regreso."

["How are you going to pay for school? You cannot come to America to work. You're a (female) child. You must return to Cuba. Wait there for the next plane to return."]

I was separated from all the other passengers and sent to a waiting room for the return flight to Havana. Even though I had a current valid passport, the proper student visa, the college acceptance letter, and a paid ticket for the Greyhound bus ride from Key West to Salt Lake City, the immigration officer did not believe that I was qualified to enter the United States. He had never heard of an underage Cuban, not speaking or understanding English, venturing off to the far west of America all by himself. Once the customs and immigration officers finished processing all the remaining airplane passengers, I was called back for what appeared to be the final arrangements to send me back to Cuba. Suddenly, I remembered the letter on a church stationery paper, from the Reverend Sergio Arce, a presbyterian minister trained in the U.S., in which he made laudatory remarks about me as a capable person along with praising my educational achievements. He assured the reader that he would be committed as a guarantor of the validity of all my travel documents, as well as his taking responsibility for making sure that I would be able to pay for college tuition and living expenses. Thankfully, the letter was the final ticket for a welcome into the U.S., and I breathed a loud sigh of relief when I was given the green light to proceed on to the Greyhound Bus area where the newly arrived plane passengers were anxiously waiting to begin their final ride to Miami. There, by the Greyhound door, for the first time, I encountered an American – that did not look at all like the American stereotypes I carried in my head - the beautiful Hollywood star Doris Day, with her blue eyes and blond hair, next to her handsome lean and mean beau Rock Hudson. This *Americano* was also tall, but a stocky black man, reaching out to me with an extended hand in what I thought was a request for money or a ticket to enter the bus -- I simply squeezed passed him, showed my ticket to the driver, and in that moment of desperation – took my seat. I later realized that he was simply asking for a tip in payment for recovering my luggage. After all, he had served as the baggage handler, who stored my beat up *maleta vieja* and brought it to the bus for me.

The Ride Through Florida – *Viaje En La Florida*

I took the bus from Key West to Miami, where all the passengers got off, and finally I had a chance to meet *Tío* Benjamín's wife, Sylvia Carbonell, and enjoy one last meal with her parents while waiting for the night bus that would take me on to Georgia and through the Deep South. But lucky for me, before catching the bus I was given a peacoat, as a most valuable present from my uncle Eddie to deal with the cold weather awaiting me in the far West. *Tío* Benjamín, known as Eddie, was stationed at a Navy base in Jacksonville, so on my second day on that great journey west, the bus came to a rest stop in that northern Florida city; there I managed to make my first payphone call and had one last chance to communicate in Spanish with my uncle who went over a list of dos and don'ts on how to behave in the more formal and quieter environment of the US. He had aspired to be a singer and movie

My *Tío* Benjamín (Known as Eddie) With US navy uniform during the 1950s

star, so had left Cuba two years earlier, but mainly as a result of receiving death threats to his life. Eddie Benjamin was the second family member that was in the U.S. Long before his departure, another family member on my father's side, back in the 1940s, Pedrito Gómez, also known as Preston Gómez, had come to the U.S. and ended up playing baseball for major and minor league teams, which in later life led him to become a manager for the San Diego Padres and the LA Dodgers.

In a rush to get to the bus, I placed a navy peacoat in the suitcase – a present left by Uncle Benjamín for the cold weather I would encounter in Utah. But unfortunately, I had trouble closing the decrepit old suitcase and had to tie a rope around it to secure my belongings, and without noticing, a shoe was dropped on the ground, under the bus, and left behind as we scurried to push the suitcase into the luggage compartment. Once I was sitting on the bus, already nighttime, I tried to sleep, but my head was filled with thoughts of nostalgia and a sense of loneliness in this strange land with no friends, and disappointment in not seeing my uncle. This unfamiliar environment was far from my expectations of what I had thought I would find in *Los Estados Unidos*. My ideas and views of the U.S. were based mostly on American movies, images of huge cities like New York or Chicago, and of course, the old cowboy pictures with scenes of the Wild West, which I was looking forward to once we reached Utah.

The bus depot cafeterias and the food choices offered were totally new and unknown to me. I was used to eating black beans and rice on a daily basis for lunch and dinner along with other wonderfully flavorful items. It was fixed and served by a member of the family, and I had never even experienced eating at a restaurant nor visited a cafeteria. All I ate for breakfast was a piece of Cuban bread cut in thin slices and dipped into a glass with *café con leche* (just a little strong Cuban coffee with mostly hot milk). It always had a lot of *azúcar prieta,* un-dissolved and unrefined raw sugar in the bottom of the glass, that I scooped out with my bread. So, during my first stop at a cafeteria with a long counter, and all sorts of food choices that I had never seen, I simply did not know what or how to order. What a dilemma I faced - How and what was I to select? and do I have enough money to pay for it? - were questions always present in my mind. I had a very poor diet for those reasons on my five-day trip. I always looked for the cheapest items as I counted every penny. I often simply pointed to the item the person sitting next to me had as my choice, and quickly learned that sugary, bready items like pancakes, French toast, and waffles, were most filling and satisfied my sweet tooth. These were food items I had never seen or eaten in Cuba, and thoroughly enjoyed, but unfortunately, the overindulgence of these choices gave me a lot of digestive problems, including diarrhea, and terrible stomach pains during most of the bus trip.

IN THE DEEP SOUTH – *EN LO HONDO DEL SUR*

Through the length of Florida, travelling from south to north, I finally reached Jacksonville and shortly after I experience the first rest stop in Georgia, at a bus station in the "Deep South" of the 1950s. There I came face-to-face with two baffling signs on top of the entry doors to the waiting rooms for passengers: one read "COLORED" and the other read "WHITE." I stared at the signs in bewilderment as to how to proceed and hesitated before entering a room in search of the restroom. Where was I supposed to go? I noticed a guard near the entrance door, so I was even more intimidated about how to proceed. My lack of English prevented me from asking questions from strangers about what the right place for me was. After a few minutes of watching people coming in and out, I extended my arm in front of my eyes in order to get a description of my skin coloring – tanned from the Cuban sun -- as either *"blanco"* or *"de color."* Not sure about where to go, I peeked inside each

of the waiting rooms and noticed that the room for *blancos* had a refrigerated cold-water fountain, an air conditioner, and easy stuffed chairs for resting. The room for those described as "colored" was crowded and smaller, opened to the humidity and hot outside air, plus it lacked a sitting area for relaxing or taking a nap. It did not appear clean, and only had a drinking faucet with room temperature water. Needless to say, my choice was made clear, I was thirsty and extremely tired, in need of rest, so I took a chance and moved right past the security guard into the "Whites-Only" domain. Luckily, I slipped by as he spoke to someone else, and he did not even notice.

My First American Friend -- *Mi Primer Amigo Americano*

I was an odd bird in an alien zone, developing communication skills by gesturing with my hands, winking, smiling, and acting as politely as possible with whoever made eye contact with me. Most of the bus passengers seemed to be older citizens, or couples with children, but rarely student-age boys or girls close to my age. Luckily, when I re-entered the bus for a continuation trip in Savannah, for a ride that would take me through Macon and Atlanta, I met a young man who was on his way to a school in Birmingham, Alabama. I sat next to him and built enough courage to begin speaking English, introducing myself by saying something that may have sounded like: *"No espeek eengleech, I espeek espaneech"* - I don't speak English, I speak Spanish. Shortly after my attempt to communicate, he smiled and pulled out a little book from his pocket along with a paper pad, and a pencil. To my surprise, since I had never seen such a small Spanish-English dictionary, I discovered a marvelous little tool through which I could expand my communication skills, ask questions and at last, felt welcomed by my first *amigo americano*. I was so excited after almost two days surrounded by people I could not speak to. We exchanged names and information about our birth places, where we were going, what we liked to study, what to eat in the cafeterias, what to expect and how to deal with work and the school challenges ahead, and even ventured into a few heavy questions about the segregation signs around us. All this communication was done rapidly looking for words in the small dictionary and putting a jumble of words on the writing pad. As strange as it may seem, we had a great time "talking" with words and sometimes with gestures like monkeys in a cage. Johnny was a super nice guy, a skinny tall blonde kid with a pleasant smile, I followed behind him in the cafeterias, imitating his moves, ordering food, and carefully watching every penny to make sure the money would last for the entire trip. At one time he even bought me an ice-cream cone for dessert – a most enjoyable treat – my first in the U.S.

Near his final stop, the bus was quite full of short-distance passengers going from town to town in Alabama. An elderly woman carrying a heavy bag was standing right in front of me, so I stood to give her my seat. At that moment from behind I felt Johnny with gorilla strength, pulling my arm down till I fell back into my seat. His friendly smile had disappeared and instead, I saw a stern face with the harsh words that I clearly understood to mean "Don't do that." He pointed to the back of the bus, as she sheepishly walked back "where she belonged." No consideration was given to her age, her gender nor her heavy load – the back of the bus was the place for "colored" folks and that was the law. That incident really came as a shock to me, and I was amazed not only to realize how that law worked, but to realize how callously my new 'friendly' seatmate accepted and enforced that law.

Through Farmlands of Arkansas, Kansas, and Missouri
Por Las Tierras Agrícolas de Arkansas, Kansas, y Missouri

Once my new friend Johnny left the bus in Birmingham, Alabama, I was again feeling lonely and filled with doubts and questions about the decision to leave my *amada tierra*. Now I had no one to converse with and distract me from the negative thoughts swarming in my brain.

We entered the flat lands of Arkansas, Kansas, and Missouri where at times it seemed like an unnatural landscape, totally designed by some robotic humans. The fields, that seem to go forever, were straight as an arrow with neatly determined and defined boundaries. The towns and cities along the bus route also seemed to follow the same pattern, with carefully planned street that formed a geometrical grid. It was a land to admire for its neatness and cleanness, but so far from my concept of what a town or field should be, with interesting twists and turns. These towns reminded me of Preston, a sugar mill village run by the American United Fruit Company in Eastern Cuba that I had frequently visited. But instead of the Preston I knew, in my crazy mind searching for the familiar, I imagined towns like Preston but that had been hit by a natural disaster, which had erased the lush tropical green landscape, knocked down all the majestic royal palms, and illuminated the blue ocean waters and sandy beaches caressing the coast lines – all that was left of my imaginary towns were neatly designed plain blocks lined up on the surreal grids with little beauty left to look at.

THE ROCKY MOUNTAINS – *La Montañas Rocosas*

As we entered the state of Colorado, I felt I had been hit by thunder and lightning as I marveled at the incredible Rocky Mountains. From the window of the bus, I saw the biggest and most impressive, rugged landscape I had ever seen. The mountain tops were covered with snowy white caps as if some god like creature had poured paint upon them down from a perch high in the sky. I did not know how to enjoy this awesome landscape as again I fearfully felt that I had been transported to a distant planet far from Earth. The mountains seemed barren, with little vegetation of any kind, and one mountain intertwined with another in continuity that never came to an end. For me this was truly an amazing sight of the diversity of landscapes and power of nature. Soothing crisp air and incredible sights finally inspired a good night of sleep in a tight fetal position on my bus seat. I awoke warm and cozy at daybreak, ready to see more of the Rockies as we had reached Wyoming.

When we entered the unforgettable town of Laramie, Wyoming, I felt I had arrived at my American Western movie in the Wild West. I was anxious to experience it all, so I combed my hair and buttoned my shirt which was a thin Cuban one that Mami had hand made for my travel. I stepped off the bus to be hit by cold air which felt like a thousand arrows penetrating my skin straight to my bones. It was the coldest air I had ever felt in my entire life and did not even know that kind of weather existed on this earth. I was totally unprepared for the Wyoming morning temperatures, so I jumped right back on the bus, took several deep breaths, and ran as fast as I could to the warmth of the Greyhound bus station. Once back on the bus, I was cold and miserable for a long time. My frozen brain and body were filled with strong doubts as to the possibility that I would even survive this decision to come to this unlivable land. I had read that Utah had white snow in the winter months - what was winter and what would snow be like? So, a school, even in the land of Zion, where it might be that cold was almost beyond my imagination. My money was almost gone from so many waffles, and my worry about how I would pay for books was now compounded with worry about buying warmer clothing, as I realized the tropical shirts and thin pants from Cuba would be far from what I was going to need in Utah, especially in the coming winter, which had already arrived.

9

IN THE LAND OF ZION
En la Tierra de Sión

THE LAST LEG OF MY JOURNEY

After travelling through the southern part of Wyoming, the bus headed south and crossed into the state of Utah, the land of Zion, within sight of an immense valley and a huge lake that for me looked more like a vision of extraterrestrial lands, I imagined the awesome allure and power that such a scene of grandeur and majesty must have had on the wandering Mormons in the 19th century, after months of trekking over a continent in search of "God's Promised Land" to build a community and come to the end of their epical journey.

The Promised Land
Views from the bus window as it entered the majestic Rocky Mountains

The terrain seemed arid, like an imagined desert from the Middle East, as I stared through the bus window at the immense expanse of The Great Salt Lake, smooth as glass for as far as the eye could see. The distant towering mountains grew greater the closer we got to the final destination. I was in absolute awe, finding it hard to believe that this was real, and that I was really here. The Cuba I knew offered country scenery of bright green plants that one could smell, touch, and delight in the sampling of tropical fruits. M*angos, platanitos, and guayabas* were always plentiful as you, meander by the side of a *manigua* thicket, or plunge into a trickling arroyo where the refreshing water ponds were always calling, I had never seen nor imagined that such immense arid land existed in our world. Even though I enjoyed the grand *paisajes*, my mind kept wandering back to the Cuba I had left behind, making comparisons to get a sense of my future dwelling place.

My Royal Palms beneath a clear blue sky

Evocative poems and sayings came to my mind; cherished since grade school, by Cubans who had confronted the wonderment of new lands and nature with agonizing feelings about their native land. A Cuban poet in contemplation of the Niagara Falls, described with exhilaration the torrential cataracts and thunderous natural wonder, while yearning for the royal palms beneath a clear blue Cuban sky.

Excerpt from The Ode to Niagara Falls
Selección de "Oda al Niágara"
by José María Heredia

Why don't I look here,	*¿Por qué no miro*
About the jaws of this abyss the palms	*Alrededor de tu caverna inmensa*
Ah, the delicious palms, that on the plains	*Las palmas ¡ay! las palmas deliciosas*
of my own native Cuba spring and spread	*Que en las llanuras de mi ardiente patria*
Their thickly foliaged summits to the sun,	*Nacen del sol a la sonrisa, y crecen*
And, in the breathings of the ocean air,	*Y al soplo de las brisas del Océano*
Wave soft beneath the heaven's clear blue?	*Bajo un cielo purísimo se mecen?*

Verses of José Martí in the song Guantanamera

I am a sincere man	*Yo soy un hombre sincero*
From where palm trees grow	*De donde crecen las palmas*
And before I die, I want	*Y antes de morirme quiero*
To pour out verses from my soul	*Echar mis versos del alma*
With the poor of this earth,	*Con los pobres de la tierra*
I throw my fate,	*Quiero yo mi suerte echar*
For the brooks of the mountains	*El arroyo de la sierra*
Please me more than the sea	*Me complace más que el mar*

As enjoyable as the views were around me, I was facing great despair since my only suitcase had been lost – no tag in the baggage room of the Greyhound station in Salt Lake City matched my luggage receipt. I searched my pockets for an address to Westminster College and looked for money to pay a taxi driver. When I pulled everything, I had out of my pockets, and showed him the money I had left, he felt sorry for the trials and tribulations of this homeless creature after a five-day journey, now trembling, undernourished, poorly dressed, with not a single item of clothing, except for what I was wearing. So, he agreed to take me to Westminster as an act of charity, perhaps encouraged by the Greyhound employees in the baggage room, who felt sorry for the lonely Cuban kid with no suitcase.

ARRIVAL AT WESTMINSTER COLLEGE

Arrival time was around noon on a weekend, in early September 1957. The taxi went from the bottom of the grand valley, in downtown Salt Lake City, through wide streets up a hill with homes surrounded by neatly manicured lawns, edged with flowers and well cared plants. We finally entered a grand welcoming arch with the words Westminster College. We stopped at the main school building with the name Converse Hall, a structure that reminded me of images from picture books I had seen of

Converse Hall of Westminster College

grand gothic English castles, certainly not a school building I was expecting nor had imagined. Finally, the taxi driver found out that the place to go for boys was a dormitory called Foster Hall, which to me seemed like a place from European lands, far from anything I had seen from the Greyhound bus window. He left me and said "goodbye." I mustered the biggest smile I could and effusively repeated, "Thank You, Thank You," which with my poor English sounded more like *"Senk Joo, Senk Joo."* I went up two flights of stairs of Foster Hall, which was to be my first home. I found a smiling couple in a wide-open room who greeted me, they knew right away who I was, and immediately took me into a reception type room where young men

were attentively watching TV. The couple introduced me to everyone, and all shouted back at me, which I assumed was their greeting. This group of macho guys all look older than I, and definitely bigger and stronger.

Foster Hall My New Home at Westminster College

A FOOTBALL WELCOME

I was given a place of "honor," sitting on a straight chair, front row centered, amongst a group of about twenty hefty, excited students, right in front of a small TV screen. For me, I was witnessing a strange happening on and out of the flat screen. I did not know what to say or do, the actions on the screen showed robotic like humans with big shoulders pushing each other, running wild, and at times kicking or holding and caressing against their chest a double pointed flattened, elliptical object. There was excitement with lots of shouts in the room, but I was frozen on my chair, without any knowledge of what was happening, afraid to make eye contact, for hours looking straight at the images, and feeling caged in a room surrounded by wild creatures, without being able to communicate, and with a total lack of understanding of what was happening around me. Days later, I discovered that I was simply "enjoying" a game of the most popular sport in the U.S. – Great American football – surrounded by future friends and the members of the Parsons Football Team of Westminster College.

Pauline and Leonard Fields "Mom" and "Pop" heads of Foster Hall

Hours later, the very friendly welcoming couple, Mr. and Mrs. Fields – whom I later discovered were the Dorm Parents, that students referred to as "Pop" and "Mom" - took me to a room and introduced me to an assigned roommate by the name of Tony Ferguson. As far as I could tell, there was no one in the dorm that spoke Spanish, but Tony appeared as a super nice guy ready to show me the ropes and guide me through the "Dos and don'ts" in my new home. I was immersed in a totally foreign culture; but since I was filled with a strong desire to learn, I developed my own sign language by winking, smiling, dancing, and helping people in any way I could. *"Yo sí puedo"* – "Yes I can" was my motto and response to any request for help or attempt to get a job done, even if I didn't know how to do it, I was always ready to sacrifice, cope, and learn. The dorm parents tried their best to make the transition into my new Westminster environment, as easy as possible, so they introduced me to what I thought were foreign students in the dorm. There was only one foreign student, but due to ignorance, I assumed that all the students appearing to have Asian features were foreigners as well.

Tony Ferguson First Roommate And guide at Westminster

After meeting my roommate, Tony Ferguson, I was introduced to a student from Greece by the name of George Ieromnimon. He was called by everyone "George I" because his last name was so difficult to pronounce by English speakers, so I took great pride in pronouncing his name correctly without any problem and no accent. When I met George, he reached out for a Spanish textbook and began to read a story in perfect Spanish, with no foreign accent at all. This was the first time after travelling for days through the U.S. that I had a chance to hear my language so well enunciated. I was so excited, that I saw him as a long lost relative and began to speak to him non-stop in Spanish, detailing my travel experiences, when he finally stopped me with a smile, the expression on his face was letting me know – *Yo no hablo español* – I don't speak Spanish. He was faking knowledge of Spanish to make

My First Friend at Westminster College
George Ieromnimon

me feel welcomed, he could read almost perfectly but he did not know the meaning of what he was reading since Greek like Spanish is a phonetic language. George was getting ready to take a Spanish class and could guess the meaning of some of the words he read. Although we did not have a common language at first for communication, we developed a special friendship, we discovered lots of common issues between Spanish and Greek culture. We both worked on all kinds of low paying jobs on Campus: from dish washers to gardeners and members of janitorial cleaning crews. Above all we also had fun at parties, and he gave me lessons on American dating customs - what was acceptable, how to ask a girl out, where to go on dates, who was and who was not available. Coming from a provincial town in Cuba, I was filled with stereotypes that were far from the mores of American society. My views of Americans were so falsely ingrained in my brain, that when I met a dear friend, Elwyn Wong, a student from San Francisco, California with Chinese ancestry, I simply assumed, that he was a foreigner from China. It took me a while to understand the multiethnic complexities of American society. Hollywood had done a number on me - there was

Elwyn Wong
First friend who expanded my views of American society.

a lot more diversity than the stereotypes portrayed by Doris Day and Rock Hudson in Hollywood movies.

FIRST WEEK AT WESTMINSTER COLLEGE
La Primera Semana en Westminster

Once I retired to my new room for what I hoped would be a good night's rest, on a soft bed after five days crouched on a bus seat, I stood in front of the window of my second-floor room, marveling at the immense Salt Lake Valley. The scene was so peaceful and quiet, and the ground appeared dotted with flickering night lights that reminded me of stars from heaven. I stared at the huge Wasatch Mountains, which I imagined were a gigantic wall of nature for my new domain of confinement. I did not admire their grandeur, but felt lost, lonely, and bewildered within that grand valley. Tears ran down my face uncontrollably, as I stared out the window, searching in vain for a sign that would indicate where I had come from – where is my Cuban homeland? The mountains, to me were seen not for their impressive beauty, but as barriers that deprived me of family and my loving home surroundings – condemned to a place of hopelessness and uncertainties. All my family, my home, and friends were forever lost in a distant land, that I might never see. Yet frozen in my mind, were their nurturing lessons of love and care, which would prove to be a source of strength and power for adapting and survival on the road ahead.

Wasatch Mountain Range

The next day, I got up and proceeded to go to breakfast at the nearby school cafeteria. Many students were busily socializing and moving on the walkways between campus buildings. Everyone appeared engaged in conversation, but I did not know how to interpret their words and facial expressions. I kept greeting people with the formal mispronunciations of *Hell-Loh! Hou Ahrr Joo?* (Hello! How're You) But in response I was greeted with giggles, smiles, and always the first sound out of their mouths was "HI," a word for informal greetings, a short abrupt one-word greeting, so I felt utterly confused as to what message was being conveyed – perhaps making fun of my strange clothing, my looks, or some other weird, possibly offensive message. Soon I found out that no harm was intended; on the contrary people were nice and probably responding with giggles at my winking, and overly expressive, formal greetings, out of a foreign language textbook.

During that first week, in the evening, I was exposed to a new dance – square dancing – where everyone on the dance floor was following directions from a big guy wearing a cowboy hat, shouting over a microphone, to steady country music beat; too monotonous for my Cuban sense of rhythm. The words came out fast and were totally confusing, but I noticed that everyone was laughing and having a great time. Being daring and anxious for acceptance, I joined the dance, in my own way, not following directions I couldn't understand, but synchronizing the steady country music beats to syncopated conga steps - clowning and dancing between the students, as if I were in a carnival parade. This was the beginning of developing a new personality far from the shy and wimpy kid I was in Cuba. I was now a bit of a clown, imitating the humor of a Ricky Ricardo in "I Love Lucy," or trying to pass for César Romero, the Latin lover character, or just a debonair guy hoping to gain admiration and acceptance among my newly acquired friends and acquaintances. Dancing became the key to my popularity among students and later a great advantage for dating girls. By the time, orientation week was over, I felt accepted and, on my way, ready to develop strong friendships. Serious and worrisome school problems were still lurking around me.

A FRESHMAN - Entrance Exams and Registration

That first week, I was called to a large room in the gymnasium, with all the freshman students, for orientation about what classes I would be able to take based on my scores in the placement exams. I was given a seat, right in the front row, within clear view of the faculty monitors. Soon after receiving the exam sheets, I stared at the paper in front of me, without being able to make any sense of the questions, or instructions about what I was supposed to do. I was lost, and after a few minutes of total confusion, one of the monitors recognized my sense of despair, and took me by the arm out of the room. I do not know what was said, but a faculty member monitoring the exam appeared befuddled by my lack of response to her questions. I walked outside and was now lost in an empty football field with no one to talk to or inquire about what was going on. All the incoming students had to take placement exams and were there busily moving about for their course enrollment. But knowing what was going on, I thought in a panic, "this is it! They will throw me out for sure, I am not qualified to be at this place, a college in the U.S., and the school administrators will have to send me back to Cuba." In those days, there were no remedial courses, no awareness of multiculturalism, nor ESL classes (English as a Second Language). On the following day after my placement exam ended in total failure, a gentle lady came to see me, speaking a few words of Spanish, and asked me to follow her into an office. I was pleased to hear someone speaking Spanish, but fearful that she was the designated administrator making final arrangements to put me back on a bus to Florida, for a final Havana destination.

She identified herself as *"la Doctora Myra Yancey,"* who was not an administrator, but a professor of Spanish language and a student advisor. Immediately, she put me at ease by saying *"se puede quedar un semestre"* -- the college would let you stay for one semester as a trial before sending me back to Cuba – so there was no need to worry. With nodding for agreements on course selections, she bypassed the required freshman courses, and created an unofficial curriculum for my first semester with the following classes: Intermediate Spanish, Engineering Drawing, Intermediate Algebra, and Physical Education. Also added to the schedule, I had to audit the Freshman Composition and Reading class required for all entering students. At

Dr. Myra L. Yancey
My first advisor and most important guide like a caring family member during times of need and despair.

that first meeting she alerted me to a dollar bill sticking up from my pants small front pocket and inquired if that was the money for school tuition. I showed her what amounted to less than five dollars, so she proceeded to ask the hard question – *¿cómo vas a pagar por la escuela, el dormitorio y la comida?* - how are you going to pay for school, the dorm and food? My answer was – *voy a trabajar, pero necesito ayuda* – I am going to work but I need help.

How weird to be taking a Spanish class, I thought, when that was the only thing, I did know well, and better than anyone around me. But from the beginning, she let me know that she was not using this class to teach me Spanish, but to teach me *Inglés* - English. I was required to translate the Spanish textbook lessons into English, and explain in class, whenever she would request, issues of culture, idiomatic expressions, or words appearing in the text, *sólo en Inglés* - speaking only in English. This was my first amazing class, where I was not only a student, but I was informally recognized as a teacher's assistant by allowing me to explain the meaning of Spanish words, idiomatic expressions, and the similarities and differences in cultural nuances between Anglos and Latinos. Lucky for me, the class came at no extra charge since the text came as a gift from *La Doctora Yancey* herself.

The second assigned class was Intermediate Algebra, a class for which I was well prepared due to my days of study with cousin *maestra* Guiselda Fernández, and my math tutor in Santa Clara, *el Señor Ocaña*. Thanks to a fuzzy business deal arranged by my *Papá* with him, and my dedication to home study, I was able to pass the exams and graduate as a *Bachiller del Instituto de Segunda Enseñaza* -- a high school equivalent degree with an extra fifth year to enroll at a university. I could not solve word problems since they were written in English – but again math provided a clever way, and a major incentive to learn English through careful and detailed accurate translations of word problems into Spanish.

Furthermore, I became somewhat of an academic clown as well, frantically waiving my hands at any opportunity, volunteering to show on the blackboard a way to solve an equation, factor any polynomial, or do whatever was needed to succeed in my algebra class. The third class was Engineering Drawing, which could be easily understood by just looking at pictures without too much need for English communication or translations. Fortunately, my roommate, Tony, was also taking this class, so he helped me through drawings, and, above all, let me borrow all the required tools: rulers, papers, pens, ink, etc. I simply did not have money to buy any of that "expensive" material, so often while he slept or was busy with his hobbies, I managed to slave over this course with his book and tools. The professor

Burgess Evans
A friend who shared appreciation for basketball and American football

also allowed me to repeat any assignment where I received less than an A grade, thus being able to obtain the best grades possible for all my drawings. The homework was so demanding and time consuming that it gave me second thoughts as to my plans of becoming an engineer. I had long ago abandoned the idea of becoming a physician, due to the sick feeling I got just at the sight of blood or seeing anyone seriously injured. Now, I feared I was encountering another field of rejection - engineering was too demanding – so how was I to make a living in my Cuba or in this strange land.

Finally, my most challenging class was Physical Education with an emphasis on basketball and taught by none other than the college basketball coach, Mr. Richardson. I knew about this game but had never played it, nor had I ever been on a basketball court -- this sport was only available to members of private clubs in my hometown of Santa Clara. Mr. Richardson appeared challenged with me as a player, shouting directions that I did not understand, as I ran from hoop to hoop without even recognizing which team I was playing for, or how I was to throw the ball in an attempt to put it through the hoop.

That first week ended with a search for a Presbyterian Church, so as best as I could I asked for directions. Someone pointed to East 1700 South Street – "What?" I said?" *¿Qué cosa tan rara?* What a strange name for a street, I had never heard of a street with numbers instead of a name, so I was not sure where I was to go. I walked for a few blocks up the street and there was a building with a spike steeple, and people milling around, so I assumed it must be the church. Once inside the sanctuary, people appeared very friendly and welcoming, but I could not understand their greeting words. On my way out I discovered that my first religious adventure was in a Mormon Church which is referred to as an LDS Ward - LDS is commonly used as an acronym for Latter-Day Saints. What struck me as different from the churches I had attended was the friendly atmosphere and apparent freedom to interact with people around you with anyone standing up to speak. I felt exhilarated and as if I had been blessed, so I was ready to tackle the arduous road ahead of study and finding work to earn my way.

MY FIRST JOB

A couple of days after my arrival, without a suitcase, I received a big box delivered from the Greyhound station that contained about 20 pairs of army boots. That was a major mistake, and it was obvious to everyone at the college that those boots could not belong to the Cuban kid. So, with the help of Mom and Pop Fields we took the boots back to the bus station, and *lo and behold!* my own beat-up black suitcase was there for me to pick up. *¡Qué felicidad!* At last, I could change my smelly sweaty clothing. The following day I was taken to the kitchen for instructions on how to wash dishes, and all the pots and pans. Scared and excited about my new job I followed attentively the instructions on how to team up, for what I thought were the very complicated tasks of kitchen work. The pay was 85 cents an hour, 15 cents below the minim wage in those days and tuition alone was around $400. So, my first math problem to solve simply related to "the number of hours I must work to pay for tuition" – excluding the cost of books and living expenses. I clearly concluded that it was nearly impossible since students were not allowed to work more than 20 hours per week, which would amount to only $17.00.

I do not remember how, but with the help of *La Doctora* Yancey and my newly acquired friends, I managed to get a "work permit" added to my student visa for the kitchen job, which also included sweeping and mopping the floors, in addition to washing dishes, and whatever else they asked me to do. This was my first real "paying job" – worrisome because I had no experience, and exciting because I was meeting older folks from the city who were not students, with diverse ethnic and religious backgrounds. An older Mormon lady who worked as a cook was the first person who invited me to meet her family in town along with a long discourse of their faith, which was the prevalent LDS religion in Utah. Somehow, I learned enough English to share my Cuban cultural experience with African Americans, Asian Americans, and others within the happy kitchen compound.

I also expanded my 20 hours per week, bypassing the college regulations and getting weekend gardening jobs at private homes. Gifts came to me in the form of coats and clothing – some very old and worn out, but certainly better than my thin tropical shirts that my *mami* (Mother Sara) had made and I loved but did not serve for the coldest weather I had ever experienced. Dressed in old fashioned hand-me-down overcoats and over-sized clothes, I must have looked quite strange, but who cared, I felt warm and ready to tackle any job as I proudly paraded through campus with my weird attire that kept me warm and shielded me from the bitter cold of winter which had already begun.

From then on *Doctora* Yancey was my savior and mentor, as well as advisor, with whom I shared my insecurities about future pursuits. She was a strong advocate for learning a foreign language through immersion, and although her Spanish was flawless, she avoided speaking to me in my native tongue, unless it was necessary. She went to extremes in trying to get me to learn English as quickly as possible. Almost a year after my arrival, I discovered that a nice, friendly upper division student from El Paso, Texas, Mary Ann Taylor, that had always appeared attentive to my daily problems around the school, had been asked to avoid speaking Spanish to me. She was fluent in Spanish, and confessed to me a year later, that Dr. Yancey had told her to treat me with "tough love," forcing me to struggle with whatever English words I could muster. As painful as it was, I was able to understand most commands and even discussions in the dorm or at the dining table after just a couple of months.

Mable Darwin, Norean Jefferson, Lillian Fritz, Alice Christiansen, and Mary Woods
Most valuable guides during my first job as kitchen helper and dishwasher
Westminster College Kitchen in 1957

However, the more I learned the more frustrated I became, since a basic understanding of the meaning of spoken words came long before I was able to find words to express myself. There was deep frustration in not being able to buy the required textbooks or enjoy refreshments and snacks from the candy machines at the dorm like all the other students, or asking girls to go out on dates, unless they drove and paid for all the expenses. But all around me I experienced a great deal of sympathy and a caring attitude for my daily problems and lack of connection with family and country. There was a great deal of ignorance about Cuba – some students thought that it was a distant place in the Pacific Ocean near Hawaii, and the "better informed ones" recognized it as a place mentioned in the "I Love Lucy" TV show. There was a lot of frustration trying to bring people up to date on the *Revolución* and happenings in my homeland during the 1950s, on top of the dilemmas faced with schoolwork late at night, laboring over my work tasks until near exhaustion, and counting every penny to pay for school tuition and living expenses. Due to this lack of money for books, I was forced to bother my classmates in search of a time when I could come by their rooms to do whatever homework was required. As bad as my situation was, I was lucky to develop strong friendships that helped in times of anguish and offered me the possibility of success in all my undertakings.

By midterm, I was getting accolades in my math class and praised for my dancing abilities. However, I was a dummy in the Physical Education class run by Mr. Richardson, the Basketball coach. My math professor called me a "math star," perhaps, not for my numerical abilities, but due to my overly enthusiastic displays of hand waving, volunteering to solve problems on the blackboard whenever he asked questions from the students in class. I was moving so far ahead that a month after arriving in Utah, my name appeared in the Salt Lake Tribune as a recipient of a scholarship from an honorary fraternity called, Sigma Pi Alpha; and by semester's end I received the highest grades possible in all academic subjects, thus becoming a member in the honorary fraternity - The Stevenson Memorial Society – that awarded me a $50 scholarship to pay for textbooks. Since those first four months in the U.S., I do not remember working so hard and achieving so much with such little resources. Once I was beginning to feel accepted and secure in my scholastic pursuits, it was time to venture into the social life of young and restless people.

Newly acquired friends were ready to introduce me to their families and show me their homes and places where they lived. My first trip away from Westminster was to be to an Idaho farm for a Thanksgiving celebration with my friend Kenny Funk and his family, followed by my first American Christmas in beautiful California.

MY FIRST VACATION
Thanksgiving in Idaho - *Día de Acción de Gracias*
Wonderful Family Celebration

This was my first trip out of Salt Lake City, after my arrival in early September. I felt locked up in the college within my dorm room, the kitchen, and attending classes, but never with a chance to experience the outside world. It was exciting to venture into the homes of American families and travel to a farm area – that I was sure would bring back memories of my Cuban *finca* with trickling arroyos,

farm animals and fresh fruits.

Senior students Kenny Funk and Gary Johnston took me on a memorable ride days before the 1957-year Thanksgiving for a trip to Gary's family home in Logan, Utah. We first made our way through Ogden, a nice quiet town with the usual grid –North to South, East to West city layout, and many blocks highlighted with the ever-present Mormon Wards (Churches) throughout towns and villages of Utah. The country scenery was quite impressive with Mountain tops already capped with snow, but with slopes appearing barren in a monotone grayish color tone.

Pocatello was our first stop in Idaho, a good size city, neatly organized but appearing more diverse in churches, far from the recurring Mormon Wards of Utah. Less than a half hour later we were in Aberdeen, a small village enclave, reminiscent of the tiny villages of the American West, surrounded by huge potato fields.

As Thanksgiving Day approached, I was happy in a family home and ready to give thanks for the generosity and compassion of my dear friend Kenny Funk and his family. He was a psychology senior student who became interested in helping me to learn and assimilate to the new college environment. Kenny's family lived in a rural area of southern Idaho, not far from the village of Aberdeen. There I enjoyed traditional Thanksgiving dinner, with a huge, browned turkey and enhanced with a heavy dosage of potato-based foods: mashed or baked, breads, pancakes and even desserts. It was all very strange and far from the rice and beans followed by sugary Cuban desserts, but nevertheless quite enjoyable, mainly because of being surrounded by a loving family, in a warm country home with older folks, visiting neighbors, and happy toddlers. Kenny helped to make the holidays special for me, playing some Cuban piano pieces I had received as gifts from my favorite cousin Inaita prior to our departure from Salt Lake City. Since early childhood I was captivated by piano music. Despite our poor living conditions, I was privileged to have a piano at home and a mother who exposed me to the classics of composers like Bach, Paderewski and the Cuban Ernesto Lecuona. But on the sad side, my Papá would not allow me to play the piano; he would hit the roof whenever he would catch me struggling at the piano, trying to hit the ivory keys to make a pretty sound -- he would shout *"¡Coño! No seas mariquita"* ("Damn it! Don't act like a sissy queer"). So, I would hide whenever I tried to play, having my cousin Inaita as the watchdog to alert me whenever he was coming home. At the Funk's home, I was free for the first time in my life, as I listened to that beautiful piano music – to engage in trying to make music myself, with the encouragement of people nearby.

Outside the home everything was neatly organized with irrigation pipes, expansive linear demarcations of potato, hay, wheat fields, and a fairly large home garden that had all kinds of salad and fresh vegetables. Nearby there was a huge enclosure for all kinds of farm machineries – like tractors, trucks, land tillers, hay packers, and so on. Unlike in the *finca*, the chickens and turkeys were enclosed in cages, while other farm animals like cows and sheep were free to roam within large, fenced areas. The farm was impressive; it seemed to expand forever into the horizon or out to the edges of mountains miles away. I was enthralled with the farm and its surroundings, listening to Mr. and Mrs. Funk as they explained the running of the farm, not only for their food consumption but going out to markets and selling cattle through betting auctions in town. They must have also been so impressed with my desire to learn that I was offered a summer job – despite the fact I knew nothing about farm work, had never seen a tractor or any kind of farm machinery. At *Tío* Patricio's finca he and the *bueyes* (oxen) did all the work. So, I returned after Thanksgiving with high hopes of having a secure job for the next summer. Little did I know, it would be an amazing learning experience, but a far cry from helping with my financial situation for the following sophomore year.

ROAD TRIP ALL THE WAY TO CALIFORNIA

Once again, I was in despair as a student who could not return home for Christmas vacation. But lucky for me, my dear roommate Tony Ferguson as a kind soul extended an invitation to his home in a rural area near Citrus Heights, California for my first U.S.A. Christmas Holidays in 1957. Tony, more than a roommate, served as a guide and a caring brother who helped me to understand the customs of accepted rules of American behavior. I always looked up to him for guidance in what it meant to be a decent person from his exemplary behavior in this strange land. How lucky I felt when he invited me to enjoy the holidays with his family.

The Bonneville Salt Flats near the Nevada-Utah border

Several students crammed into Tony's car to travel through the big state of Nevada all the way to the outskirts of the small village near Sacramento, the capital city of California. As we drove, I now had a full view of the greatest span of eerie land I had ever seen. The Bonneville Salt Flats, an expanse of flat land just beyond Salt Lake City going out into eternity, over 30,000 acres, covered with a monotone off white colored fine sand. At times along the shore, we would see a strangely altered vehicle racing at incredible speeds – faster than anything I had ever seen. We were going into another world, as this was the last bit of Utah before entering the state of Nevada. Surprise, surprise!! The city grids and Mormon wards were now replaced with a Grand Casino and a Bordello along the highway. All through the state of Nevada there were neon signs and big board advertisements for gambling and carousing -- a side of the U.S. I had not seen. After the rigid laws of Utah on sex and drinking, these displays went beyond anything I had seen in Cuba promoting "sinful" behavior.

After a long and tiring ride going west, we reached Reno and shortly after we came into full view of Lake Tahoe at the California-Nevada border; I marveled at the Sierra Nevada as a sign that we were about to enter a Golden Gem of a State. The car struggled going up a mountain slope where we stopped along the side of the road for me to have a chance to roll and play in the newly discovered magical snow. The Sierra Nevada, at that time, became my favorite landscape in the U.S. – it wasn't Cuba – but I was in awe at the natural beauty of the mountains with snowy peaks and trees rarely seen before this trip: aspens, giant sequoias, and pines that I could touch and sense their pleasant aroma. We were entering into an area of dreams and fantasies claimed by Native Americans, migrants in search of gold, Spanish and Mexican settlers, and all those who continue to roam and venture into the American Far West, a land of wealth and inspiration to poets, writers, naturalists and artists like John Muir and Ansel Adams.

The Ferguson Family - *La Familia Ferguson*

Here I am with Tony's younger sister

We made it to the Ferguson family compound located in an open farm area, outside what was then the small village of Citrus Heights. The family appeared anxiously waiting for Tony, and I was welcomed with open arms as if I were a long lost relative. The entire Ferguson Family made me feel at home, but as an alien from another world, I had to struggle with my heavily accented English speech. They treated me like a dear member of the family, not just a visitor – even with presents under the Christmas tree and catering to my desires of places to visit and things to eat and do in Northern California. I recall that Citrus Heights was so small that the hub for activities, movies, church, and shopping, was in the nearby town of Roseville; and at times we would venture into the capital city of Sacramento. Looking at a map of California at the Ferguson's home, memories of Cuban towns came to the forefront of my mind; there was a Santa Clara, a San José, a Trinidad, and a Santa Cruz, plus many sites whose names made me laugh, but I could not share what was funny about them: *Punta Gorda* (Fat Point), *Avenida de Las Pulgas* (Avenue of the Fleas), *Atascadero* (Stuck in the Mud), *Oso Flaco* (Skinny Bear), To my way of thinking at that time, English speakers had mangled the pronunciation of their towns, so I also had to learn to mispronounce Spanish names that were familiar to me in order to be understood.

The opening of presents under a heavily decorated tree was my first experience of Christmas celebration with a large family. Everything was so different from the celebrations in Cuba with phantasy images of the three Magic Kings on Camels who placed one or two gifts under my bed. It was truly surprising to see that the Ferguson family had managed for "Santa Claus" to place some gifts for me under their Christmas tree. Tony and his family will be remembered for my most memorable holiday experience in the U.S.

I Left My Heart in San Francisco
Dejé mi corazón en San Francisco

My first choice of places to go was San Francisco. I had seen pictures of a city on rolling hills near the sea, which made me dream of the Cuban waters and refreshing ocean air. So early one morning, we left Citrus Heights, drove through, Sacramento, the state capital city, without a stop, and about an hour later reached San Francisco. But first we passed through Berkeley, before crossing the Oakland Bay Bridge. From a distance, the city of San Francisco appeared to be in a dense fog, so I was disappointed by not being able to see much of the surrounding area. Then suddenly we passed through a dark, scary tunnel – the first tunnel I had ever seen - and to my amazement, as we emerged coming out into full view of the Bay Bridge; my entire body was covered with goose bumps and my mouth fell open. It was an immense bridge and the heavy, hanging cables that held it, made me think of a huge musical lyre. The city of San Francisco with its buildings and nearby hills came popping up through a misty fog that day.

The bridge appeared to go for miles and the fog gave an aura of mystery to our place of destiny - I had never witnessed such an amazing sight. As we came closer and closer to the end of the bridge, the city seemed to have sprung from nature inserted on a huge bay with island views and lively folks walking and carousing on hilly streets. When I saw and heard a clanging cable car, I immediately requested to go on a ride – wow! I was so energized that I wanted to race all over town.

We rested for just a minute over Chinese fried rice for lunch, and then I wanted to visit all of China Town, a place I had heard about from *el Chino Julio*, our dear family friend, who had migrated from China to Cuba via California. Julio had given me a letter for a nephew who lived in a neighborhood of San Francisco called China Town, but all I had on the envelope was a name without an address. Once again, my dear friend Tony abided by my request to take me to a place to investigate where we might find Julio's nephew. This shows my naiveté in not realizing how large and complex the city was, with its multiple ethnic neighborhoods – Italian, African American, Latino, Japanese, and of course the famous China Town. San Francisco seemed like a welcoming site where a person from far away could find a place of acceptance and settle to build a homey nest. To my surprise Tony took me to the Cameron House Presbyterian Community Center; a place in the thick of China Town filled with students from various countries of the world. There I met María, the first Cuban I had seen since leaving Havana, she was also a student attending a college in California. I got so frantic and crazy in my behavior that I forgot to speak English for at least an hour – it was a nonstop conversation telling of my adventures since arriving in the U.S. Tony looked at me in total amazement since my mind was blocked from English and I kept speaking to him in Spanish, unaware that he understood nothing of what I was saying. Once I calmed down, we found an administrator of the Cameron House and gave him the letter from my old Cuban friend, *El Chino Julio.* That day was one of the craziest times of my life, we drove back to Tony's home for holiday parties before the drudgery of starting out very early for a long, all-day trip through mostly desert lands as we returned to Salt Lake City. I dozed off and on, but my head was so full of all my new experiences, that I kept waking to relive them.

Dragon Gate in San Francisco Chinatown

SPRING SEMESTER – *LA PRIMAVERA*
Am I Accepted? Maybe, Maybe Not
¿Me aceptan? Quizás

By the end of my first semester, I felt secured – I belonged here - at Westminster with new friends, excellent grades, and trips to Idaho, Nevada and California to meet families that treated me like one of their own. With a job and a scholarship, I had all the necessary help to pay for tuition, textbooks, and school materials. I continued taking Intermediate Spanish, as a primary source for learning English, thanks to verbal agreements with my advisor, *La Doctora* Yancey. Although I had not declared a subject for a major, Professor Donald Wittig encouraged me to consider mathematics as a possibility, after a praise in my freshman yearbook, calling me "the star math student." On the other hand, the world was still suffering from common stereotypes that interfered with career choices and learning possibilities for minority students. Other cultural hang ups were also deterrents for developing a sense of belonging in the milieu of youth and social activities – the concept of dating was still baffling to me. But eventually I managed to become quite popular with my dancing ability and the smile and wink which always expressed my friendly attitude.

MARDI GRAS HUGE SUCCESS!!

The Parson

Mardi Gras King with Cuban Dancing

Rey del Carnaval con Bailes Cubanos

King and Queen of the Mardi Gras Delvis Fernández and Vicki Cushing are being congratulated by Bill Holman, past king, just after the official crowning.

Spring Festival
To Be Long Remembered

Excerpts from The Parson Newspaper of Westminster College, March 21, 1958

The "International" Mardi Gras held in the lounge and gym was a festival to be long remembered, for it was pretty much the consensus that it was one of the gayest affairs held in many years.

A sumptuous Mexican dinner started the evening's festivities …, students, faculty, alumni, and friends of the College flocked into the gym for an evening of revelry at a dozen or more booths, some gaily decorated to represent various nations, and to enthuse over an hour-long floor show consisting of music, Greek, Japanese and Cuban dancing …Flags representing many nations waved from the bars of the balcony, which lent a real international air to the evening.

King and Queen Preside – To get the ball rolling for the floor show … the first and main feature of the evening was an announcement of the title of King of Mirth to reign over the festivities, and his selection of the Queen. Elected was Delvis Fernández, our popular student from Cuba, with Vicki Cushing as his selection for Queen. They were escorted to the platform, duly crowned, presided over the festivities, and also did the Cuban dance.

**Vicki Cushing
The Mardi Gras
Queen at
Westminster
College**

**Cheerleaders
Left to Right: Jani
Weaver, Judy Miller,
Diane Tuck, Judy
Nilsson, Karen Hunter,
and at the center
Joy Wigfall who
surprised me by coming
on stage to dance with
me like a *Cuban Lady***

Before arriving in the U.S.A., I took great efforts to polish my Cuban dancing steps. During most of my teen years, my parents had their first small family home near the *Bar Rojo* (The Red Bar), outside of Santa Clara – a place for men to bring their *queridas* (mistresses) or perhaps meet a sassy lady for a night of drinking and carousing. The bar had a friendly atmosphere with many regular customers, a cozy counter with stools where people would sit for hours quite animated or passing out from too much *ron y cerveza* (rum and beer). There was also a good size dance floor with a *Traga Nickel* – a jukebox where for five-cents one could play old long-playing records with popular or traditional Cuban music until wee hours of the night. The bar was open, within view of my home, to anyone regardless of age, race, or gender; friends and acquaintances made sure that children did not get involved in alcoholic drinking, although we, as adolescents, were not prevented from observing adults drinking to excess and the preliminary moves towards sexual encounter. The owners were friends of my parents, so I was able to watch and at times even shake by body to the traditional and latest dance from *danzones, boleros, cha-cha-chás, rumbas,* rock-and-roll, and even popular American jazz or love songs of the 1950s. By the time I had decided to come to the U.S., I wanted to fit in as much as possible, based on Hollywood promoted stereotypes on what was popular. I went as far as getting a crew-cut hair style with lots of Vaseline to make the hair stand up for the long ride to Salt Lake City – trying to fit into a totally new home base, after thinking that I had mastered dancing steps of rock-and-roll by Elvis Presley, Bill Haley and His Comets, and other famous artists of those days.

My exposures to the *Bar Rojo* clientele and their lively dances paid off so well, indirectly teaching me the latest dance moves, resulting in being elected as Mardi Gras King and crowd entertainer with a performance of an Afro-Cuban dancer. That carnival celebration encouraged other students to approach me for fun lessons on various Latin dances that involved not only moving feet but also shaking hips and shoulders, freeing oneself to musical rhythms, unafraid of appearing too sexy. From then on, I had the unmerited reputation of being a lover boy, who could easily get dates and socialize during school events or even slip away from campus to see what the strict rules in Mormon Land encouraged.

That second semester ended quite successful grade wise, but I still had doubts about being able to make it through college with my severely limited English. Ahead of me were difficult challenges since Westminster was a liberal arts school that required philosophy, bible, and English courses enmeshed with a great deal of reading, essay writings, and lively challenging discussions taught by some of the toughest teachers on campus. I continued with the Spanish class as a way to learn English and enrolled in an engineering course plus two math classes. I attempted a vocabulary building class but had to drop out early due to a lack of sufficient knowledge of English grammar. Finally, I continued with the required Physical

Education, playing unfamiliar games like touch football and badminton. And last but not least, I attempted, by auditing, to enroll in the great Westminster choir directed by Mr. Hodges, a man who helped me to tame down my heavy Cuban accented English coming through my boisterous "near tenor" singing voice.

SUMMER WORK IN IDAHO POTATO LAND
Verano de Trabajo en Tierra de las Papas de Idaho

Once I had finished my first school year at Westminster, I was quite fortunate to have employment for the summer at the Funk farm with a promise of 600 dollars in earnings that would have paid for part of the second-year tuition and living expenses. During the Thanksgiving holidays I had a chance to daydream about my days at the *finca,* and how much I would enjoy expanding on that experience by working under the fresh air of an Idaho farm – eating potatoes galore! It was all an untested fantasy based more on my feelings of nostalgia for my days with *Tío* Patricio as he milked the cows and tilled the land while I climbed mango trees and refresh myself swimming in the ponds of the arroyos.

The home was a model of orderliness with close attention to timeliness for all the necessary tasks to optimize the harvest reaping and general running of the farm. The family showed deeply religious commitments through their daily bible readings and prayers before every meal. They would drive to the nearest town to attend a Mennonite Church every Sunday where I was impressed by the simplicity and lack of decorations or images on their walls – the religious service was mostly silent, humble without bombastic sermonizing. I had never seen such discipline and serenity of quiet behavior at a family home. No alcoholic drinking, no smoking, mostly peace, and abidance to duties were the norms around the farm. But underneath the puritanical norms of behavior there was also wild sinful side.

While working on the hay fields, with sweat on his brows, the supervisor turned his head away from me, pulled out a flat bottle from his front coat pocket and took several swallows. He was obviously trying to hide the bottle from me, but as he attempted to place it back in his pocket, it fell to the ground. I picked it up and noticed it was clearly marked as Irish whisky. My boss smiled and showed a human side perhaps unknown to his family, but now willing to share it with me. He did not offer me any whiskey, but from then on felt free to abide in moments of pleasure away from the drudgery of hard work. This was so different from my exposure to bars and drinking by my *Papá* and his friends – a marked revelation of cultural divide and family interactions. Another manifestation of behavior away from the family occurred when Kenny's two cousins took me around the 4th of July for celebrations in Jackson Hole, Wyoming. One of them drove for about three hours through pasture lands and curvy mountain passes with beautiful snowy capped peaks and greenery unlike the arid lands the Bonneville Salt Flats in Utah. Jackson Hole was a tourist town that reminded me of the old Western movies I had seen in Cuba, while the majestic scenery of the Teton Mountains recalled pictures of the European Alps –

an interesting contrast that I could never imagine as being part of the Wild American West. I was a bit scared driving over mountains and curvy roads with kids younger than I, filled with a spirit of daringness and wild behavior to scare a foreign kid from a distant land; this was unexpected from the quiet sedate atmosphere of their puritanical upbringings. They had beer and cigarettes, and worst yet lots of firecrackers in the car. Once in Jackson Hole, a town bursting with tourists, my dear companions began to light firecrackers and throw them near the feet of pedestrians on the sidewalks or crossing the streets – shouting, laughing, calling them names, and appearing to have a time of their lives, but I, as the scary-cat boy in the car, did

The Grand Teton Mountains near Jackson Hole in Wyoming

not approve of such rumblings and super wild behavior. Eventually a police car made us come to a stop and we were taken to a police station where we were placed in a cell and later asked lots of questions. I recalled the boys praising me and testifying that I was not involved in the pranks in any way or form, along with suggestions that I was an important foreign student with whom they were celebrating America's Day of Independence along with bringing him to enjoy the gorgeous, beautiful scenery around Jackson Hole and the Grand Teton. There were hours of deep anxiety, since I feared that we were going to be kept in jail, thus ending my chances to work at the farm to pay for tuition, and possibly destroy my plans for returning to college in Salt Lake City.

139

Eventually the police officer read us "the riot act" and let me know, that I had saved the day, since they did not want to punish me for the bad behavior of others. The officer escorted us to the city limits and told us in no uncertain terms to "get the hell out of Jackson Hole." From then on, the boys behaved like angels and drove me back to the Idaho farm and the peaceful quiet home. This western adventure showed me a wild side of American youth, never experienced, or seen with my old friends from Santa Clara. It seems that bad behavior existed among my Cuban friends, but they were less daring and more transparent in how they would perform their youthful pranks, certainly respectful of older people. I could not believe that my newly acquired companions, raised within strict discipline, outstanding work ethics, and religious teachings would conduct themselves in such a strange way scaring older citizens and coming close to causing traffic accidents.

A Workday – *Una Jornada de Trabajo*

A regular workday involved getting up at 4 a.m. to move irrigation pipes to insure even moisture throughout the potato fields. The pipes were extra heavy at times due to the remaining water in them from previous irrigation sessions. I had to pull my feet from the mud while balancing a pipe to avoid falling on the ground. Around 10 am we would rest and return to

Daily labor moving irrigation pipes in potato fields.

the house for a big breakfast that always included juice, bacon, potato pancakes or bread, and fresh milk. After eating and resting we would go out to the fields to move bales of hay, feed the farm animals, or gather vegetables for an evening meal. Work was almost constant from early morning to sunset, there were no fun activities – just early to bed for early to rise and work, work, work. I coped with all the heavy duties with dreams of insuring my tuition for my second year of college. In Idaho I learned that there was a large community of Basque immigrants from Spain. I met a shepherd, Fermín Echeverría, working in the fields, who delighted me with family stories and sometimes sharing foods like *croquetas* that filled my stomach with the Cuban flavors I yearned for. Fermín's family seemed well established in the U.S. since coming all the way from Spain and given preferential immigration status due to their reputation for being good shepherds who were willing to work in isolated areas of Idaho and Nevada.

But despite all my learning in the school of hard knocks and doing all kinds of farm labor, when September came, I was only paid $300. Little did I know that Mr. Funk eldest son was supposed to have come up with the other $300, but that never happened. So, there I was, heading back to Salt Lake City after a summer of the hardest work I had ever done in my life, without sufficient money for my tuition. The only solution to my despair was to get back to my old kitchen job of washing dishes and hustling for weekend work as a handy man in private homes. What lesson did I learn?

Never trust a job based on the provincial handshake and verbal agreement. Make sure you have a signed and written contract.

Back on campus after that first hard summer for more work and studies. Here in front of our dorm, I am with my new roommate Walid (Frank) Zeidan, and another student from Jordan, Fawzi Kharoub to the right.

10

MY SOPHOMORE YEAR
New Lessons to Learn

I was saddened to learn after my experience in Idaho doing arduous farm labor during the summer of 1958 and receiving only half of the promised salary, that there were similar stories from other students who were not aware of the system of contractual job obligations. It was a very sad lesson, but worthwhile for all my days ahead in my new land.

Ended my first year with honor and high grades – Selected as member of the Stevenson Memorial Society

I learned another truth that fall as I was the only student, and perhaps the first, from a Latin American country, with Spanish as his primary language. Some administrators saw me as a test case for expanding the college outreach to Latino students. I recall when a college dean called me to his office to praise me for my accomplishments; and then went on to tell me that I had opened the road for other students from Latin America -- furthermore, the college had accepted an applicant from Peru because of my outstanding grades and competence as a university student. In some ways, I was honored but at the same time I felt bewildered and somewhat offended by the "compliment" of seeing me as a general gate opener for students from other Latin American countries. Even with my mentor *La Doctora* Yancey I had to disagree, when she tried to steer me away from pursuing an engineering or math degree, probably due to a lack of role models with my background in those fields of learning. She advised me to work on a career involving Spanish – perhaps as a writer or a teacher. Spanish came easy to me, and she had no examples of students with similar background to mine succeeding in math or engineering.

In my selection of courses for that fall semester of my second college year, I opted for a class that I hoped would help me to procure a good paying job – at least minimum wage - outside the chores of dish washer and garbage collector. So, I enrolled in a surveying class in hopes of gaining the necessary skills that would get me on the road to a professional career as an engineer or a land surveyor. With limited resources of books and drawing tools for the assignments, I managed to get an excellent grade, thus allowing me to gain confidence that for the coming summer break I would get a job as a surveyor assistant or work for an engineering company. While other students in the class managed to get good paying jobs in surveying, the professor said he could not recommend me for any job, outside the college, in spite of my top grades. My destiny appeared to continue as a dishwasher, trash collector, along with other menial jobs offering below minimum wage earnings.

I did not feel in any way that these people were offensive, I accepted the fact that I was in a strange foreign world transitioning into adulthood. At that time, we lived in a social environment where college professors with Spanish surnames did not exist. I was well liked, and someone who indirectly helped to break stereotypes, yet all I could tell was that I lived in a white Anglo dominated environment. I had achieved an impossible dream by being able to pay for school and dealing with my living expenses, but the world around me still had some barriers due more to ignorance, I thought, than to evil discriminatory practices.

During my second year as a sophomore at the college, I was deeply involved in standard college courses that were quite difficult for me, like English Composition, History of Civilization, and Introduction to the Bible; as well as other less difficult courses like Calculus, Surveying, Engineering Problems, and the delightful Choir. My English had improved but I do not remember ever working as hard as I did over assignments that involved writing essays in English – while my roommate would get a top grade for a composition, he would write within a few minutes before breakfast, I would end up with a low grade for the same assignment on which I had labored over the whole weekend.

Carnival at Westminster

College Readies Global Date

Lending international air to Westminster's annual carnival, from left, Cuban Delvis Fernández, Peruvian Eduardo Merino, with event general chairman, Stewart M. Hanson

During my third college year, thanks to **Eduardo Merino**, the newly accepted student from Peru, who was also a gifted musician, I discovered another "city" within Salt Lake City, on the other side of the railroad tracks. There I came face to face with Mexicans, Puerto Ricans, and other Latinos in a *barrio* – neighborhood - where everyone spoke Spanish – now ready for a night-out at a music club that provided a blissful escape from my obsessive quest for acceptance and assimilation in the dominant Anglo-culture.

RETURN TO CUBA, Not quite!
Regreso a Cuba ¡Todavía No!

During my first semester at Westminster College, I was totally consumed with learning English, adapting to a new environment, and coping with deep feelings of nostalgia for the family and country left behind. But as time went on and I was able to communicate in English, I searched intently for news about the escalating struggles in the *Sierra Maestra* of Eastern Cuba, expanding throughout cities and now into the *Escambray* Mountains near my hometown of Santa Clara. I visited the school library almost daily in search of articles about the Revolution in newspapers and magazines; and made it a ritual to visit friends with short wave radios to try to hear news from Cuba itself. It was a major challenge that ended mostly in failure, but around September of 1958 I received a disturbing call from Miami, Florida that left me totally confounded. My *Papá* and *Mamá* had left Cuba and were now living in Miami. Instead of feeling glad, I felt rather sad and disappointed that they were not in the homeland of my dreams – where I was planning to return and live happily ever after, near sparkling blue ocean waters.

My father Delvis Rafael (alias *Vive*) had lost his garage business, was about to lose the house, and worse yet had received threats to his life. *Mamá y Papá* contacted my uncle Benjamin who was already established in Miami, and was able to get jobs for them and visas to enter the U.S. They left two daughters behind – five-year-old Puchy and 14-year-old Sarita -- under the care of my dad's family, for what they thought would be a brief one or two years stay. They were already in their forties and suffering from serious health problems. My mother suffered from very poor vision, while my 43-year-old father had long-term mobility impairments. He suffered from serious ailments causing severe pains due to rheumatism and gout diseases, on top of having to cope with addiction to daily drinking of beer and rum. They were not the typical immigrants coming to the "land of liberty" – they imagined that they would earn enough money to save family home in Santa Clara, also send money to feed their two daughters and grand *familia*, as well as make it possible for Sarita to attend the private *Academia de Antolín González del Valle* for her high school education. They fantasized that once they were able to meet their goals, and when peace was to return to Cuba, they would go back home.

Papá (Dad), with *Mamá Sara* (Mom) had carefully saved some money, running *El Relámpago*, a Sinclair gas station and auto repair business on the *Carretera de Camajuaní* (highway) outside of Santa Clara. However, during the days of rebellion, Batista's rural guards and soldiers would come to the station for tools and repairs, fill their jeeps and trucks with gas and never pay a cent, so when I left Cuba in 1957, he was struggling with keeping the business afloat. Finally, in 1958, a friend was assassinated, *Papá* received life threats, the garage was lost, and the home was about to be lost as well. He was too old and insolvent financially to care for his dear *familia*, so leaving Cuba was the only option he could see on his plate. My *Mamá* Sara as usual came to the rescue with some money hidden in weird places, so along with help from her brother Benjamin, who was already in the U.S., and assisted them, they managed to come to Florida for what they thought would be a "short stay." I was totally astonished and had not seen this move coming at all. With little word from them about this trauma, I could not even imagine how hard things must have been to make this difficult decision.

A Second Greyhound Ride – Another Long Round Trip
Un Segundo Viaje en Guaguas de la Greyhound
Esta Vez de Ida-y-Vuelta

I felt deeply compelled to be with my parents but was also confused as to what would be in all of our best interest: (1) Should I quit school and join them in Florida? (2) Should I leave the U.S. to join the rebels in Cuba? or (3) Should I stay at Westminster College until completing my studies for a college degree? Before making a rush decision, I waited until the Christmas school break, so I could go and have a serious discussion with *Mami* and *Papá* to seek advice on what to do and where to go next – moving back to Cuba being a strong possibility. The beginning of my sophomore year was filled with personal anxiety -- not only about my *bona fide* college courses but with fear of the chaos and rebellion taking place all around Cuba, now aggravated with concerns about my parent's well-being in Florida - their strange new land.

A dilemma emerged due to my low paying jobs, and all my expenses -- how was I to save money for a trip to Florida? I had only two weeks of vacation, so ideally, I would fly there and back, but taking an airplane was far too expensive and it was not possible to borrow money for such an adventure. That gave me only one option: to board a Greyhound again, and depending on the situation in which I would find my parents, seek their advice about what course of action I should take – stay in Miami, return to Cuba, or ride back to Salt Lake City?

As soon as school was out for the two weeks of Christmas Holidays, I rushed to buy the ticket and get on a Greyhound bus for the five-day trip to Miami. This time, for me, it was misery through and through, with hardly any money to buy meals and filled with confusing thoughts about what to do once I was there. I was not interested in socializing with the bus passengers, nor had any desire to enjoy, let alone, observe the passing scenery which I had already seen on my first bus trip. I was tormented, crying in silence, huddled in a fetal position, drowsy, half awake and half asleep during the long excruciating ride.

Finally, in mid-morning I arrived in Miami, feeling lost and bewildered. It seemed like no one was waiting for me, but then all of a sudden, I heard someone shouting – the shrill sound I had not heard since leaving Cuba – *"¡PUPY, PUPY, CHICO MIRA PA'CÁ!"* (Poop-ee, Poop-ee, Cheeco, Look this way!) After more than a year in the quiet land of Zion, I was embarrassed by my *Papá's* Cuban accented Spanish and loud shouting just down the block *en Los Estados Unidos* (in the U.S.) *como un loco* (like a mad man). Now I was an odd ball once again, but this time within my own rough culture, after more than a year away. My *Papá* was all sweaty from the heavy humidity, wearing an open shirt, showing his hairy chest and somewhat disheveled from whatever work he was doing. He hugged and kissed me while I wiped tears off my cheeks.

We got into a car and drove straight to a restaurant that was part of the Desert Inn, a motel in the northern section of Miami. I was not only happy to see him but looked forward in anticipation to a real Cuban cook meal. However, to my surprise – he was not taking me to a sumptuous meal of *picadillo con arroz, frijoles negros, y platanitos* – he was simply taking me to his job, where he worked more than full time as a dishwasher. He had been given permission to leave just long enough to get his son at the Greyhound Bus station. Immediately, behind the kitchen, I was given some restaurant leftovers, which I quickly devoured while standing with an apron next to a dishwashing machine much bigger than the ones I had witnessed at Westminster College with hoses and sprinklers, ready for washing just about everything used in the kitchen – pots, pans, plates, bowls, silverware, etc.

Finally, we were able to leave the restaurant after *Papá* finished his duties as we were replaced with a night crew of hotel workers. At last, in the late evening, we made it back and climbed the stairs to his tiny apartment where my *Mami* Sara was anxiously waiting for me.

The Desert Inn
First place visited in Miami after a 5-day bus ride from Salt Lake City to serve with my *Papá* as a kitchen dishwasher.

147

First Home in Miami – *La Primera Casa en Miami*

They lived in an attic, above a house, that served as a studio apartment with a double bed for them and they had managed to also get a temporary small *catre* (an army cot) for me to use as a bed during my short 4-day visit. They introduced me to nearby neighbors, Cuban families with whom we passed the time laughing, telling jokes and listening and discussing the troublesome news from Cuba. And at long last I felt fully welcomed in a humble place, where I lay on the small bed, but pleased to fully stretch out my entire body after five days of crouching on a bus seat. Morning arrived, stretched my arms wide, sat up in bed, and bang! -- I received a rude awakening with a bump on my head. The attic slanted ceiling was so low that I had to literally roll out of the *catre* onto the attic floor before being able to sit or fully stand up. Unlike my Cuban experiences, there was a "hurry, hurry" attitude -- *¡Hay que moverse! Vamos a llegar tarde al trabajo* – "we've got to move; we'll be late for work." My mother was working too, in a factory wrapping pizzas with plastic saran paper, or making stuffed toy alligators for tourists, and sometimes as a nanny taking care of a toddler. In his new life, in Miami my *Papá* was a househusband, a driver for her to and from work, and a full-time dishwasher at the hotel in North Dade County.

Between chores, at night, we found time to meet other Cuban neighbors who sat closely by a short-wave radio to hear news from Cuba. It was worrisome to hear about so much strife, reports of bombings, death, and destruction near Santa Clara, and at one time we even heard the roaring sounds of planes and bombings within the city. As agonizing and tiring as the work was around us, the radio gave us an escape route for the reality confronted by families and friends back home *en la Amada Tierra* – in our beloved land.

They put me to work too, helping my *Papá* as a dishwasher, but when New Year's Eve came, I looked forward to being paid a little money for a ride back to Utah or whatever was to come. First, I had to take a bus to Miami Beach with a young neighbor who worked at a same hotel. Since he knew that I was an experienced dishwasher, the hotel hired me for just a one-night job during the New Year's celebration. The work was unreal – towers of plates, pots, pans, and utensils crashing to the floor; waiters and bosses screaming and rushing around us demanding to speed up the delivery of clean plates and utensils. I have never forgotten the sweat all over my body nor the pain in my legs from standing up for hours on end, without a moment of rest. It was around 3:00 in the morning when we were finally able to leave the hotel after signing papers and giving my address to send my earnings to Utah for that night, at last, we could take a breath of fresh air, feel the rushing ocean waters of Miami Beach, and look forward to a good night rest on my *catre* in the attic home. But NO! That was not possible, right away; the buses were not running at that early morning hour in the dark. So, my newly acquired friend and I had to walk for hours along city and canal streets stretching for miles and miles back to our homes in Miami.

Once again, following my foolish instincts, I was denied any promised pay for the most intense night of work in my life – the check never came. Now, after a five-day bus trip, followed by four intense days of "vacation," with my parents - my decision was made: take another five-day trip back to peaceful and quiet Salt Lake City and study, study, study and work, work, work to get ahead in life with a college degree. So, I rummaged into every pocket to find only a few dollars, but *Mamá* came to the rescue again with money wrapped in aluminum foil in her freezer, I was able to buy the return bus ticket to the Land of Zion, with just enough left for the cheapest meal on the menu – pancakes, or an occasional snack bag from the machine at the Greyhound Bus station cafeteria for my five-day return.

I arrived in Salt Lake City five days later, thinner, and more tired than I had ever thought possible – an ordeal of 10 days round trip by bus plus four days of hard labor in Miami during my 14 days of college "vacation" time. Again, I had to get ready to tackle a new year of poverty, lots of manual labor, and intense studies that required good knowledge of English. But despite all my tribulations, I had some of the best times of my life that spring semester, as I had joined the Westminster Choir, which traveled throughout much of the Southwest, on their tours, thus enabling me to really make close new friends and see many states I had never dreamed of.

SUMMER of WORK and FUN
Verano de Trabajo y Divirtiéndome

During the 1959 summer break, I was invited by Dr. Parker Pontz, a college President's assistant, to watch over his home during the summer months while he went on vacation with his family. I was deeply moved by his trust in me, a foreign student without access to family and in dire need to pay for living and school expenses. His home basement was my home, free of charge during the summer months, with no particular tasks around the house; it was a blessing to have a place to live, next to the college. In a modest way, Dr. Pontz was helping me, a homeless poor student, so that I could save money for food and college tuition. In addition, I had another job on campus. Sometimes I worked every single day of the week without a day of rest; as the campus work was full time, doing all kinds of cleaning, painting, and general maintenance work, and gardening at private faculty homes. I was a "jack of all trades," always ready and able to do whatever was asked of me. I felt compelled to never turn a job down, as I so desperately needed the money, even if I had no idea as to what I was doing, nor how to do it. When my boss Leonard Clark, the maintenance supervisor at the college, asked me if I knew how to drive a jeep, I eagerly jumped at the chance and said, "yes I can," (*"Yo, Sí Puedo"*) - my response to every request. Within a matter of minutes, with help from my working buddies, I was chugging myself all over the campus, as a first-time driver with no license. That summer I was lucky to learn how to drive, and by the end of the year I took the exams for a valid driver's license.

That summer on campus, we were a motley crew of mostly foreign students – from Hungary, Jordan, Greece, China, Peru, and Cuba -- helping each other and involved in all kinds of low-paying jobs but enjoying each other's company. We developed strong friendships, shared ideas for success in the new land, discussed our different mores and customs, and discussed our common traditions of respect and human values. More than work, it was a valuable extension of learning beyond the school curriculum, by developing strong bonds with people from various parts of the world - one of the best education experiences of my life.

The Cosmopolitan Club - Learning Beyond the Classroom

Seated Left to Right: **Eduardo Merino** (Perú), **President Henry Hecker** (Hungary),
Sponsor Dr. May Schwender (Germany), **Vice-President Delvis Fernández** (Cuba),
and **Treasurer Walid Frank Zeidan** (Jordan).
Standing: **Fawzi Kharouba (Jordan)**, **Allan Lee** (China),
Radi Hadaddin (Jordan), and **Ted Xenakis** (Greece).

During my third year at Westminster College, I joined other foreign students to form **The Cosmopolitan Club** in order to meet and learn about our cultures as well as broaden our understanding of the United States of America.

Walid (Frank) Zeidan, my roommate, a brilliant young man from Jordan, only sixteen years-old when he finished high school and fluent in three languages. Walid filled me with histories about events in Jordan, Palestine, and the Middle East, enriched with family anecdotes. He was like a younger brother that I guided to abide by American work ethics, especially making sure that he would get to work on time.

George Ieromnimon, my first Greek friend, who was older and more experienced in the nuances of American culture. Perhaps more than any other friend he offered sound advice about dating college girls and social behavior in general.

Henry Hecker, my dear Hungarian friend, had tremendous joie *de vivre* and would always find the beautiful side of any life experience, even sharing stressful family stories and reasons for leaving his home in Europe.

John Russell was an American friend whom I secretly admired, as a role model for his musical talents. Music playing was always in my heart and soul; so much so, that I often fantasized about joining him at a musical concert with the Utah Symphony at the marvelous Mormon Tabernacle.

Callings of the revolution
Llamados de la Revolución

On the negative side, when I was all alone, I was feeling quite depressed after my bad experiences "dating" and frustrated for being detached from the family back in Cuba with the calls of *La Revolución*. The Revolution was in its heydays after years of rebellion that extended from the Sierra Maestra in Eastern Cuba to towns and villages all over the Island. Since my days in Cuba, family and friends were in support of government changes and some went as far as joining in the struggle for ending the Batista dictatorship. Later in 1959 after the triumph of the Revolution, I received news about my 14-year-old sister Sarita getting involved in the literacy campaign helping to teach older adults how to read and write. Also, my aging grandmother **Felicia Rodríguez Marzall**, whom I called *Mamá Vieja*, appeared dressed as a *miliciana* holding a rifle guarding the Santa Clara post office. Sister and Grandma worked with a vision of a better world, building a society with expanded opportunities for all Cubans, eradicating illiteracy, with vast agrarian and urban reforms that would attempt to level the playing field for all *cubanas y cubanos* without regards to race, ethnicity or class distinctions. My total existence appeared disconnected from the world around me, yearning for a real *familia* and home environment of loving parents and extended family, involved with a noble cause challenging the evils from our past.

Mr. Gunn's Daughter – *La Hija de Míster Gunn*

During that summer there was only one girl working on campus anywhere near my age. She worked as the switchboard operator and receptionist in the Administration building, which was also where Mr. Gunn's office was located right in front of her work area. I would always smile and wink as I passed her, but never anything more, especially for fear of Mr. Gunn's watchful eye. He was the Business Manager of the college and had always been the boss of my boss since my arrival at Westminster. He also was the person who handled payment for all the employees of that school, including me as lowly lower than minimum wage paid worker. As the man in his position of authority, he appeared very serious and handled all situations with a

Ralph S. Gunn
Business Manager and exemplary guide to students on campus

very strict and stern manner. His daughter, Norine, was the only young female on campus and a beautiful girl who posed on a grassy slope in front of the main gothic-Administration building as she ate her lunch and moved as if she were on a catwalk reminiscent of a model on a *pasarela*. She was surrounded by a small group of detached foreign male students, including myself, who stayed on campus to work,

Norine Gunn
In 1959

as none could afford to go back to their countries of origin just for a summer. She had many prospective beaus anxious to take her out on dates, and I was crazy about her but did not want to get involved, since she appeared well beyond my reach – a young man without a car, no money for going anywhere, yet starting to hope for a steady, loyal relationship. I was aware that she had dates with several of my friends and co-workers on campus, which made me think that the idea of becoming my *novia,* my concept of having a steady girl, was not part of her life experiences or anything she would consider. As a newcomer to the college, she probably had no inklings of bonding in a steady relationship with any one in particular – the American way, but very foreign for me.

Suddenly, one week at the end of summer just before school was to start *La Doctora* Yancey, acting more like *familia* than faculty advisor, invited me to a faculty get together at her home; and whispered in my ear "be sure to bring a date." Well, who was I going to ask? There was only that one girl, and although I was crazy about her, I was filled with anxiety about her as a forbidden fruit – she was not only on another social scale, but she was, as well, the daughter of the feared, ultimate boss Mr. Gunn, the business administrator, and the super boss of all my bosses on campus.

Given my dire situation, feeling the urge from my dear mentor to bring someone to her party, I had no choice but to ask Norine Gunn for a date. To my surprise, she accepted, so I immediately looked at the bad side, thinking she was not so much interested in me, but looking forward to rubbing shoulders with members of the Westminster faculty - her future teachers! To my surprise, Norine was a sweet, simple woman who never projected a sense of superiority as I had imagined. Her modeling and haughty image were simply attempting to practice her assignments at the John Robert Powers Finishing School – a school paid by her stylish grandma, as a high school graduation gift in hopes of moving her away from her tomboyish mannerisms. She did let me know, however, that she had placed fifth in the Miss Utah competition through that school. Over the years I have often teased her that only four others participated, to which she always insists there were at least twenty. The date was a revelation of a girl I could fall in love with – or perhaps I had already

Offensive cartoon drawing by a "friend" after announcing my engagement to Mr. Gunn's daughter

fallen for her during the summer without even knowing it.

I do not remember the exact timeline, but I asked her to go out on a second date for the following Saturday, but in a somewhat equivocal answer I was told that she already had a date for that evening. In a rather rude tone, I let her know about my negative views on American dating, asserting that she either "went with me, and me alone, or forget the whole thing." In shocked confusion, she asked, "What are you talking about, are you asking me to go steady with you after just one date?" to which I answered with my heavy accented English of frustration: *"Estedy, what is dat? joo go only wis me o nada!"* Somehow my rudeness paid off and she remained my loyal steady friend throughout my third year at Westminster – and far beyond.

11

FOUND MY *NOVIA* AND NEW JOB

As I began my third year in the Fall of 1959, I was adjusting to sharing a room with a new roommate named John H. Stewart. By this time, I was able to speak English quite well and to a large degree had overcome the anxieties of coping and adapting to the college surroundings – in short, I felt I was assimilating to the "American Way."

John added a new side to my life, a higher sense of duty, extra hard work and discipline. He had just left the military, so he was still immersed with a high sense of neatness and getting his work done properly and on time for the daily battle grind. Thanks to him I was trained in a valuable skill at the time as a multi-lithography operator. In those days, copying machines and computers were not available to faculty and administrators of the college. From letters to brochures and class exams, everything had to be sent to the copying center which was run by an expert printer – referred to as a *multilith* machine operator. Of course, I could not see private documents like exams or personal letters but everything else was in my hands. As I well recall, this meant a 15-cent increase in salary, now up to a minimum wage of $1 per hour – which was further increased to $1.20 once I perfected my printing skills. This was definitely a sign that I was moving up in the world, even with inky oily dirty hands from the printer; I was now in an environment where I got

John H. Stewart
My last college roommate who also served as guide in learning new labor skills and culture assimilation.

to associate with secretaries, faculty, and school administrators. Forever I cherish my friend John's contribution to improving my life. He was also an avid listener of short-wave radio stations from around the world. So, at night, free from our work duties he would give me a chance to listen to stations in Spanish, and for the first time I was able to hear news directly from *La Habana*, Cuba.

Developing new friendships
Desarrollando nuevas amistades

Now I was entering into a more secure existence, being able to argue, debate, have fun, and socialize using the English language without fear of making mistakes, or having students approach me to practice Spanish or to teach them movements for Latin dances. There were many other friends, students with whom I would socialize in school venues or in the nearby shopping center of Sugar House. At that time, I had finally found a physical education class in which I managed to receive a high grade. In Cuba I used to enjoy roller skating around the streets of Santa Clara, and now unbeknownst to me I could adapt those skills to ice skating – and better yet the college offered a class in dancing on ice, where I could incorporate new steps based on my ability to shake my body to vibrating rhythms.

Westminster Choir with Norine in front row, sixth from right
Delvis in top row 2nd from right

That fall was filled with new places to explore due to touring with the choir. Norine also had joined the choir, so the experiences were made even more enjoyable. I got to visit San Francisco again and share it with her as the 'expert' since she had never been there. Two good friends from choir also come to mind, first was Lou Campbell– a very dynamic young man with sparkly eyes who introduced himself as a person of Native American ancestry, and Eduardo Merino, from Lima, Peru.

Delvis with two choir members: Roberta McKean and Mary Anne Taylor, visiting the Grand Canyon in Arizona for the first time, with a Westminster Choir tour the southwest.

Lou Campbell was very interested in dancing and Spanish/*Latino* culture, so we were special friends who sang and travelled with the Choir to small and large towns through the Western U.S. He was a real joker and always added a light side to those long trips. Lou was crazy about Latin dances, so he looked at me as a motivational shaker for mambos, rhumbas, and cha-cha-chas. This made me feel wanted for my unique "talent" as a dancer. By right, I had no formal musical training, only the exposure I had been lucky to have, with the daily sounds and moves all over my Island, in homes with cousins, and the forbidden *Bar Rojo.*

Eduardo Merino was a skillful percussion player of Latin Music - conga drums, bongos, maracas, claves, etc. He was more in touch with the nuances of Cuban music and rhythms than I was. So, at times, in the cafeteria when hardly anyone was around, he would start tapping familiar tunes on the tables. For me it was like fresh air – hearing musical sounds with a clear beat from my dear land. Eduardo was quite interested in my Cuban roots and assumed that I, as well, must be a skillful conga player. I still remember his reaction when he asked me to play with him, what I thought was a rather complicated rhythmic pattern, and I could not even get started. So, to his amazement he asked: *"¿Y tú dices ser cubano?"* -- And you say you are a Cuban? Well, Eduardo was already an accomplished musician with a South American Combo started in Salt Lake City – a place where I thought I was the only *Latino*.

I was so isolated in my Anglo-American cocoon, working hard to blend in, that I could only imagine a Salt Lake City as an ethnically homogeneous place, mostly Mormon, with a sprinkling of other religions. But to my surprise, Eduardo took me to a lively club on the "other side of the railroad tracks." It was a revelation of a hidden side of the city, and above all made me feel that this corner of Utah was not that far removed from my cultural roots.

Jim Smith was the only friend and only person that I had met who had been in Cuba. He had visited Havana before coming to Utah, so that gave him a special place in my heart. Jim also had *La Doctora* Yancey as college advisor and, like me, was very interested in following the debates on TV occurring for the first time between the presidential candidates, John F. Kennedy and Richard M. Nixon. The issue of what to do with Cuba, was prominent in their political discourse. He was a diplomat par excellence, giving opinions, showing other points of views but always with tact and respect. He was a little older and much more experienced in life than I was, so that made me look up to him. I saw him as a compassionate person who with modesty and sincerity recognized injustices and quietly, but firmly, came to the forefront to help people in need.

Here I digress to go back to my days in Cuba as a teenager. My *Papá*, as I have stated earlier, was a clever provincial negotiator, sociable to extremes, seldom signing a contract but dealing with people face-to-face. The services provided by doctors, schoolteachers, tutors, and dentists for his *familia* were arranged through a system of favor exchanges, involving work exchange, verbal promises and always *tabaco y ron* (cigars, beer, and rum). As a youngster I suffered from dental problems that seemed to be ignored by those around me, perhaps due to the lack of tooth paste and at times having to brush my teeth simply with plain water and with my own fingers. It was assumed that teeth were a commodity that would be lost in life, so perhaps the best recourse was to let them rot and in due time replace them with false dentures. But bless my *Papá*, he tried to decide with a dentist friend to take care of my expanding number of cavities. When I was around 15 years old, I would stop in the dental office of *el Doctor Tramposo* (name changed to Dr. Cheater), a man with whom my *Papá* had made a deal in exchange for mechanical work on his car, for taking care of problems occurring with my teeth. Dr. Tramposo would place a *motica* (a tiny cotton ball) saturated with a liquid anesthetic in the holes of some of my molars to alleviate the tooth aches -- a phony cure that went on for weeks without solving the real problem of filling my multiple cavities.

My Ten Cavities – *Mis Diez Caries*

Once living in Salt Lake City, I was suffering from excruciating tooth pains, but the cost of dental care was far beyond my means to pay. Again, through the intervention of *La Doctora Yancey*, I found a dentist in town who was willing to work on my rotten teeth, he also agreed to allow me to spread the payments over the course of a year. At the time this was still too much for me to handle since I was again always near being penniless. In addition to my college expenses, I was sending $11 dollars every month to my parents in Miami, who would send them on to a family in Spain. Eventually the money made its way to the family of Dr. Manolito Fernández, to pay for my sister, Sarita's, high school education at the *Colegio Academia Antolín González del Valle* in Santa Clara. This complicated approach of helping families in Cuba was necessary, and one of the few recourses left for Cubans in the U.S., to help our families back in Cuba. Our situation was dismissed as - collateral damage, during the Cold War days in the battle of ideas to prevent the expansion of communism throughout Latin America.

When I went to make my first payment to the dentist in Salt Lake City, I was informed that the bill had already been paid. I approached *La Doctora Yancey*, thinking that she had something to do with such extraordinary help. In a quiet tone, she informed me that Jim had paid it all! Wow, that gesture, by Jim Smith, meant a great deal to me, and revealed what a true, caring, and devoted friend he was, and so I always treated him with great admiration. Later I also realized that Jim was a deeply religious person, with a sense of respect for other people's beliefs, as he never tried to convert anyone to his religious creed.

MEXICAN AMERICAN DISCOVERY
Mi Primer Amigo con Raíces Mexicanas

One of the most pleasant discoveries came while on choir tour in the form of awareness of well-established communities of Mexican origin in towns and villages of the Southwestern United States: in Colorado, Nevada, New Mexico, Arizona, and the super large states of Texas and California. People of Mexican background along Native Americans had lived on these lands prior to the arrival of European settlers, and their presence even preceded the formation of the United States of America as a nation. However, throughout my years of education in Cuba and now in the U.S., little or nothing was discussed about their history and cultural contributions in schools and universities. I had met a few students with

Spanish surnames but seldom anyone approached me speaking Spanish – I assumed that whatever was left of the Old Mexico, had been totally assimilated into a so called "American Anglo culture and way of life."

An exception came with one of my dearest friends, **Leoncio Reyes**, from Elko, Nevada. **Leon** and I had rooms near each other in the dormitory referred to as Foster Hall; like birds of a feather, we spoke Spanish and discovered that we had a lot in common even though he had never lived in Mexico or any other Latin American country. We bonded like two lost brothers reaching out to each other in the middle of our strange surroundings. Unlike me, he could act as "American as apple pie," fully knowledgeable of the cultural mores. He was a gifted athlete

and player for the Parsons Football Team, and through him I learned to like and appreciate the rules of the game. He was a well-liked and admired young man, but there was also a hidden side to him, as he had strong Mexican roots. Sharing family anecdotes and tales of the past, he was the first person who made it possible for me to experience and enjoy authentic, super-hot Mexican food as we laugh and spoke in our native Spanish language. I became so intrigued with him and his background that when the Christmas break came, he warmly invited me to his home in Elko, Nevada to meet *toda su familia, el papá y su mamá, tíos y tías, primos y primas* and many friends from the surrounding area with similar cultural backgrounds. I was dropped at his home in Elko by my sweetheart Norine's family on their way back to Utah from a memorable Christmas visit with their other daughter Clarice in California.

Leoncio Reyes
Leon with his cousin and Delvis in Elko, Nevada

I could not believe what I was witnessing, a large American family – *pero Mexicanos todos, hablando español* – eating delicious foods with *picante* that brought tears to my eyes. Leon was bound and determined to share the humble origins of his *familia* and how they lived. As we entered his home, there was a bedroom, not a living room, and everywhere else there were beds for other family members. The home of his aunt and uncle was larger and served as a place for fun and lively family gatherings and celebrations. The day before our departure back to Salt Lake City, I was helping to cut a tree by his aunt's house – a rare specimen of nature in arid Nevada – and something I had never done before. In my clumsy way I failed to step aside as the tree came falling down, and I instead kneeled down, and the tree trunk hit my thigh causing a fracture of the femur bone. It required a cast from the hip all the way to my ankle. A mad ride to emergency was the order of the day – for my first and only fracture with a huge cast. Although for years I lost contact with Leon, he remained in my heart as a dear friend who exposed me to a rich culture outside the dominant world around me. The memories he created were revisited years later at Chabot College in Hayward, California when I worked with the Chicano students to expand the educational opportunities for underrepresented students at the college where I was teaching.

CEMENTING A RELATIONSHIP
Are we "going steady"? *¿Somos Novios?*

After the party *en la casa de la Doctora Yancey* and breaking a date just to go out again with me, Norine and I became *novios* – we declared loyalty and trust for each other, in an attempt by me to establish a steady relationship with an American woman. After my negative experiences dating, I was in a trial mode – yearning for developing closer relations beyond being mere friends.

Not being a Mormon gave her a unique place in Utah and a remarkable perspective on life there. She was born in Mount Pleasant; smack in the center of the state, where her family worked at The Wasatch Academy, a private Presbyterian boarding high school catering mainly to students from Utah and neighboring states, that lived in remote areas or for some reason needed that type of school. In her hometown she was often the odd one out – as the only child of a different religious persuasion in her public grade school, named Hamilton, where all the pupils were Mormons with blue eyes and blond hair. She tried to pass for a person of Native American ancestry with some Italian and Greek mixed in – an idea she got from pictures in the encyclopedia of people with dark eyes and dark brown hair -- like hers. Neither Norine nor I fit into the dominant culture of Utah, so although we had very little in common, we were two rare birds in the Land of Zion. Norine in her clever way, also showed me an unexpected side of her life interests, as she had two Cuban LPs - long playing vinyl records - a rare find in that part of the world: Pérez Prado, the mambo King, playing *Bésame Mucho* with a Cuban swing, and another recording of traditional country song titled, "A Hot Night in Cuba." For me, finding a gorgeous woman from a remote area of Utah, with interest in Cuban music, was like a call from Heaven for the establishment of a long-term relationship.

Although we were only "going steady," she took me to her home, where I met in a friendly family atmosphere: her parents, Ralph and Alice Gunn, her paternal grandmother Grace, as well as their neighbors with strong Mormon roots, Mr. and Mrs. Simmons and their two adorable children Annette and Steve – kids that were often under Norine's care as a babysitter. When the December school-break arrived, to my total surprise, Mr. & Mrs Gunn invited me to come with Norine to meet their other daughter Clarice in Whittier, California. This was a sign of acceptance beyond anything I had ever imagined. The long drive was uneventful, but the trip gave me a chance to witness a rare family interaction; parents who appeared deeply religious, praying, and reading inspirational books at every meal. Their voices were quiet with never an argument let alone a fight, and always under, what seemed, total emotional control, even under the closed quarters of a car for hours and hours from Utah, through Nevada all the way to Los Angeles, California.

Once at the home of Norine's sister, Clarice with her husband Blaine Paetsch, I had the opportunity to meet a young family, celebrating the holidays with their six-month daughter, Renée. A family that appeared more relaxed in meeting the obligations of parenting, as they told jokes, laughed, and prayed together. Their undivided attention went out to this new family addition – cute little Renee who looked like a doll

Baby Renee telling me: "Join the *Familia*"

under the Christmas tree. This was my first encounter with holding, playing, and interacting with such an adorable baby who seemed to smile at every chance and feeling welcomed by these people who had such a strong *familia* – it was perhaps my moment of realization that the time had arrived to settle down and build a long-lasting family relation with Norine.

Decision Makings & Heavy Commitments
Tomando Deciciones – Compromisos Profundos

During that third year at Westminster, as a Junior, I felt that I had achieved proficiency in English to tackle just about any course in the language arts and music fields. I had been singing and traveling with the choir through large and small towns in adjacent states to Utah and as far as California, with opportunities to marvel in amazement at the sight of the Grand Canyon in Arizona. These trips helped to destroy many stereotypes I had of the *Americanos*. Again, although "well educated" in Cuba and now with access to a "good" college education, I was oblivious to the diversity of peoples and cultures of the Southwest. I was aware of Columbus, the Pilgrims, and the European settlers that had conquered the Americas, but I was ignorant of Utes, Zunis, Hopis, Olmecs, New Mexico Hispanos, Chicanos, Asians and many other cultures that were missing from any classroom instruction I had experienced.

Sometimes as we travelled with the choir, we would stay with families in private homes that offered a hidden side of the North American continent. In the town of Las Vegas, New Mexico, I had the good fortune of staying with a family that identified themselves as *Hispanos*. Even though they were all born and raised in the U.S., at home they spoke a form of Old Spanish going back to the 16th century when Spanish and Mexican settlers had mingled with Native Americans and come to the Southwest. I was taken aback when I heard them speaking a Spanish I had long forgotten – words I deemed as coming from uneducated persons but sounding of words I had kept hidden in my head from my A*buelo Papá Viejo* and his Jewish-Turkish *familia* in Cuba. After doing some investigation, I discovered that there was a language coming out of Spain referred to as Ladino, with roots based on Old Castilian – the basic language for modern Spanish. Instead of the word *toalla* for towel they would say *tuballa*. A question like *¿que dijiste?* ("what did you say?") would become *ki dijites* – with the s-sound transferred to the end of the word; and a greeting like *¿que hiciste?* (a form of greeting like "how are you doing?" or "what's happening"), would sound more like *kisite* – precisely, the nickname given to my *abuelo Papá Viejo* back in Cuba. I was moved by the sudden connection of sounds and words I had not heard in years. They rang out in my ears like a call from my past and from the dear family members I might never see again.

In California with Norine's Sister Clarice, Mother Alice, and adorable baby Renee

Other exciting moments came to mind as I sang with the choir at the Native American Menaul School in Albuquerque, New Mexico. There I had a chance to socialize with students that reminded me of friends back in Cuba. Their smiles and warm receptions made me feel like a member of the tribe. I kept asking myself - "Where did these people come from, why was it that I had never known they existed, and what kind of an education I was receiving?" These and other questions tormented me during the Choir tour underneath the calming sounds of pure European and Baroque classical music pieces. New Mexico gave me a humbling encounter with a history and a people so close to my roots yet missing or far removed from my "educated" upbringings.

Mathematics Calling – *El Llamado de las Matemáticas*

As I gained fluency in English, I became fascinated with writings in philosophy, politics, and religion; but I was still struggling with the meanings of slang terms, idiomatic expressions, and searching for precision with words. Unlike the undergraduate math courses, where I could show off my talents by simply solving an equation, I was now required to discuss and reach logical conclusions with words to solve a complex problem dealing with the meanings of life and human existence. These courses helped me to develop a fighting spirit and a sense of confidence of my likes and dislikes, as well as find a direction to center my attention as I worked on developing a career for my future. My first philosophy instructor, that I nicknamed Dr. Smart, played like an actor in class; he would assume the role of the philosopher that was being studied, and asked the students, through exams or class discussions, to knock down his assumed role or defend the views of the philosopher in question. At times I was baffled and anxious to come up with arguments that made perfect sense but failed miserably. A textbook being used was *History of Western Philosophy,* written by the British philosopher and mathematician Bertrand Russell – a prolific and controversial author of many books that challenged the accepted religious and political dogmas of his times. His writings inspired me to look into books like *The Principles of Mathematics, Why I Am Not a Christian* and search for other philosophical currents outside Europe.

It was through my erudite philosophy professor Dr. Smart and Bertrand Russell's writings about the great Greek philosopher Pythagoras, that I decided to concentrate on Mathematics for my future career, with music as the object of my passion, which I kept in the background for a future life's quest. However, I was still not satisfied with what was available at Westminster for me. In one of the textbooks for a philosophy class I had enrolled in, the index listed a chapter on, "Philosophy in Latin America." I was excited and looking forward to studying that particular chapter on philosophical views arising from the great lands to the south of the U.S., along with sharing my knowledge with then professor Dr. Skipper (not his real name) and other students. But to my shock and utter disappointment, when we came to that particular chapter, Dr. Skipper announced to the class that we did not have to learn anything about philosophy in Latin America, that it was enough to learn about the contributions of "Western" European philosophers. I was so upset that from then on, I simply went through the motions of attending class and taking exams, foolishly daydreaming with total lack of respect for Dr. Skipper – thus resulting in my one and only poor grade in my college career.

During this stage of my life, I became a strong defender of the need for changes, not only in Cuba but in the U.S. as well -- arguing in favor of educational reforms, reaching out to becoming knowledgeable and aware of cultures outside the dominant classes. I was in search of laws that would make possible the expansion of educational and artistic opportunities for all citizens, regardless of their skin color, gender, and social or economic classes. From my experiences in Cuba on how humans were treated on the *finca*, with the gross injustices in the sugar mills in Preston owned by the United Fruit Company, in the segregated schools and clubs in Santa Clara, in the neighborhoods singled out for *chulos y putas* (pimps and whores), in the segregated public parks and clubs, and for the ignored child labor of *sirvientas y limpiabotas* (child maids and shoe shining boys); these were signs of a society crying out for justice and revolutionary changes.

Looking back, I realize what a wonderful campus Westminster was then and is now with many improvements. It took me many years, on a return visit in 2009, to also realize the beauty of the magnificent Wasatch Mountains that surround the valley of Salt Lake City.

12

SEARCHING FOR FAMILY
En Busca de Familia

Not only was I interested in learning about the world around me, now it was time to think of my future as a human being building a family and bonding with my sweetheart for a lifetime. After dating Norine for a few months, I was gaining a deep appreciation for her artistic and domestic qualities. She washed my shirts and actually ironed them, she made exotic avocado and bacon sandwiches for my lunches, and she even presented me with Colonel Sander's Kentucky Fried Chicken in a flowery picnic basket on an idyllic Wasatch Mountain excursion. It was so delicious, and I told her it was the best I had ever eaten. She claims, to this day, that she told me why she removed it from the Colonel's bucket and placed it in her picnic basket - just to keep it warm, not to fool me into thinking she had prepared it – but it has been more fun to not remember that, so I could tease her for years to come.

As I met with her family: a highly efficient business manager for a father, a sweet and gifted pianist for a mother, and a sister with an adorable child, living near blue ocean waters in California, I looked at her as a gift that I wanted to claim and bond with. Norine had been in college with me, as a freshman that fall semester, studying together, going to movies in Mr. Gunn's little VW bug, and having the cheapest thing available after – Chinese fried rice. We were dating and enjoying Cuban music at her home and singing our way through new experiences as we traveled with choir friends. But by early spring she felt compelled to help with the care of her dying grandmother, who lived in their home with her parents. Norine's mother, Alice, taught piano lessons all day in their living room and could not attend to Grandma Gunn's needs, so Norine dropped out of school that spring semester of 1960. Norine's grandmother, Grace Smith Gunn, who lived off and on in the Salt Lake City family home had a recurrence of cancer from years before and quickly but steadily became very ill. Her decision to drop out of school to care for her dying grandmother put a new strain on our relationship, but also a new light on her character. I missed seeing her daily for classes and at work in the mail room. Unlike the very visual bookstore/reception area where she had worked on the telephone switchboard the past summer when we met, her fall campus job of distributing the mail in each student's mail slot was located in a tiny, enclosed space in the basement of the Administration building, very much out of the way. It had provided the perfect hide-away for stolen moments and quick kisses. Grandma Gunn passed away in May of that year and this, perhaps more than anything else, showed me a true side of Norine in the way she cared for and then coped with the loss of a deeply loved family member.

Norine shared stories of stopping almost daily at Grandma's house after grade school to play the card game, Canasta, and enjoy cookies and ice cream. Her grandmother appeared to be a very serious and stern woman, who always walked tall and straight as the elegantly lady she was. She worried that Norine was too much a "tom boy" and would grow up to have a "widow's hump" if she did not stand straight and sit properly with perfect posture. She would punch Norine in the back between her shoulder blades, as she pulled the shoulders back ordering Norine to "stand tall and straight." She also had to walk around the house balancing a book on her head to insure good stance and attitude. As a child, Norine rebelled against her wishes, of course, and often complained, as she slouched in a chair, about what a "really mean grandma" she had. Yet the love and admiration Norine showed for this important figure in her life came through that spring with the selflessness, and total devotion she had for her grandmother. I was so impressed with the kindness Norine exhibited for the wellbeing of those around her, that I made the important decision and with a gutsy move – asked her to be my future wife and life companion.

**Grandmother
Grace Smith Gunn**

I only had one more year of school before leaving Utah, so I also felt compelled to "test the waters" and try to build a strong family relationship before leaving Salt Lake – it was time to build a future *familia* with roots in my adopted Land of Zion. So, I mustered all my courage and met with the scary and stern Mr. Ralph S. Gunn, my boss and dominant Business Manager, to ask for the hand in marriage of his precious young daughter. After a few words of advice, he gave me his blessings, and from then on, he was always firm and fair and no longer the scary supervisor. I came to appreciate his gentle side, as a true *miembro de mi familia* (a true family member). Norine's mother, Alice Dix Gunn, always delighted me with her piano playing of classics and her incredible gift for sight reading any piece of music, including the unfamiliar sheet music my cousin had sent me from Cuba of old favorite Cuban classics, which seared the desire to learn to play them myself someday. It brought back memories of *Mami* Sara playing on her piano when I was young, which seemed to cement my place with this new family even more. So, this was it! – she was to be my mate for life, the potential caretaker in times of need, and the mother of my future children.

My family, still in Cuba, did not meet her for almost twenty years and my parents, now in Miami had to wait over a year before meeting my bride. I do remember a letter from Chicha, our family matriarch, trying to steer me away from marrying *una americana*. My father on the telephone from Miami, made some shocking remarks about her name – claiming that it sounded like "do not urinate" *(No orine)* and asked about her family coming from *"Si-Cago"* (a mispronunciation of the Illinois town of Chicago which literally meant "Yes-I do-shit"). My dad's intentions were not the least bit offensive, but it did take a good deal of effort to explain to Norine that he was simply following the loose ways of Cuban joking to the extreme with his excessive teasing of family loved ones and friends. No one from my *familia* was present at the wedding – from Cuba due to the political tensions existing at the time nor from Miami due to financial distance involved. Even

worse, and so very sad to me, was the lack of any written best wishes nor congratulations. Despite his jokes, my *Papá* and *Mamá* learned to like her through my stories, and Norine was accepted as a dear member of the *gran familia* long before our wedding date. My folks came to home plate for me as a 20-year-old, vouching under a notary public on paper that they agreed to my choice of a bride. Utah had strict rules about marriage under the age of 21 years - a rule which seemed rather hypocritical to me, since there were areas in the state where older polygamists married girls at a very tender age.

The wedding took place on August 26, 1960, near the end of the summer before moving into my fourth year at Westminster College. Norine wore the same dress her sister had worn in her wedding a few years before, her bouquet of flowers was mounted on a lace fan Dr. Yancey had given her, and her hair was a pile of curls in a tierra just as Princes Di had done for her recent wedding. Norine was a beautiful vision.

Most of my foreign friends participated as ushers in our international wedding: George Ieromnimon, from Greece; Walid Sa'd Zeidan from Jordan; Henry Hecker from Hungary; and from the U.S. my best man Jim Smith and the musical marvel John Russell. Norine had a school friend from grade school, Karen Thursby, her roommate from her senior year at Wasatch Academy, Ruth Ann LaFrenz as maids of honor and her sister Clarice as matron of honor. The wedding also had the participation of her good Mormon neighbors, Ann as the organizer, with her husband Paul Simmons as the professional photographer. Their adorable children Steve and Annette, who Norine had cared for as a "babysitter" for several years acted as ring boy and flower girl.

L to R: Karen Thursby, Ruth Ann LaFrenz, Clarice Gunn Paetsch, Dr. Myra Yancey, Alice and Ralph Gunn, Norine, Delvis, Jim Smith, George Ieromnimon, John Russell, Walid Zeidan, and Henry Hecker. In front the Simmons Children Annette and Steve

There were just a few friends of Norine and her sister but having been away for her junior and senior year of high school, and so consumed with dating me that first year of college, she had only few friends from Salt Lake City. However, Wasatch Presbyterian Church was filled, as her mother Alice had placed an invitation announcement in the Sunday church bulletin, so most of the attendees were folks from the congregation that were her parent's friends. After the service they all filled the church recreation hall for the reception. We were blessed with the music from my new in-laws' long-time friends from Wasatch Academy, where both Ralph and Alice had taught for most of their lives. Roger Hansen played a variety of musical styles at the piano, but mostly classical with his talented wife, Katy, accompanying him on the violin.as we cut the cake.

Close Friends and New *Familia*
L to R: Myra Yancey, Alice and Ralph Gunn, Norine and Delvis,
Jim Smith, Clarice, Ruth Ann LaFrenz

The Church did not allow any alcoholic drinks at the reception, nor was there any dancing *¿en la boda de un cubano?* A Cuban wedding with no rum, no Latin rhythms, and no family. It was a spectacular event in many ways, but I must admit, a sad day for me without my Cuban family and culture. I was entering a new chapter of life with my sweetheart and filled with anticipation.

That evening, after most of the guest had left, in the dark of night, I ventured into driving her father's big, borrowed Buick, his main car not the VW bug we had always used for dates. We ventured into the hinterlands of southern Utah where we

visited the magnificently beautiful and famous Bryce and Zion National Parks for our honeymoon.

Upon our return I had to concentrate on getting ready for what I hoped would be my last year at Westminster as Norine looked for a job and decorated our small one-bedroom apartment.

Not All Was Love and Roses - *No Todo Fue de Maravillas*

The ceremony and reception surrounded by a few friends plus many well-wishers with hugs, gifts and congratulations was like nothing I had experienced. There was also a negative side to this important celebration as I entered into a new life commitment with Norine. Not a single family member from my side was present - *nadie de mi familia.* Something understood in my head due to the existing tensions between Cuba and theU.S. Government but far from my heart since I did not receive a single message from the family here or back in Cuba. *La Doctora* Myra Yancey, (fourth from left in pervious page wedding picture) served as the sole representative of my family, she kept my parents in Miami informed through letters – thus, she will always have a special place in my heart, not only for being a clever curriculum organizer for a kid without the proper academic requirements, but also as a caring advisor that went the extra mile by serving as a guide and acting as a caring substitute for family members during times of uncertainties and tribulations.

There were also attempts to place suspicions in Norine's mind about her choice of a young Cuban, detached from family, without direct knowledge of his background, and without having access to his racial/ethnic composition – attempts to distance her from me, that she dismissed as racist and as being "none of their business." Everywhere I went, it seemed that I was the first *cubano* in town, and for example, when I took the test for a driver's license, the accompanying friend informed me that I should not mark "white" in the application form, which surprised and confused me. At that time Mormons did not fully accept people of African ancestry – there had been recent examples of not allowing two of our most admired singers, Nat King Cole and Marian Anderson, to stay at the magnificent Hotel Utah in downtown Salt Lake City, next to the Mormon Tabernacle when they came to Utah to perform. We also had been told by an LDS member that while the church accepted Native Americans as a lost tribe of Israel, they did not have missionaries in the neighboring island of Cuba, due to the heavily interracial composition with Africans of the Cuban population. To make matters worse, Norine was directly asked when she excitedly had told a Mormon neighbor of her engagement, "Aren't you afraid that you'll have a black baby?" I admired her steadfast and righteous attitude in responding to the neighbor "so what if we do, I love him and I will love his babies and furthermore, it is really none of your business."

The wedding preparations and the troubling news reports about Cuba and the U.S., weighed heavily on my mind and slowed my academic progress that spring semester of my junior year. When I had finished my third year of college, I was missing a few credits, so I was still considered a sophomore (a second-year student). As I faced that fourth year of college with my new bride by my side, I felt compelled to study as hard as I could to catch up in order to graduate by that fourth year. I basically skipped many junior year classes, reminiscent of my junior high experience in Cuba, and move right ahead with the senior requirements to earn my B.A. degree in Math with a minor in Physics.

We had a unique apartment for our first home which was high on the hill of "A" street, overlooking Salt Lake City, and perched on the top corner of an old Victorian house, which had been converted into six apartments. To get to our entrance you had to go to the opposite side of the house, climb some wrought iron stairs to a walkway that wound all around the roof, finally dropping down a few stairs to our kitchen door entry. The walkway and the "A" Street hill were such fun and so unusual, that Norine had fallen in love when she found the small place in late summer, however, when the first snow arrived, I definitely gave second thoughts to this adventuresome home. The main street up the hill above the Utah capital was C Street so two blocks over from us. They always snow plowed "C" Street early in the morning, but to get to it from our street was a major challenge. As I shoveled snow from our roof walkway at the crack of dawn, I would fantasize upon my dream of returning to Cuba, with sunny skies and cool ocean breezes, with a decent

paying job (at least $500 a month) and having a small house near the beach to watch the sunsets every night with my sweetie - where we would live happily ever after.

At the same time, I was always keenly aware of difference within the society I thought they were building back in Cuba and the society I was experiencing in the United States. So, in addition to the incredible challenges I faced as I struggled to accomplish all my course work for graduation plus providing a loving home for my new bride, I found time to give much thought to the injustices I saw around me. One piece I wrote was printed in the school newspaper, which I was extremely proud of. Not only because it gave my beliefs a platform, but especially realizing my English was now good enough to express my ideas and have them published. I had no idea, at that time, that it was an indication of the many "op ed" pieces and "letters to editors" that I would write in the years ahead in addition to solving math problems, as well as dealing with all of life's challenges.

MOVING FORWARD with POLITICS - *Foreign Views*

Congratulations! CLASS of 1961 **THE PARSON** Have a Safe and Sane Vacation... So We'll see You Next Year!

Opinion published in the school newspaper about the emergent Peace Corps.

What help can the peace corps give other countries? Will it be the help they need and can most fruitfully use? Let us first discuss these needs in order to conclude and answer.

The backward areas that we propose to aid, need desperately a social reform covering many areas. A land reform must come about, giving each man the right to provide food for his family. Schools must be built and equipped with teachers giving each child, rich or poor, the right to learn. Trained medical people must be available, giving each mother the right to care properly for her sick child. A reform in government must come about eliminating the five or ten per cent aristocracy that usually rules, thus enabling the people to benefit from their government. These are the things the poor people of the world need. The right to feed a child, to clothe a family, to give medical attention to a sick and aged grandmother. These are the rights they hope for, not the right to vote freely.

If the United States would send people who could answer this cry, a great purpose would be achieved. To answer this cry, however, involves a great many problems. It means a thorough understanding of the people, their language, their history, their culture, their religion, and their way of life. In order to gain this understanding an applicant for the Peace Corps would have to undergo a study program of several years. When this study has been completed and he has a thorough knowledge of the language, he would be ready to go to a foreign land. Once there, his purpose should be to better their way of life not to change it to the American way.

Perhaps you are thinking that a training and study program of three or four years would delay the peace corps program too greatly. Well, in the meantime, since all of the applicants already speak English and know our customs and history, let us first send the peace corps to the south, the reservation and to the slums that are right in front of our eyes.

Delvis A. Fernández Levy

13

LAST YEAR in ZION
El Último Año en Sión

All the heavy decisions had been made -- I was building a family with Norine while she undertook multiple responsibilities of being the wage-earner and a caring for her doll house. I abandoned engineering as a major pursuit and concentrated on math as my preferred subject with a minor in physics. Norine did not return to college following the wedding and her grandma's death. Instead, she got a full-time job at the Federal Reserve Bank of Salt Lake City, a tightly controlled workplace which required all the workers to stay until they "balanced to the penny," occasionally preventing her from coming home on time to make our daily dose of *picadillo con arroz y frijoles negros.* My work was still on campus as the multilith operator and if study time permitted, I was always eager to mow a lawn or prune trees as a gardener on weekends.

Our tiny bedroom was fitted with a small study desk leaving just inches to get around the bed. The apartment was basically an attic with sloping ceilings, which required care in rising from the bed and standing at the bathroom sink to ensure not hitting your head. I remembered my parent's tiny apartment in Miami with a similar ceiling over my bed on that first visit. The living room was more spacious, with the circular "tower" surrounded by windows overlooking areas of the downtown city below. The snow was always beautiful and something that still amazed me, but I had to clear our path to leave and drive praying that our old Chevy's wheels would grab enough traction to move up the hill to that cleared intersection for the main street. Now we looked forward to spring and blossoms instead of snowflakes.

Our rent was very reasonable even for those day, $85 a month, but our salaries were meager. After rent and utility bills were paid, Norine figured we had just $7 per week for our food budget. Vegan and veggie diets were unheard of and the cheapest meat was hamburger, which I did not care for in a bun nor a meatloaf pan. So, instead I showed my new bride how to cook Cuban picadillo, which used the hamburger meat but in a much more appealing way to my taste. She learned quickly, and simple Cuban cuisine became our daily fare. For variety, we took advantage of Sunday dinners after church with Ralph and Alice, my new in-laws. We thoroughly enjoyed a free meal and the change of pace from our home menu, going to the popular KFC Colonel Sanders Chicken spot in the Sugar House Mall, also one of Ralph's favorites. We never did explain to them why the meal delivered in the bucket brought on a giggle and a smile to our faces as we remembered that fun picnic day. On rare occasions we would splurge with a bowl of fried rice for 80 cents at our favorite Chinese restaurant where we often ended up after the movie when we were dating. We got along very well as our honeymoon lasted all year, and I don't remember ever getting into any fights, not because we did not have issues of disagreement, but probably due to the fact that we were both so totally consumed with our daily grind of work and study.

The Bay of Pigs -- A Worrisome Time
Un Tiempo de Angustias

Around April 17, 1961, the Bay of Pigs Invasion was at its climatic moments. I had little knowledge of what was going on but thanks to my old roommate, John Stewart, an avid shortwave radio operator, I was able to find a station that brought news directly from Cuba, thus getting the news "from the horse's mouth." To Norine's dismay, I spent countless hours in John's room at Westminster's Foster Hall, sometimes late into the evening, sitting by a small crackly radio, struggling to make sense of what was happening in my province not far from Santa Clara. News from Miami gave the impression of victory, *fait accompli,* by the U.S./CIA trained invaders, but finally the news from Cuba seemed to concentrate more on major warnings and encouragements to the population for the defense of the Revolution. Early on April 20 it seemed clear that the invasion – referred by Cubans as *La Invasión de Playa Girón* – had suffered a major defeat. For me it was time to rest and concentrate on the daily routine of work and study, along with hopes of peace and progress for my Cuban Homeland and *Gran Familia.*

My mathematics professors continued to encourage me on expanding my education, perhaps seeing me as a young man that could achieve higher degrees. I was gaining a love for the subject with the upper division courses, away from the toils of courses like Differential Equations and Calculus that are essential in areas of applied mathematics. Now I was allowed to shine through logic-based arguments in proving theorems from axiomatic assumptions. For me mathematics was a universal language not only for science, but for music and the arts to build new worlds and create fantasies through Non-Euclidean Geometry, Topology, and other unknown areas waiting to be developed. Without a doubt I had found a future and a life journey for work and enjoyment.

At that time, I did not know about the complexities of American education. Master's degrees, doctorates, and PhD's did not mean anything to me – I simply did not know what they were or what was involved in achieving them, although I had definitely learned they would be the key to American success. The time had come to make another major decision: should I stay in Utah, get a job, apply to schools for the next degree, perhaps move back to Cuba, but where are Norine and her parents in all of this? It was a time of major whirlwinds of uncertainty in my brain. But lucky for me, I had good advisors, with teachers and above all *La Doctora Yancey* as a trusted mother figure, who urged me to keep building on the education I had received at Westminster. I applied to major universities in theU.S., and after being accepted in several of them, I chose the University of Miami to be near my parents and possibly make the move back to my Island of Love.

It was a sad moment for Norine, but as a good and sacrificial mate, she of course chose to support and move with me to Miami - the first time for her to reside outside of Utah. She was familiar with California and areas of Illinois where her father's family lived but had never visited Florida nor sections of the Deep South. Her grandmother had spent several winters in Florida and had once invited her granddaughter, Norine's sister, Clarice, to visit as a high school graduation gift. The most interesting story Clarice had shared of that adventure, was of their visit to a nudist colony with the men and women separated by a wooden fence that had many round knot "peek" holes. I convinced her that my parents had never mentioned seeing such a place, and only spoke of warm, sunny, inviting beaches. We cuddled late into the evenings after our Cuban meal of picadillo, which she now could make like a Cuban, and listening to her album "A Hot Night in Cuba" plus the love songs from our dating days of Johnny Mathis and her favorite, Nat King Cole. One lucky night we indulged in tickets to see him in person at a nearby concert. We enjoyed his warm voice and tender love songs in a ballroom which was located outside of Salt Lake City at the Lagoon Amusement Park. Despite being underage, we were able to enter the night club where with hidden rum for our cokes through a "Jack Mormon," friend - a reference used for an LDS member who did not strictly observe the faith's rules and therefore was willing to take extra money to buy a bottle for us. In the state of Utah at that time, people were required to have a license to buy alcoholic drinks, and only in designated liquor stores with tiny windows. Drinks were not sold in any other type of stores or at social clubs. Once inside a night club there were small compartment under the tables where you had to keep the bottle in hiding – never out on display. I always found that to be a curious law which only encouraged more drinking, as I had witnessed over my four years in Utah. Instead of enjoying just one drink while relaxing at a club, you had to drink several in order to finish the bottle. As a college kid I had seen far more drinking, on a mountain picnic or snow trip to a lodge, than I had ever seen in Cuba. Utah had many strange behaviors and activities which, once I had moved away, I realized were unique to the state due to the influence of the Mormon church. Norine too, has shared many stories of being raised in a small town, where for her entire six years of grade school, she was the only non-Mormon child. Perhaps her experiences of being an outsider encouraged her to mate with me – always the odd balls. I certainly think those experiences molded the persons we were to become.

I did graduate from Westminster in June of 1961 with honors and with the distinction of being selected to the hall of fame of "Who's Who Among Students in American Universities & Colleges." For me, an incredibly proud achievement after years of strife and struggle, but also with times joy and sadness.

We had friends over to celebrate and to bid them and our wonderful little first home, good-bye. Norine cleaned out the apartment and packed the few things we could fit into our little Chevy coupe for the trip ahead.

A Time to celebrate with friends in our apartment with the newly graduation picture behind us: Beautiful Norine on the left and best Hungarian friend Henry Hecker on the right side.

Four Graduating Seniors Get Awards

(From the Utah Westminster Paper, May 1961)

Four of the college's graduating students this year have received awards from four universities and colleges, effective at the beginning of the next school year. The four are James F. Engel, Diane Victoria Phillips, Delvis A. Fernández, and Wallace R. Stealey.

A mathematics major Mr. Fernández has received a $2000 teaching fellowship at the University of Miami.

Mr. Engel   Miss Phillips

Mr. Fernandez   Mr. Stealey

WHO'S WHO in American Colleges and Universities

Delvis Fernández one of the nine students selected by the Faculty, the Academic Council, and the Dean of Students on the basis of their high scholastic achievement and their outstanding leadership ability.
(From the Westminster College Yearbook, The ETOSIAN of 1961)

Once I had been accepted at the University of Miami, Norine arranged for a portrait by her neighbor Paul Simmons, who was also our wedding photographer. On our last night in Salt Lake City, we invited her parents out to dinner, at Ralph's favorite Col. Sander's Kentucky Fried Chicken Restaurant in the Sugar House Mall. We said our farewells and gave them our portrait as a parting gift. My father-in-law insisted on paying for dinner even though it had been our invitation.

GOODBYE ZION
FLORIDA! HERE WE COME!

I was finally ready for new challenges: learning to move on with my *Americana* sweetheart to a new living experience - no longer under the watchful eye of my boss and father-in-law, and all the strict, strange codes of Utah. Instead, we would be engulfed in the Cuban sounds and smells and practices of my parents. I was excited with the prospect of being so near my homeland, and familiar cultural ways, but also concerned about introducing Norine to it all, and wondering how she would adjust. In addition, I was experiencing my own anxiety of entering a world of difficult advanced graduate courses and teaching as a T.A. (Teaching Assistant) where in addition to being a student, I had responsibilities as teacher of my own students.

A Memorable Travel Adventure
Summer of 1961

Salt Lake City, Utah ➤ Wyoming Rockies➤

Slopes of Nebraska ➤ Cornfields of Iowa➤

In *Tierra de Lincoln* with family at Smithshire & Monmouth, Illinois ➤

Familia with Cuban surroundings in North Miami ➤

Work and study at University of Miami in Coral Gables, Florida

14

MIAMI: A World of Surprises
Un Mundo de Sorpresas

Goodbye to Zion -- *Adiós a Sión*

My last days in Salt Lake City were filled with doubts and anxiety. I had made a solid commitment to continue my education, in search of a master's degree in Mathematics, at the University of Miami, but beyond that, there were many unknowns regarding future employment, where would we build our family, and more immediately, how was Norine going to manage living away from her family and familiar ways. On the other hand, I felt more secure in terms of my acceptance as a student at the University with a job as a teaching assistant, where I would be totally in charge of lecturing and running a math class all by myself. Financially, I thought I would have no worries as my teaching job was secure and an integral part of my field of study.

We dedicated a month prior to the beginning of school for the trip with a visit with Norine's paternal grandfather, Frank Gunn, and her sweet great-aunt Pearl, the only sister of her Grandma Grace. She had spent many summers as a youngster visiting "Aunt Pearl" and had many fond memories, so she was looking forward to showing off the old family home on the farm in Illinois. It was a trip full of discovery about my wife's ancestry and religious roots: Presbyterian sandwiched between Anglican and Mormon with a bit of Jewish on her mother's side. The family welcomed me as one of their own, telling me stories about their experiences at the farm while I shared tales of my happy days at my family *finca* in Cuba. We stayed in the old but elegant family house from the 19th century which was full of charm and every room filled with antiques. This was my closest incorporation into a family of *americanos* with well-established roots in the United States.

We left Salt Lake City in July of 1961, ready for a long journey across the Midwest and the Deep South, through the Florida Peninsula and ending at our destination in Miami. Since we were quite limited on money for travelling expenses, Norine and I took turns driving for hours on end, trying to make it, as quickly as possible, to our first stop, the family farmhouse in Illinois. We slept inside the car and at rest stops, never daring to stay in a motel for fear of running out of money before reaching Miami.

In Search of Lincoln's Land
En Busca de La Tierra de Lincoln

After making it through the Wyoming Rockies, we began to gain confidence in the Old Chevy as it rolled down the gentle slopes of Nebraska, and finally felt enjoyment with the scenery as our car chugged along roads with views of cornfields that seemed to blend with the sky's horizons and stretch on forever. We were now in Iowa ready to cross into Illinois in search of the small settlement of Smithshire, the nearest town to the farm of the old family home. The tiny town had one restaurant, one church and a post office, with a population, that I would guess was not much more than 50 inhabitants. This was the birthplace of my *suegro* – father-in-law – with lots of family history. We somehow made it to the farmhouse on a dirt

Farmhouse in Illinois that Norine remembers from childhood

Aunt Pearl showing off her hats

road, without having an address and just Norine's memories and help from a few farmers along the way, who all knew old Pearl Anderson's place. We were warmly welcomed with many hugs and kisses by a short. stout, little old lady – Norine's sweet and dearest Great-Aunt Pearl, who always wore hats as pictured here in her youth.

The farm was far from anything I had seen in my Cuban *finca* or the Idaho farm. The main house looked more like a museum filled with decorations and objects kept from centuries ago: ornate roll top desks, a heavily decorated piano with ivory keys turning yellow, embroidered tablecloths in every room. There were many pictures with finished wooden frames from the days when photography was being invented, which told the whole family history. An old Singer sewing machine sat on an enclosed porch, and upstairs bedrooms were all decked out with beautifully hand carved wooden headboards and dressers that seemed more apropos for palatial mansions of colonial days.

One afternoon we drove to nearby Monmouth for a short visit with Norine's grandfather who still lived in the town where her father had spent school age years after moving from the farm. He also had received his college degree there in accounting and business management right at the end of the great depression. A strange major for that time when jobs were very rare, which resulted in his going far off to Utah where he accepted his only offer. Although her grandpa no longer lived in the magnificent house Norine remembered visiting as a youngster, she found it easily standing proudly on a corner, so took a picture and headed home. She shared many memories of chasing lightening bugs in the evenings, of the horrific thunder and lightning storms in the middle of the night, and the swarm of bees flying into her open bedroom window when the chimney cleaner accidently disturbed their nest. Norine could have walked down memory lane all night, but we had to leave early the next morning to continue our journey, so we climbed up the little two step ladder and sank into the high feather bed for the night.

Magnificent grandfather's home visited by Norine back in the 1940s

The next morning, Aunt Pearl had gotten up long before us and had a full farmhouse breakfast ready, with a tall stack of potato pancakes, eggs, and bacon to fill us up for a long day of driving. After hugs and kisses we were ready to continue our travels with the prospect of many new adventures and to be near *Mi Tierra*. The landscape of the Midwest and deep South seemed vaguely familiar from my Greyhound escapades, but it was all new to my bride as she had never been so far from Utah. Two days later we reached the Florida peninsula with plenty of swamps, but not a mountain in sight. Norine began to experience for the first time the sticky feeling of sweat from the humidity – her home state of Utah had often below freezing temperatures with snow in winter, and though it was hot in summer, it was a very, dry heat, where you seldom break a sweat no matter how hard you try. Now we were certainly in flat Florida, with lakes and abundant greenery, plus humidity and bugs, bugs, bugs, which was all new to her. With so little money we were unable to stop at any tourist area and just drove on, to get to my parent's home as quickly as possible.

Our Arrival in Miami
Arribo a Miami

We had less than a month to get acquainted with our new surroundings and the University of Miami campus where I needed to prepare for my first teaching adventure at a university, plus engage in finding a paying job for Norine. We were planning to stay with my folks for at least a year to save money; but as we approached their address in the far northern area of Miami, we realized it was far from the University, which was in Coral Gables, south of Miami. As we pulled into the carport near an open door, we could hear loud voices coming from inside. As we entered the kitchen Norine saw her new in-laws, both at the stove arguing loudly over a frying pan, which she recognized as having picadillo. It took them several minutes to even realize we were there, but once our presence was noticed, we were smothered with hugs and *besitos* - kisses. I later explained to her that it was not really a fight, but just a 'Cuban discussion as to whether the picadillo needed diced potatoes, my *Papi's* idea or not my *Mami's* way of preparation. They quickly showed us our prepared bedroom and then we sat down to eat. The meal was just delicious, and I was filled with the fullness of real Cuban food, and so grateful that Norine had this chance to eat authentic picadillo.

They seemed excited and very happy to have their son, Pupy, in their home with their new *nuera* – daughter-in-law. They tried to acquaint us with our new social environment, giving us welcoming parties almost every night with delicious meals and a lot of teasing jokes with *amigos y amigas* in nonstop conversations. *Como de costumbre* – as usual *Mami y Papi* seemed to be arguing about any and all subjects, with every bit of minutia in their brains, and all the while, *Mami* kept her watchful eye over her mate's excessive drinking. I was very happy to see the way Norine was being treated as another *miembro de la familia*, but she was quietly suffering from cultural shock in that Cuban environment.

Mis padres, my parents upon arrival at their home in Miami: *Papa* Delvis (nicknamed *Vive*) and *Mami* Sara

No one spoke English, and instead the fast-paced Cuban accented Spanish was loud and bombastic, and non-stop. Norine quickly stopped trying to say anything in Spanish at those party evenings, as the minute she would open her mouth, a heavy silence would fall over the room as everyone strained to understand her and would joke about what they thought she had said. Every evening in the quiet privacy of our bedroom, I would try to assure her that no harm was intended, and it was just a cultural difference far from the Anglo ways she had always known. I reminded her of my father's joking comments over the phone the first time I told him her name was Norine (in Spanish pronounced *no reeneh* (do not urinate) as well as mentioned that her family was from Chicago, pronounced Chee-Cahgo (Yes, I do shit). It would make her smile, but the tension was growing, and we often ended our evenings intensely arguing about what would be the best course to take for building -- our nest. After just a week or so, we came to the realization that their home was too far from the university and not a place with any prospects for Norine to look for a job. It was totally residential with only one huge Walmart type store that sold anything and everything a few blocks away. My parents were very sociable with friends dropping by every single day for drinks and boisterous conversations. So, it was decided that the living conditions were not in my best interest for mathematical studies, teaching, and career building and not for Norine's sanity, at least until she became more acclimated to Cuban life.

Cutie little sister Puchy - Guiselda Fernández Levy - near the time of my parent's departure from Santa Clara, Cuba leaving their daughters behind in 1958.

It was a very painful decision to leave my parents again, and I felt badly as they seemed pleased to have family in their home. They too were still in a strange land, after their tragic departure from Cuba where they faced bankruptcy, the killings and tortures of friends, life threats from Batista thugs, and forced to leave their two adorable young daughters behind – Sarita, 13 years, and Guiselda, (nicknamed Puchy) at the tender age of just 5, during that summer of 1958, under the care of the unmarried sister-in-law, Chicha, who was not fully trusted by my mother as her daughters' caretaker – but with no other choice.

Their lives were filled with trauma, trying to make a living and in search of

Sister Sarita between my parents in Miami Beach on her only visit to Florida back during the summer of 1959.

Sarita in Santa Clara, Cuba at her secondary school Antolín González del Valle -honored in a parade at the right-hand corner.

friends arriving from Cuba and other parts of Latin America, and in despair about how to get their youngest daughter to be with them. During the summer of 1959, after the triumph of the Cuban Revolution, the older daughter, my sister Sarita, had visited Miami for a few weeks, but she had decided to go back to Cuba, ready to give her life for a new Cuba.

While my mother was in turmoil over the division of our family my dad was able to ease the pain through his addiction, although it now appeared to be more under control than at any other time in his life, he had mastered the role as a working alcoholic. We promised profusely to come visit weekly and take them to the beach often, hoping to ease their displeasure in our departure, and we did continue to have a warm loving relation with them by visiting every Sunday for *Arroz con Pollo*, or some other delicious Cuban dish with a cooking lesson for Norine mixed with a lot of jokes, Cuban music, and storytelling with their friends. So, it all worked out well, but when we made the decision to find our own place, it seemed our only choice, as I simple could not fathom actually living with them - not for my new wife, and not even for myself after four years in Utah's Anglo Mormon Culture. How could I possibly immerse myself in teaching and studying math, along with building a strong relationship with Norine, if we lived in their world. We decided to move nearer to the university where Norine could find a job, and I could find peace and quiet to concentrate on preparing for teaching - beginning algebra and math of finance – my assigned courses while learning about esoteric fields of pure mathematics.

Norine's Job, Her Home, and More
Su Trabajo, su Casa y Más

Luck came our way when we found a completely furnished apartment, even down to dinnerware, pots & pans for cooking, and even towels and sheets. This was a fairly common thing in Miami as housing often catered to and wanted to attract the many temporary folks from the north who came to Miami in winter to escape the cold snowy north. We were ecstatic at this unexpected, good find, as we had come all the way from Utah in our little old Chevy coupe that would only hold our two suitcases of clothing, a couple of boxes with math book and a few family photos. The apartment building, The Pines was on a broad street called Ponce de Leon, at the far north end, but still within the beautiful town of Coral Gables, which was where the University of Miami was located on the south side. We both fell in love with the area as everything was very green with palm trees lining many streets and colorful tropical flowers in full bloom with many homes and buildings in a magnificent Spanish style of architecture.

After the long hard trip, we feared the car would just come to a stop at any minute but hoped that my *Papi* would always have some old clunker at his garage for us to use. Still, we felt we needed to keep walking distance in mind, just in case. The Pines Apartment was a good walk, but certainly doable to "The Miracle Mile," which was the downtown shopping strip of Coral Gables with numerous banks and places of business, which looked promising for Norine's job search. She had a lot of work experience since her teen years when she worked two summers, at the Mormon LDS Genealogical Society, had secretarial experience working for her father, and of course her most recent job at the Federal Reserve Bank of Salt Lake City. Within just a few days she was hired at the City National Bank of Coral Gables, guided by none other than Connie Arnaz – the sister of Desi Arnaz, the only Cuban that Utah folks might have known from "I Love Lucy" fame – Connie served as a mentor in developing Norine's skills as our future family financial expert, which was fortune for me since I had so little interest in keeping the checking account straight or doing yearly taxes.

We moved in and got settled very quickly so had a few days to relax and enjoy the beaches. We would often meet Uncle Eddie and his wife with their two adorable little girls for a BBQ on a Sunday afternoon outing. Something we enjoyed over the next two years, but always with no invitation or mention made to my parents, as Mami was not on speaking terms with her brother and had given the edict to us that we were not to speak to him either. I do not remember what the problem was, but within just a week or two of our arrival they had a major disagreement, which lasted almost two years – the whole time we were in Miami. Norine found this behavior very strange and very sad. She was completely baffled and kept falling back to thinking that it must be a Cuban thing.

Home in Ogden, Utah sold by Norine's mother to venture into travel and paying tuition to attend the Boston Conservatory of Music, c. late 1920's

186

I easily dispelled the theory that family disputes were not present in American culture when I reminded her of old family traumas. Her mother Alice had almost no contact with her half siblings. Although Norine never met her grandparents, she was aware of their history and old family conflicts.

Alice's father, Edwin Dix, had nine daughters from a previous marriage, all of whom were adults, and her mother, Anne Rebecca, also had three adult children. Norine's mother, Alice was their only child, born when he was 68 and Annie was 32. Although her mother was considerably younger, she died first when Alice was a senior in High School. Her father soon went completely blind in his final years, and not only did Alice have to care for his every need and run the house, but also read every line of the newspaper daily, and other favorite books for 8 years until he died at 91. All of his daughters were married and busy with their own families, a few were living there

Maternal grandparents: Edwin Dix and Anne Rebecca with their only child Alice - Norine's mother c. 1912

in Ogden, Utah but others had scattered about. After death, his Living-Will was read to the family, declaring that the stately house was to be left to Alice, and Alice alone. Very shortly upon graduation she sold the house using the money for train fare and tuition in far off Boston where she had been accepted at the Boston Conservatory of Music. Needless to say, the siblings were infuriated at not getting anything, and it basically ruined any family relationships for many, many years. This was the tale of a fine, mostly Mormon family, that had its share of traumas, which can and does happen to any family, anywhere. Norine was fiercely proud of her mother's bold independent action, especially taking place back in the late 1920s, but she also realized, that my mother's behavior was not just a - Cuban trait.

The young couple Norine and Delvis bonding in their new place near the University of Miami.

We were finally settled and adjusting to life in Miami, so we found there was little time for anything other than work and study. We did meet a fun couple that had an apartment above us. They were French Canadian and about our age which was all we had in common, but we enjoyed their company and became good friends, then and for years even after we moved away. We loved the beaches and spent one day almost every

My in-laws Ralph and Alice coming from Utah to our new place in Coral Gables, Florida

weekend soaking up the sun, often with Gemma and Marcel if not meeting Uncle Eddie. She was a tall thin beauty who had worked as a model and he was a great chef, so we often ate together, and I improved my limited French with her tutoring. Norine ordered a few sexy outfits by mail from Gemma's favorite catalog in Hollywood where she bought all of her clothing.

The following summer Norine's parents came to visit, so we did take a little time off to act like tourists. We got a decent car from *Papi* to move around in, so drove to the middle of the state to visit Cyprus Gardens, a relaxing and beautiful spot with gorgeous 'southern bells' sitting amongst the flowers on the sloping green grass (reminiscent of my first sight of Norine) with their huge skirts of every color spread around them. We also enjoyed the water-skiing display with amazing gymnastics that was part of the show. One evening we all got dressed up for a night on the town and took them to a swanky Las Vegas type show with dinner at a big hotel in Miami Beach, - the same place we had celebrated our first anniversary. Norine seemed so pleased to spend that time with her folks, who she had been missing. They also were happy to finally meet my parents and seemed to get a kick out of their crazy ways even though they had to communicate totally through my translation. My folks had now been in Miami for three years, but their English was almost nonexistent, simply because there was absolutely no need for it in their circle. He had picked up just enough 'ghetto garage' language to get by each day at DELSA (his garage workplace) named after himself, DELvis and my *Mami*, SAra. She, on the other hand, spoke no English, which was true until her dying day 60 plus years later.

The Miami Challenges: Thefts, Interrogation, and Parenthood
Desafíos: Robos, Interrogatorio y Paternidad en Miami

Almost coinciding with my efforts to shine in my teaching and studying that second fall, the ultimate challenge of my life happened when Norine informed me that she was pregnant. Now, I was near the end of finishing my studies for a master's degree in Math, but there was no more time for fooling around with studying and low wages beyond that degree; I felt compelled to get serious about finding a job soon and settling down in view of becoming a father.

My salary as a TA was $2000 for the nine-month school year, and Norine's bank job paid a bit over $300 per month, which would end in April. She needed to concentrate on raising our first child, so I definitely would need full employment, which would make me the family breadwinner. While tormented with a whirlwind of decisions and filled with excitement about becoming a father, which was far from worrying about the ongoing news from Cuba, yet we were faced with acts of theft and vandalism in our peaceful surroundings, both in my Coral Gables apartment and my parent's home in north Miami.

Our very sweet landlady, who kept a careful watchful eye over everyone, and everything was anxiously waiting for us one late afternoon, to informed us that there had been a van in front of the building, identified as a moving company with two uniformed men that came into our apartment and left with the TV and several boxes, giving the impression that they worked for a moving company. She was very concerned about us moving without having yet given her proper notice -- something we were obliged to do soon, since the apartment owners did not allow children in the premises, and Norine's condition was becoming obvious. When we entered our apartment, at first everything seemed to be in order except that our small TV was gone – the one and only thing we had saved up to buy. In the bedroom, however, there were memento items like photos, jewelry, letters and postcards from family and friends spread all over the bed and floor. Upon careful study we realized that certain photos were missing, and all of the letters from my family in Cuba were missing as well. Similarly, at my parent's house that same day, letters and photos had been taken in what appeared to be an act of burglary, yet nothing of monetary value was taken.

Photo arousing trouble in Miami Delvis and Norine dressed as Cuban Rebels for a Westminster Carnival in 1961

Almost coinciding with the thefts, I was called for questioning at what I assumed were FBI offices on Biscayne Boulevard. I was placed in a room with a woman taking notes and a man asking questions over and over for about three hours. As I recall, I felt confident but highly concerned about what they were seeking from me, as I was not involved in any questionable activities nor any politics, I saw myself as a seriously studious and ambitious student immersed only in proving math theorems. The questions were obviously based on the stolen photos and letters.

1.) The first questions were based on pictures where Norine and I were dressed in Cuban rebel attire. The photographs had been taken when we dressed for a Mardi Gras Party the first year we were dating. There were many other students that year, dressed in olive green rebel attires with fake beards, since that was the year of the triumph of the Cuban Revolution and the Bay of Pigs fiasco. Pictures of *rebeldes cubanos* were front page news in major newspapers and magazines, so dressing like rebels was the most popular costume for those celebrations. Norine's neighbor Paul, our wedding photographer, had taken our pictures in their home as we were leaving for the party, but for the questioning officer, I as a Cuban, must have had some hidden meaning in mind, and it was the investigators proof that I was suspect of something.

2.) Another set of questions dealt with the reforms and ongoing projects in Cuba during the early years of the Revolution. I was ordered to: "Define the Agrarian reform"; "Define the Urban Reform"; "What is the meaning of the Literacy Campaign? These were questions that baffled me since I was oblivious to these changes taking place in Cuba, and my sole concern at the time was finishing my math degree and teaching math to the best of my ability. But the questions were repeated in a demanding fashion again and again in search of answers that would satisfy the investigator, but that I did not have.

First Anniversary at the Fontainebleau in Miami Beach

3.) The final set of questions dealt with my family's involvement with the rebels. My grandmother, Felicia Rodríguez Marzall, had served as a *miliciana* standing guard in front of the Post Office in Santa Clara. After the triumph of the Revolution, my sister Sarita had stayed in the United States a few weeks during the summer of 1959 visiting my parents in Miami, but soon after her arrival, she decided to return to Cuba, committed to shine as a student and preparing for the role she would play in the *Campaña de Alfabetización* – Literacy Campaign and later to become the first female mechanical engineer on the Island.

This whole experience was a very uncomfortable and troubling ordeal, but with so much on my plate, I simply pushed it to the back of my mind and moved on. I do not remember the exact month of this interview, but it was in the early spring when Norine was appearing more and more pregnant, and as children were not allowed in our apartment building, we needed to quickly find a new place to live. I was also facing the final weeks before graduation, so my head was filled with heavy concerns.

Our FIRST day at the beach

Our FIRST home in Miami, Florida

Our FIRST child due, so Coke to celebrate Norine's 22nd Birthday.

191

15

Unto Us a Child Is Born
Nace Nuestro Hijo

On Thursday, April 9, 1963, Norine appeared all agitated, shakes me out of bed and tells me that she is having terrible stomach pains and uncontrollable bladder problems – water running down her thighs. She wants me to take her to the bank and does not want to call in sick for fears of ruining her perfect attendance record at the bank -- Friday would be her last workday before starting her pregnancy leave. She claimed that the baby was not about to be born, since according to her calculations she still had three or four more weeks before the due date. We were both naïve and ill-informed about labor pains and breaking of water sacs. Her behavior showing signs of excruciating pains was rather unusual, so I took the macho leadership role and insisted in no uncertain terms to head straight to her obstetrician. When we arrived at Dr. Fox's office, he looked at us in disbelief and ordered us to go immediately to the Doctors Hospital as soon as possible as the baby was definitely on its way and we had no time to lose.

When we arrived at the Hospital, we were sent straight to a financial office for what seemed to be a set of unending questions about how we were going to pay for the delivery and the postpartum care. The feeling of stress was over whelming, I tried my best to answer the hospital financial officer's inquiries while the mother-to-be sat on a straight chair, squirming with tears running her cheeks, and letting out cries of pain from time to time as the labor intensified. This was a side of stoic Norine I had never witnessed since we first met. Once the officer was convinced that we had the means to pay, she showed some sympathy and took her to a delivery room while I followed behind but was stopped at the entrance, being ordered to wait outside. I was feeling nervous and filled with anxiety while I heard her screeching cries, imagining the worst, since I could not hold her hands during those precious agonizing moments. I appeared so weak and pale that a nurse thought I was about to pass out as she put a hand on my shoulder guiding me to a seat, assuring me that everything was fine. Suddenly there was silence, and a caring nurse came to lead me down the hall to a room where I could see a tiny baby through a glass window -- a slimy baby, with a lot of black hair, all wet with a squinty face -- getting cuter and cuter as the nurse dried him and clean off the bloody streaks from his skin. This was the first newly born infant I had ever seen, and he did not look like the babies I had seen in movies. Later that day my parents along with many excited Cuban friends came to the hospital to celebrate the birth of our baby boy *Davisito*-David Iván Fernández. Norine was looking so much better and was pleased with the enthusiasm everyone showed her. The nursing staff, however, were not pleased with the excess noise, the excess number of visitors and the excess time they spent far beyond the end of visiting hours, so eventually they had to get tough asking our guests to all leave.

Norine begged to let one friend stay as she had not been able to visit with Pat due to chatter from all the other visitors. Pat Duckworth was Norine's very best friend from the bank where they worked together. Pat also happened to be the daughter of Dr. Fox, and he had talked to her after we had been in his office that morning. To our surprise he apparently was just amazed that we had not gotten to the hospital much earlier, as the office visit was close to ten and the baby was born just two hours later – at noon. Pat also mentioned that she had explained to all the friends at work that the baby shower scheduled for that very night would be postponed for a couple of weeks. Norine also mentioned to Pat that she suspected her labor had actually started the day before there at work, which was all news to me. The fact that it was too early, she assumed she was just having a really bad stomachache. She had

Mother Norine with her first baby David Iván Fernández born April 9, 1963.

not missed a single day of work during her pregnancy, and finished that afternoon off at quitting time, just to keep her record clean and so she asked Pat to apologize to their boss, Connie Arnaz, for the fact that she had missed work today - her final day of work. Wow, what a trouper my sweetie was. We were both exhausted after that very big day, but also bursting with pride and happiness as we said our good night to little Davisito.

Around the birth of my son, I came face to face with an incident of ugly racism in Florida. I recall signs in South Florida denoting "colored" only beaches, and even places with signs stating that "no dogs or Puerto Ricans" were allowed, and the Coral Gables Movie Theater, had certain hours and days when "colored" people could watch the films. However, I had never encountered face-to-face the ugliness of racism until I went out to a restaurant with friends to celebrate the birth of my son. Among my math friends there was a young student from New Orleans, he was a talented graduate student from Xavier University in Louisiana – also my only African American friend and acquaintance at the University of Miami. About five of us sat at a table and waited in vain until the headwaiter finally came to tell us that we had to leave, while pointing to this student. I was very upset, in disbelief of what I was witnessing but realized that making a scene would not help, so instead quickly came up with the idea of telling the waiter that if he kicked us out of the restaurant, he would be creating an international fracas since my friend was the son of a Jamaican diplomat visiting Miami. The headwaiter then agreed to let us stay but required that we move to a booth at the back, where my Louisiana friend had to sit at the corner of the booth out of sight of other patrons.

An Upside Down World
Un mundo virado al revés

Before arriving in Miami and during my two years at the University I received letters from my family in Cuba filled with excitement and optimism about the newly liberated island with ambitious plans to bring government representation, and full access to education and justice to the disenfranchised masses. My sister Sarita had been deeply affected by the breakup of the family with her brother in faraway Utah and her parents in Florida; and from her letters, I got the impression that she and most of my *familia* were committed to building a more secure and stable life for future generations. Through my parent's friends and acquaintances, there was a constant barrage of troublesome news about terrorist actions attributed to Cuban exiles under directions of the U.S. Central Intelligence Agency – we were living in the midst of the Cold War with the old Soviet Union and the changes in Cuba were seen as a major threat to U.S. interests in Latin America. So, the simplest course of action was to use the involvement and enthusiasm to empower the exiled immigrants to bring down the Cuba government.

Not only the letters and reports from family and friends were alarming but the mainstream papers in the U.S. often had news about acts of terrorism that brought pain and suffering, not only to Cubans on the Island but also to folks in Miami including myself and my family. While finishing my graduate studies in hopes of getting a stable job to care for our family, I was consumed with worries about our family's future and how to take care of our baby Davisito.

Prior to coming to Miami, I had received the news of an explosion on a ship in the Havana harbor that caused the death of about 100 persons. Later the Bay of Pigs Invasion followed by the Missile Crisis in 1962 put the world at the brink of a nuclear holocaust. Further news about bombings from airplanes originating in the US, and the killings and tortures of teenagers involved in teaching *campesinos* how to read and write made me feel threatened and uncomfortable in South Florida. These acts of terror created travel prohibitions which prevented us from being with our families and loved ones during times of death and stress.

Getting the Math Degree and Looking for a Job
El Título de Matemático y en busca de trabajo

New *Papá* Delvis learning to care for his baby son *Davisito*.

We had found a new apartment and had settled in at the university housing for graduate students before the birth. I was sure of getting my math degree within a couple of weeks, so I dedicated a lot of time sending letters of inquiry to companies that hired mathematicians. I had sufficient knowledge after teaching math of finance to aim high in search of a job as a financial actuary, with plans to stay in Florida near my parents, rebuilding an extended family, and returning to the Island I held in my dreams. But since the job inquiries were not getting results, I reached out to the university dean's office for some sound advice. He was very helpful in advising me on how to get a job. As far as he knew I was the only Latino in Math, and to my surprise I learned he was aware of the investigations about my political leanings by Cuban exiles and U.S. intelligence. In plain terms he told me that I would not be able to get the security clearance for a job in a big company. The illegal entry into my home, not by common thugs but by someone associated with a U.S. Government agency was seen as a direct threat to me and my family. He strongly and clearly advised me to leave South Florida and to consider applying for a job far off, perhaps at a California university, where I could take advantage of my unique standings as a person fluent in Spanish with an advanced Math degree. The dean had received information about a cluster college being developed by the University of the Pacific in Stockton, California that aimed at attracting Spanish speaking students from the U.S., Spain, and Latin America, which sounded promising.

Once again, I felt at a crossroad, but this time the decision to make was obvious. I had to abandon the pursuit of getting a job with a well-established American company. I had loved my teaching as a TA, and the opportunity of using my native tongue with math and my acquired English was like a gift sent from heaven. Norine and I wrote to the Stockton Chamber of Commerce requesting information about the area. The brochures sent offered impressive pictures of the surrounding area with highlights of the Sierra Nevada's snowy peaks, nearby San Francisco Bay Area, and the impressive Burns Tower on the University of the Pacific Campus. I quickly contacted my professors and administrators to obtain letters of recommendation from of the University of Miami and filled all the necessary application forms. This was the place to go! And, lo and behold - I was offered a full-time paying job to teach at both the University and at the emerging cluster college, Elbert Covell College as their first math instructor with multiple responsibilities: teach in both English and Spanish, develop a math curriculum for Spanish speaking students, and serve as a faculty advisor. As a 22-year-old near graduation, I was in awe and full of fear and excitement about the prospects of this new career, in a beautiful land near the high Sierras, as well as my new responsibilities as a father. Our bad fortune with threats and facing an end of the road in Miami, led to our good fortune of deciding to abandon our Florida dreams and head back out west, this time to Stockton, a town in the grand San Joaquín Valley of California.

Back on the home front, our sweet little boy was finally gaining some weight and doing well after a rocky start. He developed jaundice almost immediately after bringing him home form the hospital. He would not nurse and was obviously losing weight, although his thick head of hair was growing well and covered his eyes when brushed forward, so Norine gave him his first haircut at age three days. He was so fussy and thin that by his fourth day we took him in early for his 7-day checkup. To our great dismay the pediatrician told us to take him immediately to the children's hospital for observation. Any other troubles we had experienced in life up to that point were paled by this frightening experience.

Norine stayed with him night and day and I stayed as much as my classes would allow. He was placed in a regular crib with heavy netting over the top, which was to prevent older children from climbing out. They constantly reassured us that it was not a terribly serious condition but needed constant care to ensure he was improving. I do not remember exactly how long the stay was, but it was at least three or four days, and perhaps the hardest part was seeing the other children that shared his room. They were all older with much graver medical situations. One in particular was a little three or four-year-old boy, who suffered from Macrocephaly, which caused him to have an extremely large head and suffer from seizures and constant crying. All of the little ones had something very serious wrong and did not smile or laugh, but rather just cried off and on at all times. It was the most pitiful thing to experience and made that time with our tiny little boy almost unbearable. After a few days he did start gaining back the weight he had lost, was eating better, and slowly his coloring became more normal, so we were finally allowed to take him home.

Other troubles at home were not as serious, but still were driving poor Norine crazy. Since her arrival in Miami, she had a constant running battle with all the cockroaches and giant Palmetto bugs that insisted on living in our pleasant homes. In the dry Utah climate, there were seldom problems with any sort of bugs in your

196

house, unless, as her mother had taught her, you did not clean well. So, for her entire Florida stay she was constantly cleaning and then cleaning again, but in that hot sticky climate it was all to no avail. Yet, with our tiny newborn snuggled in his bed, she became even more fanatic about eliminating the varmints (as she called them). I'm sure the teasing from myself and her Cuban father-in-law as to how those critters might climb into *Davisito's* ears and find a warm home there – did not help at all. In fact, she even went so far as to buy some 'magic' paint that claimed bugs would not crawl over it and proceeded to paint a thick line on the floor in a large circle around his bed.

Four generations of the GUNN *familia*: Great-Grandfather Frank holding baby David next to Grandfather Ralph and mother Norine (Gunn) Fernández

My parents spent as much time as they could visiting their only *nieto,* as they were dreading our departure once my graduation had taken place. All went well and I finished my University of Miami career and the first graduation my parents got to attend. After Norine and *Davisito* had an emotional goodbye with them, which was filled with tears, and hugs and promises to return the next summer, I took her to the airport for her visit with her grandfather and dear Aunt Pearl. It was a night flight to Chicago, thinking the baby would sleep all the way, but not realizing she would

Abuela Sara Levy holding her first grandchild David Iván with *Abuelo* Delvis Rafael Fernández in admiration of his *nietecito*

have to walk a very long distance in the Chicago airport with baby in hand and all the baby gear she was carrying with not a soul in sight to help at that early morning hour. The gate for the small plane on to Moline, Illinois was on the far side of that huge O'Hare Airport, and she dragged in just as they were closing the door. It was a very short flight and she had just gotten settled when the plane landed at an airport with large letters over the terminal, which read "Five City

Airport." The baby had just fallen asleep, so she sat there quietly waiting for takeoff for the last leg of her journey.

After sitting several minutes on the empty plane, the attendant came to inquire and to informed her that this was indeed the Moline airport and she needed to get off. The woman begrudgingly helped her gathered all her many belongings to carry down the stairs to the tarmac where she finally saw a very distraught Mary Loree searching for her. Her second cousin, "Cuz" Mary, was Aunt Pearl's granddaughter and just a few years older with whom she had spent many wonderful times during her childhood visits to the farm. As everyone had deplaned, Mary was in a mild panic not seeing Norine fearing they had missed the connecting flight from Chicago, or some other tragedy. Squeals with hugs and kisses filled the early morning air as mama and baby appeared, and although Norine was exhausted from the all-night ordeal she was very happy to visit all the Illinois relatives. Great Grandpa Gunn and Grandpa Ralph along with Alice were thrilled to meet little David – it was a joyful reunion. A few days later there was another round of sad goodbyes as Ralph headed the car out for the long drive back to Utah. Norine's family, especially dear Aunt Pearl, would accept nothing less than a solemn promise of a return visit the next summer, which Norine later tried to convince me would be just a few additional

Norine flies to Illinois with baby David. Here he is with Aunt Pearl before I picked them up in a decrepit car to continue our final journey to the West.

miles out of the way on the way to Miami. While all of the trauma and happiness of that visit was taking place, I had stayed at our university housing apartment for a couple of more days wrapping our few possessions and putting them a in U-Haul trailer for the long drive. My *Papá* convinced me to get rid of my old '52 Chevy, (which was running like a charm), and instead buy a newer '57 Ford that he had been repairing for a friend. and was sure would do better on a cross country trip. It was time for my goodbyes and at that last Cuban dinner, I was delighted to see my parents had invited *Mami's* brother Benjamin (Uncle Eddie) and his family along with her sister, Elvira and young Maruchi, a favorite niece. To my surprise all of the troubles of the past two years seemed to have been erased and forgotten, and there was nothing but joy and loud laughter at that family gathering. It felt so great to know that my *Mami* and her brother had each other, once again, especially since I was leaving and taking Norine and their *nieto, Davisito.*

A Troublesome Journey Across the USA
Un viaje problemático por los EEUU

Soon after leaving Miami in my Ford pulling the trailer, I had to stop due to clouds of heavy smoke billowing out of the engine. My first hunch was to turn around and head back to Miami, but I called my *Papá* instead in search of advice, to hear shouts and laughter over the phone, as he assured me that it was nothing and the car would make it – *"¡Héchale agua y pa'lante!"* was his advice. (Fill it with water and just keep on going!). I suspected that he had not the slightest idea about the vast lands I had to traverse with long dessert valleys and huge mountains to climb, the likes of which he had never seen in Cuba. My dad was gifted when it came to fixing cars, and every vehicle he would drive never got to its final destination without having to stop here and there for quick repairs that only he could perform. My new Ford was that kind of car with smoke and overheating problems on a daily basis for that trip. Lucky for me, the drive through Florida was on flat ground with many lakes for water to cool the engine and give me a chance to rest and muster the strength to carry on, after all, what choice did I have.

[As a sideline to the story, I am reminded of the first and only car we had while living in Santa Clara, Cuba. It was so bizarre that as we drove through the town, people would come out of their homes staring at us with shouts and laughter in total amazement. This *cacharro* (jalopy) had no roof, no doors, no sides, and no seats; it only had the steering wheel with a break and acceleration pedals plus a shifting gear. There was a dashboard for riders to hang on to, and a floor to place *taburetes* (rustic chairs). Although this would be considered totally unacceptable and unsafe by today's standards, my *Papá* drove slowly and carefully through city streets while all the other drivers, as well as pedestrians, kept their distance, in awe of the strange contraption.]

I made it through the Deep South with all its strict abhorrent segregation signs. The car was still giving me problems, but I learned to cope and adjusted' by frequently checking the oil, adding water to the radiator and stopping to cool the engine. However, in Nebraska I began to sense a slight climb as I was approaching the amazing Rocky Mountains – the car came to a stop and nothing I did would allow me to restart the engine. I rested on the side of the road, fell asleep and early in the morning, I was able to start the engine and chugged along to the nearest town for a quick repair. The mechanic filled me with fears about the car not being able to make it through the Rockies – but I had only a few dollars to pay for the least expensive fix up possible. After a day in a strange village, I ventured once again, this time acutely aware of the sounds coming from under the hood and driving not much more than an hour or two at a time before resting the engine, usually driving at night when the weather was cooler.

After a week of trials and tribulations in the rickety clunker pulling a trailer on a 2500-mile drive, I again marveled at the majestic Rocky Mountains of Colorado and Wyoming and cried with excitement upon seeing the grand Salt Lake Valley stretch out in front of me with the expectation of being reunited with my sweetheart and adorable baby boy.

To Southern California
And on North to Our Final Destination
Adelante hacia el Sur de Califas
Y luego hacia nuestro destino final

The growing *familia* in California
From Left to Right: Grandparents Ralph and Alice, Auntie Clarice holding her new baby Dana, Mama Norine with her baby David, Papa Delvis, and cutie Renee in the middle.

Arriving at the home of my in-laws, I rested and filled my stomach with lots of mashed potatoes and gravy - foods I do not particularly care for but know they are great for satisfying hunger. We rushed about madly trying to visit showing off Davisito to family and as many old friends as we could find. Norine's old neighbor who had been so concerned about her having "a black baby" was pleased to see his fair skin but could not help questioning his dark thick hair. Clarice had driven from California with her two little girls, Renee, and Dana. We all crowded into their parent's home for just a couple of nights before continuing our journey in tandem. One-night Clarice went out with some old high school chums and came home in the wee small hours of the morning.

A married woman with two children was greeted by her angry father as if she were in her teens again, driving him crazy with her pranks. At Wasatch Academy she had always strived to be the "badest of the bad" to prove to all her high school friends that just because her father was the superintendent of that school, they could be sure she would go along with whatever wild scheme they cooked up. Being a private school in a small Utah town, where students lived in dorms, eating, studying, and working on campus, there were many restrictions about going to town. Girls especially were certainly not allowed to date any "town boys" and riding in their cars was the greatest of all sins. Clarice and Norine were caught in the middle as they were both born and raised in Mount Pleasant, Utah, a small town of about 2000, where they went to grade school and had many town friends. Nothing infuriated Pop Gunn more than Clarice's constant breaking of those rules, which she did more and more – the more he objected. Norine on the other hand, had secretly witnessed his furry and so learned to be much more secretive, always appearing with her folks to be the sweet, obedient daughter. She had often mentioned how her mother would bring out the Bible and start reading a passage to calm everything down during those trying years. So sure, enough with their two grown daughters sitting at the breakfast table during that visit, Alice started reading a random passage from the Bible when Ralph's temper was flaring; it worked like a charm and all voices lowered down to a restrained mutter. I sat quietly observing this family dynamic for the first time in person and was absolutely astounded at the difference of our cultures and the way we had been raised. That incident alone gave me greater appreciation for Norine's ability to adjust to the Cuban environment we had just left.

Clarice was anxious to move away from that breakfast table and so offered to drive me downtown to pick up my car, which did require repairs being paid for by my generous father-in-law to insure our safe travels. The next morning, we packed the car quickly so we could leave immediately upon completion of the mandatory Church service and traditional fried chicken lunch at Col. Sander's KFC in Sugar House Mall. Clarice and I coordinated the route, as I was anxious to start and enjoy the gorgeous scenery along the way to California. We slept in a cheap motel in some little town not far from Grand Canyon, which ensured a beautiful sunrise the next morning over that magnificent sight. We made a quick stop as we drove through Las Vegas, which I had visited before Norine had joined the college choir, but she had never been there. From there we made a beeline on to Clarice's home in West Covina, and when Blaine got home, we shared all our stories as he sat on the floor happily playing with the children. He was a gifted tech expert working for Motorola and a highly dedicated golf player who tried to educate me as to the distinction between Irish and Scotch whiskey. I never learned how to tell them apart, but my head was in a swirling whirl all that evening as I nodded in agreement with whatever he said.

Heaviness and worried anticipation surrounded us as we headed north the next evening, driving for hours in the cool of night while our baby peacefully slept. As driver and co-pilot navigating our way out of the maze of freeways around Los Angeles, we were far from peaceful and had to retrace our steps several times as we would head off in the wrong direction when a freeway split without enough warning for novices like ourselves to get in the proper lane. We finally reached a wide stretch with many, many lanes as we climbed up "the Grapevine," so we pulled over to calm our nerves and catch our breath. Little did we know that years later the drive over that pass would become a well-traveled path. As we descended there was just enough light left to reveal the biggest valley I had ever seen (over 10,000-square miles) with the Sierra Nevada mountains to the east and the coastal range to the west. The great San Joaquin Valley stretched on for miles with agricultural lands and animal farms, which we later learned was a valley that fed much of the world. For us in the dark, we only knew there must be garlic fields and a lot of cattle pens which filled the night air with their pungent aroma.

We approached Stockton in expectation of the gorgeous scenery displayed in the brochures of snowcapped mountains, which had been sent to us in Miami. Instead, as we entered the town around seven am. on El Dorado Street, we saw blocks and blocks of strewn bodies pressed against the buildings and in every store doorway, where the poor and homeless vagrants were sleeping. The sun was trying to come up, but the grey gloom of both the sky and sidewalks left us both in silent disbelief. As we drove further away from the railroad tracks and that town center, there was a little improvement and by the time we finally reached the University of Pacific Campus, everything, was bathed in sunshine and looking much more attractive. It was a disappointing entrance to our new hometown, Stockton, but we were delighted with the school's surroundings, and hopeful we would find pleasant areas, which surely might be more in line with what the brochures had depicted – after all this was California, how could we not love it.

16

The University of the Pacific
La Universidad del Pacífico

Settling in California - *Estableciéndonos en California*

After two years of traumas with thefts, government interrogations, and being advised by a university administrator to apply for a job outside Miami, I became an exile, not from Cuba, but from a place in turmoil where crimes against my family were dismissed and ignored. Now I had to face a life far away from my parents, without access to their delightful Cuban cuisine and friends, and without the daily dosage of *pastelitos y café con leche* – California was the place to settle, work, and build my new *familia* with a full-time paying job. Norine for the first time since we met back during the summer of 1959, was free to dedicate her time to caring for our baby *Davisito* and study at the university to develop her writing and artistic talents and get on the road towards a secondary teaching credential. We rented a small house on the outskirts of Stockton with a big tree that provided so many walnuts that she was able to make delicious breads and cookies as Christmas gifts for all our family and friends at hardly any cost to us. Our seven-month-old baby was in one of the cutest stages of life, very active, laughing and moving about as an early crawler.

With hardly any furniture, we spent many happy hours in the shade of that huge walnut tree. We spent any free time on weekends exploring the beautiful and exciting places near-by that had been pictured in Stockton's Chamber of Commerce brochures, which had lured us to Stockton in the first place: the majesty of the grand Sierra Mountains with their snow covered ski resorts and historic Gold Country; the excitement of the city we grew to love the most of all U.S. cities – San Francisco; the spread of the great San Joaquin Valley, with its green veggies reminding me of Cuba's green vegetation.

Delvis enjoys the mild weather under the walnut tree with 5-month-old Davisito in the first Stockton home

The brochures did not show the bent farm laborers – who spoke in hushed Spanish as they whispered their wants for change. In fact, the picture in our minds of Stockton was far from what we discovered upon arrival. My job was highly demanding but for the first time in my life I was getting a full salary ($6,500 a year) with responsibilities well beyond what I had learned at Westminster College and the University of Miami. My work required good knowledge of mathematics, teaching skills with universal English and Spanish fluency, tactfulness in advising the most culturally diverse group of students I have ever encountered – foreign and U.S. natives from various ethnic groups, from the needy poor to those from very wealthy social classes. It was exciting as well as gratifying to have such an opportunity to learn and expand my views of the world, especially my Latin American world with its rich diversity well beyond the world I had mostly experienced in Utah and at the University of Miami.

The Elbert Covell College - Unforgettable Times
Elbert Covell College –Tiempos Inolvidables

The objective of the Elbert Covell College was to train Inter-American Specialists-both North American and Latin American-who are "specialists" in one of the critical areas of all the Americas of the twentieth century; that is, in the sciences or mathematics, economics or business administration, teaching or administration in the elementary or secondary schools. These specialists must be bilingual in Spanish and English, able to transmit their professional training in both the English-speaking and Spanish-speaking Americas. They must succeed in understanding the culture with its values, traditions, way-of-life, un-familiar to them until they chose to share their knowledge and experience with the countries of their second language. They must study and understand their own culture with its values, traditions, way-of-life and accept the responsibility of reflecting and interpreting it to those who speak the other principal language of the Americas.

The Elbert Covell College was a liberal arts and sciences college established in 1963 as an adjunct institution to the University of the Pacific (UOP) in Stockton, California. UOP broke from a well-established tradition in American universities that required incoming students to be proficient in English in order to be accepted at colleges and universities – now at Covell College all the courses were taught in Spanish, except for a class to learn English.

Of the 250 students for planned maximum enrollment, the following ratio is projected: one-third, North Americans; one-third, Latin Americans who without financial help could not obtain an education in the United States; one-third, Latin Americans who can afford to pay their educational expenses in the United States. In the Elbert Covell College Latin Americans of extreme financial situations will be able to study together, to live together, to get to know each other in an educational atmosphere where North Americans who represent the same extreme financial conditions can serve as the mixing element in this blend of varied social and financial levels.

Source: Hispania, Vol. 47, No. 4 (Dec. 1964), pp. 788-794 Published by The American Association of Teachers of Spanish and Portuguese.

**University of the Pacific
Stockton, California**

About half of the students and faculty members came from Latin American countries, two were from Spain, while the other half came from the U.S. – some were related to U.S. citizens who had been or worked in Latin America. Among the countries represented were Argentina, Chile, Perú, Bolivia, Ecuador, Colombia, Venezuela, Cuba, Costa Rica, Nicaragua, El Salvador, Spain, and the United States. Despite the fact that Stockton had a large Hispanic/Latino/Mexican population, they were not represented among the students, faculty, and college administration.

My assigned duties went well beyond the teaching of mathematics. As the first and only mathematics instructor of the Elbert Covell College, I had to develop a unique curriculum for teaching in a bilingual environment, become a faculty advisor for students with various academic areas of interest as well as a highly diverse cultural, ethnic, and national backgrounds. Latin America is quite heterogeneous in terms of ethnicity, languages, accents, cultures, and social classes. Covell was a major undertaking by the University of the Pacific, based on "American stereotypes" of "Latinos" and inspired by the Alliance for Progress as a way to seek and nurture future leaders in the American Continent.

In March 1961, two years after the triumph of the Cuban Revolution, President Kennedy proposed a plan for Latin America aimed at the elimination of adult illiteracy, more equitable income distribution, and land reform, through what he referred to as "Our American Revolution." This was a grandiose plan to influence in the calls for changes in Latin America – from national leaders like Augusto César Sandino of Nicaragua, Guatemalan President Jacobo Árbenz, and the Cuban Argentinian Ernesto "Che" Guevara. At that time, I was naïve and ignorant about the complexity of cultures and populations of the Americas. In the Cuba where I had been raised and educated, native cultures of our Western Hemisphere were mostly ignored, while history lessons were in the exclusive domains of European civilizations and achievements. Not only was I an educator but had to be open minded and willing to be educated by my students outside the daily routine of math lectures and homework.

The University of the Pacific was ahead of the times when it came to innovations in education. During the early 1960s two distinct colleges were developed – Raymond College and the Elbert Covell College. The students at Raymond could graduate in three years with a major in interdisciplinary studies, while Covell College followed the norms of traditional curricula except that instruction was offered in Spanish. As such, the new faculty members had rich backgrounds in education and life experiences outside what may be found in most educational institutions of higher learning.

There was a wealth of histories, cultures, and traditions among the ethnic groups, far from the stereotypes of "what is a Latino": students of Chinese ancestry from Ecuador; Quechua speakers from Peru; a Polish young man residing in Chile; a Jewish student from Argentina; a student from Spain whose mother had been born in my hometown of Santa Clara, Cuba; a secretly married couple from Nicaragua hoping to stay and work in the US. Every student had a wealth of history lessons about their families, ancestors, languages spoken, traditions, and present-day political situations in their homelands.

A financially poor, Quechua speaking student from the Andean Altiplano near Lake Titicaca found himself in severe cultural shock, to the point of having to be confined at a mental hospital near the university. Other students with high financial means had an easy time adjusting to the college environment. Some came from a world of wealth and high social classes with servants at every beckoning call, well above the needs and poverty endured by vast populations in Latin America. I recall feeling the need to bringing financially needy students to my home during summer vacation, while some of the financially affluent were able to take round trips to faraway places in South America for a Thanksgiving weekend or a Christmas holiday. Due to financial constraints, with or without U.S. work permit, most of the students had to stay away from their home countries, find jobs and remain in Stockton during times of family gatherings and holiday celebrations.

My Math Classroom at Covell College c. 1964

My Role as Professor and Faculty Advisor
Mi papel como profesor y consejero de estudiantes

My responsibilities as a faculty advisor were quite challenging and complex. I did not find out until coming to UOP that the *Covelianos* (Covell College Students) from Latin America were expected to return to their countries of origin after graduation. So, my major role was to make sure that they knew the order in which they were supposed to take their courses for whatever major they might choose. But as one of the few native speakers, raised within a Cuban environment, they shared with me problems beyond their worries about courses, such as possible majors to choose, opportunities for employment, and rules and regulations they deemed unfair. As a new teacher of math in Spanish I was challenged by my pronunciation and usage of certain words, and I felt compelled to offer consolation to students suffering from cultural shock and misunderstandings. Although the college founders had altruistic motives, they lacked understanding of the cultural and social class diversity within the countries of Latin America.

New Friendships - *Nuevas Amistades*

My wife, Norine, and I developed strong friendships with many faculty members, and as such we had a unique opportunity to learn about the wide span of cultures in the Americas and other parts of the world. One of my best friends was an American, I called Cap, of Scandinavian descent who had been raised in Mexico City and spoke perfect English as well as beautiful *chilango (Mexico City)* accented Spanish. Other friends and professors as well came from Ecuador, Bolivia, Colombia, Argentina, and Cuba. Americans from the U.S. on the faculty also shared anecdotes from their life experiences living in Puerto Rico, Guatemala and various other countries.

Profesores de Covell con familias June 1964

L. Fred Nunn holding Mariana with his wife Diana, & Prof Rivas standing behind him.
R. Mathematics Profesor Delvis Fernández with the Nunn family and María Rivas

One of the most memorable friends was a mixed couple that had met in Ecuador – an *Americano* married to an *Ecuatoriana*. We used to visit them for meals that reminded me of my Cuban cuisine – *patacones* (fried green plantains), mangos and guavas plus a wide variety of delightful foods. There for the first time I enjoyed ceviche without knowing that it was made with raw fish. They also surprised us with their pets, so well behaved – two tiny animals I had never seen before, they were Titi monkeys from the tropical forests of Ecuador. I discovered that one of the smallest countries of South America had a tremendous diversity of landscapes – from Amazon jungles to *altiplanos* of the Andes mountains to the pristine Galápagos Islands in the Pacific – along with a wide diversity of peoples, languages, and cultures. Thanks to our friends, Ecuador remained in the forefront of our minds as a place to visit and explore.

Rekindling My Cuban Roots - *En busca de mis raíces*

By the end of that first year of work at the University of the Pacific (UOP), I was again suffering from deep nostalgia about my Cuban roots and culture. Now with a one-year-old and wife far from my Island, I yearned to expose them to *mi cultura cubana*. We had made it from Miami the summer before in an old Ford, which was so bad, I had to actually pay someone to get rid of it. So, by total impulse, I huddled them in my new small black VW Karmann Ghia and drove all the way to Miami – this time via Illinois where we visited with Norine's grandfather during the

Great Aunt Pearl, Davisito and Norine in Illinois family home

twilight of his life and stayed at the old family farm of her dearest great-aunt Pearl.

***Davisito, Abuelo* Delvis and *Abuela* Sara**

Once in Florida we found my parents in their new home in a rather unusual neighborhood of Northwest Miami, a neighborhood populated by *snowbirds* - elderly people from the north who came to Florida to escape the cold winter months. This was a well-manicured neighborhood with lawns, palms, and lush tropical fruit trees. African Americans, poor Cubans, Haitians and Dominicans were moving in, buying or renting from the snowbirds as they were in the process of moving out. *Papá y Mamá* were now renting from an elderly couple who were anxious to move out of Miami, since their dear neighborhood was not seen as a peaceful place for retirement. They claimed that the new residents were far from being retirees, spoke louder in foreign tongues and did not seem to appreciate the well-groomed gardens and surroundings. This situation gave my parents a unique opportunity to buy a home that was in the process of being abandoned for only $6,000 in 1964. Over a short period of time the home was divided into a duplex with an adjacent garage turned into an efficiency apartment. The grassy area around the house seemed to my parents as *un terreno baldío* (a wasted land), so shortly after buying the home, they replaced the front lawn with cement, removed several unfamiliar trees, but kept the sweet mango and *toronja* (grapefruit) trees. For them, a good house was a *finca bohío* (poor country hut) or family home with a wall separating their neighbor's dwelling.

The Neighborhood of My Parents
El Vecindario de mis padres

My parent's neighborhood soon transitioned from a retirement community for "whites only" to a highly diverse neighborhood far from what I had seen in the segregated town of Coral Gables during my teaching and studies days at the University of Miami.

● On one side of my parents' house lived an African American family where one of their resident friends had been killed by a gardener, slitting her throat with a butcher's knife.

● On the other side lived a Cuban family that had expensive autos – Mercedes, Jaguars, etc. They practiced a *Santería* religion which involved playing drums, chanting late into night hours, and sacrificing chickens. The young son, who was around seven-years old was in the process of being inducted into becoming a *santería* saint – this required sitting for hours on end, which he often did on his bed in the Florida Room, an enclosed front porch. On one occasion there was a drive-by shooting that made bullet holes all along the front of the house. Thankfully, the young son was in the backyard participating in a religious ceremony. Later it was discovered that a member of the family worked for the Florida Department of Motor Vehicles and was in the illegal business of making cars disappear in lagoons near Miami in order to collect the owner's insurance money.

● One of the biggest residences at the corner of the street had been bought by a person who covered all the windows with plaster and painted the place with a bright pink color. The place was totally quiet during the day but busy at night with rumors in the neighborhood that it had been turned into a bordello.

● On the opposite corner there was a holy-roller church that filled the air with lively shouts and praises to the Lord.

One may get the impression that all was bad, but that is far from the truth. Everyone in the area went about their business and learned to cope with the rhythmic sounds of drums mixed with Christian holy-roller chants. Most neighbors were decent, trustworthy caring human beings ready to come to anyone's aid during times of need or simply for social gatherings.

Hurricane Cleo - *El Huracán Cleo*

That summer we had to postpone our departure from Miami due to hurricane Cleo, scheduled to strike on August 27, 1964, near our time of departure for our drive back to California. Despite the fact that I had lived in Cuba for seventeen years with *ciclones* affecting Cuba almost on a yearly basis, my home in Santa Clara had always been spared of their fierce winds. Only once I remember a hurricane coming through our *Las Villas* central province of Cuba, without striking our family home; only causing heavy rains that provided my cousins and childhood friends with a time of total enjoyment -- getting soaking wet while playing in flooded streets as if they were huge swimming pools filled up to our ankles. Here in Miami the situation was quite different with hurricane Cleo, projected to arrive in Miami that evening. My parents' home did not seem well suited for heavy rains and winds of over 100 miles per hour, so I felt compelled to help my *Papá*, suffering with chronic gout and rheumatism, to prepare the house by sealing as much as we could with wood planks and tapes around windows and filling any crevices we could find. My *Mami* Sara was busy filling the bathtub with water and checking canned food supplies.

My American wife from Utah, who was totally oblivious to the disaster potential of hurricanes, had taken our little Davisito to visit her old friend, from her banking days in Coral Gables. It was now late afternoon with a radio swarming with warnings and announcements to residents as to the projected strike time of the hurricane -- "take precautions, don't leave home, traffic is at a standstill on roads with raised bridges" was heard over and over. So, my dear wife and baby were

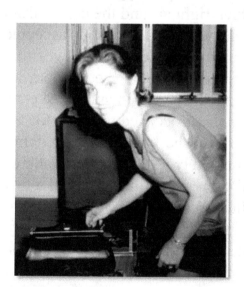

Patricia Duckworth, Norine's friend from bank work in Coral Gables, Florida

nowhere to be seen, they were stuck in heavy traffic over canal streets with raised open bridges, as sea crafts had the right of way to come inland for protection. *Al fin, qué Dios los bendiga!* was our cry when we finally saw Norine and the precious *criatura* enter the home. It was already dark, and we huddled around the living room in total darkness. We were awake all night while the heavy winds, rain, and noises from trees and falling objects kept us in a state of deep fear, as we watched the metal awnings from the neighbor's house fly by while worrying about what to do if the house were to blow apart. Suddenly, in an aura of mystery, everything was silent around us – the eye of the hurricane was passing by! I ran to peek through a hole, not daring to open a door, and saw fallen trees and damage to nearby homes. The rest of the hurricane then came and left, and to our amazement we were safe and sound. As dawn arrived, we were in a whirlwind of work taking off the planks and tapes from the windows. We tried to take naps here and there without much success, so decided on one last beach jaunt to relax in preparation for our long drive back to our home in Stockton, California.

After that wild summer vacation, which did little to rejuvenate us, but filled us with interesting stories, we felt the need to live close to the university, so immediately started a new home search. Luckily, we quickly found a charming, converted garage which worked for our second Stockton home. The lower floor had an interesting bamboo squared covering which was tough on the knees, so the baby quickly improved his walking skills. That level consisted of a living and dining area, with a counter separating the small kitchen. Up the narrow staircase was a tiny bath with a huge bedroom which provided room for our bed, the baby's crib, and a desk for lecture preparations, as Norine was always spread out on the kitchen table working on art projects. That stairway was also a learning experience for our baby, as well as an incredible scare and prediction of his adventuresome ways to come. Without any coxing or experimental steps, he quietly and quickly ventured all the way up to the top as Norine and I talked in the kitchen right around the corner from the stairs. He almost as quickly learned to back down the stairs, so we soon accepted trusting his agile athletic ways and gave him full reign of exploring that two-story dwelling. There was only one adventure later that made us regret the freedom we had given him. One afternoon as Norine was consumed with a pen and ink sketch, he climbed and entered the upstairs bathroom, where he proceeded to climb for the first time up on the toilet, which meant he could reach the bathroom sink items. Norine heard him calling and entered the room immediately to find blood splattered all over his shirt, the shower curtain, the walls and even the ceiling. He had a tiny cut on his pinkie finger from my razor, which had splattered everywhere as he rapidly, shook his hand in pain. He never cried out and only called for help. Luckily, having our land lady, Clem, living in the house just steps away, was often a comfort when Norine needed the calming wise advice of a mother figure since our mothers were just a phone call away, but not on the spot.

A Day of Infamy
Un Día de Infamia

On the morning of Friday, the 22nd of November of 1963, life at the university came to a standstill – this date is etched in my memory as a "Day of Infamy." President John F. Kennedy was killed by an assassin's bullet while travelling on a Presidential motorcade in Dallas, Texas. I felt a great sense of loss since after the Bay of Pigs fiasco and the Missile Crisis of previous years, he filled me with hopes about starting a new era in US/Cuba diplomatic relations – an era of travel and engagements with the people of Cuba, free of threats and acts of terror and intimidations, on both sides of the Florida Straits.

Life in the U.S. entered a period of uncertainty about political discourse through peace and dialogue. Evening news often reported on American casualties in Vietnam and ended with pictures of coffins arriving on U.S. soil. There was turmoil at universities as student protestors rallied against the continuance of what appeared to be a lost cause that only brought death and destruction. While the end of the war was in sight, the struggle of Blacks and Latinos for justice was developing as new leaders and organizations emerged. Martin Luther King, César Chávez and many others called for labor and social changes that resonated as well among disenfranchised minorities who were highly underrepresented in educational institutions.

The assassinations of **President John F. Kennedy** (1963) followed by the murders of his brother **Robert F. Kennedy** (1968) and the **Reverend Martin Luther King, Jr.** (1968), **Malcolm X** (1965), instead of silencing their voices, gave impetus to calls for change among Mexican American leaders. From **Reyes Tijerina** in New Mexico to **César Chávez** and **Dolores Huerta** in California, young Chicanos were mobilized in search of expanding their access to their history and fair

President John F. Kennedy with first Lady Jackie Kennedy riding in Dallas, Texas moments before his assassination, 22nd of November 1963

representation in schools, and colleges. Although the University of the Pacific was trying to attract students from the rest of the Americas, those enrolled sensed the unjust biases incorporated into the development of Covell College. As far as I recall, there were no students from Mexico, Stockton, or from areas in the U.S. with high Latino-Chicano populations.

PART III

Teacher and Family Builder

17

HERE TO STAY
Aquí Nos Quedamos

Keeping Up with Math -- *Al Ritmo De Las Matemáticas*

The UOP Mathematics Professor Floyd Helton gave me continued support and guidance during my second year in Stockton as a full-time instructor. He provided me with books and materials, showed me useful teaching techniques, and encouraged me to expand and continue my education towards a doctorate degree. I was still smitten with the idea of going beyond teaching and engage in pure mathematical research, so his words of encouragement and trust in my abilities were like blessings from heaven. To keep the quest alive, I first enrolled at the San Joaquín Community College for a course in Russian, in hopes of learning enough to pass the exam for one of the languages required to obtain a PhD degree in Mathematics. Soon I found that the complexities involved with the Cyrillic alphabet and grammar were too much for me to handle. I already had sufficient knowledge of French, but needed another language, as Spanish was not accepted since there is not enough mathematical research done in my native tongue. So, as a madman, during the summer 1965, I rushed to enroll at the University of California in Berkeley for a course in analysis and worked to learn German, translating math articles into English, and learning enough to pass the required exams for the pursuit of a PhD. My friend, Joel (Cap) Hancock, also wanted to expand on his studies, so we shared a summer rental near the university. His single life seemed simple and uncomplicated but for me as a husband and father it was a period of pure lunacy, so much so, that after coming home for weekends, I would say to my sweet welcoming Norine: "if you can't say it in *Deutsch, sprechen nicht!*" – don't speak!

Delvis and Joel Hancock at The University of California in Berkeley.

The summer was memorable for Norine as well, as she was able to enroll our two-year old Davisito in his first day care center, so she could take art classes during the day. By then we were living in our third home, a one-bedroom house just blocks from UOP and Covell College on Euclid Avenue. She met new friends, and one in particular named Patty, who was also in her art classes and kept her entertained that lonely summer when I moved to Berkeley for three months of intense studies at the University of California. Through newly acquired friends at day care, Davisito picked up several common illnesses. On a Monday after a weekend home visit, Norine called to inform me that he had come down with the mumps, which I had not had as a child, and so I was forced to spend the rest of that week quarantined at the university clinic, but luckily did not get the disease, just missed class lectures and homework. Once released from quarantine, I called Norine to give her the good news, only to learn she was living in nightly fear of a crazy neighbor who she had seen lurking around the house and peering in her windows. She informed me she slept with the fireplace poker beside her bed.

There was always stress from school studies, and the home front, but occasionally happy stress. On one early weekend visit, Norine had given me the news that a second child was on its way, due by the end of December, so a larger place was needed. We both realized that yet another move, our fourth in Stockton, would have to take place before the beginning of the fall semester. Luckily, the early months of her pregnancy went smoothly, which meant she was able to continue her classes and look for a new 2-bedroom rental.

A New Child Is Born - *Nace nuestro nuevo hijo*

As the fall quarter began, we settled into our new place on Euclid Avenue but on the other side of the University. It had insane wallpaper with huge colorful flowers and a garage with a scary history but served our purpose with the baby coming. There was discontent brewing with the Administration of Covell College, and we were facing such important personal life changes, so I realized the seriousness of finding a secure job, possibly nearer to Berkeley to continue my education. I continued my hectic teaching pace and caring for Davisito several evenings each week, while Norine struggled through the thick Stockton fog to attend her evening art classes at UOP and San Joaquín Delta Community College.

Just as with *Davisito's* 1963 birth when she had finished her last day of work before going into labor even though he came 21 days early-- again with this 1965 birth, she waited until her last day of fall art classes before going into labor, which again was exactly 21 days early. The Christmas decorations were all in place early just in case and when suddenly, on Sunday evening, December 12, while watching TV at the end of our favorite 8:00 pm Ed Sullivan Show, she started grimacing in despair. Again, she simply thought that it was stomach problems from the Cuban food with *tostones, picadillo y arroz con frijoles negros* that I had helped to prepare for dinner that evening after returning from a bumpy mountain car trip with some friends to the California Gold country. As usual she showed signs of her stoic nature and tried to avoid getting me too excited about the prospect of having to run to emergency, especially since it was three weeks before the forecasted delivery date. At last, I convinced her to start timing the pains and based on her previous pregnancy we concluded that the baby was on its way. With no family nearby, I reached out to my friend Cap Hancock calling him by phone to give him the news - with a sense of panic about what was happening. I asked him to come to our home as fast as possible to take care of *Davisito* for the night, while I took Norine to the hospital. She acted as if there was ample time before birth – accepting the intensity and frequency of her labor pains. She insisted on taking a shower and shampooing her hair before leaving, so once she finally came out of the bathroom, Cap dashed in to use the facilities. When she went back in to dry her hair, she discovered he had apparently clogged the toilet and water was all over the floor.

Cap and I sat nervously waiting, wondering what in the world was taking her so long, and he even debating whether he should drive back home looking for his shoe along the way, which seemed to be missing. As he had dashed out with his Monday teaching outfit in hand, he had placed the shoes on top of the car while he searched for the keys, then drove right off – losing one shoe on the drive over. I convinced him it was not a good idea, as I knew it was obviously time to go to St. Joseph Hospital. On that drive Norine explained to me the problem of cleaning the floor on her hands and knees, which made me wonder about her sanity in that moment. The midnight hour was approaching, which was almost three hours since her labor had begun, and remembering David's record three-hour entrance, I was very nervous. Still before leaving the house, I had thought it might be a long wait, so I took a backpack with books to prepare my lectures, and a set of homework papers to grade. Immediately, she had been swept away, so after that goodbye kiss I slumped into a waiting room chair to unwind, chill out, and wait for another *criaturita*, as everything seemed under control. No sooner had I pulled out my papers to grade, when a nurse came with a blue blanket wrapped around a tiny bald-headed baby. She simply stated, "here is your boy." Even over my protest of "no, it couldn't be, I just brought my wife in, and our other baby had a full head of long black hair." She insisted the child was mine and invited me to come into the delivery room where Norine was grinning from ear to ear, very tired but reassuring me that he was our baby Danny. He was already cleaned up and after watching him closely, I thought I could see a little family resemblance and realized *"éste sí es mi hijo."*

A day or two later, Norine was well enough to come home, but our sweet little boy, *Danielito* had the same problem with jaundice that his big brother, *Davisito* had at birth, so needed to stay three more days in the hospital for observation. Grandma Alice Gunn had come from southern California to help out with the new baby, so her presence helped to take Norine's mind of the sadness of not bringing her baby home -- and there was all the re-doing of the Christmas decorations, as Alice's help in vacuuming the living room had resulted in the toppling of the Christmas tree with a tangled cord. Many of the balls were broken and needed replacing, although Norine's carefully and perfectly placed tinsel was never redone. Grandma Alice did help by doing the missed Monday's laundry, which Norine always hated to do out in our garage -- with its history. Unfortunately, we had learned after move-in day, that a previous renter had hung herself in that garage, which was a vision always present upon entering that garage. We did not mention that to Alice, but when the washer water line clogged and water spilled out all over the garage floor, we quietly wondered about yet another strange thing happening in our "haunted" garage. Poor Alice, she was trying so hard yet having so many mishaps. She did do a fine job of fixing the second bedroom and happily, things were all set up and in perfect order in *Davisito's* room when our newborn finally came home. Even though he had very good length and weight for his early birth, he looked very small in the big crib which we'd gotten – by-passing the bassinet stage to save money.

Davisito chose a teddy bear and a soft bunny, as his gifts for his new baby brother
Daniel Rubén (Danny)

Our dear friends, Brenda and Cap Hancock, and Norine's art buddy, Patty Bristowe,

By springtime, our backyard provided a wonderful play area for our boys and children of other faculty members, with BBQs and Davisito's third Birthday party. We managed to squeeze in some really wonderful memories that spring and early summer. One weekend we decided to go to Mark Twain's Frog Jumping Contest in Calaveras County with Cap and Brenda. To camp with a new born was not a good plan, so against everyone's advise, Norine asked her wild and crazy friend from her art classes, Patty Bristowe, to stay with him for one night. We drove to the mountains arriving well after dark and dead tired, so we found a flat spot to roll out our sleeping bag and collapse. Very early the next morning we were all abruptly awakened by the loud horn of a semi-truck just feet away, as we were sleeping right on the road. Patty got along fine and only shocked us by telling us that she had let the baby sleep in bed with her, which according to Dr. Spoke, in those days, was "absolutely no-no," in case you rolled over and smothered the child. It was a great spring, but the minute summer vacation arrived we made a beeline for Miami for our beach fix with a good dose of Cuban excitement and food, as my parents met their newest little *nieto, Danny.*

***Danielito & Davisito* loved time with their *Abuela* and with their *Papá* on Miami Beach.**

221

BREAK with COVELL
En desacuerdo con Covell

The main objective of the college was to bring people from different countries and social classes under student visas and then to have them return to their homelands. During my third year, problems began to emerge when students were not allowed to mingle in a normal way, which prevented social interaction – Education YES, Assimilation NO! My moment of decision came when I discovered that one of the administrators had been involved in intelligence work after the American sponsored coup d'état of the democratically elected government of Jacobo Arbenz in Guatemala. It seemed obvious that there was a dishonest portrayal of the college which I found intolerable, so I decided once again to search for another place to earn a living and to continue my education while raising my family.

The experimental cluster colleges showed signs of having a short existence. Covell College was conceived during the Cold War period after major setbacks in American foreign policy; with the Bay of Pigs, being in the midst of a quagmire as a result of the unending war in Vietnam, and rising concerns about calls for change in Latin America. The college had altruistic goals inspired by the newly emerging Alliance for Progress and Peace Corps initiatives of President Kennedy. The founders did have deep concern about social inequities but lacked knowledge and understanding of the complexities of life in Latin America. They were all Anglo Americans, although some had government and foreign travel experience. I, on the other hand, was the only "Latino," but as a mere faculty member was not involved in tracing out the general goals and simply took care of teaching mathematics along with the development of curricula and serving as student advisor in both languages.

The students were free to experience campus life but were obviously encouraged to return to their countries of origin. *Covellianos* were somewhat segregated and not allowed, for example, to sit next to other students during dining hours. This in itself was a rather strange policy, aimed at insuring an education in Spanish for Latin American students, yet with avoidance of contact with students from the adjacent College of the Pacific. I came to the conclusion that UOP with Covell could become a recruitment center of foreign agents as Inter-American Specialists.

Towards the Oakland-San Francisco Bay
Hacia la Bahía de Oakland-San Francisco

Once again, I was on the move, running from San Diego to Los Angeles and on to San Francisco for meetings and job interviews. I very much enjoyed teaching and flirting with math theorems, but I also had a strong attraction to activism, perhaps influenced by the changes called by the *revolucionarios* around the World and by my exposures to the isolation of Latinos in Salt Lake City, the unfair treatments of people of African ancestry in Florida, and the callous ignorance of administrators at a university that ignored the expansion of educational opportunities to a major ethnic group of *Californianos*. Here. near the center of the San Joaquin Valley, Covell College back in 1966 was totally without representation of the Hispanic/Latino/Chicano population. Years later in 2010, according to the U.S. Census, Stockton had a population of 291,707 with a Hispanic or Latino of any race of 117, 590 persons (40.3%). I was definitely sold on the new idea of getting a job at a **community** college as a means to provide educational opportunities for all, and to be near a major university for my continued expansion in learning and doing research in pure mathematics.

After getting a job offer from Chabot College, a community college in Hayward, I did not hesitate to accept it. Norine was thrilled and very happy, even though in Stockton she found beautiful oak trees to sketch, the fog in winter and black peat dust in summer were easy to leave behind. The San Francisco Bay Area, near the misty ocean waters, was the place to be and still close enough to the great Sierras for a day's trip. Now I could teach and be within a short distance of two of the greatest universities in the world for doing research, UC Berkeley and Stanford University. Towards the end of the summer of 1966 after our quick Florida trip, Norine and I with our two precious boys, Danny and Davisito, and our few belongings, crammed everything into our small VW Karmann Ghia pulling a small trailer, to continue our final westward move searching for a new home. We were filled with excitement and enthusiastic hope, as we became acquainted with our new surroundings, for what was to be our home for the next thirty-eight years, as we enjoyed our hilltop view of Hayward and the San Francisco Bay Area. But as time passes, our friends, the students, and my learning experiences at Covell College and the University of the Pacific are forever etched in my heart, my mind, and my soul.

18

Onward to Our New Home
The San Francisco Bay Area

Revelations from Job Interviews at Chabot College

After travelling all around California interviewing for jobs as a math teacher, I decided on Chabot College in Hayward, at the heart of the Oakland-San Francisco Bay Area. There were various points of attraction: (1) Outstanding colleges and universities near-by for expanding my education; (2) Wide diversity of populations that included Asians, Latinos, and African Americans for my teaching experience; and (3) A seemingly peaceful environment for raising my family. This was to be my extended homeland.

In late 1965, I was called for interviews at a community college that served a large section of the Bay Area: Chabot College had opened in San Leandro, a town near Oakland in 1961, but four years later, in 1965, moved to a new campus within the city limits of Hayward. Although parking lots and some buildings were still under construction, I was impressed with the surroundings and the modern architectural design – reminiscent of a mathematical creation with the aim of bringing harmony to learning and community. The campus had an elliptical path enclosing a library and the amphitheater as major focal points while the classrooms, offices and theater had entrances outside the orbit delineated by the walkway. Unlike other colleges I had attended, Chabot was truly embedded within the city limits with easy access to students and community members for lectures, meetings, plus music and theater performances.

Chabot College Campus in Hayward, California.

224

On the surface the college appeared to have a fair representation of students, faculty, and administration. However, a different reality was discovered through my job interviews with the college president and administrators. During my first encounter with an administrator, I was given the name "Del," as a designation for easier pronunciation for the English speakers, the administrator explained. As a person seeking a job, I did not object, but found it rather irrelevant and somewhat offensive to be baptized with a nickname. It was reminiscent of the customs official in Key West who insisted I change my signature, so he could read it. Other questions and comments by administrators appeared to be significantly based on my education and teaching experiences, nothing was asked about my math teaching experience nor my educational background. It was a very short encounter yet etched forever in my mind - he simply asked about my background as a representative of the "Mexican" people, which at the time, I did not find offensive, but definitely took it as showing a level of ignorance from a community leader in an educational institution.

It was not a good beginning but at the same time, it brought awareness of an environment that needed wider openings and changes in leadership. Although cultural, ethnic, and racial diversity were present in Hayward and its surrounding Bay Area, Chabot had almost no representation of women and ethnic minorities in its faculty and administration. On a personal note, when I began my teaching job in 1966, six years after the founding of Chabot, Chicanos/Latinos, Asians, and African Americans had no representation in the Math/Science Division faculty. The counseling and administration offices also had nearly zero representation of women and ethnic minorities. According to a 1970 census in Sothern Alameda County, 16.8% of the population had Spanish surnames but the Hispanics (Latinos) were only 4% of the student population at Chabot.

We looked at several towns nearby for a rental, but the actual city of Hayward had the most appeal mainly because I did not want to waste time commuting, which so many Bay Area residence seemed to do. Hayward had attractive neighborhoods, especially in the hilly area above the town, and although we could only afford rentals in the flat lands, at that time, the hills looked pleasant and promising for our future home. Staying in a motel with the two boys was not that comfortable and certainly a waste of money, so Norine very quickly found a two-bedroom duplex just a block above a main street through town, Mission Boulevard. It was just a couple of blocks from a beautiful small park where a huge indoor swimming pool, The Plunge, was located and just blocks from the downtown shops. It was a split-level duplex and lucky for us our downstairs neighbors were very friendly and grew quickly to be like an extended family ready to care for our boys and help in anything we needed. They were eager to celebrate their Jewish festivals like Purim and Hanukkah and enjoyed sharing their little boy's traditions with our sons. He was very close in age to our boys, so became their playmate, and best of all he had a little, adorable dog.

I was immersed in my new classes and fitting into the scene of teaching at Chabot, while Norine was busy making new traditions for our family. Decorating of cakes began with the clown cake that year for David's third birthday and became her trademark for many years to come. And another tradition for several years was that first Christmas tree for our little apartment, which was a 'six-foot tall, thin weed, she pulled up from the backyard, refusing to pay the $9 (yes, in 1966) for a real tree off the lot. Once we bought our own home and the boys started to bring friends home, she was teased so much that she gave into a regular tree, and the boys no longer had to explain what was up with their mom's weird tree. Sitting at our kitchen table, after putting the boys to bed, both in David's twin bed, we started making plans for our first real vacation – a summer trip to Europe. Danny had had a brief stay in the hospital in a crib with bars

Norine's first Birthday Cake creation – a 'Clown" for David's third party with his little brother, Danny.

on top, like a cage, and was so traumatized that he refused to sleep in or be placed in his own crib, even for naps, and he would only fall asleep in a "big kid's bed" next to his brother and always with a storybook. Spring brought wonderful weather and with summer not far off, we began dreaming seriously of a fantasy we had for several years. A trip to Europe crept into our conversation after I learned that a new friend and colleague was planning to return to his homeland in Germany come summer.

We felt that if we were to make such an amazingly long trip, we needed to make it worthwhile by spending most of the summer traveling. The 64-thousand-dollar question simply was – what to do concerning our boys? To my great surprise Norine was the one who suggested they spend the time in Miami with my folks. Her father was still working daily, and her mother's days were filled with piano students in their home, which would make care of the boys impossible. My mother, on the other hand, although she often went to the garage to help my dad with his work, was not essential and if needed she could take the boys along with her to experience it all. Norine shared my belief in the value and importance of their exposure to everything on my side of the family, which pleased me, so we went ahead with planning how we could work it all out. We called my parents and presented the idea, and to our delight they were thrilled with the plan.

Being well into that first year at Chabot, I was starting to feel comfortable, and I was also pleased to meet several instructors who were to become longtime friends. The very first friend, Hans, was a biology instructor born in Germany who spoke fluent Spanish and was acquainted with Latin culture. We talked of his desire to take a trip the following summer, which for him would be his first return to see family and a country he had left as a teenager in the early 1950s. It sounded like an impossible dream, but Norine made a list, as she always did, and we started working our way down through the items. Travel visas were needed, so numerous trips had to be made to European consulates in San Francisco, since I was not a U.S. citizen, it turned out to be much more complicated for me than it was for Norine. While working on the visas, we had contacted my parents with the idea and they were thrilled to death, so plane reservations were made for *Mami* to fly to California to pick them up and take them back to Miami. I was happy about my boys having the opportunity to be immersed in Cuban Culture, but as both Norine and I look back all these years later, we can't help but think that it was a very crazy thing. Fortunately, I can jump ahead and also say, that the boys had a great time and came back all in one piece, and Davisito was chattering away in Spanish. Unfortunately, one minor side effect that Danny suffered was a slowdown in his speech development. He had just started talking before leaving for Miami, and to then be thrown in with only Spanish, seemed to have had its effect, and he did not really talk much upon their return to Hayward. Thankfully, it did not last long and with nightly story time and constant playtime with his brother and Joey, he soon started talking a blue streak and never stopped.

David and Danny ready for their flight with Abuela to Miami

Somehow with my busy teaching load I managed to press through grading the final exams I had given and finished up grades to turn in ahead of schedule. *Mami* arrived to spend a few days of getting acquainted with the kids, while Norine and I finished packing their things and two small bags for ourselves. It was amazing that we could work out just one suitcase for each of us for the whole summer but figured we would be doing a good deal of walking, dragging our own suitcase behind us. We had been reading a popular book of that time called "Europe on 5 Dollars a Day," so already knew that the best way to see it all, and also travel cheaply was to do it by foot as much as possible.

The boys were all dressed up for the flight, so with hugs and many, many kisses, we tearfully watched as they climbed aboard the plane with my mother headed for Miami. We then walked across the big San Francisco airport to the opposite side to wait for our international night flight to Amsterdam. Having that long wait was not too smart, which we had not considered in trying to simplify and save money with just one trip to the airport. We were both feeling very conflicted about the goodbyes and questioning what in the world we were doing. The boys were 18 months and just four years and sitting all afternoon gave us far too much time to consider bad scenarios and worry about the sadness we were going to experience over the next two and half month. Finally, they announced our flight, and the excitement grew as we boarded the plane for what turned out to be -- the adventure of a lifetime.

19
Our Travel Adventures Begin

AMSTERDAM, an Impressive Start

We arrived in Amsterdam, way past midnight their time, but were so excited that we began to explore the neighborhoods without thoughts of sleep. Norine, as an art lover, delighted seeing Van Gogh originals and the Rijksmuseum was the first, and so forever a favorite. Later, she insisted on going to museums and art venues in every city. We had planned our trip based on an old travel book - "Europe on Five Dollars a Day" – which I interpreted to mean as a five-dollar maximum for both. Even back in the sixties it was a challenge, but walking was free, and we could see many things other tourists might not, and thankfully we could each manage our one suitcase.

Delvis admires Amsterdam.

The next day we found a cheaper hotel, which when night fell, we found that we were right in the center of the red-light district with prostitutes sitting on every windowsill, with their long shapely legs dangling down as they tempted passersby with their wares. It was a wild awakening for a quiet lad from Cuba and a naïve lass from Utah. It was a rich experience, yet a cheap price to pay for a tiny room on the very top floor with its narrow spiral staircase. Despite the climb and inconvenience, of that room, we thoroughly enjoyed the beauty of Amsterdam with its amazing canals and found that eating cheese with bread and fresh fruits from local markets was wonderful and would be our main stay diet that summer. Hans and his wife Shirley had immediately left for Germany upon our arrival in Amsterdam. We were to meet later and continue the trip together, all the way to Madrid by way of Switzerland, Southern France and on into Spain in the car he was planning to purchase in Cologne. Before leaving Amsterdam, we visited the home of Anne Frank, which was on our list of "musts." After that moving afternoon, we realized that the things we had heard or read about, but were now seeing with our own eyes, were going to make this trip the most memorable and profound experience of our lives.

On To GERMANY, But for Too Long of a Stay

Delvis' suit and tie matched the elegance of *Kölner Dom*.

We left Amsterdam by train and made a stop in Köln. The majesty of the great *Kölner Dom*, the Cathedral of Cologne was an amazing preview of the many cathedrals to come throughout Europe. We were to have a brief yet very memorable encounter, with Hans' family, whom he had not seen for over 15 years. The family was cordial, and our visit was a very personal view into the home and life of the German people. However, for me it was also filled with tension, as Hans had identified me as a person with a Jewish background when he introduced me to his family. It goes without saying that I avoided any discussion or questions as to how they lived during the times of persecution of Jews and other minorities in Nazi Germany.

The next morning Han's uncle Karl, took us to an immense shopping type mall, with store after store and all closed off to traffic. With their help, Norine bought a very good German camera for next to nothing, and to her delight, small sized lederhosen (leather type short pants) for my son David, which they were able to bargain for in German, thus keeping her shopping within our strict budget. A visit to an immense zoo gave her the chance to try out the new *Voigtländer* camera. Hans had worked there as a boy, and his uncle knew the lay out of the zoo like the back of his hand. All the animals roamed around freely in very large natural habitat areas, so we were able to get 'up close and personal,' something we had never seen in a U.S. zoo.

AUGSBURG -- Our Home Base for Weeks

We traveled on by train to Augsburg where we thought we had a place to stay and family to visit. Norine's favorite second cousin, Aunt Pearl's granddaughter from Illinois, was stationed with her husband at an American Army base between Augsburg and Munich. However, when we knocked at the door, the cousin's husband, whom Norine had never met, answered, and informed us that her cousin Mary Loree was back in the U.S. for the summer. He graciously invited us to stay anyway, not knowing it would turn into a 3 week's visit, while we waited for Hans to finalize the purchase of his used Mercedes in Cologne. That first day we took a trolley into Munich, which was the nearest big town, to explore and see the sights and learn the tricks to getting around by trolley and by foot for the next several weeks. The wait for Hans turned into a long ordeal, so we got to know Augsburg well and enjoyed the culture of Munich.

Very memorable was an afternoon at the largest opera house in Germany, which was only $1.50 for standing room on the very top balcony level. The performance of "Der Rosenkavalier" was so amazing and unlike anything either of us had ever seen or dreamed of that we were oblivious of the four hours standing. In Munich we also enjoyed the Royal Ballet's performance of "Romeo and Juliet" and an absolutely amazing performance by a Boys choir from Spain.

Every evening, there with Mary's husband at the army compound, Ed would claim to be a great gourmet chef. He would prepare an appetizer with our first glass of wine and explain what amazing things he had planned for the second, third, and fourth courses. However, he enjoyed his second, then third, then fourth glass of wine so much that he would pass out in his chair before we would get to the main course. So, we quickly realized the need to eat a good hardy lunch wherever we were for the day before returning to Ed's apartment. He did take us out to a fine restaurant one evening with a typical German dish made with venison – all for $1.25 each, which was the American serviceman's perk. To our surprise, we learned that evening that even though he had spent many years in Germany, Ed could not speak German well enough to order, to pay, nor even give the directions for taking us home. The following weekend Ed took us on a jaunt to the south which became more beautiful and greener the further south we went. We got to Oberammergau midafternoon and although it was not the year for the "Passion Play," we found many interesting shops with wood carvings and flowers everywhere.

We continued to Garmisch for a night's stay at a quaint hotel and the following day took the "cog train" to Germany's highest peak where we could see the peaks of the Alps in four different countries peeking through the clouds. That afternoon on the return to Munich we passed through a small village filled with the music and the excitement of a local parade. That evening we topped off a marvelous weekend with a visit to the "Hofbräuhaus" for a true German experience in the beer hall where the servers carried an unbelievable number of huge steins of beer in each hand and everyone enjoyed far too much drinking and singing of the "oompah" songs.

The First View of the Alps in Four Different Countries

231

When we finally reached Augsburg the next day, we were exhausted from our marvelous adventures yet absolutely delighted to learn that Hans was on his way. We were more than ready to finally move on to places beyond the Bavarian region of Germany. There was only one more "must see" which we hurriedly planned. That last day of our saga proved to be the most interesting with a trip by train, then bus to see Dachau, one of the worst concentration camps. We started off, on what we had been told would be a long trek after the bus ride, but eventually became concerned as to our directions. We saw two middle aged women, dressed in typical German garb, working in a garden, so as we passed, we politely with broad friendly smiles asked for directions. They were sternly serious with a reply indicating they had never heard of such a place. Finally, a man who heard us asking for directions, identified himself as being from Pakistan, now living in Germany, and he explained in a whisper where to go. He warned us not to inquire from the locals about the concentration camps. He implied that the shame or denial of those massive killings during the Nazi regime were still very raw and town's people in that small village right next to one of the worst camps, Dachau, would "know nothing." We finally made our way to the broad unwelcoming gate and upon entering the camp – observed the long rows of indications as to where the barracks had been. The museum was open, but empty of other travelers, making the stark pictures and horrifying silence even more profoundly chilling. The sight of the crematorium was perhaps the most moving and sadly profound experience of that summer.

A somber visit to Dachau: The Museum and The Crematorium.

On to SOUTHERN FRANCE with Our Friends

Once Hans finally arrived with his newly purchased 'used' Mercedes Benz, we travelled with him and his wife all the way to Madrid, visiting various sites along the way in Switzerland, Southern France, and Spain. The sights along the way were spectacular, but the drives were long and tiresome and often stressful, due to what Hans found to be rather fast and unfamiliar driving habits. Such a "road trip" presented many interesting situations, some positively hilarious and some sadly negative, but all were never to be forgotten.

One afternoon in southern France, we had stopped early and found a charming café for wine and dinner. Norine and Shirley were restless, so wandered about as Hans and I engaged in heavy conversation. When they returned to the café, which had a long bar filled with local fellows who had stopped for a drink after their day's work, they inquired about the location of the lady's restroom, to learn it was in the corner straight down from that bar. It had swinging, saloon type doors with a gap below the door down to the floor. To their amazement, the cement floor of the small 5x5 space, which had a raised lip on all four sides, and sloped to a drain in the center had absolutely no other facilities, other than a chain hanging from the ceiling. Luckily, they were both wearing skirts, and finally concluded, that a slight bend of the knees to a somewhat squatting position was the only solution. After which, when they pulled the chain, water poured out from every direction of the small lip around the floor, flooding the whole area as it rushed to the drain. They hopped and jumped out of the space as quickly as they could, only to realize the gentlemen at the bar, had observed - from beneath the swinging doors - the entire spectacle of their dancing feet. Unfortunately, neither Hans nor I were fluent enough in French to interpret the men's boisterous shouts but knew from the laughter and back slapping that we had missed a very funny show. Later, all was explained in good fun with a free round of fine French wine and the food was wonderful, so it all became one of those marvelous nights etched in our memory.

From our first day in Amsterdam, Norine had been writing a daily journal account of our experiences in the form of letters for her parents, which we mailed every few weeks. This bathroom joke was one story she failed to share with them in her letter for fear of misinterpretation. The next day we were sitting at a lovely outdoor spot enjoying our morning coffee and croissant. Hans was explaining how badly the morning had gone as there was no hot water for his wife's shampoo, which she had complained about bitterly. Their stay with family had obviously not exposed them to the same minor inconveniences to which we were growing accustomed: lack of hot water, lack of towels, lack of toilet paper and pillows often hard as rocks. We also were concerned that their budget for hotels might not jive with our low allowance. Another possible problem became apparent that morning, as Shirley

Norine always well dressed, her grandmother would have been proud.

approached our table. Her head was piled high with huge rollers to set her hairdo for later that day. Norine had seen a movie not long before our trip, which portrayed American travelers as very unaware of their disrespectful behavior when it came to customs and dress, in the foreign land they might visit. Therefore, she had carefully packed her suitcase with not a single pair of pants nor sneakers, but instead skirts or dresses and always low pump shoes. She hoped not to be the "ugly American," as she had read, that European women of that time did not wear pants and certainly never appeared in public with their hair in rollers. Both Norine and I were always dressed to the tee in hopes of blending in, but it had become clear that our travel companions did not share our concern. In conversation with natives who occasionally mistook us for Europeans, we did learn that the dead giveaway was always our shoes.

At Long Last – SPAIN

Our entrance into Spain after enjoying the majesty of the Alps and the lush green vegetation of Switzerland was quite surprising, perhaps due to my ignorance about the complexities of Spanish cultures and languages - a country that as a Cuban I always referred to as *La Madre Patria* (The Mother Land). During that first month in Europe, we faced difficulties speaking in French and German, and now I was looking forward to crossing the border into Spain so that I could speak my native tongue. But to my surprise I heard people speaking an incomprehensible language, *Catalán*. After many hours on the road in the confined car space, we were excited about spending a few days in Barcelona as planned. We stopped for coffee as we entered town and immediately Hans became upset as he interpreted the waiter's slow manners as rudeness, which escalated to a full-blown argument, and he stormed out. Once in the car he had a complete melt-down as the memories came flooding back to him about the tragedy, he experienced upon leaving his home and family in Germany with a first stop in Barcelona. He took off driving straight through the town without a single stop. Norine had her window rolled down and was frantically taking pictures from the moving car, as our overnight stay in Barcelona flew by. Sadly, all the pictures were just a blur as was our memory of that magnificent city.

Once out on the open road again, we did stop on a green slope, where Hans finally relaxed in admiration of the beautiful country landscape with birds, insects, and butterflies. Norine fixed a bread and cheese lunch while Hans embarked on a photo safari snapping colorful flowers and a big black bumblebee, which to our amazement, he spotted on a flower in a far-off field. That was my discovery of another side of my friend that went beyond just teaching biology -- his passion for painting in great detail the beauty of birds and animal life in nature.

Norine fixes lunch as Hans unwinds and admires the beauty of Spain.

Han's artistic ability shown in the Christmas cards sent to us in later years.

VALENCIA -- As we entered Valencia, the regret of missing out on the architecture and wonders of Barcelona was soon forgotten, however, to this day the magic of seeing that grand city remains on my bucket list. Once in Valencia we found a wonderful little hotel with a view of the town and beach from our balcony, so we grabbed our swim wear to lay in the warm Spanish sunshine on a wonderful beach. We soon engaged in conversation with a very interesting local character, which turned into a wild adventure. He was a very short, stout little priest, who looked the part but certainly did not sound nor act his proper role; Hans and I could understand his Spanish, but we were rather surprised at his foul language to describe anything and everything. He definitely enjoyed the wine as we sat for hours on tall stools at a high table listening to the sea and his endless stories. Eventually he invited us to come to his "humble" home where his treasure of fine Spanish wines could be enjoyed. We agreed but were surprised when Norine and Shirley seemed uncertain and far from eager to go. We later learned that his wandering hands under that high table where the women sat in their swim wear was the reason for their hesitation. We did follow him, as we were all anxious to see the inside of the picturesque homes that lined the streets. The house was simple, but the inner patio with the walls covered with plants was amazing. Norine fell in love with this, and every patio of Spain covered with greenery and colorful potted plants. After one glass of wine, we quickly excused ourselves and thanked him for his hospitality.

MADRID -- Upon reaching Madrid we had decided, after our long drive that it would be best to say goodbye to our friends, so that we could enjoy and discover things, on our own time and in our own way. We were so excited about the prospect of seeing the cultures of Spain in Madrid, *Andalucía, Castilla La Vieja* (Old Castille) and the Basque Country, we did not want to take any chance of spoiling it. There were museums and cathedrals to explore, colorful patios and interesting shops to admire, dance festivals and music to experience, and friends of the family to meet. Every day in Spain was filled with wonder and excitement and love of a country neither of us could have imagined. In Madrid we looked forward to meeting and visiting some acquaintances of my parents, José González Cienfuegos and his wife, Piedad. Manolo Fernández, the son, of our doctor in Cuba, was studying medicine in Spain, so through one of those bizarre back and forth exchanges that was made necessary due to the complicated relationship (or rather lack of) between the U.S. and Cuba, my folks would send money to these friends in Spain to help pay for Manolo's education and in exchange, his family back in Cuba helped pay for my sister's private schooling. It reminded me and gave me a renewed appreciation of the bartering my father had done years ago, to make my whole schooling experience back in Cuba a positive one.

We met them and enjoyed their kind hospitality with an offer to take shopping at the 'thieves' market' the next day and to help me purchase a handmade guitar. So early the next morning, we went for our coffee and pastry, then Norine and the wife took off for a shopping adventure. She was an energetic little lady that ran circles around Norine as they dashed from shop to shop. Poor Norine was completely exhausted by day's end, mainly because the woman was so much shorter in statue which meant that holding her hand, which was at least a foot lower than Norine's, caused a sideways bend that was very uncomfortable. Apparently, it was customary for the older woman to hang on tight to the hand of the younger, naïve, guest shopper to ensure she did not get lost. Norine did her best to comply with tradition but paid the price all night with her aching back. I also had a fascinating day learning to order my guitar in the "Spanish way," which involved hours of bartering back and forth, unlike a straightforward order back home. It would take at least a week, to make the guitar, so we excitedly made our plans for traveling on to southern Spain for adventures we had read and dreamed of.

AVILA & SEGOVIA -- With Norine's study of art, she had a acquired a great love and admiration for the Moorish influence she had seen pictured in *Andalucía*. The entire area did not disappoint, and we both found southern Spain to be a favorite. We loved the art, the architecture, the food, the people, the music, the dancing – we just loved everything about Spain! We hitched a ride with Hans and Shirley as far as Avila and Segovia as they had decided to go back and spend more time in Germany, where they felt more "comfortable," because of the language we assumed, and as they stated, "more safe." So, from there on we were on our own experiencing trains or bus and even one hitch hiking adventure. Norine was enthralled with the art and architecture, and I with the music and dance. So many beautiful and amazing experiences, that I can only highlight a few of the marvels. In Segovia, the Roman aqueduct took our breath away. It was built by hand during the second half of the 1st century A.D., and adjusts to the contours of the valley, the hills, and the city along 14 kilometers of rolling landscape. The pillars and arches of its tall, two-story arcades were made of solid blocks of stone, fitted closely together with little or no mortar. It remains one of the most intact Roman aqueducts in Europe and was magnificently monumental. Also, in Segovia was the *Alcázar*

Castle, which Disney copied for Disneyland, and of course a magnificent cathedral. Here we said our good-byes to our travel companions and headed to the train station for our tickets back to Madrid. We had our first experience, but not our last, with a small fire on the train in our car, so everyone had to move up one car which meant standing for the entire journey. We had not been

The ancient Aqueducts in Segovia.

sure about the wisdom of keeping our Madrid hotel for that night but were so very grateful when we finally arrived and had a familiar bed to fall into after an exhausting day.

TOLEDO -- We had planned to leave for Toledo early the next morning, but there was no train till midafternoon, so we decided to give the bus a try. We always travelled third class to get the cheapest tickets, but with a bus it turned out there was little difference. We walked and walked for hours and Norine's choice was to visit El Greco's home and seeing several incredible original works that she had studied. **Santa María la Blanca** was my choice which was a beautifully moving Jewish Synagogue and now museum. It was erected in 1180, according to an inscription on a beam, and is considered by some to be the oldest synagogue building in Europe which is still standing. I insisted Norine take my picture with the street sign of Calle Samuel Levi in the 'old' Jewish quarter. Toledo is an ancient city set on a hill, erected in 1180, according to an inscription on a beam, it is disputably considered the oldest synagogue building in Europe still standing above the plains of Castilla-La-Mancha in central Spain, and as the capital of the region, it is known for the medieval Christian, Arab, and Jewish monuments in its walled old city. But it was not an edifice nor a monument that filled me with emotions and speechless, but rather looking down as we stood above cliffs, realizing that this was the very place where Jews were flung to their deaths during the Inquisition.

Jewish Synagogue in Toledo

We could easily have filled a whole week exploring Toledo, but we knew the next destination would probably be just as great, so we tore ourselves away with a promise to each other, that one day we would return. We had saved our hotel reservation for the room in Madrid for one more night but found there was neither a bus nor a train at that hour, so decided to try our luck at hitch hiking - something that did not have a bad reputation back in those days. Luckily, we quickly got a ride from a very talkative, young man from Cordoba, which was coming up on our list of places to go, so we pumped him for a local's scoop on things to do and see. Next morning, we cleared out of the room and took one suitcase to leave with our friends but learned there was no train to Cordoba until eight that evening, so we had a delightful lunch with them and did a little shopping for gifts to take back to friends at home.

Cliffs above Rio Tajo in Toledo

CORDOBA -- The evening train to Cordoba was fairly comfortable as we had splurged for first class tickets since we would have to try sleeping while traveling. We arrived in Cordoba at three in the morning, tired but very excited so immediately started walking about and even in the dark we could tell it was going to be an absolutely charming town. We found a pleasant hotel early and to our great surprise were invited to have coffee and pastries, when the matron learned we had traveled all night. She told us of many things we could do but emphasized strongly that visiting *La Mezquita* should be our first priority. It is called "Mosque – Cathedral." because it displays the cohabitation of three important religions. The Arabic style of the structure of the Mosque blends beautifully with the Gothic, Renaissance and Baroque style of the Christian architecture, with one built right on top of and/or around another. We spent hours wandering in wonderment of this amazing site. Norine's photos below show the stark difference in architecture detail and all under one roof. Finally, hunger overtook our thrill of further investigation, so we found *Del Caballo Rojo* and had perhaps the most delicious meal of our entire trip. It had just opened after the afternoon siesta and still had very few customers, so we received their full friendly attention and learned a great deal about the many different types of Paella, depending on the region where they are made. In all of Spain, we had found that having a big lunch in late afternoon suited our needs so much better.

The next stop was to be Seville but there was no train until the next day, so

Capilla Real   **Capilla Teresa**   **Puerta del   Puerta de la
                                              Espíritu Santo   Grada Redonda**

**Norine's photos show the remarkable contrast of architecture,
all found under "one roof."**

we wandered around in the cool of evening admiring many **inner patios** through open doorways. We grew tired of walking, so enjoyed a romantic carriage ride before retiring. We had experienced the afternoon heat in southern Spain, but it became more bearable when we learned that due to the excruciating heat, the early inhabitants of Cordoba started building their houses with a central patio, decorated with water fountains and wells for a cool place to relax. During the Muslim kingdom, plants, and trees, were added to keep local homes even cooler and more sheltered from the hot sun rays. Eventually, the patios were decorated with colorful flowers, giving birth to the gorgeous patios that we enjoyed everywhere.

Our train did not leave until late afternoon, so we went walking through a colorful street faire. It was fun but resulted in an argument about spending too much for some little souvenir - I do not remember what. Norine went storming off in one direction and I in another, which led to a wild adventure for her. She was so captivated with the many items for sale that she did not grasp how far she had walked and suddenly was just weaving in and out of the narrow streets with no sight of me anywhere. After a bit she realized there were two young men walking quite far from her, yet on the same path, which made her fear they might be following her. She said she quickened her pace, clutching her bag and camera tightly. As she rounded a corner, she saw three elderly women, dressed entirely in black, sitting in front of an open doorway with one empty chair. As she approached them, she smiled sweetly, greeted them in her broken Spanish and then quickly sad down on the empty chair. She tried to explain what was happening, she thought without much success, but when the two men rounded that corner, and the women saw them hesitate, they stood up shouting and screaming and shaking their fists, at which point the two men turned and took off running. Immediately she had made three friends and joined them for a *cafecito*. As we had checked out of our hotel, she had no idea how to find me, but the women were able to understand that we were headed for Seville, so the youngest one walked all the way to the train station to show her the way and there they found me patiently waiting. What a relieved and happy reunion with promises never to argue again.

SEVILLE -- Upon arrival in Seville we checked our $5 a Day book and found a great little hotel right away and only for $1.40 with the bath down the hall. Today as I look back over Norine's letters from that summer, I can hardly believe the prices we paid for many things, mostly hotel rooms and how very thankful we are to have had the experience of that amazing journey when we could afford it. We did have one great experience with music and dance in Madrid but had not encounter the real flamenco I was craving. So that night we headed out to a restaurant and club in the "caves," which our tourist brochures bragged about as being wonderful. Unfortunately, we were highly disappointed, but while enjoying our meal, I struck up a conversation with the waiter, and he quietly whispered that this spot was considered by locals to be a real tourist trap and far from the "real" thing. When he realized our interest in experiencing authentic entertainment, he excitedly shared news of a local festival in a very small town that was not too far away. He warned that it might be difficult for us to find, yet he was so assuring and encouraging that it would be well worth our time, so our anticipation and determination grew. The next morning, we investigated buses and found one later that afternoon, but nothing returning until the next afternoon. In spite of that, we decided to take our chances for such an unusual adventure. We started walking to take in as much as we could before the bus departure. Everyone advised and agreed that the grandeur of *La Giralda* Cathedral was a must.

La Giralda is the belltower right next-door to the Cathedral, and has Moorish origins, being the minaret for the former mosque. We were informed that the tower had 34 ramps leading to the top instead of a stairway, so a horse could be ridden to

the top. With such limited time we decided to pass on that exercise and just admired it all from the ground. By the late afternoon heat all the Spaniards were taking their siestas, but we found a helpful man behind the ticket counter, so were able to purchase our bus tickets to the village of Mairena, but with no return later that night. Our excitement at the prospect of a fun adventure ruled, and we climbed on the bus, having no idea what an amazing experience we were to have, let alone how we would get back. The festival was scheduled to begin at 11:00 p.m. that night, so we had plenty of time to explore the village and enjoy the local cuisine of Mairena.

La Giralda bell tower in Seville

By ten that evening we headed over to the venue for the festival, and I immediately engaged in pleasant conversation with those sitting nearby. Within two minutes of the opening song, we forgot the chill with no jackets and only our unsightly sandals nor the discomfort of the hard, straight wooden bench. The thrill of this authentic singing and dancing in that perfect setting was exhilarating and obviously an experience never to be forgotten. It lasted until around four in the morning, and we were enthralled every single minute. Having made several new seating friends, we had no problem hitching a ride, in spite of the hour, back to Madrid. It was only an hour to sunrise when we finally fell into bed in our little hotel, but it was impossible to sleep with our heads and hearts so filled with the beauty and excitement of the dance and the drama and joy of the authentic music.

GRANADA -- We had one more town to visit before heading to France and it was spectacular. Granada's sights had splashed across Norine's art history books, and she was filled with anticipation that one day for exploring "The Red One - *La Alhambra*," a palace and fortress complex with a long history.  Its beginning was near the end of year 880, and largely ignored until its ruins were renovated and rebuilt in the mid-13 century and converted into a royal palace in 1333. By 1492 it had become the Royal Court of Ferdinand and Isabella where they gave endorsement to Christopher Columbus for his expedition. A Moorish poet described it as "a pearl set in emeralds" which alluded to its brilliant color set in the lush green woods and flowers around it. The sound of running water from all the fountains was cool and calming and the dancing light and attention to detail was unreal – it reminded us of fine lace. Granada was the perfect ending to our journey through *Andalucía*, the region of southern Spain that will always be our favorite.

The *Palacio Nazariés y Generalife* in Granada

The Court of the Lions in *La Alhambra* in Granada, Spain

Upon our return to Madrid, we took an easy day off to rest but did find a shop that carried posters, and to our delight they had one depicting the festival in Mairena, which we bought without hesitation. Our only sadness was not receiving the expected letter from Miami, telling us how our boys were doing. We had made very elaborate plans for places and dates to receive letters about every two to three weeks, but somehow the plans did not work well and here in mid-August, we had only received one letter from my mother during the entire trip. It had been written only days after her arrival in Miami, so she spoke mostly about the airplane ride with no real news as to how they were all getting along. We put on a brave face and just hoped for the best, but the concern for our two little boys was the one and only thing that gave us real sorrow. Our other complaint in every town and every country was the red tape and difficulty of getting -- anything done -- that was a necessity. For example: purchasing tickets for travel whether by train or bus was always an awful ordeal that took a great deal of our time; arranging the simple task of mailing my letters let alone a package was unbelievably complicated, always involving a trip to the actual post office just to have things weighed; buying the right film for our new camera was a nightmare and Norine's constant fear that she wasn't using it properly and might not be getting any pictures (we developed them all at home after the trip, and thankfully they pleased her. Also, shopping for food and wine was sometimes problematic for if you dared to touch or 'squeeze' any of the fruits in the market, you were immediately reprimanded, yet the low prices of wine always made the shopping spree worthwhile and it never disappointed.

We stopped at our friends and got the second suitcase we had left with them.

**MUSEO
NACIONAL
del
PRADO
Madrid,
Spain**

José and I went to arrange for the shipment home of my magnificent guitar by boat which would take several weeks. Norine with Piedad headed for ***El Prado* Museum** for one last dash through that favorite museum. We then met up for lunch of authentic tapas in a restaurant reminiscent of Seville. Next, we were off to the post office, which took several hours, just to mail her weeks' worth of diary letter to her parents, a post card for my folks to show the boys, several rolls of film, and a package with the hand carved wooden bookends we found as a wedding gift for Cap and Brenda, our dear friends from Stockton. By late evening we met them again for a farewell dinner of *Paella Valenciana*. We had been on such a sparse budget that these two invitations for fantastic meals could not be resisted. However, we both over indulged and paid all that night with stomach problems and anxiety for the long train ride the next morning.

SAN SEBASTIÁN -- The train ride from Madrid to San Sebastián was exhilarating with a completely different landscape and amazing new colors. It was much cooler, quite mountainous and much greener with threatening afternoon clouds but with no rain. We passed through and stopped in several small, picturesque towns with interesting sights to entertain us and camera calls for Norine. We found the bread and oranges with plenty of water plus the beauty of northern Spain did wonders for our ailments, and we both forgot our troubles as we looked to our next adventure – Gay Paree.

A working donkey in Spain

When we arrived late in the evening at our destination, we found throngs of people everywhere as it happened to be a week of *fiestas*, for what, I do remember. We had a great deal of trouble finding a decent room and finally accepted going well over budget just to find a bed for the night. And once again, we finally found something to eat, close to midnight, and just in time for the most amazing fireworks display over the water. San Sebastián had a real resort feel to the city with many French and Spanish tourists as well as from all of Europe. They were all enjoying the famous beach, *La Concha* (The Seashell) which was absolutely packed both day and night. We had to try some of the Basque food before our afternoon departure,

La Concha **Beach in San Sebastián, Spain.**

so splurged again assuming we would eat bread and water for our entire French stay, as we'd heard that the food in Paris was very pricy. The train was very late which added to our anxiety of arriving late with needing a hotel and to change money. But excitement overtook our concerns, and we were off to Gay Paree. We had also been told that the French could be a bit rude if you ask too many questions, and certainly if you did not use good French to ask. I had learned a little French from my friend, Gemma in Miami, but that had been quite a few years back, and I noticed immediately that I picked up a few words here and there but was amazed at how fast they seemed to speak. Those concerns were softened next to our excitement and absolute awe that we were headed for the city of romance.

AH, GAY PAREE in FRANCE!!

We had fallen in love with another great city of Europe. If you have been to Paris, France, you know exactly what I am talking about – if you have not, you must go. Our only regret was not allowing much more time, as we could have spent weeks. The highlight for us both was the Louvre and Norine was there from dawn to dusk. Food was pricy and very particular, as we were asked to leave our indoor table in a small café when we ordered only French onion soup for lunch, which could only be ordered from the outdoor tables, so of course we left in a huff. After an extravagant show at the Lido, we did have our soup for breakfast. We had sat at the bar to avoid the table charge, perched on two high stools as we grew dizzy with the swirling dancers and raucous music. When we had left around three in the morning all of the final metro trains had left, so we walked for hours heading back to our little hotel. We passed *Les Halles*, the food and flower market, just at the perfect hour early in the morning as they were unloading their trucks for blocks and blocks. There we also found a wonderful little spot serving morning pastries and when the kind matron heard our sad tale of the previous days lunch, she immediately disappeared into her kitchen, returning with two overflowing bowls of onion soup covered with French bread and dripping with cheese.

Our hotel was central to everything on the Left Bank right in the heart of the University crowd - for only $3.40 a night. The shower was down the hall, but there was a bidet and the strange sensation caused by the tilting floor was ignored by Norine as there was a basin with hot running water, her first for that entire summer. There were many 'beatnik caves' in the dark cellars all around us, slow dancing to jazz and French poetry made us think we were actors in a foreign flick. We enjoyed the place when we went in search of the brother of one of Norine's cousins, Genevieve. Unfortunately, he had gone off for a month of holiday in southern France, but his sweet landlady invited us in for a sip of sweet liquor with some marvelous homemade *Patisserie Française*: eclairs and madeleines. I finally got to practice my French with a sympathetic tutor, and we were ecstatic to find she had a letter from my Mama in Florida tucked away in a drawer that had arrived a few days earlier. Our boys were fine and loving the beach as well as "working" in the garage with their *Abuelo*. To her delight they were understanding everything she said to them in Spanish although Davisito usually answered in English and Danielito only in his nearly two-year-old "gibberish."

We had not quite a week in Paris and considered staying longer, but we did want to see London for at least a couple of days and make it to Brussels for our flight home. So, our last day was a twenty-four-hour whirl wind of seeing everything left on our list, even if only to take a picture. Our final dinner before the night train consisted of wine, French bread and cheese at the Luxembourg Gardens.

Enjoying the colors, the sounds and especially the children of Paris

Every sight in Paris was magnificent, as was Sacre Coeur

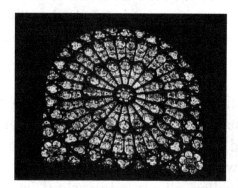

The Rose Window at Notre-Dame

Winged Victory of Samothrace and Venus de Milo at the Louvre Museum

The Eiffel Tower in Paris

LONDON, ENGLAND

At last, Norine was so relaxed and pleased, as we were headed for England where she would understand the language. We crossed by boat at Dover and then boarded the train for the last leg into London. Two elderly little ladies were sitting behind us, chattering away without a pause the entire trip. We paid no attention as they were rather quiet, but as we pulled into the station, Norine looked at me with absolute astonishment, stating that those two were actually speaking English. Their cockney accent was so strong, that until we arrived, and they more loudly exclaimed "Well, home at last," did we realize they had been speaking English all along. It was a rude awakening for what was to come and reminiscent of my difficulty in understanding the heavy Spanish Castilian accent when we first arrived in Spain.

Being so near the end of our summer travels, we took stock of our money situation and decided to splurge a bit more for a room with a full bath, which actually had a shower in the tub for our enjoyment. I also realized that we had enough money left that we could probably do some shopping, which up until that point had only been for the very rarest of small special items. Norine immediately bought three wool coats, a very fashionable one for herself and one for each of our boys with little caps to match. She had heard that Belgium was the place for fine lace and beautiful carpets, so tucked the rest away for our final shopping spree in Brussels. She did have several requests since all her relatives were from England, so we spent time looking in the phone book for the name Dix – perhaps a distant descendant of her grandfather, Edwin or his brother, who was (she thought) a famous architect in London or perhaps his daughter, Dorothea Dix, a Shakespearean actress. Sadly, we found pages and pages with the name Dix, and with no other clues it was a wasted effort. As a young lad, her grandfather had labored carrying water to the workers during the midnight shift in Madame Tussaud's famous Wax Museum, and he had told her mother tales of the dread of walking through the darkness with hideous figures looming around many corners. Needless to say, that Museum was on her list and most interesting and so very different from the many, many museums we had seem all across Europe.

I quickly grew tired of the pomp and circumstance, which appeared to be the main tourist attraction. I have never understood the American's fascination with the Royal Family and found other attraction much more interesting. Even back in the late sixties there seemed to be more diversity of people and language than in other countries we had visited. The food also reflected that variety, as long as you stayed away from, in my opinion, the very bland typical English cuisine. One of our most delicious and interesting meals was from Indonesia called Rijsttafel, which consisted of many -sometimes as many as forty – side dishes served in small portions accompanied by rice prepared in several different ways. A few I remember included fish, egg rolls, various fruits, and vegetables, with pickles and nuts. We spent the entire evening enjoying the amazing flavors and conversing with those who served us. The longer we stayed, the more I came to enjoy, mainly due to interesting discussions with natives and tourists alike. As always however, there was too little time for all the sights we wanted to see, so after just our few days, we headed to the dreaded train station to arrange for our departure.

The Royal Guard,

Big Ben and

The Thames.

FAREWELL from BRUSSELS, BELGIUM

We only had one full day to see Brussels and since we had plenty of money left, we really wanted to take the time to find a few things that would always remind us of this amazing summer's trip. We inquired about the best place to find a magnificent Belgium carpet and at the very first recommended shop we both fell in love with a stunning piece. Arrangements for shipping it home was an ordeal and required several of our precious hours. Next, Norine's last wish was for some Belgium lace, and she found a lovely curtain with a valance, which she was able to fit into her bulging suitcase. There were so many beautiful things to see, yet our energy was running low, and our concentration was now on just getting home and seeing our family. So,

Grand Palace in Brussels

after taking care of our shopping, we were perfectly happy just sitting in the magnificent square, Grand Palace, surrounded by and soaking in our last look at the glorious architecture of Europe. We slowly sipped their coconut beer from a coconut shell, had a leisurely dinner in an outdoor café and sank into bed early to prepare for the next day's long flight home. Neither of us could sleep on the plane, as we were far too excited about all the adventures we had had and the prospects of seeing our little boys. Norine had not written one of her descriptive *diary* letters to her folks since details about Paris with only a postcard sent from London, so to avoid forgetting a single detail, she entertained me with an *interview*, as she jotted down my feelings and reaction to the entire experience. Overall, I was almost in disbelief of the vast array of experiences we had had, and how much we had seen and learned.

***Davisito y Danielito* enjoying a summer with *Abuela* Sara and *Abuelo* Delvis.**

CALIFORNIA WELCOMES US HOME

Upon our return home to Hayward, we had been so thrifty, even with our shopping sprees those last days in London and Brussels, that we had enough money left over for my flight to Miami to bring our boys back home. Seeing our boys at the Miami airport was a happiness unlike any other. I spent just a few days visiting, as I knew how badly their mother wanted them home. They were healthy, happy, a little plumper, nicely tanned and *Cuban* in many ways. All my concerns, as to whether we had done the right thing vanished, and I was sure my folks had done a wonderful job caring for them. The only thing that did concern us for a short period of time was Danny's speech development. He seemed to understand things said to him in either language, but just didn't respond much. Norine was terribly concerned that we had hampered his speaking progress by confusing him with the new language at such a crucial time. Thankfully, it was not too long before he started talking constantly, and all our fears were put to rest. That was the beginning of many trips to Miami, almost every summer over the next few years, which were very memorable times for our boys. They usually spent several weeks there, learned Spanish well, and cemented a strong bond with their *Abuelos*. It was a completely unique experience as they learned a way of life with many cultural differences, which contrasted dramatically from the upbringing they were learning with us in Hayward.

The following school year was filled to the fullest. A new home to make our own, my beginning involvement with the Chabot Chicano students, my pursuit of my citizenship, and seriously thinking of my quest for higher learning at Berkeley. Our travel all over Europe was fresh in our minds, but quickly pushed back as we moved forward with the 1967-1968 school year.

My mother returned with us and Norine's mother had to come too for a visit, as she'd not seen the boys since early summer.

20

A Memorable Home

BUYING OUR FIRST HOUSE,
Our Home in the Hills of Hayward.

That fall after winding down from our amazing travels we dreamed of our own home, so instead of throwing more money away on rent, Norine began the search. With the small savings we had put away while living in the rental and some help from my father-in-law Ralph Gunn, who was managing Norine's small inheritance from her grandmother, we managed to buy a home in a hilly unincorporated area above Hayward called Hill and Dale. In those days, realtors had printed descriptions of homes on 5 by 7 cards with pictures on the backside. Norine spent hours and days looking and reading them carefully, as I was immersed in my teaching schedule, and we didn't want to waste time driving all over town. Out of hundreds of cards, she had finally narrowed it down to just a couple with her first pick being home straight up steep East Avenue above Hayward. So, we headed off in the realtor's car early one Saturday morning. He took us to her first pick and as we neared the top of the hill, a sign to the left said, "Hill and Dale." The agent bragged about the eighty-three different kinds of trees on the property, and best of all only "white folks" lived in the Hill and Dale neighborhood. His vulgar comment of "n---- free" area shocked us both, and in disbelief I did not open my mouth from that point on – I let Norine do all the talking. I feared he might think that with my accent, I would not be accepted in such a "pure neighborhood." As we pulled into the drive the towering eucalyptus trees filled the backdrop behind the entire house, and before she even got out of the car, she pinched me and said that this was the house for us. Before entering, she insisted we go to the back yard, where we discovered not only a whole forest, but a creek with a bridge, huge boulders scattered over the hill and even a rusty swing set. We finally entered the house which was roomy with huge windows for a lot of light and full views of the forest of trees, right in a regular city neighborhood. When she called her parents a few days later to tell them we had found "the' house of our dreams," she did not mention the bigoted comments the realtor had made, but instead told them of the great variety of trees, the creek, the fireplaces, one upstairs and one down, both with roaring flames dancing as reflected in the wall of windows which brought the outside scenery into our living space. As we left the house, we marveled at the magnificent view of the

San Francisco Bay Area every time we left home to drive down to town or work. However, when Norine's mother asked mundane questions about how many bedrooms or baths there were, what the floor coverings were, whether the kitchen was up or downstairs, etc etc., Norine could not remember any of those mundane

details. As with every house we have ever lived in, she has always been more impressed with the outside vegetation and the windows to let that outside beauty come in. I on the other hand, had trouble with that realtor's comments and hated having to give him a cent as his finder's fee, and I never forgot the experience. His description proved to be true in the beginning, but thankfully only for a few more years.

On Bridle Drive, our first house and home for the next 37 years.

During the first few years as homeowners, we were both so busy, Norine making the house into our home as well as always taking night classes in art, and I carving out my career at Chabot College. We were pretty oblivious of our new town and spent almost every weekend exploring the wonders of the entire Bay Area. Yet as the boys grew and entered into school, we realized that things were far from ideal. We came to realize that Hayward had a bad reputation for being a city with high levels of crime and racial divisions back in the early 1960s, which showed little to no improvement over the years we lived there. During all of the 1960s I experienced some of the most exciting and at the same time traumatic times of my life. There I was, away from my loving Cuban *familia* and not allowed by my new homeland to visit, or even travel to share in the sorrow of losing so many loved ones. We were surrounded by a world in turmoil dominated by the Vietnam War, a blockade of my homeland, and the assassinations of several American leaders that had shown hope. Math was a marvelous refuge, and I did find promise and peace by studying and teaching math, as well as caring for my precious family. As always, however, the wrongs of the world weighed heavily on my mind and keeping involved with causes that were important to my beliefs and passion for what I felt was "right" held importance to me and constantly influenced the path I took.

We now had our very own home and our family of four was settling in and growing with cats and dogs and beginning a lifetime of memories. Daily life settled into daily activities with each of us developing along our own path. My time was consumed with my teaching, my involvement with the Chicano's effort for recognition and my effort to manage the rigor of research and study for my advanced degree. I realized that financially I would not be able to take "time off" for that endeavor, so gradually slid into an insane schedule of doing it all at once. I continued with a full load of classes while I worked on my Ph.D. at Berkeley.

By late spring, we realized there would not be time for a long vacation, but definitely felt the need to start our plans for short summer fix and decided on something very different. Norine had been dying to show off the beauty of the Utah mountains she had enjoyed as a child. We had already done a few weekends camping trips, which we thoroughly enjoyed, so decided camping above her hometown of Mt. Pleasant would be an exciting adventure. We now had our little black Karmann Ghia, so careful planning was needed to fit everything in. Mama Sara was visiting and begged to take Davisito home with her, so it was decided that only Danny would join us for the camping trip.

The following is an account of that camping trip we tried to take to the majestic Wasatch Mountains in central Utah. Danny was two and a half and David just over five years old, but more than ready for a driving lesson behind *Abuelo's* garage in Miami. Norine wrote about the events of that experience as a short story for a writing class years later. Because I was pretty well "out of it" - as you will soon see - I asked Norine to include her story here.

**Davisito visiting in Miami
with his Abuelos.**

THE NEVADA SAGA
Norine Fernández' account of the summer of 1968

Even with the rain, we had nowhere else to sleep, so we put the three sleeping bags under a picnic table, buried our heads and tried to sleep through the night. At first light, I gave up on the idea of rest, even though the rain had stopped, and got up to figure out breakfast. Delvis yawned and stretched, then brought the heavy food box from the car. The smell of bacon on an open fire awakened Danielito, and as always, the toddler jumped up hungry and eager to face the day's excitement. The Nevada air was clean and fresh, everything glistened bright green from the rain, and the expanse of blue sky seemed to go forever. We should have stayed and hiked a bit, but the dessert sand was soggy and slippery. We could have stayed and read a bit, but the picnic bench was wet and had already soaked through yesterday's newspaper. We would have been wise to try and sleep a bit longer in the car, but the open road called, so we prepared to leave. Our sleeping bags were soaking wet, so we carefully folded them back and forth in the small Karmann Ghia's front trunk. I hoped that by not rolling them up, they would dry more quickly and be ready for the

The straight stretch of highway typical in Nevada that seems to

next night's camp out. How were we to know we would never use them again.

The boring black asphalt ahead was as straight as an arrow, across the flat desert, then climbed the looming mountain as far as the eye could see, up to nowhere. The beauty of the landscape varied just enough in hue and color to capture my attention, as I tried to think of my next game move as Delvis teased with a brilliant checkmate move that ended the game. As I squirmed to straighten out my position in the seat of our tiny little black car, a huge, grey concrete block loomed straight in front of me.

I squeezed my eyes shut, an instinct I had acquired whenever I feared danger was imminent. Delvis held firm to the steering wheel as he jerked it to the left, and the grayness was replaced with that blackness of the asphalt as we slid from side to side, around and around in circles, and finally turning completely over – once, maybe twice. How surreal it all was, and how bizarre those brief seconds were, as they stretched out in slow motion for what seemed forever.

We sat motionless once the car stopped many feet from that concrete block and on the opposite side of the highway. It seemed forever, but finally, I glanced over to see Delvis staggering out of the car. I pushed with all my might to open my door, but to no avail. When I turned my head to see the back seat, Danny was nowhere to be seen and instead the Heinz catchup and mayonnaise from our food box were dripping from the roof and all over the side windows, but not the back window which was completely gone. As the adrenalin was pumping, I somehow crawled over the center brake stick and cups in their holders to fall out of the open driver's door. I staggered across the shiny black pavement toward the tiny body of our little boy whose face was turned away as Delvis knelt over him. Just as I too knelt down, he turned his head and flashed a sweet smile. Delvis stretched his arms upward and let out a piercing cry of relief, then slumped down to the pavement in a heap there in the middle of the highway. I grabbed the baby into my arms, and as he shook his small hand back and forth, the blood from a teeny tiny cut on his little finger splattered all over my white sweatshirt. I hugged him tightly and rocked him back and forth as I sat stroking each familiar hair on Delvis' motionless head. My mind flashed back to that bathroom scene in Stockton when David had his first climbing experience and cut his little finger with Papa's razor. I remembered how much blood there was from the cut, but also thankfully remembered it was very tiny and did no real harm.

My mind jolted back to the present and I was suddenly aware of cars, and trucks, and people stopping but all shrouded in the grey clouds that seemed to have covered the sun. I felt no pain, yet everyone who stopped to help insisted that I lay down, only because my white sweatshirt was splattered with blood for which they could see no source. They tried to take Danny from my arms, but I hung on tightly, as I hysterically pushed them away screaming at them to check on my husband. I could not understand why everyone was fussing and pulling at me, when it was so obvious, he was the one who needed their help.

Then I heard a big burly truck driver talking on his walkie talkie. He was giving directions saying, "Right, about thirty miles east of Elko on the main highway, right, okay, this is Love Handle, over and out." Finally, someone had called for help, and although I still felt no pain, the helpful onlookers kept insisting that I sit quietly with my baby in my arms and not stand up. Delvis was awake now, but they would not let him move either. So much fuss and attention as my mind flashed back to my childhood home with Mother, talking, talking, talking on the phone when I had cut my leg so badly and the blood pooled on the floor while I pulled at her apron strings to get her attention. The tears streamed down my face then as now sitting on the asphalt. As I wiped them away my eyes wandered across the road trying to distinguish the black crumpled heap of metal that was our beautiful Karmann Ghia from the blacktop. Although years later, I remembered the sweet smell of new upholstery, and I cringed in disbelief when a woman commented on the weird smell coming from the blood covered interior, as she handed me my purse. This made no sense as I knew why my shirt was bloody, but none of us were really bleeding that I could see.

The huge clock hanging on the hospital waiting room wall said 4:33. It had to be afternoon as the sun was shining once again, but how was that possible. We had left the makeshift campground at 7:45 in the morning. Where had this day gone? The long wait for the ambulance seemed to have taken forever, and the long ride in the makeshift ambulance, seemed to take even longer. But where had this day gone. The nurse had bandaged Daniel's little finger and assured me that he was perfectly fine. And, she had said the same thing about me, after a lot of poking and prodding, but then I already knew that. It was their examination of Delvis that kept me waiting and wondering, waiting, and worrying.

It was well past seven when a very, very old man dressed in a white doctor's coat came into the waiting room and told me to "sit down for he had some very serious news." His voice quivered with his years as he calmly informed me that my husband might be paralyzed from his neck down for the rest of his life! What? What had he just said? He calmly continued that they would not know for sure until an expert could read the x-rays and there was no such person in this small-town hospital. He informed me that the x-rays were to be sent off to Salt Lake City on the next plane. He was hopeful there would be more positive news from Salt Lake "within a week." A week? How could that be possible? At that moment I was the one who felt paralyzed and sick to my stomach. Yet I had to gathered strength from somewhere and push the cloudy, swimming, swirling feelings far back in my head, so I could smile at the sweet little boy on my lap.

The nurse convinced me that sleep was sorely needed for both of us, so I kissed my bedridden sweetie good night with no comment of the news the doctor had given me and started out on foot toward the motel the nurse had called. Only a short distance, she had said, but it was the longest, darkest walk I had ever taken in my life, and my poor tired baby seemed to have gained the weight of the world as I carried him with the heavy burden of that day. He fell asleep again immediately once I laid him on the clean white sheets in his dirty, dusty clothing. I made a mental note that I would buy some clothing the next day. I stepped into the shower, to the rude realization that my entire right side, from my shoulder to my ankle bone, was one solid bruise with every color of the stormiest rainbow. Despite the pain that I was now suddenly aware of, I fell asleep instantly and slept with my baby through the night.

As the bright Nevada sun streamed in through the thin curtain at our window. Danielito's squealing and happy smile as he jumped on the bed, made me question if I had just awakened from a horrible nightmare. But without my sweetheart next to me I quickly jumped into action, and we hurried out the door. Within a block or two we came across a diner with worn but bright red leather stools and booths, so we sat at the counter to order Danny's favorite – pancakes. I told him his father's favorite pancake story of riding for five days and five nights in a Greyhound bus from Key West, Florida to Westminster College in Utah. Every morning, as the waitress in the bus depot café came for his order, he would point to the stack of pancakes that the guys next to him had ordered. With no knowledge of English to read the menu, so knowing nothing of the foods that were typical of an American breakfast the tall stack of sweet bread seemed a good choice. He was in a strange new land and had to "make do" as best he could. I hoped to explain to him that we too were in a strange land with new experiences as we had to wait for news from Salt Lake City, ironically Papa's first American home in the United States. My story was over the top of his little head, and he was much more intrigued with the attire of those around us. All the men at the counter had broad band cowboy hats and I uncomfortably noticed that several had guns in the holsters on their sides, which frightened me, but only filled Danny with questions.

The following seven days in Elko were an unbelievable yet unforgettable blur. Due to the uncertainty of the severity of Delvis' possible neck and back injuries, they had him flat on his back with a strange contraption across his forehead with several weights hanging off the edge of the bed to keep his head motionless. He could only stare directly above at the blank ceiling, which proved not always to be boring. He did always know when the tray of food had been delivered due to the smell of pancake and bacon - if

Norine's sketch of me while in traction for seven days

he were lucky. I quickly realized that I would always need to be nearby at mealtime, as no one else seemed to realize nor care that he could not feed himself.

Although there was a loudly hooting owl in a giant tree right outside the hospital window, Danny soon grew tired of stepping outside to try and spot the owl only to realize we always had to go back inside. I remembered that an old high school chum had lived in Elko, so I looked for Robert Zorko in the phone book. To my absolute delight, that call resulted in an offer to watch Danny for several hours each day. I frankly do not remember if Bob and his wife had children, but I do remember their wonderful big gentle dog that Danny fell in love with and rode around on like a pony. Bob also assured me that simply because it happened to be Rodeo Week, the craziness I had noticed was just in good fun and nothing to worry about. Unfortunately, I still felt uncomfortable walking back and forth to my motel, as the local cowboys filled their pickup trucks and were "dragging" up and down main street late into the night shooting their guns in the air and setting off firecrackers. Several mornings while walking to the hospital, I would notice new gunshot holes in the windows of stores, so I knew the merchants probably didn't think it was all in fun. I also realized I needed my little 'man' by my side whenever eating at the diner to keep their flirtatious comments to a minimum, which was not the case if I were eating alone.

On the third morning of poor Delvis' ordeal, I found a sheriff waiting to speak with me when I arrived at the hospital. He asked several questions regarding my memory of the accident and had a rough drawing of what had occurred based on the tire marks left on the road. His sketch did not jog my memory at all, but certainly came as a shock and did help to explain a few things. The black tire marks indicated that the car had headed from the far-right side of the road across the highway, where it spun around in two circles, and then the break in the black streaks indicated that we rolled over twice and landed on the opposite shoulder in an upright position. The fact it had roll over on my passenger side explained why my door was so crushed and not operable, and why my right side was still aching and black and blue. The back window was completely broken out, which gave rise to their speculation that Danny had slid out of that open window during the first roll over when the top of the car was on the road. This would explain his being so far from the final resting place of the car and with no serious injuries other than the small cut on his pinkie finger.

He asked me to go to the garage that afternoon where they had towed the car, and the officer thought I might want to claim some of the items remaining in the car. He did warn me that the car was completely totaled, and that after being parked in the hot sun for three days, it might be a very unpleasant chore. I did not mention any of this to Delvis, as I tried my best not to burden him beyond what he had to bear. He did not really seem to be in any great pain, but the challenge was to downplay my answers to the questions he had about his condition. I tried my best to eliminate the stress of what might yet be to come, as I feared his reaction and knew that the boredom and lack of any activity were all he could handle as he lay there staring up at the ceiling.

After helping him to eat his lunch I made up an excuse of needing to shop for some toiletries and headed out to find the garage. It was on the other side of town, and I was hot and exhausted by the time I finally arrived. Luckily, there was a well-worn, dirty old easy seat from a car just outside of the office door, and upon spotting our car, my legs gave way, and I slumped into the seat, like a wet rag, unable to move or think or even focus for several minutes. Finally, the patient mechanic said he had to get back to work if I didn't want to see the contents of the car. This motivated me to slowly stand and putting one foot in front of the other, I moved toward the black wreckage. He opened the driver's door and the unbelievable stench -- blew us both back a few steps. The catsup and mayonnaise hung from the roof like stalactites and other food stuffs spread over the back seat looked like smashed stalagmites. I realized that the red catsup explained why several people at the accident site had mentioned so much blood in the car. When he opened the front hood, the strong smell of mold from the sleeping bags and other wet clothing was overwhelming, so I slammed the hood down and walked away. Everything was lost and I wanted none of it! Luckily, a good Samaritan who had stopped on the road had retrieved my purse and given it to me as I sat on the road. It contained our credit cards, all the cash we thought we'd need for our trip, a small bag with our three folding toothbrushes, and best of all, my prized camera which I had gotten in Germany, although I had not taken a single picture at our first camp site because of the rain, so have no visual record of that fateful week.

The next morning upon my arrival at the hospital, Delvis was very agitated and begged me to find out what in the world had happened during the night and early morning hours. He spoke of a loud commotion and much shouting in the dark of night and then, just as the sun was coming up, a man flew overhead swinging on a bar, which he was dying to tell Danny about, as it reminded him of the monkeys at the zoo. His room had eight beds with a bar above each for a curtain to be pulled around the bed for visual privacy, although sounds were obvious and sometimes very strange. It also had two large swinging doors with the word EXIT above, which opened to the outside world. After much inquiry, one sweet young nurse whispered in absolute confidence the events of that night. Apparently one of the more vocal male patients feared his wife might be enjoying Rodeo Week too much and was fooling around while he was confined to the hospital. So soon after midnight he slipped quietly out of the exit doors, which were also the emergency entrance doors, with his hospital gown gaping open in the back, but with shoes and just no socks.

He ran to town entering several bars in search of his wife before finally being apprehended by the local sheriff. He was returned to his hospital bed in handcuffs, which did create a disturbance for his fellow patients, as they chattered in the dark with their theories. He too was highly excited, but finally just near dawn, quieted down, so they removed his handcuffs. To everyone's surprise and shock, he leaped up and out of the bed, grabbing onto the curtain bars and began swinging from bar to bar over the beds just above the patient's heads. Delvis, of course, was the only one who could not turn his head from side to side to watch this entire show, and only saw him fly by when he was directly above his bed. The nurse pointed to the guilty patient's bed, although I had already guessed who he was from several previous strange shouts and sound I had heard. As I walked by later, I could see he was finally sound asleep but wearing a straitjacket with his hands cuffed to the edge of his bed.

Each day did not have that kind of excitement for Delvis as he just laid there, bored to death while waiting, waiting, waiting. For me, on the other hand, every day seemed bizarre and unreal, and by the end of that week I was greatly relieved when the nurse came in telling us the x-ray report had arrived that morning. My head was swimming as I anxiously waited to hear the results, which could bring the drama of this week's saga to an end or change our lives forever. I was petrified of the results, which we had refused to think about or even talk about all week. When the same aging doctor came into the room, he pulled up a chair for himself and one for me. My mind flashed back to that awful moment, a week ago, when he said I had better sit down to hear his bad news. This time he barely whispered, and I had to lean forward to hear his quivering voice, saying that the x-ray showed -- he paused, "No bad signs, so it's probably just whiplash." Delvis and I were both numbed at that moment and could not speak. My mind swirled with doubts as to whether I was going to scream and lash out at the old fool for the ordeal he had put us through, or hug and kiss him with great relief. Finally, a soft "Thank you" slipped past my lips, and I leaned down to kiss my precious husband.

Two nurses came to the bed as soon as the doctor left and proceeded to remove his head gear with the hanging weights, telling him he could -- get up and go. Delvis just laid there, unable to move or even lift his head, and Danny's puzzled look expressed the fear we were all feeling. Within the next few moments, he appeared to be trying to sit up, but to no avail, so each nurse took one arm and pulled him to a sitting position. It was obvious, as his legs dangled to the floor, that he could not stand nor even take a few steps. After seven days in that motionless state, his body just would not function, and it became clear that only with time would he heal. So, no more of their Nevada crazy care, except for the final act of offering a wheelchair.

We piled into an old brown sedan taxi and headed for the small airport, where I arranged for our flight through Salt Lake City on to Orange, California where my parents were living. Once I had the tickets in hand, I slowly walked to the pay phone to make the dreaded call. I had thought a hundred times that week about calling my parents, but with nothing definite to tell them, I simply could not do it. The concern of their worry that my husband might be paralyzed for life was just unthinkable. Mother's cheery voice answered with the question if we were back home in Hayward so soon, but by the time the conversation ended, her cheeriness was replaced with low, soft sighs and sobs. I could hear the worry through the tears, even though I had told only the bare minimum with many gruesome details left for later. My father, on the other hand who heard me repeat the news, was absolutely furious, and would not buy any excuse or apology I made. He simply could not understand nor believe we had not reached out to them for help. When we met at the airport in Orange, mother was still in tears, but Daddy, who was very thankful we were alright and in one piece, was still fuming. For many, many years after that incident, he would make me take a solemn oath, even for the shortest of trips, that I would call him every single night until we were home. *End of The Nevada Saga by Norine*

After that insane summer trip, we needed time to relax and catch our breath. We stayed in Orange with Norine's folks for a while looking for a new car and doing a few fun things, so our summer vacation time was not a total loss. We went to Disneyland, but David felt no loss as he went to Disneyworld near Orlando with his Abuelos in Florida. After a few days of calm, I flew to Miami to visit with my folks and bring David back home. He had talked by phone with us several times and Norine was always amazed that he would answer her English questions in Spanish. Once home again in late summer, he spoke almost entirely in Spanish and apparently continued doing so for a few weeks into his first school days, as he started Kindergarten with the always to be remembered, Miss Isler. Within just a few weeks, we were invited to the first teacher–parent night meeting and when we entered the classroom, found almost life size stuffed figures sitting in the little chairs, with signs hanging around the necks with each child's name to identify where they sat. We immediately noticed there were three or four tables together with only one off to one side. At that particular table, we found David's mannequin with four or five others and from the parents standing behind each chair, we realized they were all black. It was the first year of "busing" in our school district, when they brought children by bus from another school in a neighborhood that had a majority of black families. We were informed that the seating assignments were based on the child's knowledge of the letters of the alphabet, and supposedly those sitting with David at that table were not familiar with the entire alphabet letters. This came as such a shock, as David had learned to read with Norine's nightly bedtime stories, so not only knew the alphabet letters well, but could also read quite well. We stayed after the meeting to speak with Miss Isler and ask why our son had been so classified. She informed us that the problem with David *Fur-nan-deeez* was his lack of speaking English as he was using only Spanish, so he obviously, in her eyes, would not know the English alphabet letters. We certainly set her straight that night as we were absolutely flabbergasted at the naiveté and lack of awareness of this woman, who frequently "corrected him," on how to pronounce his own last name - so he thought she should learn some Spanish pronunciation. It was a rude awakening and an unforgettable lesson to us and to our child about the world we lived in.

21

At Chabot College
Teaching and Learning

Expanding Learning from Students

In the fall of 1967, after our amazing European summer, during my second year at Chabot College I had one of the most rewarding experiences of my teaching career. More than just being a math teacher, I was also a "learner" from students and community residents who lacked representation in the administration and faculty of an improperly named "Community" College. Chabot College was

- **Without a single Chicanx on the Faculty.**
- **Lacking community programs relevant to the Chicanx population.**
- **Without counselors for assistance to minority students, and an educational center that excluded the Chicanx from every aspect of college life with no consideration to their educational needs.**

Up to that time no African American or Chicano/Latino had ever held a full-time position at Chabot. It was on my first day at the job that a colleague in the Science-Math Division called me to his office, closed the door, extended his hand in friendship, and welcomed me with the following words: "Welcome to our Division, *you people* can work here now but Negroes are not quite ready." Without protesting, but in shock I swallowed my pride and went about my business as well as I could. Insults followed and incidents of exclusion in the affairs of the Division let me know that I was not seen as a peer, but as one *of those others*.

The world around us in the sixties was in turmoil, with daily news reports on the number of deaths in Viet Nam with daily pictures on TV's evening news of the returning caskets, anti-war demonstrations, and the killings of President John F. Kennedy and his brother Robert Kennedy followed by the assassination of admired and revered leader Martin Luther King, Jr. Our own César Chávez and Dolores Huerta were in an extremely difficult struggle organizing farm workers in the nearby San Joaquín Valley.

As the newest and only faculty member who spoke Spanish, I discovered many gardeners and maintenance workers who conversed in my native language, and would greet me with warm smiles, handshakes, and *Buenos Días*. On one morning, etched in my mind, as I finished teaching a math class, a maintenance worker came to me and introduced himself as Ray Marchán. He inquired if I would be willing to serve as faculty advisor to a group of students who were trying to form a new organization. He said, "*Señor Fernández, usted parece 'gachupín' pero necesitamos un maestro de Chabot para formar una organización.*" I assumed that he was referring to a group of students dealing with Hispanic, Latinos or Mexican/American issues. The word "Chicano" was not widely used at that time; and I later found that "*gachupín*" was a Mexican term applied to a person of lighter skin or to a Spanish immigrant. I replied that I would be honored to

Ray Marchán on the right A humble organizer behind the scenes – 26 years later

serve as a faculty advisor but informed him that the students would be my teachers and true advisors." Ray was a leader without recognition who played a major role in cementing the Chicano Movement at his place of work. He impressed me as a valiant pioneer willing to fight in the struggle for opening the college to a disenfranchised and marginalized community.

WORKING TO ORGANIZE, An Awakening –*Un Despertar*

The organizational meetings were a source of learning for me about a people whose presence and history were ignored at Chabot and other centers of learning. They were a small group of students, ten or less, that came together for a month to discuss a name or identification for the organization. For example, certain issues addressed were:

- Common bonds – what brings us together?
- Problems in the college – cultural presentations, faculty representation, unfair treatment.
- Family histories - places of origin.
- A title name for the organization.

Stereotypes persisted in society and at the college about the Spanish-speaking groups, Mexican Americans, Latin American immigrants, and other ethnic groups that were difficult to address but with persistence and high motivation the word "CHICANO" rang as a common bond for all those present. The meetings were a tremendous source of learning due to the sharing of family anecdotes and testimonials. Some students had lived in Texas, New Mexico, and other places of the American Southwest; but of course, now were attending Chabot and living in Hayward or in the nearby towns of San Leandro, Union City, or Fremont.

Delvis attends an administrative meeting where Rudy Triviso, as President, presides demands.

At last, after several weeks of discussions the word CHICANO was accepted by the organizers as an all-inclusive bonding term to identify people who previously had been referred to as Mexican, Mexican Americans, or Spanish-Americans. Now it was time to select a leader and planners, to begin major undertakings for expanding education opportunities as well as bring awareness to injustices towards groups within the bounds of the college campus and its surrounding community. Many students joined in *La Causa*, and despite the passing of over 50 years, their presence is still etched in my mind and soul for their courage in joining the fight for improvements in education and to address the need for support of workers – both for teachers and field workers. Our struggle reached far beyond Chabot with César Chávez, Dolores Huerta in California, Reyes Tijerina in New Mexico, "Corky" Gonzales in Colorado, Rubén Salazar in Los Angeles, and many more across the United States of America.

AT CHABOT COLLEGE:

- Chicanos were at the forefront for the establishment of the Chicano Movement that later transition into MEChA or *Movimiento Estudiantil Chicano de Aztlán*. Among the key players were **Paz Flores**, **María Elena Ramírez**, **Theresa Beltrán**, **Jessica Hart** who raised their voices in meetings with students, faculty and administration.

- **Rudy Zapata Triviso**, was a key player in the development of the organization. He was a courageous young man and a dedicated fighter in the struggle for expanding educational opportunities and bringing justice to underrepresented and disenfranchised minorities in our schools. Through his leadership and family stories in New Mexico, we learned about an American side of history absent in textbooks and ignored by educators in our surroundings. His legacy is a source of inspiration for future generations.

- The brothers **Pedro and Raúl Bonilla** with many more students and community residents, challenged the administration establishment by setting a large tent, LA CARPA, in front of the college, to provide a place for classes, tutoring, counseling, and mentoring. **John Gonzales, José Dorado, Antonio Abarca**, and **Abel Cota** served in leadership positions and gave legal advice to the newly emerging organization. **Félix Galaviz** was a courageous fighter for developmental education, offering advice for career development. Years later in 1981 he and faculty member **Pat McGrath** started the **Puente Program** with the mission to increase the number of students transferring from high-schools and community colleges to four-year colleges and universities.

- **Emalie (Webb) Monárrez Ortega** came to Chabot in 1969 to serve as an English instructor. Soon after her arrival she became a co-advisor of the newly formed Chicano Student Union. She was a dynamic leader offering her home for meetings and social gatherings as well as participating in demonstrations for expanding access to education. After her days at Chabot, she obtained a law degree from the prestigious Stanford University.

Through years of involvement seeking expansion of education and justice for the entire community, I collected historic documents that served me to write a book about the Chicano Movement. A book that is dedicated to the courageous students and faculty members who expanded education. **Ray Marchán**, a maintenance worker at Chabot College, who invited me to form part of the newly emerging Chicano Movement as a faculty advisor, lives forever in my heart and soul.

Delvis and Emalie Ortega working together for *La Causa.*

Our struggle was part and parcel of the fight for awareness and calls for changes in a world coming out of strict rules of segregation. From the examples of Martin Luther King, Jr. to César Chávez and Dolores Huerta, Chabot transformed into a college that offered more inclusive opportunities to all members of its surrounding population.

DIFFICULT TIMES AHEAD

During my involvement as advisor for the Chicano Student Union (CSU), I also had to struggle with acceptance by faculty members and college administrators. A lack of knowledge about the culture and history of wide segments of the community were absent from the college environment. Dr. Buffington, the top administrator and president of Chabot, used the term - "chicanery" –referring to the on-going work of the CSU. I found his comments offensive and disrespectful and thus refused to answer his questions. As a result, he never spoke to me again during my years at Chabot. It was obvious to students that my position as a math instructor was in danger of termination. The following heartfelt letter was received from the Chicano Studies Committee.

TO: Delvis Fernández
From: Chicano Studies Committee C.S.U.
Subject: Contractual status of Chicano Faculty

The Chicano Student Union is concerned with the status of your contract with Chabot College. We understand that some instructors will not be teaching next year, because their contracts have terminated and will not be renewed due to a lack of funds. We also believe that some instructors hired on a part-time basis will also be terminated.

If all or part of this is true, we would like to hear from you! The C.S.U. is interested in increasing the number of Chicano faculty on campus regardless of the costs. Costs can be eliminated elsewhere!

Inform us on administrative hiring practices as opposed to the hiring policy. We are interested in the general welfare of all our Chicano instructors. How can we help?

Please write me a memo addressed to Raul Bonilla. We will regard the information as confidential and will refer to it only with your approval.

Viva la Raza!
Raul M. Bonilla
Tri-Council
Chicano Student Union

TENSION, DISTRUST, AND EXCLUSION

Presentation by Delvis Fernández to the faculty and administration of Chabot College at a Faculty Meeting

Here today we represent over 100 years of service to Chabot. We bring unique talents in our teaching and yet we share a strong commitment to the welfare of our students.

I would like to explain why I agreed to a meeting with Dr. Morrow, Eric, Ken, and Lloyd. I came to Chabot almost 30 years ago – although well trained and qualified to teach math, some colleagues appeared more interested in other aspects of my life. Up to that time no African American or Latino had ever held a full-time teaching position at Chabot. It was on my first day at the job that a colleague in the Division called me to his office, closed the door, extended his hand in friendship and welcomed me with the following words: "Welcome to our Division, 'you people' can work here now, but Negroes are not quite ready." With no protestation, I swallowed my pride and wet about my business as well as I could. Insults followed and incidents of exclusion in the affairs of the Division let me know that I was not seen as a peer but as an "other."

Despite the negatives, I never lost hope that a day would come when we treat each other with respect, tolerance, and appreciation for our unique styles and philosophies of teaching and reaching students.

Today, I am concerned about recent incidents in our Division that create a climate of tension – some might use words such as racist, intolerant or slanderous. But I think that these sources of tension real or perceived must be aired among ourselves and then we must try to reach harmony and mutual respect.

1. In December an anonymous note with accusations and a derogatory name was place in a faculty member's car, apparently by a member(s) of the Division.

2. At a recent math conference in Monterey, statements, in the presence of new math instructors, were made about:
   An ex-faculty member being incompetent and having done much harm to her students.
   A teacher who fails miserably to cover course outlines.

A colleague who deserves no respect and inclusion in the affairs of the Department.

Disparaging statements about the application Affirmative-Action at Chabot.

3. A Mexican American teacher is stopped by police on his way to Chabot (for no infraction) only to check his identification card.

4. An African American teacher claims that he was singled out for questioning after the theft of computer equipment in the division.

   I think that these events create a climate of tension, distrust, and exclusion and I appeal to our sense of decency in refraining from making accusation about our colleagues. If a grievance is due, let us use established channels and not the hallways of Chabot.

Today more than 50 years later, Chabot is a center of hope for inclusive education and a better future for Our struggle was part and parcel of the fight for awareness and calls for changes in a world coming out of strict rules of segregation. Many individuals have learned from the *Lucha por La Causa* -- the struggles by César Chávez, Dolores Huerta, Philip Vera Cruz, Martin Luther King, Jr., and many others – that will continue to inspire new generations for education and awareness of injustices in their surroundings.

Marching in protest by the Administration building at Chabot with Emalie Ortega carrying a sign "Taxation without Representation

With my son Davisito, getting ready for taking assistance to the grape worker in Delano.

Letter of Appreciation
To Dr. Delvis Fernández

My departure from Chabot College was a sad and agonizing time in my life. Here I was, leaving behind my love for teaching mathematics and saying goodbye to my admired colleagues, faculty, and administrators of an exemplary school, that grew beyond expectations and offered educational opportunities to all members of my second home in Hayward and surrounding communities. Chabot lives forever in my heart and soul.

We the undersigned members of the Mathematics Subdivision at Chabot College, express our deep appreciation to you for your dedicated service as our Coordinator from autumn 1990 to autumn 1992. For over two years, you have gone well beyond the call of duty to establish or strengthen many programs or projects of the Math Subdivision including the Math Lab Innovation in teaching statistics and basic skills, establishing contact with local high schools and colleges, hiring and evaluation of many full-time and part-time instructors, computerizing course scheduling, calculator and other workshops, and various other activities such as the Faculty Assistants and Math Mentor Programs designed to bring women and ethnic minorities into math-related disciplines and careers. WE will miss your leadership as our Math Coordinator, but still look forward to working with you as a colleague and friend.

The Letter was signed by the members of the Science and Mathematics Division of Chabot College.

My Letter of Thanks - *GRACIAS*
To M.E.Ch.A. and The Chicano Student Union

25555 Hesperian Boulevard
Hayward, California 94545
(510) 786-6600
FAX (510) 782-9315

15 May, 1994

Movimiento Estudiantil Chicano de Aztlán
c/o Luís Molina
Chabot College
Hayward, California

Dear Students:

De todo corazón I want to say *GRACIAS* to each and every one of you for the very special evening on Friday, May 6th, 1994. Everything that night was presented so well, and your hard work, time, and effort was obvious in a wonderful event.

The recognition of the part I played in the foundation of the Chicano Student Union/MECHA, was greatly appreciated, and I was very touched by the importance you placed on remembering past history.

My best wishes in your education -- MECHA is a beacon of hope and your continued presence on Campus for the past twenty-five years is a testimonial to your success.

Sinceramente y en solidaridad con LA CAUSA,

Delvis Fernández, PhD
Mathematics Department

c. Mr. Ramón Parada, MECHA Faculty Advisor
   Dr. Raúl Cardoza, Chabot College President

270

My SPEECH at the 25th Year Reunion

Cinco de Mayo speech
May 3, 1994
1. Importance of Cinco de Mayo

At the battle of Puebla 132 years ago The Mexican Nation in one of the most difficult moments of its history, after losing half of its territory a few years earlier, a nation divided under civil war, besieged by the superpowers of the day: Spain, France, and Britain and invaded by one of the most powerful armies of that world; Mexico wrote one of the most glorious pages of its history at the battle of Puebla *El Cinco de Mayo de 1862* – May 5th, 1862.

2. Inspiration to Continue the Struggle for Justice

Today this example serves as inspiration in our continued struggle to advance our quest for justice in schools and in our community.

Twenty-five years ago, I had the most rewarding experience of my teaching career at Chabot, for I the teacher became the learner, and the students became the *maestros* of a history in the making, and a history that wasn't taught.

- Not a single Chicano on the faculty
- No community programs relevant to our culture
- No counselors on our staff
- Excluded from practically every aspect of college life with little or no consideration given to the educational needs.

Our country was led by President Nixon, every night on TV we listened to Walter Cronkite giving a report on the deaths in faraway Vietnam, the revered an admired leader of the civil rights movement Dr. Martin Luther King, Jr. had been assassinated in Memphis Tennessee. Our own César Chávez and Dolores Huerta were organizing farm workers.

So even here at Chabot we could not escape the changes taking place around us and we organized the CHICANO STUDENT UNION.

The students tried to talk to the same administrators who had not directly addressed the educational needs of the *Mexicano*. It was stated that no problem existed and that we were trying to make something out of nothing.

Massive action took place, students in solidarity with community leaders were able to make changes. Among the accomplishments:

- *Centro de Información*
- Tutorial Center
- Hiring of counselors
- Programs for the community

3. **Today the struggle continues.**

- We must not remain quiet on the attacks against immigrants when we all know that to be a code word for Mexican or Latino.

- The *Chicano Mexicano* must be recognized as an indigenous people to this continent, not an *immigrante*, with long and solid roots in the history and culture of Califas and AZTLAN.

- We must combat *Las drogas en las escuelas*.

- Our youth needs Role models recognized by the community at large. We have role models, but much education is needed to convince the City Council to name our Hayward library or a major thoroughfare after César Chávez.

In honor of the courageous students who founded the Chicano Student Union I wrote the following poem which I entitled *DESPERTAR* - Awakenings

Despertar

By Delvis Fernández Levy for the 25th Year Reunion
Dedicated to the courageous students who founded
The Chicano Student Union

Back in nineteen sixty-nine
Veinticinco años atrás
Nixon Commander in Chief
And Cronkite on CBS-TV
Body counts they brought.
From far away Viet-Nam
Dr. King – I dream … --
The flame was gone.
Nuestros César y Dolores
¡BASTA YA! They say.
Campesinos organize.
Winds of change
Will not escape us,
¿Quién soy yo?
And who are we?
In the mythic melting pot
Invisible strangers
En tierras de Aztlán
Raza Cósmica – soy de aquí
Por La Causa – I'll live and fight
Chican@ Latin@ Mexican@ Soy

Latest Celebration of The Chicano Movement Forever in our Hearts and Soul – *Sí Se Puede*

Again, for the 50th Reunion we gathered with a panel of founders, and I presented the book I have written, which is filled with anecdotes and historical documents about the roots of Chicano Movement and its accomplishments. A movement that continues to serve as a force that brings awareness to unjust treatment of major segments of our population. On the positive side, it also brought an expansion of opportunities and a more inclusive education for women, ethnic minorities and those affected with physical or learning disabilities. Its legacy lives forever and for me, it provided knowledge of a history well beyond anything I learned in schools and universities. It inspires our fight and search for justice.

Chicano Student Union presenters at a panel for the 50th Anniversary

Current professors Francisco Zermeño and Jaime Flores at Chabot with Mariana Triviso

Friends enjoying lunch after the conference: Theresa Beltrán, María Elena Ramírez, Jessica Hart, Jaime Flores, Delvis Fernández, Paz Flores, and Félix Galaviz

During my third year at Chabot, I was filled with anxiety and doubts about being able to keep my job as a teacher. The president of the college had called me to his office to inquire about my role as advisor of a student organization along with details about national background and ethnicity of the students. My reply as I remember was: "If you want to find out, come to a meeting." The president told me to leave his office and from that moment on, he never talked to me again. Some students were also aware that my job was insecure. So once again I felt the urgency to continue work on expanding my education by seeking entrance into a university to work on obtaining higher levels of education.

John Brunn

On top of my dilemma, my status as a resident of the U.S. was still unsecured. My application for citizenship was in limbo, so thanks to another math teacher by the name of **John Brunn**, I was connected with a lawyer of the American Civil Liberties Union who was able to expedite my application. I also gained acceptance at the University of California in Berkeley to do research in pure mathematics leading down the arduous road for a PhD while I continued my full-time teaching load at Chabot College.

Lloyd Rochon

Despite my sense of rejection at Chabot from the administration, I was always pleased with the community, the students, and the dear friends I did have in the faculty family. One of my best friends was **Lloyd Rochon**, a young man with deep cultural roots in New Orleans. He brought to me a sense of reality and knowledge about the similarities between Creole culture and cuisine with my Cuban background. Lloyd and I were like brothers who enjoyed family dinners, political discussions, and interaction for improvements of our mathematics education.

I learned so much from these students and the experiences of those years. The awareness I gained strengthened my deep feeling of the major loss to humanity for the destruction of art and achievements of the Aztec and Mayan civilizations by Spanish colonizers. A destruction that continued through the U.S. expansion and usurpation of Mexican territories during the mid-19th Century and continues to this day through lack of awareness and ignorance.

22

ENCHANTING AND DEAR MEXICO
México Lindo y Querido

As a result of my new awareness of the vast Latino population in the United States of America, a population that surpasses that of most Latin countries, my wife and I shared a need to explore México. We took many amazing trips over several summers – fun and educational journeys from north to south - always in search of places beyond the tourist areas. One summer we travelled down Mexico City by car along the Pacific coast by way of Guadalajara with our two little boys. The return trip had to cover the exact same route due to an unforeseen incident in Mexico City. Other summers, we went on to Oaxaca, into the Yucatan peninsula; and returned through central Mexico by way of Guanajuato, San Luis Potosi, and Chihuahua. Driving with the boys or just the two of us flying, it was my summer "fix" of Spanish, which I could not have with a trip to my homeland with the strain between Cuba and the United State for so many years. Museums, pyramids, and historical sites were always in our travel agenda, where we discovered a history and culture and wonderful people, which neither one of us had been aware of.

MEXICO

The Maya Calendar

"Man of Fire" in Guadalajara, fresco by José Clement Orozco

Mathematics was always on my mind, and I marveled at the development of numbers and calendars by the Maya civilization. Norine's studies of Mexican art came to life in a vivid and real way on our travels. Our journeys were enmeshed with learning about the culture and ancient civilizations of Mayas, Aztecs, and the rich ethnic diversity of Mexico. We wanted to expose our children to a culture beyond their California surroundings. My Chicano involvement sparked in me an interest and hunger for learning about a people and culture that was ignored by the mainstream media and schools in the United States. So, we travelled on several occasions from Hayward to Tijuana and deep into remote areas of Mexico driving through Sonora, Sinaloa, Nayarit, Jalisco, Mexico City, Oaxaca, Guerrero, Yucatán, and back through Chihuahua before reentering into the United States. Highlighted in our journeys were visits to the Xochimilcan Lake, Teotihuacán, Chichen Itza, Tulum, the Mummies of Guanajuato, and rich displays of Maya civilization in the Yucatán peninsula. Great enjoyment was always discovered in Oaxaca cuisine with the largest variety of Mexican *mole* sauces and learning the difference of "real" Mexican food and what we thought was Mexican food in California.

Our boys in front of artist Siqueiros mural, Universidad de México & Teotihuacán Pyramid

Years later we expanded our search in Ecuador, climbing the Cotopaxi volcano and visiting Inca ruins with *familia* in Quito and Guayaquil.

OUR FIRST TRIP to MEXICO – Summmer 1969

One of the most memorable with our two boys.

Our summer in Europe was a lifetime experience, but now we wanted to share the wonderment of travel with our boys, so we set off on the long drive from Hayward in California for Mexico City. Our first real stops with time for fun were the beach towns on Mazatlán and Puerto Vallarta, and needless to say the boys saw no need to continue in the hot dusty car for hours on the road, as they loved the beach fun. However, new adventures awaited so we moved on down the coast to Guadalajara where are dear friends, Cap and Brenda from Stockton days, were living for the summer. They had visited us a few times in Hayward, so the boys knew them well and were excited to rough house and goof around with them. A highlight was the main plaza with many mariachi bands and local boys their age, playfully running all around. Cap and Brenda were full of good ideas to show off their city and spent happy hours showing us local sights most tourist do not get to see.

Sun and fun on the beaches of Mazatlán

Cap and Brenda entertained us in the Mariachi Plaza of Guadalajara.

278

Danny proudly climbed to the top of the pyramid.

Our next stop would be Mexico City, which was exciting and wonderful, but had its share of unexpected surprises as well. Discovering the wonders of the pyramids and civilization of Teotihuacan was perhaps the greatest marvel. Every museum and ancient site were a marvel to us, and we soaked in the wonderment of it all. The boys dashed from place to place with excitement and enjoyment and loved discovering new sights, sounds and smells even just walking along the streets. Unfortunately, Danny picked up some sort of stomach bug (Montezuma's revenge**)**, so h**e** and Norine had to spend a miserable day in the hotel room.

Davisito and I went off to some scary caves with mummies inside at Guanajuato, and then to the great National Museum, which was an incredible experience even for a boy as young as David, although I probably learned as much as he did, and certainly came to appreciate the need for more awareness of that fantastic culture with all its achievements. While she was in the hotel room attending to Danielito, the woman came in to clean the room. Norine watched in absolute amazement as she picked up the glass water pitcher from the writing table and proceeded to fill it tap water from the bathroom faucet. We had been drinking from that pitcher, assuming it was filled with bottled water, so we feared that water was the culprit and cause of all our ills.

Davisito and I explored the *Museo Nacional*.

Our last night of that week's stay, had a sad ending. Our Volkswagen Squareback had been parked on the street right under our hotel window, which we thought would be safe as we could see it well and hear the sounds from the street. However, that last night, someone broke into the car taking a huge black bag that was probably mistaken for a purse, which had no money or anything of value to anyone but us. Instead, it contained several rolls of unused film, but most tragically, many more rolls of used film that Norine had already taken of our travels up until that point of our trip. A few incidental items were taken also, but the other missing tragedy was the complete dinnerware set which she had gotten in the quaint little town of Tonalá near Guadalajara, which was well known for their beautiful ceramic ware. Having studied both photography and ceramics as part of her art major, Norine was absolutely devastated, and insisted that we must return home along the very same path on which we had come, so she could retake photos that were lost, and hopefully buy, at least a few, replacement ceramic pieces. Sadly, we could only afford to replace a setting for four, not the original twelve place set. She spent many of our following trips to Mexico looking for that particular pattern, occasionally finding them in the airport gift shop where she could only buy a few pieces at a time, due to the expense and lack of room in her carry on. After many, many years on that same search, she did acquire a complete setting for twelve, which graced many of our celebration tables throughout our lives till this day.

Ceramics in Tonalá.

The VW Squareback, which had replaced our Karmann Ghia after the Nevada accident, was broken into on the street in Mexico City.

23

EMBRACING MATH

CALLS FROM CHILDHOOD

Mathematics was a difficult subject for which I had a love-hate relation through childhood. I remember as a grade school kid, when my *Papá* came home slightly intoxicated and demanded in a loud angry tone: *¿Cuánto es ocho por siete?* **– What is 8 times 7?** Since I could not give him an answer, he was upset and shouted *"¡Ay! ¡Qué estúpido!"*- Oh! How stupid! It took me a while to realize that his abnormal behavior for a father was due to his overconsumption of alcoholic drinks.

Later in life when I was in a public secondary school during times of strikes and civil war, *Papá* managed to provide me with a math tutor and gave me a small book with math tables dealing with logarithms, trigonometric functions, and many more. My *Papá* never paid for my tutoring or schools, since he was a clever sociable person who managed to barter favors from teachers, dentists, and physicians. Some of them were dishonest but lucky for me, *Papá* linked me with a tutor, *Maestro* Ocaña who helped me to pass the necessary math exams and become a graduate of the *Instituto de Bachillerato* (High School plus an extra 5th year). During my last year, I had my first experience as an unofficial algebra tutor of an older female student whose mother paid me with snacks and desserts. Although being a math teacher was not in my plans for earning a living, mathematics more than Spanish or English provided me with a means to survive during my last year in Cuba and expand my education in my new land of Utah and later through Florida and California.

During my freshman year at Westminster College, my math teacher Professor Donald Wittig, referred to me as "The Math Star" in the college yearbook, the Etosian of 1958. Mathematics provided me with a tool to show off by solving problems on the blackboard, while enduring difficult times writing essays in English. The final call for seeking a degree in Math came via a philosophy class along with upper division math courses that convinced me of the beauty and expanse of a subject that served as a language and gave connectivity with music and art. My success at Westminster gave me a chance to obtain my first teaching job with a scholarship to pursue a master's degree at the University of Miami. There I came face to face with the first professor that encouraged me to move on to the area of pure research in math.

My First Math Challenges
Primeros Desafíos de Matemáticas

The two years at the University of Miami were very intense – I was the only Spanish speaking student, as far as I could tell in the master's program, and as far as I was concerned, the only minority student, despite the fact that South Florida had a large Latino and African American population. Some students from cold climates referred to the university as "Suntan U." These students came more for the fun and sun on Miami's warm beaches, and then would drop out just before the deadline, so they would not get penalized with a bad mark on their record. Most students, however, especially those studying for a graduate degree were quite serious and totally dedicated to their educational pursuits. When I entered the classroom for my first teaching assignment, I had to state loudly and clearly that "I am the professor here," a statement received with raised eyebrows and quiet giggles, since at barely 21 years of age, I appeared younger than many of my students. One of the courses I was assigned to teach was Math of Finance. It was the ultimate teaching challenge – as many business majors disliked math and had postponed their enrollment, in this required class for graduation, until their last year, definitely making them older than I was. Unlike all the professors around me, I still had a strong Cuban accent, and I had never taken courses involving the financial vocabulary for everyday applications. So, I madly struggled to learn good pronunciation and even figure out myself what that class was all about. It not only required solving math problems, but also knowledge of the essential applications in banking, loans, mortgages, and interest rates, which had never been of much interest to me.

To make matters even more difficult, one of my students, a young woman, had a total hearing impairment and had to read lips – imagine reading lips of a teacher with a strong Spanish accent! I had to constantly look straight at her, face-to-face, ignoring all the other students - but that was not enough, I also had to write on the blackboard any statement made that might be needed to solve a particular problem. She often came to my office to clarify what she had missed, asking me to explain the entire lecture carefully and clearly for a second time. Through the school of hard-knocks I probably learned more in that class about teaching and helping students with impairments than at any other time in my teaching career.

Another challenge came to my life when one of my professors started the class with a brief handout of about four pages filled with statements that upon several readings appeared meaningless. The statements consisted of definitions of certain weird terms followed by axioms (basic math assumptions) from the world of Topology, and unproven theorems. This was the strangest class I had ever taken, there were no lectures given, but the students were required to give presentations and would be graded by their ability to prove the theorems and be subjected to challenges and criticisms from the professor and the other students in class. If no one had anything to present we would sit consulting with each other or in silence, struggling with the logic of proving theorems. Some days I felt the class was a total waste of time, but on other days there was the excitement and exhilaration typical of mathematicians when they come to a logical conclusion of a theorem, proven beyond a doubt, convincing everyone in class and ending with "QED" *Quod Erat Demonstrandum*– What was to be proved -- my final blessing!!

In hindsight this was the best class to prepare a student for moving on to do research in pure mathematics. It filled me with confidence and accepting mathematical studies as a road to take; in particular when the professor called me into his office to praise me for my abilities and encouraged me to continue my work in pursuit of a PhD in math. At that time, I had no idea what that entailed, but of course, I felt honored and more secure than ever with my chosen subject. That message stayed in my mind but due to lack of finance and facing the duties of family life I chose to continue as a teacher at the newly emerging bilingual Covell College and the University of the Pacific in Stockton, California. Towards the end of the 1960s I felt very insecure with my teaching job and intense activism as advisor to the emerging Chicano Movement at Chabot College. I kept up with mathematics by taking classes at University of California in Berkeley since coming to California. At the University of Miami, the professor that encouraged me to continue my education and work doing research in pure math, had a tremendous impact on my life. During my second year as a graduate student, he showed me what pure math was all about, and that led me to discover my talents for theorem proofs and research.

The traumas at Chabot College and the insecurities of my status as an immigrant brought the call for expanding my education. My wife Norine gave me full support by also obtaining a teaching credential which helped to provide financial support for our family and permitted me to apply at UC Berkeley as a graduate student for a PhD degree. The early 1970s was a time of protest due to the ongoing Viet Nam war and the heavy number of casualties. Never before had I worked with such intensity, keeping my job at Chabot and going to Berkeley on a daily basis to the top floor of Evans Hall. I was on an ivory tower, hidden from a world in turmoil and totally devoted to pure math, meeting with some of the smartest minds I have ever encounter, discussing in small groups topics related to mathematical analysis, probability, and ergodic theory. Sometimes even going to Stanford University to meet with Professor Donald S. Ornstein, a memorable advisor who gave me a real vision of my abstract mathematical research. Dr. Ornstein open doors to my research by suggesting a funny image of dogs along a line with flees jumping among them.

After years of research, often staying in an office on the top floor of Evans Hall in UC Berkeley, my advisor and research guide, Dr. Jacob Feldman, assured me that for a year I had done all the discoveries necessary for a PhD in mathematics. The final dissertation was titled:

"Some velocity changes on ergodic flows and a skew product of a Poisson flow and a Bernoulli shift."

Pi Mu Epsilon Mathematics Fraternity - Delvis Alejandro Fernández Levy at the top row center among students and professors. In the second row from left to right: my inspirational professors Edwin Duda, Bernard E. Howard, and Emmet E. Low. Photo from the IBIS '63 Yearbook, Vol 37. Thanks to assistance from Marcia Tyrrell Heath and Charles Eckman from the University Archives of the Otto G. Richter Library at the University of Miami.

My Hiding Place for Research
Evans Hall - my "Ivory Tower" at **UC Berkeley** during times of unrest in the 1960s and 1970s - the statistics, economics, and mathematics building.

Doctor Fernández Levy - A *Fait Accompli*

THE REGENTS OF THE

University of California

ON THE NOMINATION OF THE
GRADUATE COUNCIL OF THE BERKELEY DIVISION
HAVE CONFERRED UPON

DELVIS ALEJANDRO FERNÁNDEZ-LEVY

WHO HAS PROVED HIS ABILITY BY ORIGINAL RESEARCH
IN MATHEMATICS
THE DEGREE OF DOCTOR OF PHILOSOPHY
WITH ALL THE RIGHTS AND PRIVILEGES THERETO PERTAINING

GIVEN AT BERKELEY
THIS TWENTIETH DAY OF DECEMBER IN THE YEAR
NINETEEN HUNDRED AND SEVENTY-FIVE

GOVERNOR OF CALIFORNIA AND
PRESIDENT OF THE REGENTS

CHANCELLOR AT BERKELEY

PRESIDENT OF THE UNIVERSITY

DEAN OF THE GRADUATE DIVISION
AT BERKELEY

Research in pure math also brought an interest in music and physical activities. Piano playing was a venue for inspiration and serenity, away from times of total absorption in trying to expand on theorems and axioms. Also, I ran on a daily basis to give my body mobility and a chance to detach the brain from just mathematical research. On top of my activities as a dedicated student and researcher of mathematics, I still had to teach at Chabot College, but lucky for me I was now on a tenure path that allowed me to take time off under sabbaticals and reduction of courses to teach. The accomplishment of a doctorate was a major highlight of my life. It gave me a sense of security as a teacher and mathematician.

There was a call for moving to a major university as a professor but family responsibilities and changes at Chabot sparked by Chicano/a/s, African Americans, women, students affected by physical disabilities, and many others influenced my decision to remain and continue my job as an activist and teacher at Chabot. Among the changes in which I managed to get involved were:

- The Math Lab for teaching statistics and basic skills,
- The establishment of contacts with local high schools and colleges,
- Hiring and evaluation of instructors; Calculator and computer workshops,
- Tutorials Center,
- *Centro de Información,*
- Expansion of Counselors,
- Programs for the Community,
- Inclusion of Faculty Assistants and Math Mentor Programs designed to bring women and ethnic minorities into math-related disciplines and careers.

Turmoils of Life

Being an Absent Father
Difficult Times of Decision after reaching a Ph.D.
Should I Get a Job at a University in another state?
Stay in our Home Base near Chabot College?

My children were now reaching teen-age years. My wife Norine took good care of the family, home, and finances. But I remain deeply affected by the separation I suffered from my Cuban homeland, due to government policies that prevented freedom to travel for family visits. Attempts to visit my only grandfather, and main paternal role model during the twilight of his life, filled me with a strong desire to be with him and visit the *familia* and friends I had not seen for over 20 years.

24

FAMILY LIFE
Behind My Teaching Scene (1970-1994)

Visits with Friends and Family

My entire life had been consumed with math while I worked toward the PhD. At the same time, I was teaching full time at Chabot College and marching with my sons and Chicano friends to protest the selling of grapes. Also, enjoying the wedding of our friends, Alida and Lloyd, with the birth of their first child, Lanissa, who was to become Norine's Goddaughter, and seriously becoming more involved with piano classes at Chabot as a student. The denial of being allowed to visit family in Cuba at the sad time of my beloved grandfather's death and no prospect of any visits for my wife and sons to meet my side of our family, weighed heavily on my mind. Looking back, I wonder how I managed to do it all, yet at the time I was filled with concern that I was not devoting enough time to our family life.

I did find relaxation from the heavy load and peace of mind in my pursuit of learning to play the piano. At the beginning, I only dabbled with beginner's books my mother-in-law had given us for our boys, but I soon realized I needed a class and teacher for discipline and improvement, which I found on the Chabot campus. After a few years and once I had completed my math degree, I was fortunate to find an outstanding teacher, Mrs. Trula Whelan, who set me on the path of becoming a classical pianist. Her teaching approach and guidance was and is greatly appreciated, and only the Sunday afternoon recitals in her home were dreaded as my father's objecting voice echoed in my head making me very nervous in front of all the adoring parents of Mrs. Whelan's pupils, who were all so much younger than I. She also helped to find a magnificent German *Ibach* baby grand piano from the 1910s, in beautiful condition, which I have treasured and loved even to this day.

Norine too was working on her art degree but managed to take care of the kids and everything at home at the same time – an amazing multi-tasker. When Danny had started kindergarten, she finally had her mornings free, so had enrolled in daytime classes at Cal State Hayward – a first, after all those night classes for eight years. She loved art, so continued with that as her major, yet as the end-goal approached, she could not imagine how she could make a living with art. So, she decided to continue one more year to earn her secondary teaching credential, which sadly was a waste, as teaching jobs were very hard to come by in those days. She had a wild experience doing student teaching in a continuation high school in Oakland with her classroom window just two feet from the new Bart rapid transit tracks. The real purpose of her drama class (something she herself had never studied) was to teach the students, all ages from teens to late twenties, to read. They saw through it all and were a terribly undisciplined 'gang' with young women coming late to class still in their skimpy nighttime professional wear, and guys who threatened to throw the teachers out of the window onto the train tracks, and on and on. That situation did not fill her with any excitement for her approaching teaching profession. She initially could only find substitute teaching jobs, which were not quite as dramatically bad, but not enjoyable, as in those days the troublemakers were always sent to shop or art classes. She suffered through one year in a junior high then quit – never to return.

The summer after all that trauma turned out to be one of her high lights. We had planned to send the boys for their usual summer in Miami, and we decided it was an ideal chance for her to learn more about my culture, my language and even how to cook Cuban food. It would give me full time to devote to my Berkeley studies, so TV dinners became the cuisine of my days. They stayed in Miami for five or six weeks with daily trips to the beach in the old clunkers that my dad provided for wildly exciting and harrowing drives. Upon their return home, she

David and Danny loved trips to the beach and parks with Maruchi.

always sat on a stool in the kitchen as my mother prepared the evening meal, taking notes hoping to discover the secret to real Cuban cooking. Of course, *Mami* never measured any of the ingredients and often added a bit of this or that depending on the taste or her mood, so poor Norine found it very difficult to follow. When my father would arrive after a stop at the bodega, he always brought caramels for the boys and a big bag of *chicharrones* - the fried fat from the pig which was the favorite snack for this man that would not touch a single vegetable nor salad. There was also a loud explosion of banter back and forth with he and *mami* as a sneaky wink would let Norine know he was just doing it to drive her crazy. Norine had become accustomed to their 'loving behavior' when we lived in Miami but now listening to it on a nightly basis brought it to a new level, as did the constant flow of visiting friends. Her refuge was with my dearest cousin, Maruchi, who was several years younger, but always full of ideas for fun things to do together. By the end of the visit the two had come up with the idea of a 'road trip' back to California along with *Mami* and the boys, and just as when I had left Miami after my master's degree in one of *Papá*'s spare cars, they had only gone twenty miles or so, north on the Florida turnpike when the steam billowed up and engulfed the entire car, he had given them. A quick phone call to my father resulted in the same advice, "just pour water over the engine, and give it ten or fifteen minutes." That was to be the routine across the entire country, yet somehow, they

Maruchi's 1st visit to Hayward with my *Mami* Sara.

managed to arrive in California in one piece. As with many road trips, she could have written an entire book about their escapades, mostly centered on the behavior of my mother, who always provided entertainment in the most bizarre ways. Highlights were the long quiet conversations as they drove early in the morning while *Mami* and the boys still slept and there was very little traffic, which cemented their bond and deep friendship.

That was the beginning of almost yearly visits from my cousin for several years and always filled with fun and excitement as we shared the west coast with Maruchi. It seemed everything we would do with her was new and filled her with delight, which made each visit a profoundly marvelous time. She too was in awe as we passed under the towering cables of the Oakland-Bay bridge as we shared the beauty of San Francisco and enjoyed the cool spray on the boat past San Quentin to Marin County. We stayed in a log cabin where my old friend Patty was living in the Santa Cruz mountains where she fed the racoons and marveled at the giant Sequoias. On a rare winter visit, we built a snowman near Tahoe and in summer took camping trips up the Oregon coast with stops in the grand Redwoods of northern California.

Camping was one of our most enjoyable family activities when the boys were young, and our trip to Yosemite with her was perhaps the most memorable. We had packed all the gear and Norine had made my favorite carrot cake to celebrate my birthday that first night by the campfire. We had just finished our meal with our mouths watering for the cake sitting on the table. Danny and David were climbing on a huge rock formation in our camp site, when David started yelling excitedly about seeing a bear. Having learned the fine art of telling fibs in grade school, we assumed it was just another one of his tall tales, but suddenly a huge brown bear came lumbering out from behind the boulders toward our table. The excitement of our actions to save our lives and giving up the yummy cake was all recounted in Norine's memorial book written for Maruchi's family upon her death in 2015 which came much too early.

Other regular summer and often Thanksgiving Dinner or Christmas gift opening visits were from my sister-in-law, Clarice, and her three girls. The oldest, Renee, was always the one in charge and entertained us on every visit by organizing and directing an amazing production of song and dance and drama on their final day. Unfortunately, I find no pictures of these artistic creations, but luckily, we made videos, so we do have keepsakes. Our dearest family friends, the Rochons, spent many a Christmas eve for the traditional carol sing-along, which always gave me great purpose much of December, as I practiced playing the carols on piano in preparation. The *Nochebuena* meal with all of the traditional Cuban dishes of *carne de puerco, arroz con frijoles negros, yuca, plátanos, flan, y turrón* from Spain. Lloyd and Alida were from New Orleans and although their typical fare when we went to enjoy a meal at their house was often gumbo, they thoroughly loved Cuban food and all my traditions. Poor Norine would labor cooking all that day, and then again, the next day after the kids opened their gifts, to make the typical American fare for our big Christmas dinner. Once her folks had moved to the Bay Area, they would always join us and often her sister and family would also come from Arizona.

Our life was very family oriented from Norine's side and with good dear friends, but not with any of my family. I only remember my folks coming from Florida once during the winter months, but the joy they expressed with experiencing snow for the first time was very memorable. My *Mami* visited more frequently, often around taking or bringing the boys back from their Miami summer stay. My father owned his own garage and worked there every single day for all his years in Miami. Although he had good friends that worked with him, he never trusted them to completely take charge. The kids

My parents Delvis Sr. and Sara with my son Daniel on their visit to the Sierra Nevada

absolutely loved going to the garage with him – 'helping him', playing with his guard dog named King, learning to drive in some old clunker in the empty lot between the garage and the railroad tracks, and most of all - counting the piles and piles of dollar bills on the kitchen table at the end of a hard day's work. My father, for all the years in Miami, always carried out his business in a very provincial way, which was often in cash and with a handshake. The piles of money were many but not much as it was mostly dollar bills, which *Mami* would often wrap in aluminum foil then hide in the freezer – banking and credit cards were foreign to them.

Years later when my father passed away and I brought my mother to live with us in California, we found hidden money in the ceiling lights, behind walls, under floorboards and probably places we missed entirely. His poor eating habits, his drinking and his lack of exercise had caused poor circulation resulting in the removal of one leg. Then in the early months of 1989 I made many trips flying back and forth to help with his care and then finally planning to close out his business and sell their home after he passed away in March. Those two daunting tasks proved just how much he had retained "his way" of doing things, as I searched through his little black book to see who had borrowed money, that was never to be retrieved, and finally accepting that both the business and the house were to be lost causes, because the proper legal paperwork did not exist. Both had good value as he had built an apartment in the separate garage out back and turned the house into a duplex. The business had grown into a body and paint shop along with the auto repair and gas pump garage. We ended up spending more money on attorneys than we ever received, so eventually just gave up the fight. Bringing my mother to California from her world in Miami was very difficult for her, and until her dying day, twenty-five plus years later, she always referred to *"mi gente en Miami"* -my people in Miami.

My First Trip Home - *Twenty-one years later*

Left to Right: Brother-in-law Arturo López-Calleja, sister Gilda Sara (*Sarita*), *Tía* Évora (*Chicha*), sister Guiselda (*Puchi*) with daughter Ania, Brother-in law Ramón González with daughter Nadia, myself Delvis (*Pupy*).
In front Sarita's four boys: Twins Ernesto & Enrique, Jorge, and Arturo.

In early summer of 1978, I made my first trip back to my beloved land after twenty-one years. My sisters, who were four and thirteen years old when I left, were now grown women with children of their own and both with high level university degrees in engineering. They and their husbands all held teaching positions at the University of Marta Abreu in Santa Clara, Cuba. My initial arrival at the airport was not too pleasant, as they were all waiting outside, but through the lengthy custom's ordeal I had to stay in a hotel the first night rather than heading home with them. Once I did get to Santa Clara, it was a wonderful whirl wind of visiting everyone, but a heavy sorrow of missing all those who were now gone – several close family members. It was exciting to hear about all their accomplishments and to share their enthusiasm for positive changes, yet sad to see the hardships they had to bear and to realize my great cost of lost years. I remember talking with two tall young men who had been barefooted kids back on the farm, who never raised their heads when talking to me as the owner's grandson, but that day they stood towering above me and looked me straight in the eye as they told of their college education and achievements as doctor and engineer. It was an amazing journey in many ways.

The following spring, when Jimmy Carter was president, there was a small window open for travel, Norine saw an ad in the San Francisco newspaper for a Berkeley agency planning a two-week tour of Cuba in early May. She excitedly convinced me she wanted to go even though I could not join her due to my school schedule. The boys were then thirteen and sixteen, and as teenagers they were sure that being on their own was completely doable. We were not quite ready to share that belief, but she wanted so badly to go and meet her Cuban family, that we just plunged ahead hoping for the best. Norine remembers standing in a line to get cash for the trip at the bank and when the teller suggested traveler checks instead, she

Norine joined this amazing crowd for May Day on her first day in Havana, Cuba- in 1979.

proudly stated it had to be cash for Cuba. In shock, the teller asked if she did not fear she might be arrested and detained there, to which Norine stated that the only fear of arrest might be when she entered the airport on her return at a city in the USA.

Her first full day in Havana was May Day of 1957, and the tour group joined the thousands in Revolutionary Square under the towering statue of the country's great patriot, José Martí, for their May Day celebration. I hope she will write a book on this life changing journey, but I will just mention her meeting with all my family. The second day the group boarded a plane and flew to the far eastern part of Cuba to start a return trip by bus all the way from Santiago de Cuba back to Havana. It had been arranged that halfway through the trek, at a resort nearest my hometown of Santa Clara, she would call the family and they would come to pick her up for an overnight stay with them. It took several minutes for Sarita to come to the neighbor's phone, and when Norine heard her sisters-in-law's voice, she chocked up and then finally blurted out, "*Ay, Dios mío*" and Sarita immediately responded, "*Mami?*" Norine's knowledge of the Spanish language was very limited at that time, but she had picked up many of my mother's expressions along with her

Sisters Sarita and Puchi with their husbands Arturo and Ramón.

Cuban accent, and therefore sounded to my sister just like our mother. Within an hour she was riding in their little white VW bug with Sarita's oldest ten-year-old son, Arturito, and Puchy's husband, Ramón, as driver. The boy knew quite a bit of English, and suggested they play an easy game for her about U.S. history. He would ask a question, and if she answered correctly, then she would have a turn to ask him a question. To her absolute amazement and embarrassment, she had to admit that he knew more about U.S. history than she.

Once in the family home they had a typical meal with all the immediate family present, which led into a long conversation into the wee small hours of the morning. With only an hour or so of sleep, Norine joined Ramón for a whirl wind tour of their town as they visit many, many relatives. In each home, regardless of the early hour, she was given a shot of rum along with some delightful edibles. I had given her a long list with all the names and what their relationship was to me to use in trying to keep everything straight. To my astonishment she had met and checked off almost every name after that brief

Norine tries "to pass" in her Cuban garb.

time in my hometown. By late afternoon they drove her back to the arranged spot on the central highway where she was to meet the tour bus. The kissing and crying and hugs with more kisses went on for several minutes as they all bid her good-bye, and once back on the bus, she blocked out the foolish and ignorant questions from many as they ask what that tremendous, emotional display was with folks she had just met the day before. There was no explanation nor any way of making them understand the importance and magnitude of her encounter.

Later, she would dress in the wrap around skirt and colorful blouse along with a kerchief on her head, which were her gifts from Sarita and Puchy. She would then sit on many a central plaza bench with smiles and no words, hoping the passing school children, might think she was a Cuban. After great debate and much staring, the kids would always giggle and point out she did not fool them, and it was always because of her American shoes. It was so reminiscent of my attempt to pass as a Spaniard when we were in Madrid, and the shoes gave me away. She told me many such stories of her experiences on that trip, and we bonded more strongly than ever with this newly found connection.

Exercise Becomes My Obsession

After our two amazing trips to Cuba, I was falsely filled with hope that perhaps changes were coming. We had made trips to Mexico almost on a yearly basis many summers to have, as we put it, "my Spanish fix." Now I hoped for the possibility of more frequent trips to the homeland of Cuba. My teaching was quite satisfying as well as my family responsibilities. When the 1980s rolled in, and I was in my forties, I felt a new calling. The PhD and years of intense study that had been on my mind, made me realize that my physical well-being had been sorely ignored during my youth. When Danny was just eight, Norine convinced me we should put the boys in swimming lessons. My old method for teaching to swim by throwing a person in a pool was not working. So, we agreed to enroll our sons in swimming lessons. Within the first week, the coach asked if he could enter Danny in a swim meet that coming weekend. To our absolute amazement, he took first place in the eight-year-old free style race, obviously he was a natural born fish. David also soon entered his first meet and showed great promise, so our life changed drastically as we became "swim parents." Driving back and forth to swim practice every single weekday all year around with judging or timing at swim meets almost every weekend – many out of town which meant weekend camping. Unlike other sports that your kids might get involved with – flag football, basketball, baseball, etc. – swimming was a year-round activity, and therefore I felt so much more demanding. As a Cuban kid I should have been good at baseball, but sadly I was the last one chosen for any team and just never enjoyed nor was any good at it or any other sport, so I was proud that my sons were becoming such amazing swim champs. By my fortieth birthday David was seventeen and had pretty much dropped out of swimming, but Danny at fifteen was still going strong. He rode his bike every morning from our house on the Hayward Hills to the Chabot pool, which was about fourteen miles round trips, for daily morning workouts before school started at 8:30. He also had workouts after school, but rode the bike and carpooled, so we were not as involved. Their involvement was a constant reminder of how lacking exercise was in my own life, so I decided to take up running. My first half-marathon was around the city of Oakland during the early 1980s. I continued my running routines and eventually did the full San Francisco Marathon and accomplished the challenging Bay to Breakers Race in 1990. Because of living a couple of miles straight up East Avenue in the East Bay, my return home after any exercise routine was a difficult challenge, but a great source for training. Once on a visit to Miami I entered an advertised run and zoomed ahead on every causeway overpass, which was nothing to me, but caused huffing and puffing from all the other runners. It was one of my finest hours, as I received a first-place trophies for my age group, however the race was far from a true challenge. Several colleagues at Chabot were involved with biking and so invited me to join them. I met a young cyclist in his twenties who became my training buddy, where again my ride home made me very strong whenever faced with a hill. Summer rides with my Chabot cronies when we rode round trip up Highway 1 from the Bay Area well into Oregon were very memorable. Those intense rides became my preferred sport for quite a few years. In training for the Davis Double (200 miles in one day) I would get up very early and ride through the Oakland hills to the original Peet's Coffee, which was on the far side of Berkeley, then ride home in time to shower and make it to teach my 8:00 a.m. class. Perhaps the high point on the bike was doing the Markleeville Death Ride. Markleeville was a little town not too far from the Kirkland Ski Resort in the Sierra Nevada. It was

the crossroad for several mountain passes, so riders started off from Markleeville going up and coming back down each of five passes. A ride of about 120 miles over beautiful scenic mountains going up and down five mountain passes reaching 14,200 feet of climb. I remember it resulted in extreme exhaustion and ecstatic exhilaration for its triumph. The ride, considered one of the best in the world celebrates its 40th Anniversary in 2021.

California Alps Death Ride

During this crazy period of my life, my wife was working as an entrepreneur with her own franchise business. After her Cuba trip she was approaching her dreaded forties, and had added several unwanted pounds, so joined a very sensible program which monitored her exercise and diet program with daily advice and counseling. Her own counselor was moving away and convinced her that it was a very good business opportunity, so in 1981 she bought the franchise and after the necessary training period, reopened the Hayward Diet Center. Over the next ten years she turned her one little center into three with several employees in each. I helped in the computer area by writing a manual and program to communicate with her client's physicians; and also benefitted with some wonderful travel almost every summer to the yearly conventions: Acapulco, Mexico; Florida with Caribbean Cruise; Santa Barbara, California; Honolulu, Hawaii; Jacksonville,

The Computer in Action
by
Delvis A. Fernandez, Ph.D.

A Business Guide for the Diet Center Computer System

Wyoming; and others. However, the death of my father and bringing my mother to live with us, and then the death of Norine's mother just a few months later, created some major changes in her responsibility, and she decided to sell her three franchises and returned to the home front in 1991.

David, our oldest son, had returned home after working and living in Tucson, Arizona for several years with his cousins and visiting his aunt Clarice in Phoenix. He had decided to move on to a college education by enrolling at Chabot College in Hayward. So that Christmas break we decided to take him along with my mother Sara, who was now living with us, on a trip to Ecuador where her brother Eddie was then living. The social misfortunes and inequalities were a real eye opener for all of us, but especially for David. He had taken his first trip to Cuba a few years before and now he was expanding his knowledge about people, life, and culture in Latin America. Eddie had an Afro-Ecuadorian maid from the Province of Esmeraldas who prepared all their meals and had charge of the kitchen. When David walked into her domain to get a glass of water, he was strongly reprimanded and told that she would fetch anything and everything he needed. A few days later while shopping at an open market he was constantly pestered by elderly women, completely bent over after years of carrying heavy loads of woven goods on their backs. He was holding a plastic bag of veggies, which was something a man of his stature should not do, and therefore they insisted on carrying it for him. The poverty was unbearable to see and the lack of respect for your fellow human beings was shocking. We did enjoy the magnificent scenery and our climb of the Volcano to the Cotopaxi Glacier was an unforgettable and surreal experience we shared.

The altitude of Cotopaxi, at well over 15,000 feet was the excruciating challenge of the climb. Family time was wonderful and connecting with my Uncle Eddie, cousin Magda, and their families was a remarkable experience for us all. *Mami* Sara had not seen her brother and his wife, Xiomara, nor her niece, for several years and had never traveled outside of Cuba and the United States, which was so exciting for her. David too, was thrilled to spend time and learn to know his cousin,

Magda as well as her husband, Rodrigo, and little boy, also named, David. Finally, we were sharing 'family time' with my side of the family.

The following summer we took *Mami* to Mexico City for her first trip there.

Traveling with her was fun and worthwhile yet had its share of difficulties. She was apt to wander away, like a child, if you took your eye off her for a minute and she often said crazy things loudly that were embarrassing. At her age, we had hoped she would need to rest in the room by afternoon, allowing us to go off for a little alone time, but she was so energized and always wanted to go everywhere and do everything. The last straw was when she absolutely insisted on the foolishness of spending money on two rooms, so shared our room and snored loudly all night. We had fantasized about taking her to Spain and Turkey to see the lands of her father, however after Ecuador and Mexico we needed a break. Back home she had completely taken over the kitchen, which was perfectly fine with Norine, and enticed our sons to share many more meals with us, although they were both out of the house by then, so they not only enjoyed her fantastic cooking, but both learned and became remarkable Cuban cooks, thanks to her. Her delicious *crème de vie* (drink like eggnog) became a great addition to our traditional *Nochebuena* meal.

Near Guayaquil, Ecuador
L to R: Magda with her son David, Delvis, my son also named David, and Rodrigo Carrión (Magda's husband); my *Mamá* Sara in front.

Near Quito, Ecuador
L to R: Uncle Eddie Levy, Delvis, wife Norine, son David. Aunt Xiomara & *Mamá* Sara in front.

Running   Cycling   Skiing   Hiking
Dancing   Windsurfing   Skating

1ˢᵗ Place Trophies for running in The Rites of Spring Race (March 22, 1980)
The Vietnam Veterans Day 15K Classic (April 26, 1981).
Trophy for AQUADUCKS 50s Dancing with Norine.
HEART of CALIFORNIA Double Century (200 Miles in One Day in 1984)
Markleeville Death Ride (1983 & 1984), 120 miles and 14,200 feet of climb
Marathon Races in Oakland and San Francisco.
Century Bicycle Rides (100 miles cycling) in various areas of California

Marathon in San Francisco Bay Area

Getting ready for Century and Double Century Rides with my son David

A cross country skiing adventure in the Sierra Nevada

Backpacking and hiking in the Sierra Nevada and Oregon

Climbing the Cotopaxi Volcano in Ecuador

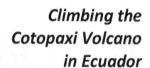

Exciting windsurfing days in California and in Hood River, Oregon

Weddings and the First Birth as the Family Grows

My duties at Chabot College had a new twist in the early nineties as we adjusted to life with my mother and our sons coming and going. I was asked to organize and lead a mentoring program, which presented new challenges with the Chicano students that I had worked with through my entire career at Chabot. I was thrilled with this new task and gladly added it to my list of "to dos." I continued with some running, but did more cycling, as I did the Markleeville Death Ride for a second time as well as the Davis Double (two hundred miles around Sacramento and Davis). My oldest son had gotten involved with a great new sport – wind surfing – which looked like fun, so I gave it a try. After my first attempt in the calm Bay just off Alameda, I was completely hooked. Mastering the necessary skills were the most difficult thing I had ever done physically, but rewarding, and although I never conquered the control and fine ability that son David had, I always enjoyed the time spent - doing what I could do. The only disadvantage was the waiting and watching for the wind to 'pick up,' so again I took up a new activity, rollerblading, to pass the wait time. *Mami* had made a wonderful new friend, Obdulia, who was a sweet, loving Cuban widower who lived in Hayward with Orlando, her adult son. She was often invited to spend the weekend with them, which gave Norine and I an opportunity for one-night trips to many wonderful Bay Area hideaways. Driving north of San Francisco along the coast to Gualala became a favorite and taking my bike to ride on inland country roads was very pleasurable. Norine would drive ahead, stop in gorgeous areas and roam about taking photos until I caught up.

First wedding of son Daniel Rubén with Teresa Margarita Peña

By then both boys were dating seriously, and by November of 1992 Dan announced the plans to marry his beautiful sweetie, MariTere. She spoke Spanish fluently having been born in Guadalajara, Mexico, and we were all thrilled. Her mother Margarita worked very long hours down in San Jose, California, so had little time for wedding plans, and Norine excitedly volunteered to help. The two spent hours looking for 'the perfect setting,' and finally settled on an elegant resort style home right on our high hill. They carefully calculated the ceremony time, so a sunset over the San Francisco Bay would be the backdrop. Norine's entire family came for Thanksgiving that year with the wedding two days later, and the sky did not disappoint as it turned orange and pink just as they said their vows.

Within months, David too, announced a forth coming wedding. Norine's father had become dear friends with a woman who had graduated from Mills College in the Oakland Hills, so had access to using many of their facilities on the beautiful campus. Summer rolled around quickly and like Dan and MariTere's ceremony, David and Deborah had a darling group of children as participants, lovely weather for the outdoor reception in a splendid venue, and all the family members on Norine's side were present, but no one on my side except my mother. *Mami* and I had traveled to Cuba several times since my father's death, Norine had gone back a second time with a group from Global Exchange, and both boys had gone with me to meet my family. It was not an easy thing to do, and neither of my sisters were able to travel as tourist family visitors to California. So again, I could not share these moments with my *familia*.

Big Changes, but the Biggest Yet to Come

After all the excitement of weddings with so many family guests, we needed a break. *Mami* Sara's trip to Europe was still in the back of our heads, but when David mentioned driving up the coast through Oregon for a windsurfing trip on the Columbia River, a favorite and one of the best spots in the country, we could not resist. He had finished his studies at Chabot and had been accepted as a student by the Architecture Department at California Polytechnic University in San Luis Obispo, so we knew a move was coming. The campsite at the Hood River Gorge was the perfect place to relax, enjoying the beauty and excitement as we had to bid our son good-bye. The following year brought many trips to San Luis Obispo to visit and to get acquainted with our first granddaughter. They also came to our home in Hayward often, and one weekend in late spring after a fun visit to San Francisco, we received shocking word from Cuba, that would change my life dramatically from that day forward.

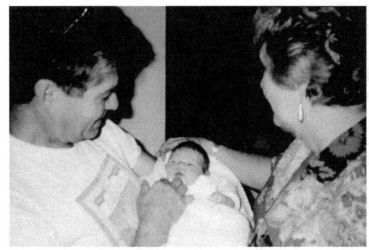

First addition to the family from our oldest son David Iván, our adored *nietecita* Dariella Arianna

25

CALLS OF MY DEAR FAMILY
Llamados de Mi Querida Familia

From Days of Hope to Reality

On my journey *"Hacia El Norte"* – to the U.S. – I fantasized about getting an engineering degree for a return to Cuba with a secure job in an idyllic place near my hometown of Santa Clara. But the outcome of that journey was far from my plans and dreams for the future. Away from family and friends, in a foreign cultural domain as a teenager, I felt a call for learning a language and building a new *familia*. At times letters from my loved ones in Cuba also burned calls in my heart and soul for return to the beloved homeland.

During the summer of 1958, a year after arriving in Salt Lake City, Utah, I received news about my parents coming to Miami, Florida. It was unbelievable, since I had assumed that they were cemented in the homeland with family, a secure business, and friendly surroundings. It was also shocking to learn that my *Papá* had lost his garage business due to thefts from Batista's forces coming by to steal gas from his Sinclair Service Station on the Camajuaní Highway. On top of losing his business, his life was threatened after the loss of a friend, nicknamed "Mosquito," who was found dead after being tortured.

My parent's arrival in the U.S. was my first call for a return to the homeland, and join forces in the struggle for justice, peace, and a democratic society after the end of the Batista Regime. After receiving the news, I saved all the money I could from my days as a farm worker and as a college dishwasher (at 85 cents an hour) to pay for a 10-day Greyhound bus round-trip to Miami and back to Salt Lake City, during my 14-day Christmas vacation in 1958. This was the most agonizing "vacation" in my life, also working as a dishwasher in a Miami hotel followed by nights glued next to a short-wave radio with family and friends listening to news about the warfare in Cuba, along with the sound of bombings in my Santa Clara hometown. These were days of uncertainty about the demise of the Batista regime and the possible triumph of the revolution led by Fidel Castro.

My *Tío* Benjamín (Uncle Eddie Levy) had been in the U.S. for several years and as far as I knew, served as an anchor for my parent's safe migration to the U.S. *Tío* Benjamín was also a victim of the Batista regime since he had received death threats while working in Havana during his youth. Although I was tempted with the idea of returning to Cuba, it was also painful to abandon the pursuit of a college education after a successful year with high grades and accolades from faculty and new friends. Everyone, among family and friends in Miami advised me to return to Westminster College in Utah and keep on working to obtain a college degree.

A Second Call - News about *Mamá-Ramona's* Death

During my third year in the U.S., I visited California with my *novia* Norine and her parents Ralph and Alice Gunn. This was perhaps the beginning of bonding with Norine and her family, when I met Norine's sister Clarice and her adorable baby daughter Renee in Whittier, California. After the trip her parents dropped me off at the home of my friend Leoncio Reyes in Elko, Nevada. "Leon," as he was called, and his grand *familia* enriched my life with the discovery of a side of American culture ignored in those days by teachers in schools. There I was, in the Far West enjoying deliciously hot foods, with family stories about Mexicans living for centuries in the American West. After returning to Westminster College, with a fractured leg, due to an accident in Nevada, I received news about the death of my paternal Grandmother, *Abuela Mamá-Ramona*. My Aunt Évora *(Tía Chicha)* had sent a letter for me through my college mentor and advisor *La Doctora* Myra Yancey with details about the last days of my dear *Mamá-Ramona*. She died on Tuesday, December 15, 1959, at 2:30 am at the home in Santa Clara surrounded by family and friends, but Dr. Yancey kept the news hidden from me until my return in order to avoid spoiling my vacation days with Norine's family and my dear friend Leon Reyes.

This news filled me with sadness for being far away from my adored *familia*. I cried uncontrollably, hiding in the dark, feeling unable to share my pain with my new friends. Although I was not in touch with family left behind, I did not expect the reality of their death. This experience brought awareness of major family losses that were yet to come, along with the suffering resulting from the denial of travel permits to be with loved ones during times of crisis and despair. This personal tragedy brought to mind family histories from my *Abuelo Papá-Viejo* (Salvador Levy). Similar to my story, he left home in Turkey all alone when he was a teenager and later received the tragic news about family loss. His mother also named Sara Levy, died after his departure, and a sister left Turkey and eloped with a Bulgarian soldier. Family disputes resulting from migrations, deaths, and lack of contact, caused divisions and the discovery of unknown relatives within the family. Years after my first return to Cuba I discovered cousins via an unknown Great Aunt who had left Santa Clara after a dispute with my *abuelo Papá-Viejo*. The tragedy of family separation may never heal.

"Where common memory is lacking, where people do not share in the same past, there can be no real community. Where community is to be formed, common memory must be created." Quote by Georges Erasmus, a Canadian Native Aboriginal Leader.

Working on a Travel Permit
Llamados de mi Querida Familia

In my hometown of Santa Clara, near the time of departure from Cuba with my *abuelo Papá-Viejo* on my last goodbye. The US government did not consider him a close relative despite the fact I saw him on a daily basis, and he played a most significant role raising me and providing access to my educational achievements.

Since leaving Cuba in 1957, I wanted to be with my grandfather within a family surrounding during his last days on Earth - before death. My dear *abuelo Papá-Viejo* – Grandpa Salvador Levy - was very close to me as a role model, a mentor and father figure throughout my entire childhood. In 1970, after 13 years far from him and my dear *familia*, I received the sad news about his poor health as imminent signs of the end of life. Several family members had died or were out of sight from my Grandparents *Papá-Viejo & Mamá-Vieja*. Two of their daughters, my aunts Siomara and Alegrina as well as Uncle Rubén had passed away. Other daughters, like my *Mamá* Sara, my *Tía* Elvira and his young son, my *Tío* Benjamín were living outside of Cuba, unable to be with him near his time of death. Several grandchildren, like myself, were no longer living near the grand *familia* in Santa Clara. For me it was a devastating call while I was heavily involved with teaching, serving as advisor, doing research in mathematics, on top of assisting my wife, Norine to care for our precious boys – Danny and Davisito. Here I offer details from a letter by my sister Sarita (Gilda Sara).

"I went to Immigration; they told me that you must head to the Czech Embassy in Washington to ask permission to come to Cuba. They will take a series of data, send it to Cuba, to analyze and decide if you can come. Must ask at the U.S. State Department for permission because Cuba, as well as Albania, China, Korea, and North Vietnam are prohibited countries for traveling from the U.S. If you come without permission, you run the risk of not being able to return. When you arrive in Mexico and leave for Cuba, a big stamp will be placed on your passport stating that you are traveling to Cuba; your passport will be copied and sent to the U.S. Once these requirements are completed, they send permission to Mexico, for acceptance of your ticket."

Permission denied from the U.S. Government as indicated in the following letter:
"It is the policy of the Department to grant passport validation for travel to Cuba for the purpose of visiting relatives when there is evidence that an immediate relative is seriously ill. ...your request to visit your grandfather does not meet the criteria ...on travel to Cuba."

DEPARTMENT OF STATE

Washington, D.C. 20520

In reply refer to:
PT/D - Fernandez, Delvis A.

JUN 8 1970

Mr. Delvis A. Fernandez

Hayward, California 94541

Dear Mr. Fernandez:

I refer to your letter of May 15 regarding your request
for permission to travel to Cuba to visit your ailing
grandfather.

It is the policy of the Department to grant passport
validation for travel to Cuba for the purpose of visiting
relatives when there is evidence that an immediate
relative is seriously ill. The term "immediate relative"
refers to the mother, father, sister, brother or child
of the traveler.

In this respect, I regret to inform you that your request
to visit your grandfather does not meet the criteria for
exceptions to the general restriction on travel to Cuba.

I am sorry a more favorable reply cannot be made.

Sincerely,

Frances G. Knight
Director, Passport Office

305

Parents Trip back to Cuba – *Papá* Ends in a Hospital

My mother asked me to go to Washington, D.C. to request a travel permit to Cuba, through the Czech Embassy. Although I was successful in getting the necessary permits, their trip was very difficult since my *Papá* suffered from chronic illness and was under serious mobility impairments. In a letter later in 1977 *Mamá* described their trip as a complicated journey since my father had to travel in a wheelchair and she had full responsibility for all the details of checking in and paying multiple fees for their many suitcases. Once in Havana they stayed with *Tío* Benjamín in a hotel, where many family members came to visit.

In Santa Clara, my father spent most of his days at a hospital under care of doctors and nurses. They wanted to stay more time in Cuba for recovery as was recommended by family and physicians but were quite worried about losing their service station and repair garage in Miami. Sister Sarita bought around ten medications that were prescribed to *Papá* in Cuba. He was allowed to leave the airport in his wheelchair, but *Mamá* Sara had to stay behind dealing with checking out details; without being able to see family on her side, although my sisters Sarita and Puchy were present with their husbands Arturo and Ramón. They also had a chance to see other family members in Santa Clara, nephews, and nieces as well as Raúl and Guiselda, the attentive godparents of their daughters Puchy and Sarita. *Mamá* Sara was highly impressed with the facilities available in schools and the level of educational achievements reached by her daughters, family, and friends.

First Trip to My Cuban Homeland

During the late 1970s President Jimmy Carter brought hope for the establishment of normal relations between the U.S. and Cuba. Travel restrictions were less severe and I was able to arrange a trip to Cuba through Mexico. This was one of the most emotional, together with joy and sadness times of my life. After seen from the plane the verdant landscape with royal palms, tears flowed from my eyes at the José Martí Airport. But as I walked out of the airport the sight of family waiting for me brought one of the happiest and joyful moments in my life.

Here I am, more than 20 years later between my sisters, **Gilda Sara (Sarita)** to my right and **Guiselda (Puchy)** to my left, with our dear **Aunt Évora (*Tía* Chicha)** in the front.

Sisters Guiselda (Puchy) 4 years-old and Gilda Sara (Sarita) 13 years-old, in 1957 when I left Cuba.

All the family celebrations: graduations, weddings, birthdays, etc. were absent from common memories, but letters and pictures had a tremendous impact on my life. To the left there is a picture of my sisters near the time of departure in 1957, and below there is also a family picture from 1959 of Sarita's 15th year birthday.

Sarita the *Quinceañera*, September 1st, 1959

Between her *Padrino* Raúl Hernández and *Madrina* Guiselda Fernández
- after whom my little sister Puchy was also named Guiselda.
From left to right: cousins Alegrinita and Elbita; *Tías* Chicha and Ana;
Godfather Raúl, Sarita, and Godmother Guiselda; little cousin Olguita
with her mother (our aunt) *Tía* Estrella and her husband (our uncle) *Tío*
Victor Noemí. The children in front from left to right are: Little sister
Puchy, and cousins María Elena (Maruchi), Mayra and Grisell.

At least eight of the people shown in the picture have died. When I first made it back to Cuba in 1977, besides *abuela Mamá-Ramona* and *abuelo Papá-Viejo*, my dear uncle *Tío* Rubén, adored *Tía* Ana (Anatolia), as well as *tías* Siomara and Alegrina, among others had died or were no longer within the family surroundings.

Taking Care of My Parents

Family problems were also present with my parents in Miami during the late 1980s. In Florida far from my home in California, my *Papá* was affected by a chronic illness referred to as gout, that led to having a leg amputated. This new phase of life prevented him from taking care of his garage business, while my *Mamá* was also having problems related to her visual impairments that eventually developed into total blindness. As their only son in the U.S., I felt compelled to help in any way possible. So, around 1988 I manage to get a month leave-time permission from my teaching job and travel from San Francisco to Miami to assist my mother while my father laid in intensive care at a hospital far from their home. Although he appeared to be totally unresponsive, I got near him and asked him to move his fingers if he could hear me. To my surprise he responded to my words by moving his little finger on my arm; eventually the sign on the intensive care monitor indicated that his heart had stopped. This was the first death I experienced in my life. A very sad occasion and a final call for helping my mother to transition to a life without her loving companion at our home in California.

DEATH OF SISTER

Although I had not seen her for more than 20 years, she was present in my life as an exemplary human figure and role model for family and friends as well as an educator and the first woman engineer in Cuba. Due to the travel restriction imposed by U.S. policies, I had not been able to take my mother to Cuba to be with her daughter during her last days on this earth. Dealing with the trauma of death and facing direct damage to my *familia*, I felt a final call to give my passion and energy in calling and demanding changes in U.S. policies that cause pain and suffering to innocent human beings.

Six years after my *Papá's* death, and now taking care of my mother in faraway California, I received the sad news that my sister Sarita was under intensive care at a hospital in Havana. She was deeply affected by a brain aneurysm which she suffered on the road while driving after work back to her home. I was in total shock since my dear sister appeared to be a healthy active person, approaching her 50th year on Earth. My mother and I were in disbelief, and I worked incessantly to get in contact with family and do everything possible to go to Cuba. We managed to establish phone contact with a person in Canada that made it possible to connect people in the U.S. with families in Cuba. For about 10 days we made phone calls, but family and doctors assured us that the end of her life was in sight. My mother Sara, wife Norine and I were in total disbelief when we received the news of her final departure on March 21st, 1994.

My dear sister Sarita was a woman of strength and full commitment to her family and to her country. Although she came to the U.S. in 1959 to be with her parents and had possibilities for joining me at a college in Utah, she went back to the homeland to work during the literacy campaign in hopes of expanding education for all. Here is a summary of her accomplishment as a path opener for women through Latin America, followed with an English translation.

GILDA SARA FERNÁNDEZ LEVY
PRIMERA MUJER
INGENIERA MECÁNICA
EN CUBA

José Roberto Marty Delgado*,
Pedro Pablo Hidalgo Reina**

Existen pocos estudios en Latinoamérica, y particularmente en Cuba, sobre la presencia y contribución de la mujer a la historia de la ingeniería mecánica. La Escuela de Ingeniería Mecánica en Cuba, comenzó sus actividades en la Universidad de Oriente en el año 1949. Gilda Fernández Levy (1/09/1944- 21/03/1994) fue la primera graduada como Ingeniera Mecánica en Cuba y muy pronto se destacó por sus dotes organizativas, su capacidad de trabajo, valores humanos y su aguda inteligencia. Fue profesora a tiempo completo de la Facultad de Ingeniería Mecánica en la Universidad Central "Marta Abreu" de Las Villas, donde desempeñó diversas responsabilidades. En reconocimiento a sus aportes y ejemplar trayectoria, la presente resume la vida y obra de esta singular figura de la ingeniería mecánica en Cuba, como una muestra de los logros y resultados que ha obtenido la participación de las mujeres en la ingeniería, un área de conocimiento históricamente considerada masculina, pero que durante los últimos años ha mostrado una favorable evolución en el número de mujeres que se matriculan en esta carrera.

Proyecto para un capítulo del libro:
Figuras ilustres de la Ingeniería Mecáncia en Iberoamérica II
(*English translation on the following page)

GILDA SARA FERNÁNDEZ LEVY
FIRST WOMAN MECHANICAL ENGINEER IN CUBA

There are few studies in Latin America, and particularly in Cuba, on the presence and contribution of women to the history of mechanical engineering. The School of Mechanical Engineering in Cuba began its activities at the University of Oriente in 1949. Gilda Fernández Levy was the first graduate as a Mechanical Engineer in Cuba and soon stood out for her organizational skills, her ability to work, human values and her acute intelligence. She was a full-time professor at the Faculty of Mechanical Engineering at the Central University "Marta Abreu" of Las Villas Province, where she held various responsibilities. In recognition of her contributions and exemplary career, the book named below, summarizes the life and work of this unique figure of mechanical engineering in Cuba, as a sample of the achievements and results that have gained the participation of women in engineering, an area of knowledge historically considered masculine, but that in recent years has shown a favorable evolution in the number of women who enroll in this career.

Reported by José Roberto Marty Delgado and Pedro Pablo Hidalgo Reina
Project for a chapter of the book:
Illustrious Figures of Mechanical Engineering in Ibero-America II

In Santa Clara, Cuba as children: *Pupy* **(Delvis Alejandro) and sister Sarita c. 1949**

Photo with Sarita at Lake Hanabanilla in Las Villas Province near my departure from Cuba in 1957

In Cuba after more than 20 years with my two sisters: Puchy (Guiselda) and Sarita (Gilda Sara) c. 1990

GREEN LIGHT FOR PLANNING A TRIP

Excerpts from a press release by the Freedom to Travel Campaign December 13th, 1994. Four generations of Cuban American family to challenge the restrictions against travel to Cuba! from 76-year-old great grandmother, 12-month-old baby, family of eight will attend family reunion call, as part of the Freedom to Travel Campaign.

On December 27, more than sixty U.S. citizens who will again risk 10 years in prison and $250,000 in fines as they visit the Island of Cuba for one week. The trip is organized by the freedom to travel campaign which has taken over 500 U.S. citizens to Cuba in the last year, asserting the constitutional right of US citizens to travel. Of the 70 people "ringing in the new year in Havana, eight of them will be the four generations of the Fernández family, including a year-old child and a 76-year-old great grandmother, who will participate in a long-awaited family reunion. "In this holiday season, when the chorus of family values has been ringing out so loud and clear across the country, we think it is cruel and hypocritical of the U.S. government to deny Cuban Americans the right to visit with our family members in Cuba," said Cuban American Delvis Fernández of Hayward, California.

"When we started the Freedom to Travel Campaign, we were trying to expand the categories of citizens who could travel to Cuba. We never imagined we'd one day be fighting for the right of Cuban Americans to visit their families. Many Cuban Americans have responded to this outrageous violation of their human rights by secretly traveling to Cuba through third countries," says coordinator of the freedom to travel campaign Pam Montanaro. "We believe along with the Fernández family that it is important to openly challenge this cruel and unjust law." The Freedom to Travel Campaign is a diverse coalition of over fifty organizations nationwide, including Global Exchange, the National Emergency Civil Liberties Foundation, the Latin American Studies Association, and the Center for International Policy, that work to end all restrictions on the rights of US citizens to travel.

The challenge this December is the 4th trip organized by the campaign. Participants on all of the previous trips have been harassed by the Treasury Department. When the first trip (October 1993) returned from Cuba, 65 of the 175 participants had passports confiscated by customs officials and the government threatened prosecution. In June 1994, one week before the second trip was set to leave, the US Treasury Department froze the $48,000 bank account of the Freedom to Travel Campaign.

311

News about our Family Trip

The Daily Review Hayward, California ▪ Saturday, December 24, 1995
By Carolyn Jones, Staff Writer

Family risks embargo to visit Cuban kin

The restrictions are the last thing on my mind.
The consequences are certainly very serious, but we're willing to take the risk."

Delvis Fernández

A math professor at Chabot College who came to the U.S. from Cuba in 1957

EXTRACTS

Eight family members - ranging from 76-year old Sara Levy-Fernández to her great granddaughter Dariella will join about 60 other people with the San Francisco-based Freedom to Travel Campaign which organizes family trips to Cuba.

The risk lies not in flying to Cuba but in returning to the United States. Previous trips organized by this group have resulted in temporary passport confiscation, questioning, and bank accounts frozen by the U.S. Treasury Department, which enforces the embargo forbidding American residents from spending money in Cuba.

"We respect the right of our country to impose regulations, but I find it intolerable that there are restrictions on mothers seeing their children," said Delvis Fernández. "Some things go beyond politics."

In the 1950s, when he was growing up in Cuba civil war shut down most of the schools and universities. So Delvis Fernández came to the United States to finish his education. After finishing school in Utah, he planned to return to Cuba. But the 1961 Bay of Pigs crisis -- which triggered the U.S. embargo -- interfered with his plans.

The whole family has never been able to meet. Waiting in the central town of Santa Clara are a sister, aunt, four nephews, and two nieces.

"The one thing Aunt Chicha said she wanted more than anything in the world is to have the family together," said Delvis' wife Norine about a recent call from Cuba. "She said, 'I'm 88 years old, so you'd better hurry up and do this'."

In addition to photographs and memories, the Fernández family is bringing boxfulls of medical supplies that are scarce in Cuba.

"I'm not worried at all," said Delvis. "It's a fundamental right to maintain contacts with sisters, mothers, brothers."

The Daily Review

Hayward, California • Friday, January 6, 1996
By Carolyn Jones, Staff Writer

Customs halts family on return from Cuba

U.S. customs agents confiscated a toy windmill, coffee cups and other gifts from a Hayward family returning home from Cuba.

In defiance of U.S. travel restrictions, eight Fernández family members spanning four generations were on their way home Tuesday from visiting their Cuban relatives when U.S. Customs Service officials stopped them at Sky Harbor International Airport in Phoenix. "It was just ridiculous," said Delvis Fernández, a math professor at Chabot College. "The gifts were of no monetary value but great sentimental value." The Fernándezes, spent a week in central Cuba visiting family members they rarely get a chance to see.

Family members, ranging in age from 13 months to 76 years, knew they were risking $250,000 in fines and 10 years imprison by defining the travel restrictions, but planned the trip anyway because they felt the law is unfair.

At a stopover in Phoenix on the return home, the family was taken aside by customs officials, read their Miranda rights, briefly interrogated, and told that any items brought back from Cuba would either be confiscated or destroyed.

Marcia Boardley, a spokeswoman for the U.S. Customs Service, said the Fernándezes and others returning from Cuba were stopped at the airport because "it's illegal to bring back items purchased in Cuba. Actually, Americans are prohibited from traveling to Cuba at all."

Sorting through the luggage of all eight family members, officials took a bottle of rum, a box of cigars, toys and other mementos given by Cuban family members. "Even though the gifts are mostly just little trinkets, they have great meaning to us."

One item was rescued however: a book of Cuban flora and fauna dating from before Fernández's move to the United States in 1957. When customs officials took the book, Fernández wife Norine began to cry.

"The man was moved by that and went to check with his supervisor," said Fernández. When the official returned, Fernández was told he could keep the book. Sissy Wood, who coordinated the trip for the Freedom to Travel Campaign, said the group promotes the Cuban trips to draw public attention to what it considers unfair laws. "We think we should have the right to travel the world especially to Cuba, which is no longer a real threat to the U.S.," she said. "The fact that families are not allowed to see each other is appalling."

ARIZONA REPUBLIC

azcentral.com

A GANNETT COMPANY

Phoenix, Arizona, January 4, 1995

Extract from article by Kelly Pearce

Cuban American clan braves U.S. law to visit homeland

Tears of joy mingled with tears of frustration Tuesday as the Fernández family emerged from the depths of Sky harbor International Airport after a weeklong trip to Cuba. With many eyes, Delvis Fernández, 54, told how he had brought gifts of car brakes and stove burners to his relatives.

His Cuban relatives had gifts for the family as well. Among them were a set of coffee cups Sara Fernández's daughter gave her as a keepsake to mark their precious reunion, which could be their last. The cups are now the property of the U.S. customs service.

The Trading with the Enemy Act prohibits U.S. citizens from bringing items from communist Cuba. Articles from such embargoed countries are confiscated. "These are things that cost (their relatives) upward of a month's salary," said David Fernández, 31. "They have no monetary value but so much sentimental value.

Delayed by Customs, the Fernándezes missed their 7:30 PM flight from Phoenix to San Francisco. Clarice Black, Delvis Fernández's sister-in-law couldn't have been happier, however. The clan was expected to spend the night at her Phoenix home, where she was sure to pump them for details about the visit. It was a trip that Delvis Fernández will never forget. "The emotion is so intense," he said. His son, Dan Fernández, 29, said he journeyed to Cuba when he was 15. "I went there when I wasn't nearly the man I am now," he said. "It's just a simple right to see your family. Life is too short."

During their recent trip they had to travel first to Mexico City and then catch a flight to Cuba. The Fernándezes said they were questioned for almost two hours about what they had done in the country and where they had traveled. It was a frustrating conclusion to an emotional trip. But it won't be the bureaucracy the clan will remember. "We have an 88-year-old aunt who wanted more than anything to see her whole family, said Norine Fernández, Delvis' wife

San Jose Mercury News

Chabot prof quits quiet life to buck U.S.-Cuba impasse

Extract from article bY T. T. NHU Mercury News Staff Writer

Since 1962 families like the Fernández-Levy's have been separated by a U.S. foreign policy. In April 1994, Fernández's sister Sarita suffered an aneurysm. Fernández and his 78-year-old mother, Sara, desperately sought permission to travel to Cuba. They appealed to their congressional representative, the State Department, the Red Cross and other humanitarian agencies. By the time they got to Cuba, his sister was dead.

Monday, January 6, 1997 • SAN JOSE MERCURY

Delvis Fernández Levy next month will move to Washington, D.C., as director of the Cuban American Alliance Education Fund, working to restore harmonious Cuba-U.S. relations

Even though travel was officially banned for Cuban Americans, the Fernández-Levy family decided it was time to go to Cuba. In December 1995, four generations of the family set off for Cuba.

Fernández said he's received a great deal of tacit support among Cuban Americans despite their sometimes-hostile public demeanor.

"I haven't met a single Cuban, even during a debate, who disagrees with the idea of family reconciliation and assistance."

"As Cubans, we are victims of the Cold War and have been under relentless attack."

"I can't see how a small island such as Cuba can be a threat to the U.S. national security. It is up to us Cuban Americans and our families to break those barriers."

315

A FINAL CALL TO ACTION

Despite years of separation from our Homeland -- our culture, family, and friends – "cubanness" or a sense of Cuban identity continues to be an integral part of our very being and soul. I came to the United States nearly 50 years ago, one of less than a dozen graduates from the only public high school in the central capital city of Las Villas province. I wrote a bus for five days and nights from Key West Florida to Salt Lake City Utah, dreaming of becoming an engineer for a quick return to a job and secure livelihood in my beloved island. Twenty-two years later I finally returned filled with emotion to sights and sounds of the past and in hopes of rekindling the love of family and friends who nurtured me into the person I am today. But the dream soon gave way to the reality of bygone friends, children, who are now adults, and grandparents who no longer live.

Like so many Cubans in the United States, I thought we would be free to travel to our Homeland within a matter of days. It was mere illusion and a denial of a reality we could not comprehend. For years we waited, caught in a time warp, victims of government policies that later drove us into a frenzy of expectations about the imminent demise of the Cuban Revolution.

The time has come for a reality check on behalf of our children and those who follow us, leave pain behind, heal the wounds and work for a better future. Respectful engagement is the only way to achieve this goal.

For over 20 years I had not seen my family in Cuba – *La Gran familia* that gave me love, daily care, and nurtured me into the person I am today. Somehow, I managed to visit my hometown of Santa Clara in the late 1970s but by then my grandparents and most of my dear aunts and uncles had passed away. It was one of the saddest and most emotional journeys of my life.

In 1994, The California Fernández Team on a trip of defiance joins 4 generations of *Familia* in Santa Clara. Cuba

I was filled with meaningful work and care with my new *familia* in California, immersed in math teaching along with advocacy for expanding education for disenfranchised minorities. Although expected changes came my way with the death of my *Papá* Delvis Rafael and caring for my mother Sara, we were deeply affected by the sudden death of my sister *Sarita* (Gilda Sara) on March 21st, 1994.

My mother and I in California managed to communicate with the *familia* in Cuba through phone contacts in Canada. During Sarita's final days, we desperately sought permission to travel to Cuba, appealing to congressional representatives, the State Department, the Red Cross and other humanitarian agencies. For immediate family visits we were given only a legal right to travel once a year.

The death of my sister Sarita was the final call to defy cruel laws, by four generation of my dear *familia*. My California Fernández family risked $250,000 in fines per person and 10 years in prison. This gave rise to joining other Cuban Americans to form an organization to advocate for changes in U.S. laws that create collateral damage on innocent people in both Cuba and the United States.

Here was a call years later after forming an organization – **The Cuban American Alliance** - with chapters throughout the United States back in 1995, moving to New Jersey and Washington, D.C., as well as working from California; reaching out to people throughout the U.S. as well as to major international groups in New York City; Geneva, Switzerland; and Brussels, Belgium.

PART IV

Advocacy and Passion
Search for Justice and Human Rights

26

THE CUBAN AMERICAN ALLIANCE

In 1994 after the death of my dear Sister *Sarita* I felt a call to bring awareness to the pain and suffering of Americans due to laws that separate families. My first concerns were about a place to center an organization for outreach to political leaders and the public at large. However, I soon realize that our search for justice went beyond a particular region and affected all of humanity.

The trip of defiance provided a place to start in San Francisco, California through Global Exchange, an organization dedicated to promoting justice and served as the main anchor for the Freedom to Travel Campaign. After a month of work trying to decide where to set our base, I managed to meet in Washington D.C. with a group of Cuban Americans from various parts of the U.S. This gave a start to a network of Cuban Americans to educate the public at large on issues related to hardships resulting from current United States-Cuba relations. The Alliance was formed as a vehicle for the development of mutually beneficial engagements which promote understanding and human compassion. It was formally named "Cuban American Alliance Education Fund," known as CAAEF and chartered as a (501c3) non-profit organization, working outside ideological constraints, in compliance with U.S. law, and respectful of Cuba's sovereignty and independence. CAAEF calls for a reassessment of U.S. policies that may be outside the best interests of the American people and cause undue harm to Cubans and Americans. Among the work of CAAEF we include the following activities:

Humanitarian Travel through *La Familia* project establishes direct links of support and friendship with the Cuban Association for the Disabled.

Relief Efforts carried out with other national-based organizations to assist victims of natural disasters in Cuba.

Social Work Projects to compare practice and efforts to meet human basic needs and enhance human well-being.

U.S.-Cuba Sister-City Ties to promote and facilitate people-to-people engagements of mutual benefit.

Cultural Exchanges, art exhibits, music, dance, cinema, and festival events to promote Cuban culture and raise funds for humanitarian projects.

Forums and Debates at schools and universities, the National Press Club, and U.S. and foreign conference sites.

Press Outreach, Op-Ed pieces, radio and newspaper interviews through U.S. and foreign media outlets.

Congressional Visits and distribution of educational material regarding perspectives of Cuban Americans on U.S.-Cuba Relations.

Joint Action and Advocacy Work with business, religious, human rights, cultural, and humanitarian groups to monitor legislation that may adversely impact on the well-being of both Cubans and Americans.

Busiest Times of My Life

With my retirement as a full-time math faculty member at Chabot College, I started going to various places in the United States in search of learning and engaging with Cuban Americans to form an organization to bring awareness about our traumas and suffering due to the unfriendly relations between our two countries: The Republic of Cuba and The United States of America.

The word "Alliance" as a primary term developed into the Cuban American National Alliance (CANA) and then transitioning into the Cuban American Alliance Education Fund, Inc. (CAAEF) as a nonprofit (501-c3) organization in 1995. Along with the primary efforts to meet and involve Cuban Americans throughout the U.S. came multiple meetings with political leaders in Congress and the White House. Also, priority was given to debates with well-established organizations in the U.S., primarily in Florida and New Jersey, plus interviews, press outreach in order to bring a voice of strength and awareness to our emerging Alliance.

Besides visiting people in many cities of the U.S., journeys to other parts of the world were at the forefront of our efforts with participation at the European Parliament in Brussels, Belgium and at The United Nations Commission for Human Rights in Geneva, Switzerland. In Mexico, Cuba, Canada, Europe, and the U.S, participation in major gatherings were at the forefront of organizing the Cuban American Alliance. Sharing testimonials about our lives was as a way to educate and bring awareness to the suffering caused by the lack of normal relations between Cuba and the U.S. Reaching out to political leaders face-to-face, writing letters to the press, and meeting with people on all sides of the political spectrum, was part of the struggle to promote changes on American policies towards our citizens and people of our beloved Cuban nation.

East Bay Professor Targets Cuba Policy

Excerpts from an article in the San Francisco Examiner Newspaper in California.
By Wendy Koch, Examiner Washington Bureau, Saturday, July 22, 1995

WASHINGTON - Delvis Fernández, an East Bay math professor, is challenging U.S. policy toward his native land, Cuba.

He met with senior White House aides Richard Nuccio and Morton Halperin this week to discuss goals of his new nonpartisan group, the Cuban American National Alliance

"They are willing to listen -- and to me, that's encouraging," Fernández said. "They're looking for voices, pressure, out there in the Cuban American community that says current policy isn't right."

Most Cuban American groups favor maintaining Cuba's pariah status. But Fernández's new Alliance wants the United States to end its 34-year-old trade embargo against Cuba, begin a dialogue with Fidel Castro's government and lift its year-old ban on Americans who want to travel there. Nuccio, the White House's Cuba coordinator, said the Clinton administration still supported the trade embargo and the travel ban, but welcomed the different points of view. "Basically, we have an open-door policy with the Cuban American exile community," he said.

Fernández's Alliance, which has at least 150 members nationwide, is a diverse group – doctors, lawyers, blue-collar workers, many of whom live outside Miami, the base for most Cuban American groups. It is just one of the Cuban American groups formed in recent years to push for changes in U.S. policy.

The more moderate groups are trying to counter the power exerted by the Cuban American National Foundation, a conservative Miami-based group that wants to tighten the economic noose around Cuba to isolate Castro. The Foundation, led by Jorge Mas Canosa, opposed the White House's May decision to return to Cuba refugees fleeing by sea.

Fernández, 55, a Cuban-born U.S. citizen, has been a professor at Chabot College in Hayward since 1966. He arrived alone in the United States in 1957, washing dishes to put himself through college. He married an American woman, earned a doctorate in mathematics from UC Berkeley and raised two sons.

Fernández pushes forward, he says, because he believes greater contact with Cuba is the best way to help relatives there. He has a sister, an aunt, nieces and nephews still in Cuba. "I've been a good citizen to the United States and my future is here," he said. "But there's a part of me that's in Cuba."

Major Move to New Jersey

After the fall quarter of 1995, I arranged for only one semester of teaching, so in January 1996, almost a year after the establishment of CAAEF, I joined other activists in choosing New Jersey/New York as a good area for reaching out to the press and political leaders in the U.S. This area has the second largest population of Cubans after the state of Florida. It was quite a challenge for me, to leave my adored family and wonderful teaching job in California, but I found a great friend, Frank Scofi, who along with his wife Marina and their adorable baby Alex, allowed me to stay at their home, while the Alliance office got established. Norine came to help me look for a place to live and find a space to set up CAAEF office. We missed our adorable little Dariella terribly but reading a story every night to Alex, who was exactly the same age, helped and gave us pleasure after each insane day of work in the dead of winter with snow knee deep. Somehow everything fell into place and my tiny studio apartment was right at the base of the George Washington Bridge in Fort Lee, which provided an interesting walk into New York on an occasional Sunday afternoon. The office too was in Fort Lee, so driving was not a problem except when there was snow. Within weeks I was able to open the office and start making connections with the large Cuban population. Frank was an incredibly dedicated worker who helped tirelessly, and Raymundo del Toro was the Cuban American who filled me with education about the community and how to reach out to the press and political leaders.

My New Jersey office with pictures on the wall of our family trip of defiance.
<<Frank Scofi with his son Alex and Delvis

RESPONSES IN DEBATE

Encounter with leaders of organizations that included the Cuban American National Foundation and the 30th of November Movement came through an interview sponsored by The Jersey Journal on Saturday March 16,1996. There I was enclosed in a room with four other *Cubanos* entrapped in disagreements through questions by a civil and polite journalist.

Leaders agree on purpose, but not on method.
Article by Journal staff writer Miri Ascarelli
Where do they stand?

The Jersey Journal recently asked 4 local Cuban leaders where they stand on four controversial positions involving the island nation serious here are my answers not in line with the other 3 debaters.

▪ TRAVEL RESTRICTIONS
President Clinton canceled all charter flights from Miami to Havana following the February 24 downing of two Brothers to the Rescue planes by Cuban fighter jets. Prior to that, visits were limited to one per year for a sick or dying relative.

Delvis Fernández, executive director of the East Coast office of the Cuban American Alliance: Opposes; says restrictions hurt families and don't work; notes thousands of Cuban Americans circumvent rules by flying through third countries.

▪ U.S. NAVAL BLOCKADE OF CUBA
Fernández: Opposes; it's an act of war that would isolate Cuba and add to the suffering; would infringe on sovereignty of Cuban people.

▪HELMS-BURTON LAW
Signed into law Tuesday, the measure allows American citizens to sue foreign investors who are using property that was expropriated by the Castro regime.

Fernández: Opposes; argues provisions will jeopardize the legitimate claims of American companies that have been already filed with the Foreign Claims Settlement Commission; creates new precedent not given any other immigrant group.

▪EMBARGO
Fernández: Opposes; says embargo hasn't worked; U.S. has no international support.

I was the only one that supported the end of travel restrictions to Cuba. President Clinton had canceled all charter flights to Cuba following the downing of the two Brothers to the Rescue planes on February 24th, prior to that, Cuban Americans were limited to one visit per year to visit sick or dying relatives. The old restrictions were already too stringent because they prevent Cuban Americans from visiting and caring for their families in Cuba. In addition, I claimed that they do not work since thousands of Cuban Americans circumvent them by flying to Cuba through third countries.

This meeting was extremely disturbing for me, since I was all alone without any friend nearby, and I had never met the organizers or been in that area, but more importantly, distressed since I was all alone in presenting my opinions. Once the meeting had ended, a guard stood by me and waited for everyone to leave the room. He appeared to be worried and escorted me to the garage where my car had been parked. The guard stopped me from getting in the car and checked all around and under the car to make sure there were no explosive devices. Despite the fact that there were intense disagreements, I did feel that everyone was in favor of continuing support for family reunification. After that incident and given a green light by the friendly guard, I drove straight to Frank's house in Teaneck, knowing that a big hug from Alex was what I needed, and a nice glass of red wine could not hurt. As usual, however, Frank wasted no time to immediately scribble off a piece for the next day's paper emphasizing the positives that had come out of that meeting. Since my days in English classes back at Westminster College, I have always found that writing does not come easily. I would labor for hours over a short op-ed piece, making sure it expressed my thoughts exactly and precisely. Frank, on the other hand, could scratch out a brilliant statement anywhere and everywhere in just a free moment, that more often than not, would make it into print the next day. I always admired and so greatly appreciated his skills and help during those early, difficult days of the Alliance.

Standing by the George Washington Bridge connecting Fort Lee, NJ with New York City. Our first CAAEF office was within walking distance for roaming into Manhattan.

PRECURSORS OF CAAEF

The emerging organizations working for changes in US policy toward Cuba were growing around states like New Jersey, New York, California, and Washington, D.C. According to a careful research done by Dr. Indira Rampersad, for her dissertation at the University of Florida, the current organizations during early years of the new millennium numbered around 100 and could be divided into three categories.

1. Organizations run by international activists which do not have Cuba as a special project but have taken up the Cuban cause. These include the American Civil Liberties Union, Human Rights Watch, Madre (an international human rights organization), Global Exchange, Oxfam America and faith-based groups like the World Council of Churches, Church World Service, the United States Conference of Catholic Bishops and the Episcopal Church.

2. Organizations dealing with other Latin American/Caribbean issues but dealing with specific Cuba projects. These include the Center for International Policy (CIP), the Washington Office on Latin America (WOLA), the Latin American Working Group (LAWG), the World Policy Institute and the Lexington Institute.

3. Organizations concerned only with U.S. Cuba policy such as Venceremos Brigade, the Center for Cuban Studies, the Emergency Coalition to Defend Education Travel (ECDET), Pastors for Peace, the Alliance for Responsible Cuba Policy, U.S. Women and Cuba Collaboration; and the business interests including USA Engage and the U.S.-Cuba Trade Association. It also includes a host of moderate Cuban American organization. The most prominent are the Cuban Committee for Democracy, Cambio Cubano, the Emergency Network of Cuban American Scholars and Artists (ENCASA), the Cuban American Alliance Education Fund (CAAEF), the Cuba Study Group, and the Cuban American Commission for Family Rights. Among this third group there were organizations based in Washington, D.C. like the Center for Cuban Studies, the Washington Office on Latin America, the Latin American Working Group, along with groups advocating for business and travel/education connections with Cuba like Emergency Coalition to Defend Education Travel, the business coalitions, USA Engage and the U.S.-Cuba Trade Association and the New York based Center for Cuban Studies.

The Primarily based Cuban American organizations included

The Cuban Committee for Democracy

The Cuban American Alliance Education Fund

And others like Puentes Cubanos, the Cuba Study Group, the Emergency Network of Cuban American Scholars and Artists, and the Cuban American Commission for Family Rights.

Introduction Summary for CAAEF

There are a number of policy-issues being addressed by the Cuban American Alliance Education Fund, Inc. (CAAEF or the Alliance) in its pursuit for constructive engagements and a peaceful resolution to the differendum between the United States of America and the Republic of Cuba. Although problems and crises continue to arise within the dynamics of U.S.-Cuban affairs, we have set utmost priority to the education of policymakers on the following issues:

- The Right of Cuban Americans to Travel to Cuba
- Reunification and Reconciliation of Families Restrictions on Family Assistance
- Prohibition of Commerce in Food Staples
- Licensing Requirements for Medical Trade
- Establishment of Forums for Interaction and Dialogue

As a general strategy, the Alliance seeks common points of advocacy with Cuban American organizations and individuals to promote changes in current United States policy toward Cuba. We strive for the formation of action-based coalitions with religious, labor, humanitarian, and business associations to raise public awareness to the effects of U.S.-Cuba policies that are detrimental to the welfare of Cubans and Americans.

As vehicles to expand links with Cuban Americans nationwide, we have established a humanitarian assistance program, *La Gran Familia,* for disabled children in Cuba; a newsletter, *La Alborada;* and a WebPage (www.cubamer.com). Our offices serve as bases for press outreach and for the development of legislative strategies to educate policy makers at the local, state, and national levels on issues that directly impact on the lives of Cuban Americans and their families.

Policy-Issues Being Addressed

THE RIGHT OF CUBAN AMERICANS TO TRAVEL TO CUBA

Under United States government regulations pertaining to the Cuban trade embargo, travel to Cuba by Cuban Americans is severely restricted. American citizens or residents with close family members on the island are granted a general travel license to Cuba only once over a twelve-month period for cases involving extreme hardship, such as terminal illness or severe medical emergency. For a second visit to Cuba within a twelve-month period, U.S. citizens or residents must obtain a license from the Office of Foreign Assets Control (OFAC), to see a terminally ill close family member living in Cuba. These travel licenses may be denied by OFAC without documentation from Cuba of a terminal illness or extreme humanitarian emergency. Criminal penalties for violating the regulations which are enforced by OFAC, range up to 10 years in prison,

$1,000,000 in corporate, $250,000 in individual fines, and $50,000 in individual civil penalties.

REUNIFICATION AND RECONCILIATION OF FAMILIES

Normal family visits -- family gatherings of any kind among Cubans and Cuban Americans -are not authorized by current presidential decree. And furthermore, under the Helms-Burton Act of 1996 (L1BERTAD), the President is urged not to grant a general travel license to Cuba until certain conditions are met by the Cuban government. Despite the restrictions, tens of thousands of Cuban Americans, at the risk of criminal prosecution, circumvent the travel restrictions through third countries in order to spend time and provide assistance to their relatives in Cuba.

RESTRICTIONS ON FAMILY ASSISTANCE

Under current U.S. law, Cuban Americans may only send $300 per quarter to their family in Cuba. This limitation on family assistance discriminates against Cubans and is not applied to any other U.S. minority group.

In order to send medicines or medical supplies to a seriously ill family member, a person must obtain an export license, rely on someone travelling to Cuba, or pay a minimum of $10 per pound to an agency approved by the U.S. Department of Commerce. While someone waits for approval or a carrier to send medical assistance to a dying relative, the approval may be denied, or the medicines arrive after the relative's death.

PROHIBITION OF COMMERCE IN FOOD STAPLES

Cuba is the only country prohibited from purchasing food from U.S. markets. This situation is further exacerbated by the Cuban Democracy Act of 1992 (CDA) which forbids ships that dock in Cuban ports from docking in U.S. ports for six months, thus restricting the delivery of life sustaining food and basic medical supplies to people living in Cuba.

LICENSING REQUIREMENTS FOR MEDICAL TRADE

Restrictions imposed by the CDA also limit Cubans' access to medicine, medical equipment, spare parts for medical equipment, and raw material for the manufacture of rehabilitation equipment.

ESTABLISHMENT OF FORUMS FOR INTERACTION AND DIALOGUE

Since 1959 an adversarial relationship has existed between the Republic of Cuba and the United States of America. Tensions and hostilities between the two countries have left deep emotional wounds among Cubans on both sides of the Florida Straits. This enmity continues to exist despite the end of the Cold War and the establishment of diplomatic relations with Vietnam -- a former war adversary -- and the granting of "Most Favored Nation" status to the People's Republic of China.

As a precursor to the normalization of relations between our two countries, we believe it is imperative to begin people-to-people and government-to-government dialogue and interactions. CAAEF proposes that these engagements be conducted within a framework of full compliance with U.S. law and utmost respect for the independence and sovereignty of the Republic of Cuba.

Approach to the Problem and Specific Goals

Objective: To form coalitions with existing organizations to advocate for family reunification and to educate legislators on issues that have a negative impact on the welfare of Cuban Americans and Cubans on the island.

Specific Goals: Build **support nationwide.** Continue to expand a national data bank to identify individual Cuban Americans and organizations working with Cuba related issues to seek common points of advocacy.

Operate a national outreach office in Washington, D.C. Expand CAAEF chapters in California, Florida, and Texas. Set up contacts with Cuban Americans to **disseminate information** about issues that impact on their lives and the well-being of their families. **Expand coalition** to promote changes in U.S. policy toward Cuba, and **execute a humanitarian assistance program,** *La Gran Familia,* that ties Cuban American families and disabled children in Cuba.

Form **coalitions** with other groups and individuals to advocate for the right of Cuban Americans to reunite and work toward reconciliation with Cubans on the island.

Target the following spheres of influence to disseminate advocacy tools in an effort to change U.S.-Cuba policy:

The U.S. Nationwide. Assist Cuban Americans in arranging meetings with their families in Cuba within a framework of U.S. and Cuban Law. Assist in forming discussion groups nationwide to combat the negative effects of U.S.-Cuba policy on Cuban Americans and their families. Assist other organizations in the execution of action plans to advocate for changes in U.S. law that negatively impact on Cuban Americans and their families.

New Jersey/New York. Expand a base of support in the Cuban American communities of New Jersey and New York to reach out to the press and legislators in areas of heavy Cuban American concentration, e.g., Union City and Elizabeth, NJ.

Florida. Put into effect strategies to reach out to Cuban Americans through action-based coalitions with existing organizations in South Florida. Establish a CAAEF chapter to disseminate information and strengthen cultural ties with other minority communities and immigrants from the Caribbean region.

California. Continue to set up forums on U.S.-Cuba relations and develop "Sister City" ties between communities in Cuba and in the U.S. In particular, strengthen the ties between Oakland, CA and Santiago de Cuba. Explore the development of ties between Santa Maria, CA and a city in Oriente, Cuba. Continue to forge cooperation with Cuban American organizations in the Los Angeles and San Francisco Bay Area to strengthen cultural and family ties.

Washington, D.C. Area (Virginia, Maryland, Delaware). Work with existing groups and individuals to develop an on-going presence in Congress, the State Department, and the White House through education and distribution of information to legislators and government officials. Coordinate and facilitate contacts between Cuban Americans and lawmakers in Washington, D.C. to:

Work for lifting the U.S. ban on the sale of food staples to Cuba: rice, wheat, beans, etc.

Urge a relaxation of the licensing requirements for trade in medicine, medical equipment, spare parts for existing medical equipment, and raw materials for building rehabilitation equipment for the disabled and chronically ill in Cuba.

Educate the general public on the regulations in U.S.-Cuba policy that affect the normal development of family life, such as, travel and remittances restrictions, as well as the issuance of travel permits for Cubans to visit family members in the United States.

Heighten public awareness to the negative effects of current U.S.-Cuba policy on the lives of ordinary Cuban citizens and Cuban Americans, such as, lack of medicine for the chronically ill and the cumbersome licensing requirements for the delivery of humanitarian assistance to Cuba.

Dispel the myth that Cuban Americans support current restrictions on family assistance and travel to Cuba. Invite members of Congress and their aides to conferences and fact-finding visits to Cuba.

Raise public awareness about the effects of U.S.-Cuba policy on Cuban Americans through presentations in churches, schools, city councils, neighborhood meetings, and press outreach.

Facilitate media access for Cuban Americans on issues that affect their daily lives through letters to the editor, Op-Ed articles, and radio, newspaper, and television interviews.

Publish a quarterly newsletter for distribution with-up-to-date government regulatory and legislative activity on issues of concern to Cuban Americans such as: contacts between families; the delivery of food, medicine, and medical equipment; family remittances; humanitarian assistance; travel regulations; legislation updates; travel information; news items; and information about *La Gran Familia* project with The Cuban Association for the Physically Limited (ACLIFIM).

Upkeep CAAEF's web site: www.cubamer.org with news, information about upcoming events, humanitarian assistance projects, travel information, legislative updates and relevant information to people interested in U.S.-Cuba affairs.

Operations and Support for Carrying Out the Program

Operations will be directed by Delvis Fernández Levy in collaboration with the directors of the following organizations: Amerindia, Inc., the Cuban American Women of the United States, *Cubanos Mano-a-Mano,* and the Central Coast and Bay Area Alliance Chapters, in California; the *Alianza de Trabajadores Cubanos (ATC),* the Cuban Committee for Democracy, the Cuban American Defense League, the Caribbean Children Foundation, and *Cambio Cuban,* in Florida; Participative Democracy and the Alliance Advisory Council of Maryland; *TPC-Todo por Cuba* in Alabama; *JIRIBILLA* Cultural Association, *Cubanos Contra el Bloqueo,* and *Fundación Amistad* in NY; the Cuban American Committee for Peace in New Jersey; the Latin America Studies Project of DePaul University in Chicago; and the Cuban Association for the Disabled (ACLIFIM) in Cuba.

We seek coordination of efforts from the following organizations: ALAMAR Associates, the Center for International Policy, the Latin America Working Group, the National Security Archive, OXFAM-America, and the Washington Office on Latin America in Washington, D.C.; Global Links of Pittsburgh; Catholic Relief Services and the Howard County Friends of Central America and the Caribbean in Maryland; Global Exchange, the Association for Free Trade with Cuba, the Political Science Department of Chabot College, the Office of the Americas, and Operation U.S.A. in California; the Cuban Research Institute of Florida International University in Florida; the U.S. Cuba Trade and Economic Council, Inc., Disarm, and the U.S.+Cuba Medical Information Project in New York.

• Directors

DELVIS FERNÁNDEZ LEVY, PH.D. is a Cuban American educator who is fluent in both English and Spanish. He is the founder and president of the Cuban American Alliance Education Fund, Inc. He has organized and led trips to Cuba. He organized forums on U.S.-Cuba policy in several cities of California and most recently organized a conference in Congress to discuss religious, cultural and humanitarian aspects of life in Cuba. He has been a speaker at several conferences in California, New York, New Jersey and Washington, D.C. He has led delegations of Cuban Americans to meetings with representatives and officials of the U.S. Congress, the State Department, the Pentagon, and the White House. He obtained licenses for CAAEF from the U.S. Department of Commerce for travel to Cuba and for sending humanitarian assistance to disabled children. He is the publisher and editor of CAAEF's *La Alborada* and the web site www.cubarner.org. He has had letters, Op-Ed articles, and interviews published in major national newspapers. He has had interviews aired by several TV and Radio stations locally and nationwide in Cuba and in the United States. He has been featured in two movies and documentaries about the Cuban American community. He has been a speaker and moderator at press conferences in Washington and California.

Dr. Fernández Levy came from Cuba in 1957 to do undergraduate work at Westminster College in Salt Lake City, Utah, from which he graduated in 1961, and was married the same year. He received a master's degree from the University of Miami in 1963, and a Ph.D. in Mathematics from the University of California, Berkely in 1974. He retired from teaching in 1998 after having taught in the California University and College system for 35 years.

NORINE GUNN FERNANDEZ is a graphic artist, photographer, and general office organizer. She owned and ran two businesses for eleven years where she managed employees as well as all operations in marketing and advertising, inventory: and ordering, computer data input, general secretarial work, and all work related to accounting and tax records. She studied at Westminster College in Salt Lake City, Utah; the University of the Pacific in Stockton, California; and received a secondary teaching credential from California State University in Hayward,

California. Norine was among the first group of women who traveled to Cuba during President Carter's administration. This past spring, she helped to organize a trip by college students and teachers to Cuba. On a previous occasion, in 1994, she organized the first family trip of defiance to Cuba by eight members of her family to assert their right to visit with their Cuban relatives. She assists in editing, artwork, and layout for the CAAEF newsletter, *La Alborada*. Prior to owning a business, she had experience in all phases of office work: secretarial, computer data input, typing, receptionist, phone operator, and filing clerk.

Board of Directors

Luly Alcebo-Duke
Fundación Amistad, President
New York City, NY

Hugo Cancio
Director of Family Services and Charters
Miami, FL

Regino Diaz
Owner of Graphics Services Unlimited
Houston, TX

Delvis Fernández Levy, PhD
CAAEF President
Washington; D.C. and Hayward, CA

Anamaria Goicochea-Balbona, PhD
Department of Social Work
University of Maryland
Columbia, MD

Dr. Alberto Jones, DVM
Ortho Medical Waste Management,
Caribbean Children Foundation President
Palm Coast, FL

Reverend Gustavo Vinajeras
Vicar of Saint Paul Lutheran Church,
Union City, NJ

Advisory Committee

Daniel Aguirre
TPC -Todo Por Cuba
Ashland, AL

Sandra Alfonso
President of the Louisiana, Hispanic American Council
Baton Rouge, LA

Xiomara Almaguer-Levy
President Cuban American Defense League Miami, FL

Tania Álvarez Guerra, Esq
San Francisco, CA

Abelardo Arteaga
Cuba Vive
Tampa, FL

Barbara Curbelo-Cusack
Miami, FL

Jose Estevez, Esq.
Pres. Amerindia, Inc.
Upland, CA

Francisco Aruca
Marazul Charter, Inc., Miami, FL

Dagmaris Cabezas
Cuban American Research & Ed. Fund
Tobyhanna, PA

Lorenzo Cañizares
Cuban Committee for Democracy
Trenton, NJ

David Cibrian, Esq
Jenkins & Gilchrist
San Antonio, TX

Enrique Conill
CAAEF Maryland Advisory Council,
Columbia, MD

Maria I. Marquez
CAAEF Bay Area Chapter
Oakland, CA

Prof. Felix Masud-Piloto

Freddy Fajardo
Director Cubanos Mano a Mano
Oakland, CA
Margarita Fazzolari
Pres. Jiribilla Cultural Association
New. York, NY
Iris Fernández
Executive Director Cubanos Contra el Bloqueo
New York, NY
David I. Fernández
CAAEF Central Coast Chapter
San Luis Obispo, CA
Dr. Pedro Ferreira
Wilmington, DE
Prof. Maricela Fleites-Lear
University of Peuget Sound
Tacoma, WA
Ricardo A. González
Madison, WI,
Ruben Honik, Esq.
Jewish Solidarity Pennsylvania Chapter
Philadelphia, PA
Eddie Levy
Founder of Jewish Solidarity
Miami, FL
Prof. Nelson Valdes
Latin America Data Bank
University of New Mexico,
Albuquerque, NM
Luis Seguí
Pres. CAAEF Central Coast Chapter
Santa Maria, CA

Center for Latino Research, DePaul
University, Chicago, IL
Dr. Concha Mendoza
Dir. of Geriatrics
Long Island College Hospital
New York, NY
Carlos Molina
Woodland Hills, CA
Dr. Guillermo Pérez-Mesa, M.D
New York, NY
Joe Perez
Gentle Home Healthcare
Culver City, CA
Berta Porro
Democracia Participativa
Olney, MD
Irene M. Recio, Esq.
Magda Montiel Davis Law Offices
Springfield, VA
Luis E. Rumbaut
Washington, D.C.
Carmen Rumbaut
Intercambio Cultural Cuba/USA
San Antonio, TX
Leslie Salgado
Pres. Howard County Friends of Central
America and the Caribbean
Columbia, MD
Dr. Milton Sánchez-Parodi, M.D
Cambio Cubano
Poland, OH

27

The Alliance in Action

La Alianza en Acción

CAAEF organized and set up appointments in the State Department, the White House and Congress for Cuban Americans to discuss specific impacts of U.S. impediments to family travel, remittances, and general restrictions on humanitarian trade, as well as obstacles affecting Cuban American businesspeople representing major travel agencies.

Letters to the Press

When I moved to New Jersey, I chose the opinion sections of newspapers as a way to link with Cubans and people in general throughout the U.S. Lessons were hard to learn in "The Land of the Free and the Home of the Brave."

In order to get letters published in major newspapers I had to abandon my trainings as a mathematician who searched for truths and opined through logical arguments and conclusions based on axioms and facts. For example, when referred to the policies of the U.S. or the naming of government leaders, I had to abide by common words used by the American ruling class in newspapers and government discussions:

1. We have a "democracy" whose leaders are elected by a minority of citizens who vote; in addition to a population of voiceless residents considered "illegal" that surpasses the populations of most Latin American countries.
2. "Blockade" must be referred to as an "embargo," and "leaders" of countries with different systems are called "dictators" of their "regimes."

Access to the press required education outside schools and teachings, mainly through personal face-to-face contacts with editors, publishers, and newspaper staff writers. But my New Jersey friends, Frank Scofi and Raymundo del Toro would take my written messages and replace taboo words with terms fully accepted by the "American free press" to insure publication. My letters to the editor and op-ed pieces

336

achieved the highest levels of publication in major newspapers: from the New York Times to The Star Ledger, The Jersey Journal, *El Nuevo Hudson*, *Diario La Prensa*, The Daily Review, *El Nuevo Herald*, USA Today, and other newspapers from major U.S. cities.

Through The maze, Through the tears, A glimpse of Cuba

By DELVIS FERNÁNDEZ LEVY

The serenity of a quiet Sunday afternoon is suddenly broken by the persistent ringing of a phone I try to avoid.

Hello.

Cuba calling…Accept the charges?

Of course!

Brother. *Tía* is not well... Sure would be nice if you could come, but for now, I guess it's impossible.

Two days later, hours before leaving for Havana, I run through the house opening drawers looking for things to take to *la familia en* Cuba - toilet paper, old shirt, anything I can stuff into a suitcase before my dash to the airport. On the way there, I must stop at the Fed-Ex office for my permit to enter Cuba. Yes! I'm going home ...for the visit I'm allowed once every 12 months to see a close relative in circumstances of extreme humanitarian need. Hours later, in Mexico City, I'm taking a taxi to a hotel for a good night's rest before the final flight to Havana.

TIA, MY CLOSE relative, is an aunt who remained in Cuba and is now living in extreme humanitarian need due to the lack of basic necessities and the ravages of her 90 years of life.

The dark green landscape dotted with swaying palms on a background of bright blue sky splashed with puffy white clouds fills me with intense emotions as the plane lands at Havana's José Martí Airport. *La familia* is waiting to share hugs and kisses, laughs, tears and stories to bridge years of separation.

The ride to Tia's home through the streets of Old Havana reveals baroque ornamented walls recalling the grandeur of a bygone era. Young and old in an array of colors are seen moving in every imaginable mode of transportation: a Chinese bicycle transporting a family. A '50sh-vintage American cars and *guaguas* (buses) filled to capacity being pulled by tractors. Along Havana's Fifth Avenue, we pass grand old mansions being restored and storefront signs for foreign companies doing business in Cuba.

ALMOST 24 HOURS since leaving New Jersey, I arrive at a house full of relatives I hardly recognize, although they all seem familiar. Tia's living room buzzes with conversations that at first are like incomprehensible sounds. But after a short time of acclimating to the fast pace of Cuban-accented Spanish, I become fully engrossed in two or three simultaneous discussions. The hot topic is the recent downing of the planes from Miami and the ensuing tightening of the embargo.

Will Fidel Castro be able to weather Jesse Helms' storm as he has Robert Torricelli's and others for 37 years? (The embargo has existed through nine US. administrations since President Dwight Eisenhower first imposed trade restrictions on Cuba in 1960. Torricelli's legislation in 1992 and Helms' in 1996 strengthened the trade embargo.)

MY NEPHEW JOSÉ, a nuclear engineer laid off when construction at the Juraguá nuclear power plant stopped, foresees hard times ahead for his family. He wants to leave Cuba but fears that his teenage son will be enlisted in the army. José thinks that the hard-core, *patria-o-muerte* (fatherland-or-death) Castro supporters are consolidating forces under what they perceive as a reinforced economic war from El Norte. He waits for better times and supports the family with odd teaching jobs.

COUSIN MARTA, who years ago had begged me to help her pregnant daughter get out of Cuba after her live-in boyfriend took off for Florida in a raft, expressed indifference and resignation about the effects of the tightened embargo. A modest display of affluence was evident in her house since my last visit: new furniture and a fresh coat of paint - rare sights in any Cuban home. Marta proudly tells me, "I rent the place for $15 a night, and with dollars I buy anything I want."

While Marta enjoys the fruits of her tenuous capitalist venture (her business is at the margins of Cuban law), her sister María, a teacher, lives on a meager salary of about $10 a month plus the *"beneficios socialistas"* of free school and medical care — benefits that her "wealthy" sister Marta also receives.

Finally, it was Sunday again and time for my teary goodbyes and hugs for Tia, my sister, nieces and nephews. This time, I was lucky to get ground transportation and connecting flights from Havana to Mexico City to Newark, all in a span of 16 hours.

The Continental flight from Mexico City touched down in Newark after midnight Monday morning. Now only U.S. Customs stood between me and my wife.

WHAT I EXPECTED to be a routine check turned out to be an unpleasant two-hour ordeal. Upon seeing "Cuba" written on my customs declaration form, the officer in charge sternly warned me that travel to Cuba was forbidden and followed his admonition with a series of questions: Where is your license to travel? How much money are you carrying? How much money did you take to Cuba? Then he placed me at the mercy of two other officers, who told me that they were only following

338

rules. A computer check of my passport was followed by more questions and photocopies of driver's license, business cards and car registration. I left Customs with bags and passport in hand minus my two boxes of Churchill's Romeo y Julieta Cuban cigars. My wife, after two hours of waiting and being told that everyone had been processed, returned home thinking that I had missed my connecting flight from Mexico City.

At 2:30 a.m., I was in a nearly empty airport with no wife, no ride and no cigars, but my Cuban soul was recharged with memories of *Tia* and *la familia*.

A Crime to Denounce

Every human being has the legitimate right to contact family and loved ones - a human foundation through which one acquires the values and nurturing that makes us who we are. It does not matter what conditions of war or peace may exist between nations; each human being has that divine right which is key to the survival of the human species.

Policies by the Bush Administration have redefined "family," by excluding aunts, uncles, and first cousins. It is absurd to have to ask permission to visit a family member in Cuba, and beyond that be limited to a single visit in a three-year period through a truly cumbersome and inhumane process. Limitations have also been imposed on the material aid one may give to our families, thus creating conflicts within ourselves when raised as respectful law-abiding citizens. In dealing with a family emergency, a person may have no other option but to travel to Cuba through a third country, hiding when one returns, or claiming that one is fulfilling a religious mission.

There are cases of family members who fall gravely ill and die, and then the Bush Administration prevents us from visiting the burial site to mourn with loved ones, because of a family visit within the previous three-years. Emotional conflicts generate terrible dramas for people with families in Cuba -- unprecedented in World history.

Why the law

President Bush explains that the ill-conceived legislation aims to eliminate all monies entering Cuba. But this is simply unacceptable to anyone with family on the island. It is a cruelty that must be denounced and be known by the entire world, in particular by the vast majority of Americans who believe they live in a free and democratic country. Nevertheless, when one explains the restrictions imposed by the Bush Administration, people appear perplexed because it is difficult to think that such restriction happen in their own country.

Cuban Immigrants are burdened with double suffering because if one were free to travel -- when and wherever one decides -- family separation would be less painful but when that is forbidden, a conflict, a trauma arises that may be quite detrimental to one's emotional stability. The immigrant leaves a place and family where he/she was nurtured with love from infancy, carrying countless memories, frozen in time, deprived of internal evolution. He/she may remember better the birthday of someone not seen in decades than the birthday of family members presently near. It is terrible to accept one's reality if on top of that, a law is engendered to increase pain, the situation then becomes frustrating and unbearable.

But sadly, the U.S. media appears distant from that reality. The truth about Cuba is distorted, blaming only the Cuban government for the policy of family separation. But if the press were to pay attention to the human drama around them, it would bring light to confused people who would otherwise be ready and willing to repeal such an absurd policy.

Most U.S. citizens may trace their history to a voluntary or involuntary Diaspora, but the trauma of family separation is part of all humanity. It does not matter where one comes from, a Cuban, Mexican or African American family, we must, and we will demand respect for our right to family ties. An African woman in Rwanda, separated from her son, feels as much pain as a Cuban mother with a son on the other side of the Florida Straits. We must rise in defense of our families. We can and we have the right to be part of that humanity because Humanity itself is our *Gran Familia.*

Letter to His Holiness Pope John Paul II

Hand-delivered at the Office of the Holy See in Havana, Cuba

We, Cubans who reside in the United States of America, are joyful for your pilgrimage to our beloved island. And we feel deeply moved by your blessings and message of love and hope brought to the people of Cuba.

Vicar of Christ, we implore that you intercede on behalf of the Cuban family and invoke maximum respect for the following human rights:

- The right of all residents in the United States to visit their loved ones in Cuba.
- The right of all immigrants to care for the welfare of their family by sending monetary remittances and basic necessities for their families' survival.
- The right of all citizens of the United States to export medicines, food and medical equipment to Cuba, particularly to be able to have humanitarian commerce with Cuba.

We plead for your solidarity and support in the construction of a new future for our beloved people. With our maximum respect and admiration,

Cuban American Alliance Education Fund Inc., Washington, D.C.

Meetings with a highly admired religious leader: His Eminence Jaime Lucas Ortega y Alamino, Archbishop of Havana, appointed as Cardinal in 1994.

SISTER CITIES
U.S.-CUBA Sister City Association

In March, we were welcomed in the Council Chambers of Pittsburgh by President Emeritus Jim Ferlo to assist in forming the U.S.-Cuba Sister City Association (USCSCA). The association fosters understanding through mutually beneficial exchanges between individuals, community groups, organizations, and institutions in the U.S. with counterparts in Cuba.

Then in late May we traveled to Santa Clara, Cuba with Mr. and Mrs. Jack and Katherine Hopkins of Bloomington, Indiana to lay down sister-city agreements between those two cities. From Mobile/Havana to Bloomington/Santa Clara, the U.S.-Cuba Sister City Association helps to expand friendship links between U.S. and Cuban cities.

SISTER CITY PROJECTS

The Cuban American Alliance Education Fund is an active participant in the U.S.-Cuba Sister City Association (USCSCA). The association fosters understanding through mutually beneficial exchanges between individuals, community groups, organizations, and institutions in the U.S. with counterparts in Cuba. CAAEF Board members Ricardo González, Alberto Jones, Delvis Fernández Levy, and financial officer Norine Fernandez were among the founding members of USCSCA. As an organization CAAEF has helped facilitate several sister city relationships. In May of this year, Board members Ricardo González was one of over 100 individuals who traveled to Cuba to participate in bilateral meetings with mayors and provincial officials to explore and discuss sister city relationships with U.S. counterparts. So far agreements have been established or are near completion between the following U.S. and Cuban cities: **Bloomington, Indiana & Santa Clara; Mobile, Alabama & Havana; Madison, Wisconsin & Camagüey; Pittsburgh, Pennsylvania & Matanzas; Richmond, California & Regla; Oakland, California. & Santiago de Cuba; Tacoma, Washington & Cienfuegos; Philadelphia, Pennsylvania.**

& Cárdenas; Milwaukee, Wisconsin & Nuevitas; and the mayors of the oldest cities in the U.S. and Cuba have met to discuss friendship relationships between their cities of **St. Augustine, Florida, and Baracoa, Cuba**.

Last March 19th, the U.S.-Cuba Sisters City Association (USCSCA) was founded in Pittsburgh, Pennsylvania for the purpose of fostering exchanges between individuals, community groups, organizations, and institutions in the United States with counterparts in Cuba. Pittsburgh's City Council under the leadership of Councilman Jim Ferlo has spearheaded efforts to develop ties of peace and friendship under respect and recognition of Cuba's national sovereignty. Pittsburgh, which formalized a sister city project with Matanzas a year ago, sent 600 students to Cuba in March for a "Semester at Sea" program.

Founders of the Association of Sister Cities Cuba-USA in the meeting room of the municipal government of Pittsburgh, Pennsylvania on March 19, 1999.

Madison-Camagüey Sister-City Association

The city of Camagüey, founded in 1515, is the capital of Camagüey Province — Cuba's "Dairy-land." Like Madison, the city is a center of culture, education, technical research, and agriculture. The people of Camagüey are especially proud of their progressive traditions, dating back to 1826 when Frasquito Agüero Velazco became the first martyr of the Cuban struggle for independence from Spain. In 1868 another *camagüeyano,* Ignacio Agramonte fell in the "Ten Years' War" fighting to free Cuba from foreign control.

Educational Delegation Travels to Camagüey

From August 16-23 a group of High School students from Madison traveled to Camagüey to learn about Cuba's educational system and exchange experiences about the use of computers in the classroom.

Ricardo González became a main organizer of

The Madison-Camagüey Sister-City Association.

Society Mobile-Havana

Mobile, Alabama was the first U.S. city to establish fraternal ties with a city in Cuba. The City of Mobile, with ancient historical ties to Havana, has developed exemplary relations with the Cuban capital. The Society was organized in the spring of 1993 and the fraternal management officially began in October 1993 when Mobile's mayor and council and Havana's mayor signed the twinning agreement. Several exchanges of delegations have taken place, including scholars, artists, religious figures, and musicians. The Cuban ecumenical choir SHALOM gave concerts at schools, City Hall and various churches, including the Mobile Cathedral. Several ministers, the Bishop of Cuba, Cuba's representative in Washington and noted historian Eusebio Leal, among others, have visited Mobile. The mayor of Mobile, along with other city officials and members of the Society have traveled to Havana to visit hospitals, schools, museums, and public agencies.

Philadelphia - Santiago de Cuba Ties

Reported by George I. Fernández of Philadelphia, Pennsylvania.

A proclamation for a Philadelphia-Santiago sister city relationship was introduced and passed by the Philadelphia City Council on March 11. This was followed by a tour of Cuba by the Philadelphia Boys Choir, 88 boys.

The Choir's founder and director Robert G. Hamilton stated that in 30 years of world tours he had never witnessed such a group of warm, loving and kind people as the Cubans. There was a long-standing ovation at the Dolores Hall performance in Santiago when the Sister City resolution and the letter of friendship from the City Council and Mayor Ed Rendel was introduced.

"To watch these little 'Ambassadors of Music' sing at each school, church, synagogue, cigar factory, park, town square, and interact with children and people in Cuba was something I will remember the rest of my life. For 10 days, they created a bridge between two countries, and created music and harmony with the people of Cuba."

Bloomington-Santa Clara Friendship Ties

Reported by Jack and Katherine Hopkins of CUBAMISTAD Bloomington, Indiana

On Wednesday, May 26 we traveled to Santa Clara, Cuba, to finalize sister-city links with Bloomington, Indiana. We toured the Ernesto "Che" Guevara monument, an imposing and beautiful monument that also houses a museum. Later we visited the Medical Science Institute to learn from its director, Dr. Fernando González, and faculty about the work of the institute and allied hospitals.

This was followed by a delightful lunch with Arece Guerra Mesa, President of Santa Clara's Municipal Assembly, Alexander Rodríguez Rosada, Vice-President of the Municipal Assembly, and other officials. The luncheon was preceded by toasts and exchanges of gifts: H. Upmann cigars and flowers, a scrapbook about Bloomington and Dillman Farms fruit preserves from Monroe County, Indiana.

After lunch we visited Cuba's Central University for a meeting with the Vice-Rector Dr. Lee Tenorio and department heads. The university has departments in biotechnology and in research on several crops such as bananas, sugar cane, potatoes, and flowers. We visited the Rostroso Rodríguez Pérez school for visually impaired children, where children explained the school's mission and entertained us with songs. Our final visit was to the association for the physically impaired.

In the evening, we went on a tour of historical sites, including the *Parque Vidal,* a lovely plaza in the city's center; the *Teatro La Caridad,* a theater build during Spanish colonial times for the poor (Enrico Caruso sang there!); the *Casa de la Cultura-,* the *Boulevard,* a wide pedestrian street near the plaza; the old Provincial Palace, now the library; and the statue of the "boy with the unfortunate boot," a charming statue of a little drummer boy from the American Civil War -- the little drummer boy whose boot is so worn that no longer holds water, water was often given to wounded soldiers in this way.

Early the next day, we toured the INPUD plant, which produces refrigerators, ovens and other kitchen items. And finally, we went to the headquarters of ICAP, the Cuban Friendship with People Institute for the signing ceremony. First, we met in the back garden with ICAP's provincial director Iris Menéndez Pérez to discuss our project and how we had come to select Santa Clara as our Sister City. Then in ICAP'S conference room, President and Secretary signed the letter of friendship and certificate reaffirming the new relation between Santa Clara and Bloomington, concluding with a toast of Cuban rum.

Highlights of Activities
The first 3-years of CAAEF

January to April 1995 -- Interviews were conducted nationwide with leaders of Cuban American organizations and individuals in order to seek **consensus points** with regards to U.S.-Cuba Policy and its effects on the Cuban American community. Agreement was reached on:

- Lifting the travel ban on family visits to Cuba imposed in August 1994.
- Support for normalization of migration from Cuba to the United States.
- Opposition to the U.S. embargo against Cuba as it relates to the sending of food, medicine, and humanitarian assistance.
- Support for freedom of expression and an end to intimidation and harassment in the Cuban American community

May to July 1995 -- The points of consensus above were discussed at **a meeting in the US state Department** with Ms. Anne Patterson, Deputy Assistant Secretary of Inter-American Affairs and Mr. Kevin Sullivan, Economic Officer in the office of Cuban Affairs. Meetings were conducted in the offices of Senator Dodd, Representative Gilman and Senator Boxer. **Met in the White House** with Richard Nuccio and Morton Halperin, Special Advisor and Special Assistant to the President, respectively.

August to December 1995 -- Joined other organizations of Cuban Americans on the first anniversary of President Clinton's imposed restriction on family travel and remittances to Cuba at a **press conference** on the steps of the Federal Building in Newark NJ.

Members of the Alliance converged in Washington D.C., for meetings with congressional legislators and pentagon officials to address issues of family travel, remittances, and the embargo on foods and medicines to Cuba. Met with Cuban Foreign Minister Robaina and Americans investors at the First Anniversary Luncheon sponsored by the U.S.-Cuba Trade and Economic Council, Inc.

Mailed letters to supporters, members of Congress and President Clinton to express concerns about the Helms-Burton legislation.

Attended the **Nation and Emigration II Conference in Havana.** Presented letter to delegation from the European Union advocating respect for the sovereignty of Cuba in reaching economic agreements. Helped to organize a **conference at The World Affairs Council** in San Francisco with delegates of the White House, Global Exchange, and the Center for International Policy.

January 1996 -- Alliance Board of Directors attended **advocacy training** seminars in Musgrove, Georgia sponsored by ARCA Foundation and the Advocacy

Institute of Washington, D.C. Spoke with President Clinton's special advisor in Cuba, Richard Nuccio, about current U.S. policy on family travel. Planned day of advocacy for March 5, 1996, in Washington D.C. with the Cuban Committee for Democracy, *Cambio Cubano, Cubanos Contra el Bloqueo*, Jewish Solidarity, the Cuban American Defense League, the Latin American Working Group, the Center for International Policy, and unaffiliated Cuban Americans.

February 1996 -- Opened office in New Jersey to work with Cuban American organizations and individuals from the New York New Jersey area. Miami -- Updated members of the World Affairs Council for their fact-finding trip to Cuba.

March 1996 -- Four mass mailings of over 500 pieces each were sent. The **Alliance newsletter** *La Alborada* with news and articles in English and Spanish made its debut on March 15, 1996.

...y hemos de poner la justicia tan alta como las palmas, José Martí
(...and we must place justice as high as palm trees)
Volume 1. Número 1 Boletín de la Alianza Cubana Americana Spring 1996

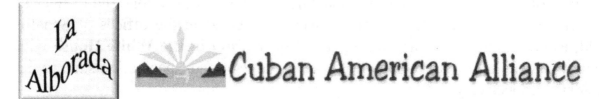

The Alliance president participated in various **press interviews**: NY Fox TV; CBS UN news correspondent Moses Schonfeld, radio WCAC of New Brunswick, NJ; Telemundo of NY/NJ; and NY's WBAI debate with José Basulto of Brothers to the Rescue.

Alliance president participated in the following **press conferences**: New York Labor Union Hall; Jersey Journal roundtable with the Cuban American National Foundation and others who favor increased hostilities toward Cuba; in office of Representative Joe Moakley on Capitol Hill with representatives of other Cuban American organizations; and at the United Nations.

A fifteen member Alliance delegation participated with *Cambio Cubano*, the Cuban Committee for Democracy, Jewish Solidarity, and the Cuban American Defense League in a **Day of Advocacy in Washington D.C**. One hundred packets of information were distributed, and personal visits were conducted with several members of Congress and their aides.

Participated in **conference at the University of Havana** to continue process of examination of Cuba's relation with its émigré community. Met with Cuban government officials (ministers Alarcón, Robaina, Cabrizas, and Balaguer among others) to discuss status of US-Cuba relations.

April 1996 – Dinner-meeting with members of the NY/NJ Cuban American community representing ten different organizations. **Meetings in Washington** at the State Department office of Cuban Affairs, with Economic Officer Kevin Sullivan to discuss the recently approved Helms-Burton bill and current presidential decrees on travel to Cuba; at the office of the Secretary of Defense in the Pentagon with Raimundo Ruga to discuss impact of current legislation and downing of planes on our family reunification efforts; at the US Treasury Department with Clara David for specific guidelines on obtaining licenses for sending humanitarian aid to Cuba; in office Representative Dick Zimmer, R-NJ.

May 1996 -- Press conference on Capitol Hill grounds with representatives Charles Rangel and Esteban Torres, church leaders and representatives of four Cuban American organizations asking for release of computers confiscated from Pastors for Peace that were destined for medical facilities in Cuba. Discussed strategies on how to reach legislators with Representative Nydia Velazquez of Brooklyn, NY.

Met and discussed humanitarian assistance projects in Cuba with representatives of Catholic Relief Services, the Lutheran Church, the United Methodist Church, and the Cuban Jewish Friendship Committee.

Prepared, in English and Spanish, **chronologies of US-Cuba relations** and an **analysis of the Helms Burton legislation**.

June 1996 -- Met with Cuban American leaders in Los Angeles at the **Participatory Democracy Seminar** sponsored by the Hans Seidel Foundation. Mailed the second issue of our **newsletter *La Alborada*,** to over 900 homes. Appealed to representative Robert Menéndez for easing travel restrictions to Cuba. Met in Washington, D.C. with the Cuba Coalition Steering Committee to advocate for waiver of provisions of the US-Cuba embargo.

July 1996 -- Traveled to Cuba with license from the US Treasury Department to select a Cuban non-governmental organization for the delivery of **humanitarian assistance** to disabled children. Met with representatives of various Cuban organizations: Director of the Julito Díaz Hospital; representatives of MINSAP (Ministry of Public Health); neighborhood family physicians; and members of ACLIFIM (Cuban Association for the physically limited). Met with the US consul at the US Interests Section in Havana with regards to restrictions on sending humanitarian assistance to Cuba. Traveled to Santa Clara province for fact finding meetings with children and their parents, and representatives of ACLIFIM.

August 1996 -- San Francisco, CA -- met with Cuban American community leaders in California -- Cuban rafters, the Cuban American Women of the US exiles from the 60s, arrivals through the "Peter Pan" program, arrivals during the Mariel boatlift, and recent immigrants -- to explain work of the Alliance, to network educating policymakers, and to coordinate the sending of humanitarian assistance to Cuba and family reunification.

Freddy Fajardo con su linda Familia

September 1996 -- Washington D.C. -- Met with the US Commerce Department official to investigate application procedures for export licenses for sending humanitarian assistance to Cuba.

Assisted in the **reunification of Cuban families** through the *Instituto Cubano de Amistad con los Pueblos* (ICAP) and rafter's organization *Cubanos Mano-a-Mano*.

October 1996 -- Meeting with disabled activists in Oakland, CA to (1) send assistance to disabled children in Cuba and (2) to set up **fraternal ties between the cities of Oakland and Santiago de Cuba**. Washington -- met with Mr. Michael Ranneberger, special adviser to the President at the US State Department.

November 1996 – Univisión TV interview on **hurricane relief assistance** for victims of Hurricane Lily. Meeting with **McWorld CEO** to request stopping promotion of computer program "Cuba attack."

December 1996 -- **Keynote speaker and Organizer of Symposium** on United States Cuba-Policy at the Office of the Americas in Los Angeles, CA. Met with Thomas Miller, President of the US-Cuba Trade Association, Cuban Vice-Consul Eugenio Martínez, business executives of San Francisco, and assistant to Mayor Willie Brown of San Francisco. Filming of interview with David Brown Productions for submission to PBS for program on Cuban Americans.

January 1997 -- **Speeches at Laney College in Oakland and Chabot College in Hayward**, California on the work of the Alliance, human rights, and US-Cuba relations. Meeting with Oakland City Council to present project to **explore sister city ties between Oakland and Santiago de Cuba.** Gave presentation at *Cubanos Contra la Ley Helms-Burton* **Conference** in Havana on impacts of the US law on Cuban Americans. **Met with delegation of American disables** on tour of Cuba sponsored by the US+Cuba Medical Project to coordinate assistance. Gave **Keynote speech at forum in Occidental College** sponsored by the United Nations Association of Pasadena and Foothills and the office of the Mayor of Pasadena. **Advised in organizing trip of educators to Cuba** from Chabot College.

February 1997 – Published and mailed **4th issue of CAAEF newsletter,** *La Alborada* to over 1000 homes and organizations.

March 1997 -- **Opened a CAAEF Office in Washington, D.C., on** Sixth Street SE. **Met with Michael Ranneberger,** assistant to President Clinton on Cuban Affairs to discuss difficulties with the licensing process for sending humanitarian assistance to Cuba. **Traveled to Cuba** with a group of 32 students and educators as part of a course on Cuban History and to deliver medicines and rehabilitation equipment to the Cuban Association for the Physically Disabled (ACLIFIM).

April 1997 -- **Met with the President and Vice President of ACLIFIM** for our first delivery of assistance -- medicines, and equipments for the disabled. **Met with Enrique Comendeiro, Advisor to the Cuban Ministry of Public Health (MINSAP),** to obtain permission from Cuban government authorities for the delivery of donations of medicines and rehabilitation equipment. **Gave talk at Temple Emeth** in Teaneck, NJ, about Jewish Life in Cuba. **Prepared information packets** for legislators and made visits to Congress for advocacy work on trying to lift the ban on trade with Cuba in food, medicine, and medical equipment.

May 1997 -- **Led delegation of Cuban Americans from Maryland to Congress.** Met with representatives of *Democracia Participativa* and the Cuban Committee for Democracy to plan congressional visits. Published and mailed the **fifth issue of CAAEF newsletter - *La Alborada,*** to over 1500 homes and organizations.

June 1997 -- **Led delegations of Cuban Americans** from Texas, California, Ohio, New York, Maryland, and Florida to visits in the House and the Senate. **Led delegations of disabled women** (two from Cuba, one Mexican, and three Americans) to thank supporters of the Cuban Humanitarian Trade Act of 1997. **Spoke and moderated for the second half of a press conference** called by representatives Esteban Torres (D-CA) and Jim Leach (R-IA) for the introduction of the Cuban Trade Humanitarian Act of 1997 (H.R. 1951). **Met with the ex-mayor of Pasadena, Bill Paparian** to plan congressional visits in July and to plan a cargo of humanitarian assistance to Cuba. Met with members of CAAEF in Washington, D.C., to set up a plan of action for the remainder of 1997.

July 1997 (9th) Meeting in Baltimore with Howard County Friends of Central America and the Caribbean (HOCOFOCA) to discuss work with CAAEF. (11th) Meeting with Sen. Dodd's aide Janice O'Connell and others to discuss progress on legislation to exempt food and medicine from the embargo. (21st) CAAEF's secretary travelled to Petaluma, CA to receive donations (Wheelchair and other equipment) for ACLIFIM.

In Washington, D.C. (21st) Meeting with Pasadena city councilman Bill Paparian to plan humanitarian assistance through Operation U.S.A. (22nd) In Virginia, meeting with Juan Romagosa, President of The Bridge for Historical Preservation, Inc., of

Kissimmee, Florida to plan tour of Historical Sites in Cuba and encourage preservation of Cuba's historical and cultural sites. (26th) Travel to Philadelphia for Cuban Film Festival, meeting of Maryland Advisory Council. (28th) Planning meeting for congressional visits with president of The Cuban American Women of the U.S.A. (28th) Meeting with Rabbi Saks of Washington to give assessment of the Jewish Community of Cuba.

August 1997 — Meeting with June Safran, of Berkeley, California and two visiting youth leaders of Santiago Synagogue in Cuba to discuss the status of religion in their community. (29th) Hosted two Cuban Scientists (Aimee Robaina and Eduardo) with Sebastián Aguilera of the Alliance Chapter in the Bay Area. (30th) Bay Area Chapter meeting to discuss participation in Dialogue with Cuba Conference.

September 1997 -- (2nd) Working session with Sady Morales in San Francisco to discuss layout of Web Page. (10th - 11th) Meetings in White House and with 12 congressional representatives. (12 - 13) Travel to Miami to meet with directors of Cuban American Defense League and *Alianza de Trabajadores Cubanos.* (14th) Travel to Houston, TX to meet with board member Regino Diaz and plan for assistance to ACLIFIM in Matanzas, Cuba. (19th) Meeting with Cong. Xavier Becerra in San Francisco. Visited office of Congresswoman Nancy Pelosi with CAAEF member Sebastián Aguilera. (24th) Planning session with Global Exchange rep Michael O'Heanny and Ira Sugarman to plan for Hundredth Anniversary of U.S. intervention in Cuba's War of Independence. (27th) Meeting in Glendale, CA with board members of Amerindia, Inc. to coordinate activities with immigrant advocacy groups in Los Angeles. (28th) Board meeting of Bay Area Alliance Chapter to discuss website progress and work on publication of La Alborada.

October 1997 -- (8th) Dialogue with Cuba Conference planning session at the University of California at Berkeley. (10th - 12th) CAAEF's president and Amerindia president, José Estévez travelled to Washington, D.C. and New York to participate in a march for immigrant rights. (16th) Participated in CIP conference in Miami. (23rd) Planning meeting for Dialogue with Cuba Conference. There were other meetings with Amerindia and Centennial Planning Committee. (31st) Planning meeting of Student/Teacher Tour of Cuba with Prof. Rick Moniz of Chabot College Political Science Department and others.

November 1997 -- (7th & 18th) Working sessions on Web Page with Sady Morales. (19th) TV interview with Chauncey Bailey of the Oakland Tribune for program Soul Beat to finalize details on Web Page. (20th) Planning session for Dialogue with Cuba Conference.

December 1997 -- (8th & 9th) Congressional visits with Maryland Chapter members. Meeting Stephen Rosenfeldt and editorial board of Washington Post.

January 1998 -- (Th. 9) Bay Area Alliance Chapter sponsored presentation at Laney College in Oakland California. Presentation of sister-city arrangement between

Oakland and Santiago de Cuba. (Sat. 10th) Bay Area Chapter Meeting to prepare for Dialogue with Cuba Conference. (Wed 14th) Travel to Havana for Pope's visit and to deliver humanitarian cargo to ACLIFIM. In Cuba delivered letter for Pope at the Vatican Embassy in Havana. Obtain ample coverage for - CAAEF's work in over 20 news media.

ACCOMPLISHMENTS
From February 1998 to September 1998

New Headquarters in Washington, D.C. As of June 1, 1998, we have an office entirely dedicated to the work of the Alliance. Our headquarters have been relocated to Capitol Hill on Maryland Avenue,

In collaboration with business, academic, Cuban American, religious, developmental, and humanitarian groups, the Alliance took an active role in organizing and carrying out the following projects:

- **Education and Advocacy Work in Washington.** On March 31, we joined with various Cuban American organizations, religious, business and trade union groups to express support for an end to the ban on food as well as the restrictions on medicine and medical equipment sales to Cuba. Hundreds of Cuban Americans and friends walked the Halls of Congress for a Day of Education about the reality of the Cuban family.

- **Vote by The Commission on Social Action of Reform Judaism.** After we made an appeal at the Spring 1998 meeting of the Commission, it passed a resolution urging the U.S. Congress to pass and the President to sign the Cuban Humanitarian Trade Act of 1997 (H.R. 1951) and also urging the federal government to take other appropriate measures to make an exception to the United States embargo on Cuba for the provision of humanitarian relief.

- **Over 1000 People Attended "Dialogue with Cuba" at The University of California at Berkeley.** Last March over 20 Cubans were able to come to a conference in the U.S. — making that the largest gathering of Cubans to attend a U.S. conference since 1959. The Alliance hosted a party reception at which over 100 Cuban Americans from the Oakland/San Francisco Bay Area welcomed the visitors. The conference lasted over two days, but the visitors stayed in the U.S. for a week to participate in spin off conferences at schools, universities, city councils, and community organizations in California.

The Cuban Academics had a day of rest and enjoyment on a tour of the San Francisco/Oakland Bay Area after the "Dialogue with Cuba Conference"

- **Links with Cuba and Delivery of Humanitarian Aid.** We are currently expanding contacts with the Cuban Association of Disabled People (ACLIFIM). Dr. Bill Atchinson of Flint, Michigan will travel to Ciego de Avila Province in Cuba to assess the needs of amputees and persons with disabilities in that province. Businessman Regino Diaz, our Texas representative, will assist in forming ACLIFIM partnerships in Matanzas province. So far this year, we have sent three cargos of humanitarian aid to ACLIFIM — during the Pope's visit last January, in late July, and most recently in September.

- **Conference on Culture, Religion, and Health.** We prepared and moderated at a one-day conference in the U.S. Congress, September 16, for Jewish Solidarity, a religious/humanitarian organization that channels medical assistance to Cubans through the Jewish Community on the island. In conjunction with this conference, we coordinated meetings with legislators and State Department officers for the President of the Jewish Community of Cuba and the President of Cuba Hadassah. We also held a meeting with the president and board members of B'nai B'rith to request among other things their support for family right-to-travel and the lifting of restrictions on humanitarian trade with Cuba.

- **Central California Coast Chapter.** We established a Central California Coast Chapter of CAAEF under the direction of Luis Seguí of Santa Maria, Cal. and David Fernández of San Luis Obispo, Cal.

- They just conducted their first event on September 11 with a presentation at the San Luis Obispo Library. Luis Seguí is a Cuban American lay leader at a local parish in Santa Maria where he ushers and teaches ESL classes. David Fernández is a Cuban American architect who has travelled to Cuba on several occasions and wrote a dissertation on the remodeling of Centro Habana.

- **Advocacy Work with Other Organizations.** This past July we conducted visits to the White House, Congress and the State Department in cooperation with the U.S. Council of Churches, Disarm, OXFAM America, and Global Links.

Letters to the editor, op-ed pieces, and articles have appeared on major national and local newspapers: The New York Times, USA TODAY, the Christian Science Monitor, The Jersey Journal, The Star-Ledger, *El Nuevo Hudson*, and the Record of New Jersey; The San Francisco Examiner, The Miami Herald, The Oakland Tribune, The Daily Review of California, The San José Mercury, (Chabot College) The Spectator. TV interviews for Northern California ABC and Telemundo affiliates, *Univisión*. Radio interview for CNN, Radio Fe in Miami, WBAI in New York, WCAC in New Jersey, CBS, ABC in Phoenix.

YEAR 2000 COLLABORATIVE RELATIONSHIPS

CAAEF has fostered, built, and maintained working relationships with organizations striving to improve US/Cuba relations. The members of our Advisory Council serve as important links to many of the most prominent Cuba-American groups in the United States. Members of our Board of Directors also serve on the board of other Cuban American organizations, or of other organizations that work towards improving relations between the US and Cuba. Examples of such links include the already mentioned participation in the **US-Cuba Sister City Association**, as well as the **Caribbean American Children Foundation**; the **Wisconsin/Camagüey Friendship Committee**; **TransAfrica**; **Americans for Humanitarian Trade with Cuba**; **US-Cuba Business Council**; and the **National Network on Cuba**. The organization **Global Exchange** has arranged several national speaking engagements for CAAEF's President under the title **"The Realities of the U.S. Embargo Against Cuba."**

CAAEF's presentations assess the trade embargo of Cuba from a moral standpoint and stress the importance of promoting mutually beneficial exchanges between Cubans and Americans. CAAEF's president offered lectures and panel discussions at The University of California in Los Angeles (UCLA), Fordham University, the Institute of Foreign Relations, and the World Affairs Council of Portland among others. CAAEF is a cofounder and an active participant in the **Cuba Steering Committee** - a coalition that meets at least once a month to examine, monitor, and take part in the development of legislative initiatives that may affect U.S./Cuba relations. **This coalition includes The Washington Office on Latin America, The Latin America Working Group, Global Exchange, OXFAM, Americans for Humanitarian Trade with Cuba, the Center for International Policy, the World Policy Institute, the Cuban Committee for Democracy, Catholic Relief Services, and other organizations.**

MISSION STATEMENT OF CAAEF:

The Cuban American Alliance Education Fund, Inc. educates the public at large on issues related to hardships caused by current U.S.-Cuba relations. It is a vehicle for the development of mutually beneficial engagements which promote understanding and human compassion.

THE GOALS AND PURPOSE OF CAAEF

Working outside ideological constraints, within the dynamics of the Cuban American Community, in cooperation with more than 40 U.S. organizations, in compliance with U.S. law, and respectful of the sovereignty and independence of Cuba, we strive to put a human face on the ongoing hardships caused by the lack of normal relations between the U.S. and Cuba. **CAAEF** calls for a reassessment of U.S. policies that are outside the best interests of the American people and that also carry undue harm toward Cubans and Americans. Our sphere of action includes congressional visits, family linking, and engagements of mutual benefit to Cubans and Americans. Our board members assist in the establishment of sister-city projects, community assistance programs, visits by Cuban professionals, student exchange programs, ties between Cubans and African American organizations, and fund-raising events for medical projects. Thus, forging engagements that promote understanding and human compassion between the people of both nations:

In order for us to have an effective voice within the body of American politics and public opinion, we strengthen ties between Cuban American organizations, academics, health professionals, the business community, religious organizations, and individuals across the U.S. We strive to facilitate coalition building effort between organizations and individuals who share these common goals.

Memorable Meetings with Legislators

Shortly after CAAEF developed as an organization in California, I decided to move to a place with a large population of Cuban Americans in order to discuss U.S. policies of common impact on our friends and families in Cuba and in the United States. The northeastern area around the states of New York and New Jersey with the second highest Cuban American population would be the most desirable places to advocate for changes in policies that bring harm to our families.

One of the first attempts to meet a legislator revolved around Mr. Robert Menéndez, who at that time was a congressman from Union City, New Jersey. There I was able to arrange and obtain permission for a meeting with him and a group of his constituents. We were accepted to come to his office, but once we arrived, we were taken to a different room and were unable to meet with him since he was meeting with a group of lobbyists from Florida. This was a lesson on politics and a major disappointment since I had left my own family behind and moved to a faraway place on the East Coast to advocate for easing restrictions on families for constituents in the Menéndez of New Jersey. Later on, I felt fortunate to be invited for a debate on FOX TV with Representative Menéndez, but there he advocated to the separation of a father from Cuba after his 6-year-old son had been brought illegally into the U.S.

Jeff Flake from Arizona

Among my positive experiences, I managed to meet with many legislators of both political parties who treated me with courtesy and support for the uplift of family values. I was fortunate to open an office for CAAEF withing walking distance of the U.S. Senate, Congress, and the White House, so I had a chance to see many legislators and their aides in their offices or walking by the neighborhood. One of the most uplifting and appreciative meetings took place in the office of Republican representative Jeff Flake from Arizona, a man who later became a senator. Although I was not in total agreement with his political ideas, I felt welcome by a true human being in his office, a person willing to listen. The office went beyond politics with a person who projected love for his constituents and high values for his family displayed in numerous photographs in every room.

Ileana Ros-Lehtinen

One of the most memorable visits along the halls of congress took place with a republican representative from Florida, Ileana Ros-Lehtinen - a hardcore advocate for policies that were contrary to my values. I never imagined being able to meet with her despite the fact that we had some family connection. There I was with Carlos Lazo, a man who was visiting congressional offices with me. Carlos was a remarkable human, a *Cubano* who had served as a medic in Iraq, dressed in his Marine uniform discussing where we should go for our visits. All of a sudden, we smelled a strong coffee and followed the wonderful aroma in total surprise right to the office of Miami Florida Representative Ileana Ros-Lehtinen. We both were welcomed; Carlos in his marine uniform, and I for my family connection to the congresswoman with a photo in my front pocket of her grandfather Jacobo Adato next to my *Abuelo* Salvador Levy near the time of their arrival in Cuba from Turkey/Greece. The aide immediately brought Ileana Ros-Lehtinen to meet me and when I mentioned our family connection, she put me on a phone call with her mother in Florida and I had the distinct opportunity to share with her our family connection.

She appeared pleased and brought back memories of her times with my mother Sara, who was her cousin and friend from their days in the town of Sagua La Grande of central Cuba. There they grew and lived as children near their fathers Salvador and Jacobo. Carlos and I were able to convey messages about family values and the need to build of bridges of love between our two countries and distant families.

At the White House

A third meeting in memory occurred at the

Unique opportunity to meet with Carlos Lazo in Washington D.C., c.2000

Carlos Lazo in his marine/medic uniform ready for meetings in the U.S. Congress

My (Grandfather) Salvador Levy sitting next to Jacobo Adato, Congresswoman Ros-Lehtinen's grandfather in Cuba c. 1920

White House with an assistant to President Clinton, Richard Nuccio. There we were with a group of Cuban Americans. We talked and listened but to my surprise I felt that he agreed with our points of view and that U.S. policies were not in the best interest of American and Cuban families. I tried to expand through our conversation by asking why U.S. policy was so unique and different towards Cuba when compared to other countries like Vietnam or China. His answer was direct in placing Cuba in the backyard of the U.S. Thus, using versions of the Monroe Doctrine of colonial days going back to the early 19th century to justify present lack of normal relations with Cuba. This provided a from the White House about the extent of exceptionalism and dominance of US imperialism towards my homeland of Cuba and all Latin American/Caribbean nations.

A SAD GOODBYE due to Heart Problems

Subject: about CAAEF and my present situation
Sunday, September 16, 2012,

To My Dear Friends:

It has been almost twenty years since we founded the Cuban American Alliance Education Fund (CAAEF) in an effort to change the aggressive policy of the United States government towards the Cuban people. Your work in collaboration with organizations and people of Cuban origin living outside our dear Homeland have inspired all those who yearn for full freedom to travel; an end to terrorists acts; an end to the inhumane extraterritorial blockade of Cuba; the granting of full freedom to the five Cubans who were ready to sacrifice their lives to protect the Cuban Nation against terrorists and who are unjustly kept in prison; and the bringing to justice the nefarious terrorists who have caused, and continue to cause death, destruction and sufferings to families and innocent human beings.

Luis Rumbaut, in particular, has contributed through the publication of *La Alborada*, with firm resolve, and without financial interests, to keep us informed on current news, on-going events, and with opinion articles about important issues often ignored by the mainstream press.

Alberto Jones has written valuable testimonials about his life and has collaborated extensively with visits to members of the US Congress, as well as bringing humanitarian assistance to Cuba through the Caribbean American Children Foundation and the San Augustine – Baracoa Friendship Association.

Patricia Morán together with others has collaborated with her participation in meetings with senators and representatives, offering testimonials about the negative effects of the policies directed from Washington, D.C. towards her family in Cuba and other regions of the Caribbean.

José Pertierra has been at the forefront of the struggle, persevering with dignity and profound energy for the liberation of the Five Cuban Heroes unjustly imprisoned and kept far from their families, fighting as well for bringing proven terrorists to justice, such as the now deceased Orlando Bosch and his accomplice Luis Posada Carriles, executors of acts that have caused dozens of deaths and destruction, in and out of Cuba.

And among other accomplishments, for almost a decade, in spite of multiple impediments imposed by the Office of Foreign Assets Control (OFAC), we were able to become a main source of assistance to the Cuban

Association for those suffering from lack of physical mobility (known in Spanish under the acronym of ACLIFIM – *Asociación Cubana de Limitados Físico-Motores*).

I am sending this letter because I find myself at a crossroad, unable to continue a work that has given fulfillment to my life, so therefore, I am requesting from each of you, guidance, and advice to determine the future and roads to be followed by CAAEF.

Since the beginnings of the decade of the 1990s, I have suffered from cardiac problems that at the beginning were relatively simple to keep under control through a series of medications. I have had more than ten cardio versions (electro shocks to maintain the heart in rhythm), and when these procedures failed, I was kept on the maximum of medical prescriptions, but once again these medications failed. So, my two cardiologists opted for a new medical procedure referred to as ablation – a process through which certain cells near the heart that emit false signals are destroyed. The first ablation worked well for four years, but unfortunately had to be repeated a second time last spring and within a month ended in failure.

Today, after staying in a hospital for a couple of days, a pacemaker was inserted near my heart. I am still feeling some painful discomfort but maintain hopes for improvement - so much so, that I am deeply involved in writing a book about my life's journey: beginning in Lengua de Pájaro, Preston, Mayarí, and Holguín, through Santa Clara and my life at the family *finca*, moving on to Salt Lake City and then Miami to study, teaching and studying to earn a PhD in Math in the San Francisco Bay area, following with the Alliance efforts in New Jersey, New York, Washington, D.C., and ending with my adventures in various towns of California.

My health situation limits me severely from carrying out the work that I was able to perform through trips to centers of government and meetings in various U.S. cities, plus my jaunts in Brussels at the European Union and the Human Rights Organization in Geneva, where I was able to bring testimonials of *cubanos y cubanas* whose families have been deeply affected by cruel U. S. policies.

As a result, I feel obliged to pass the leadership to a person you may be able to advice and recommend, and to give guidance or suggestions as to what new path the Alliance is to pursue. I have all the legal documents and with the assistance of José or Luis, who are both lawyers, I could send them these documents in hopes of continuing to gather voices in the U.S. to help in the fulfillment of our goals.

This letter has been sent only to the CAAEF Board Members, but feel free to share with anyone who you think might be able to help. Your assistance is essential and will be greatly appreciated.

I send you warm fraternal greetings and my eternal gratitude for your collaboration in search for a peaceful future for our dear Land and its people.

Delvis Fernández Levy

WORDS from my Dear Friend, Luis Rumbaut

This is painful news, although not unexpected. You have been carrying on despite the recurring bouts of heart trouble, but by natural law none of us gets any younger. Sooner or later, organizations change because people change. For CAAEF, this is that time. We all had hoped that the blockade would be on the way out by now, but it continues. It's time for a new person, or even generation, to take over an effort to undo a policy that stubbornly remains in place. This will take some more years, I think.

Of course, you should prioritize your health, and then your life-history project. The pacemaker may well put you back on your feet once your body gets used to it, but that would not argue for your continuing to maintain the stress of managing the organization. Norine has been for many years the other part of the dynamic duo of CAAEF, and I am sure that she agrees. She herself should be taking it easier now.

You have shown the rare ability to get along with people and to keep the work moving forward without the personal dramas that characterize some other organizations. Alberto, Patricia, and José also have been able to help CAAEF remain an organization that is respected among the anti-blockade forces. It has been a fruitful cooperation, enough to have motivated me to keep the newsletter going 5 days a week. Next February will be the 9th year of existence of La Alborada on the Web, and in all that time it has been a pleasure to work with you and Norine.

A salute to you, Delvis. You've made a big difference in creating and leading CAAEF to this point.

Un abrazo, Luis

28

WORLD CONFERENCES
Europe, Mexico, Cuba, and The U.S.

European Parliament Conference
1898-1998 Cuba Independence and Sovereignty
The Alliance seeks support at European Parliament.

In November 1997, we traveled to Brussels, Belgium seeking support from the European Parliament for the removal of impediments that hinder the development of family relations among Cubans, such as restrictions on travel and the meeting of financial responsibilities towards our children and family dependents.

Summary of the alliance appeal for support. In 1963 the U.S. Treasury Department produced the Cuban Assets Control regulations which include a freeze on all Cuban owned assets in the U.S. and the imposition of restrictions on spending money in the course of travel to Cuba.

During president Carter's administration restrictions on travel were removed, thus giving Cuban Americans a window of opportunity to rekindle family relations that had been shattered for more than 20 years. During the Reagan administration trouble diminished or came to a halt.

Under the Torricelli and Helm-Burton Acts, the U.S. codified into law a unilateral embargo with extraterritorial implications, the banning of food sales and restrictions on travel and remittances that have dire consequences on Cuban families.

What restrictions and climate of intolerance affect the development of healthy relations with our loved ones?

- Under the Cuban assets control regulations, issued on July 8, 1963, U.S. citizens and permanent residents wherever they are located are subject to criminal penalties that range up to 10 years in prison $1,000,000 in corporate, $250,000 in individual fines and civil penalties of up to $55,000 per violation.

▪**Cuban Americans are permitted one visit every 12 months to see a close family member who is under circumstances of extreme humanitarian need.** This policy is so incomprehensible, that tens of thousands of Cuban Americans circumvent U.S. law by traveling to Cuba via third countries. There is a false perception that since massive number of people violate the remittances and travel restrictions, no one gets hurt because enforcement of the law seems to be ignored. However, enforcement of the law is used selectively to intimidate and harass travelers on their way to Cuba and upon their return to the U.S. Precious family gifts have been confiscated and destroyed, travelers are detained at airports -- detentions that cause economic hardships due to missed flight connections and the need for extra hotel accommodations.

▪Cuban Americans are encouraged to make anonymous accusations through a phone hotline of the office of foreign assets control in Miami to accuse suspected violators of the embargo. This hideous practice should have no place in a society where one is presumed innocent unless proven guilty. Individuals have been detained on their way to third countries for being suspected travelers to Cuba, and their money and travel tickets have been confiscated. Cubans coming to the U.S. are placed in a paradoxical situation, while receiving special privileges over other immigrants in securing resident status, they are restricted in meeting responsibilities to support and visit the families left behind.

▪Under the eye of law enforcement authorities at the Miami airport Cuban Americans have been kicked, spat upon, photographed, and showered with epithets by sign carrying demonstrators upon their return from Cuba. These activities have been encouraged with impunity by local radio announcers.

The Cuban American alliance has embarked on a project to examine all aspects of US Cuba policy that hinder the development of family relations. We are collecting testimonials to present them to Congress and human rights organization. What can you do to help?

Request for Testimonials for the U.S. Congress, the European Parliament, and the Geneva Commission on Human Rights

-- DO YOU KNOW ANYONE WHO

1. Has had family gifts confiscated upon departure for or arrival from Cuba?
2. Has been prevented from supporting a child or an aging parent by the restrictions on money remittances?
3. Has had a medical emergency in Cuba and being unable to receive money from the US?
4. Has been detained or harassed at a U.S. airport for being a suspected traveler to Cuba?
5. Has received letters threatening with fines or imprisonment from a U.S. government agency?

Partial view during the closing session at the
**European Parliament Conference
1898-1998 Cuba Independence and Sovereignty**

Among the Participants at European Parliament Hearing

Delvis Fernández-Levy
Cuban American Alliance Education Fund (CAAEF)
Washington, D.C., U.S.A.

Paul Davidson
Cuba Solidarity Campaign
London, United Kingdom

Lisa Valanti
Interreligious Foundation for Community Organization
IFCO Pastors for Peace
Pittsburgh, Pennsylvania, U.S.A.

Wayne S. Smith
Center for International Policy
Washington, D.C., U.S.A.

Esteban Cobas Puente
United Nations Educational, Scientific and Cultural Organization (UNESCO)
Cuba & Paris, France

Alberto Montano
CubaAids Project
Miami Beach, Florida, U.S.A.

Commission on Human Rights
Geneva, Switzerland
Statement of **Dr. Delvis Alejandro Fernández Levy**
President of The Cuban American Alliance Education Fund, Inc.
(Agenda Item 10 – Economic, Social and Cultural Rights)

Mr. President,

Since July 1, 2004, the Government of the United States of America under the Administration of President George W. Bush, in contravention of The Universal Declaration of Human Rights, The United Nations International Covenant on Civil and Political Rights, The Convention on the Rights of the Child, and the International Covenant on Economic, Social and Cultural Rights, has imposed further restrictions on people having familial, cultural, and religious bonds with residents of Cuba, such as, limitations on:

- **Visitation Rights,**
  - **Financial Assistance,**
    - **Humanitarian Assistance, and**
      - **Religious Assistance**

Testimonials and press reports abound that illustrate infringements of the United Nations covenants on: (1) The protection of the family as the natural and fundamental group unit of society, (2) the rights of parents and children, and (3) the civil, economic and cultural rights of ethnic minorities in the United States linked through familial and cultural ties with Cuba.

A 103-year-old grandmother of Cuban origin who resides in the United States was anxious to see her son, a resident of Cuba in a grave life-threatening situation, suffering from lung-cancer. The family contacted their United States Congressional representatives but was told she could not obtain an exception to travel with an accompanying family member.

In another case a U.S. citizen, serving the United States Armed Forces as a medic in Iraq, while on leave from service tried to visit his two teenaged sons who live in Havana but was not allowed to travel to see his beloved children before returning to active duty.

Disabled Cubans are also casualties of policies by the Government of the United States of America that impede assistance to Cubans in vulnerable situations of human existence.

For over seven years, *La Familia* -- the Cuban American Alliance humanitarian project -- has secured licenses from both the United States Department of Commerce and the Office of Foreign Assets Control for the delivery and exportation of donations to the Cuban Association for the Physically Disabled.

Our project is unique in two respects: (1) Deliveries are made on a regular basis to meet current needs and (2) Assessments are made with each delivery for future assistance. Participants in *La Familia* mission strive to assist the physically impaired to reach new levels of independent living and empowerment.

Today, *La Familia* is held hostage waiting for a license placed on hold since August 15, 2004. Neither aid nor assistance has been sent for seven months while officials of the United State Government deliberate on granting a humanitarian travel permit to deliver donations already licensed by the United States Commerce Department.

We appeal to the Commission on Human rights to consider these violations of human rights and fundamental freedoms and request from the U.S. Government under President George W. Bush to refrain from inflicting further suffering on our families and loved ones.

Thank you.

Statement Read at
The United Nations Commission for Human Rights
From Norine Gunn Fernández
Director of *La Familia* Project with the Cuban American Alliance
(March 23, 2005)

Eight years ago, after a trip to Cuba with my husband, we returned to our home in California having been made aware of the very desperate need of one of the most vulnerable segments of Cuban society - the disabled. It was not our first trip, as we had been there on several previous occasions to deliver medications and other badly needed staples to my husband's family members. However, that particular trip was the most significant in creating a new direction we would follow which was to totally consume my energy and time in providing humanitarian aid to these very needy people.

My husband, who came from Cuba at the age of seventeen, had founded a nationwide organization of Cuban Americans, who are working for a change in United States policy toward Cuba with the purpose of making the support of their families and family relationships possible and normal. I had helped him with the work of CAAEF (Cuban American Alliance Education Fund), but after being so profoundly moved by the great hardships I realized the disabled in Cuba had to bear, we decided that my efforts could best be served by directing a new project, *La Familia*, to deliver humanitarian aid to ACLIFIM (the Association of the Physically Disabled in Cuba).

Our help started with very small steps due to the difficult restrictions in trying to do anything or help Cuba in anyway. We finally did obtain the two needed licenses; one from the U.S. Department of Commerce to export medicines and needed equipment, and one from the U.S. Department of Treasury to travel to deliver that aid. We were allowed to extend our license to anyone who was willing to help our organization with that delivery. Originally, we started gathering donations from generous Americans who wanted to help, and would then ask for volunteers who, at their own expense, would travel to make the deliveries. The first year we only had a hand full of people, mostly from our immediate area, who hand carried and hand delivered the badly needed material. However, upon their return, they were so moved by the importance of the experience, they told others and by sharing their enthusiasm, the project quickly began to grow and spread. The cost of shipping the collected aid for delivery to the many new volunteers across the nation became prohibitive for our nonprofit organization, so we began sending a list of the needed items requested by ACLIFIM and asking the volunteers travelers to collect the aid themselves. The great effort of donating their own time, energy and money to gather this aid in addition to their effort towards making the delivery possible, was indeed a strong testimony to the importance they felt this help could be and a demonstration of the true American spirit.

The program rapidly grew and to our great surprise and satisfaction, we learned from ACLIFIM's 2002 annual report, that CAAEF had become their largest donor of humanitarian aid, not only from the United States, but worldwide as well. This proud distinction continued, and our network of medical and health workers expanded until August of 2004, when the work of *La Familia* came to a halt. Our project had benefited the 60,000 members of ACLIFIM in two unique ways. We were able to fulfill urgent request for materials or medicines that were needed immediately, and to provide medicines on a consistent basis over a long period of time. This was possible due to the constant flow and the number of travelers who made the deliveries for our organization. But also, of importance was the benefit the American volunteers experienced themselves. People returned from Cuba with a profound feeling of satisfaction in the good they had done, their own increased firsthand knowledge of the reality of Cuba, and the pride of acting as an ambassador for their homeland.

To carry out this program, we continually faced one difficult hurdle after another due to the harsh restrictions the U.S. has placed on any dealings with Cuba. These challenges have only grown more and more profound each year until ultimately this past August our license for travel expired and has not been renewed. This incredible program has come to a screeching halt with the current administration's refusal to grant the new license.

As an American mother and grandmother with several disabled family members, I find it so unbelievable and unacceptable that this nation, which professes to place such great importance on family values and the sanctity of a quality life for every human being, should refuse aid and assistance to our brothers and sisters. The American people have the means and the desire to extend these values and share them with their fellow human beings. What an inhuman and criminal shame that our government does not reflect the values of the American people. I find the harsh behavior of this administration and the cruel policies of the United States toward Cuba to be unsurpassed as a human rights abuse.

On a personal note, I feel equally outraged at the inhuman restrictions placed upon our own family. The dear ninety-eight-year-old aunt, who raised my husband, is no longer defined as family, and can never be visited again! The Cuban cousins of my California sons are no longer family and can never be visited again! My only remaining sister-in-law, who supports her government, can no longer receive our financial help! Through our work with Cuban Americans across this land, I have come to know the many tragic and heart-breaking stories of families that have been separated, that have become dysfunctional, and that have actually been destroyed. I have read that dividing the family is the most effective form of war. How very sad that the obsession of the U.S. government to bring down just one man, results in over forty years of waging a war against the warm and wonderful people of that entire nation.

Norine Fernandez interacts with Cuban school children, telling of the work she does with ACLIFIM

PRESS REPORTS

In French and Spanish about my Presentation at the UN Commission for Human Rights

UNITED NATIONS OFFICE IN GENEVA, SWITZERLAND

Des organisations de Cubano-américains dénoncent les restrictions de leurs droits

05/04/2005

La Havane, Des organisations regroupant des ressortissants cubains resident aux Etats-Unis et des Nord-américains d'origine cubaine ont denonce devant la Commission de l'ONU pour les droits de l'homme (CDH) les restrictions que l'administration Bush impose a leur droit d'avoir des contacts avec leurs families a Cuba.

Delvis Fernández Levy, president de l'Alliance cubano-americaine pour l'Education, a dénoncé devant la CDH, actuellement en session a Genève, une serie de mesures mises en vigueur en juillet dernier par l'administration Bush.

Ces restrictions stipulent, entre autres, que les personnes resident aux Etats-Unis ne peuvent rendre visite à leurs families à Cuba qu'une fois tous les trois ans.

Après avoir fait remarquer que ces restrictions violent la Déclaration universelle des droits de l'Homme et d'autres conventions des Nations Unies, Delvis Fernández Levy, a appelé la CDH à tenir compte de « ces violations des libertés et des droits de l'homme fondamentaux » et à « enjoindre le Gouvernernent du president George W. Bush à mettre fin aux souffrances auxquelles donnent lieu » ces mesures de Washington.

Il a déclaré ensuite à la presse cubaine que c'est la premiere fois que des Cubano-americains ont recours a la Commission de l'ONU pour les droits de l'homme pour denoncer ce qu'il a appele les « cruelles dispositions anticubaines » du gouvernement des Etats-Unis.

Le president de l'Alliance cubano-americaine pour l'Education a annoncé en outre que des cubano-américains qui desirent voir leurs families à Cuba ainsi que des ressortissants nord-americains ayant des liens avec l'île se rendront le 27 avril a Washington pour manifester contre la politique anticubaine des Etats-Unis.

[Partial Translation: Cuban-American organizations denounce restrictions on their rights. Organizations of Cuban nationals residing in the United States and North Americans of Cuban origin have denounced before the UN Commission on Human Rights (HRC) the restrictions that the Bush administration imposes on their right to have contact with their families in Cuba. Delvis Fernández Levy, president of the Cuban American Alliance Education Fund, denounced before the HRC, currently in session in Geneva, a series of measures put into effect last July by the Bush administration.]

Denuncian en la CDH prohibiciones a residentes cubanos en EE.UU.
(Tomado de Granma)

Agrupaciones de cubano-americanos denunciaron hoy en la Comisión de Derechos Humanos (CDH) las medidas tomadas por el presidente George W. Bush para restringir los contactos con sus familiares en la Isla, que calificaron de criminales, informó PL.

Delvis Fernández Levy, presidente de la Fundación de la Alianza Cubano-Americana para la Educación, intervino en la sesión de este jueves donde se debatió el tema 10 relativo a los derechos económicos, sociales y culturales.

Apuntó que desde julio del pasado año la Casa Blanca puso en ejecución tales disposiciones, que contravienen la Declaración Universal de los Derechos Humanos y otras convenciones adoptadas por Naciones Unidas.

Liamó a la CDH a "considerar estas violaciones a las libertades y derechos humanos fundamentales" e "instar al Gobierno del presidente George W. Bush a poner fin a los sufrimientos provocados por tales políticas."

Fernández Levy dijo a Prensa Latina que es la primera vez que ciudadanos cubano-americanos concurren a este foro de la ONU para reclamar a Estados Unidos "por sus crueles disposiciones anticubanas".

[Partial translation: Fernández Levy told Prensa Latina that this is the first time that Cuban American citizens have come to this UN forum to complain to the United States "for its cruel anti-Cuban provisions." He urged the CHR to "consider these violations of fundamental human rights and freedoms" and "urge the Administration of President George W. Bush to put an end to the suffering caused by such policies." Fernández Levy told Prensa Latina that this is the first time that Cuban American citizens have come to this UN forum to complain to the United States "for its cruel anti-Cuban provisions."]*

Se trata de algo histórico. Tenemos por lo menos representaciones de cuatro agrupaciones de California, Orlando y Miami. Ya es hora de que más personas salgan a la calle y hagan masiva esta denuncia, afirmó.

Comentó que el 27 de abril próximo habrá una manifestación grande en Washington en la que participarán cubano-americanos y otros ciudadanos estadounidenses que tienen vínculos culturales, de amistad y de otro tipo con Cuba. "Allá tendrán que oírnos," concluyó.

EVENTS IN CUBA

Every year Cuba holds several world-class events that attract thousands U.S. citizens.

Sharing a productive time with Ricardo Alarcón de Quesada, Cuban Minister of Foreign Affairs

- On the occasion of the 150th Anniversary of José Martí's Birthday, on January 27(* through the 29th, Cuba is cosponsoring with UNESCO an international conference under the title: ***Conferencia International por el Equilibrio del Mundo.*** José Martí along with Antonio Maceo, represent the two inspirational leaders of Cuba's struggle for nationhood and independence from foreign domination.

- **The annual U.S.-Cuba Business Conference is slated for February 17-18** in Cancún, Mexico with a fully hosted day trip to Havana, Cuba on February 19. Summit, in which as in the past, major U.S. companies are expected to participate.

- **U.S.-Cuba Sister-City Conference** is scheduled for early April for promoters of people-to-people engagement through city-government and state-to-province links.

- **The 3rd Conference of The Nation and its Emigres,** *La Nación y La Emigración*, is being planned for April 11-13. Discussions will take place on issues that impact the worldwide Cuban immigrant community.
- **The Association for the Disabled in Cuba (*ACLIFIM*),** has scheduled an international conference on the Rights of Disabled People for May 5-9.
- Annual back-to-back **Jazz and Film festival** are scheduled for early December in Havana.

U.S. Cuba Business Summit

In the year 2000, at the beginning of a new millennium, filled with optimism about changes in U.S. – Cuba policy, we participated in the **U.S.-Cuba Business Summit** held in Cancún, Mexico to discuss issues and policies that affect the Cuban American community: immigration, money remittances, sister city arrangements, legislative initiatives, and cultural and sport exchanges.

Our meetings in México included the participation of representatives from several major U.S. industries who also met with foreign counterparts investing in Cuba. Open and frank discussions took place with the President of Cuba's National Assembly, Ricardo Alarcón, and several of Cuba's ministers dealing with economic affairs.

Americans for Humanitarian Trade with Cuba

Americans for Humanitarian Trade with Cuba (AHTC), organized under the auspices of the U.S. Chamber of Commerce, is a coalition of prominent business, Cuban American, religious, medical and humanitarian leaders interested in the flow of food and medicines to the people of Cuba.

At a news conference last January in the chamber's headquarters, Willard A. Workman, its international vice president, pledged to run a "grass-roots campaign" to enlist support for legislation introduced in both houses of Congress to modify the trade ban.

Joining Workman at the news conference were former House Ways and Means Committee chairman Sam Gibbons (D-Fla.); former senator Malcolm Wallop (R-Wyo.); and retired Marine Corps General and former NATO supreme commander, Gen. John J. Sheehan. The advisory council includes former Treasury Secretary Lloyd Bentsen; former Federal Reserve Chairman Paul A. Volcker; former World Bank president A.W. Clausen; Benjamin Spock; David Rockefeller; former U.S. Trade Representative Carla A. Hills; and Dwayne Andreas, chairman of the giant Archer Daniels Midland agribusiness company.

Delvis Fernández Levy, a member of the group's executive committee stated: "There is a perceived division in the Cuban American community. To some, weakening the weapon that was supposed to get rid of Castro is heresy. But it gets to a point where many of us agree that the policy is counterproductive: It is not getting rid of Castro, and it is creating pain and misery for people in Cuba."

US • CUBA Business Summit. - The business potential between US and Cuba will mark the pace in the agenda of a meeting of entrepreneurs from both countries to be held in Cancún, Mexico and in Havana the upcoming 4-6 of March.

Delvis Fernández Levy, PhD, *Washington, District of Columbia*

Delvis Fernández was born and raised in Santa Clara, Cuba, where he attended public schools up to the high school level. He holds a BA from Westminster College, in Salt Lake City, Utah, a master's degree from the University of Miami, and a PhD in mathematics from the University of California at Berkeley. Since 1995 he has organized forums on U.S.-Cuba policy in various parts of the U.S. has led delegations of Cuban Americans to meetings with government officials in Washington. He is the publisher of *La Alborada,* CAAEF's Spanish/English newsletter. He has had opinion letters and editorials published in several newspapers. He has participated in radio and TV interviews across the United States and has been featured in several documentary films about U.S.-Cuban affairs. He has been a speaker and organizer of various press conferences. He has been a speaker and has helped to organized conferences at various U.S. universities, from UCLA to Fordham University. He has taught at the University of Miami, at the University of the Pacific, California State University at Hayward, and Chabot College in Hayward (from 1966 to 1997). In the mid-sixties, he developed the mathematics program for the first Spanish speaking college in the U.S. for Latin Americans at the University of the Pacific in Stockton, California. He served as advisor to the Chicano Student Union and developed programs to expand educational opportunities in California.

He is currently the president of the Cuban American Alliance Education Fund, Inc. and serves on the board of directors of American for Humanitarian Trade with Cuba, the U.S.-Cuba Sister City Association, and the U.S.-Cuba Business Association.

"Latinos USA" National Meeting. - Announces a founding meeting of Latino community-based organizations to formulate the post Coordinadora 96 platform.

When: March27, 28, and29, 1998
Where: National Education Association (NEA),
Headquarters Building - News Conference Room

CAAEF at LASA Congress in Chicago

Over 4000 delegates were present at the XXI International Congress of the Latin American Studies Association (LASA) in Chicago, Sept. 24 - 26. Twenty delegates came from Cuba, and Cuban affairs dominated in more than a dozen panels. This was the first time that LASA had sponsored a delegation from outside the U.S.A. The Alliance was represented by Enrique Conill and Prof. Anamaría Goicoechea of the University of Maryland.

At the Dawn – *La Alborada*
A New Era in U.S. – Cuba Relations

**At the U.S. Cuba Business Summit Meeting
Cancún México, June 8, 2000
Also published in the Millenium Edition of La Alborada, November 2000**

One of the panels at the U.S.-Cuba Business Summit in Cancún, Mexico this Spring. Kirby Jones, President of ALAMAR leads a discussion on changes in U.S.-Cuba policy and the potential for U.S. investments in Cuba.

There are indications that the United States and Cuba are moving towards closer contacts and in due course the establishment of full diplomatic relations. However, it will be years before relations reach a state of "normalcy" -- one that permits open trade, travel, and in due course the establishment of full diplomatic ties.

Although no legislation has been approved to ease any of the restrictions of the embargo the Senate in 1999 voted 70 to 28 in favor of a legislative initiative known as the Ashcroft Amendment, to lift unilaterally imposed U.S. trade sanctions on agricultural commodities. This marked the shift of forces and emboldened those working to lift the embargo on food and medicine – farmers, business and religious groups together with Cuban Americans as well. Despite the fact that there were sufficient votes to move the amendment forward to a full congressional vote, it stalled in conference committee due to unprecedented intervention by representative Tom DeLay of Texas and senator Trent Lott of Mississippi. A companion house bill, under sponsorship by Representative Nethercutt of Washington State is expected to receive wide approval in Congress later this month.

Congressional advocates

Advocates in Congress for the lifting of trade sanctions now span a wide range of the American political spectrum. Last year over 30 Cuban related bills were introduced by the 106th Congress, and over 20 of them called for major changes in the U.S. Embargo, such as an overhaul of the entire policy or the lifting of trade and travel restrictions. So far this year, a letter to Speaker Hastert asking for an end to sanctions on food and medicine has been endorsed by 220 representatives. But despite an unlikely probability that legislative advancement will be made during an election year, the sheer number of congressional advocates for change plus the issues they raise are clear indications that a serious intent is under way to ease, and perhaps lift, the embargo in the near future.

The Clinton Administration

The Clinton Administration has gone on record in opposition to the use of trade sanctions as weapons of U.S. foreign policy, and has liberalized some restrictions, on money remittances, travel, and commercial contacts with Cuba. Furthermore, it carries out immigration talks and favors the pursuit of joint maneuvers with Cuba for drug interdiction -- changes that seem to occur more as a result of U.S. commercial and security concerns. But while trade talks and commerce develop with former U.S. adversaries, for example China and Vietnam, Cuba continues to be an exception to, and a contradiction in, the application of U.S. foreign policy.

The Senate approved a version of the Agriculture Appropriations bill **by a vote of 79 to 13,** without objection to a sanction provision offered by Democratic Senator Byron Dorgan of North Dakota **to lift all unilateral sanctions on the sale of food and medicine.** And the House Appropriations committee approved a similar language initially submitted by Republican Congressman George Nethercutt of Washington state.

• The Senate Foreign Relations Committee, chaired by Republican Senator Jesse Helms of North Carolina, approved similar language, offered by Republican Senator John Ashcroft of Missouri, in a foreign aid bill.

• Most significantly, on July 20, 2000, **the House of Representatives decisively voted 301 to 116 to ban Treasury Department funding for the enforcement of**

U.S. restrictions on the sale of food and medicine to Cuba, an amendment offered by Republican Congressman Jerry Moran of Kansas. **The House also voted 232 to 186 to prohibit funding for enforcement of the restrictions on travel by U.S. citizens to Cuba.** An amendment was offered by another Republican congressman, Mark Sanford of South Carolina. Language for both of these amendments was later removed from the bill by the House Republican leadership.

The American Public. Americans, across party lines and geographical areas, are finding common ground to push for changes in policy. The case of 6-year-old Elián González, who after losing his mother when she attempted to come to the United States, was kept in Miami against the wishes of his father and grandparents in Cuba, served to bring new voices into the political debate about Cuba.

- **A Gallup poll conducted in May 1999. concluded that 71% of Americans support the reestablishment of diplomatic relations with Cuba.**
- **Musical, sports and academic exchanges are increasing.** Cuban bands from the island play to packed audiences in US festival from coast to coast. Students spanning wide geographical areas from Oregon to Massachusetts visit and interact with their Cuban counterparts. And even in Miami, 100 Cuban academics, the largest ever in the US since 1959, participated in the Latin American Studies Association last March.
- **Americans and Cuban Americans travel to Cuba in increasing numbers.** Despite travel restrictions, in 1999 alone about 180,000 Americans traveled to Cuba. 124,000 of these were Cuban Americans who are limited by U.S. law to one visit every 12 months for family emergencies.
- **Citizen Exchanges** are being developed across the U.S. Nearly 200 colleges and universities are licensed by the U.S. government to send people to Cuba. 100 Cuban academics, the largest ever since 1959, participated in a congress of the Latin American Studies Association in Miami. High school students from Oregon held debates in Havana with their Cuban counterparts; and now those same students plan to bring a delegation of students from Cuba for debates in the U.S. Sports exchanges by professional and amateur athletes are taking place between Cubans and Americans from Baltimore to Havana and from Oakland to Santiago.
- **City-to-city and people-to-people contacts continue to expand.** City councils and mayor from cities such as Mobile, Alabama; Oakland, Hayward, and West Hollywood in California; Pittsburgh and Philadelphia in Pennsylvania; Madison and Milwaukee in Wisconsin; Seattle and Tacoma in Washington; Tampa and Saint Augustine in Florida; and others have reached

out to Cuba to explore and engage in sister-city associations or projects of mutual benefit with Cuba.

What is the Cuban Embargo?

In 1963 the US Treasury Department produced the Cuban Assets Control Regulations which embodied the essential features of the U.S. Economic Embargo against Cuba that has been in effect ever since. This includes a freeze on all Cuban owned assets in the U.S. and a prohibition on all non-licensed financial transactions between the U.S. and Cuba, and between Cuba and U.S. nationals (including the spending of money by U.S. citizens in the course of travel to the island).

The embargo was relaxed during the Carter administration when restrictions on travel by U.S. citizens were removed. Then President Ronald Reagan severely restricted travel by U.S. citizens and developed a lobby group of Cuban Americans émigrés hostile to the Cuban Government.

President George Bush under the Torricelli Act restricted ships that visit Cuba from visiting the U.S. and in 1996 President Clinton signed the Helms-Burton Bill into law, thus codifying the embargo into law and curtailing his own presidential powers to bring about changes in U.S.- Cuba policy.

Today the embargo referred to us a "blockade" in Cuba is perhaps the harshest embargo in U.S. history.

- Bars any ship that docks in Cuba from docking at any US board for six months.
- Stipulates on site verification for medical sales.
- Bans medical exports that could be used by Cuba's pharmaceutical industry.
- Completely bans food sales. The free flow of medicine and food was allowed in the multilateral embargoes against North Korea, Vietnam, South Africa, Chile, El Salvador, the Soviet Union, and Haiti. In recent U.N. supported embargoes against Iraq and the former Yugoslavia, the U.N. upheld the principle that medicine, and food must be allowed to serve the basic needs of the civilian population.

Why it should be lifted.

From the perspective of those who want to get rid of Castro and the Cuban Revolution the policy simply has not worked. It is essentially a unilateral U.S. policy condemned by the United Nations for over 9 years. It is essentially a unilateral policy with no support from U.S. friends and allies. For nine years the United Nations has voted against the U.S. and the only nation that consistently votes with the U.S., Israel, has investments in Cuba.

It penalizes investors and entrepreneurs. While Cuba is open to investors from all over the world, Americans are not allowed to take advantage of lucrative business possibilities in tourism, biotechnology, and agriculture.

It creates a state of siege in the Cuban population, thus handling the Cuban government a ready excuse for any failed economic policy or measures it might take against groups deemed U.S. nurtured subversives. And as an added consequence, it closes doors and possibilities to Cubans everywhere to address issues of common interest for the good of the Cuban nation.

From a purely American perspective, it creates a threat to U.S. national security by having U.S. policy in the hands of a vociferous lobby based in Florida that can muffle the Pentagon and force it to hide defects of U.S. – Cuba policy. In other words, it denies access to the public and lawmakers of necessary information to promote a national policy towards Cuba.

From a human perspective it causes pain and suffering to innocent human beings and has been deemed as immoral and ethically unacceptable by religious leaders.

The Cuban Adjustment Act

As the central piece of U.S.- Cuba policy stands the Cuban Adjustment Act of 1966, an act that excepts Cubans from general U.S. migration laws. Virtually any Cuban who reaches U.S. soil has a work permit, permanent residence and in due course full U.S. citizenship rights.

This policy stands in sharp contrast to what is offered to the millions of undocumented immigrants who reach the US from all parts of the world. These people live lives outside the political system, deprived of voting rights and access to the press, often scarred by family breakups and the abandonment of cultural surroundings. Many come to the U.S. to escape poverty, human rights abuse, and in search of economic opportunities.

But the privileges granted to Cubans come with imposition of laws that directly affect Cuban families and that many find impossible to abide by.

- Once in the U.S., Cubans are restricted to a single visit to Cuba every 12 months for reason of close family emergencies.

- Unlike other immigrants they are limited as to the amount and frequency of money remittances that may be sent to family dependents (who may not be deducted from their income tax reports) back in Cuba

For the reasons listed above, it is evident that profound changes will take place in U.S.-Cuba relations in the near future.

CAAEF HOLDS ORGANIZATIONAL WORKSHOPS ON CAPITOL HILL

Directors of CAAEF together with Cuban American leaders from Florida, California, Texas, Maryland, and Washington, DC held workshop meetings aimed at strengthening the Alliance. During two days of intense work, we analyzed the work of the Alliance and developed strategies and a two-year plan. Prior to our meetings, we visited over 20 congressional offices and held an open- house reception in our office on Capitol Hill.

During the months of June and July, we conducted a revision of our Bylaws and the structure of CAAEF. We held an election for our new Board of Directors, and at present are in the process of selecting candidates for our Advisory Council. of CAAEF.

THE CUBA MILLENNIUM SUMMIT
A PARTNERSHIP WITH FAMILY RIGHTS ADVOCATES AND
BUSINESS, RELIGIOUS AND CUBAN AMERICAN ORGANIZATIONS

Cuban Americans came to the steps of the U.S. Supreme Court at the end of their visits and briefings to Congress asking for justice in lifting the travel ban to Cuba. CAAEF was assisted in organizing The Cuban American Advocacy Day in partnership with Puentes Cubanos, Cambio Cubano, The Cuban Committee for Democracy, and the US/Cuba Legal Forum. The events in Washington were also supported by West Coast Cuban American Alliance, The Dante Fascell Center for Peace and Conflict Resolution, Fundación Amistad, and Cuban American Defense League

CAAEF MEETING IN TAMPA, FLORIDA
OCTOBER 2- 3, 1999

The Alliance for Responsible Cuba Policy, The Latin American Working Group, The Washington Office on Latin America, The Center for International Policy, The World Policy Institute, Americans for Humanitarian Trade with Cuba, The Tampa-Cuba Alliance, U.S.-Cuba Sister Cities Association, The Caribbean American Children Foundation, *Alianza Martiana Asociación Martiana*, The Time Is Now Coalition and a host of other organizations hosted the Tampa meeting.

Center for International Policy Conference in Miami
U.S.-Cuba Policy - A New Look

CAAEF Board member and executive director of the Caribbean-American Children Foundation, Alberto Jones gave a presentation on "The Views of the Afro-Cuban Community" at the CIP conference in Miami. Delvis Fernández-Levy, CAAEF President, also spoke on the effects of the embargo on Cuban families.

Next to Sylvia Wilhelm, a Cuban American advocate for democracy, family reunification and changes in US/Cuba policy,

29

ENCUENTRO ENTRE CUBANOS
MEETING WITH CUBANS

In May of 2000, CAAEF organized a conference entitled U.S.-Cuba Relations at the Threshold of the New Millennium with religious, academic, business, and political leaders in South Florida. In the late spring, CAAEF also led panel discussions on the impact of U.S. policy on the Cuban American community at the U.S.-Cuba Business Summit held in Cancun, Mexico and Havana, Cuba, which included participation by representatives from major American and foreign companies with investments in Cuba.

Our work within Cuba itself, in addition to ongoing citizen exchanges, has included organizing a meeting in Havana in July of this year (as detailed in this full report) to promote a dialogue between leaders in the Cuban American community and representatives of the Cuban government. Over 50 Cuban Americans and Cubans from the island participated in several workshops to explore obstacles to family reunification; potential investment in Cuba; and prospects for increased citizen exchanges.

A Memorable Meeting in Cuba

Our group of about 20 Cuban emigrants, residents in the United States, members of the Cuban American Alliance, visited the island from July 24 to 27 of 2000. The Alliance is recognized in North America as a non-profit organization that works within constructive and respectful schemes in the search for solutions to problems faced by Cubans residing in the United States. Our mission is to educate the American people and their leaders about the adverse impact on Cubans, inside or outside the island, of current United States policy and the consequent lack of normal relations between Cuba and the United States. To carry out that mission, we make efforts to serve as a vehicle or bridge for the development of links between people in our two nations that promote human understanding and compassion. Our meeting among Cubans was based on the full recognition of the integrity and independence of the Cuban Nation as well as our unconditional support for the economic and social well-being of all Cubans.

What We Expected from the Conversations

• Exchange views on U.S. policy toward Cuba. In particular, to talk about the current situation: after the reunification of little Elian with his family in Cuba, and by virtue of substantive changes in American public opinion in favor of trade and travel to Cuba.

• Deepen knowledge about the Cuban economy and advance our potential and possibilities to cooperate in its different areas of development: tourism, agriculture, mining, etc.

• Explore and participate in liaison projects with Cuba. Update our knowledge of projects at the people-to-people level, such as sister-city partnerships between Cuba and the U.S.; family reunification and impediments to its realization; academic, medical, cultural, and humanitarian exchanges; and the renovation and architectural rescue of our historical and cultural heritage.

THE PROGRAM

The visit began on the morning of July 24 with a welcome ceremony at the Cuban Institute of Friendship with Peoples (ICAP) in which José Ramon Cabañas, director of the Department of Assistance to Cubans Living Abroad (DACCRE), expressed his gratitude for the efforts we made in the search for just relations between the country of residence and our country of origin. For our part, the Alliance also thanked the DACCRE leadership for this first step in enabling a frank, cordial, and respectful conversation among Cubans.

For a second session we moved to a meeting with Osvaldo Martínez, President of the Economic Affairs Committee of the National Assembly, where he gave us a summary of the serious consequences for Cuba of the disintegration of the socialist bloc together with the intensification of the United States economic blockade during the decade of the 1990s through laws such as the Torricelli and the Helms-Burton. During the meeting, recovery rate statistics and sustainable economic growth rates were shown. We exchanged views on the effect that family remittances could have on that growth and the possibilities for us to insert into future economic and financial development. In the afternoon we also participated in extensive exchanges of views and debates on issues affecting Cubans in the United States and the current policy of the United States Government towards Cuba. Along with the representatives of the Alliance were delegates from the following organizations: National Assembly of People's Power, Center for the Study of Political Alternatives (CEAP), DACCRE, Center for Studies on the United States of the University of Havana, ICAP and other guests. In particular, we conveyed to the MINREX (Ministry of Foreign Affairs) authorities our concerns and problems that we faced in order to be able to travel to Cuba.

The next day, on July 25, we continued with a tour and detailed report about the redevelopment project for *La Habana Vieja* (Old Havana) next to the social work that is developed there to rescue one of the most beautiful architectural areas of the world, declared a "Heritage of Universal Culture" by the United Nations. From there we went to the Ameijeiras Hospital to learn about the Cuban health system and the medical assistance projects that Cuba develops in several countries of Africa, Latin America and the Caribbean.

On July 26, we were able to witness the march for the Day of national rebellion with more than a million Cubans and participants from various countries of the world who carried flags as a sign of support and solidarity with Cuba. That night we attended a Gala event at the Karl Marx Theater where an emotional account of Cuba's history was held through dances, music, and poetry -- an event that filled everyone there with inspiration and *Cubanness*.

On Thursday, July 27, we left Havana on a trip to Matanzas, crossing green valleys and mountains with their ubiquitous royal palms and sugar-cane fields to reach a meeting with representatives of the National Association of Small Farmers (ANAP), at the Ramón Martell Cooperative in the Limonar region. Topics were discussed on the different forms of land tenure by the *campesino* (agricultural worker) sector in Cuba. With typical peasant hospitality we were dismissed with the *trinar* of guitars, *guajiros* points and a rich snack of varied Cuban fruits, full of joy and friendship in the middle of a green countryside, under a beautiful blue and white sky and an immense tricolor flag with its lone star.

We left for Varadero to end our visit with representatives of the Ministry of Tourism and a broad explanation about the tourist development in Cuba. The next day, members of the Alliance traveled to Matanzas, Cienfuegos, Camagüey, Santiago, and Baracoa to strengthen family relations and deepen academic projects, architectural restoration, sister cities, and to strengthen the ties between the Alliance and the Cuban Association of Limited Physical-Motor (ACLIFIM).

After several hours of debate, a resolution was unanimously adopted, calling on congress and the President of the United States to end restrictions on trade and travel to Cuba, and beyond, to work diligently to establish full normalization of relations between the United States of America and the Republic of Cuba.

IMPRESSIONS ABOUT THE MEETING.

"I was moved by the strength of the Cuban people, and I appreciate everything I could witness there. At first, I didn't know what to expect. I developed a great appreciation for my cultural heritage and the way of life of the Cubans. The embargo is harmful to everyone. I think it's time to reach a political understanding between the United States and Cuba. That is; our countries must respect the sovereignty of each to enjoy their natural resources and the beauty of their lands and people, and above all, to enjoy peace."

Cristina Ferreira, *a young student from the state of Pennsylvania, on her first trip to the land of her ancestors.*

"I paid a visit to an aunt who for me highly important and appreciated. Tía Acela is like the 'griot* of the people' — someone who knows my family's history and can relate the stories her father had made since the war on the Hill of San Juan. As an African-American my family heritage is an essential part of knowing who I am."

Patricia Morán, *resides in the Washington metropolitan area and tells us about the needs to visit her Grandmother's Land.*
* 'Griot' is a word of African origin meaning historian of the people. In the oral tradition these people are responsible for transmitting the history of their people from one generation to another.

"When the plane took off from Havana, I remembered what I had witnessed during that week, I was more convinced than ever that U.S. policy toward Cuba must change. And if it is, we Cuban Americans who have been responsible for maintaining that embargo, it is up to us to bring it to an end."

Ricardo González, *resides in Madison, Wisconsin, member of the board of directors of the Cuban American Alliance and president of the Madison-Camagüey Association.*

"I will continue to fight to meet with anyone who wants to close the gap that artificially divides our people. I will continue to fight to expose all this inhumane policy that causes pain and suffering to our people."

Alberto Jones, resides in Palm Coast, Florida, a member of the board of directors of the Cuban American Alliance and leader of the Caribbean American Children's Foundation -- an association that strengthens fraternal and cultural ties with Cuban communities of Anglo-Caribbean descent.

Meetings in Cuba - Highlights

On the heels of a congressional vote, last July 20th, that favored trade and travel to Cuba, 20 members of the Cuban American Alliance Education Fund (CAAEF) held meetings in Cuba from the 24th to the 27th of July. A broad representation of the Cuban American community from Florida, Texas, Illinois, Wisconsin, Delaware, Pennsylvania, New York, New Jersey and California conducted meetings and debates with Cuban authorities on issues that impact on the lives of Cubans on both sides of the Florida Straits. Some stayed longer to visit family and friends in different parts of the island: Havana, Matanzas, Santa Clara, Cienfuegos, Camagüey, Santiago, and Baracoa.

CAAEF (or the Alliance) is recognized as a nonprofit organization that functions within a framework of respect and constructive engagements in search of solutions to problems facing Cuban Americans. Our mission is to educate Americans about the adverse impact that U.S./Cuba policy and the ensuing state of abnormal relations between the U.S. and Cuba have on the Cuban people, both in the U.S. and in Cuba. We strive to serve as vehicles or bridges to develop engagements that promote understanding and human compassion. Our *Encuentro entre Cubanos,* "Meeting among Cubans," had as a basis the full recognition of the integrity and independence of the Cuban Nation as well as our unconditional support for the social and economic well-being of all Cubans.

THE PROGRAM
EXPECTATIONS AND ACCOMPLISHMENTS

- To exchange opinions about U.S. policy towards Cuba, particularly at this political juncture: following the reunification of young Elián González with his family in Cuba, and in view of substantive changes taking place in U.S. public opinion in favor of permitting trade, travel and contacts between Cubans and Americans.
- To deepen our knowledge about the Cuban economy and to advance our potential and possibilities for future involvement in Cuba's economic development in areas, such as, tourism, agriculture, and mining.

- To explore and engage in projects of mutual benefit between Cubans and Americans, in particular to update our knowledge about: **1)** the implementation of sister city projects; **2)** impediments that hinder family reunification; **3)** citizen exchange projects in areas such as education, culture, the legal profession, and humanitarian assistance; **4)** projects for the restoration of buildings and historic sites in Old Havana and other parts of Cuba.

WELCOME

Our visit began on Monday, July 24th with a welcoming ceremony at the Cuban Institute for Friendship with People (ICAP) led by Cuban Officials of the Ministry of Foreign Relations (MINREX). **José Ramón Cabañas, Director of the Department of Cuban Residents Overseas (DACCRE)** expressed recognition for the work that the Cuban American Alliance carried out on behalf of the reunification of Elián González with his family in Cuba. He also expressed thanks for our efforts in seeking just relations between the U.S. and Cuba. We, as members of CAAEF thanked the representatives of DACCRE and ICAP for facilitating a space and a forum where Cubans may have cordial, frank and respectful conversations.

José Ramón Cabañas extends a welcoming message to the Encuentro entre Cubanos

THE ECONOMY

Later that morning, we met with **Osvaldo Martínez, President of the Commission on Economics of the National Assembly**. Mr. Martínez sum marized the grave consequences fallen on Cuba due to the disintegration of the Soviet Block along with the intensification of the U.S. embargo as manifested by the Torricelli and Helms-Burton Acts.

The Crisis of 1993

In 1993 Cuba's GNP was 35% less than in 1989. At that time very few analysts gave the Cuban government any chance to survive. Petroleum imported from the old Soviet Union at low prices declined from $13\frac{1}{2}$ million tons in 1989 to 6 million in 1993 -- transportation was nearly paralyzed, there were frequent black-outs, some for as long as 16 hours in Havana and 20 to 24 hours in other municipalities. Total imports of $8 billion in 1989 fell down to $2 billion in 1993. Level of imports in 1993 was 25% of what had been in 1989.

The Recovery

By 1995 there were signs of recovery. The GNP increased by 2.5% and later in 1999 by 6.5%. Foreign financing has a limiting effect on Cuba's economic growth. Cuba is not allowed to obtain financing from the World Bank or the International Monetary Fund. It can only get private short-term loans at rates of 30% above normal -- and here is where Helms-Burton hits the hardest. The total financial cost of the blockade up to1998 is figured at $67 billion U.S. dollars, a crushing 4 times Cuba's GNP.

The exchange rate of Cuban pesos to U.S. dollars which went as high as 150 to 1, now has stabilized at 20 to 1. Foreign investments in 1990 amounted to $100 million U.S. dollars and in 1999 they reached $2.5 billion dollars, of which 80% were due to tourism. The official revenue figure from dollar stores, *paladares* (small family-owned restaurants), and bed & breakfast accommodations, is $500 million. Revenues from sugar exports are $400 million and from tobacco amount to $200 million. Petroleum production is up to three million tons, which includes the equivalent of 400,000 tons in gas, being now used as kitchen fuel. Offshore exploration is being parceled out to foreign companies, up to 200 miles out to sea. 80% of the Electric power is generated with Cuban oil.

Some in the U.S. have estimated the **remittances** from abroad to be around $1 billion U.S. dollars, but no one can truly be certain of that amount. Remittances are not considered in the national budget, but they play an important role in the recovery of the economy.

Other Statistics. State enterprises were operating at a loss. The number of ministries has been reduced from 50 down to 32. Unemployment is recognized at 6%, although it is not alarming, e.g., in Spain it is 16% and in Latin America it is 10%. Cost of housing is 10% of a person's salary, 6 % of which applies to the purchase of the house or apartment, millions already own their places of residence. A new tax system has been enacted for self-employed people.

Outlook for the Year 2000. The greatest problem lies in obtaining foreign financing — every country in the world obtains financing. The cost of the U.S. economic blockade of Cuba is estimated at $67 billion U.S. dollars, more than 4 times its GNP, and more than 6 times its present debt. For the year 2000 economic growth is estimated to be at least 4%.

Remarks. The cost of imports for basic human consumption would change drastically, if trade were permitted by the U.S. For example, rice which comes from-Vietnam, powdered milk from New Zealand, bicycles from China, and soybean products, could be easily obtained from nearby U.S. markets. Some see the present situation as an economic war being waged by the U.S. against the Cuban people.

OPINION EXCHANGES

On Tuesday, July 25th, we met with representatives from the National Assembly, the Center for the Study of Alternative Policies (CEAP), American (U.S.) Studies Faculty at the University of Havana, ICAP and other invited guests, we participated in a wide exchange of opinions and debates. Issues ranged from specific policies that impact on the lives of ordinary Cuban Americans to citizen exchange projects for students, academic faculty, medical workers, and legal professionals.

THE CUBAN HEALTH CARE SYSTEM

After that lively discussion, we went to the Ameijeiras Hospital to learn about the Cuban health care system. The hospital is housed in a tall imposing building overlooking the Havana waterfront. It was inaugurated in 1982 and currently has 42 medical specialties, 500 physicians (70 are foreign residents), and 950 beds. Twenty-two thousand surgeries are performed per year, and 80% of the personnel are women. It has the most modern medical technology in Cuba. We held talks with two physicians and hospital administrators, Drs. Martínez and Gillian.

Comments and Statistics. According to Dr. Gillian, a young woman physician, "The health of a country is not necessarily measured in terms of hospital buildings. Health is not just absence of sickness, but well-being." They presented the following statistics:

- In Cuba there are 65,000 doctors, that is 1 doctor per 172 inhabitants -- in Africa the ratio is 1 doctor per 100,000 persons.
- 98.3% of the Cuban population is covered by family doctors.
- Infant mortality has been reduced to 6.4 per 1000.
- 95% of pregnant women are under care during their first trimester. Maternal homes are located near the hospitals.
- 100% of children are protected against 12 common childhood diseases - Polio was eradicated in 1962.
- 98% of deaths are from non-infectious diseases.

Cuba's Medical Assistance Overseas. Cuba is presently sending 1724 doctors and nurses to 13 underdeveloped countries around the world, including 470 to Guatemala, 420 to Haiti, and 150 to Gambia. Cuban medical personnel overseas have performed over 14,000 surgeries. Cuba opened a medical school for Latin Americans where approximately 5000 doctors will graduate in the next ten years to work in regions of Central America and the Caribbean.

In Gambia alone, before the arrival of the Cuban medical professionals, there were only 18 physicians for a 7 million population and infant mortality stood at 121 per 1000 inhabitants -today, it has now been reduced by 34%.

TOUR OF *LA HABANA VIEJA*

The same day we went on a tour of La Habana Vieja, Old Havana, led by a historian and an architect who carefully explained the on-going restoration of buildings and the humane social work carried out as they temporarily relocate residents nearby until the restoration work is completed. Old Havana has been declared a Heritage for Humanity by the United Nations and is one of the most beautiful architectural regions of the world.

Restoration in progress in Old Historic Section of Havana

Tropical fruits from the Ramón Martell Cooperative
Delicious *Cocos, Guayabas, Mangos y Platanitos*

A MEETING WITH AGRICULTURAL WORKERS

On July 27, we departed Havana for Matanzas Province crossing lush valleys and green mountains splashed with the ever-present royal palms, sugar cane and banana plantations. Oil pumps dotted parts of the land scape signaling an energy resource that reaches over 2 million tons and fuels 70% of the electric power needs of Cuba.

Three hours later we arrived at the Ramón Martell Cooperative in Limonar, Matanzas where we met with members of the National Association of Small Farmers (ANAP) to discuss their work, the incorporation of farmers into the national economy, and the different forms of land ownership in Cuba. The cooperative produces sugar cane for a nearby sugar mill, *Central Horacio Rodríguez.* Also fruits and vegetables are grown, and milk and beef are produced for the 45 families associated with the cooperative -- 70% of their production is sold while the remaining 30% goes for local consumption.

With typical *campesino* hospitality, we were treated to a delicious lunch with papayas, mangos, bananas, oranges; local cheeses, fruit juices, rum and a strong local coffee called *café carretero.* This was a festive and friendly occasion with families, the singing of traditional songs, *puntos guajiros,* and Cuban country music amid a verdant landscape under a brilliant mottled blue sky.

MEETING WITH TOURISM INDUSTRY OFFICIALS AT VARADERO BEACH

On our last afternoon as a group, we were received at the Varadero Golf Club, the old DuPont mansion, that now offers first class accommodation in rooms built of Cuban mahogany and Italian marble. The Club is open daily for full services, including the rental of golf clubs, practice ranges, trolley and cart's rental, caddie service, lockers, and lessons. The total length is 6,850 yards. At the time of our visit, a vacation package was offered for $1000 per week, including all meals, drinks, beach access and golf facilities (this alone usually runs at $180 per day).

Later that evening we said our goodbyes and went our separate ways to renew family ties and strengthen our projects in education, historic site restoration, sister-city relationships, and our work with the Cuban Association for the Disabled. Each participant came away from the conference with a positive and powerful new commitment for the work that lies ahead.

Discovering My Cuban Soul
by Christine Ferreira

I longed for it, to be a part of it. A voice inside of me kept saying, "Go, follow your heart." I discovered my Cuban soul the week of July 23, 2000. It was as beautiful as I had imagined. My father never went back, remembering all the hardship and chaos of the revolution. But after thirty-eight years since that time, what I saw was a rich, beautiful land, a well-cared for people, and educational opportunities available to all who wanted them.

My journey took me from Havana to Varadero on this large Caribbean Island. My uncle, Dr. Pedro Ferreira, his wife, and I traveled to Arroyo Naranjo to meet Sara Diaz Ferreira and Juan Falcon Ferreira, members of my extended family, who I never had the opportunity of meeting. They became dear to me right from the start.

Through my travels and educational experiences with the Cuban American Alliance, I developed a heightened awareness of the intense political confrontation between the United States and Cuba. It is now my quest to educate and share my experiences with other Americans.

To me, Cuba was a new frontier worth every second of my time spent there. I was touched by the strength of the Cuban people, and I value all that I experienced. At first, I had no idea what to expect. I looked forward to eating authentic Cuban food and listening to the music that I love. I did so, but my trip was much more than that. I developed a sense of my heritage and an appreciation for the Cuban way of life. I was assimilated into the culture of Cuba on the 26th of July when I participated in a march calling for an end to the 40-year U.S. economic blockade on Cuba. I shared the same views as all the participants in the march; that the embargo is harmful to all Cubans, preventing them from purchasing necessary food and medicine from the United States.

I believe that now is the time to come to a political understanding, between the United States and Cuba. This means that our nations should respect each other's sovereignty so that they may enjoy the resources and beauty of their lands and people, and above all, enjoy peace.

Discovery of Paradise and a Trip Cut Short
by Anita Núñez

After accompanying Luis Seguí to visit family in Santiago, I traveled by bus to Baracoa, an idyllic small town on the north coast near the eastern most tip of Cuba, the oldest colonial town in the Americas, founded in 1512. The town is surrounded by pristine forests and mountains, coconut and cacao plantations, big rivers and black-sand beaches. One may stay at a private home for $15 a day including breakfast. There are also small hotels, discos, and a few foreign tourists, but the townsfolk remain among the friendliest in Cuba, still unspoiled by urban life and contact with the outside world. For centuries it was difficult to travel to Baracoa by land due to the lack of roads. The town has been made accessible to the rest of Cuba by a ribbon of a highway carved from mountain sides, a major feat of engineering developed by the Cuban Revolution. The entire region, referred to as "Sagua/Moa/Baracoa," is a National Park that has been declared an "international preserve" by UNESCO.

I planned for a two or three-day visit but fell in love with the place and decided to stay for about 9 days, leaving only because I ran out of cash thanks to Bank of America and Western Union. Luis and I had planned on a fourth week to visit family on the island and had foreseen the need to withdraw additional funds from our personal accounts in Bank of America, using a VISA card.

However, when on August 9, Luis went with his bank card to a bank in Santiago, *Banco Nacional,* and I did likewise in Baracoa, we both obtained a slip from a computer stating: *operación denegada,* transaction denied. Luis' wife in Santa Maria, California tried to transfer $300 from their California Office, but was informed that Cuba was not in the list of countries for money transfers. Western Union had been making those transfers since

Luís Seguí and Anita Núñez

January 1, 1999, when President Clinton authorized them but apparently these actions were now part of a new U.S. policy to further block the entry of dollars into the Cuban economy. For us, it meant a family trip cut short, we had to return quickly to Havana by bus, an all-day trip, to catch a flight out of Cuba, thus limiting our time with friends and loved ones and unable to complete our mission of assessing the needs of the disabled in Santiago.

My Grandmother's Country
by Patricia Morán

On route to Cuba with the Cuban American Alliance Education Fund (CAAEF), memories of family stories start to fill my mind. From the moment the plane touches down, I am anxious to walk along Malecón Avenue to look over the wall and see the beautiful shades of blue-green water on a clear blue-sky sunny summer day. The very same waters where my *Abuela* (grandmother) Mercedes watched her nephews take a swim to cool off from the tropical heat, noise, hustle and bustle of city life in *La Habana.* As I bend over the wall looking into the water, I'm reminded of Cousin Pedro's story about a fishing trip to Havana when he was nine years old. After coming down from San Joaquin with his father to fish, he stood on the rocks directly under the Malecón wall with a make-shift fishing rod and decided to swim out as far as possible but

then could not get back to shore easily. He had to be rescued and consequently -- got a spanking from Papi José for not listening to his warnings about engaging in such risky behavior. "That was a lesson learned the hard way," he says after sharing the story.

These and many stories of my family's life in Cuba answer those important questions about my life that give meaningful connections to my beginnings and culture. As a second-generation Afro-Cuban American, my family's heritage is an essential part of knowing "who I am."

I visited a very important aunt in Habana, *Tia Asela.* She is important because like the village *griot* she knows the history of our family going back to stories her father related about the war of San Juan Hill. She also had pictures which were priceless. Unfortunately, quite a few of the photos were destroyed in the floods caused by hurricane

Hugo. But the ones I brought back were like "gold" to my family. Pedro, who lives close

to my neighborhood in Maryland, is nostalgic and yet realistic about the changes that have occurred since he left. He and his family are planning to make the pilgrimage back home to visit family, the old block, and especially *Tia Asela*. The break-up of our Cuban family was a traumatic and unfortunate occurrence. They came to Washington 32 years ago to escape the economic hardships caused by a U.S. policy that prevents the sale of food and medicine to their country. I was 14 years old when they arrived and was able to see how being uprooted from their culture, home and family took a toll on their lives.

Our group visited the Cuban Institute for Friendship with People (ICAP) and I was moved by the warm welcome and recognition of our contribution in helping to reunite Elián González with his family and his return to his homeland. They also acknowledged our efforts to improve family relations for Cubans on both sides of the Florida straits.

We were able to hear firsthand reports from José Cabañas, Director of the Office Attending Cuban Residents Overseas, attached to the Ministry of Foreign Affairs, about the many obstacles hindering normal relations between the two countries. Our visits to the Ministry of Foreign Investments, Cuban Chamber of Commerce, Ministry of Tourism and the Public Health Sector informed our group on the grave economic difficulties faced by the country over the past 10 years due to the collapse of the Soviet Union and the tightening of the U.S. embargo through the Torricelli and Helms-Burton legislation. But I am amazed and encouraged by how humane and creative Cuban policy responds to the needs of the people who have sacrificed above and beyond for their country's sovereignty. For example, during CAAEF's tour of the renovation and conservation of Old Havana, we saw that the habitants of these historical landmark buildings in such disrepair (once used exclusively by the rich) were temporarily housed nearby while renovation is taking place. Once the work is completed, they will move back into their renovated housing at an unbelievably low cost. I was thoroughly impressed by this because in most countries the prime real estate of such historical buildings once improved, is rarely financially affordable to the people who have been forced to leave.

Visits to Cuba are so important to understand what the "Cuban experience" is and what it has been. The food and medicine embargo has to be lifted immediately. Babies and children are not receiving the essential nutrients needed for healthy development. As a result, Cuba has started to lose ground on having the lowest infant mortality rate in Latin America.

The information from this trip is invaluable because here in the U.S. we are so deprived of accurate news from Cuba. My family was both surprised and happy to hear about the information from my visit. They feel news about Cuba is never positive, is unbalanced, and is dominated by propaganda from Miami. I was delighted to know that my trip influenced their plans to visit Cuba soon. It is a definite "go-see-for-yourself experience" and then return determined to do the "right thing" by voting to lift this inhumane blockade on my Grandmother's country.

Thoughts on the 26th of July

by Ricardo González

The last time I had been in Cuba on the 26th of July was in 1979 when, as part of a group of *norteamericanos* from Wisconsin and Ohio, we watched the festivities on TV in the lobby of the Hotel Camagüey. It was a huge rally and Fidel Castro spoke for hours. We all commented later on his qualities as an orator, especially his delivery style -- how he repeated his points to drive them home -- and how it seemed the crowd was mesmerized yet responsive to his every call.

This year I participated in two separate activities commemorating the 26th of July. I was in Cuba attending a conference sponsored by the Cuban American Alliance, a network of Cuban Americans dedicated to promoting understanding between the U.S. and Cuba, and we were invited to take part in the march held in Havana on the morning of the 26th. People began to gather on the Malecón, Havana's seaside boulevard, very early in the morning. We arrived around 7:30 a.m. and I was impressed to see so many people arriving and taking their place. Little did I know then just how many people!

We walked behind the delegation of Americans who had traveled with Pastors for Peace, an American church group led by the Reverend Lucius Walker who for the past 10 years has taken humanitarian shipments to Cuba (and other Latin American Countries) in defiance of U.S. government restrictions. We were surrounded by people of various nationalities carrying their country's flags and signs of solidarity with Cuba. The atmosphere was festive and confident. It was a beautiful morning with a brilliant sun, yet without the humidity so common at this time of year. We walked for about a mile, passing by the old American Embassy, where the march ended. It was later, watching the news on TV, that I learned that one million people had taken part and that Fidel himself had been at the head of the throng, just forty steps ahead of us!

That evening, we were invited to attend a more formal cultural presentation at the Karl Marx Theater. Also attending were many of Cuba's leaders, members of the ruling Central Committee, as well as provincial rank and file members of the Communist Party. One minister after another began to come in from a side door and finally Fidel Castro himself appeared dressed in a dark blue suit and welcomed by sustained applause. Again, it was obvious that a genuine feeling of goodwill and respect reigned in the air. I found myself applauding with enthusiasm and thinking to myself how fortunate I was to be a part of this event and to be able to witness another moment in the history of Cuba.

As the plane took off from Havana a few days later and I reminisced about my week there, I came away more convinced than ever that U.S. policy toward Cuba must change. And if Cuban Americans have been responsible for maintaining the embargo in place, then it behooves us now to be the ones to bring an end to it. The Cuban American Alliance provides us with the opportunity to join in an unprecedented effort to bring our case before Congress and the American people. The more our elected officials hear from us as Cuban Americans, the more they will start believing that a growing majority of our people want normalization of relations.

The Resolution drafted and approved by our group in Havana should only be the first step in a sustained effort to change U.S. policy. Each and every one of us ought to do what he/she can to follow up with more letters and calls to our representatives. We cannot stop until the embargo is ended, and Cuba is recognized as a sovereign nation, regardless of who is the head of its government.

Elisa Greenberg, Mariana Gastón, Ricardo González and Juan Romagosa

Reaching out to Cuba - A Moral Imperative

by Elisa Greenberg

As a Cuban American who deeply loves both my country of birth and my adopted country, I am pained by the fact that it is precisely my government which bears the responsibility and/or lends itself as the excuse for the scarcities of food and medicine-that so hurt the Cuban people.

Elisa Apfel Greenberg
in Washinton, D.C.

At the same time, while helping to establish academic exchanges between American and Cuban universities I have witnessed the kind of clarity of vision, mutual understanding and respect that comes from honest dialogue while recognizing philosophical disagreements. In order for these types of exchanges to take place, it is imperative that our laws do not hinder the kind of travel to which we, as American citizens, are entitled, even to Cuba. It is also important to remember that this people with whom we are exchanging important ideas are entitled to negotiate as best they can, the extremely necessary purchases of their food and medicine without impediments from our country. These impediments are WRONG.

One must also bear in mind, that a healthier stronger Cuban citizenry (both of mind and body) could also lead to a stronger healthier civil society better able to realize their aspirations, which of course, may not necessarily be what some of us envision. Here again they are entitled, as any sovereign people should be, to forge the course of their history. Cubans in and out of the island are not a homogeneous group, and as in most other societies each member has a vision of what ought to be. I suggest that it is precisely through the dialectic process that this vision, or rather the multiple visions could combine in new and exciting concepts. Our current policies toward Cuba are not conducive to an environment of mutual trust and respect where these intellectual interactions may take place.

Cubans sometimes mistrust even a well-intentioned hand extended in friendship. Considering our hurtful policy, who can blame them? In the spirit of our vision for an America that is just, whose foreign policy is guided by a sense of responsibility as a world leader, whose power is used to help nations less fortunate than our own; let us put to rest the petulant adolescent years when a temper tantrum in the form of an embargo or blockade met those who dared to confront us; let us have the courage to be mature, responsible citizens of the world. Cuba would be a good place to start.

A Cuban Encounter --My Impressions
by Maura Barrios

This was my first hosted visit to Cuba; I have traveled there for family visits in the past. I was most impressed with the quality of the tour organized by the Cuban Institute for Friendship with People (ICAP) facilitated by its bright and energetic staff. The tour included meetings with high-level economists, Havana restoration officials, health practitioners, University of Havana faculty members, farm cooperative administrators and officials in the tourism industry. We also participated in the march on July 26th with more than 1 million persons, including many from other nations. The march protested the United States embargo of Cuba; not a comfortable sight for we Americans.

I was also impressed with the dialogues that took place between Cuban government officials and Cuban Americans. The Cubans were open, honest, and direct. The Cuban Americans raised important questions about future relations between the U.S. and Cuba and reconciliation of the split communities. All are committed to dialogue, reconciliation, and improved relations with the United States.

Cuban economists described their economic situation as one "miraculously in recovery." (I noted great improvements since my first visit in 1992). All spoke of the U.S. embargo in severely negative terms, as a deterrent to providing better services to the Cuban people. They honestly stated that family remittances are a major source of income, surpassing sugar or tobacco revenues. Tourism is booming, even in the hottest month of July! People that I met outside the government official circles also expressed that things have improved, although prices are very high. Capitalism and entrepreneurship are now common practice and even encouraged in many sectors.

I was surprised by the support displayed by the vast majority of Cubans for their government, their leaders and their Revolution. There is a rekindled pride following the reunification of Elián González with his nation and family. Cubans are proud that they have survived all of the difficulties imposed by U.S. policies and enjoy favorable economic relations with many nations. There remains a strong commitment to social-human values among all sectors of Cuban society, even when they complain about limitations in other areas.

My particular interests in Cuba are academic and cultural exchanges. I am very pleased that U.S. policies are allowing more of these kinds of exchanges; and the Cubans welcome these exchanges also. These exchanges allow Americans to learn about our close neighbor's fascinating and unique culture(s) and history. They also allow Cubans to learn more about American culture(s) and values, after so many years of isolation and misinformation. The exchange is mutually beneficial, it is an exchange of philosophy as well as values and both parties gain deeper insights. For those of us interested in. U.S.-Latin American relations and cooperation, there is much to learn from the Cuban experiment.

I am very grateful to the Cuban American Alliance and to the *Instituto Cubano de Amistad con los Pueblos* (ICAP) for this learning experience and this opportunity to meet Cubans from so many diverse back grounds.

The U.S. Embargo and Afro Cubans
by Dr. Alberto Jones

For the past 40 years, there has been an ongoing debate by many cubanologists about the existence or not of an embargo on Cuba by the U.S. Government. Some argue it exists while others insist that it does not exist, because Cuba can purchase their goods in other markets around the world. These discussions in an academic setting, are always interesting, enlightening, but usually devoid of a human face and its tragic results.

I lived through the first half of this issue in Cuba, and I have observed the second half from the United States. One needs only to look at this tragic man-made conflict, with an impartial, honest and sincere attempt to establish what is right from wrong, irrespective of our individual educational level, religious affiliation, social stratification, political inclination, sexual orientation or racial, ethnic or age group.

I should begin by saying that I have supported and will continue to support each, and every effort taken by everyone, anywhere around the world, that may lead to the weakening or abolition of this legislation, in order that we may be able to explain our actions to future generations or a higher authority. This reasoning led me to the recent meeting held in Havana, Cuba, by the Cuban American Alliance Education Fund.

The United States Embargo on Cuba and its intensification through the Torricelli and Helms-Burton Bill, have literally placed the Afro Cuban community on the verge of its breaking point. Because of the limited tendency to migrate, most Afro Cuban families have no family members abroad, limiting their ability to receive material support through family remittances, which is an imperative to survive today in Cuba.

What makes this fact much more painful, is that the architects of these laws are acutely aware that this sector of the Cuban society is suffering the brunt of these measures. Yet, the laws are kept in place intentionally, hoping that the increased pain and suffering may lead the victims to a social explosion. Here are a few examples:

1. The United States Naval Base in Guantanamo Bay, Cuba, had employed over the years, thousands of emigrants and descendants of the English-speaking Caribbean islands living in Cuba, who performed all sorts of duties faithfully for 20, 30, 40 or more years. Suddenly in 1964 they were presented with the option of requesting political asylum on the Base and abandon their families in Cuba or, return to their families and be on their own. And on their own they have been since when most of their retirement payment have been arbitrarily withheld by the U.S. Treasury Department. Although hundreds of them have tens of thousands of dollars frozen in banks in Pennsylvania, many have died hungry, suffering from a lack of medication, their homes in disrepair or bitter with their fanner employee, who unilaterally attempted to turn them into deadbeats.

2. The extreme lack of cooking fuel in Cuba, has led families to resort to all sorts of makeshift ranges capable of burning kerosene, petroleum, alcohol, or any other flammable material. These highly hazardous burners blow up frequently, creating one of the highest injury indexes of partially burnt or burnt to death women in this hemisphere. In a predominantly Black country with a near absolute lack of hard currency that would enable the acquisition of a hazardous free industrial appliance, the burnt limb and the massive painful keloid formation that deforms and instills in the victims a permanent inferiority complex, points an accusatory index finger to each of the perpetrators of her misfortune.

3. And finally, in the name of thousands of people that have paid the ultimate price due to a lack of a simple anti-asthmatic inhaler, people have died. They have also died in indignity due to the lack of pain killers or have died unnecessarily because the emergency vehicle did not have sufficient fuel or broke down due to lack of spare parts. These are a constant reminder that we must all do whatever is within our power to end this inhumane situation.

There will never be any acceptable reason to explain such barbaric behavior that demeans all of us. I will therefore continue to travel to these meetings, hoping to close the gap that has artificially divides our people. I will continue to struggle to expose and hopefully put an end to the policies that have made all of us guilty by association.

Let each of us continue to work toward restoring human decency. Let us all be able to say in our final hour, **"We Tried!"**

Children are the hope of the World
"Los niños son la esperanza del mundo," José Martí

.

The First National Games for the Disabled
In Santiago de Cuba, Cuba - July 31, 2000 - photos by Luis Seguí

The First National Games for the Disabled
A Report from Santiago de Cuba
by Luis Segui

The Cuban Association for the Disabled is known in Cuba by the acronym ACLIFIM, *Asociación Cubana de Limitados Físico-Motores*. ACLIFIM has a chapter in each of the 14 provinces of Cuba and a national association headquartered in Havana.

The Santiago chapter was founded on March 14, 1980, and about a week later on the Day of the Disabled, March 22, it had only 32 members. Today it has a membership of 3,995 individuals in different stages of physical disabilities: prostrated, quadriplegic, hemiplegic, paraplegic, amputees, and others. ACLIFIM assists the disabled and their families in education, culture, sports, and the obtainment of meaningful employment. The association advocates for the removal of barriers that may hinder mobility or participation in society. It also promotes exchanges of experiences on the rights of the disabled in different parts of the world. ACLIFIM has a close working relationship with two other sister organizations: ANCI (the National Association for the Blind and Visually Impaired) and ANSOC (the National Association for the Deaf). In Santiago the association Administrator, Dinorah Tamayo Acosta stated that "We have signed work contracts with the Federation of Cuban Women, the National Assembly, and the Commerce and Public Health Departments to keep our personnel gainfully employed and being an important part of our society."

During my stay in Santiago, I had the privilege of watching the inauguration ceremony of the **First National Games for the Disabled,** held on July 31, 2000, with more than 1,000 brightly uniformed athletes representing all the provinces of Cuba, marching with precision into the Antonio Maceo Plaza of Santiago, some in their wheelchairs, others with crutches, some with no apparent disability.

The reporter of the local newspaper, *Sierra Maestra,* called them "Champions of Life." Furthermore, he stated, "Appreciating their willpower, optimism, sheer will to live, to be useful and not a burden to society, made our hearts palpitate at a fast pace." The Avenue of the Americas was filled for the first time with representatives from the three organizations: ANCI, ACLIFIM, and ANSOC, including Olympic pre-selections. Several high government officials addressed the public and welcomed the athletes with emotional and eloquent words.

Charmed by the colorful pageant, I was busily capturing snapshot images with my little compact camera. Many national records were established in the ensuing competitions between provinces, including weightlifting, swimming, baseball, volleyball, basketball, ping-pong, goal ball and badminton. First place went to Granma Province followed by my province of Santiago. The whole conglomerate of disabled citizens had just made a great contribution to the national holiday.

Biographical Data of Contributors to This Report

Elisa Apfel Greenberg, *Miami, Florida*

Elisa Greenberg was born in Camagüey Province, Cuba. She is the founder of an academic program involving students from Hampshire College in Amherst, Massachusetts and the University of Camagüey. She has also developed assistance projects for the Jewish community of her native province. She is a member of CAAEF's Advisory Council.

Maura Barrios, *Tampa, Florida*

Latin community. While at Utah State, she worked as a Minority Recruiter and Upward Bound Counselor. She also served as Vice President of MECHA, a Chicano student organization.

From 1986 to 1989, she worked at the Kennedy School of Government, Harvard University, at the Center on Press and Politics where she directed an International Visiting Fellows program and lecture series. She was active in the Status of Women and Minorities Committee of Harvard University. In 1995, she joined the University of South Florida International Affairs Center as Assistant Director for the Latin American and Caribbean Studies program. She organized the campus-wide Committee for Cuban Studies in 1996 and recruited more than thirty faculty members to the Committee. The group has arranged several visits to USF by Cuban artists and academics, to assist USF faculty and students who want to travel to Cuba.

She wrote *Memoirs of a Tampeña,* to be published in a collection of Cuban American *testimonios*. She is founding editor of *Oye Latino,* a Latin American music program for community Radio, and a founding member of *Cuba Vive,* a group that promotes the normalization of relations between the U.S. and Cuba. She is an Advisory Board member of the Cuban American Alliance Education Fund, the League of United Latin American Citizens, and the Council of La Raza. Maura received the City of Tampa Hispanic Woman of the Year in Education category award in 1999.

Delvis Fernández Levy, PhD, *Washington, District of Columbia*

Delvis Fernández was born and raised in Santa Clara, Cuba, where he attended public schools up to the high school level. He holds a BA from Westminster College, in Salt Lake City, Utah, a master's degree from the University of Miami, and a PhD in mathematics from the University of California at Berkeley. Since 1995 he has organized forums on U.S.-Cuba policy in various parts of the U.S., has led delegations of Cuban Americans to meetings with government officials in Washington. He is the publisher of *La Alborada,* CAAEF's Spanish/English newsletter. He has had opinion letters and editorials published in several newspapers. He has participated in radio and TV interviews across the United States and has been featured in several documentary films about U.S.-Cuban affairs. He has been a speaker and has helped to organized conferences at various

U.S. universities, from UCLA to Fordham University. He has taught at the University of Miami, at the University of the Pacific, California State University, and Chabot College in Hayward (from 1966 to 1997). In the mid-sixties, he developed the mathematics program for the first Spanish speaking college in the U.S. for Latin Americans at the University of the Pacific in Stockton, California. He served as advisor to the Chicano Student Union and developed programs to expand educational opportunities in California.

He is currently the president of the Cuban American Alliance Education Fund, Inc. and serves on the board of directors of American for Humanitarian Trade with Cuba, the U.S.-Cuba Sister City Association, and the U.S.-Cuba Business Association.

Christine Ferreira, *Millersville University, Pennsylvania*

Christine Ferreira is an eighteen-year-old student at Millersville University in Pennsylvania pursuing a degree in Meteorology. As a second generation Cuban American, she feels passionately about the land of her family, just as her father and uncle who were both refugees of Operation Peter Pan. Christine's mother is a high school Spanish teacher. She hopes to work as a Broadcast Meteorologist in the United States or in a Spanish-speaking country. She is particularly interested in the phenomenon of hurricanes and would love to travel to Cuba as an intern to study and forecast weather for the island.

Ricardo González, *Madison, Wisconsin*

A native of Camagüey, Cuba, Ricardo González came to the U.S. in 1960. He attended college in Oklahoma and has lived in Wisconsin since 1968. Mr. González served on the Madison City Council for six years and has been deeply involved in community affairs for nearly three decades through his Cardinal Bar in Madison. Currently he is the President of the Madison-Camagüey Sister City Association. Mr. González is a founding member and Trustee of the Cuban Committee for Democracy and serves on the Board of Directors and executive committee of the Cuban American Alliance Education Fund, Inc.

Alberto Jones, DVM, *Palm Coast, Florida*

Dr. Alberto Jones was raised in Banes, Cuba and spent much of his life in Guantanamo. He left Cuba in 1980 and now resides in Palm Coast, Florida where he is the owner of OrthoMedical Waste Company. Dr. Jones is a member of the Board of Director of the Cuban American Alliance Education Fund, Inc. and presides over the Caribbean American Children Foundation. His writings have been published in several newspapers, and he has appeared in various television and radio shows as an advocate for a reassessment of U.S. policy towards Cuba.

Félix Masud-Piloto, PhD *Chicago, Illinois*

Dr. Masud-Piloto was born and raised in Havana, Cuba and immigrated to the U.S. in 1961. He received a Ph.D. in history from Florida State University in 1985 and is currently Associate Professor of history and Director of the Center for Latino Research at DePaul University in Chicago. He is the editor of ***Dialogo,*** a multidisciplinary journal of Latin American and Latino affairs and the author of numerous academic articles. His most recent book, ***From Welcomed Exiles to Illegal Immigrants: The Cuban Migration to the U.S., 1959-1995,*** has been praised as a "well documented, thoughtful, and timely" history of U.S-Cuba relations of the past forty years. He is presently working on a history of the Mariel boatlift of 1980 and its impact on U.S.-Cuba relations. Masud-Piloto travels frequently to Cuba for research and has participated in three major meetings between the Cuban Government and the Cuban community in the U.S. Dr. Masud-Piloto is on the advisory council of CAAEF.

Patricia Morán, *Silver Springs, Maryland*

Patricia Morán works in the department of Infrastructure and Urban Development at the World Bank as Administrative and Circulation Manager to the Urban Age Magazine. She also works with the Washington's D.C. chapter of TransAfrica on policy in Africa and the Caribbean. She presently is a board member of the Cuban American Alliance Education Fund, Inc. and serves as secretary on the executive committee. Her cultural heritage contribution appears in **"I Come Back Home: Perspectives on the Trinidad and Tobago Festival"** edited by Prof. Isidore Smart and Prof. Kimani Nehusi.

Luís Seguí, *Santa Maria, California*

Born 1921 in Central Miranda, Oriente, Cuba. He left Cuba in 1968 with his wife and 3 children, Mr. Seguí graduated from Havana University in 1945 from the School of Business & Public Accounting.

In Cuba he worked at the Miranda Sugar Estates, American Sugar Plantation from 1940 to 1960 and from 1960 to 1968 for *Ministerio de la Industria Azucarera* (MINAZ) as Chief of Cost and Finances for the Cuban Government. In the U.S. he worked for 18 years as an accountant and/or Controller in Santa Maria California.

Currently he serves as a tutor for English as a Second Language (ESL) and is a lay leader at a local Catholic Parrish. Since 1998, he has served as the Director of the California Central Coast Chapter of CAAEF and is an advisory council member.

CAAEF YEAR 2000
PROGRAMS AND ACCOMPLISHMENTS

HUMANITARIAN SUPPORT: In order to support our humanitarian efforts, our organization has secured licenses from the U.S. Department of Commerce and from the Office of Foreign Assets Control (OFAC) for travel and for the delivery of medicine, rehabilitation and health equipment to Cuba. With this license, the US government allows us to take up to $ 300,000 worth of medicine and equipment to Cuba. Under our license, American citizens from throughout the U.S. have been able to visit, assess, and exchange views on medical care as well as assist in the delivery of much needed medical and rehabilitation equipment. Groups in Cuba helped by our efforts include the National Association for the Physically Disabled, and their 14 provincial affiliates as well as religious and educational centers on the island.

Each year, CAAEF also organizes a *Fiesta Cubana*. Last year on the central Coast of California almost three hundred adults and children enjoyed supervised games, Cuban food and dancing to an authentic Cuban Band. In the spring of this year, we held our Fiesta at the California Democratic Party Convention in San José where Congresswoman Maxine Waters was the featured speaker. The objective of the Fiesta is twofold: 1) to educate Americans about the effects of US/Cuba policy and 2) to raise funds for medicine and medical equipment that will be sent to Cuba.

In order to assist family and neighbors in Cuba who may be affected by natural disasters, CAAEF established the *Cuban-to-Cuban Relief Fund*. The latter was created in the summer of 1998 to assist the victims of a severe drought that hit the eastern provinces of Cuba, followed by the devastating effects of Hurricane Georges. This project was carried out in cooperation with the United Nations World Food Program (WFP). The Fund can quickly be reactivated in times of extreme need or natural disasters.

CITIZEN EXCHANGES: The Cuban American Alliance Education Fund is an active participant in the U.S.-Cuba Sister City Association (USCSCA). The association fosters understanding through mutually beneficial exchanges between individuals, community groups, organizations, and institutions in the U.S. with counterparts in Cuba. CAAEF Board members Ricardo González, Alberto Jones, Delvis Fernández Levy, and financial officer Norine Fernandez were among the founding members of USCSCA. As an organization CAAEF has helped to facilitate several sister city relationships. In May of this year, Board members Ricardo González was one of over 100 individuals who traveled to Cuba to participate in bilateral meetings with mayors and provincial officials to explore and discuss sister city relationships with U.S. counterparts. So far agreements have been established or are near completion between the following U.S. and Cuban cities: Bloomington, Indiana & Santa Clara; Mobile, Alabama & Havana; Madison, Wisconsin

& Camagüey; Pittsburgh, Pennsylvania & Matanzas; Richmond, California & Regla; Oakland, California & Santiago de Cuba; Tacoma, Washington & Cienfuegos; Philadelphia, Pennsylvania & Cárdenas; Milwaukee, Wisconsin & Nuevitas; and the mayors of the oldest cities in the U.S. and Cuba have met to discuss friendship relationships between their cities of St. Augustine, Florida, and Baracoa, Cuba.

Current efforts to increase citizen exchange initiatives have included: 1) Visits to Cuba by a delegation from Florida to explore Cuba's African heritage and by a group of Houston lawyers interested in learning about Cuban culture and tracing their Cuban ancestry. These trips were led by CAAEF board members Alberto Jones and Regino Diaz, respectively; 2) Organizing a town hall meeting in Oakland, California. as a follow up to a fact-finding mission to Cuba by U.S. Congresswoman Barbara Lee. 3) Hosting a breakfast dialogue between Cuban Americans and Cuban delegates to the WTO trade talks in Seattle, Washington last December; 4) Board member Anamaria Goicoechea and Advisory Council member Enrique Conill, have presented a proposal to establish a social work research project in conjunction with the University of Havana. They have also established bonds of friendship with a Catholic home for the aged in Havana.

PUBLIC EDUCATION: These activities target changes in public opinion and U.S. policy towards Cuba. This year we launched an extensive campaign to reunite Elián. González, the 6-year-old boy found floating off the coast of Florida, with his family in Cuba. Activities in this regard included daily updates to our network of constituents, both by telephone and e-mail, participation in over 100 interviews in both the print and electronic media urging Elián's return to Cuba, and the placing of numerous letters and editorials in the print media written by CAAEF friends in support of our cause. In addition to national media outlets, CAAEF's campaign was carried by the BBC of London, KBS of Korea, CBS of Canada, and CNN in Latin America as well as Cuban radio and TV.

CAAEF has organized and set up appointments in the State Department, the White House and Congress for Cuban Americans to discuss specific impacts of US impediments to family travel, remittances, and general restrictions on humanitarian trade, as well as obstacles affecting Cuban American businesspeople representing major travel agencies.

In May of 2000, CAAEF organized a conference entitled U.S.-Cuba Relations at the Threshold of the New Millennium with religious, academic, business, and political leaders in South Florida. In the late spring, CAAEF also led panel discussions on the impact of U.S. policy on the Cuban American community at the U.S.-Cuba Business Summit held in Cancun, Mexico and Havana, Cuba, which included participation by representatives from major American and foreign companies with investments in Cuba.

Our work within Cuba itself, in addition to ongoing citizen exchanges, has included organizing a meeting in Havana in July of this year (as detailed in this full report) to promote a dialogue between leaders in the Cuban American community and representatives of the Cuban government. Over 50 Cuban Americans and Cubans from the island participated in several workshops to explore obstacles to family reunification; potential investment in Cuba; and prospects for increased citizen exchanges.

This year, CAAEF launched an e-group: CubanAmericanAlliance@egroups.com and improved its web site: www.cubamer.org.

~

YEAR 2000 COLLABORATIVE RELATIONSHIPS

CAAEF has fostered, built, and maintained working relationships with organizations striving to improve US/Cuba relations. The members of our Advisory Council serve as important links to many of the most prominent Cuba American groups in the United States. Members of our Board of Directors also serve on the board of other Cuban American organizations, or of other organizations that work towards improving relations between the US and Cuba. Examples of such links include the already mentioned participation in the US-Cuba Sister City Association, as well as the Caribbean American Children Foundation; the Wisconsin/Camagüey Friendship Committee; TransAfrica; Americans for Humanitarian Trade with Cuba; US-Cuba Business Council; and the National Network on Cuba. The organization Global Exchange has arranged several national speaking engagements for CAAEF's President under the title "The Realities of the U.S. Embargo Against Cuba." CAAEF's presentations assess the trade embargo of Cuba from a moral standpoint and stress the importance of promoting mutually beneficial exchanges between Cubans and Americans. CAAEF's president offered lectures and panel discussions at UCLA, Fordham University, the Institute of Foreign Relations, and the World Affairs Council of Portland among others. CAAEF is a cofounder and an active participant in the Cuba Steering Committee - a coalition that meets at least once a month to examine, monitor, and take part in the development of legislative initiatives that may affect U.S./Cuba relations. This coalition includes the Washington Office on Latin America, the Latin America Working Group, Global Exchange, OXFAM, Americans for Humanitarian Trade with Cuba, the Center for International Policy, the World Policy Institute, the Cuban Committee for Democracy, Catholic Relief Services, and other organizations.

THE MISSION STATEMENT OF CAAEF: THE CUBAN AMERICAN ALIANCE EUCATION FUND, INC. EDUCATES THE PUBLIC AT LARGE ON ISSUES RELATED TO HARDSHIPS CAUSED BY CURRENT U.S.-CUBA RELATIONS. IT IS A VEHICLE FOR THE DEVELOPMENT OF MUTUALLY BENEFICIAL ENGAGEMENTS WHICH PROMOTE UNDERSTANDING AND HUMAN COMPASSION.

THE GOALS AND PURPOSE OF CAAEF: Working outside ideological constraints, within the dynamics of the Cuban American Community, in cooperation with more than 40 U.S. organizations, in compliance with U.S. law, and respectful of the sovereignty and independence of Cuba, we strive to put a human face on the ongoing hardships caused by the lack of normal relations between the U.S. and Cuba. CAAEF calls for a reassessment of U.S. policies that are outside the best interests of the American people and that also carry undue harm toward Cubans and Americans. Our sphere of action includes congressional visits, family linking, and engagements of mutual benefit to Cubans and Americans. Our board members assist in the establishment of sister-city projects, community assistance programs, visits by Cuban professionals, student exchange programs, ties between Cubans and African American organizations, and fund-raising events for medical projects. Thus, forging engagements that promote understanding and human compassion between the people of both nations:

In order for us to have an effective voice within the body of American politics and public opinion, we strengthen ties between Cuban American organizations, academics, health professionals, the business community, religious organizations, and individuals across the U.S. We strive to facilitate coalition building effort between organizations and individuals who share these common goals. The following resolution was unanimously adopted at our meeting.

RESOLUTION
CUBAN AMERICAN ALLIANCE
July 27, 2000

WE members of the Cuban American Alliance, United States citizens residing in various parts of the nation, encouraged by recent events such as the reunification of Elián González with his family in Cuba and by recent votes taken in the House of Representatives affecting United States trade and travel policy towards Cuba; and

KNOWING that the people of Cuba and the United States have geographical, cultural, historical and economic ties which make them neighbors and natural friends; and

CONSIDERING that an overwhelming majority of the American people have stated through recent polls their support for the normalization of relations with Cuba; and

BEING deeply concerned about the forty-year-old embargo that

- Restricts free trade and travel;
- Deprives the Cuban people of access to medicines and basic necessities;
- Prolongs and exacerbates divisions between families and neighbors;
- Compels Cubans to risk their lives through dangerous and illegal migration; and
- Limits cooperation on issues of national and hemispheric concern such as drug trafficking.

THEREFORE, we, Cuban Americans, resolve to petition Congress and the President of the United States to end the policy of trade and travel restrictions and to work diligently towards the goal of full normalization of relations between the United States of America and the Republic of Cuba.

PARTICIPANTS (*Partial List*)

Elisa Apfel Greenberg
Miami, Florida
Maura Barrios
Tampa, Florida
Regino Díaz
Houston, Texas
Delvis Fernández Levy
Washington, District of Columbia
José Fernández
Miami, Florida
Norine Fernández
Hayward, California
Christine Ferreira
Millersville University, Pennsylvania
Margaret Ferreira
Willmington, Delaware
Dr. Pedro Ferreira
Willmington, Delaware

Mariana Gastón
Brooklyn, New York
Ricardo González
Madison, Wisconsin
Alberto Jones, DVM
Palm Coast, Florida
Felix Masud-Piloto, PhD
Chicago, Illinois
Patricia Morán
Silver Springs, Maryland
Anita Núñez
Nipomo, California
Juan Romagosa
Kissimmee, Florida
Luis Seguí
Santa Maria, California
Bárbaro Rafael Vázquez
Kew Gardens, New York

ORGANIZATIONS VISITED

Ministry of Foreign Relations
Ministerio de Relaciones Exteriores
(MINREX)

**Department of Consular Affairs
for Cuban Overseas Residents**
*Departamento de Asuntos Consulares
para Cubanos Residentes en el Exterior*
(DACCRE)

**Cuban Institute of Friendship with
People**
*Instituto Cubano de Amistad con los
Pueblos* **(ICAP)**

**Economic Affairs Department
of the National Assembly**
*Comité de Asuntos Económicos de la
Asamblea del Poder Popular*

**Center for the Study of Alternative
Policies**
*Centro para el Estudio de Alternativas
Políticas* **(CEAP)**

**Ministry of Foreign Investments and
Collaboration**
*Ministerio de Inversiones Extranjeras y
Colaboración*

**United States Studies Department
of the University of Havana**
*Centro de Estudios sobre Estados
Unidos de la
Universidad de La Habana*

**Office of the Havana Historian
(Historical Restorations)**
*Oficiana del Historiador de La
Habana*

**National Association of Small
Farmers**
*Asociación Nacional de Pequeños
Agricultores* **(ANAP)**

**Cuban Association for the Physically
Disabled**
*Asociación Cubana de Limitados Fisico-
Motores* **(ACLIFIM)**

Ameijeiras Brothers Hospital
Hospital Hermanos Ameijeiras

Ministry of Tourism
Ministerio del Turismo

The Cuban American Alliance Education Fund, Inc. (CAAEF) is a nonprofit [501(c)(3)] national network of Cuban Americans that educates the public at large on issues related to hardships caused by current United States-Cuba relations. The Alliance is a vehicle for the development of mutually beneficial engagements, which promote understanding and human compassion. The Alliance publishes a Spanish/English newsletter, *La Alborada,* which is distributed to individuals interested in U.S.-Cuban affairs.

Executive Committee: Delvis Fernández Levy, PhD, President, D.C.; Patricia Morán, Secretary, Maryland; Ricardo González, Treasurer, Wisconsin. **Members at Large:** Regino Díaz, Texas; Anamaría Goicoechea, PhD, Maryland; Dr. Alberto N. Jones, Florida

ENCUENTRO ENTRE CUBANOS
CAAEF CUBA CONFERENCE JULY 2000

Photo taken at the San Francisco Convent in Old Havana

Chapter 29 taken from CAAEF's La Alborada Publication
Washington, D.C.
Editor and Publisher, Delvis Fernández Levy
Assistant Editor, Félix Masud-Piloto, PhD
Layout and Photos, Norine Fernández
Printing and Mailing, Graphics Services Unlimited

30

PRESENTATIONS
Universities and Public Forums

A Reality Check for U.S./Cuba Policy
Cuba and the U.S. in the 21ˢᵗ Century

By Delvis Fernández Levy, President
Cuban American Alliance Education Fund

Presentation at The James A. Baker Institute for Public Policy at Rice University in Houston, Texas   October 12, 2005

Cuba and the United States in the 21st Century

WORLD STAGE AT THE TIME OF THE CUBAN REVOLUTION

The Cuban Revolution triumphed on the heels of two successful CIA-sponsored "regime- changes." Over fifty years ago, in 1953, Iran's Prime Minister Mohammad Mossadegh was overthrown, and later, a coup was staged against the president of Guatemala Jacobo Arbenz Guzmán, a democratically elected president with 67% of the vote. The social-nationalistic agendas promoted by these leaders and their governments were beyond what the U.S. was willing to tolerate: land reform in Latin America and the nationalization of oil wells under British control in the Middle East. Although viewed as American foreign policy successes, these interventions bore cataclysmic long-term consequences for the people of these nations.

These regime-changes along with U.S. Government acquiescence in the coup led and organized by Fulgencio Batista against a democratically elected president of Cuba back in 1952, have kept many Cuban Americans in constant expectation of the demise of Fidel Castro and the Cuban Revolution.

PREMISES

For many Cubans, it was unthinkable to expect a Cuban government outside the careful tutelage of the U.S. And even up to the present there is an aura of expectation that the collapse of the Cuban Government is a foregone conclusion, be it through cadres of internal dissenters led and financed by the U.S. Government conjoined with Cuban American controlled enterprises funded by U.S. taxpayers.

DOMINANT FORCES

Cuban exiles of 1959 and those of the early 60s, enmeshed in the Batista Government, were to spearhead the recovery of bounties left behind in the American brokered Cuban Republic. Their minions were part and parcel of CIA covert incursions, which culminated with the Bay of Pigs invasion of 1961 and continued with terrorist acts against Cubans on both sides of the Florida Straits.

TERRORISM

The bombing of a *Cubana Airline* in 1976 in midflight instilled terror and suffering in scores of Cuban families. All 73 passengers including the entire youth fencing team of Cuba were killed. The accused masterminds of this dastardly act, Luis Posada Carriles and Orlando Bosh live in the U.S. [1]. The former crossed into the U.S. from Mexico with a bogus passport, snubbed his nose at Homeland Security and held a press conference in Miami [2]. Today he is in custody awaiting a presidential pardon. Orlando Bosch, an escapee from a Venezuelan jail, while awaiting trial for this dastardly act, now roams freely in South Florida despite recommendations by the Justice Department to exclude him from living in the U.S.

[1] Luis Posada Carriles died in May 2018 at age 90 in Miami, Florida, as a free man. According to scholar Peter Kornbluh of the U.S. National Security Archive he was one of the most dangerous terrorists in recent history."

[2] Orlando Bosch died in April 2011. In 1987, he was arrested for illegally entering the U.S. Upon direct intervention of Jeb Bush, he was granted permission to stay by the administration of George H. W. Bush.

Among many acts of terror, it is worthy to note the assassination in Washington of Chilean Ambassador Orlando Letelier and his assistant Ronni Moffit also carried out in 1976 by extremists in the Cuban exile community. On a gentler vein, President Nixon had to resign the U.S. presidency as a result of the Watergate scandal, where at least one Cuban American was on the payroll of the CIA.

The ascendancy to the U.S. Presidency by George W. Bush also involved extremists in the exile community. In the 2000 elections mob tactics were used to prevent vote counting. *Radio Mambí*, a Cuban American radio station called on its listeners to shut down the vote count in Miami-Dade. Election officials were intimidated by fears that a large mob of Cuban Americans was on the way.

Today five Cubans languish in prison with sentences of 15 years to two life sentences for monitoring groups that have committed acts of terror against Cuba. They were tried and convicted by a Miami court without the opportunity to change their trial venue to a city where they could receive a fair and impartial trial. Their convictions were reversed on August 9 of this year by the 11th Circuit Appellate Court in Atlanta. A UN report noted that "the trial did not take place in a climate of objectivity and impartiality" and furthermore stated that they were wrongfully held for 17 months in solitary confinement and their lawyers were deprived from examining available evidence. [3]

[3]A prisoner exchange for the Cuban Five: **Gerardo Hernández, Antonio Guerrero, Ramón Labañino, Fernando González,** and **René González**, took place in December 2014. The exchange coincided with Cuba's release of U.S. contractor **Alan Gross**.

THE COMMUNITY

There are approximately 1.2 million Cuban Americans according to the 2000 Census. We are less than 0.4% of the U.S. population and only 4% of the Hispanic/Latino population.

> [84% live in Florida, New Jersey - New York and California. The vast majority, 650,000, live in Miami-Dade. 56% in Miami- Ft. Lauderdale, 11% in NY-NJ, 4% in LA-Orange County, and 3% in Tampa]

We have a unique immigrant status vis-à-vis other immigrants from Latin America: (1) No Cuban American is an undocumented immigrant, we have access to the courts and highest levels of politics without fear of deportation thanks to the Cuban Adjustment Act of 1966; (2) The Cuban Refugee Program, initiated in 1961 went beyond what any affirmative action program has done for minorities in the U.S. The program provided a broad range of financial, educational, professional retraining and other services to incoming Cubans. At present Cuban American representation in government includes four representatives in Congress and 34 in the George W. Bush Administration. [10 Republican Cuban Americans are in the Florida legislature.]

CHARGED UP EXPECTATION

With the collapse of the Soviet Union in 1991 renewed expectations were fueled in Congress for the final demise of the Cuban Government. New Jersey representative Robert Torricelli, who had previously praised Cuba for social advances, changed his tune after receiving donations from hard-liner exiles. In promoting the Cuban Democracy Act back in 1992, a bill that bans business between Cuba and U.S. subsidiaries, then Representative Torricelli asserted that "Within a brief time, it's a matter of months; the U.S. will destroy Fidel Castro, the Cuban Revolution along with the political system established." Elected to the U.S. Senate,

Torricelli later had to drop out of a senate race in shame for failing to report gifts and political contributions from an individual with business ties to North Korea.

Later in 1996 Senator Jesse Helms referred to his bill to codify the U.S. embargo as the "Farewell Fidel Act" and also asserted that this bill would drive the final nail in Castro's coffin by punishing overseas companies and executives who do business with Cuba.

The war in Iraq renewed hopes among certain elements of the Cuban American community for a military solution or a much tougher stance for solving the "Castro Problem." The Administration has embarked on a program to erase all vestiges of the Cuban Revolution from the face of the Earth. The pronouncements for the new policy are enshrined in a report to the President by the Commission for Assistance to a Free Cuba in 2004.

Since July 1, 2004, the Government of the United States of America under the Administration of President George W. Bush has imposed further restrictions on people having familial, cultural, and religious bonds with residents of Cuba, such as, limitations on:

THE HUMAN TOLL -- Visitation rights, financial assistance, and humanitarian and religious assistance

Testimonials and press reports abound that illustrate infringements of United Nations covenants on: (1) The protection of the family as the natural and fundamental group unit of society, (2) the rights of parents and children, and (3) the civil, economic, and cultural rights of ethnic minorities in the United States linked through familial and cultural ties with Cuba.

A 103-year-old grandmother of Cuban origin who resides in the United States was anxious to see her son, a resident of Cuba in a grave life-threatening situation, suffering from lung-cancer. The family contacted their United States Congressional representatives but was told she could not obtain an exception to travel with an accompanying family member.

In another case a U.S. citizen, serving the United States Armed Forces as a medic in Iraq, while on leave from service tried to visit his two teenaged sons who live in Havana but was not allowed to travel to see his beloved children before returning to active duty.

Disabled Cubans are also casualties of policies by the Government of the United States of America that impede assistance to Cubans in vulnerable situations of human existence.

Humanitarian Assistance

For over seven years, *La Familia* -- the Cuban American Alliance humanitarian project -- has secured licenses from both the United States Department of Commerce and the Office of Foreign Assets Control for the delivery and exportation of donations to the Cuban Association for the Physically Disabled.

Our project is unique in two respects: (1) Deliveries are made on a regular basis to meet current needs and (2) Assessments are made with each delivery for future assistance. Participants in *La Familia* mission strive to assist the physically impaired to reach new levels of independent living and empowerment.

Today, *La Familia* is held hostage waiting for a license placed on hold since August 15, 2004. Neither aid nor assistance has been sent while officials of the U.S. Government deliberate on granting a humanitarian travel permit to deliver donations previously licensed by the United States Commerce Department. [4]

[4] *La Familia*, CAAEF humanitarian project, was <u>not</u> granted permission to continue after that date in 2004. A program which according to the 2003 records of **the Cuban Association for the Physically Disabled (known as ACLIFIM)** had provided more aid than any other organization.

A COMMUNITY IN FLUX

Through a forty-five-year period of waiting for Castro's demise, our community continues to be an essential component in the dynamics of U.S. policy toward Cuba. Remaining elements of the historical exile of the 1960s and their descendants are still the most loyal supporters of a policy of total trade and travel embargo of Cuba.

Support for Cuba policy is fueled by perks and turf protection of federally financed interests based in the Cuban American enclave of South Florida. Radio and TV Martí are examples of more sophisticated enterprises subsidized by U.S. taxpayers to ensure a steady stream of millions of dollars to the community, money which is lavished through a patronage system to pro-embargo ideologues, in spite of the fact that TV Marti is a ghost station virtually unseen in Cuba. U.S. Government largesse toward Cuban Americans is intrinsically attached to the pursuit of a Cuba policy that has a corrupting effect on all levels of community life, thus negating one's basic freedom to express views against policies that stands in sharp contradiction to American family values and principles of free trade and travel.

Despite acts of coercion and intimidation, new organizations and individuals in our community have emerged as beacons of hope that signal a future regime change, not in Cuba but in the vortex of Cuban American political control in South Florida.

Indications abound of attitudinal changes in our community toward current U.S.-Cuba policy

• The Pope's visit to Cuba back in 1998 made it Kosher for Cuban Americans to visit the Island.

• The histrionics of extremists in the Cuban American enclave of Miami who used six-year-old Elián González as political fodder for their political agenda projected the debate on U.S.-Cuba policy to a nationwide audience. [5]

[5] Many Cuban Americans were in favor of the return of Elián Gonzáles to his father, but a few had the opportunity to speak out publicly. I was fortunate to advocate through interviews in major TV stations and through opinion letters in various newspapers across the nation.

• President Carter's visit to Cuba again created debate as to whether dialogue offers a better alternative to hostile confrontation.

• The lack of substantive changes in George W. Bush policy toward Cuba has created major fractures in the Cuban American National Foundation, the most effective promoter of a hardline policy toward the Island. Their leadership is now endorsing a policy of partial engagement, somewhat like moderate Cuban American organizations were offering 10 years ago. Their more extreme faction would like to provoke a U.S. invasion of the Island.

• Our Cuban American Alliance works today with a wide spectrum of organizations and Cuban Americans with diverse political views. We promote peaceful respectful engagement and projects of mutual benefit with the Cuban people.

CONCLUSION

A majority of American citizens want to see an end to the embargo on Cuba. Bipartisan majorities of Members of Congress have repeatedly voted in favor of easing the embargo on Cuba.

The goal of current U.S.-Cuba policy is an affront to Cuba's sovereignty and right to self-determination. Restrictions on travel to Cuba are inconsistent with U.S. policy and in violation of basic human rights. The Cuban people are fully capable of guiding the Cuban Republic. Let us not ignore our historical bonds in our search for a future of democracy, peace, and social justice.

I invite you to seek a truly humane policy toward the Cuba and its people, in tandem with what's in America's best interests, and with adherence to the lofty ideals of this Great Nation.

Those who cannot remember the past are condemned to repeat it.
George Santayana, Spanish American Philosopher
Life of Reason, Reason in Common Sense, 1906

Conferences on US-CUBA Policy

Cuban Americans held conferences in several US cities (From New York to Los Angeles, and from Miami to Seattle) to analyze the Helms-Burton Law and its impact on the Cuban community in the U.S. In all the meetings the law was examined and reviewed within the context of U.S.-Cuba historical relations. In strategy group meetings, Cuban Americans met to identify specific actions to advocate for changes in U.S.-Cuba policy.

At a symposium at **DePaul University**, participants expressed rejection of Helms-Burton and demonstrated how it lies outside current norms of international law.

All the speakers emphasized the need for respect to Cuba's sovereignty and the right of Cubans to work toward building their own political structures without sanctions or external coercion.

Attorney José Estévez and Delvis Fernández Levy preside over panel at the Office of the Americas

In **Youngstown, Ohio**, residents from Ohio and Pennsylvania, representatives of pharmaceutical firms, and academicians from Youngstown State and Pittsburgh Universities discussed some negative impacts of the law on Cuban and American citizens. Extraterritorial applications of U.S. law and interference in Cuban and other foreign nations affairs were also outlined. "This law does not represent American principles, it was written by Cubans outside of the island who seek foreign intervention against their country of origin," stated Dr. Milton Sánchez-Parodi, organizer of the Ohio conference.

OUTREACH and PRESENTATIONS

Cuba at the Crossroads

Conference at Occidental College, in Los Angeles, attended by over 300 people. The Alliance president assisted as a panelist in giving a keynote address. This conference served as a springboard for Congressman Esteban Torres introduction of the Cuban Humanitarian Trade Bill (H.R. 1951).

A DIALOGUE with CUBA -- March 19-21, 1998

Initiated by the University of California at Berkeley, this conference will facilitate an open, interdisciplinary dialogue with leading individuals broadly representative of Cuban society. We have invited the largest and most representative group of Cubans to visit the United States in the past 39 years. Each session, plenary and workshop will probe a different field of human endeavor, including U.S.-Cuba relations, Health Care, Literature, Science Education, Agriculture, Religion, Tourism, Sports and Society, Filmmaking, and others. Panelists – Cuban Americans – will probe vital issues of our time, seeking to learn and understand.

Over 1000 people attended this conference, and over 20 Cubans, who live on the Island, came to be present and participate, making that the largest gathering of Cubans to attend a U.S. conference. The Alliance hosted a reception and an opening concert where hundreds of Cubans living in the Oakland/San Francisco Bay Area met to enjoy an evening of food, and *ambiente cubano*. The conference lasted over two days, but the visitors stayed with us for a week during which spin off conferences were also held at schools, universities, city councils, and community organizations in California.

The Future of US-Cuban Relations

Excerpts from a keynote address published in La Alborada, by Delvis Fernández Levy in Pasadena, California, January 25, 1997. **The conference was sponsored by the United Nations Association-USA, the Southwest Voter Research Institute, and the Department of Diplomacy and World Affairs of Occidental College.**

A Cuban American Awakening

Despite years of separation from our beloved Island -- the land, our culture, the struggle of nation building, its people and their aspirations for social justice -- *la cubanía* or "cubanness" for us continues to be an integral part of our very being and soul.

The son scurries up a flight of marble steps and into a barren looking living room. First there are shouts, then screams. His mother and sister frantically embrace him. His mother is at a loss for words. "No tears, no tears," she says hysterically, but in a moment, she is weeping like her son has returned from the dead. He has. "My life, my life," she cries. "You are here now."

Despite much investigation of current US-Cuba policy for its extraterritoriality and interference in other nation's affairs, there seems to be little analysis of the sections in Helms-Burton that most profoundly affect Cubans, Cuban Americans, and the grand Cuban family in general.

Scanning through this law, we read section 2, subsection 10 (of the Conference Report):

"The Congress has historically and consistently manifested its solidarity and the solidarity of the American people with the democratic aspirations of the Cuban people." We have no doubt that many Americans have manifested their solidarity with the democratic and social justice aspirations of the Cuban people.

However, it is clear that since the days of Thomas Jefferson, on through the Monroe Doctrine, the Manifest Destiny Theory, the Platt Amendment, Torricelli's Law, military interventions, and collaboration with corrupt regimes — **Congress' solidarity with the democratic aspirations of the Cuban people lie more in the realm of fiction than fact.**

Moreover, we notice, one, two..., nineteen times! that the American President, whoever he may be at the time, shall determine what constitutes a "democratically elected government in Cuba."

We read in Title II, sections 201 and 202 that the policy of the US shall also include assistance in preparing the Cuban military forces to adjust to an appropriate role in a democracy. In other words, a Cuba envisioned by US authorities would be doomed to a dictated military pact by a single nation.

And further we read that in this US imposed "Cuban democracy," the US would have the right to decide that certain Cubans, namely Fidel Castro and his brother Raúl, cannot be nominated for any government position and must not run for any elected position. Despite all the disagreements we may have with the present Cuban head of state or his relatives, this would represent the height of hypocrisy coming from a US government that places little or no conditions on people who have engendered political careers through racist campaigns, warmongering and where even Nazis, communists, or Ku Klux Klan members may run for any political office they may desire.

But the provisions in this US legislation that most directly affect us – Americans of Cuban descent – are those that include restrictions and conditions on visits to Cuba and assistance to our families.

Only after a transition government in Cuba is in power, freedom of individuals to travel to visit their relatives without any restrictions shall be permitted.

Before considering the reinstitution of general licenses for family remittances to Cuba, insist that . . . the Cuban Government permit the unfettered operation of small businesses . . .

And according to Presidential and US Treasury regulations:

- **Travel to Cuba must be done via a third country.**
- **Close family members are allowed to travel only once in a 12-month period to visit a close relative in circumstances of extreme humanitarian need; and**
- **Violators of these regulations are threatened with a quarter of a million dollars in fines and 10 years in prison.**

Despite these ominous threats, Cuban Americans, sometimes hiding or in open defiance of the law, travel to Cuba and bring assistance to their families -- assistance that has been estimated to be as much as a billion dollars per year.

For us these restrictions, acts of intimidations, and harassment represent a massive violation of human rights. It is a sin under any religion to prevent contact between mothers, fathers, and their children.

Here is a law in contraposition to our attempts (both Republican and Democrat) to promote family values. And thus, we allow a direct attack on our most sacred unit of civilization — The Family — in order to promote a foreign policy against a small nation that represents no threat to our way of life or national security.

For us to accept or collaborate with present restrictions on travel, family visits, and remittances, would be tantamount to renouncing the very essence of being Cuban and American, and to turn our backs on our brothers and sisters who toil and struggle in their land of birth.

To us it is obvious that present US-Cuba law is being violated, through a conspiracy of silence, by large numbers of Cuban Americans. It is unacceptable by the world community at large.

It causes pain and suffering on innocent people, and it violates the dignity and independence of the *Cubanos* -- no matter what their political alliance or affiliation may be.

"The hottest places in hell are reserved for those who in a period of moral crisis maintain their neutrality."

From Dante's Inferno

Cuban Culture Spices Up Campus Life at California State University at Hayward

On May 26 the university campus was infected with the heart and soul of Cuba. The university community was treated to authentic Cuban cuisine and music. The event entitled **Cuba: Good Neighbor or Evil empire,** was organized by sociology professor Michael Schutz. After detailing a brief history of Cuban American relations, Raquel Rodríguez of CAAEF Bay Area Chapter gave a moving account of her family's suffering as a result of the tense situation existing between the two countries.

Rep. Esteban Torres honored by Cuban Americans.

Amerindia, Inc., a Cuban American organization based in Los Angeles that promotes respect for the independence and the sovereignty of Cuba, honored U.S. representative Esteban Torres for his work in favor of lifting the U.S. embargo against Cuba on food and medicines. José Estévez, president of Amerindia, presented Rep. Torres with a painting of Cuban patriot José Martí by Oscar Albuerne, a Cuban artist and board member of Amerindia.

Baltimore's Kurt L. Schmoke, unveiled a bust of José Martí on Sept. 5th at the corner of Broadway and Fayette in Baltimore, Md. The mayor in his recent trip to Cuba observed how revered Martí is among Cubans. Enrique Conill, director of the Maryland Council of CAAEF was present at the unveiling ceremony.

Events for Centennial of Struggle for Independence

Representatives of Amerindia, were also present with other Latino organizations at events at Cal Tech, UCLA, Cal State Los Angeles, and Occidental College to mark 100 years of the struggle for independence by the people of Cuba, Puerto Rico and the Philippines.

Scholarly presentations were given on the Cuban economy, civil society, social justice, democratic values, policies regarding Cuban Americans, relations with the E.U. and international displeasure for the Helms Burton Law.

Noteworthy of mention was the overall cordiality towards Cuba expressed by participants at the Congress -- a noticeable improvement over previous LASA congresses. Speakers who had held high offices in the U.S. Government spoke of past errors in the formulation of U.S.-Cuba policy.

Representative Esteban Torres

After the conference, the Cuban delegation was invited to join for fun and conversation at a Latin American disco. Poetry, readings, and songs offered by Spanish speaking members of the local community helped sooth tensions after three days of hard work. Cuban Americans had an opportunity to learn about events unfolding in present-day Cuba.

Events for Centennial of Struggle for Independence

Representatives of Amerindia, were also present with other Latino organizations at events at Cal Tech, UCLA, Cal State Los Angeles, and Occidental College to mark 100 years of the struggle for independence by the people of Cuba, Puerto Rico and the Philippines.

CAAEF at LASA Congress in Chicago

Over 4000 delegates were present at the XXI International Congress of the Latin American Studies Association (LASA) in Chicago, Sept. 24 - 26. Twenty delegates came from Cuba, and Cuban affairs dominated in more than a dozen panels. This was the first time that LASA had sponsored a delegation from outside the U.S.A. The Alliance was represented by Enrique Conill and Prof. Anamaría Goicoechea of the University of Maryland.

Scholarly presentations were given on the Cuban economy, civil society, social justice, democratic values, policies regarding Cuban Americans, relations with the E.U. and international displeasure for the Helms Burton Law.

Noteworthy of mention was the overall cordiality towards Cuba expressed by participants at the Congress -- a noticeable improvement over previous LASA congresses. Speakers who had held high offices in the U.S. Government spoke of past errors in the formulation of U.S.-Cuba policy.'

After the conference, the Cuban delegation was invited to join for fun and conversation at a Latin American disco. Poetry, readings, and songs offered by Spanish speaking members of the local community helped sooth tensions after three days of hard work.

Cuban Americans had an opportunity to learn about events unfolding in present-day Cuba.

31

PRESS OUTREACH

Press Conference participation

FORGING AN ALLIANCE

After 1996, during the early days of CAAEF - The Cuban American Alliance Education Fund - working in conjunction with the Cuban Committee for Democracy, Cambio Cubano, Jewish Solidarity, and the Cuban American Defense League we organized a Day of Advocacy in Washington, D.C.

A delegation of 60 individuals met with representatives and senators. Alliance members met with Congressmen Rangel (D-NY) and Richardson (D-NM) and also with aides to Senator Bingaman (D-NM), Rep. Zimmer (R-NJ). We had participants from California, Florida, Ohio, New York, New Jersey, Pennsylvania, Maryland, Delaware, and Washington D.C. We were able to get printed Op-Ed pieces as well as letters to the editors in major newspapers, including the New York Times, USA Today, the San Francisco Examiner, The Star-Ledger of New Jersey, and El Diario/LaPrensa.

There was participation in press conferences in Washington, D.C., New York, and New Jersey. At the United Nations on March 7, 1996, we were interviewed by the CBS correspondent of the Security Council. Overall, we made an effort to educate the American public and legislators through voices of reason and moderation that focus on the welfare of families here and in Cuba.

In our new office in Teaneck, the Alliance brought together Cuban Americans from New York and New Jersey. We helped to organize press conferences at the United Nations, in the US Congress with other Cuban American groups, and in support of releasing the medical computers donated to Pastors for Peace. Conferences were held in several U.S. cities (From New York to Los Angeles, and from Miami to Seattle) to analyze the Helms-Burton Law and its impact on the Cuban community in the U.S. In all the meetings the law was examined and reviewed within the context of U.S.-Cuba historical relations. In strategy group meetings, Cuban Americans met to identify specific actions to advocate for changes in U.S.-Cuba policy.

At a symposium at DePaul University, participants expressed rejection of Helms-Burton and demonstrated how it lies outside current norms of international law. All the speakers emphasized the need for respect to Cuba's sovereignty and the right of Cubans to work toward building their own political structures without sanctions or external coercion. In Youngstown, Ohio, residents from Ohio and Pennsylvania, representatives of pharmaceutical firms, and academicians from Youngstown State and Pittsburgh Universities discussed some negative impacts of the law on Cuban and American citizens. Extraterritorial applications of U.S. law and interference in Cuban and other foreign nations affairs were also outlined.

"This law does not represent American principles, it was written by Cubans outside of the island who seek foreign intervention against their country of origin," stated Dr. Milton Sánchez-Parodi, organizer of the Ohio conference.

PUBLIC EDUCATION: These activities target changes in public opinion and U.S. policy towards Cuba. This year we launched an extensive campaign to reunite Elián. González, the 6-year-old boy found floating off the coast of Florida, with his family in Cuba. Activities in this regard included daily updates to our network of constituents, both by telephone and e-mail, participation in over 100 interviews in both the print and electronic media urging Elián's return to Cuba, and the placing of numerous letters and editorials in the print media written by CAAEF friends in support of our cause. In addition to national media outlets, CAAEF's campaign was carried by the BBC of London, KBS of Korea, CBS of Canada, and CNN in Latin America as well as Cuban radio and TV.

MEETINGS in CUBA

In an unprecedented event, over 130 Cuban émigrés, most of them from the U.S., met in Havana in 1997, to examine how Helms-Burton affects their relations with Cuba. All the participants have declared their opposition to said U.S. law. They have appeared in school presentations, public forums, or have sent editorial letters to newspapers.

The initiative for the meeting derived from Cubans who live outside Cuba. This meeting was the pinnacle in a cycle of regional meetings across the US and other countries. In the U.S., conferences were held in Miami, Los Angeles, Houston, Youngstown, New York, San Francisco, Seattle and in many other cities. During the month of January, meetings took place in Mexico and Venezuela. Future conferences were also announced for other cities in the U.S. and Madrid, Spain —just about anywhere there is a group of Cuban émigrés interested in how this law affects their relations with their land of origin.

People acquired greater consciousness of the law and expressed their commitment to carry out actions to expose the anti-Cuban character of the law. There was also general agreement on the need to develop strategies to mobilize other Cubans and Americans.

REACHING OUT TO THE PRESS

THE HERALD, THURSDAY, JULY 9, 1998

The Miami Herald

Let Cuban Americans help Their loved ones back home

Delvis Fernández Levy is president of the Cuban American Alliance Education Fund in Washington, D.C.

DELVIS
FERNANDEZ LEVY

WITH THE recent Defense Department assessment that "Cuba's military does not pose a national-security threat to the United States," isn't it time to lift all restrictions on family travel and humanitarian trade with Cuba?

Even after President Clinton's announced relaxation of policies on travel and remittances, we Cuban Americans continue to be treated as second class citizens when it comes to assistance and contact with our loved ones on the island.

Under a global travel license granted by the President, Cuban Americans are permitted one emergency visit every 12 months to see a sick or dying relative. We aren't allowed to be with their mothers, brothers, or sisters for normal family activities -- weddings, baptisms, birthdays, or just a simple gathering to share our love. This policy is deeply injurious to Cubans and represents a direct effort to destabilize our families.

An injury to one family is an injury to our entire nation. For what is a nation without the protection of our most basic unit of civilization-- the family?

There is a false perception that because the restrictions on visits are being violated by tens of thousands of Cuban Americans, no one gets hurt because enforcement of the policy is ignored. However, the policy has been used to intimidate and harass travelers in route to Cuba and those returning to the United States.

After long, arduous trips, precious family gifts have been confiscated or destroyed, and travelers have been subjected to hours of detention in airports -- causing physical and emotional pain as well as additional expenses due to missed flight connections and hotel accommodations.

Some of us have had travel savings confiscated. We've been detained just for "looking Cuban." Imagine the outrage if an American citizen were harassed for being suspected of visiting people who cared for him or her as a child.

Unlike all other immigrants, we have severe restrictions on sending money to our loved ones. Although Clinton recently relaxed the remittance restrictions in response to Pope John Paul II's condemnation of the embargo, Cuban Americans still are treated as second class citizens.

It has been a tradition that those who migrate to the United States make strong efforts to send regular assistance to support their families back home. The assistance money, on which we have paid taxes, often represents meager earnings obtained by the sweat of our brow. It is criminal to attempt artificially to separate families and to deprived us of the God-given right to provide assistance to our loved ones.

Finally, in what might be the most egregious violation of our human rights, Cuban Americans and Americans in general are prohibited from selling life-sustaining food medicine, and much-needed medical equipment to the people of Cuba.

These restrictions violate basic international charters and conventions, including the United Nations charter, the charter of the Organization of American States and the articles of the Geneva Convention governing the treatment of civilians during wartime.

On March 31, after the Pope's visit and the Pentagon report, hundreds of Cuban Americans joined religious, business, human rights, and Hispanic organizations in Washington, D.C., for a National Day of Education and Advocacy to press for family rights. Indeed, there is a rising tide of indignation in the Cuban American community. Many of us are saying: Enough is enough! *¡Basta!* Stop using their families as pawns to fight a relic of the Cold War.

Early Days of The Cuban American Alliance
Buscaran alianza grupos que abogan por fin del embargo

Por PABLO ALFONSO *Redactor de El Nuevo Herald*
Viernes 7 de Julio de 1995

Exiliados cubanos que abogan por la normalización de relaciones entre Estados Unidos y Cuba y por la suspensión del embargo norteamericano se reunirán en Washington la próxima semana, para constituir una alianza que coordine una estrategia común.

El primer congreso de la Alianza Nacional Cubano Americana sesionará del 14 al 16 de julio en el hotel Holiday Inn Central, de Washington, D.C., y al mismo han sido invitados el canciller cubano Roberto Robaina y varios congresistas estadounidenses, de acuerdo con la agenda de la reunión.

"Hemos podido unir bajo unos cuantos puntos comunes a una docena de organizaciones de exiliados progresistas y moderados que asistirán al evento," afirmó Luis Martín, secretario del comité provisional de la Alianza.

Martín, diseñador mecánico que reside en Portland, Oregón, dijo que el trabajo organizativo de la reunión comenzó en enero con encuentros entre grupos afines en distintas regiones de Estados Unidos. "Durante esos contactos pudimos comprobar que existen suficientes organizaciones que quieren participar en una Alianza nacional, que coordine los esfuerzos ante el Congreso y el gobierno de Estados Unidos por un cambio de política hacia Cuba," afirmó Martín.

Entre esas organizaciones Martín citó al Grupo Cubano de Acción, de Ohio; el Comité por la Amistad entre Estados Unidos y Cuba, de Nuevo México; Cubanos contra el Bloqueo, de Nueva Jersey; el Comité Cubano por la Paz, de Nueva York, Pastores por la Paz, la Alianza de Trabajadores de la Comunidad, Ciudadanos Preocupados, Profesionales y Empresarios Cubano Americanos y la Brigada Antonio Maceo.

Martín dijo que esperan un total de 100 asistentes, en su mayoría cubanos residentes en la Florida, California, Nueva York, Nueva Jersey, Illinois, Ohio, Oregón, Nuevo México y Washington, D.C.

La reunión se inaugurará el viernes por la noche y según la agenda, el sábado está programado un panel de conferencistas entre los que figuran los congresistas demócratas Charles Rangel, José Serrano y Nydia Velázquez. El orador invitado para el almuerzo será el exdiplomático norteamericano Wayne Smith; por la tarde se anuncia la presencia de Robaina o, en su lugar, de Hugo Yedra, funcionario de la Sección de Intereses de Cuba en Estados Unidos.

"El Canciller ha sido invitado, pero todavía no podemos confirmar su participación," dijo desde La Habana el jueves un vocero del Ministerio de Relaciones Exteriores.

Los puntos principales de la agenda son el acuerdo migratorio entre Cuba y Estados Unidos; la reunificación de la familia, la libertad de viajes y envíos, el levantamiento del embargo y la libertad de expresión de la comunidad cubana que reside en Estados Unidos. Martín dijo que este se refería a las dificultades de expresión de sectores del exilio favorables a la normalización de relaciones entre ambos Países.

"En la isla no lo hemos tocado porque eso es parte del diálogo abierto que proponemos. Hemos decidido no dictarle al gobierno cubano lo que tiene que hacer," afirmó Martí.

Delvis Fernández-Levy, profesor universitario residente en San Francisco y otro de los miembros del comité provisional, dijo que representantes de la Alianza se reunieron en mayo con Kevin Sullivan y Ann

Patterson, de la oficina de asuntos cubanos del Departamento de Estado, para apoyar la nueva política migratoria hacia Cuba del presidente Bill Clinton y exponer los planes de la mencionada reunión.

"También nos reunimos con Richard Nuccio y Morton Halperin," afirmó Fernández-Levy.

Fue imposible comunicarse el jueves con Nuccio, asesor de asuntos cubanos de la Casa Blanca, o con Halperin, miembro del Consejo Nacional de Seguridad.

Fernández-Levy añadió que ambos funcionarios se reunirán el viernes con miembros del comité organizador.

Quotes from Letters in Newspapers

Letters, op-ed pieces, and quotes from interviews have appeared on major national and local newspapers: The New York Times, USA TODAY, the Christian Science Monitor, The Jersey Journal, The Star-Ledger, *El Nuevo Hudson*, and the Record of New Jersey; The San Francisco Examiner, The Miami Herald, The Oakland Tribune, The Daily Review of California, The San José Mercury, (Chabot College) The Spectator. TV interviews for Northern California ABC and Telemundo affiliates, *Univisión*. Radio interview for CNN, Radio Fe in Miami, WBAI in New York, WCAC in New Jersey, CBS, ABC in Phoenix.

The Record of New Jersey
Early Days of CAAEF – August 22, 1995

End embargo, say Cuban American (Excerpts)   The Associated Press

NEWARK – A Cuban American group on Monday implored the Clinton administration to ease restrictions on travel to Cuba and to end the curbs on sending money, food, and medicine to relatives there.

The Cuban American Committee for Peace made the request a year and a day after the United States imposed limits on family visits and money transfers. ....

"An embargo is not in the interests of the American people or the United Sates," Marshall Garcia, vice president of the Cuban American Committee for Peace said during a news conference outside the federal building.

The group's president, Raymundo Del Toro, said it is ironic that the United States can normalize relations with Vietnam, but not with Cuba. "Fidel Castro is not Cuba," said Del Toro of Linden, referring to the president of the island nation. "Cuba is the people," Del Toro, 43 said he last saw his 19-year-old son who lives in Cuba two years ago.

A math professor from a community college near San Francisco also criticized travel restrictions. "How can we say we are for human rights when my mother, who is almost blind, has to travel to Mexico, and commit an illegal act to see her six grandchildren," said Delvis Fernández Levy, 55, who teaches at Chabot College in Hayward, Calif.

The New York Times **Now Take Steps to Cuba Dialogue**
Wednesday, October 11, 1995

(Excerpts from letter)

We are pleased that President Clinton is giving back to United States citizens of Cuban origin our right to visit our families, but to impose a limit of one visit a year to see a sick or dying relative is an affront to human dignity.

Considering the visit of Pope John Paul II, who called for lifting the United States trade embargo against Cuba, as well as the recent trip to Cuba by 47 Fortune 500 company executives, the United States appears to be laying the groundwork for normalized relation with Cuba. It is time for engagement and dialogue. We hope the Administration will continue in this direction for us and our loved ones in Cuba

Delvis Fernández Levy
Exec. Director, Cuban American Alliance Education Fund

USA TODAY **U.S. travel ban hurts Cubans**
January 17, 1996

...as a Cuban American and writing from the perspective of someone who still has close family living in Cuba, I have to add that Cuba is not only Fidel Castro but also 11 million individuals. They – our sons and daughter, brothers and sisters, parents and grandparents – have suffered immensely due to policies of separation and a punitive U.S. trade embargo that includes even food and medicine.

Delvis Fernández Levy, President of CAAEF

Oakland Tribune — Don't block Cuban visits

October 13, 1995

How can we deny American citizens the right to visit any family member ... We are deeply concerned with our family values, our rights as human beings to visit and care for the wellbeing of our mothers, fathers, brothers, sisters or children...It is time for a policy of engagement and dialogue.

"We've really been overwhelmed by support from people who before would never have supported sending a single aspirin to Cuba."

Delvis Fernández Levy
Cuban activist

The Daily Review — Hurricane Lili helps reunite divided Cuban Americans

Monday, November 25, 1996 & Sunday, December 1, 1996

(Quote)

After the hurricane, the Clinton administration approved a permit for Baltimore-based Catholic Relief Services to make direct aid flights to Cuba. Fernández Levy flew to Washington, D.C., Wednesday to submit a permit application for the Cuban American Alliance to make direct shipments.

"The hurricane happened a month ago, and people are just getting organized for sending goods because of all the complications associated with it," said **Norine Fernandez**, English editor of the Cuban American Alliances' newsletter.

...the Cuban American Alliance met with **Cubanos Mano-a-Mano** of Oakland to plan the logistics of shipping donated goods to Cuba.

For the moment, the two groups plan to funnel donations through organizations that already have flight permits ...

Press Release from Congressman Jose E. Serrano – July 27, 1999

(Excerpt)

The "Cuban Food and Medicine Security Act of 1999," legislation to give the Cuban people access to food, including agricultural products, medicines, and medical equipment from the United States, has been co-sponsored by 147 members of the House of Representatives.... "The current United States policy toward Cuba continues to hurt the Cuban people and has not succeeded in winning the support of the international community."

Open Forum of The San Francisco Chronicle – August 4, 1999
Excerpts from letter

...Any Afro Cuban today can stand on his/her own two feet and compete in any field of knowledge with their cohorts ... seeing the first Latin American astronaut was a Cuban son of Africa; that slave's descendants have now produced more individuals with higher education that those of our former masters; and that black nuns are no longer forced into different religious order and a different dress code...They must accept that Blacks in Cuba can walk on any street or neighborhood without being detained for "Walking While Black," go to beaches ... or enjoy a Cuban park without having to walk on different paths...

Mariana Grajales, the black woman that exemplifies the best of Cuban motherhood, said to her youngest son on learning of the death of an older brother during the struggle for Cuba's independence, *Empínate* – "Grow tall quickly to meet the needs of our country!" This statement is more valid today than ever.

Dr. Alberto N. Jones
Director of the Cuban American Alliance
President of the Caribbean American Children Foundation

32

LA FAMILIA PROJECT

Humble beginnings in my hometown

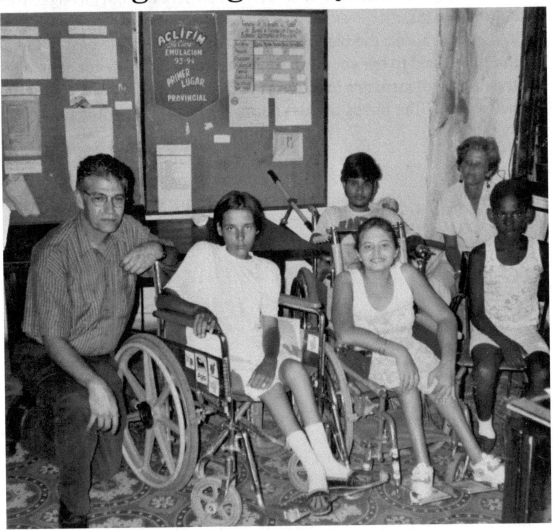

First meeting in my hometown of Santa Clara with members of ACLIFIM
The Cuban Association of the Physically Disabled – A CALL for *La FAMILIA*

On a visit to family in Santa Clara not long after establishing CAAEF, I was invited to attend a meeting with neighbors who were creating a local chapter of the national organization of ACLIFIM (The Cuban Association of the Physically Disabled). I was so impressed with their enthusiasm, yet painfully aware of the struggle they were having to build a chapter along with the difficulties they faced on a daily basis. CAAEF had been trying to come up with a

Delvis and Norine meet in Havana with directors of ACLIFIM Mabel Ballesteros and Luciana Valle, in an office surrounded by impressive painting by one of their members

plan for a worthwhile project we could carry out in Cuba, in conjunction with our work in Washington, D.C., I realized that this might be a perfect fit.

Since opening our office in New Jersey, our work had focused on Congress and on our outreach program to Cuban Americans nationwide in the United States. Our base of support was growing, as we established contacts with Cuban Americans and friends from Hawaii to Florida, and from Maine to Alaska, and I felt this idea of compassionate work would be well received. We were carrying out our advocacy work in Congress in D.C. where we brough Cuban Americans to visit hundreds of legislators. These constituents were diverse in thought and ideology but united in a common quest for changes in U.S. policies that negatively affect the lives of our families and friends in Cuba. Having a project of taking humanitarian aid to the group that ACLIFIM represented, would add personal meaning to our work and give the Cuban Americans an important way of getting involved with their fellow citizen and family in the homeland.

I discussed my ideas at length, first with Norine, thinking that it was a project she could carry out from our California home office, when not in D.C. helping me set up congressional visits. She was excited and full of ideas, so we approached the CAAEF board and got their full support, not having a clue as to how we would carry it out, but knowing it was the right thing to do.

CONFERENCE PARTICIPATION

By the fall of 1997, our office in D.C. had opened and we had made inquiries as to how to carry out our delivery of humanitarian goods. The process was complicated but doable, so we applied and received the two necessary licenses – one from the Treasury Department for travel, and the second from the Commerce Department to export the goods. When we learned of two major conferences in Cuba related to this subject, we attended both which gave us many great contacts and made our presence known. In October of 1997, the "Second International Conference on the Rights of Disabled People" was held in Havana in conjunction with the National Association for the Deaf and the National Association for the Blind and Visually Impaired. The conference was attended by 219 persons representing 18 countries from Europe as well as Venezuela, Canada, Belize, Panama, Bolivia, Guatemala, Brazil, Cuba and several international organizations were also in attendance. The agenda of the conference also included visits to special schools for deaf children. In plenary sessions, they focused on issues dealing with sexuality, education, physical disability in general, children with cerebral palsy, Down Syndrome, and mental retardation. The conference also dealt with employment, architectural barriers, rehabilitation, and the integration into society of disabled people.

We met a group of young people participating in fun activities at their special school in the town of Regla.

CAAEF president, Delvis Fernández Levy had a warm working relationship with **Dr.Raúl Gil Sánchez**, Director of the Community Mental Health Center of Regla.

At that conference there was also an explanation and recommitment to the goals of the association, stating: ACLIFIM works for the total integration into society of people with disabilities and the elimination of barriers that segregate them. It also works for the empowerment of disabled people through the use of available technology, education, and the attainment of meaningful employment. With love and a deep desire for peace among all nations, in their final declaration, they asked for:

- An end to the Helms-Burton and Torricelli laws that support the embargo and violate the rights, not only of those who live in Cuba and the U.S., but also of people around the world who want to have relations with both countries.

- An end to terrorism that negatively impacts on the growing tourist industry of Cuba as well as maims and kills innocent people.

- The delivery of food, especially for the very young and the very old; the delivery of desperately needed medicines and medical supplies and equipment that Cuba is not allowed to purchase due to the U.S. embargo; and to encourage world leaders to exert pressure on the U.S. Congress to approve legislation that would permit humanitarian commerce with Cuba.

From Cuba, representing ACLIFIM, Mabel Ballesteros and Luciana Valle, visited Congress with La Familia supporters from the U.S.

IN WASHINGTON, D.C.

At home in Washington, we were making many visits in the offices of Congress to educate and make Congresspeople aware of our work and the great need in Cuba. On a special day, accompanied by two members of the Cuban Association for the Disabled, Mabel Ballesteros and Luciana Valle, we conveyed our first-hand knowledge about the effects of the embargo on the scarcity of life sustaining medicine, rehabilitation equipment, and materials for building prosthesis and wheelchairs. One of the major highlights of our activities in D.C., was the privilege we had to speak and moderate at a press conference in the House for the introduction of the Cuban Humanitarian Trade Act (HR 1951) (the 105th Congress - 1997-1998). The bill dealt with trying to exempt from the embargo on trade with Cuba the export of food, medicines, or medical supplies, instruments, or equipment, or any travel incident to delivery.

Norine on the steps of the U.S. Capitol with a group of Cuban Americans from Florida and California, ready for congressional visits .

As is common, the bill had been tacked on to a much bigger bill that dealt with many other things. While working in Washington we quickly learned the bill had to "go into committee" to resolve those slight differences. While sitting in a Congressional office with the four Cubans, the word came out that the bill had not passed, which completely baffled and sadly disappointed them all. Norine asked the aide of the congress person they were visiting, to please explain how that was possible when it had gotten the majority vote. The aide explained, "going into committee" meant that just a handful of Congress people (usually only 5-6) joined in a private discussion, often late into the night and in this case into the wee hours of the morning, to iron out the differences in language. The aide explained that there were no notes taken nor any recorded record of who says what. But on this day when the "committee" immerged from this privately held meeting, the bill had changed slightly in things having nothing to do with Cuba, but the portion of the bill dealing with Cuba – had been completely and totally removed. In absolute shock, Norine asked the aide if those Congressional members who had voted in favor of the bill (the majority in both houses) would not object and rise up to repudiate the committee's results. The aide calmly answered, "No, it is accepted by everyone, as that is just the way this works." We later learned that a Cuban American Representative, who fought anything and everything having to do with Cuba was on that particular committee and obviously influenced the others. To this day Norine feels that this example of how "democracy works," was the saddest and strongest message she learned while living in Washington, D.C.

More and more disability Rights Advocates were visiting Cuba, as word of our project was spreading. The U.S.+Cuba Medical Project took a delegation of disability rights advocates to Cuba to meet with members of ACLIFIM. At a seminar U.S. and Cuban participants discussed a wide range of issues such as integration, sexuality, disability rights, education, employment, health care, and the impact of the embargo on disabled people in Cuba. Representatives from ANSI (the Cuban Association for the Blind) and ANSOC (the Cuban Association for the Deaf) were also present to share their experiences. The seminar was followed by visits to *Los Cocos*, an AIDS sanatorium, the psychiatric hospital, *La Castellana*, a center for the developmentally disabled and mentally retarded, and Havana's School for the Blind. CAAEF participated in the opening session of this seminar, and we made new friends and gathered valuable information for our project of assistance to disabled children with their physical rehabilitation needs. We were excited and so appreciative of the support the U.S.+Cuba Medical Project was giving in its humanitarian efforts on behalf of the Cuban people and give thanks to **Stephanie Davies**

with U.S.+Cuba Medical Project in New York. Shortly after that seminar another important delivery was made to ACLIFIM, which consisted of 17 boxes of precious medical supplies. Special thanks went out to **Leslie Salgado** of the Howard County Friends of Latin America in Maryland, to **Yvonne Rose** in Miami, Florida, and to the folks at **ABC Charters in Miami** for their help in that delivery.

Operation USA, a Los Angeles-based international relief and development agency, sent a major shipment of medical supplies and hospital equipment in the following year. Two 40-foot sea containers were sent on board the Nuevitas of Cuba's Coral Line out of Montreal, and they promised many shipments to follow over the next few years. The group had licenses from the U.S. government departments of Treasury and Commerce to assist pediatric hospitals in Cuba with up to $1 million in aid. Operation USA had worked in 67 countries providing disaster relief and long-term development assistance, including major development programs in Vietnam. The organization was the first U.S. group back into Vietnam and Cambodia after the end of the Vietnam War.

The Cuba Medical Project of Operation USA had been coordinated by **William Paparian,** a former mayor and City Council member of Pasadena, California, who was also an Operation USA volunteer. Paparian had traveled to Cuba on several occasions, hand-carrying medicine and antibiotics for local pediatric hospitals. **Richard Walden**, with Operation USA, president at the time, had announced: "The purpose of the shipment of medical assistance is to help Cuba's children overcome the shortages of medical supplies resulting from the 38-year-long U.S. trade embargo. We hope that the Congress and the Clinton administration will work together for a saner and more compassionate U.S. policy towards Cuba which will not penalize its children. We regret that humanitarian aid for children is still part of the politics of U.S.-Cuba relations, making relief efforts like ours necessary."

CAAEF asked our friends in the U.S. to send donations for needed medicines and equipment plus money for transportation, to write and visit legislators, especially their local representative and two state senators in Congress, and to ask the U.S. Commerce Department to drop restrictions on sending computers for the education of people with disabilities as well as the restrictions on sending materials for building rehabilitation equipment. Above all, we requested that they ask Congress to repeal all the inhumane restrictions on trading in food, medicine, and medical equipment with Cuba.

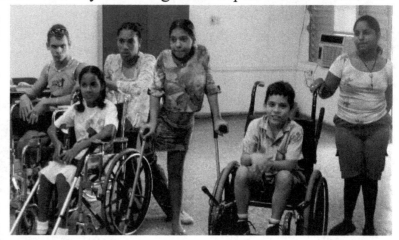

Our efforts were severely curtailed by the prohibitive costs of transportation and the inhumane restrictions on the items we were allowed to take. For example: while we could get a license from the Commerce Department to take computers for a religious group, we were not allowed to take computers for the education and employment of disabled people; while we were allowed to take a wheelchair suitable for the streets of New York we were not allowed to take materials to build a wheelchair sturdy enough for a country road in Matanzas or an old cobblestone street.

**Mr. William Paparian, (left) former mayor and councilor of Pasadena, California, with a group of Cuban doctors at the Pediatric Hospital in Havana, Cuba.
Photo was taken by Delvis Fernández Levy, who accompanied Mr. Paparian in the delivery of medicines and medical equipment.**

ACLIFIM always expressed their appreciation for donations but explained they could not depend entirely on the sporadic arrival of charity. They also emphasized their need for computers, to assist them on their road to integration and empowerment for their education, and materials to build their own equipment for mobility.

MEDICAL PROGRESS IN CUBA

MENINGITIS VACCINE TO BE MARKETED IN THE U.S.

SmithKline Beecham and the Finlay Institute of Cuba have reached agreement to market Cuban developed vaccine for meningitis B. The U.S. government is allowing SmithKline Beecham to commercialize the vaccine worldwide. Bacterial meningitis is an inflammation of the membranes enveloping the brain. (July 29, PR Newswire)

CUBAN SCIENTISTS DEVELOPED A NEW AIDS VACCINE

Tested on animals and by the end of this year in humans. Cuba is one of five countries whose scientists have managed to obtain a formula that has been authorized by the World Health Organization to be tested on humans. The other countries are the United States, England, France and Switzerland. As of Last April, 2,223 people infected with the HIV virus had been detected in Cuba, 856 of whom have become ill and 614 patients have died. 72 per cent of HIV-positive people on the island are male and the highest incidence of the disease is among young people. (AFP, 17 May)

A TOTAL PELVIS AND HIP TRANSPLANT WAS PERFORMED FOR THE FIRST TIME IN CUBA

Performed by a team of surgeons from hospital Frank País, led by Dr. Rodrigo Álvarez Cambras. The 17-year-old patient, Naela Piloto Alameda, was successfully evolving. No reports of similar intervention have been found in any other country in the world. (Miami Post, May 26, 1999)

Dr. Álvarez Cambras at the recepción in his honor by the San Francisco Global Trade Council and Guzik Technical at the Fairmont Hotel late December.

CUBA TO OPEN MEDICAL SCHOOL
FOR CENTRAL AMERICANS

Under full scholarship 1,200 students from Central America and other parts of Latin America are studying medicine at the new Latin American Medical School in Cuba. Late last year Cuba sent 2,000 doctors and other medical worker to remote regions of Central America hit hard by Hurricane Mitch. With the new medical school, the Cuban government hopes to train 5,000 doctors from throughout Latin America over the next decade. Students without scholarship pay a tuition of $7500 to attend other medical schools. (AP 6/27).

SAVVY CUBAN EXPORT:
HEALTH REVOLUTIONARIES

Since last October, Cuba - with the world's highest number of doctors per capita - has dispatched 698 doctors to five countries. It sent 292 physicians to Haiti, 121 to Honduras, 63 to Nicaragua, 16 to Colombia and 206 to Guatemala. Forty years ago, Cuba had only 6,000 doctors. Half of them fled the country when Castro came to power. Today it has 64,000 physicians, virtually all of whom were trained in one of Cuba's 21 medical schools. (USA Today 5/3).

EDUCATIONAL TOURS

Health and Healing in Cuba
With The Real Patch Adams
And his performance partner Susan Parenti

When: December 10 - 20, 1999

Contact: Global Exchange

What: Visit with Cubans in hospitals, family doctor and natural medicine clinics, schools, day care centers, farms and factories to discuss their holistic health care system and programs in sustainable development. Attend the Havana premier of the film Patch Adams starring Robin Williams.

"Visiting Cuba's Health Care System was like seeing my dream realized on a nation-wide basis There are many things our society can learn from Cubans. The strongest is their vital *sense of community."*

LETTER FROM DR. PATCH ADAMS TO THE CUBAN AMERICAN ALLIANCE

[**Hunter Doherty "Patch" Adams** (born May 28, 1945) is an American physician, comedian, social activist, clown, and author. He founded the Gesundheit! Institute in 1971. Each year he organizes volunteers from around the world to travel to various countries where they dress as clowns to bring humor to orphans, patients, and other people. Copied from Wikipedia]

good health is a laughing matter — and that's nothing to sneeze at!

4-18-04

DEAR friends of CAAEf,

Well, we had A fabulous trip to cuba April 3-10, 2004 with 20 clowns and medical AID. We delivered it to the headquarters of the ASSOC that cares for the desabeled from all of Cuba. We also visited 4 of there institutions and as a physician feel that they do a remarkable job - given the embargo. We could see and heard that - meds and supplies are scarce and still, we saw impressive care to all in the institutions. Thank you for letting us take part in humanitarian efforts in cuba.

in peace

patch Adams MD

GESUNDHEIT INSTITUTE
6855 Washington Blvd., Arlington, VA 22213
Phone : (703) 525-8169, Fax : (703) 532-6132

The 'PERSONAL TOUCH' for DELIVERY of AID

When the following message was received at our CAAEF headquarters, we realized a different and better approach was needed for our delivery of aid. For one thing, large shipments were not realistic as funds were just not available. Secondly, time was of the absolute essence, and many times when medications were sent, the long wait destroyed their efficiency or created a huge gap in taking that medication regularly.

A Special Urgent Request from Cuba. - *The wife of an ACLIFIM leader, a young psychiatric patient is in desperate need of medications. Let us know if you can assist in obtaining and/or transporting (legally) the following medicines: Triperidol, Pimozida, Nortriptilina, Nobrium (Medazepam), Alprazolam, Clonazepan. Gracias.*

We ran through many ideas, and it took many months to implement, but we finally came up with a plan that finally seemed to work well. We double checked and realized that our license could be extended to any group or individual who was willing to make a specific delivery for us and fulfill our extremely strict requirements. The majority of these rules came from the U.S. government, as folks were allowed to travel under our license for the sole purpose of making the delivery and nothing else. So Norine came up with our "packet of materials" to cover all the bases and started personally contacting "friends" and sending them the needed information.

The packet explained:

- Who we were and what the project was all about;
- Instructions for the items they must deliver - an extremely detailed list of medications that constantly changed depending on requested needs;
- How to go about obtaining these medications and equipment from professional medical donators;
- A list of facilities they must visit to learn about ACLIFIM's activities while in Cuba;
- The labels showing where each package was going and what it contained;
- The documentation for their proof of delivering with the ACLIFIM official stamp of delivery, and most important to us;
- The required 'return report' which was to be sent to CAAEF within days of their return detailing their activity around the delivery, but of real value to us was their information regarding any new or additional items that were urgently needed.

Norine had a network of doctors and nurses all across the country, which she could call on to help provide what was needed, plus getting it to a traveler who was scheduled to leave within a day or two. It was an incredibly complicated procedure and involved a great deal of paperwork back and forth, which Norine and her daughter-in-law, MariTere carried out mainly from our CAAEF home office in Hayward. As the interest grew and more and more "friends of Cuba" became aware of our project and wanted to help, we were absolutely amazed at the amount of material we were able to send, the speed with which we could get needed items to the Island, and the beneficial "side effect" that many

Americans traveled to Cuba to see the situation there with their own eyes to make their own decisions about what they saw.

Norine and I were also allowed (required by licensing officials) to make two trips a year to meet with our friends at ACLIFIM to confirm that everything was being done according to the U.S. requirements. We were also pleased and honored when we were given the official ACLIFIM report from the 2002 World Conference, which listed the CAAEF organization's efforts, as the greatest contributor of humanitarian aid to the island. Here is the quote from the report of 2002: "*Se realizaron cartas de agradecimientos a todos los donantes. La mayoría de las donaciones provienen de Estados Unidos, a través de* Cuban American Alliance Education Fund, Inc." (Letters of thanks were sent to all donors. Most donations come from the United States, through the Cuban American Alliance Education Fund.)

It was a very satisfying effort, and one that to this day, Norine says was the most rewarding project she has ever been involved with in her entire life. Countries or large organizations would send very large donations, but usually only a time or two each year, whereas the friends that helped with our approach, would arrive frequently bringing medication that was desperately needed as well as prosthesis and other equipment. At the height of our activity, small groups or individuals were going every week, with the average number participant between nine or ten. On one occasion we learned there was absolutely no hernia mesh for needed operations, a condition often afflicting those within the ACLIFIM community, as well as the general population. A call went out immediately to our dear reliable Cuban American friend, **Dr. John Padilla**, who was a physician in Santa Barbara and always quick to respond to any need we had. The next day, a large overnight envelope arrived in Hayward containing six sheets of hernia mesh. It was immediately overnighted to one of our travelers and arrived in Cuba three days later. Apparently, each sheet is cut into small pieces, sometimes only one inch square, for each repair operation. On our next visit, just a few months later, we were told that the packet of mesh took care of every single needed hernia operation in all of Cuba at that time, and several that had been waiting for their surgery for many months.

After such a successful campaign, we were very saddened and shockingly distraught when we were abruptly informed by the United States government, under the Bush administration, that our necessary licenses would no longer be available for our work. We continued our effort trying to obtain these licenses with letters from many, many folks who had participated in addition to several Congress people who appealed on our behalf. It was all to no avail, so soon after our move to San Luis Obispo in the fall of 2004, we had to accept the end of our *La Familia* Project.

33

ELIÁN GONZÁLEZ

During the year 2000, I helped to launch an extensive campaign through CAAEF (Cuban American Alliance Education Fund) to reunite Elián González, the 6-year-old boy found floating off the coast of Florida, with his family in Cuba. Activities in this regard included daily updates to our network of constituents, both by telephone and e-mail, participation in over 100 interviews in both the print and electronic media urging Elián's return to Cuba, and the placing of numerous letters and editorials in the print media, written by supporters of our cause. In addition to national media outlets, our campaign was carried by the BBC of London, KBS of Korea, CBS of Canada, CNN in Latin America as well as U.S. and Cuban radio and TV.

To help jog my memory in writing the events of the intense and difficult happenings surrounding the "Elián Saga" of early 2000, I have used much of the documentation, which we compiled in a three-ring binder with 100s of pages and gave to Elián's father, when they finally headed home to Cuba. It contains a very complete and accurate picture of our CAAEF efforts and activities to give support for returning his son. There were original photos and many documents: personal letters written by Cubans and Americans, then living in the United States, who gave support; letters written to members of Congress, government officials, including the President; 'letters to the editor' and 'op ed' pieces which had been published in major newspaper from Boston to San Diego and Seattle to Miami; radio interviews as well as TV news coverage which kept me on an incredibly hectic and chaotic schedule.

In writing, we had strong support from Cuban Americans in almost every state, yet there were some afraid to speak out in public due to fear and intimidation from extremists among the Cuban American community. As their representative, in a leadership position and as President of CAAEF, I was compelled to bring that message forth. Interviews with supposedly right-wing news anchors, were especially trying, but I did learn that their extreme views were sometimes all for 'ratings.' For example, during a makeup session in preparation for an interview with a news anchored on Fox News, I was told that behind the scenes, he was much more in agreement with my views, but would never say that on the air.

Thankfully, we were eventually rewarded for our efforts when Elián returned to his homeland with his father, his stepmother, his little baby brother and his two grandmothers. Unfortunately, once the media blitz of this story died down –

relations between Cuba and the United States have remained almost the same - sometimes better under the Obama administration, but often very bad under Trump's regime.

Delvis meeting with Elián's father Juan Miguel at the Cuban Interests Section in Washington, D.C.

RESOLUTION
By the CUBAN AMERICAN ALLIANCE

July 27, 2000

WE members of the Cuban American Alliance, United States citizens residing in various parts of the nation, encouraged by recent events such as the reunification of Elián González with his family in Cuba and by recent votes taken in the House of Representatives affecting United States trade and travel policy towards Cuba; and

KNOWING that the people of Cuba and the United States have geographical, cultural, historical, and economic ties which make them neighbors and natural friends; and

CONSIDERING that an overwhelming majority of the American people have stated through recent polls their support for the normalization of relations with Cuba; and

BEING deeply concerned about the forty-year-old embargo that

- Restricts free trade and travel.
- Deprives the Cuban people of access to medicines and basic necessities.
- Prolongs and exacerbates divisions between families and neighbors.

- Compels Cubans to risk their lives through dangerous and illegal migration; and
- Limits cooperation on issues of national and hemispheric concern such as drug trafficking.

THEREFORE, We, Cuban Americans, resolve to petition Congress and the President of the United States to end the policy of trade and travel restrictions and to work diligently towards the goal of full normalization of relations between the United States of America and the Republic of Cuba.

Presentation Given by Delvis Fernández Levy At the World Affairs Council of Oregon
Published in the Oregonian Newspaper

On March 2000, I had the privilege to be invited to speak at the Governor Hotel before the World Affairs Council of Portland, Oregon. Here is a summary of my presentation under the title **"Revising Our Policy Toward Cuba – Overhaul Needed."**

The case of Elián González, the five-year-old boy found clinging to an inner tube off the coast of Florida, underscores a need for a thorough re-examination of U.S. policy toward Cuba.

As a central piece to that policy stands the Cuban Adjustment Act of 1966, an act that excepts Cubans from general U.S. migration laws. Virtually any Cuban who reaches U.S. soil has guaranteed permanent resident status and in due course full citizenship rights. This unique privilege, taken in conjunction with the harsh realities of life in Cuba plus an economic embargo that bans food sales as well as curtails trade in medical supplies, offers major incentives to come to the mythical and bountiful *El Norte*, the United States of America.

There are millions of undocumented immigrants in the United States from all parts of the world. They live outside the political system, deprived of voting rights, without access to a free press, scarred by family breakups, and the abandonment of cultural surroundings. They come for many reasons: to escape grinding poverty and human rights abuse, and in search of economic opportunities for their families.

But what if we were to offer Mexicans and Chinese an adjustment act like the Cubans have? Of course, then the America we know would cease to exist.

Cuban families have suffered undue hardships as a result of a civil war still frozen under their island nation.

Today, while migration privileges are granted to Cubans, once in the United States they are restricted to a single visit to Cuba every 12 months for reasons of close family emergencies. Unlike other immigrants, they are also limited as to the amount of money and frequency that it may be sent to family dependents back in Cuba.

Added to these hardships is the apparent disinclination of Florida authorities to prosecute people who carry out and profit from alien smuggling through perilous journeys across open seas, charging thousands of dollars per person or indentured servitude for their human traffic.

Elián and his family, on both sides of the Florida Straits, are the latest casualties of the Cuban Cold War. A child who suffered the tragic loss of his mother and separation from father, grandparents, and baby brother, now became a poster child for lobby groups in their desperate attempt to keep U.S. policy and the Cuban Embargo in place.

Elián's case and our Cuban migration policy will ultimately harm U.S. prestige as a promoter of family values and human rights. We must not let anachronistic profiteers of a 40-year failed embargo hijack U.S. foreign policy and continue to use the life of a little boy for their nefarious shenanigans.

Delvis Fernández Levy is president of the Cuban American Alliance Education Fund in Washington, which is dedicated to educating the public on issues that impact the lives of Cubans and Americans.

**Delvis with the *Abuelas* of Elián:
Mariela Quintana y Raquel Rodríguez**

**Eliáncito with his
Papito Juan Miguel**

Muestras de Amor

y

Solidaridad

para

Juan Miguel y Familia

de

Cubanos

Residentes en Estados Unidos

Messages of Love and Solidarity
for
Juan Miguel and *Familia*
of
Cuban Residents in the U.S.

Letter of introduction to Juan Miguel (In Spanish)

Washington, D.C.,
Domingo 16 de abril del año 2000

Queridos compatriotas
Juan Miguel, Nercy, Eliancito y Hianny:

Esta carpeta contiene muestras del apoyo que muchos cubanos y otros residentes en Estados Unidos han aportado para lograr la reunificación del pequeño Elián con su verdadera familia y la Patria que ansiosa lo espera.

Nuestros corazones y nuestros pensamientos están con ustedes. A pesar del ambiente hostil hacia nuestra querida Cuba, aquí estamos en pie de lucha por todos los niños y familias cubanas que hoy son víctimas de uno de los más crueles e inhumanos bloqueos de la historia.

Abrazos a cada uno de Uds.

Delvis

Introductory Letter (In English)

Dear compatriots
Juan Miguel, Nercy, Eliancito and Hianny:

This folder contains samples of the support that many Cubans and others residing in the United States have provided to achieve the reunification of Elián with his true family at the Homeland that longs for him.

Our hearts and thoughts are with you. Despite the hostile atmosphere towards our beloved Cuba, here we stand in struggle for all Cuban children and families who today are victims of one of the cruelest and most inhumane blockades in history.

Hugs to each of you,

Delvis

Quotes from letters of support to Juan Miguel
(Spanish in italics)

Here are a few sample quotes from the many letters CAAEF received which were presented in the binder to Elián's father Juan Miguel.

- **My Granddaughter Dariella**, the same age as Elián, and **Grandson Cian** near the time of Elián's tragedy. Great motivation for the struggle for the return of Elián to his Cuban *familia*. Before starting first grade, Dariella wrote:

Dear Juan,
I think Elián
should go home
with you. Elián
shouldn't stay
in the u.s.a.

"I think Elián should go home with you. Elián shouldn't stay in the U.S.A."

- **Juan Pablo Cabrera, from California**

"Soy Cubano-Americano y nací aquí pero me encanta Cuba y creo que Elián debe estar contigo Señor González. Yo llamé al presidente Bill Clinton, Vicepresidente Al Gore y a Janet Reno para decirles que Elián debe estar en Cuba."

"I am Cuban American, and I was born here but I love Cuba and I think Elián should be with you Mr. González. I called President Bill Clinton, Vice President Al Gore and Janet Reno to tell them that Elián must be in Cuba."

- **Abelardo and Consuelo Arteaga, from Florida**

"Les escribo a nombre mío, mi señora Consuelo y toda mi familia, para expresarles nuestro profundo apoyo y unidad con Uds. ..."

"I am writing to you on behalf of me, my Wife Consuelo and my whole family, to express our deep support and unity with you..."

452

- **Adela Hirsch, from Maryland**

"Estamos siguiendo muy de cerca los acontecimientos que desgraciadamente son tan tristes para ti y tu familia...Espero que pronto puedas actuar libremente y volver a Cuba con Elián y tu familia...Soy uruguaya."

"We are following very closely the events that are unfortunately so sad for you and your family. I hope that soon you can act freely and return to Cuba with Elián and your family... I'm from Uruguay."

- **Len Antal and Dra. Ivania del Pozo, from Ohio**

"...hemos estado con ustedes esta batalla por recobrar a su niño Elián...Siempre los tendremos en nuestros corazones aquí en el estado de Ohio."

"... we have been with you in this battle to recover your child Elián. You will always be in our hearts here in the state of Ohio."

- **Rubén G. Rumbaut, from Michigan**

" mi hijo de 6 años ...que conmigo y su mamá pasamos por Cárdenas el mismo 20 de noviembre ...desde que se enteró de lo que pasó ha insistido en que devuelvan a Elián a su papá..."

...my 6-year-old son ... that with me and his mother we passed through Cárdenas on November 20th ... since he found out what happened, he's insisted that Elián be returned to his father..."

- **Mariana R. Gastón, from New York**

"Ya es hora que su hijo tenga la oportunidad de sanar esa gran herida que lleva dentro al naufragar en el mar y perder a su madre. Quien mejor que Uds. Junto con sus abuelas, los amiguitos de Cárdenas y el calor del pueblo cubano para ayudarlo a sobreponerse a esta trágica odisea."

"It is high time your child had the opportunity to heal that great wound inside as he is shipwrecked at sea and losing his mother. Who better than you along with his grandmothers, the friends of Cárdenas and the warmth of the Cuban people to help you overcome this tragic odyssey."

- **Waldo Parravicini and family, from California**

"Estimado coterráneo; no estás solo en estos momentos tan duros para tu familia y especialmente tu hijo Elián. Nuestra familia está con ustedes y como tu luchamos por justicia, honor y verdad."

"Dear Compatriot; you're not alone now during these hard times for your family, and especially for your son Elián. Our family is with you, and as you, we fight for justice, honor and truth."

- **Ruby Pratka and Frank Pratka, from Maryland**

My family and I strongly support the INS (Immigration and Naturalization Service) decision to return Elián to you in Cuba. We have written many letters to our elected officials urging them to do the right thing."

- **Michael P. Wright, from Oklahoma**

"…I would like to express my profound sympathy for you, your son, and your family, in the face of the ordeal you have experienced these last four months. This has been a grave injustice, and as a U.S. citizen I apologize for the behavior of my government. Your son should have been returned to you in December."

A memorable day meeting with Juan Miguel and the outstanding Washington immigration attorney José Pertierra, April 9, 2000

The little brother Hianny, Juan Miguel, and his stepmother Nercy at a reception in the Cuban Embassy, April 9, 2000

Song for Elián

Words and Music by Dave Welsh

Let little Elián González go
Home to Cuba, let the little boy go
Back home to his papa,
His grandmas and his grandpas
Time to send the little boy back home.

1ST CHORUS	2ND CHORUS (AFTER 1ST & 3RD VERSE ONLY)
Time to let Eliancito go	**We gotta stop–stop the blockade of Cuba**
Can you imagine just how sad he	**Stop-stop-the blockade of Cuba**
Feels without his Daddy	**Stop-stop-the blockade of Cuba**
(Time to) let Eliancito go	**Time to let Eliancito go.**

Washed overboard on the stormy sea
A long way from his family
Holdin on and inner tube
With the fightin spirit of a Cuban
That was his destiny.

Chorus

Elián survived the waters cold
And he's only six years old
And after all that danger
He's kidnapped by some strangers
Held hostage by the Gusanos

1st and 2nd Chorus

Elián was rescued from the deep
Now he's surrounded by Republican creeps
The crazies in Miami
Don't care about the family
Time to set little Elián free (home to Cuba)

Chorus

It's time to learn to live and let live now
It's time to love thy neighbor somehow
Uncle Sam throws his weight around
The Cold War has stayed around
Forty-seven years long.

Last chorus ends: The embargo is a crime, and now is the time to let little Eliancito go.

PRESS CONFERENCE
CUBAN AMERICAN AND RELIGIOUS LEADERS
CALL FOR ELIÁN'S RETURN TO CUBA

At a Press Conference with Gloria La Riva, highly dedicated activist for Peace and Freedom and for Eliáns return to his *Familia*.

A major press conference was called for Tuesday, January 18, 2000, at the National Press conference in Washington, D.C. Our primary aims were to expedite Elián's return to his family. The following persons gave presentations connecting to religious views, legal facts, and general family values and opinions in search of justice for Elián and his family.

Rev. Dr. Joan Brown Campbell, outgoing General Secretary, National Council of Churches. She reported on meetings with Elián's father and grandparents in Cuba.

Delvis Fernández Levy, President, Cuban American Alliance Education Fund, an umbrella group of 36 different Cuban American organizations from across the U.S. focused on improving the situation of the Cuban family. Members of the organization received death threats when organizing a counter-protest in Miami.

José Pertierra, Cuban American Human Rights / Immigration Attorney discussed how conferring U.S. citizenship on Elián could have a tragic impact on the boy and his family.

Michael McCormick, Director American Coalition for Fathers and Children. This group filed a 'friend of the court' brief with the INS stating the legal argument for returning Elián to his father which contributed to the INS determination to send Elián back to his family in Cuba.

A simultaneous press conference took place in Chicago organized by the Chicago Cuba Coalition with representatives of several Midwest Cuban American groups, legal experts and U.S. Representative Jan Schakowsky and Danny K. Davis, members of the House Government Reform and Oversight Committee. **Gisela López** was the contact person to reach for that press conference.

Messages and letters calling for the return of Elián were received along with testimonials for publication. For our press presentations, as president of the Cuban American Alliance, I received letters from lawyers, students, university professors, medical professionals, psychiatrists, and psychologists. Protests against Elián's abduction took place throughout the United States. In some of these protests, all of which were conducted peacefully, dozens of protesters were arrested. Here is a <u>partial list</u> of the states and cities in which protests, and messages of support were carried out:

California -> San Francisco, Los Angeles, Santa Maria, San Diego, Inglewood, Monterey Park, Lake Forest, Oakland, Hayward, San Luis Obispo, San Gabriel
Connecticut -> New Haven
Delaware -> Wilmington
Florida ->Tampa, Dade City, Safety Harbor, Gainesville, St. Petersburg and Miami
Illinois -> Chicago
Louisiana ->Baton Rouge
Maryland -> Baltimore, Columbia, Bethesda
New Jersey -> Teaneck
New Mexico -> Albuquerque
New York -> New York City, Brooklyn, East Hampton
Ohio -> Canfield
Oklahoma -> Norman
Oregon -> Portland
Texas - > Houston
Washington -> Seattle and Tacoma
Washington District of Columbia
    Wisconsin -> Milwaukee.

Rev. Dr. Joan Brown Campbell, outgoing General Secretary, National Council of Churches. Pictured in Washington, D.C. with Elián's brother

Rev. Lucius Walker calls for Peace and Justice and the Return of Elián to his loving Cuban family.

Praise for Attorney General Janet Reno

Miami – January 13, 2000

The Cuban American Alliance Education Fund praised Attorney General Janet Reno for her decision to uphold INS ruling to send Elián González home to his father. CAAEF will hold a rally in support of this decision Friday January 14, 2000, at 2:00 PM in front of the INS building in Miami.

Since Elián's rescue from the trauma suffered at sea and the loss of his mother he has been denied the physical and emotional contact he so badly needs with his father, grandparents, stepmother, baby brother and friends. This little boy has been further traumatized and abused by parading him before hordes of reporters, politicians and television cameras in Miami. The INS conducted exhaustive private interviews with Elián's father, Mr. Juan Miguel González in Cuba and reached the conclusion that he has the sole legal authority to speak on behalf of Elián regarding his immigration status in the United States.

While fully endorsing the INS decision to return Elián to his home, CAAEF will continue to work for a reassessment of U.S. policies that are injurious to the welfare of Cuban families.

But now the bad news

Due to an overwhelming amount of harassment, CAAEF has decided to cancel the rally in support of Elián González's return to Cuba. We fear for the safety and well-being of our members in the city of Miami. While fully endorsing the INS decision to return Elián to his home, CAAEF will continue to work for a reassessment of U.S. policies that are injurious to the welfare of Cuban families.

URGENT APPEAL

A young Cuban American and a member of our Advisory Council who despite harassment raised her voice in the trenches of Miami in favor of the prompt reunification of Elián González with his family in Cuba.

In particular, **if you're a Cuban American**, or have visited Cuba and witnessed how children are nurtured and cared for by their families, <u>praise</u> the INS for their wise decision and <u>insist</u> on the prompt return of Elián to his family in Cuba. The longer they delay in complying with their decision, the greater the danger that unscrupulous politicians will try to score points on the plight of little Elián.

HERE IS A GLIMPSE OF LIFE IN TODAY'S MIAMI

Our Advisory Council member was present at the demonstrations and reported that there were more police and reporters than actual demonstrators. When she and her dad were stopped by a handful of people stopping traffic on the expressway, her father called the nearby police for help, and they simply took the side of the demonstrators. On another incident, later that day, she was scheduled for a TV appearance and when it was discovered that she supported the view of returning the boy to his family and home in Cuba, the interview was canceled before it got started...

For Cuban Americans in Miami, it takes a lot of courage to come out and openly express their views on Elián's case. All they have is the strength of their conviction that keeping Elián here is an egregious and immoral act against the sanctity and unity of the Cuban family.

Press conference in San Francisco
Mission Culture Center for Latino Arts
Tuesday January 25, 2000
Norine Fernández for the Cuban American Alliance Education Fund

Unfortunately, my husband Delvis Fernández Levy is now in Washington, D.C. and regretfully unable to join us today. He asked me to present this rational and thoughtful discourse and asked that I inform you that the angry mob of anarchistic hate mongers that have been so visibly portrayed on your television sets do not speak for all Cuban Americans. He works endlessly to give a voice to the vast majority of Cuban Americans across this land who quietly want this insanity to end by reuniting this child with his family in Cuba, in the country that all Cuban Americans love.

The Elián González case is a battle for the hearts and minds of the American people. As a Cuban American speaking for many Cuban Americans who make up our Alliance, we want to raise our voices in favor of the prompt return of Elián to his real family. We as a people are witnessing child abuse, human rights abuse, and a gross violation of family unit. This is an issue that should unite people everywhere, outside of political constraints and in favor of family values and parental rights.

Please consider the following facts:

1. A 5-year-old Elián González was placed in an unsafe boat by his mother, Elizabeth Brotons, following (according to her own mother) the dictate of her domineering boyfriend Lázaro Munero. On a first attempt to leave Cuba the boat had engine trouble and had to return to the island. At that time, another child of 4-years was left behind. After repairs, the boat which was designed for 6 passengers set off again. It was overloaded with 14 people paying between $1000 to $2000 apiece to this man, Lázaro.

2. The mother's boyfriend (not her husband and certainly not his stepfather) was a convicted alien smuggler who could not have entered the U.S. legally due to his previous convictions. He should have been prosecuted by U.S. authorities but instead, he continued to make unsafe trips back and forth from Cuba - receiving between $1000 to $2000 per head - a bargain fare considering the price of $8000 to $10,000 per person is charged by most Cuban immigrant smugglers.

3. Elián's father, four grandparents, and great grandmother all live in Cuba and have openly and strongly asserted that they want Elián back within the bosom of their family in Cuba. These assertions have been made in INS private interviews, in talks with a delegation from the National Council of Churches, and most recently by the two grandmothers themselves in New York and in Washington, D.C. Elián is also being deprived of the joy and real happiness of caring for and seeing his 4-month-old baby brother change each day back in his home in Cárdenas, Cuba.

4. There is ample evidence that Elián's father is a good father, always attentive to his son's needs. He maintained an amicable relationship with his ex-wife in all affairs regarding their child's schooling and parenting.

5. Elián has become a propaganda tool for some political leaders in Miami and in Washington, as evidenced by the camera record of the numerous visits of gifts bearing political candidates. Their statements in print and the photo-op opportunities, constitute free political advertisement at its worst and at the expense of this child's tragedy.

6. He has been enrolled in a Miami private school without his father's consent and without his father's knowledge of what is being taught. That school has exploited Elián's attendance by receiving a bonanza of free advertisements.

7. Elián is under the custody of distant relatives against the wishes of his real family in Cuba.

8. A judge in Miami, Rosa Rodríguez, granted custody to a great uncle that was basically unknown to Elián and had played no role in his upbringing. The judge is under investigation for improprieties in campaign contribution due to a conflict of interests regarding the custody case. She hired the spokesperson for Elián's Miami relatives, during her election bid for judgeship to the rate of $63,000. The first federal judge assigned did remove himself for the very same reason.

9. Elián's Miami relatives seem to be living off the child's tragedy. They have left their jobs; yet drive a brand-new Lexus automobile, dress in new designer clothing and appeared to be profiting from the media frenzy and the coffers of the Cuban American National Foundation. The pictures of a little boy being coached and coaxed into uttering words and raising his thumb or hands to make victory signs he doesn't understand, to take a boat ride at Disney World when his mother drowned at sea, these are evidence of child abuse by his Miami handlers for all to see.

10. As a fatherless child in the United States, many would argue that Elián's future will not be better than as a loved son in arms of his family in Cuba.

Additional closing statement by Norine Fernández
Secretary and CFO of CAAEF

In closing, I personally would like to say that people around the world and the vast majority of Americans in this great land understand the tragedy and the damage of Elián's long separation from his home and family. And so, we must stand firm and not let a small angry mob in Miami dominate our news waves. We must not let those who bask in the Florida sun determine unacceptable grey rules to run that beautiful city based on their hateful and resentful memories of the past. We must not let their old Mafia money direct those who are supposed to represent us. We must not let these loud wishes of the few dictate the moral behavior of the many.

As a grandmother of three with one being a 6-year-old and as a mother of two sons, I join Elián's grandmother's plea to all Americans. And I state here before you that we must provide the child's return to peace and a normal quiet atmosphere where his immediate relatives can soothe his tears of sorrow to let his healing begin. We must insist that the schoolboy be returned to his little friends and schoolmates, where he can develop as just a regular kid. We must demand that Elián be returned and allowed to grow in his own land, in his own town, for it is very true and, in this case, as in any case – 'this' child must be raised by 'his' village.

We must act now, as the great Cuban Patriot José Martí wrote,

Ver en calma un crimen es cometerlo
To watch a crime in silence is to commit it.

Migration policy towards Cuba harms US prestige

The case of Elián González the five-year-old boy found clinging to an inner tube off the coast of Florida on Thanksgiving Day underscores the need to reexamine US migration policy towards Cuba.

Incentives for Cuban migration to the U.S.

Under the Cuban Adjustment Act in effect since 1966 any Cuban who reaches U.S. soil is virtually granted permanent residence and in due time full citizenship rights. While granting this privileges U.S. policy restricts Cuban Americans with close family members on the island to a single visit every 12 months to deal with an emergency. An American citizen of Cuban descent must also endure the most stringent conditions imposed on any immigrant group as to the amount and frequency with which money may be sent to a family member living in Cuba. At times, these remittances were limited to expenditure incurred on departures out of Cuba. Added to these conditions there is an apparent disregard by Florida authorities for bringing to justice people who profit from alien smuggling in speedboats at the tune of $8,000 to $10,000 per person.

No matter what one may think of the Cuban government and the harsh realities of life in Cuba these U.S. imposed conditions taken in conjunction with an economic embargo that bans the sale of food and severely curtails the sale of medical supplies are clear incentives for massive and uncontrolled migration from Cuba to the mythical and bountiful *El Norte*.

Coming to America is more than a search for freedom and democracy.

In the United States there are millions of undocumented immigrants from Latin America thousands of them face forced repatriation each year and still they continue to use every conceivable means to come to the U.S. They live lives outside the U.S. political system without voting rights nor freedom to openly plead their case or tell their stories to the Free Press. They live in a political Limbo where their lives are scarred with family breakups and the abandonment of cultural surroundings. Among the reasons for coming are the escape from grinding poverty and the search for a better life for them and their children. What if the U.S. were to extend the privileges granted to Cubans - legalize their status and approve an Adjustment Act for Mexico and all countries adjacent to the United States? This would put U.S. migration policy in concert with its Cuba policy but then the America we know would cease to exist.

Cuban families are used as pawns of a Cold War still frozen over Cuba.

With Cuba the U.S. applies a unique brand of foreign and migration policy: From the *Proyecto Pedro Pan* of the early 1960s that brought over 14,000 children to the U.S. from Cuba to Elián's case now, Cuban families have been used as pawns of a Cold War that he still frozen over their island nation. *Proyecto Pedro Pan,* named for the children's story character Peter Pan, was directed by the CIA in compliance with the Cuban Catholic Church during the early years of the Cuban Revolution. As a rule, parents willingly sent their children to the U.S. believing that the revolutionaries in Havana wanted to take their parental authority, the so-called *patria potestad* away from them. Operation Peter Pan targeted white, Havana based, upper middle-class children. The intent of course was not humanitarian but political, just as Elián's case is today.

The case of little Elián's is the last chapter of a migration policy gone haywire contrary to his father's wishes, the INS placed Elián in the custody of distant relative's unknown to him and acquiesced to a circus mounted around the young boy by the media, political leaders, and political groups in Miami. Had this boy been from any other country, the INS would have returned him to his surviving father and the loved ones in his home country.

As a father and as a grandfather, I appeal to the American people and the world community at large to demand that nations stop using families and children as weapons for the promotion of foreign policy objectives. As a teenager I too experienced the trauma of being separated from loved ones and as such I am outraged at the compliance of U.S. government officials with groups that use and abuse an innocent traumatized child to promote their political agenda towards Cuba.

To remain silent is tantamount to a tacit endorsement of a crime that promotes alien smuggling without regards for human life, the separation of a child from his natural parents and grandparents and the exploitation and abuse of a child to promote a foreign policy towards my homeland. Worse yet, a crime that is directed towards the most basic an essential unit of humanity - the family.

Elián's case will ultimately harm the best interests of the U.S. and will hurt America's prestige as a promoter of democracy and human rights.

I was an 'Elián' of the early '60s
(Operation Peter Pan, a testimonial appearing in the Boston Globe)

In 1962 at age 13, I too was a Cuban American child who was kept in the United States without my parents. Only recently I learned that my parents like, Elián González's father, were victims of a major political battle between the United States and Cuba and not fully free to determine my sister's future and my own.

In the late '60s, my sister aged 11, and I were among 14,000 Cuban children sent unaccompanied by parents to the United States in an operation similar to the Kindertransport that rescued German Jewish children from Nazi occupied countries in the 1930s. We Cuban children were part of Operation Pedro Pan. The Central Intelligence Agency files regarding this operation continue to be classified as national security secrets. María de los Angeles Torres, a former Pedro Pan child, was denied government files researching her new book "In the Land of Mirrors: Cuban Exile Politics in the United States," in which she states that Operation Pedro Pan was part of a State Department - CIA plan. The origins of the operation are still open to speculation but it is clear that U.S.-backed propaganda frightened Cuban parents into thinking that the Castro government was going to take their children away and send them to the Soviet Union for indoctrination, she wrote.

Half of us – 7,000 children never saw our parents again. Had we remained in Cuba, the argument went, Castro would have taken us from our parents to farm schools to pick tomatoes, make us good communists, and force us to study in the Soviet Union. My sister and I were separated from our parents for a year-and-a-half, and ended up picking plums in California to earn a little extra money.

Cuban Americans arguments claim Elián faces no future if he is returned to Cuba, the reason his mother risked her life and died for Elián to be free in the United States. When I first saw Elián's image appear on television running away from the cameras in Miami, I ached for the way he was being used and wanted to cry out: Leave the boy alone! He just lost his mother!

It was eerie to hear those same arguments that were used to justify sending my sister and me and 14,000 other Cuban children of Pedro Pan to the United States without our parents.

I constantly feel the emotional pain of my own many losses as I follow the daily news and I fear for Elián. Even now, I still feel foreign in this country where I hold citizenship even though both my sister and I are highly educated, successful people. I remember clearly the loss of my parents for that long year and a half, a time of great fear and anxiety that can never be fully healed. There were my great losses: the Spanish language, the Cuban soil, my warm extended family, and my national identity as tied to the place where I was born. I could lay blame for my sense of loss on Fidel Castro, or on the John Kennedy administration both of whom used us Pedro Pan children as political capital during the Cold War. But that doesn't heal the enduring pain.

As a mother and new grandmother, I hope to be able to continue to love my daughter and grandchild closed at hand and not far away.

This political theater that passes for news is not about Elián González, but about Little Havana against *La Habana*. I see the Cuban government exploiting Elián González absence as thousands of women wave his image with Cuban flags. Indignant Cuban Americans in Miami also waved Cuban flags holding on to Elián's fate as if they could recapture "The Cuba," they left so many years ago if the boy could stay in the land of the free.

Both the Cuban American community and the U.S. politicians concerned with their own imminent elections are reacting to the Cuban government's spectacle, not to concerns for Elián's personal fate.

As a U.S. citizen, I would like to see politicians from both parties stop using children as political fodder. As in Elián's case and mine, such political theater obscures the obvious failures of the United States and Cuban government to redefine U.S. Cuba relations.

Caring citizens must demand that leaders stop the 40-year practice of using Cuban children as proxies in their fight and start exploring ways to normalize relations between Cuba and the United States.

Cuban Emigres Are Not All of One Mind
(Excerpts from an article by Lewis Dolinsky in NOTES FROM HERE AND THERE)

For many Americans, the Elián González case is simple. The 6-year-old belongs with his father, brother and grandparents in Cárdenas, Cuba, not with relatives in Miami he had hardly met before his mother's death in the sea. For anyone unconvinced, a Los Angeles Times opinion piece by Anne Louise Bardach accused the Miami Cubans of everything but axe murder. In the New York Times sister Jeanne O'Laughlin the "neutral intermediary" between the grandmothers from Cuba and the Miami relatives told why she now thinks Elián should stay. In what others may see as Stockholm Syndrome, he has bonded with his 21-year-old cousin and looks upon her as his surrogate mother.

No surprise, says Delvis Fernández Levy. a Cuban American whose 6-year-old granddaughter just visited him in Hayward. "She didn't want to go home, and that was after two days. I give her everything she wants."

Like Fidel Castro and the Castro hating Cuban American National Foundation (both needing a poster boy) Fernández is finding the Elián affair useful, though he cringes at the idea of benefiting from it. Fernández, a retired Chabot College math professor, heads the Cuban American Alliance Education Fund, which is dedicated to ending the U.S. embargo, providing humanitarian aid and reconciling the Cubans of Havana with the Cubans of Little Havana. Before Elián, business was slow.

Now, Fernández is on radio and TV. It took the Fox network to get Rep. Robert Menendez, a Democrat who represents a heavily Cuban district in New Jersey, in the same room with Fernández. When Fernández is quoted in the press, he can point out that if Elián is granted U.S. citizenship the law will deny him the right to visit his father and grandparents except once a year in a "family emergency." If Elián stars in a miniseries or receives royalties from an Elián board game, he can send his relatives in Cuba only $300 every three months. Unless Congress enacts an Elián exemption.

In immigration, Cubans are privileged but if they want to visit their Homeland or aid relatives, they have fewer rights than other Americans. In July 1998 Fernández took one of the first flights from Miami to Havana. He had to be at the airport at noon; the plane left at 9:00 PM. Bags were searched and searched. All passengers were Cuban. Everyone was taking extra money to give to relatives. Women poured perfume on their bras to disguise the smell of cash so dogs couldn't sniff it.

Most American tourists have little trouble going to Cuba illegally, but Cuban Americans are more likely to be turned in on a U.S. government hotline. Most aid must go through a third country. You can hardly get a letter to Cuba. In a 40-year conflict, Elián, who should be above politics is the latest pawn.

Fernández met the grandmothers twice; he thought they should not go to Miami. "In a custody fight," he says, "you want both sides to have private access." In this case, people listened in and interrupted, and there was a circus outside. Fernández cannot say whether the grandmothers are manipulated by Castro as Sister Jean charged, but "I am convinced that they really love that child and want to be with him and nurture him."

A Cuban American lawyer, reached by phone in Miami agrees and says that in putting ideology over family, the hard-liners overstepped. She remembers leaving her grandparents behind in Castro's Cuba when she was 7. "No material gain, no freedom of speech could replace them," she said but why don't she and Fernández hate Castro obsessively as other emigres do?

Fernández answers: In 1950s Cuba his home shared two outhouses with three other families. On grandmother's farm, there was no outhouse and no well, just the river. "But we were privileged," he says. Other families did the work.

In this class-ridden society, one of his sisters was offered a scholarship to Catholic school. But she would have to wear a special uniform and stay away from the other girls at recess. Fernández's mother said, "This is humiliating. You are not going."

His mother put him on a plane to Key West in 1957 at age 17 after he was one of 11 public high school graduates in Santa Clara, a city whose population was 150,000. He did not return for 22 years. He was dispossessed not by Castro but by the U.S. conflict with Castro.

But for the wealthy, Batista's Cuba was paradise, and they lost it. The vendetta has never ended encouraged by U.S. administrations that became hostage to the power and myth they helped create. In Miami an "anti-Castro industry" exerts control and stifles dissent (mirroring what goes on across the water). There is more interest in preserving the Miami Cuban identity than in changing Cuba, Fernández says.

Asked about Cuba now, he sounds much like Castro's loyal opposition when they speak privately. He applauds health care and education. (His older sister became the first female engineer in Cuba; another sister has a doctorate; nieces and nephews are University graduates). But restrictions and movements are bad, as is the state's unwillingness to listen to alternative policies, especially in economics. Like Cubans in Cuba, he says that a nation under siege acts like one and that Cubans have a concern that transcends their feelings about Castro and communism. They fear losing their country. This is not something Americans easily understand.

"The revolution is over. The point is not to undo it but to grow from it." Fernández thinks free travel and free trade from America can help. Those are things that we profess to believe in.

Children Have Better Lives in Cuba

Opinion letter in the New Times April 12, 2000, by David Fernández

As a first-generation Cuban American who has traveled to Cuba several times, staying with relatives who live there, I take offense at R. Bravo's assumptions ["Free Elián," New Times Feb. 3.]

The "reality" of Elián's life in Cuba includes a culture where family connections are a primary value. Families and extended families share strong bonds. I have never felt such a depth of "family" here in the United States. In Cuba, children are revered. The educational system is one of the best in the world, and Cuba has an extremely low incidence of violence and child abuse (unlike the United States).

The right-wing radical views of a few Miami Cubans (200 to 300, not millions as Bravo suggests) are not the only Cuban American views. The majority of us believe Elián should be returned to his home, with his father. Moreover, Cuban Americans in Miami who agree with that are fearful to voice counter opinions, knowing they could experience threats to their lives and property from strong-arm Miami Cuban Americans.

In my visits to Cuba, I have not experienced "fear" in the people. They are proud, warm-hearted people eager to discuss the pros and cons of Cuba's political ideologies. Perhaps the fear the grandmothers expressed during their visit was due to an awareness of intense hostility in the Miami area.

Who are we to say that Elián would "thrive" best in the United States rather than with the family who has loved him his whole life? I have a 6-year-old and could not imagine the damage that it would do to her (and to me) if she were taken away from me - her father.   David Fernández

Re: Diane Sawyer's interview with Elián González

March 27, 2000

Dear Ms. Sawyer

I watched the interview you conducted with Elián on Monday March 27, against the wishes of his father Juan Miguel González.

You and the people at ABC responsible for conducting and airing this interview, have shown a total disregard for the bond that exists between a caring father and his six-year-old son.

Due to the level of hostilities existing between the Republic of Cuba and the United States of America, it appears that the producers of Good Morning America have decided that they accrue no legal or financial liabilities from Juan Miguel, Elián and his close family in Cuba.

Your interview is an egregious act against the entire Cuban people and a violation of internationally recognized rights of parents.

Signed   Delvis Fernández Levy.

Expressions of support in the U.S. Congress

February 6, 2000

Dear Senator

We would like to express our deep opposition to the proposal for granting U.S. citizenship to Elián González, the six-year-old Cuban child who for over 2 months has been separated from his father in Cuba. We also wish to discuss U.S. Cuba policies that have negatively impacted on the well-being of our loved ones still in Cuba.

Returning Elián to his father has received the overwhelming support of the American community as amply shown in polls by major U.S. news organizations.

Our delegation of Cuban Americans from various parts of the United States includes individual who came to the U.S. as very young children through the *Pedro Pan* project – a project during the early sixties that brought over 14,000 children from Cuba without their parents. Everyone in our delegation has suffered the trauma of family separation, some for as long as 30 years.

Elisa Apfel-Greenberg, Miami and Safety Harbor, FL. Board member of CAAEF and founder of student exchange program between Hampshire College in Amherst, Massachusetts and the University of Camagüey, Cuba.

Arturo J Robles, MPA San Francisco CA. Cytologist and Health care Administrator at Kaiser Permanente Hospital in Oakland, CA

Delvis Fernández Levy, PhD, Washington D.C. and Hayward CA. President of the Cuban American Alliance Education Fund.

Dr. Pedro Ferreira, Wilmington, Del. Private Practice Clinical Psychologist.

Miriam Pearson-Martínez, Baltimore MD youth Advisory Council for the Cuban American Alliance Education Fund.

Silvia Wilhelm, Miami, Fla. Executive Director of Americans for Humanitarian Trade with Cuba. Former Executive Director of the Cuban Committee for Democracy and Executive Director of Puentes Cubanos.

Our enclosed information packet contains:

- A letter from Elián's father, Mr. Juan Miguel González asking for the return of his son and requesting information about his son's psychological treatment in Miami.
- Legal arguments from distinguished American jurists supporting the return of Elián to his father.
- Letters from Congressional colleagues supporting the return of Elián to his home and in favor of not granting U.S. citizenship to the child.

- Other documents: letters from Cuban Americans, health professionals, clergy, major newspapers editorials, and news articles.

Please feel free to contact our office if you desire any more information on this important case. We are willing to testify or meet with you on any hearing you might deem necessary to expedite Elián's return to his family.

Sincerely,   Delvis Fernández Levy, CAAEF president.

Text of statement by Elián's Grandmothers

To Attorney General Janet Reno:

The retention of Elián in the United States adds to the tragedy of the family over the loss of Elián's mother Elizabeth. For us, the significance of returning Elián to his family will honor his mother's memory, return the family to normality and more importantly, return Elián to the normality of life with his father, brother, family friends at school, his toys, dog and parrot.

We are grateful to you for affirming Juan Miguel's paternity rights, but we have felt frustrated over delays in complying with this right. We ask that you return Elián to his immediate family and not to his distant family, where they had not been a previous relationship. This is the reason for being here, and we thank you for this interview.

We only have Sunday to see Elián, and we not only want to see him, but we also want to return with him to Cuba.

Sincerely,   Mariela Quintana and Raquel Rodríguez

Grand Day of Celebration

With Friends in Washington, D.C.
To His Loving Family
And Homeland of Cuba.
"Elián Te Recordamos"
Forever In Our Hearts And Soul

**All smiles - Cubans in Washington, D.C., Celebrate Elián's Return
Cuban Ambassador far left Pro Baseball Player Pedro Sierra fourth from
the right, and Delvis Fernández far right.**

34

Cuban Culture
Fiestas, Music, Dance, Sports

Politics and education must have music, dance, and sports as basic ingredients for spreading our rich culture. I take pride in reaching out to dancers and musicians across genres in Cuba, the U.S., and the world beyond. Our Cuban *Fiestas* brought to stage extraordinary musical talents from the old classics to current popular performers that filled us with pleasure and messages of love, joy and peace. On the first layer, our festive gatherings were infused with the *Ballet Nacional de Cuba* by the prima ballerina Alicia Alonso, the Liszt Alfonso Dance Group, and the Camerata Romeu. Search for music and dance was also nurtured by outstanding performers like guitarist Pablo Menéndez along with pianists Chucho Valdés and Frank Fernández. My aims were topped by *"La Colmenita,"* a group of gifted and talented children led by the also brilliant director Carlos Alberto Cremata. As our heroic patriot José Martí would say, this group brought hope for a better future.

La Colmenita Director Carlos Alberto Cremata and the granddaughters of María Mantilla. In Cuba c. 2003. 150th Birth Anniversary of patriot José Martí *Los niños son la esperanza del mundo* - **Children are the hope of the world.**

CAAEF on The Central Coast of California

Luis Seguí presided over our newest chapter from Santa Maria, California. The chapter organized writing campaigns to newspapers and legislators, petition drives, and medicine and money collections for Medical Projects and the Cuban-to-Cuban Relief Fund. In 1999 the chapter gave a traditional *fiesta cubana* with food music and traditional Cuban games at a coastal California ranch. More *Fiestas Cubanas* were organized on the central Coast of California where hundreds of adults and children enjoyed playful times. We also held *Fiestas* in other venues, private homes, clubs and conference centers. On one occasion we participated in a fiesta at the California Democratic Party Convention in San José, California where the **Congresswoman Maxine Waters** was the featured speaker. Among our objectives we provided awareness about the effects of U.S. policy on Cuba as well as raised funds for donations of medicine and medical equipment to assist people on the Island.

CAAEF's Central Coast Chapters in Santa Barbara, Santa Maria and San Luis Obispo announce their first annual Cuban Fiesta **on Sunday, August 15**[th] at Dr. John Padilla's "San Antonio Ranch" -- A full day of family fun in the country with games for kids, authentic Cuban food, and live music for dancing. Tax-deductible donations accepted for medical projects in Cuba. A year later we held a second Central Coast Fiesta in the quaint coastal town of Cayucos, right next to the pier. George Milanés, the board member who is a professional chef, used his three wooden boxes, which he buried in the sand on the beach to cook three pigs all day. This specialty and wonderful smell attracted a lot of attention and we feed close to 300 people who learned about our programs. The three strong supporters on the Central Coast were always **Jorge Milanés** in Morro Bay, **Dr. Padilla,** in Santa Barbara, and **Luís Seguí** in Santa María, who helped found the western chapter of CAAEF and make the two big Fiestas so successful.

Live music for entertainment at the ranch.

Sources of Inspiration and Support

- **Bill Martínez,** a lawyer from San Francisco, was also a top endorser of festivals and musical performers from Cuba. He was a leading supporter for starting concerts by Cuban artists in the U.S. as a cofounder of the Latino Entertainment Partners.

- **Billy Foppiano,** is a talented musician who studied at California Polytechnic University and was leading the group "All Occasions Live Music" from San Luis Obispo in California. Billy gave us guidance on the Central Coast and travelled to Cuba for the expansion of festivals.

- I had the good fortune to meet **Joaquín Nin-Culmell,** a Cuban-Spanish pianist composer (born in Germany). Joaquín lived in Oakland, California; and was a music professor at the University of California in Berkeley – the same place where I was a student and received my PhD in math. He brought joy and inspiration in promoting music concerts by telling me that he wanted to donate to Cuba his piano recordings and collection music by Lecuona.

- **Candi Sosa,** was a great singer and Cuban like me from the old Las Villas Province, but now living near Los Angeles, California. Candi wrote *"Cuba, Mi Corazón Te Llama"* – Cuba, My Heart Calls You - and gave support to festivals through her performances.

- **Robert W. Cole** was a main supporter for the Ballet Nacional de Cuba and my presentation of prima ballerina Alicia Alonso at the Zellerbach Hall in Berkeley near 1999.

A warm welcome to **Alicia Alonso** and
The Ballet Nacional de Cuba

- Many others from various parts of the U.S. assisted in the presentation and promotion of festivals and and concerts. I relish forever the meetings with **Hugo Cancio** from Miami, Florid. He was involved with an organization that gave priority to Family Services and Charter travel to his homeland of Cuba. It was a total surprise to discover that Hugo was the son of Miguel Cancio, a well-known Cuban singer and member of *Los Zafiros* – The Saphires – a vocal group that reminded me of The Platters from the 1950s with their highly harmonious vocal musical deliveries.
- **Marylin Greenberg** was a supporter of musicians in the area of San Luis Obispo. I knew her for a short period of time and received advice about bringing groups from Cuba to the Central Coast.
- A dear friend **Patricia Behrend "Patsy"** was also helpful in organizing trips to Cuba for festivals and to help with our project to bring medical supplies to Cuba.
- **Melissa Daar Carvajal** introduced me to **Chucho Valdés** at her home in San Francisco. She was well acquainted with Cuban culture and organized trips to Cuba under Caribbean Music and Dance led by another music expert, **Jane Anderson** from Missouri. Thanks to Melissa's work at the Cuban American Alliance, we supported travelers to Cuba for the **Caribbean Music and Dance Programs** interested in being part of any of the following events: The International Film Festival • The International Jazz Festival • Rumba and Folklore, Studies in Matanzas • Musical Traditions of Oriente · International Ballet Festival and Competition • Hanukkah or Passover celebrations -- in Havana.

OTHER FESTIVALS

A **CUBAN ALL-STAR CONCERT** was celebrated on Thursday. March 19 at the Berkeley Community Theater

With the help of the Latino Entertainment Partners of San Francisco a special concert was held Thursday featuring an all-star lineup of Cuban musicians, led by award-winning Canadian jazz artist **Jane Bunnett** and Cuba's popular youthful singer/songwriter, **Carlos Varela.** The Afro-Cuban jazz ensemble includes legendary **Pancho Quinto** (one of the original members of the Conjunto Folklórico Nacional), **Hilario Duran** (virtuoso pianist and ex-musical director for trumpeter Arturo Sandoval), Roberto Vizcaino (ex-conguero of Cubanismo), and **Raul Pineda** (percussionist extraordinaire). The program also features a poetry reading by Pulitzer Prize winning writer, **Alice Walker**, and **Nancy Morejón**, one of Cuba's leading poets.

MEMORIES OF DEAR FRIENDS
Tu visión humanista es fuente de inspiración
Siempre vivirá en NUESTROS CORAZONES

Luis Seguí, President CAAEF Chapter on the Central Coast of
California to the left of Dr. John Padilla and Delvis Fernández

Luis Mateo Seguí, a dear friend, a humanitarian and tireless fighter for changes in U.S./Cuba policy, died peacefully on Nov 13, 2013, in Santa Maria, California. Luis presided over our chapter of the Cuban American Alliance in Central California, where he organized writing campaigns to newspapers and legislators, petition drives, medicine and money collections for Disarm Cuban Medical Project, the Cuban-to-Cuban Relief Fund, *La Familia* Project of CAAEF, and Pastors for Peace. **John F. Padilla III** died as a result of an airplane crash on November 10, 2004. He was among the coordinators of CAAEF West Coast Chapters as well as one of the main contributors to donations for La Familia Project for ACLIFIM (The Cuban Association for the Physically Impaired). "Padilla" as I would call him gave assistance with visitors from Cuba. He provided lodging and a venue for an art show at the Santa Barbara Art Museum where Cuban outstanding artist Lester Campa was able to display original paintings brought from Cuba.

On one occasion I received news about the need for hernia mesh for surgeries throughout Cuba, and by contacting Dr. Padilla we were able to place enough of them in envelopes for donations through ACLIFIM.

Dr. Padilla was from the municipality of Guane in the far western province of Pinar del Río where relatives still live. In 1961, age 7 he came to the US. with his Cuban father and German mother. He provided help to people beyond the U.S. in Latin America and other countries as plastic surgeon and provider of medical services to people in need. He went to Cochabamba, Bolivia, for example, with a group of American surgeons, and advertised their plans to operate cleft lips. They had intended to work on 500 patients. They were overflowed by 800 anxious natives, some of whom had to wait for another trip. In Havana at Juan Manuel Márquez Pediatric Hospital, he operated freely on many occasions demonstrating new techniques. He offered his picturesque San Antonio ranch near Buellton, for fund raising and medical donations to Cuba. via ACLIFIM.

A friend told the Santa Barbara News press on October 10, 2003: I have known Doctor Padilla for nine years, he has uplifted and assisted the downtrodden, he has donated more professional hours than any other person I know. He gives of himself even to those that can't pay. He donates endless hours to his "Liberty Program" for free removal of tattoos from young men to facilitate their getting employment."

He had great hopes of restoring travel and trade relations between the two next door neighbors, and for that he also joined the Santa Barbara Santiago de Cuba sister city project, a recent initiative of Marty Blum Santa Barbara mayor.

He treated children with much care and love, specially one with a badly injured face in the bombing of Kosovo, his sister, an older brother, and a homeless boy from Guatemala atrocities of the 80s. They all lived in his ranch free of charge, and I saw them all around him like his biological children, holding hands with great love and respect. The young one, in December 99 underwent several critical operations to restore his nose and face.

We were very grateful to Dr. Padilla for his help in offering his Ranch as a venue for our first *Gran Fiesta Cubana*.

Patricia Ann (Patsy) Behrend Was born 19 April 1944 in Brookings, South Dakota passed away on November 2, 2009, in San Francisco, CA. Patsy was a pioneer in the formation of the National Network for Friendship with Cuba (NNOC).

She was a part of the early IFCO travel challenge trips to Cuba, organizing San Francisco caravans and programs. She arranged for many US delegations to attend conferences and events in Cuba. She organized and hosted many trips there, each trip loaded with medical supplies for those less fortunate in that country. She was an inspiration in her work with people when help was needed, always with a ready smile and a word of encouragement and a true hero to many.

Here is **Patsy Behrend** with her contagious smile next to **Clare Weaver**, also a friend supporter of US-Cuba Sister-City partnerships

Marilyn Greenberg was born in Fairmont, W.V., in January 1937, and died peacefully Thursday, May 28, 2009, at Sierra Vista Hospital, surrounded by family, friends and co-workers. She developed an insatiable appetite for Latin jazz and for

the past four years had traveled to Cuba for salsa dance instructions and the Havana Jazz Festival. Marilyn was an endless resource for local musicians seeking information on jazz tunes and history. She often said that she would have been a great jazz singer if only she could sing. Marilyn had been a treasured employee of Hospice of San Luis Obispo County for the past 12 years. Following her husband's death, she was immensely helped by their Widow-Widower Support group and soon became a pivotal part of the organization.

I was honored to play *"Milonga del Angel"* a piano piece by Argentinian composer Astor Piazzolla at her memorial celebration.

Fun fun and humanitarian aid focus on Fiesta Cubana

By John Dean, May 12, 2001
VALLEY LIFE EDITOR

Thousands of miles away, unbeknownst to the people of Cuba, close to 200 Americans came to celebrate their Cuban heritage and give their support for humanitarian aid to the island country.

Supporters of the Cuban American Alliance Education Fund, Inc. (CAAEF) converged on the ranch of Cuban born Doctor John F. Padilla just outside of Buellton for the first ever Fiesta Cubana Sunday.

Cubans and non-Cubans from as far as Los Angeles came to support the organization's fight for the people of Cuba.

The CAAEF is a national nonprofit organization that sends humanitarian assistance two disabled children in Cuba, works for family reunification, educates legislators on issues affecting the welfare of Cuban Americans and favors engagement as the best way to promote democratic values and assistance to family and friends in Cuba.

The organization, headquartered in Washington D.C. voices strongly in opposition to the embargo of humanitarian aid to the people of Cuba.

The event featured petition signing, games for children and adults, an auction, dancing to Cuban music, and politics.

Addressing the crowd, Luís Seguí, the West Coast coordinator for the organization, said "Cuba is not the enemy, and never has been the enemy."

Following Seguí at the mike was Los Olivos resident Eldon (Bud) Boothe. Boothe announced to the crowd the adoption by the Green Party of California of the following platform plank:

"The Green Party of California opposes the US government's current embargo of Cuba. We support (HR 130) 'Free Trade with Cuba' - this bill would eliminate the embargo and is the superior of the two-house bills. The Senate Bill entitled 'Cuban Women and Children Humanitarian Relief Act' also deserves our support." The addition of this statement to the party's platform was sponsored by Boothe.

The crowds then participated in an auction of Cuban goods with the proceeds going toward medical aid for the people of Cuba.

"Luís Seguí and his wife Dolores have done tremendous work for this event. It is a wondrous turn out," said Boothe.

Expanding into Sports and Surprising Meetings

In 1999 the baseball game between the Baltimore Orioles and the National Team of Cuba was played in a stadium to full capacity. I was able to extend a warm welcome to the Cuban baseball player outside the Oriole Park at Camden Yards Stadium in Baltimore, Maryland. A few years later the national baseball team of Cuba managed to make it to San Diego, California where I travelled with friends to extend our welcome along with George Milanés and family from the central coast of California.

Seeing a Cuban baseball team in San Diego, California brought excitement since I was now surrounded by Cubans in the U.S. who were passionate about their most popular game. I was also grateful to be in a stadium where my most famous cousin, Pedro Gómez (nicknamed **Preston Gómez**) was the manager of the San Diego Padres team. *Pedrito*, as I called him, had also been a major manager of the Houston Astros, and the Chicago Cubs. While living in Salt Lake City, Utah, during the early 1960s, he was the only family member I had the pleasure of meeting along with introducing him to my fiancée (now my wife) Norine. At that time, while he was manager of the Spokane Indians, he was the only Cuban family member that my wife had a chance to meet. Years later his mother Elia Martínez Fernández came to visit my new *familia* at our Hayward home. Although Pedrito is gone from our world, his example of dedication to building family bonds remains forever in my heart.

Meetings of Surprise

On my travels to Cuba, I was able to accidentally meet famous people from the U.S. The great comedian **Al Lewis of "The Munsters Show"** – a super funny guy ready to take a picture with me while we waited for departutre to the U.S.

About the year 2000 at the José Martí Airport in Havana Another fighter for freedom to travel to Cuba

Many more meetings of surprise are etched in my mind, but I choose not to identify their names since I am not sure they had licenses from the U.S. for travel to Cuba: famous journalists, well known artists, and friends.

A Memorable Concert Meetings at home in California

FROM CUBA, WITH LOVE: Pablo Menéndez **"Walking in Two Worlds Music and Culture in Todays Cuba,"** a lecture with video and music at Cuesta College. With my son Daniel (far left), Pablo far right and dear friend George Milanés to my right

Chabot College Presents "Faces of Cuba" Cultural Extravaganza, October 13-15

THE SPECTATOR · THURSDAY, OCTOBER 6, 2005

SPECIAL SECTION

A cultural connection with Cuba

A decade of vibrance is celebrated during 3-day conference on Oct. 13-15 at Chabot campus

(Hayward, CA) – Chabot College in Hayward celebrates ten years of cultural exchange and educational trips to Cuba with "Faces of Cuba: A Decade of Cultural Exchange," scheduled from Thursday, October 13 through Saturday, October 15, 2005. The event is open to the public, with an invitation to share in three days of workshops, performances, ideas and discussions about past and present issues in Cuba.

A broad range of experts and luminaries with an intimate knowledge of Cuba will participate. They include participants from past Chabot trips to Cuba, Cuban Americans living in the community, and multi-talented Cuban artists and entertainers. Among the many program highlights of the event are an authentic Cuban cooking workshop and a presentation on the history of music and dance in Cuba, both slated for Saturday; an art exhibit featuring "Portraits of Cuba" by internationally recognized photographer Jock McDonald; a Cuban film festival including *Buena Vista Social Club*; and a performance by the ultimate Latin music experience, Sapo Guapo.

"Cuban food, history, music, and dance are just a few of the topics that will be touched upon in this exciting three-day celebration of Cuba," according to **Rick Moniz, a Cuba historian and tour coordinator** from Chabot College. "We look forward to sharing some of Cuba's culture and issues with the community."

EVENT SCHEDULE
Faces of Cuba
Program Update

Thursday, October 13

Noon: Opening with Music, Dance and Calling of Orishas
Mike Spiro with drummers, Christina Velasco and Dancers
Reception with entertainment - Performance at the amphitheater
1:00-2:30 p.m.: "The Cuban Five" – Alicia Jrapko
1:00 – 6:00 p.m.: Cristina Velasco, *Santería* (Altar & Rituals)
2:30 – 3:30 p.m.: Delvis Fernández, Alberto Jones and Bob Guild
        "Freedom to Travel - Travel Restrictions to Cuba"
4:00 – 6:00 p.m.: Program Overview/Q&A - Reception and gallery opening
        Jock McDonald displaying fine arts prints
        Panel Discussion: "Faces of Cuba" with travel participants
        Art Gallery Reception/Exhibition: "The Cuban People"
6:00-10 p.m.: Cuban Film industry with Catherine Murphy
        Films: "*Guantanamera*" & "*Miel para Oshún*"("Honey for Oshun")
        Discussion: *"The Cuban Film Industry"*
7:00 – 10:00 p.m.: Critique of Cuban Theater with Carlos Barón
        Reader's Theater: Contemporary Works in Verse

Friday, October 14

10:30 – 12:00 p.m.: "The Soul of Cuba" - "The Life of José Martí"
        Speaker: Delvis Fernández
12:00 – 2:00 p.m.: Panel Discussion: "U.S.-Cuba Relations"
        Ana Pérez Moderator
        Wayne Smith, Mavis Anderson, and Bob Guild
2:00 – 3:30 p.m.: Afro Cubans and Cuban Reality
        Alberto Jones, Maurice Poplar, Catherine Hall
        Speaker: Travels with author Christopher Baker – "*Mi Moto Fidel:*
    Motorcycling through Castro's Cuba"
4:00 – 5:00 p.m.: Hurricane Preparedness with Ruth Rodríguez

Cuban Dinner hosted by U.S.- Cuba Sister Cities
        With Delvis Fernández Keynote Speaker

7:30 – 10 p.m.: Film Series continues with
    Jock McDonald photos in Gallery
8:00 – 9:30 p.m.: Christopher Baker interview with Bill Johnson

Saturday, October 15
        César Chávez Plaza, All Day Bazaar with Stalls
    Global Exchange   Artists
    Sister Cities   Food
    Casa Cuba   Cuban Five
9:00 – Noon   Chef Noda and Cuban Cuisine
          Workshop: Authentic Cuban Cooking
10:00 – Noon   Cuban Music and Dance Class
          Workshop: The History of Cuban Dance and Music
11:00 – Noon   Casa Cuba: Cuban Five & Questions on Terrorism
          Gallery and Campus Exhibitions
Noon – 1:00 p.m. U.S. Cuba Sister Cities
1:30 – 4:00 p.m.   Panel Discussions
          Travel: Wayne Smith, Mavis Anderson, and Bob Guild
          Faces of Cuba: Health Care, Housing and Education
4:30 – 5:00 p.m.   Orishas and Drummers in César Chávez Plaza
5:00 – 6:30 p.m.: Closing Concert: Sapo Guapo Popular 10-member Cuban band

Delvis with amazing talented youngsters from *La Colmenita* – The Little Beehive, Children's Theater of Cuba

Rick Moniz, historian friend from Chabot College, has organized and led over forty, "Faces of Cuba" trips. At a park in Havana with John Lennon, a "dear old friend."

35

La Alborada Publications
Bringing Hope for
A New Era in U.S./Cuba Relations

Cuban American Alliance

La Alborada began to be published during the Spring of 1996 from different cities of the United States: San Francisco, Hayward, California; Fort Lee and Teaneck, New Jersey; Washington, D.C.; and Houston, Texas.

Cuban Americans: Regino Díaz, from Texas, and Delvis Fernández, from California planning the publications of La Alborada in our Washington, D.C., CAAEF office.

With assistance from a Cuban American friend, Regino Díaz of Unlimited Printing Services in Houston, Texas, we managed to publish around ten issues of La Alborada during the late 1990s, since we had to use old fashion computer languages and mail from the newsletters free of charge to subscribers across the U.S.

As the technology advanced, we were fortunate to publish the newsletter through the careful collection of news, photos, and opinion letters; all directed and edited by by Luis Rumbaut, also a Cuban American, gifted writer and attorney from Washington, D.C.

Summary of Printed Editions
Spring 1996 to Jan 2003

La Alborada – began to be published during the Spring of 1996 shortly after the founding of the Cuban American Alliance Education Fund. All the editions had articles in English and Spanish. At first from 1996 to 2003 copies were sent out by mail with (1) Inspirational quotes of admired leaders like José Martí; (2) Explanations about U.S.-Cuba policies; (3) News Capsules about issues regarding Cuban and the U.S.; (4) Calls for action from people in general; (5) Brief reports on positions taken by legislators; (6) Education about laws from Washington, D.C. that have a dire effect on Cubans and U.S. citizens.

As time went by - with computers, webpages, e-mails, and social networks – La Alborada became part of a new age publication. This transition was due thanks to **Luis E. Rumbaut, Esq.**, and his great contribution by transitioning the Alborada to the new age of computer communication and technology. My dear friend **published more than 1500 issues of *La Alborada*,** with total dedication, at no financial cost – a tremendous achievement in a humble way to expand education and share high values in search of truth and justice.

Nearly two thousand issues of La Alborada in both Spanish and English are saved in digital format for donation to libraries and university archives. We continue to publish news in "La Alborada with the Cuban American Alliance" by way of social media in FACEBOOK on issues of interest related to the Cuban community on Planet Earth.

Here is a list of topics covered in La Alborada publication in print, through e-mail and social media. We hope to continue bringing truth and awareness to issues of concern to our grand Cuban family.

- Developments in U.S. policy towards Cuba.
- Brief news capsules from the U.S., Cuba, and the world press media.
- Reports on meetings and conferences covering a wide variety of subjects dealing with business, family, fiestas, humanitarian projects, sister cities development between the U.S. and Cuba.
- Sample letters and opinion articles to encourage wider participation of the Cuban American on promoting dialogue and understanding between our two nations.
- Bringing knowledge about Cuba's accomplishments in education, health care and assistance across the planet from: the children affected by the Chernobyl nuclear accident, to the expansion of medical education through ELAM (Latin American Medical School), and their accomplishments in worldwide literacy campaigns.

Printed Editions Of La Alborada
English Excerpts from the first publication

Volume 1, Number 1   Cuban American Alliance Newsletter   Spring 1996

... and we must place justice as high as palm trees. José Martí

We call for restraint in U.S. policy towards C U B A

President Clinton receives severe criticism from extremists in the Cuban exile for failing to respond to his heartburning calls for a naval blockade, the total breakdown of communications, and the sending of remittances to Cuba. Our community deplores the incident on February 24th and the loss of the four pilots, but decrees of harmful actions to innocent Cubans dishonor the memory of those who perished on a mission of peace. The President deserves applause for not getting carried away by pressures in an atmosphere full of passions and murky reasoning.

Monetary remittances sent to an elderly woman or child in Cuba are often decisive factors between life and death in obtaining medicines and adequate nutrition. If there is any lesson in this tragic event, it is the need to increase communications between the Cuban and American people.

The ban on chartered travel receives wide criticism from sections of the exile and Cuban émigrés who still have parents, children and siblings on the island. While Mr. Clinton in his State of the Nation address calls for the strengthening of American families, his action in ending these journeys injures the unity and sanctity of the Cuban family. Cancellation of family visits in no way harms Fidel Castro, on the contrary, these restrictions deprive us of visiting and ensuring the well-being of our loved ones. Today these restrictions are intensified by the decree of Mr. Helms and Mr. Burton in coding into law the meaning of a close relative in a certain state of gravity that can only be visited once a year - *what jury would be responsible for prosecuting that low-income elderly woman who secretly travels to Cuba to simply nurture children and grandchildren with maternal love?*

If the legislation were to fail to overthrow Castro, it would serve only as a constant irritant in future relations between Cuba, the United States and its trading partners. Without international support, with massive violations, and warnings of legal disputes by its main trading partners, the "Liberty" project is destined to be another hefty writing in the fight against Castro. In its attempt to isolate Cuba, the legislation has the opposite effect by antagonizing the United States with friendly countries of the European Community, Russia, Canada, and Mexico. Violations of international agreements such as GATT (General Tariff and Trade Agreement) and NAFTA (Free Trade Agreement) presage legal entanglements never seen internationally.

Another dilemma is posed by U.S. companies with pending cases before the Claims Adjustment Commission, the Foreign Claims Settlement Commission, against the Cuban government for expropriations in the 1960s. Under the law adopted by Congress, this legislation will jeopardize the legitimacy of these claims by allowing Cuban Americans who were not U.S. citizens to use American courts—unprecedented privilege for any group of immigrants in the United States.

The use of American courts to adjudicate cases in Cuba not only damages the sovereignty of the Cuban Nation, but also gives Castro a new weapon to bring together nationalists, anti-Castroists, and communists in his historic fight against the Northern Goliath. One can imagine the sinister threat to families on the island who fear being displaced from homes and schools. Popular campaigns already initiated in Cuba give the Cuban regime another coup of propaganda and not Senator Helms' desired Fidel goodbye.

If a *democratic transitional* government were to be achieved, it would have to contend with an avalanche of judgments at the precise times that it would need greater economic flexibility -- the President of the United States would be tied to negotiate political concessions of a Cuba in transition.

As evidenced by the thousands of Cuban Americans who each month circumvent travel restrictions, we, American citizens of Cuban heritage, affirm our fundamental human rights by visiting and monitoring for the well-being of our relatives who remain on the island. We were lost to see the most sacred unity of civilization, the family, used as a game token to promote certain foreign policy objectives. This law is harmful to the Cuban American community, a community that cares more about its well-being and reconciliation with its home country than of vendettas against Castro. The law opens old wounds and does not take into account Pandora's box that begins to open.

NEWS CAPSULES

2/5/96 Business Week's February 5th edition reports an **Australian mining company agreed to a joint venture with Cuba's Commercial Caribbean Nickel valued at $500 million.
Club Mediterranee will market and manage a 300-room resort scheduled to open in November.
2/23/96 (Xinhua) Cardinal Furno, **special envoy of Pope John Paul II, at a mass in Havana reiterated the Vatican's opposition to the embargo against Cuba.
2/24/96 **Four members of Brothers to the Rescue, led by Bay of Pigs veteran José Basulto, perished when their planes were downed by Cuban jets.
2/28/96 (Notimex) **Cuba and the Canadian province of Nova Scotia established foundations for the development of mixed enterprises in fishing, health, education and transportation.

**3/13/96 Pres. Clinton signed Cuban sanctions into law
   The Bill
-GIVES Cuban Americans the right to sue in U.S. courts for claims in Cuba worth $50,000 (not clear if valued in 1959-dollars).
-PUTS into law past sanctions imposed by the president.
-MAKES impossible for Clinton or any future president to ease sanctions without an act of Congress.

CALL TO THE UNITY OF THE GREAT CUBAN FAMILY

   - We call for voices to unite in defense of the fundamental human right to travel and ensure the well-being of our loved ones.

   - We must defend the right to nurture our lives with the cultural heritage of our ancestors and be able to transfer that legacy to future generations.

   -And above all we must defend the right of our sisters and brothers on the island to develop a society of justice in an atmosphere free from interference and hostile foreign actions.

FORGING AN ALLIANCE

   Despite passage of the Helms-Burton legislation the Cuban American Alliance did not take this slap in the face to family reunification efforts sitting down. The Alliance working in conjunction with the Cuban Committee for Democracy, Cambio Cubano, Jewish Solidarity, and the Cuban American Defense League organized a Day of Advocacy in Washington, D.C. (that was scheduled prior to the downing of the planes).

   A delegation of 60 individuals met with representatives and senators. Alliance members met with Congressmen Rangel (D-NY) and Richardson (D-NM) and also with aides to Senator Bingaman (D-NM), Rep. Zimmer (R-NJ running for senator against Torricelli), Sen. Boxer (D-CA), and Rep. Torricelli (D-NJ) among others. The lobby day included participants from California, Florida, Ohio, New York, New Jersey, Pennsylvania, Maryland, Delaware, and Washington D.C. We were able to get printed Op-Ed pieces as well as letters to the editors in major newspapers, including the New York Times, USA Today, the San Francisco Examiner, The Star-Ledger of New Jersey, and El Diario/LaPrensa.

   There was participation in press conferences in Washington, D.C., New York, and New Jersey. At the United Nations on March 7, 1996, we were interviewed by the CBS correspondent of the Security Council and presented our views prior to Mr. Basulto.

   Overall, the Alliance has made a good effort to educate the American public and legislators through voices of reason and moderation that focus on the welfare of families here and in Cuba.

SAMPLE LETTER

From José Estévez of California

A Thank You Letter for those who voted against The Helms-Burton bill.

Dear Representative

I want to thank you for having voted against the Helms-Burton legislation. You showed courage in view of the pressures brought by a radical fringe element of Cuban exiles who claim to speak for the entire Cuban American community.

As a Cuban-born American citizen, I sincerely appreciate your stand regarding this piece of legislation. It was bad law before the tragic loss of life of February 24, 1996, and today it is still bad legislation.

Those who voted for it out of pure emotion do a disservice to our Country. And those who voted for it, believing that by doing so Señor Castro would fall, have given him an extra lease on power for years to come.

As one who sought freedom in this Land, it is my sincere conviction that only through dialogue with the Cuban government, based on equal terms, democracy will flourish in that troubled land and there will be no need for President Castro to remain in power.

Sincerely,

José Estévez, Esq.

Volume 1, Number 7   Cuban American Alliance Newsletter Winter 1998

"Without comparing myself to you in value, I feel as one with you in being capable to die for our country."   **José Martí to General Antonio Maceo in 1894**

In this issue

Cuban Americans and Pope - Building a Future of Hope

We begin this edition with a quote (above) by José Martí directed to Antonio Maceo, the most distinguished military strategist of Cuba's War of Independence. These heroes, with pen and sword, left a rich legacy of ideals and examples for nation building. Martí expressed a profound solidarity and unity of purpose with Maceo in his quest for the right of Cubans to live as a free, sovereign and independent people.

Today, over a century later. Pope John Paul II called on all to demonstrate solidarity with the Cuban people and contribute to the common good as builders of peace, harmony, reconciliation and hope. Cuban Americans answered the Pontiff's call. From New Jersey and New York, Tampa and Miami, Los Angeles and San Francisco, and from many comers of the U.S., they joined their brothers and sisters in Santa Clara, Camagüey, Santiago and Havana. Together with Pope John Paul they say:

YES to hope! YES to freedom! YES to truth! YES to life!
NO to hatred! NO to the foreign siege of Cuba!
NO to isolation! NO to privations of basic necessities!

The Pope's Messages in Cuba
Selection of statements by the Pope in Cuba.

To Cuba. - I thank God, the Lord of history and of our personal destinies, that he has enabled me to come to this land which Christopher Columbus called "the most beautiful that human eyes have seen."

May Cuba, with all its magnificent potential, open itself up to the world, and may the world open itself up to Cuba, so that the people, who are working to make progress and who long for concord and peace, may look to the future with hope.

To Family. - In Cuba the institution of the family has inherited the rich patrimony of virtues which marked the Creole families of the past, whose members were so active in every aspect of life in society and who built this Country without counting the cost in sacrifices and adversities.

In married life, the service of life does not end with conception, but continues in the education of the new generations. Hence parents must be acknowledged as the first and foremost educators of their children. Their role is so decisive that scarcely anything can compensate for their failure in it (cf. *Gravissimum Educationis*)

The family [is] the fundamental cell of society and the guarantor of its stability. Cuba: take care of your families, in order to keep your heart pure!

To Youth. - When a young person lives according to "his way," idealizing that which is foreign, he allows himself to be seduced by unbridled materialism, he loses his own roots and yearns to escape. The emptiness resulting from such behavior explains many evils that beset youth: alcoholism; poorly lived sexuality; drug use; prostitution that hides under different reasons, which are not only personal; motivations based on taste or egotistical attitudes; opportunism; lack of a serious personal project in life, where there is no place for stable marriage, and where all legitimate authority is rejected; the yearning to escape and to emigrate, fleeing from obligations and responsibilities in order to seek refuge in a false world based on alienation and up rootedness.

Embargo.- In our day, no nation can live in isolation, The Cuban people therefore cannot be denied the contacts with other people necessary for economic, social and cultural development, especially when the imposed isolation strikes the population indiscriminately, making it ever more difficult for the weakest to enjoy the bare essentials of decent living, things such as food, health and education.

May nations, and especially those which share the same Christian heritage and the same language, work effectively to extend the benefits of unity and harmony, to join efforts and overcome obstacles so that the Cuban people, as the active agents of their own history, may maintain international relations which promote the common good. In this way they will be helped to overcome the suffering caused by material and moral poverty, the roots of which may be found, among other things, in unjust inequalities, in limitations to fundamental freedoms, in depersonalization and the discouragement of individuals, and in oppressive economic measures -- unjust and, ethically unacceptable -- imposed from outside the country. Economic embargos are always deplorable because they hurt the most needy.

Father Félix Varela. - Illustrious son of this land, who many consider to be the cornerstone of Cuban nationality. He was aware that, during his life, Cuba's independence was an unreachable ideal; for that reason he dedicated his life to developing men of conscience, that would neither be arrogant with the powerless nor weak with the powerful.

Jewish Community. - I want to send a special greeting to the Jewish Community here present. Your presence is eloquent proof of the dialogue aimed towards a better understanding between Jews and Christians. With you we share a common spiritual heritage, that sinks its roots in the Holy Scriptures.

Political Systems. – A modern State cannot turn atheism nor religion into one of its political ordinances. On the other hand, a certain form of neoliberal capitalism emerges anew that subordinates human beings and conditions the development of nations to blind forces of the market, thus placing unbearable burdens on the less favored nations from their centers of power. At times, unbearable economic systems are imposed on less favored nations as conditions to receive new assistance. Thus, in the concert of nations, assistance is given for the exaggerated enrichment of a few at the expense of the impoverishment of the many, in such a way that the rich gets richer and the poor gets poorer.

To Cubans in Other Lands. - To the extent that they consider themselves Cubans, they too must cooperate, peacefully and in constructive and respectful way, in the Nation's progress, avoiding useless confrontations and encouraging an atmosphere of positive dialogue and mutual understanding. As much as possible, help them through your proclamation of the highest spiritual values to be builders of peace and harmony, of reconciliation and hope, and to practice a generous solidarity with their Cuban brothers and sisters most in need; thus demonstrating their profound attachment to their homeland.

All Cubans are called to contribute to the common good in a climate of mutual respect and with a profound sense of solidarity.

Let's Take a Cue From the Vatican and Look Anew at: U.S.-Cuban Policies. - "When one of the world's pre-eminent moral leaders decides that Cuba is worthy of a papal visit, it is hard to argue that Fidel Castro is still a threat worthy of sanctions. Sanctions haven't ousted Castro in 36 years. All that the most recent steps have done is punish U.S. companies and strain relations with allies."

The Buffalo News, 21 Jan 1998

Winds of Change Headed Toward Cuba with Pope. - "...decades have exploited the role of Florida electoral votes in presidential politics to sustain an irrational influence over U.S.-Cuba relations."

The Seattle Times, 20 Jan 1998

The Pope's Message to Washington. - "If the White House cannot muster the political courage to press for the embargo's repeal, it should at least continue to delay implementing provisions in the Helms-Burton law that seek to keep foreign companies from doing business with Cuba. The Administration should also work for passage of Congressional bills that would allow the sale of food and medicine. They enjoy bipartisan support and even the approval of some emigre groups."

The New York Times, 26 Jan 1998

Follow Pope on Cuba. - "The U.S. Chamber of Commerce and a bipartisan group of prominent people called the embargo, as it applies to food and medicine, immoral. Pope John Paul called the embargo 'unjust and ethically unacceptable'."

The Palm Beach Post, 30 Jan 1998

What John Paul Wrought in Cuba. - Pope John Paul II exhorted the U.S. to end its 38-year-old economic embargo against Cuba. It's a policy that is archaic, useless and universally condemned. The U.S. should take the pope's advice and open up economic and political relations with Cuba, at least to the extent of lifting the ban on sales of food and medicine to the long-suffering people of the island."

Chicago Tribune, 25 Jan 1998

Harsh Effects of the Embargo. - "When I was in Cuba recently, I spoke with many Cubans and witnessed firsthand the effects of our embargo. The shortages of medicine, food and basic necessities have caused desperation and suffering amongst the talented and educated Cuban population. We need to leave Cuba alone. We need to end the embargo, and let the Cuban population decide their own political destiny. There are two bills before Congress to be considered in the coming session. S1391 and HR 1951 would end the embargo of food and medicine against Cuba. I hope Herald-Sun readers will write or call their members of Congress to urge passage of these bills.

"The Herald-Sun (Durham, N.C.), 28 Jan 1998

Letters from Our Readers

To His Holiness Pope John Paul II:

We, Cubans who reside in the United States of America, are joyful for your pilgrimage to our beloved island. And we feel deeply moved by your blessings and message of love and hope brought to the people of Cuba.

Vicar of Christ, we implore that you intercede on behalf of the Cuban family and invoke maximum respect for the following human rights:

- The right of all residents in the United States to visit their loved ones in Cuba.

- The right of all immigrants to care for the welfare of their family by sending monetary remittances and basic necessities for their families' survival.

- The right of all citizens of the United States to export medicines, food and medical equipment to Cuba, particularly to be able to have humanitarian commerce with Cuba.

We plead for your solidarity and support in the construction of a new future for our beloved people.

With our maximum respect and admiration,

Cuban American Alliance Education Fund, Inc.,
Washington, D.C.

Editor's Note: The letter above was hand-delivered at the Office of the Holy See in Havana, Cuba

Special Publications of *La Alborada*

Cuban American Alliance Education Fund, Inc.

Politics is the art of combining diverse and opposite factors for a nation's growing internal welfare, and of saving the nation from other people's open hostility or covetous friendships.

José Martí

La política es el arte de combinar para el bienestar creciente interior, los factores diversos u opuestos de un país, y de salvar al país de la enemistad abierta o la amistad codiciosa de los demás pueblos.

José Martí

Volume 2, Number 1 *Volumen 2, Número 1*	**Special Millennium Edition** *Edición Especial del Milenio*	November 2000 *Noviembre 2000*

Cuban American Perspectives on the Need to Normalize U.S.-Cuba Relations

Informe sobre la conferencia en Cuba: Encuentro entre Cubanos

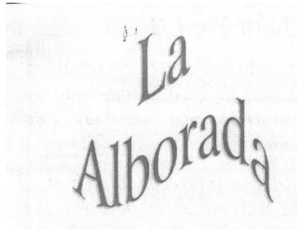

Social Work Development and Practice in Cuba and in the U.S.

Desarrollo y práctica de trabajo social en Cuba y en Estados Unidos

A Report Prepared by The Cuban American Alliance Education Fund, Inc. CAAEF

February 2002

Social Work Development and Practice in Cuba and in the U.S.

Vol 11, No. 2, February 2002, Washington, D.C

Perspectives on U.S./Cuba Policy in the Year 2003

January 2003, Vol 11, No. 3, Washington, D.C.

Martí's Soul Testament: *A Mi María*
An English translation of José Martí's
last letter to his beloved child María
Mantilla, January 2004

A Human Legacy of José Martí

Inspired by meetings with
descendants of María Mantilla in
Cuba, California, and Hawaii.
Published through Amazon,
February 14, 2018

**Carmen Miyares:
A Patriot in Silence**

Published through Amazon
February 15, 2018

An expanded English version of
La Patriota del Silencio
Carmen Miyares
de Nydia Sarabia

La Alborada Continues – Sigue Andando

Via electronic mail

Five newsletters per week by Editor and Director Luis Rumbaut reached more people than I could ever imagined – thousands of issues were composed with news, letters, and announcements about meetings and events. The newsletters were also placed in the Alliance website to reach people all over the world from 2005 to 2015.

Excerpts from La Alborada

July 29, 2005

NOTICIAS - NEWS
> Long arm of the Bush administration touches Cuba caravan
Austin Chronicle - July 29
By Cheryl Smith
Most of an 11-vehicle, 150-member caravan hauling tons of humanitarian aid to Cuba, including donations from Austin-based Bikes Across Borders, has made it to the island nation. Seven caravanistas have stayed behind in the Texas-Mexico border city of Hidalgo, however, in an attempt to reclaim 43 boxes of computer equipment seized from two yellow school buses at the front of the caravan last Thursday by U.S. Customs and Border Protection officers acting on orders from the Commerce Department.
> McCarry Named to New State Dept. Post
Washington Post - July 28
By George Gedda / The Associated Press
WASHINGTON -- Caleb McCarry, a veteran congressional staff expert on Latin America, was appointed Thursday to a new State Department post aimed at preparing for a peaceful transition to democracy in Cuba.
> Caribbean States to Strengthen Ties in Panama Summit
Prensa Latina - 26 de julio
Panama City, Jul 26 (Prensa Latina) The Association of Caribbean States (ACS) is now trying to promote new multilateral agreements that would help the dreams leading to the establishment of the group ten years ago come true.
> First Delegations to World Youth Festival Arrive in Venezuela
AIN - July 28
Havana, July 28 (AIN) The first foreign delegations to the 16th World Youth Festival arrived Thursday in Caracas, the capital of Venezuela.

EXCERPTS from LA ALBORADA
February 23, 2015

CULTURA Y ACTIVIDADES
» Relatan experiencias en traducción de libros de La India

CASAS DE CRISTAL (Titulares)
» Triple suicide blasts kill 47 in Libya's Qubbah
» Guardian Corrects Anti-Russian Story Based on 'Research" of Own Reporter / Sputnik International
» 1,500 Ukrainian soldiers are 'missing in action' – Ukraine Security Service negotiator — RT News
» Ukraine must pay for Russian gas sent to rebel areas: Medvedev - Yahoo News
» China pivots everywhere – RT Op-Edge
» European Lawmakers Demand Answers on Phone Key Theft - The Intercept
» How the CIA gets away with it: Our democracy is their real enemy - Salon.com

NEWS - *NOTICIAS*

U.S.-Cuba Talks on Re-Establishing Diplomatic Relations
US State Department - Feb 20
Media Note
Office of the Spokesperson
Washington, D.C.
February 20, 2015

On February 27, Assistant Secretary of State for Western Hemisphere Affairs Roberta S. Jacobson will host a delegation from the Cuban government led by Josefina Vidal, general director of the U.S. Division of the Ministry of Foreign Affairs, to discuss re-establishing diplomatic relations. The talks will take place at the Department of State in Washington, D.C. and will focus on matters related to reopening embassies, including the functions of diplomats in our respective countries.

Investing in Cuba: Tom Herzfeld Sizes Up the Prospects
Barron's - Feb 21
By Richard Rescigno

"Look out there!" Tom Herzfeld exclaims, pointing to the sparkling panorama of Miami and its port, visible from his condominium's rooftop terrace. "There's where cruise ships come in; the cruise lines will benefit from tourism to Cuba. There's a dredger; the Cubans need to have some of their ports dredged. There are cargo containers; container ships will be needed for U.S. trade with Cuba."

INTERNACIONALES

Cuba frees Canadian businessman after 3 years
Oman Tribune - Feb 21
HAVANA (Reuters)
Cuba has freed Canadian businessman Cy Tokmakjian after more than three years in jail, his company said on Saturday, resolving a case that had strained Cuban-Canadian relations and alarmed foreign investors.

Ecuador Cuts Wages of Top Officials to Fund Maternity Doctors
teleSUR - Feb 21

The Ecuadorean President Rafael Correa announced Saturday that he will make a reduction on high-ranked public servants' salaries — including his own — in order to fund more than two thousand physicians as part of an intensive health campaign aimed at reducing maternal mortality.

OPINIONS - OPINIONES

The 2006 report on Cuba that mentioned Venezuela a lot
La Alborada - Feb 23
EDITORIAL

In 2006, Condoleezza Rice, then Secretary of State, chaired a commission to overthrow the Cuban government. Formally named the <u>Commission for Assistance to a Free Cuba</u>, the commission foresaw a prompt collapse of Cuba, the formation of a Cuban Transition Government, and, at the latter's request for assistance, a massive intervention of the US in Cuba at all levels, to be ready for action within two weeks after a decision were made. The commission's report of 2006 (a prior report had been issued in 2004) mentioned two Latin American countries only: Cuba and Venezuela, which were described as working together to destabilize the entire continent and so on.

The frequent mentions of Venezuela stand out, given the official focus on Cuba. Here are some examples:

- The current regime in Havana is working with like-minded governments, particularly Venezuela, to build a network of political and financial support designed to forestall any external pressure to change.

- At the same time, there are clear signs the regime is using money provided by the Chávez government in Venezuela to reactivate its networks in the hemisphere to subvert democratic governments.

- The current regime in Havana is working with like-minded governments, particularly Venezuela, to build a network of political and financial support designed to forestall any external pressure to change.

- The Castro regime is actively seeking to control the policy environment on transition in concert with opponents of peaceful, democratic change, led by the Chávez government in Venezuela. The regime is implementing information and influence campaigns to develop support networks outside of Cuba to provide it additional revenue streams today, to act as advocates on its behalf against U.S. policy toward Cuba and the region, and to support and secure international legitimacy for a succession within the revolution. These networks undermine the opportunity for a democratic future for Cuba; U.S. national security interests in Cuba and in third countries; and our interest in a democratic and stable Venezuela.

- This axis also undermines our interest in a more democratic Venezuela and undermines democratic governance and institutions elsewhere in the region. Together, these countries are advancing an alternative retrograde and anti-American agenda for the hemisphere's future, and they are finding some resonance with populist governments and disenfranchised populations in the region. Castro hopes a political shift in [sic] beginning to grate on Cuban nationalist sensibilities. The more than 11 million people in Cuba are, in fact, our natural allies in breaking both the dictatorship and the Cuba-Venezuela axis that protects and sustains it.

Rice was National Security Advisor in 2002, when a coup in Venezuela succeeded for two days and then fell apart. On the day after the coup, Rice publicly hailed it and declared that the people of Venezuela had rebelled against a hated Hugo Chávez. In fact, the people faced off against the military and demanded the return of their elected president. Rice had to eat her words. The lack of objectivity of her report on Cuba-Venezuela was demonstrated when she described the fascist coup --it planned for a dictatorship to be in effect until the massive support for Chávez could be eliminated-- as "peaceful, democratic change."

Several years later, the US has recognized that the 54-year-old policy of strangulation of Cuba has failed. That does not mean, however, that its policy of regime change for Venezuela has changed. The oil is still there, and the elected government is still led by Chavistas, with Nicolas Maduro, the elected president, as leader. As the commission's report made clear, it was the view of the State Department that Venezuela was holding up the Cuban government: without that support, Washington had concluded, the Cuban government would be ripe for intervention.

Latin America and the world have changed much since 2006 and the days of "mission accomplished" in Iraq. It may be the case that the US now is willing to live with Cuba as it is, more or less. That remains to be seen in practice. The more urgent question today is whether US policy on Venezuela has changed. For now, it does not look that way.

Why Does Latin America Reject US Belligerence toward Venezuela?

teleSUR - Feb 20

By Joe Emersberger

Latin American governments have been very united in rejecting the USA's efforts to have the government of Nicolas Maduro in Venezuela overthrown – and they've also rejected the U.S. government's take on the human rights situation there. When a verifiable diplomatic record opposes U.S. policy, the corporate media (following the lead of US officials) will sometimes quote anonymous foreign "diplomats" who allegedly support the USA. But the more common tactic is to ignore the diplomatic record entirely. It's a good way to avoid an awkward question. Why is the region so united against the USA?

The Union of South American Nations (UNASUR) rejected the U.S. sanctions on Venezuela. The Community of Latin American and Caribbean States (CELAC) also rejected them. Even the OAS, until quite recently a reliable U.S. lapdog, passed a resolution of "solidarity" with Venezuela during last year's violent anti-government protests.

There are three interrelated reasons for Latin America's unity against the U.S. campaign to oust Venezuela's government.

1) U.S. government claims about the human rights situation in Venezuela are false.

Venezuela has a much higher tolerance for protest and the expression of dissent than the USA.

Code Pink activists were recently ejected from a congressional hearing for staging a symbolic "arrest" of Henry Kissinger whom they called a war criminal. Kissinger (who really should have been imprisoned for mass murder decades ago) simply chuckled, but John McCain erupted at the spectacle: "Get out of here, you low-life scum" he barked. During the 2008 presidential debates, Obama and McCain each said they had Kissinger on their side and bickered over who could really claim him as an ally. It was a sickening illustration of how remarkably constrained public debate is in the USA, and explains why Code Pink feels justified in using mildly disruptive but completely non-violent tactics.

But imagine if Code Pink leaders wrote op-eds every few weeks for leading U.S. newspapers, made regular appearances on its largest TV networks where they spoke at length and were treated respectfully, and had leaders who were governors, legislators, and mayors. Under those hypothetical conditions, anger at them for interrupting hearings (though not as much anger as McCain's) would be understandable.

Now imagine if Code Pink's tactics also included major vandalism, killing police officers and setting death traps for motorists. One can only wince contemplating the extreme violence the USA's political class would endorse against what it would unanimously call "low-life scum," especially if black men were involved. The hypothetical I've outlined still leaves one thing out that applies to the leaders of last year's violent protests in Venezuela. Imagine if Code Pink leaders had participated in the violent overthrow of the U.S. government.

Cuba Détente

President Obama's Dec. 17 statement announcing changes in U.S. Cuba policy was a mixture of historical truths and catch phrases drawn from the catalog of myths about Cuba and U.S. policy goals. The first round of rule changes, announced by Jan. 16 by the Office of Foreign Assets Control (OFAC), was significant in the areas of trade and banking. At the same time, much of the language is drawn from the old justifications for regime change. (Let us put aside the hypocrisies in Obama's speech such as the instruction — coming from a country where labor unions have been systematically destroyed — that "Cuban workers should be free to form unions.") In his speech, Obama reworked Einstein's famous definition of insanity to support his partial abandonment of the half-century attempts to destroy the Cuban revolution. "I do not believe we can keep doing the same thing for over five decades and expect a different result," said Obama. (If he means that the policy he has supported for six years is insane, what does that say about him?) Nowhere in the speech did Obama renounce the longstanding U.S. commitment to regime change in Cuba or even acknowledge that it ever existed. While implicitly recognizing that the use of sanctions to achieve political results had failed, he continues to pursue them in Korea, Russia and elsewhere. One day after making the Cuba speech, he signed a bill imposing sanctions on Venezuela alleging that the government of President Nicolas Maduro had violated the human rights of protestors during violent anti-government demonstrations last February. The demonstrations were led by right-wing representatives of the Venezuelan elite who have long been backed by the United States.

36

SOCIAL WORK PROJECT

At our Cuban American Alliance conference in July of 2000, we made several important contacts in Cuba and in the U.S. with plans for a conference on social work. For most of the following year, we were consumed with work around the project and invitations went out for September of 2001 to three faculty members at the University of Havana who were involved with the emerging Social Work Department.

Bringing Cubans to the states for any reason was very difficult, time consuming with paperwork, and often a failure at the last minute. We had experienced that with the University of California Conference in Berkeley, a few years before when over twenty Cubans had been invited to participate, but at the last minute the visas for only twelve or thirteen individuals had been granted. A major Latin American Studies Association Meeting - known as The LASA Conference - was being planned in Washington D.C for the first week of September. and several Cubans from the Social Work Department at the University of Havana had been invited. This eliminated the hurdle of our getting their visas, and only meant an extension would have to be applied for, so we set the date for our conference immediately following that official, much bigger one. It worked like a charm and a week before all the meetings were scheduled in D.C., New York City, New Jersey, and several Florida cities, they arrived.

Their meetings ended right after lunch on Friday, September 7ᵗʰ so we took our three new friends to a Cuban Restaurant for dinner and

University of Havana Professors visiting the U.S. Senate prior to the Social Work Conference. From left to right: to right: Lissette Pérez Hernández, Juan Mendoza Díaz, and Lourdes Pérez Montalvo

had a wonderful evening getting acquainted and talking about plans for their free weekend and the following week's meetings. We spent Saturday as tourist guides all around Washington, and a real highlight was a Sunday afternoon self-guided tour of the Capitol.

On Monday we visited a few Congressional offices then headed to Washington University for our first meeting which was an afternoon panel discussion with several of our CAAEF Board Members as participants and students from a Social Work class.

Norine serving as guide through Washington, D.C.

Early Tuesday morning we met at Union Station to board the 7:40 train for New York City and our first evening meeting. We had most of the day free, so Norine asked each of our guests what sites they had heard of and would really love to see in New York, giving them each two choices, which she wrote down on a snitch of paper. On her list was the Statue of Liberty, the Empire State Building, the Twin Towers, NY pizza for lunch, the Guggenheim Museum, and Time Square. When she finished writing just before nine, I pointed out how restless all the nearby passengers seemed and that every single person was talking on their cell phones in an agitated manner. It was not even six a.m. in California, but we decided to call our son David, as it was obvious something very wrong was happening. When he sleepily answered, we ask him to turn on the TV and let us know what he saw. Within seconds we heard his shouts and cries, and it took him several minutes to return to the phone. That is how we learned the shocking and unbelievable news of the attack upon the Twin Towers on that 9/11 day. The train car was filled with frantic chatter as people compared notes as to what they had heard from their phone calls. Our Cuban friends were nervously, stunned in disbelief, and we were at a loss of words unable to tell them anything.

As we approached the Philadelphia train station, an announcement informed us that everyone must get off the train, which everyone proceeded to do. The board with train information indicated that every train was "cancelled," and the comments we overheard were frightening and beyond belief: the dome of the capitol in D.C. had been blown off, the White House was on fire, Walter Reed Hospital had been destroyed, and on and on. The mass of people was wandering around in a daze constantly bumping into us as their attention was focused on their cell phones. Norine had left to use the restroom when a blaring announcement came ordering everyone to evacuate the building in an orderly manner, but as quickly as possible." We dragged our suitcases to the nearest exit, where I frantically watched and waited for Norine. She was stunned and shocked to see the vacant station when she came out but ran across the empty space once she spotted me desperately waving for her to come. The rumor was of a bomb threat, so people were

In the Philadelphia Train Station on 9/11 with my wife and three Cuban professors, being ordered to "EVACUATE!!" but SHOWING NOWHERE TO GO

weaving in and out of cars as the ran across a busy nearby bridge. Luckily, Norine and I had fairly small, light suitcases with wheels for the three days stay, but the Cubans had huge, heavy metal suitcases with everything they had brought for their entire trip, which of course, had no wheels. Once across the bridge, we were faced with a mass of cars stuck in traffic jams on every street, honking and yelling at each other. We wearily stopped under the many tall buildings of downtown when we found a solid stone wall to sit on.

After a moment of rest, I stood and with all the force I could muster, told the others to sit there without moving until I returned, as I was off to get water and some sort of provisions, for we had no idea how long we would be stranded there. Norine gave me an obedient salute and blew a kiss as she waved goodbye and begged me to be very careful. The traffic had thinned out very quickly and as I walked about, the town was deserted with no stores open. Finally, I came across a small corner market with a young man standing in the doorway, who agreed to sell some bottled water, a few fruits, and a box of crackers. When I returned almost two hours later, I saw the four forlorn people under my care on the opposite side of the street. A local guy had pointed out it was best to move, as the building behind their first wall seat was very tall and all glass. Being some sort of an important banking business, he feared it might be a target and they would be buried in glass if it were blown up and came down. I had also been able to reach a contact in Washington, D.C. who gave me the phone number of a friend, Pamela Martin, living in Philadelphia, and she was making arrangements for us to stay with a family. There were no cars on the streets and taxis were few and far between. With five of us and the many suitcases, it would take two taxis, so we had to wait quite a while for a second ride to come along. We drove forever to a far but beautiful neighborhood and finally pulled into a long driveway with a grand Tudor style home where a smiling couple with two huge dogs were waiting in the doorway.

After a wonderful pasta dinner, we turned on the TV and sitting in silence we saw for ourselves the events of that fateful day. Being exhausted we all fell into bed early having no idea what would happen the next day, but sleep did not come easily as we relived the nightmares of that day. When the sun streamed into our window, Norine started investigating a way back to Washington with absolutely no results. So, another day was spent relaxing in the beautiful surroundings of our host's home, but unable to put our minds at peace. The next

A peaceful night of rest having dinner with Pamela Martin in Philadelphia on 9/11

day we learned there would be one train to Washington, and we dashed off, having to run through the station, to luckily get on the slowly moving train as it pulled out of the station. Once in Union Station we hurried up to the top floor where cars were rented, to see one small car standing there alone. When we climbed in with the three women squeezed into the back seat, Norine realized the long drive ahead to Florida would be impossible. So, we dropped her off a few blocks away at our condo and bid her farewell. She had nothing but an opened container of ice cream in the freezer, so ate that over the next few days, being too fearful to step outside. There she could see soldiers on each corner of Maryland Ave. and 6th Street, with their rifles lifted at attention and hear the fleet of fighter jets buzzing back and forth over head of our place, close to the Supreme Court, the Hart Senate Office Building, the Capitol and the White House within walking distance. Early the next morning both Dave and Dan, our sons, had called their mother Norine from California, and when they learned their dad was head out at one in the morning in a rental car for Florida with three Cubans, they feared for his life at any blockade or even a restroom stop along the way. We reached the home of our dear friend and fellow CAAEF Board Member, Alberto Jones, in Florida to learn that they had set up a couple of meetings, the only two of the many we had planned for the conference.

THE PROJECT

Our project on comparative social work in the U.S. and Cuba, touched on various aspects of social work: history; curriculum development; attention of minors with conduct disorder; philosophy and political foundations of social work; social and clinical interventions; delinquency prevention; the penal and the juridical systems; and advocacy, social integration, education, and rehabilitation of individuals suffering from various mental and/or physical disabilities.

The project was developed over an 18-month period, and was to be highlighted with conferences, discussions, and meetings in Washington, D.C., Philadelphia, Pennsylvania, and St. Augustine, Palm Coast and Miami, Florida, from the 5th to the 15th of September 2001. Consultations were held with directors of the following Cuban institutions: the Cuban Association for the Disabled (ACLIFIM), the Group for the Integral Development of the Capital City of Havana (GDIC), the Community Mental Health Center of Regla, the Center for Studies on Migration (CEMI) at the University of Havana, and developers of the Social Worker Training College in Cojímar. In the U.S. we received advice from social workers (academics and field workers), health professionals, advocates of social policy change, experts on Cuban affairs, and Board and Advisory Council members of the Cuban American Alliance Education Fund.

Panelists at American University in Washington, D.C. Delvis Fernández, Patricia Morán, and professors Mendoza, Pérez Montalvo, and Pérez Hernández.

Our objectives were:

- To collect information and maintain a data bank with reports, videos, photos or other visual material about social work practices in Cuba.
- To provide and disseminate a written report about the development of social work practices in Cuba and in the U.S.

Social Work Development and Practice in the U.S. and Cuba

Conferences, Workshops and Congressional Presentations

Theme: Perspectives on Social Action and Interventions in Addressing Urban Problems

Discussion Topics: Ex offender Social Reintegration; Juvenile Delinquency; Housing and Urban Gentrification; Race and Gender Issues: economic disparities, family violence, social participation; Legal Training for Social Workers.

The following program had to be altered due to the September 11 tragedy.
Replacement events/actions are in bold and italics.
Cancelled events are within brackets [...]

PROGRAM

Wednesday, September 5 to Saturday, September 15

Cuban Participants: Dr. Lourdes Pérez Montalvo, Prof. Juan Mendoza Diaz, and Prof Lissette Pérez Hernández

Main Host: Cuban American Alliance Education Fund (CAAEF)

WASHINGTON, D.C.

WEDNESDAY 9/5
EVE. Arrival BWI (airport) from Havana (via Miami) Professors Juan Mendoza Diaz, and Lissette Pérez Hernández, and Lourdes Montalvo.

THURSDAY 9/6
A.M. Presentations to the Latin American Studies Association at the Marriott Hotel, 2660 Woodley Rd. NW
P.M. Presentations - House of Representatives
EVE. Cuban Embassy Reception

FRIDAY 9/7
Presentations - House of Representatives

SATURDAY 9/8
A.M. LASA conference
EVE. Reception hosted by immigration and civil rights.
    Attorney José I. Pertierra.

SUNDAY 9/9
Tour of Washington, D.C.

MONDAY 9/10
A.M. Presentations - Senate.
P.M. 1:00-5:00 Social Work Development and Practices in Cuba with Social
    Worker Walter Teague,
    Prof Phillip Brenner of American University.
    American University, 4400 Mass. Ave. NW
    Mary Graydon Center - Room # 5, Washington, D.C.

NEW YORK CITY

TUESDAY 9/11
A.M. 8:40 Leave Washington, D.C. Union Station D.C. for New York City,
Amrak Train #152
Due to the September 11 tragedy, the train was stopped around 11:00 am in Philadelphia – an evening meal was shared with host who finally took the group in for a lively discussion of the day's events and our guests social work involvement in Cuba.
[A.M. 11:30 Arrive at NYC Penn Station]
[P.M. Tour of New York City]
[EVE 6:30 Brooklyn Reception - Hosted by Mariana Gaston with members of
    Puerto Rican, Dominican, Cuban communities]
    Cosponsor by CAAEF Northeast Chapter.

WEDNESDAY 9/12
[NOON Luncheon / Roundtable, Committee for the Heights Inwood Homeless,
    10 Fort Washington Avenue "Penthouse Level, New York, NY 10032]
    Cosponsors: The Cuba Project and the Cuban American Research and
Education Fund.
[EVE. 5:30 "Roundtable with Cuban Social Scientists"
    The NY Project/Bildner Center
    C-203 (Concourse Level) The Graduate Center
    City University of New York
    365 Fifth Avenue - across from Empire State Building]

Traveled back to D.C. by train and drove in rental car to St. Augustine, Florida.

ST. AUGUSTINE / PALM COAST

THURSDAY 9/13
[A.M. 9:30 Leave New York LaGuardia Airport for Orlando, Florida.
     American Airline Flight #2085, 12:30 pm Arrive in Orlando Florida.]
P.M. 2:00 Meeting with organizers of Palm Coast Event
EVE. 6:00 The Development of Social Work Schools and Practice in Cuba
Daytona Beach Community College, Palm Coast Campus,
     Room 107, 3000 Palm Coast Parkway, SE,
     Palm Coast, Florida 9:00 pm Reception
     Hosted by The Caribbean American Children Foundation and the African American Cultural Society

MIAMI

FRIDAY 9/14
President George W. Bush declared Sept. 14 National Day of Mourning. Hurricane Gabrielle crossed Central Florida. Waited in Palm Coast for passing of storm then drove guests in rental car on to Miami.

[A.M. Orlando flight to Miami]
[P.M. 1:00 One-on-One meetings at Urban League/Social Work Centers in Liberty City, Allapattah or Little Havana]. - Coordinator: Álvaro Fernández
[P.M. 6:30 Reception/Round Table Discussion. Social Work Developments in Cuba and the US
     Graham Center of Florida International University. Cosponsor: Latin American and Caribbean Center], Coordinators: Elena Freyre and Professor Eduardo Gamarra.

SATURDAY, 9/15
AM. Family Reunification Meetings in Miami with Cuban guests -
Reencuentro familiar
P.M. Flight Miami -- Havana, Cuba

GRACIAS – Heartfelt Appreciation

The Cuban American Alliance Education Fund acknowledges their appreciation to The Ford Foundation and The Christopher Reynolds Foundation for their contributions toward this project. We also extend our deepest appreciation to the contributors and supporters who made our work possible.

After 18 months of planning, our conferences and workshops were altered due to the tragic events on September 11, 2001. Our heartfelt thanks to the organizers of meetings that were planned for New York: The Committee for the Heights Inwood Homeless and the Cuba Project/Bildner Center at City University of New York. Special thanks are due to Dagmaris Cabezas for months of work coordinating events and to Mariana Gastón for the reception she had planned for us in Brooklyn. We also extend our appreciation to the Latin American and Caribbean Center of Florida International University in Miami; our program there was cancelled out of respect for the victims of the tragedies on the National Day of Mourning declared by the President. Thanks to Elena Freyre, Álvaro Fernández, and José Fernández of the Cuban American Defense League and the Martí Alliance for their support under such difficult circumstances. A special thanks to Norine Fernández for her unwavering support throughout the entire project.

We acknowledge our warm appreciation to Mrs. Gertrude Blackwell, Dr. Alberto Jones, and Mrs. Silvia Jones, The Caribbean American Children Foundation, and the directors of the African American Cultural Society for coordinating meetings and receptions in Palm Coast, Florida, to Professor Ivan Schulman for the tour of St. Augustine and translations at the conference in Daytona Community College.

In Washington, D.C., we extend our gratitude to: Evelio Sánchez for serving as translator; José I. Pertierra for warmly receiving our Cuban guests; Patricia Moran for publicity and conference arrangements; and Daniel McDade of International Travel Planning Services for coordinating travel arrangements.

A special warm thanks to Rita Barouch of the Mental Health Center of Contra Costa County in California for her valuable advice, editing, books and contacts with social workers. Thanks also to the social workers and academicians in the U.S. who advised on project development: Dr. Ana María Sierra of Tacoma, Washington; Professors Anamaría Goicoechea, Morgan State University, and Nelson Valdés, University of New Mexico; psychotherapist Walter Teague for his insights into social work practice; and professors Nili Tannenbaum and Michael Reisch, University of Michigan, for their valuable article on the History of Social Work in the U.S. Special thanks to Regino Díaz of Graphics Services Unlimited in Houston, Texas for printing the report. On September 11, in Philadelphia we were forced to evacuate the train taking us to New York City. On that fateful day, we experienced fear but discovered warm friendships and people who housed and fed us during a time of need. Our deep appreciation to Pamela, Kitty, Bob, Bruce, and Lee for your loving care.

We extend our warmest thanks to the Cubans who gave us advice and assistance: Dr. Miriam Rodríguez, Vice Rector of the University of Havana; Luciana Valle Valdés, Vice President of the Cuban Association for the Physically Disabled; architects Miguel Coyula and Gina Rey of the Group for the Integral Development of Havana; Dr. Olga Fernández Rios of the Cuban Interests Section, Dr. Raúl Gil Sánchez, Director of the **Community Mental Health Center** of Regla, Cuba. And finally, *nuestro más ferviente agradecimiento* to our distinguished guests: professors Juan Mendoza Díaz, Lourdes Pérez Montalvo, and Lissette Pérez Hernández.

Urgent attention to children's rights
Is essential to the future of humanity.

37
OUR GROWING FAMILY

When I returned to Washington, D.C., Norine and I hunkered down in our condo for a few days until the first flight to California out of National Airport was available. We cried and laughed as we shared stories and relived everything that had happened, but we were anxious to leave it all behind and hug family members. The airport was eerily quiet with very few passengers wandering about, as obviously only those desperately in need of getting somewhere important were willing to fly. On the flight home, with only six other passengers on that huge, jumbo jet, it was easy to concentrate, so I began writing our report. The information was compelling and fresh in my mind about our very strange conference with what should have happened and what actually did happen. (The report is printed in La Alborada)

After that unbelievable event, family suddenly became so much more important, and the meaningful time we were missing out on with our grandchildren saddened me greatly. We now had four adorable grandchildren, but all our work and travels back and forth from the west coast to the east coast and beyond, had taken its toll. Norine had actively been present for every birth, and I was as well, but always for a shorter period of time. We were both losing the experience of many of the "firsts" – first smile, first steps and first words. So, once we had returned to our Hayward home after living through 9/11, we simply wanted to stay home and spend time with our family taking our first real break since the Alliance began.

Norine holds Daniel, and I hold Isabella as we visit a Big Ship in Morro Bay with Cian and Dariella in the late fall of 2001.

514

Dariella Arianna

Our first granddaughter, Dariella, had been born almost eight years before, in November of 1993. That was just, a few months before my sister Sarita's death, which changed my life so profoundly and which was one piece motivating the birth of the Alliance. She was the youngest of *La Familia Fernández* as eight of us traveled to Cuba on our Defiance Trip, during the Christmas Holiday break of 1994-95.

The adorable red head was a great hit in Cuba, and we had an amazing time, never to be forgotten, except for Dariella, who can only enjoy the photos and stories she has been told. A year later Dave and Deb took her again while he worked on his Architecture Thesis with our dear friend Miguel Coyula, a well know architect, whom many travelers have met, as he speaks several languages and often leads tours of old Havana to explain the restoration of the grand city, and show off the huge model, *La Maqueta* (Model of

Compay Segundo's trio entertained Mari Tere, Dave with Dariella and Dan in 1995

Havana*). Dariella was then just over two years of age and remembers next to nothing. The model David made of Havana's Capitol building and its surrounding area was for me, a beautiful work of art and a precious piece of memorabilia which hangs in my garage to this day.

Several years later, when Dariella was nine, she came to Washington, D.C.

for a visit. It was exciting to show her all those memorable sights and share with her what I was doing there. Being too young to remember Cuba, we have promised at her high school graduation, again at graduation from California University in Berkeley, and who knows how many other important times that we would take her to Cuba again. She is now working on her PhD. in Austin, Texas so perhaps that promise can come about before too long.

Cian Delvis

A little over three years later, Dave had his second child, born in 1997 on the birthday of my father, March 5th. I was very honored when they named him Cian Delvis. His dark brown hair was like his fathers, but with no waves or curls until he was older. Dave's hair too, had been straight, but changed in color and texture with all the years as a swimmer. Cian too got to travel with Norine and I to Washington D.C., but also New York City, which was certainly a highlight for us all. We packed each day with sights and sounds that were all new to him and many to Norine.

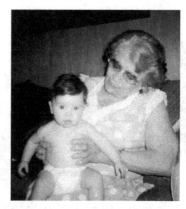

Cian with *Bisabuela*, my mother Sara.

Cian loved the Smithsonian Museums in D.C. and enjoyed New York bagels and pizza.

In 2009 at the age of 12 we took Cian to Cuba with a group from 'Faces of Cuba' under Rick Moniz, who had led these trips for many years. It was not unusual, as I ended up doing a lot of translating and explaining about anything and everything, which has always been the case when I travel with a group. Unfortunately, our journey going through Cancun was a dreadful adventure. When we headed for the gate to on to Cuba, the officials claimed there was a problem with my paperwork. I had to grab a taxi to go to an office far from the airport to fix things, and of course, pay a fee. When I finally returned, the plane for Havana had left, so I had to scramble and go through more hassles to get on the next flight early in the morning. By the time I reached our hotel, I was exhausted and furious, but even more regretful when Norine explained about Cian's great concern. She said he had fought back tears on the entire flight, and when we landed, he stepped off the plane stairway and dropped to all fours to kiss the soil of Cuba, saying he knew that is what *Abuelo* would have wanted. Once they had settled in their rooms at the Riviera Hotel, they gathered in the lobby for Rick's dinner plan which he did not have, thinking they could manage that first evening. Norine knew a woman behind the desk, so managed a reservation at *El Aljibe*, one of Delvis' favorites, with chicken and amazing black beans, which only made Cian sadder, without *Abuelo* there. Fortunately, the rest of the trip went smoothly and was an absolute success.

Daniel Alejandro

Our younger son, Dan and MariTere had also had a boy and then a girl during those hectic years of Alliance work. This second grandson was given my middle name, after his birth in Hayward on January 27th of 1999, as Daniel Alejandro. Many years later when I took Dan and Daniel to Cuba for the dedication of the José Martí Statue in 2018, we joked the evening before, on the 27th, saying all the torches carried by the great throng of people in the traditional 'March of the Torches' represented his candles for his 19th Birthday. The march is a tradition paying honor to Martí's birthday on January 28, 1853.

Dinner in the home where I grew up, myself, Daniel, his Aunt Puchi & my *Cuñado* (Brother-in-Law) Ramón González

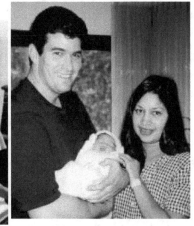

Dan and MariTere with Baby Danielito

Holiday dinner with Dan and MariTere, along with her mother, Margarita and Norine's dad Ralph Gunn.

In grand style through Havana with his father Dan, *abuelo* Delvis and great granddaughters of José Martí: Vicki and Marti Romero

517

Isabella Guadalupe

Our last grandchild, Isabella was born to Dan and MariTere just one day after their eighth wedding anniversary on November 29, 2000, so was almost one when we returned after the 9/11 tragic day. Happily, we were there for her first birthday party with all the family, together in their Hayward home including my mother, *Bisabuela* Sara, and Norine's father, Great Grandpa

The first birthday with *Mamá y Papá* giving the cake for Daniel, Dariella, and Cian to enjoy, along with the one-year-old Isabella.

Ralph. She was the absolute darling of everyone's eye, and all the grandchildren brought immense joy, and continue to be our life's greatest pride and pleasure. Isabella is fluent in Spanish, as my daughter-in-law, MariTere, is from Guadalajara, Mexico and Margarita, her mother, has always lived nearby. With that knowledge and all the stories, she has always heard, she is anxious for her visit to Cuba, a standing promise.

***Mi linda nietecita Isabelita, años más tarde en el 2012*
My youngest beautiful granddaughter Isabelita c. 2012**

I often fantasize of a trip with Dariella, since she really remembers nothing of Cuba having gone as a baby, and maybe other family members will go as well - for my farewell to my beloved homeland I often play *Adiós a Cuba*, the sentimental composition by one of Cuba's most distinguished pianists, Ignacio Cervantes.

MORE FAMILY MEMORIES

Cian with Great Uncle Ramón, Great Aunt Puchi, and Great Grand Aunt Chicha.

He jokes around reading the *Gramma* Newspaper with Chicha's thick glasses.

The playful *abuelo* in Cuba with *nietecita* Dariella trying out Cuban Hats.

Cian enjoyed music at a café with Miguel Coyula, his dad's thesis advisor in Havana.

The work continued that early winter, but closer to home, with a few speeches and interviews here and there, from San Diego to Seattle. But still, it was a wonderfully fun and relaxing break. By the New Year we were off and running again with my crazy schedule in full swing for CAAEF.

March of the Torches in Havana

January 27, 2018, on the eve of the 165th Birthday of José Martí, regarded as the Great Patriot and Apostle of Cuba. Marching in the celebration were my son Dan, myself, and my grandson, Daniel Fernández,

along with Marti and Victoria Romero, the Great Granddaughters of Martí, who had taken their first trip to Cuba with Norine and I for the worldwide conference honoring Martí's 150th birthday back in January 2003.

I was honored to be invited for the unveiling of José Martí's statue by the Presidential Palace of Havana, so I joined Martí's granddaughters with my son and grandson Danielito for a most memorable occasion. A replica of the statue displayed in the Central Park in New York City.

38

JEWISH SOLIDARITY

On September 14, 1998, The Cuban American Alliance and Jewish Solidarity organized meetings in Washington, D.C. with legislators and government officials together with representatives of the Jewish Community of Cuba. Dr. José Miller, President of the Jewish Community of Cuba; Dra. Rosa Behar, President of Hadassah-Cuba; and Jewish Solidarity Founders: Eddie Benjamín Levy and Xiomara Almaguer-Levy.

From left to right, Dr. José Miller, Eddie Levy and Xiomara Almaguer-Levy, The Levy's received an achievement award from the Center for International Policy for outstanding work in building bridges of love and understanding among Cubans.

CUBA – A Jewish Awakening

In 1492 Columbus claims Cuba for Spain and it soon became a base for the Spanish conquest in the Americas. British troops captured Havana in 1762 and later exchanged it for Florida in 1763. Slavery was abolished in 1886 and in 1895 the patriotic leaders Antonio Maceo and José Martí led revolutions against Spain. The United States declares war on Spain after the sinking of the battleship Maine. A Cuban Republic is established from 1902 to 1959 under the Aegis of U.S. dominance with a naval base at Guantanamo in Eastern Cuba. Periods of dictatorship and U.S. military interventions take place.

Jews have lived in Cuba since Christopher Columbus in 1492, but the Inquisition prevented open observance of Judaism. Luis de Torres (*Yosef Ben Ha Levy*), Columbus interpreter, came to Cuba in the first voyage, and was the first European Jew to step on the New World.

In the early 1900s the *Unión Hebrea – Shevet Ahim* was founded consisting of Sephardim from Turkey, Syria, and Mexico. My Grandfather Salvador Levy and other family members migrated to Cuba during the 1910s. Some were cloth merchants, shoe manufacturers, and tailors. Due to their knowledge of Ladino (a version of Spanish) they and their offspring were able to live in towns far from Havana and quickly assimilate into mainstream Cuban culture and society. During Spanish colonial times, Judaism was still affected by remnants of the Inquisition. Jews practiced their religion in hiding or assimilated into a Spanish Catholic religion by saying *"Soy Católico a mi manera"* (I'm Catholic, but in my own way). In 1906, the first Jewish synagogue, the United Hebrew Congregation opened in Havana under the control of American Ashkenazim.

After World War I, Jews emigrated from Eastern Europe, some settled in Havana while others moved into provincial towns. In proportion to its population, Cuba received more Jews during the 2nd World War than any other country of the Americas. For many Jews, fleeing the horrors of Nazi Germany, Cuba served as a transit point for the U.S. The community was divided into two main groups: Ashkenazy and Sephardic, referred to in slang terms as *Turcos* (Turkish) and *Polacos* (Polish). There were also people in Havana who called themselves American Jews.

Message of Pope John Paul II to the Jewish Community of Cuba: "I want to send a special greeting to the Jewish Community here present. Your presence is eloquent proof of the dialogue aimed towards a better understanding between Jews and Christians...With you we share a common spiritual heritage, that sinks its roots in the Holy Scriptures."
Pope John Paul II in Havana with Dr. José Miller and Cardinal Jaime Ortega near them.

The present

Before 1959 the community numbered around 15,000, and by the 1990s it went down to about 1500. The community has experienced a rebirth, since many children and grandchildren of the assimilated and intermarried Jews are returning to the faith of their ancestors.

There are three synagogues in Havana with existing communities in the cities of Santiago, Camagüey, and Cienfuegos. A new group has been identified in Guantanamo and a dispersed group remains in the province of Santa Clara.

Western Chapter Director
A Call to Action

In 1994, my uncle Eddie (*Tío Benjamín*) and his wife, my Aunt Xiomara Almaguer-Levy asked me to help with the expansion of Jewish Solidarity. This was a new learning experience in my life. Although I was often called *Judío* or *Morito* in my youth, as slang terms to identify people expelled from Spain around the times of the Inquisition at the end of the 15th century.

I was raised within a highly divided family with mixed cultural and religious practices. On one side, during childhood, before age of 12, I had to: recite Catholic prayers in bed with my paternal Aunt *Chicha* before going to sleep; attend catechism rituals for first communion; go for confessions on a regular basis; and attend Mass in Latin all by myself, every Sunday morning. Members of my close *familia* took pride in saying *"Soy Católico pero a mi manera,"* – "I'm a Catholic but in my own way." Iconic images of Christ on the cross and saints were in every room of the house.

On the other side, my Mother Sara considered herself *Hebrea* – Hebrew – but never tried to teach me any religious ritual. My father was not a religious man, he informed me that he was an agnostic. My Great-grandfather Salomón, according to my mother was a highly respected *Chacham (KHäKHäm),* a version of Sephardic Rabbi who often was seen praying with a string of beads that resembled a rosary. There were no synagogues in my Santa Clara hometown, but I managed to join Pesach rituals with *Tía* Raquel in the nearby town of Caibarién and Torah readings with my Behar family friend. The exposure to Jewish culture appeared sporadic and somewhat secretive. It was not until my grandmother Felicia enticed me into going to a newly formed Presbyterian Church, which for the first time allowed me to read the Old Testament. Awareness of Jewish religious practices reached a climax with deep conversations with my *Abuelo* Salvador and his taking me to receive a version of a Bar Mitzvah as a young teenager.

When my *Tío* Benjamín (Uncle Eddie) asked me to assist with the newly founded Jewish Solidarity, I felt honored and did not hesitate to provide all the assistance within my power, around California, Cuba, and Washington, D.C.

Expanding Jewish Solidarity

To my *Tío* Benjamín (Eddie Levy) and Aunt Xiomara Almaguer-Levy, August 2, 1994

Here I write about my experiences in solidarity with the Jews of Cuba. Last Friday, July 29th, I gave a presentation at The Vallejo Synagogue. My wife Norine and I went to the synagogue where we met with Rabbi David Kopstein. He informed us that the congregation's board of directors had already agreed to adopt reconstructing the Jewish community as I would suggest. The Vallejo congregation is a reconstructive Jewish community which regards Judaism not only as a religion but also as a civilization. After being introduced by the Rabbi, I spoke for about 20 minutes, and stayed much longer answering questions. The presentation was followed by a Bat Mitzvah and Kaddish prayers.

After the religious service, we went to a conference room where I met several members of the congregation: a Sephardic lady born in Atlanta, a Uruguayan, a French Moroccan, an Israelite, and many more. The Sephardic lady was of Turkish descent, born in Atlanta, and spoke English with a typical Southern accent. She also informed me that when she started grade school in Georgia, she only spoke the Ladino language prior to learning Spanish and English. She pronounced words like my grandpa, *Abuelo Papá-Viejo* Salvador. It was so exciting to hear her voice and accent taking me back to unforgettable times of my childhood.

I gave a brief history of the Jews in Cuba from 1492 to 1994, followed by anecdotes from recent history, personal experiences, and the current phase of community reconstruction throughout the Island. The talk ended up with an old Jewish story drawn from one of the articles sent to me by Rabbi Szteinhandler where he compares Cuban Judaism to "a melody sung with all my heart."

Abrazos, Hugs from your nephew, Delvis

Uncle Eddie and Xiomara with my grandbaby, Dariella, a California visit in 1994

P.S. At the end of September there will be another talk about Cuba in the same congregation of Vallejo, but with the women of Hadassah. On September 13 there will also be a presentation at the Palo Alto temple, this should be very interesting as it is in the hub Stanford University.

JEWISH SOLIDARITY
Cuba – USA Project
September 1998

Jewish Solidarity (**JS**) is a religious/humanitarian non-profit organization (founded in the summer of 1993), to help restore hope and give sustenance to the Jewish Community of Cuba. Since its creation and with the help of many activists, friends, and caring people, **JS** has delivered over 25 tons of food, medicine, school supplies, and religious items. In keeping with Jewish traditions, the community shares assistance with non-governmental institutions such as hospitals, child caring centers, schools, and senior citizen centers. Moreover, **JS** has assisted groups of American doctors and technicians to establish links with Cuba's public health system, working together towards the development of project and programs in the public health field. The work of **JS** is fundamentally a religious and humanitarian project that also offer alternatives to the government of the United States to reevaluate its policies toward Cuban society - making a first step the lifting of the embargo of foods, medicine, and medical equipment. In the context of the new millennium, advance a climate of greater tolerance, respect and peace.

Building Bridges of Hope, Love, and Understanding
"Whoever saves one life, it is as if he saved the entire world."

Mishnah Sanhedrin 4:5

Jewish Solidarity had its national headquarters in Florida with regional offices in Pennsylvania and California. Among JS most important projects is assistance in the restoration of Cuba's Jewish cemeteries and Houses of Worship. In 1995 efforts were underway to rebuild the outer walls of the Jewish Cemetery of Santa Clara and to refurbish the Hatikvah Synagogue of Santiago de Cuba.

National Headquarters
Jewish Solidarity Founders
Eddie B. Levy
Xiomara Levy, MS

Southern Regional Directors
Glenn Siesser
Pamela Siesser

Pennsylvania
Eastern Chapter Director
Ruben Honik, Esq.

California
Western Chapter Director
Delvis Fernández-Levy, PhD

MY SPIEL and *KIDDUSH* INVOCATION

Antes del Kiddush - La primera bendición sobre el vino

Before the Kiddush - The First Blessing on Wine

We are here tonight to affirm our continuity with the generations of Jews who have maintained the vision of freedom inherent in Pesach's History. We proudly claim that we descend from slaves – the first group of slaves in recorded history to have a successful rebellion against their "slave owners." Ours is the first story to fight for national liberation, and the prototype of many struggles that other nations would undertake against their oppressors.

Others would have done all they could to forget their humble pasts. Others saw themselves as descendants of gods or heroes over humans. We are proud that our people have kept the vision of seeing themselves as a slave people and has insisted on proclaiming the history of liberation as the fundamental base event on which their culture has been built.

The ruling classes have traditionally tried to convince us that domination is inevitable and is part of the universe's own structure. The Torah of the Jewish People counts the struggle of our liberation and has been a perpetual thorn on the side of these ruling classes. Pesach is not only the celebration of our freedom but a time when we are dedicated to the struggles for peace, justice, equality, and the full realization of our lives.

Beginnings of Jewish Solidary

Early in 1994, my uncle Eddie Benjamín Levy and Aunt Xiomara Almaguer-Levy had to deal with death threats in Miami, Florida as a result of their efforts to organize a group that would bring assistance to Cuba's Jewish community. Under the name of Jewish Solidarity, they managed to get a U.S. Government license to deliver humanitarian supplies to the small but now awakening Jewish community throughout the entire Cuban nation. They went to the "forbidden Island" to celebrate the Channukah Festival with 22 persons from the United States and bring foods, medicines, and toys for children. Their work inspired me to join them by opening a Western Chapter of Jewish Solidarity.

An article was written by Natalie Weinstein and published in the Jewish Bulletin of Northern California on February 17, 1995, under the title: **Activist vows Cuban Jews to get aid despite Congress.**

LIFELINE TO HAVANA

Xiomara and Eddy Levy are helping the Jews of Cuba. Are they heroes or traitors?

Announcements were made for contacts and donations through the Bay Area Chapter. The list of speaking engagement included: Congregation B'nai Shalom of Walnut Creek; Temple Beth Abraham in Oakland; University of California in Berkeley; Hillel in Santa Cruz; and Temple Israel in Alameda. There were also announcements about a trip sponsored by Caribbean Music & Dance to bring seder supplies and celebrate Passover in Cuba. In another article, **"Sí! Jews in Cuba need help!"** from the Jewish Community News of San José on March 1995, it was reported that more than 70 people showed up at congregation Beth David on a rainy Sunday morning to hear Delvis Fernández Levy. The talks were praised as heartfelt and fascinating on the history and status of the more than 1500 Jews living in Cuba today. It also stated that the Cuban community was reconnecting with its Jewish religious and cultural roots. Mentioned was made about the reactivation of B'nai B'rith and Hadassah chapters in Havana. Furthermore, there was recognition of three major Jewish communities outside of Havana in the provinces of Camagüey, Santiago and Cienfuegos.

An Unforgettable Journey

Melissa Daar came to visit in San Luis Obispo with her Cuban husband and two adorable sons

Around 1995, I became quite engaged in expanding the work of Jewish Solidarity. I met many wonderful people who guided me and gave me valuable education about the history and diversity of the Jewish community throughout the Western United States. Melissa Daar, an artistic talented person, linked me with other Cubans and expanded my knowledge of the Jewish community of the San Francisco-Oakland Bay Area. There, at her home I was fortunate to meet the famous Afro-Cuban Jazz Pianist, Chucho Valdés, and other admired Cuban musicians, as well as *Americanas* in love with the vibrant sounds of *Música Cubana*. During the early 1990s she was able to organize trips to Cuba for people to attend workshops at institutions like the *Escuela Nacional de Arte* and immerse themselves in expanding their education in dance and rhythmic sounds of Cuba and the Caribbean.

527

Later in 1995 Melissa showed me how to struggle for a travel license from the U.S. Department of Treasury. We were in the mist of planning a **Passover celebration in Cuba**, where I would assist as a translator and educator on Cuban culture and history of the Jewish community of the Grand Caribbean Island.

Two travelers, Holocaust survivors, had a tremendous impact on my life. Their stories conveyed messages of love and empathy for humans who suffered cruelties and injustices ignored by governments and people in power. Hella Roubicek, née Lövinsohn was well prepared with notes for her presentation about her life and journey to Cuba at the *Patronato* Synagogue of Havana. On the other hand, her husband Frank Roubicek did not have notes, and simply spoke from his heart as I translated the traumatic ordeals he experienced in various countries of Europe during Hitler's times.

Hella was only 12 years old when she boarded the St. Louis Ship packed with Jewish refugees coming to Cuba. Her father was already in Havana and had managed to escape Nazi persecution through Hitler's Third Reich control and expansion through much of Europe. It was a trip of a lifetime for young Hella in hopes of being able to embrace her dear *Papá*.

Frank Roubicek
  Born August 11, 1911
  In Prague,
Czechoslovakia

Hella Roubicek, née Lövinsohn
  Born June 20, 1926
  In Frankfurt / Oder,
Germany

HERE is a Brief History
The Voyage of The St. Louis

On May 13, 1939, the German transatlantic liner St. Louis sailed from Hamburg, Germany, for Havana, Cuba. On the voyage were 937 passengers. Almost all were Jews fleeing from the Third Reich. The German annexation of Austria in March 1938, the increase in personal assaults on Jews during the spring and summer, the nationwide Kristallnacht ("Night of Broken Glass") pogrom in November, and the subsequent seizure of Jewish-owned property had caused a flood of visa applications. People in the audience were in tears as she revealed seeing her father in a boat near the ship, but she was not allowed to get off the ship.

The *St. Louis Ship*, carrying more than 900 Jewish refugees, waits in the port of Hamburg. The Cuban government denied the passenger's entry. Hamburg, Germany, 1939.

After the *St. Louis* arrived in Havana, the passengers learned that the Cuban government had canceled their landing permits. The American Jewish Joint Distribution Committee (JDC) negotiated with Cuba on behalf of the passengers, but the negotiations failed, and the Cuban government forced the ship to leave the harbor.

Although the ship sailed near the Florida coast, the U.S. government did not allow the passengers to land, since they did not have U.S. immigration visas and had not passed a security screening. American newspapers publicized the saga and many Americans sympathized with the passengers.

Great Britain, France, Belgium, and the Netherlands each admitted a percentage of the passengers upon their return to Europe in June 1939. Many passengers were able to obtain immigration visas and leave for the United States before the German invasion of western Europe in May 1940, but 254 passengers of that fateful ship were killed in the Holocaust.

The voyage of the *St. Louis* attracted a great deal of media attention. Even before the ship sailed from Hamburg, right-wing Cuban newspapers deplored its impending arrival and demanded that the Cuban government cease admitting Jewish refugees. Indeed, the passengers became victims of bitter infighting within the Cuban government. The Director-General of the Cuban immigration office, Manuel Benítez González, had come under a great deal of public scrutiny for the illegal sale of landing certificates. He routinely sold such documents for $150 or more and, according to U.S. estimates, had amassed a personal fortune of $500,000 to $1,000,000. Though he was a protégé of Cuban army chief of staff (and future president) Fulgencio Batista, Benitez's self-enrichment through corruption had fueled sufficient resentment in the Cuban government to bring about his resignation.

More than money, corruption, and internal power struggles were at work in Cuba. Like the United States and the Americas in general, Cuba struggled with the Great Depression. Many Cubans resented the relatively large number of refugees (including 2,500 Jews), whom the government had already admitted into the country, because they appeared to be competitors for scarce jobs.

Hostility toward immigrants fueled both antisemitism and xenophobia. Both agents of Nazi Germany and local right-wing movements hyped the immigrant issue in their publications and demonstrations, claiming that incoming Jews were Communists. Two of the papers—*Diario de la Marina*, owned by the influential Rivero family, and *Avance*, owned by the Zayas family, had supported the Spanish fascist leader General Francisco Franco, who, after a three-year civil war, had just overthrown the Spanish Republic in the spring of 1939 with the help of Nazi Germany and Fascist Italy.

Reports about the impending voyage fueled a large antisemitic demonstration in Havana on May 8, five days before the *St. Louis* sailed from Hamburg. The rally, the largest antisemitic demonstration in Cuban history, had been sponsored by Grau San Martin, a former Cuban president. Grau spokesman Primitivo Rodríguez urged Cubans to "fight the Jews until the last one is driven out." The demonstration drew 40,000 spectators.

Information from United States Holocaust Memorial Museum Publication
The Story of the St. Louis Passengers

NEVER TO BE FORGOTTEN
A Most Impacting Testimonial

As guide and translator, I was ready for Hella's presentation about her traumatic journey from Germany, unable to step on Cuban soil, seeing her father in a small boat from the ship but never allowed to disembark or touch him, and finally heading back to Europe in the midst of war. But that same day, on the morning of her presentation, I met with Frank for breakfast at the Hotel Nacional in Havana. The two of us engaged in a deep conversation about the value and importance of sharing stories and testimonials about our lives. Frank appeared concerned about sharing traumatic experiences hidden in his soul for more than fifty years. He was ready to come out and I firmly encouraged him to speak, and I offered my services as translator and supporter for bringing out stories never to be forgotten by future generations.

Frank experienced a life of cruelty and pain difficult to explain as consequence of Nazi persecution and extended domination over European countries. He was born in Prague, Czechoslovakia and deported to various ghettos and concentration camps. He recalls the Łódź ghetto in Poland where he was sent by guards in 1941, later he was sent to Czentochowa, also in Poland, another ghetto that served as a munition's factory. From there he was moved to concentration camps, Buchenwald and Rehmsdorf in Germany, and finally to Terezín in Czechoslovakia. Frank had graduated from law school and worked as an attorney until the Nazis invaded Czechoslovakia in 1939.

A TV film crew had been invited to document Hella's story and once she had finished her emotional talk, the crew picked up their cameras and left the synagogue. At that point Frank stood up and I also stood up to introduce him and serve as a translator. This was one of the most emotional times of my life – feeling his life experiences as if they were my own, penetrating into my heart and soul. There came a time when I lost control and tears began flowing from my eyes. I recall stopping and asking the audience for help finding another translator, since I was overwhelmed with emotions and sank into my chair unable to control my feelings.

In the following paragraphs I offer excerpts from an article by William Brand about our Passover trip to Havana with Frank and Hella, that appeared in the Oakland Tribune newspaper of April 27, 1995.

531

Holocaust: 'Memories we'd prefer to forget'
A Historic trip by a dozen Bay Area Jews to spend Passover in Havana

When the group returned to the United States after a week of religious services and Passover seders at the Havana synagogue, custom agents confiscated all their Cuban purchases, took their passports and noted they made an illegal visit to the communist nation.

For Hella and Frank Roubicek, two members of the group from Berkeley, the effect of seeing their passports seized was much worse.

Both are survivors of Nazi Germany.

Standing in a U.S. customs station in Bermuda brought back all of the horrors of World War II. And Wednesday, a week later, they still wonder, if somewhere in Washington there is a dossier with their names on it.

"We would just like some reassurances from our government that everything is all right," Frank Roubicek, now an American citizen said Tuesday. "These brought back memories of things we would rather not remember."

Fifty years ago, this weekend, Roubicek, a Czechoslovakian lawyer was freed by Allied forces after a death March from the Rehmsdorf concentration camp. He weighed less than 100 pounds and could not stand, but had survived four years of slave labor, torture and starvation, and two death camps.

At the Havana synagogue, he spoke about his ordeal in public for the first time. "The Spanish translator, Delvis Fernández Levy, began to cry and had to stop his translation," said Danny Scher, who was a Passover participant.

Fifty-five years ago, Hella, born in a hamlet 50 miles East of Berlin, sat with 935 other German Jewish refugees in the heat of the Havana harbor aboard a German ship. For seven fear-filled days they waited, as first Cuba -- then under the Batista dictatorship -- then the United States and every other country in the world denied them refuge from Hitler.

Finally, the ship, the St. Louis, turn back toward Nazi Germany and certain death. "There were many suicides," Hella, who then was 13, recalled. "Finally, the ship's crew held suicide watches so the passengers could not kill themselves."

At the last moment Belgium, the Netherlands, and France offered refuge. But weeks after they arrived in Europe, Hitler's Panzer tanks rolled into those same countries and World War II began.

"Two-thirds of the people on that ship died eventually at the Nazis' hands." Hella said. "My father had gotten into America, and at the last minute my mother and I got visas. We left Rotterdam on a Dutch ship six weeks before the invasion.

"Unlike my husband, I was lucky I did not suffer. I was never hungry. I was never physically tortured. But I was humiliated and helpless," said Hella now 68 and an American citizen who recently retired after 25 years teaching at El Cerrito High School.

She said the same helpless feelings rushed through her earlier this month as an unspeaking customs agent vanished with her passport. "We were under the impression we were on a legal, religious journey. We feel we have a right to know what our status is," she said. The official returned their passports after making copies. "They kept asking us if we had any cigars," said Frank, who is now 83 and operated a health food store for many years on Telegraph Ave. "Why would we have cigars."

Michael Sheehan, a spokesman for U.S. customs in Miami, said that because the travelers had no travel permits, officials confiscated and destroyed the purchases on the spot, under terms of the trade embargo with Cuba. "We really had no choice," Shehan said. "It's the law they had no permits."

Hella and Frank Rubicek's World War II stories are on display with those of thirty other Holocaust survivors at the Judah L. Magnes Museum

THE JOURNEY CONTINUES

After the memorable Passover trip, I participated in many other activities as Jewish Solidarity representative through conferences, films and discussions across the United States and Cuba. As representative of Jewish Solidarity, I had a chance to meet President Clinton in Washington, D.C., as well as participate in the opening of the synagogue in Santiago de Cuba, *Comunidad Hebrea Hatikva*.

In the next page I offer photos of announcements for presentations at Marquette University in Wisconsin and California Polytechnic University in San Luis Obispo. I also include a picture with my sister Guiselda Fernández Levy in front of *El Patronato de la Comunidad Hebrea of Havana*.

Cuban Jewish Leaders Hold Talks with U.S. Legislators

Thanks to support from Geoff Thale of the Washington Office on Latin America (WOLA), I managed to get bring assistance from the Cuban American Alliance Education Fund and Jewish Solidarity in holding a press conference in Washington, D.C. Here are excerpts from the press release.

Washington, D.C. - On Tuesday, September 15, at 2:00 pm, leaders of the Jewish community of Cuba will speak at a press conference on the "Situation of the Jewish Community in Cuba Today." The press conference will be held at the Stewart Mott House, 122 Maryland Ave., NE, Washington, D.C.

Speakers at the press conference will include **Dr. Jose Miller Friedman, M.D., President of the *Patronato Hebreo*** and **Mr. Eddie Levy, Founder of Jewish Solidarity.**

"Cuban Jews are no longer forgotten," said Mr. Levy," we are morally bound to establish bridges of love with our brothers and sisters on the island."

Dr. Rosa Behar, M.D., a gastroenterologist, and President of Cuba Hadassah will join Dr. Miller in a series of national visits sponsored by Jewish Solidarity, a humanitarian and religious organization that provides support to the Jewish Community of Cuba.

While in Washington the group will meet with the press, legislators and leaders of Jewish organizations. Their visit will conclude with a conference on the work of Jewish Solidarity and their development of medical projects of benefit to both nations.

Quotes from Leaders in Cuba and in the U.S.

"I hope to tender alternatives to the U.S. government intended to reevaluate policies that affect all Cubans; making a first step the lifting of the embargo on food and medicine."

Xiomara Almaguer-Levy, Executive director of Jewish Solidarity

"The embargo of medicines and food has a serious impact on the health of the Cuban people, particularly on children."

Dr. Rosa Behar, President of Hadassah Cuba

"We also think that to have an embargo on food, medicine and medical equipment against any country is unethical and immoral."

Eddie Levy, Founder and Chairman, Jewish Solidarity

During the last five years, the Cuban Jewish Community has had a spiritual awakening. However, the needs of our community cannot be solved just with humanitarian donations. The U.S. must begin a process to eliminate restriction on commerce, above all those that affect nutrition and health."

Dr. Jose Miller, President Coordinating Cuban Hebrew Congregations

Present with Dr. José Miller Friedman at a celebration for the restauration of the Hatikvah Synagogue in Santiago de Cuba

Highlights of Program

O'Neill Congress Building in Washington, D.C., September 16, 1998 with

Program coordinator: Delvis Fernández Levy, Sponsors: Cuban American Alliance Education Fund, Inc.; Washington Office on Latin America; Jewish Solidarity, Philadelphia Chapter; ABC Charters, Miami, Florida; B'nai B'rith, Pittsburgh, Western Pennsylvania; Center for International Policy; Mr. And Mrs. Norman Elias; John Fisher; Mr. and Mrs. Hyman Kirsner; Jack Lieberman, Nita Manitzas; Hon. Jim McGovern.

Opening Remarks by Ruben Honik, Esq, JS Solidarity Philadelphia Chapter
- **Jewish Community of Cuba**, Dr. José Miller
- **"Tittle Pending,"** Michael E. Ranneberger, Coordinator for the Office of Cuban Affairs, U.S. Department of State
- **Presentation of Jewish Solidarity Projects:** Religious, Humanitarian, Cultural by Eddie B. Levy and Xiomara Almaguer-Levy, JS Founders; Rabbi Elliot Holin, Kol-Ami Congregation; Jay Hyman, President of the Society for the Advancement of Latin American Art; Dr. Rosa Behar, Cuba Hadassah President; Dr. David Borenstein, New York JS Representative; Dr. Richard Hirsh, President of Mammography International, Akron Ohio
- **Projections and Perspectives to Work with U.S. Jewish Communities** by Stanley Cohen, President of B'nai Brith International
- **Relations between Cuban Institutions and Religious Communities**
- **Questions and Answers**

CUBA MÍA – A PERSONAL JOURNEY

At Marquette University in Milwaukee, Wisconsin, part of International Education Week. Also, at Cal Poly University in San Luis Obispo

Cuban-born, president of the Cuban-American Alliance Education Fund, Dr. Delvis Fernández Levy, confers recent Cuban-American history and developments through his Jewish family history prior to the revolution, a re-encounter with family and culture after a 22 year absence, and current projects with Cuba's association of the disabled despite the U.S. embargo.

Alumni Memorial Union
RM 407
1442 W. Wisconsin Ave.

Part of International Education Week offered by Marquette International Studies

Free and open to the public.

Also:
Showing of film, *Next Year in Havana*, A Cuban-US documentary depicting the reawakening of the Jewish community.

Dr. Delvis covers Cuban history and development through his Jewish family history, prior to the revolution to the current time. He is the president and founder of the Cuba American Alliance Education Fund, Inc., a national not-for-profit organization dedicated to educating policy makers on issues that directly impact the lives of Cubans and Americans. The alliance works for family reunification and promotes engagements of mutual benefit between the people of Cuba and of the United States.

EVENT IS FREE AND OPEN TO THE PUBLIC
Sponsored by the Jewish Community Center of San Luis Obispo, the Ethnic Studies Department, the History Department, and the Political Science Department

More information: Ethnic Studies Department at 805.756.1707

CAL POLY

From Zion to Reality

As an epilogue to this chapter, I offer thoughts about my human roots along with touches of Jewish religion and culture.

According to the view that Jewishness is passed along from the maternal side of the family, my siblings and most members of my Grand *Familia* do not classify as Jews. My mother during her late years of life saw herself as a Hebrew but in my family, she never offered religious teachings or exposed us to Jewish rituals. She had stories about her grandfather Salomón as a highly religious person who went around praying with a version of a Jewish rosary. Also, she was encouraged by her father to marry a Jewish doctor from France before she met my father and eloped with him against the wishes of her family.

My Grandfather Salvador Levy was the main father figure in my life. He did not teach me about religion but instead served as a role model for honest work and family building. The only occasion for a religious ritual occurred when he took me to a private meeting with friends to what may be seen as a version of a Jewish Bar Mitzvah. At the home of his sister-in-law, my *Tía* Raquel in the town of Caibarién, I sat at a table with my Turkish Hebrew family for a Passover Seder and reading of the Haggadah. The first synagogue I ever visited was in Salt Lake City, thanks to an invitation by a Jewish administrator at Westminster College in Salt Lake City in the late 1950s.

Since childhood I was inspired by religion. Catholic prayers, communions, confessions, and Catholic mass attendance were part of my daily routine before my teenage years. Religion became a major part of life as a young man when I was taken to the newly founded Presbyterian Church in Santa Clara by my Grandmother Felicia Rodríguez Marzall, the wife of my Grandfather Salvador. This involvement served as a main tool for exposure to Biblical teachings and seeing religion beyond mass rituals, giving lessons for advocacy in search for justice and a peaceful world for all of humanity.

As a dream fantasy I saw the Land of Zion as a place for my future life – not in Israel but in Utah! Once in the United States I became aware of a wide diversity of people and ethnic cultures, unknown to me in Cuba through school teachings and Hollywood movies stereotypes of what it meant to be a U.S. American. But after a revealing trip through Dixieland and years living in the far West, I became aware of complexities and diversities of populations, civilizations, and cultures ignored by schools and "educated" elites. At Westminster College I had close friends not only from the U.S. with strong Mexican, Asian, and Native American roots, but also from Greece, Hungary, Perú, Jordan, Japan, and China.

My "Brother" Walid Zeidan, 2nd from right at Westminster College with the Israeli Ambassador

One of my dearest friends, Walid (Frank) Zeidan was my roommate, a recent arrival from the Middle East, during my second year in Utah. By that time, I was well acclimated to American labor practices, so I took the responsibility of directing and "educating" Walid about proper work ethics, like always arriving on time for his job assignments. I saw him as a brother and in hindsight, more than any other person, he provided me with education about the ongoing unrest in Jordan, Palestine, Syria, and Lebanon. An unforgettable debate took place with the Israeli ambassador around 1959. Walid let me know of family and friends who had been expelled from their homeland of Palestine by colonizer settlers from Europe. Sometimes I took a different position but Walid's honesty and moving stories made me question the fantasy of my quest for that promised Land of Zion.

More than fifty years later with my involvement in organizing Jewish Solidarity to bring assistance and support to the remaining Jewish community throughout Cuba, I learned about the suffering endured by survivors of the Nazi holocaust in Europe. Prior to that experience I had visited places in Spain and Germany where Jews were assassinated and forced into labor camps. I also became aware through my mother of traumas endured by my grandfather due to his escape from Turkey, the death of his mother (my great grandmother), and the loss of a sister who escaped to Bulgaria.

On a sobering side of my adventures, I witnessed behavior that I found shocking during the difficult days of the so called "Special Period" in Cuba after the fall of the Soviet Union. Being a representative of Jewish Solidarity, a person called me into his bedroom to show me his healing penis after getting a circumcision to claim Jewish identity. Another person asked me for a copy of an ancestry book that I had researched and written in which mention was made about my maternal grandfather family. The ancestry book was seen as a source to establish Israeli citizenship and gain entrance into Israel or the U.S. Some family and acquaintances went as far as displaying hyphenated or new surnames recognized as Jewish.

These were shocking experiences along with my passionate work to expand education and justice for disenfranchised populations in the U.S. Awareness of discrimination, along with my work with the Chicano Movement, during calls for racial justice were a repeat of history with pseudo-Jews, offering help to Israel for colonizing and extending the injustice of apartheid over Palestinian Lands. The following opinion piece summarizes the ongoing trauma in my dreamland of Zion.

Beautiful dream of Israel has become a nightmare

By *Gabor Maté, M.D., Author and Speaker.* Published in The Toronto Star, Tue., July 22, 2014

As a Jewish youngster growing up in Budapest, an infant survivor of the Nazi genocide, I was for years haunted by a question resounding in my brain with such force that sometimes my head would spin: "How was it possible? How could the world have let such horrors happen?"

It was a naïve question, that of a child. I know better now: such is reality. Whether in Vietnam or Rwanda or Syria, humanity stands by either complicitly or unconsciously or helplessly, as it always does. In Gaza today we find ways of justifying the bombing of hospitals, the annihilation of families at dinner, the killing of pre-adolescents playing soccer on a beach.

In Israel-Palestine the powerful party has succeeded in painting itself as the victim, while the ones being killed and maimed become the perpetrators. "They don't care about life," Israeli Prime Minister Benjamin Netanyahu says, abetted by the Obamas and Harpers of this world, "we do." Netanyahu, you who with surgical precision slaughter innocents, the young and the old, you who have cruelly blockaded Gaza for years, starving it of necessities, you who deprive Palestinians of more and more of their land, their water, their crops, their trees — you care about life?

There is no understanding Gaza out of context — Hamas rockets or unjustifiable terrorist attacks on civilians — and that context is the longest ongoing ethnic cleansing operation in the recent and present centuries, the ongoing attempt to destroy Palestinian nationhood.

The Palestinians use tunnels? So did my heroes, the poorly armed fighters of the Warsaw Ghetto. Unlike Israel, Palestinians lack Apache helicopters, guided drones, jet fighters with bombs, laser-guided artillery. Out of impotent defiance, they fire inept rockets, causing terror for innocent Israelis but rarely physical harm. With such a gross imbalance of power, there is no equivalence of culpability.

Israel wants peace? Perhaps, but as the veteran Israeli journalist Gideon Levy has pointed out, it does not want a just peace. Occupation and creeping annexation, an inhumane blockade, the destruction of olive groves, the arbitrary imprisonment of thousands, torture, daily humiliation of civilians, house demolitions: these are not policies compatible with any desire for a just peace. In Tel Aviv Gideon Levy now moves around with a bodyguard, the price of speaking the truth.

I have visited Gaza and the West Bank. I saw multi-generational Palestinian families weeping in hospitals around the bedsides of their wounded, at the graves of their dead. These are not people who do not care about life. They are like us — Canadians, Jews, like anyone: they celebrate life, family, work, education, food, peace, joy. And they are capable of hatred, they can harbour vengeance in the hearts, just like we can.

One could debate details, historical and current, back and forth. Since my days as a young Zionist and, later, as a member of Jews for a Just Peace, I have often done so. I used to believe that if people knew the facts, they would open to the truth. That, too, was naïve. This issue is far too charged with emotion. As the spiritual teacher Eckhart Tolle has pointed out, the accumulated mutual pain in the Middle East is so acute, "a significant part of the population finds itself forced to act it out in an endless cycle of perpetration and retribution."

"People's leaders have been misleaders, so they that are led have been confused," in the words of the prophet Jeremiah. The voices of justice and sanity are not heeded. Netanyahu has his reasons. Harper and Obama have theirs.

And what shall we do, we ordinary people? I pray we can listen to our hearts. My heart tells me that "never again" is not a tribal slogan, that the murder of my grandparents in Auschwitz does not justify the ongoing dispossession of Palestinians, that justice, truth, peace are not tribal prerogatives. That Israel's "right to defend itself," unarguable in principle, does not validate mass killing.

A few days ago, I met with one of my dearest friends, a comrade from Zionist days and now professor emeritus at an Israeli university. We spoke of everything but the daily savagery depicted on our TV screens. We both feared the rancor that would arise.

But, I want to say to my friend, can we not be sad together at what that beautiful old dream of Jewish redemption has come to? Can we not grieve the death of innocents? I am sad these days. Can we not at least mourn together?

Gabor Maté was born in Budapest, Hungary January 6, 1944. He is a Jewish survivor of the Holocaust. His maternal grandparents were killed in Auschwitz when he was five months old. His aunt disappeared during the war, and his father endured forced labor at the hands of the Nazis. He emigrated to Canada with his family in 1956. He has a background in family practice and a special interest in childhood development and trauma, and in their potential lifelong impacts on physical and mental health, including on autoimmune disease, cancer, attention deficit hyperactivity disorder (ADHD), addictions, and a wide range of other conditions.

39

FAMILY LEGACY OF JOSÉ MARTÍ
A Cuban Hero akin to a religious Prophet and Apostle

José Martí is the most revered figure in Cuban history. For many he is simply an icon on a wall or a statue on a pedestal devoid of human existence, but in Cuba he is referred to as *El Apóstol* – the Apostle – and with other titles that exalt him to a prophet of larger-than-life dimensions. School children memorize quotes akin to biblical verses, his poems are routinely recited at patriotic events, and his writings are used in debates by friends and foes alike across the political spectrum. Martí's thoughts encapsulate the *raison d'être* of the Cuban Nation.

Statue of José Martí

On Central Park in New York City by American sculptor Anna Hyatt Huntington. The Cuban Hero is shown as he was killed in battle on May 19, 1895, with a picture of his beloved child María Mantilla – daughter of Carmen Miyares. on his chest pocket, as a shield against Spanish bullets.

By fashioning mortals into paragons of history we pay little attention to their human legacy, disregard lessons inherent in their mere existence, and relegate their partners and collaborators to the pantheon of forgotten heroes. Martí left very valuable messages about teaching and raising a family, messages that continue to nurture the life of his descendants.

In doing research for a book about the family legacy of José Martí, I traveled to various places in Cuba, from Havana to Dos Rios in Eastern Cuba. There were many places in the U.S. where José Martí left his life imprints and further places for doing research: New York State, Southern California, Tampa and Key West in Florida, and even further west in the state of Hawaii. In Cuba I met with scholars from the *Centro de Estudios Martianos* to clarify the meaning of words appearing in 19th century documents as well as share pictures, documents, and text outlines, accompanied by the granddaughters of María Mantilla – Victoria and Marti Romero. I was fortunate to share time and meals listening to family anecdotes and marveling at the historical mementos and pictures that decorate their homes. Moreover, I graciously received copies of pictures and documents in their possession that presented me with a living history -- a little known human legacy of José Martí. I was also guided along with Victoria and Marti Margaret on a long journey through historical sites in Cuba of great relevance in the life of José Martí. In New York, I visited Central Park and other sites where Martí felt inspired to write with his adored child María by his side; and in Hawaii, I held conversations, interviews, and filming of Eduardo's recollection of stories about the life of his mother. In Southern California, Marti Margaret Romero and I gave formal presentations for the Pacific Ancient and Modern Language Association (PAMLA) at Scripps College in Pomona. Writing a book about José Martí was judged as a labor of love about a remarkable family and a human legacy that continues to nurture the life of future generations and descendants of José Martí.

There is Love among the Cuban People

Article by Delvis Fernández Levy based on conversations with Marti Margaret and Victoria Romero and an interview by Norges Martínez Montero of *Juventud Rebelde*, Feb 4, 2003.

The two granddaughters of María Mantilla through a small picture in their bedroom learned about José Martí's existence. In their first visit to Cuba, Victoria and Marti Romero discovered the enormous transcendency of this man – united through a close relationship with their grandmother. They participated in the recently concluded International Conference on World Balance, dedicated to the life and work of José Martí on his 150th Birth Anniversary.

"Where there is a will, there is a way," as the saying goes. And the saying became a reality with the recent visit to Cuba of Victoria and Marti Romero, two granddaughters of María Mantilla.

"When we requested a travel permit for the first time in the United States, it was denied," explains Victoria, the elder sister, in an interview with *Juventud Rebelde*. "It was very difficult to be able to come to Cuba. We had to reach out to the directors of the Cuban American Alliance, an organization that, among other activities, promotes events in Cuba and develops engagements between schools in both countries."

This organization established contacts with the executives of the Cuban Association for the Physically Disabled (known by its Spanish acronym, ACLIFIM), a group in charge of the procedures that made possible the entrance into the country of the Romero sisters.

"As soon as we return home, we will present our displeasure to the proper authorities. The fact that my grandmother was closely linked to José Martí's life, was apparently not a convincing reason to permit us to visit this beautiful country," stated Marti Margaret.

MARTI & VICTORIA ROMERO
(two granddaughters of Maria Mantilla)

traveling in CUBA - HAVANA & SANTIAGO
during the 151st Anniversary of JOSÉ MARTÍ - Jan. 2004

on a Humanitarian Mission for ACLIFIM
(The Association of the Disabled in Cuba)

with Delvis & Norine Fernandez of CAAEF
(Cuban American Alliance Education Fund, Inc.)

Photos by Norine Fernandez   Jan./Feb.2004

Cuban American Alliance
Education Fund, Inc.
CAAEF

Delvis Fernández Levy, PhD
President

Why did you decide to visit Cuba?

"If you allow me, I'll speak for both of us," says Marti with a wide smile. "It was a very personal decision for each of us. We were very curious to know who José Martí really was. After these days in Cuba as visitors, we are sure of two things: Cuba is not what it is said to be in the US, and José Martí, a man who loved my grandmother very much, is one the most appreciated human beings on this Island and in all of Latin America."

"We knew very little about him, although in our bedroom as children there was his picture with a medal on his chest. We had assumed that he was a very special man. We never asked grandmother who he was, but we had great respect for that image."

"That he was a patriot who wrote many political essays, who organized a war in Cuba against Spain and who was one of the best poets that Cuba has given to the

World. These things we found out now as participants in the recently concluded International Conference for World Balance."

"In this event dedicated completely to him, we realized the greatness that surrounds the figure of José Martí. We are still in awe with the brilliant discussions heard about his life. Honestly, we hadn't the slightest idea about the impact this man still has on the world scene at large."

"As an eighth-grade student in California," tells Victoria, "One of my teachers commented on the relationship of José Martí with our family. That was strange for me," adds Marti Margaret, "since in schools in the U.S. one does not hear anything about him. That particular teacher knew who we were and knew a great deal about Martí."

"From that moment on," continues Victoria, "I gave myself the task of collecting information about Martí's life. This very same teacher recommended that I read some of Martí's writings in his possession. Later, when I saw his name in an encyclopedia, my interests in learning more in depth about him were awaken even more."

You tell us that you were surprised with the friendliness of Cubans?

"The visit has surpassed our imagination," comments Marti, speaking for the two of them. "We were surprised by the way people treat each other in the streets, by the beauty of the city -- mainly by its architecture. The friendliness of Cubans toward visitors is one of the things that pleased us the most. Everywhere we went we were received as distinguished guests, in José Martí's birth house as well as in his Memorial."

"On the 27th of January, the eve of his birthday, we participated in the March of the Torches – it was surprising and marvelous. If in California we were to concentrate tens of thousands of young people carrying torches, surely there would be trouble and much property damage. But how different everything is here. That night people were walking and interacting as if they had known each other for a long time, talking in such a friendly way – I never would have imagined. During this event we realized that for Cubans, José Martí is more than a symbol, he is a paradigm."

How do you remember María Mantilla?

"My grandmother loved us very much. She was very loving with us. We had an aunt, also named María, who liked to scold us for everything, but almost always grandmother would come out to protect us, to fix things. 'If they want to wear their hair loose, let them,' she would say."

"I remember we would spend hours on end playing hide and seek or she would sit and put on very large glasses to play cards with us. She loved us so much, that each time we would decide to play hide and seek, not only she'd convince the rest of the family to let us play, but she herself would become our main ally and join in playing despite her old age," says Victoria.

"Often, she'd also share with the family a certain type of sweet wine before meals. I particularly liked it a lot – confesses Marti. Older relatives tell us that when grandmother was young, she used to sing a lot, she had received formal training as a singer. They say she had a beautiful voice for interpreting mainly romantic music."

"She loved TV soaps," explains Marti, who also adds that she remembers her grandmother as a talented person, attractive and with a pleasant personality. "Every evening before meal, she'd play some beautiful melodies on the piano. Unfortunately, no specific title comes to mind, what I do remember is that it was classical music."

And your grandmother never spoke about her special relation with Martí?

"Although it may seem strange, and it is something I've never been able to understand, my grandmother did not speak much about José Martí, nor recommended anything to read about him. However, we constantly heard our aunts and uncles mention that name."

When María Mantilla died in California in 1963, Victoria was 11 years old. But the memories of the last days with her grandmother remained etched in her mind.

"Each time I saw her with oxygen and unable to move in bed, I knew she suffered a lot. I would become horrified just from entering the room. My father, Eduardo, had to talk a lot with us to help us get rid of the fear my sister and I had of that room after grandmother's passing," she says.

Marti also treasures the sad images of those times. "Although I was only nine years old, I remember that most of my family, that had always been very united, was near the bed watching over her state of health. Her death was something I will never be able to forget."

Do you plan to visit Cuba again?

"As soon as the opportunity comes, I will be back," says Victoria. "I have a 17-year-old son whom I would love to bring to Cuba someday, so that he may appreciate what friendly and respectful people you are. If I could be here three or four months, the better, because we have much to learn."

Returning to Cuba is a matter of honor for Marti. "I leave here with beautiful memories of this Island that I would like to share with all my friends and acquaintances in the US. It needs to be known that Cubans love each other."

Reunion with Victoria and Marti Romero with Representatives of ACLIFIM

A Dream Comes to Reality
By Norine Fernández working with the Cuban American Alliance

We at the Cuban American Alliance (CAA) were contacted in the fall of 2003 that two women, granddaughters of Maria Mantilla, wanted to go to Cuba for the 150th celebration and conference of José Martí at the end of January in 2003. They had been denied permission from the US government and had learned of possible travel through our organization with its humanitarian license. At that time CAA was able to extend our license to those willing to assist with our humanitarian project. By their willingness to fulfill the requirements, we could arrange their trip from Los Angeles to Havana. In addition to physically carrying our humanitarian aid, they visited the office of a national Cuban association dealing with people affected by physical mobility, known as ACLIFIM – *Asociación Cubana de Limitados Físico-Motores*. Several clinics, schools, medical offices, and senior center facilities were visited to deliver donations and learn about their work with people affected by physical mobility limitations. We also made time for the celebrations taking place in honor of their revered family member, José Martí, on his 150th Anniversary.

I remember well the morning break on the first day of the conference, when several Martí experts sought out the two women, knowing their connection to María Mantilla. They greeted them with great excitement and enthusiasm, with one Mexican scholar dropping to his knee to kiss Victoria's hand while Marti looked on in utter disbelief. Their lack of knowledge for the prestige and admiration of Marti was quickly dispelled, and they soaked in their amazement of this man, whose name had been a household work as they were raised, yet they had no idea of his importance and the revered respect for him in the Spanish speaking world.

The entire trip, day by day with each experience was a great awakening for Victoria and Marti Romero. They marveled in the honor paid to them as they walked the path their grandmother, Maria Mantilla, had taken fifty years earlier. I remember their absolute surprise and pleasure in discovering a bust of Martí placed at the entrance of every country school as we drove through the province of Pinar del Río.

The warm attention they received when we stopped unexpectedly at one school was overwhelming. The young students rushed in from recess when the teacher announced who the visitors were. Each child proudly stood and recited a poem or verse of Marti for memory, then gleefully lined up for a group picture with the grand daughters of their beloved Maria Mantilla.

Playitas de Cajobabo

Place where José Martí landed with five companions on a stormy night on April 11, 1895, to liberate Cuba.

Vicki and Marti

At *Playitas de Cajobabo* render homage to José Martí, Máximo Gómez and all the Cuban patriots.

A Happy Time in Our First School Visit
Viñales, Pinar del Río, 29 January, 2003

The only moment of disbelief came when the two women showed the children a picture taken in their youth with their beautiful, but aged grandmother. Children in Cuba fondly remember the portrait of a young María Mantilla with José Martí sitting on a chair next to her. He was killed in battle about five years after that picture had been taken, when María was 15 years old, so the children at school were not aware of a María Mantilla as an adult; they could not believe that she had grown into a grandmother.

A year later, we again accompanied Victoria and Marti to Cuba. Although the birthday of Martí is always noted and celebrated, the 151st in late January of 2004 did not have a great world conference as had occurred on our previous trip. We were able to travel across the island giving them a much broader view to learn of the country José Martí had so loved and worked and fought for.

We flew from Havana to the eastern city of Santiago de Cuba, and visiting that area gave them an incredible new lesson and appreciation of the man. While there, we struggled along the rocky path to the remote beach, *Playitas de Cajobabo*, where Martí had landed on a black, stormy night in a small rowboat after leaving Haiti. He had been in New York City and various other locations planning the War of Independence for Cuba from Spain for over fifteen years. He had lived in the boarding house with Carmen Miyares much of that time watching over the rearing of her three children and his beloved María. The solemn importance of that treacherous beach with the appropriately stark grandeur of the moment placed there in his honor was moving to us all. We then continued to travel along the path where his body had been taken to the burial site in Santiago de Cuba. The great poet and patriot had been killed in battle just 39 days after landing in Playitas with a photo of María in his breast pocket. Every small town along the road had an impressive monument to this hero, and as Victoria and Marti Margarita honored him with floral wreaths, and spoke with the towns people and children, their knowledge of the love and reverence the Cuban people have for this great man, became cemented.

Carmen Miyares – A Patriot in Silence

In assisting Eduardo Romero, the last remaining child of María Mantilla, to write an English version of Nydia Sarabia's book, *La Patriota del Silencio*, I wanted to bring to light the life and historic contributions of Carmen Miyares. Carmen was a nearly forgotten figure of Cuban history, an indomitable, selfless woman who collaborated with José Martí in his quest for the total independence of Cuba and the Americas. *Carmita* was a trusted confidante, a refuge of love, support and inspiration to the most admired hero in Cuban history.

Mr. Romero has a wealth of family anecdotes and intimate knowledge about the lives of his mother, María Mantilla and grandmother, Carmen Miyares. He overcame many obstacles since it has been over sixty years since he had occasion to speak Spanish on a regular basis; a problem which was compounded by his failing eyesight. Therefore, in doing this work he relied on a Spanish-English dictionary and a large magnifying glass under a bright lamp attempting to make as literal a translation as possible, word by word, sentence by sentence. As I received his manuscripts, I made corrections with regards to syntax, meanings, and historical data. The new text was carefully examined against the original Spanish text in an attempt to keep the integrity of *Doña* Sarabia's Spanish writings. Furthermore, we edited the text and documents a third time, trying to end up with a book as if it had been originally written in modern English and following the advice of José Martí to his beloved child María Mantilla back in 1895, "... the text should not end up, like so many translations, in the same strange language in which it was originally written. The book should keep your interest, taking you back to the life and times of the characters ..."

A problem encountered lay in the fact that the original Spanish text had references to historical characters, events, and geographical places unknown to readers outside of Cuba and certainly most English readers. Therefore, while keeping the integrity of the Spanish text, we felt compelled to make the book accessible to a larger English readership and thus enhance it with the following:

•A table of contents, acknowledgments, and a dedication to Carmen Miyares with words from José Martí.

•Pictures and illustrations directly tied to the original Spanish text.

•A map of Martí's historical journey in Cuba right before his death.

•Expansion of footnotes from fifty-one to seventy-four in order to explain historical events and historical sites and characters.

•A bibliography augmented from nineteen to forty-two books and writings which were consulted in researching translations and English editions of books by and about José Martí.

•A glossary of over one-hundred Spanish terms, acronyms, titles, etc. used in the book.

•A detailed index of over 400 terms for easy reference to characters and events mentioned in the original Spanish text.

In doing research for the book, I traveled to Cuba, New York, Southern California, and Hawaii. In Havana I met twice with Nydia Sarabia in her home to clarify meaning of words appearing in 19th century documents as well as share pictures, documents, and text outline. In New York, I visited places where Carmen Miyares lived and other sites frequented by Martí while he lived and worked in Manhattan. In Hawaii I held several conversations with Victoria Romero and her father, Eduardo Romero. I felt fortunate to share time and meals listening to family anecdotes and marveling at the historical mementos and pictures that decorate their homes. Moreover, I graciously received copies of pictures and documents in their possession that presented me with a living history, a little-known human legacy of José Martí and Carmen Miyares. In Southern California, Marti Margaret Romero and I jointly gave formal presentations for the Pacific Ancient and Modern Language Association (PAMLA) at Scripps College in Pomona.

This book represents a labor of love about a truly remarkable woman, Carmen Miyares, whose family and descendants continue to cherish in her human legacy and that of Cuba's National Hero, José Martí.

Carmen Miyares

Between a Star
And a Palm Tree,
Heavens forever to grace,
Carmen Miyares we praise,
Angel of Our History!

MESSAGE TO THE CUBAN PEOPLE
FROM EDUARDO SALVADOR ROMERO

Hello. Today is November 2003. My name is Eduardo Salvador Romero y Mantilla. I am the only surviving child of María Mantilla, José Martí's beloved girl. My siblings, María Teresa, César, Jr., and Graciela, have all passed away.

When I was a small boy, the Romero family lived in our home in Bradley Beach, New Jersey, during the summers. We spent winters at the home of my much-loved grandmother, Carmen Miyares, at 135 W. 74th Street, New York City. Ever since I can remember, the name of José Martí was spoken in our home with reverence and love. My mother taught me about Martí when I was but a child. She told me about his place in Cuban history; how he became Cuba's National Hero, what a wonderful poet and writer he was, and that I should be proud of her relationship to Martí.

The Romero Family, c..1939
Left to right: Graciela (Grace), César Romero, Sr.,
César Romero, Jr., María Mantilla (de Romero), Eduardo (Ed),
and María Teresa.

She told me that Martí was her godfather, which, of course, is a documented fact. When I became older, I realized that her love and affection for Martí was more like what one would expect of a daughter for her father.

In our home were always many reminders of José Martí, some of which I now have in my home. One of my favorites was always the **picture of Martí as a boy**, a copy of which now hangs here in my apartment.

Next to it is an **original painting of palm trees**, which my mother willed to me, knowing I had always admired it. She told me it was a painting, which Martí had, possibly in his office in New York. He loved palm trees, she told me.

**Eduardo Salvador Romero in his home standing between a
Picture of young José Martí and a painting of Cuban Royal Palms**

On this other wall are displayed a few other items: **the poster of Martí** which was produced in quantity in Cuba on the 100th anniversary of his birth in 1953, a caricature of Martí by Sergio Rivera which depicts the Cuban flag as his hair, the shape of the island of Cuba as his eye, an inkwell as his mustache, and a feather quill pen as the side of his face.

Below them are a **framed Cuban peso and coin**, both showing Martí's likeness. Above those is a **bronzed likeness of Martí's head**. All of these are constant reminders of Martí's place in our family.

Sixty-nine years ago, in 1935, my mother wrote a letter to my elder brother, César. It was typical of what a mother would write to her son, except for one overriding factor. In this letter, she revealed to César what was believed by many, although not previously documented. She told him that José Martí was in fact her true father. That revelation in her handwriting makes the letter a historical document of some importance. Upon the death of my brother in 1994, I came into possession of the letter in which she writes to César of Martí, apparently in response to some questions he had regarding Martí's place in our family. She tells him, and I now quote in its original English,

"Do not mention that he was my uncle: I want you to know, dear, that he was <u>my father</u>, and I want you to be proud of it. Someday, we will talk a lot about this, but of course this is only for you to know, and not for the publicity. It is my secret, and Father knows it."

I believe that this letter deserves to be placed and exhibited in Cuba. I wish that I could personally come to Cuba to present the letter to La Fragua Martiana to be preserved for posterity, but my age (84), my almost total blindness and my desire to stay close to my wife who, having had a third stroke one year and a half ago, is now in a nearby nursing home where I visit her three times a day, preclude me from making what to me would be a long and arduous journey.

Therefore, I am making the presentation of the letter by means of this videotape. The letter and the video will be carried to Havana and turned over to *La Fragua Martiana* by my two daughters, Victoria Romero Zane and Marti Romero. With these items goes my salutations and very best wishes to Cubans everywhere. *Viva Cuba!*

**Expanding Knowledge About José Martí and His Family
By Marti Margaret (Romero) Timmerman**

End of a Wonderful Journey

José Julián Martí Pérez as "a biological father of María Mantilla" has been a subject burning in the hearts and minds of the Romero family and scholars attentive to the teachings and exemplary life of a Cuban Hero akin to a religious Prophet and Apostle – whose life went beyond being a human being. Heroic figures are featured as paragons of history and their human legacy is often ignored or simply hidden from research.

José Martí
Forever in our Hearts and Souls

Marti Margaret Romero has done a DNA test that confirms a high probability of biological relation to the immortal patriot José Martí.

Is María Mantilla the Biological Daughter of Martí?

There is plenty of evidence beyond the DNA tests results, without going into pure scientific research. From family anecdotes and examining the unique physical characteristics of José Martí – facial shape, broad forehead, lips, eyes, etc – plus reading María's multiple assertions that Martí was her father, it is time to move on and accept him as her biological father. *En Paz Descansen María y Martí*. Truth will be forever in our future generations.

Remmy Zane (Romero) with his Grandpa Eduardo Salvador Romero (8 Jan 1929 – 20 May 2016). Remmy was born in Hawaii and is the only son of Victoria María Romero. They may be the last biological descendant of the admired Cuban Patriot José *Martí* c. 2010

César Julio Romero, Jr. was the oldest son of María Mantilla. He became a famous Hollywood actor. His mother let him know back in 1939 that José Martí was his biological grandfather. This photo was taken in Cuba showing profiles of Martí and César c. 1950

ADDENDUM to our Two MEMORABLE JOURNEYS

A third amazing trip with Victoria and Marti took place in January of 2018, as we had been invited to the dedication of a Martí statue in Havana.

The March of the Torches in Havana, on January 27, 2018, commemorating the birth of José Martí, the great patriot of Cuba. Marching in the celebration were my son Dan, , myself, and my grandson, Daniel, along with Marti and Victoria Romero, the Great Granddaughters of Martí, who had taken their first trip to Cuba with Norine and I for the worldwide conference honoring Martí's 150th birthday back in January 2003.

The traditional visit to the bar in the Hotel Nacional to see Uncle Butch's pictures (César Romero, Jr) with the many celebs who had visit that grand hotel.

Unveiling in Havana of exact replica of the Martí statue in Central Park in New York City.

Un Adiós Riding in Grand Cuban Style through the streets of Havana with Marti & Victoria along with mi *Nieto Danielito* and mi *Hijo Daniel Rubén*

Meeting of Descendants of Revered Patriots
José Martí and Antonio Maceo

Left to right: Antonio Rizo Acuña, Lidece Duany, Santiago Grajales, Marti Margarita Romero, Nancy Rizo, and Victoria María Romero

El Titán de Bronce
Antonio Maceo y Grajales
Cuban Patriot who gave his life for
Cuban Independence
Born: June 14, 1845, Majaguabo, San
Luis, Oriente Province, Cuba
Died: December 7, 1896,
San Pedro, Punta Brava, Havana, Cuba

PART V

LIFE OF RETIREMENT
And
FINAL QUEST

40

MENDING MY HEART

Shortly after my sister Sarita's death, I began to feel heart pain and discomfort together with symptoms of irregular heartbeats. This was a scary time, thinking that perhaps the end of life was near. On one occasion I went on a hike with my son David and after walking for a short distance near my home, I had to stop and lean against a fence unable to move, thinking that I was having a cardiac stroke, I suddenly became very faint. He said I lost all of my color and was sweating, yet clammy cold which scared him to death. That was the first episode of a lifelong battle I have had ever since. I continued to have these episodes, sometimes mild and sometimes worse so went to my doctor to learn the cause. When I explained my radical exercise activity, he pretty much concluded that I was just "overdoing" it.

After that incident, I blamed my irregular heartbeat on overactivity as a result of daily exercise, running, or cycling. Finally, after too many calls from feeling that the heart was near a stopping point, I had to be taken to emergency at a hospital in my hometown of Hayward, California. At the emergency entrance of a Kaiser Hospital with my wife Norine next to me, I completely blacked out and had to be driven in an ambulance to another hospital in the town of Richmond for an exam and eventually had to ride on the ambulance to a hospital in San Francisco, where I was kept in ICU – Intensive Care Unit.

Once out of the hospital, after being diagnosed with Atrial Fibrillation, mental depression was worse than the illness itself, filling me with a conviction that death was around the corner. These events took me to hospitals in various towns from Washington, D.C., to the Oakland/San Francisco Bay Area, to a hospital near Stanford University, and finally to hospitals in my new town of San Luis Obispo, California. In summary, I have been subjected to more than fifteen cardioversions – like electric shocks to stabilize the heart beats; two ablation surgeries for monitoring the heart; and two surgeries with implants of a heart generator pacemakers.

Even though I often said to family and friends that the "end was near," I kept working and travelled across the U.S. including Hawaii, Mexico, Ecuador, Cuba, Canada, and various European countries to participate in meetings and bring awareness and testimonials about the sufferings and difficulties endured by people as a result of lack of normal relation between Cuba and the U.S. I went as far as moving for a while to Fort Lee and Teaneck, New Jersey and for years residing in Washington, D.C. This was a labor of love to bring hope for family reconciliation and promote peace and understanding between my two countries: (1) The beloved homeland of Cuba, and (2) The United States of America -- My *Nueva* and dear *Familia* homeland.

After several alarming incidents, that I tried to hide, in open meetings and at airports, I came to the full realization that it was time to work virtually from home and slow down on my activities. Although many years went by, depression took hold of me, resulting from lack of peer support and unawareness about the health problems around me. Luck and blessings came my way when my daughter-in-law Mari-Tere, an expert on hospice care, exposed me to the work of a national organization named Mended Hearts. There through empathy and people-to-people meetings, I found an organization offering hope to heart disease patients, their families, and caregivers.

I was so fascinated and filled with hope that my life took a turn with a renewal of daily activities in piano playing, writing, giving presentations, visiting patients in hospitals and care centers; without abandoning my passionate quest for normal relations between my two countries.

During my late thirties after receiving my PhD in math in 1974, I became captivated with extreme exercise, starting with running and biking, even double century rides training with an energetic guy who was half my age. I fell in love with hiking and the beauty of nature, so did a lot of backpacking often into the wilderness by myself. Later I learned the sport my son loved, which was windsurfing and became insane following the wind for the thrill of skimming across the water. This was all very new for me as I had never been physically active, even as a youngster.

A few years later, when Norine still ran her Diet Center, I was sitting at our dining room table working with my Stanford colleague on the computer program/manual we wrote for her to use in contacting client's doctors. I started feeling faint and excused myself to go downstairs and rest a bit. When Norine came down, she became very alarmed and insisted on taking me to emergency in Castro Valley - fearing it was a heart attack for sure. They poked and prodded all afternoon while I insisted it was just a bad stomachache from the green apple I had eaten for lunch. They found no evidence of an actual attack, but could not explain my symptoms, so insisted I stay overnight for observation. Norine had arrived the next morning to take me home just as the nurses in the ICU were changing shifts. A new one took one look at my vitals at her station and came dashing into my room with the crash cart and two other nurses, alarmed that my heartbeat was much too slow – in the upper thirties. I was sitting up finishing my breakfast, waiting to change into my street clothing, and assured her that my heart rate was always in the low fifties, due to my exercise activity, and I was feeling fine. Finally, I was given the OK to leave with a cardiologist's referral in hand. At the car I insisted that we drive to the nearby Lake Chabot, a favorite running spot, for a lovely long walk around the lake, since I had been so inactive for two days.

FINALLY, A DIAGNOSIS

Dr. Feldman in Castro Valley was a Godsent, as he finally diagnosed that I had Atrial Fibrillation (A-Fib) and for the first time gave me medication to thin my blood to help in the prevention of blood clots, which are the greatest danger with A-Fib. His wise advice was also included – slowing down on exercise and cutting back to no more than one cup of coffee a day, as I was easily having four or five cups of strong Peete's coffee per day. I controlled the coffee habit, and the exercise somewhat, but replaced it with the stress surrounding my father's death on May 31, 1988, in Miami. He was a very hard worker but had terrible eating habits and enjoyed drinking far too much, which eventually caught up with him. He suffered from gout and had very poor circulation for many years, actually causing the need to amputate one leg several years earlier when our sons were still doing their summer visits to Florida during grade school.

One of Norine's favorite stories about losing her inhibitions to speak her poor Spanish was the tale told on her second solo visit to Cuba as the entire family sat around the dinner table trying to make her feel welcome and asked, she talk about their grandfather. She explained that once while the boys were visiting their *abuelos* in Miami when he wore a prosthetic leg, they were crossing the street with him when a car, making a right turn, clipped him on that leg. In his usual playful manner, he winked at the boys as fell to the ground with the loosened prosthetic and shoe sticking out beyond his pant leg in an awkward position. The driver had jumped out and was shocked and stunned at his moaning and groaning in great pain as he said his leg had been cut off, which of course, was all a joke. Norine's family audience laughed so hard some had tears in their eyes, which surprised her as she didn't think her story was that funny. Well, her brother-in-law, Arturo, sitting next to her, finally explained that she had consistently confused the Spanish word for father-in-law with that for brother-in-law – making the story sound like it was all about him. They had all laughed and had such great fun with her mistake, that she realized there was no need to worry or be embarrassed about speaking "her Spanish." Since that incident she feels fluent speaking her *Español* with help from nearby listeners.

My father's death was a very trying time for months before and after. My *Mami* Sara was helpless without him, and once he was hospitalized after a long and difficult illness, she could not even figure out how to get to see him. Her dear friend Emilita, who lived in the duplex they had made with a shared wall, could drive, but also had a job so was not always available. With a full teaching load but no classes on Fridays, I made three-day weekend red-eye flights back and forth during those last months. Thankfully, I was at his bedside when he passed, which I have always appreciated as an important part of dying, in fact near the end, as I quietly talked to him, I had asked him to squeeze my hand if he heard me, which he did.

Norine and the boys flew to Miami for the funeral, which was so very sad but a warm bonding time for us all. The boys had pretty much been out of our house for some time, and we loved sharing those moments with them. David managed to say a few heartfelt words about all the happy times with his *abuelo,* and Norine managed to tell the story of her first meeting with him when he and my mother were "discussing" (she thought fighting) the need for having diced potatoes in his *picadillo.* Dan too lightened the somber mood with his imitation of various accents heard in Miami, which was a talent we had never heard before. He also jokingly, just like his *abuelo*, offered to meet some of the shady characters that owed my father money. He said he would go to the garage, right in the heart of the ghetto, with a big black briefcase (indicating the presence of a firearm) and the "little black book" which contained the history of money owed to the generous and fun-loving man.

Norine and I were left to clean up all the messes left behind. Their house required a cleaning quite like Norine had never seen but did give us the opportunity to find many bundles of cash hidden in the most unusual places. We tried to sell the home but soon learned that not a single bank would take on a loan to a buyer since so many things had been done to the house without proper permits. Eventually, acting as a banker myself, I arranged with a woman from Haiti who did pay monthly for the first year, but then disappeared into the woodwork, and years later when the house was auctioned off by the city, we spent more money on a lawyer trying to save it, than the total she had paid. The garage which consisted of a filling station, a body and paint shop and even a small luncheonette café was eventually all lost as well. After months of hassling with my dad's work partner, an agreement had been reached and he did pay, on and off (eventually more off than on) for a couple of years, but then passed away. With Miami so distant, in every way, and still with the bitter, sour taste of money lost fighting for their house, we just had to let the garage go and never looked back.

MAMI SARA ADDS A BIT OF CUBA TO OUR HOME

We brought my *Mami* to Hayward and she would live in our home for the next twenty-six years, but always lamenting that move and our taking her from "*Mi gente en Miami* – my people in Miami." Norine's mother too, passed away just eight months after my father. They had been living only forty minutes from us in Walnut Creek for several years, and with her father now alone, and her sister in far off Phoenix, Norine became a full-time care giver. We were still adjusting to having my mother with us and Norine had completely let go of her kitchen, since *Mami* was such a good Cuban cook. She only prepared five or six meals every Saturday morning for her dad's freezer which we delivered on our weekend visits. Calling him every other day also became part of the ritual, but if she missed a call, he would scold her like a child, saying he did not know "if she were dead or alive." Eventually he found a dear neighborhood friend, named Elena, and became her "caring companion. Elena was a blind woman his age, both in their eighties, she kept him busy driving her around, reading all her mail, and paying all her bills. Norine appreciated this distraction for her father. My mother had also found a wonderful, friend, a Cuban woman, named Obdulia who lived in Hayward with her son Orlando, so, we had a bit more time to ourselves, since *Mami* would often stay overnight on Saturdays, and we would take off for a one-night break. Gualala up the California coast was a favorite destination, and I would often jump out with my bike, as Norine would drive ahead stopping in a pretty spot to take arty pictures until I caught up.

This more relaxed approach to exercise along with enjoyment, seemed to suit my heart's condition kindly. I did participate in more intense activities with biking and windsurfing, but at a more sensible pace while training. We were busy too, with life's joys, a big Thanksgiving dinner for Norine's entire family just days before our youngest son's wedding, wildly wonderful Halloween parties at the house of our niece Renee, with many "Hollywood" type friends that went way beyond with incredible costumes. Also, exciting travel with the trip to Ecuador with my mother and oldest son David, as well as Cuba. The second "Markleeville Death" bike ride as well as the "Davis Double Century," and many happy family gatherings, with our first grandchild's birth, which brought joy along with the satisfaction that my teaching brought to me. However, the news in spring of 1994 of my dear sister's passing was a jolt that turned my life around and filled me with new anxiety and unrest. Many things happened that following year, which set me on a new direction, and the feeling of pain and discomfort together with symptoms of irregular heartbeats were worrisome and very scary, thinking that perhaps the end of life was near for me too.

After many warning calls, which I often dealt with in pure denial, a serious situation one evening sent us rushing to Kaiser emergency in my hometown of Hayward, California. It was decided that I needed a procedure only done at a hospital in San Francisco and with no beds available overnight there in Hayward, they prepared me for an ambulance ride to the Kaiser Hospital in Richmond, which would be closer for the morning transfer to San Francisco. While waiting on a gurney in the hallway, Norine became alarmed, later telling me I had turned absolutely greyish white, with sweat pouring down my face, but icy cold to the touch. She said that a nurse and an attendant from the ambulance were at the foot of my bed arguing about whose responsibility it was to have given me morphine for a more comfortable ride to Richmond, and she got the distinct impression they had both done it. That was never admitted and instead it was suggested that I was allergic to the drug. To this day morphine appears in capital letters on my medical information not to be used, yet never having been tested again. There has always been a question in her mind that perhaps, it was a double dose, causing the problem that night. I was unaware of the 20-minute ambulance ride (normally 30+ minutes) with Norine obeying their instructions to "drive behind and keep up, which caused her to feel she needed a bed as badly as I did once we arrived at Richmond's Kaiser. To our astonishment the following day after hours of test in the San Francisco hospital, we were told they would not perform the prescribed procedure, the cause had been A-Fib and not the blockage they had suspected. We drove home in silent disbelief, we mulled over the events of the past two days, as depression was settling in.

LIFE WITH CARDIOVERSIONS

Within weeks I experienced another similar episode, but this time went straight to Dr. Feldman, who performed my first Cardioversion the next day. That is a medical procedure that restores a normal heart rhythm in people with certain types of abnormal heartbeats (arrhythmias). A Cardioversion is usually done by sending electric shocks to your heart through electrodes placed on your chest which will put your rhythm back in "sync." We imagined the many shows we had seen on TV where a person's heart has stopped, and the paddles must be used to shock them back to life, so the imagined picture was very scary. It only takes a few minutes, but they put you completely under, so there is always a certain amount of risk and a day spent with pre-op and recovery time. For the remained of the 1990s and until our move to San Luis Obispo in 2004, I was given five cardioversions and was taking the absolute maximum of the medication that was to help control my condition. Along with the constant dark cloud of fear that hung over my head, the mental depression was worse than the illness itself, filling me with a belief that death was around the corner. These health episodes continued to flare up throughout the years I was working with the Cuban American Alliance and took me to hospitals in various towns from Washington, D.C., to the Oakland/San Francisco Bay Area depending on my location when it occurred. Even though I often said to family and friends that the "end was near," I kept working and traveling – crisscrossing the entire country as well as foreign lands. I often tried to hide my situation by saying it was just fatigue or lack of nourishment, and would break away from a speech I was giving, a conference I was attending, or a difficult panel I was participating in.

One incident that stands out more than others, was after a difficult meeting I had led in Miami with emotional tensions flaring up on both side of every discussion. On the flight back to Washington, D.C. the next morning, I realized I was definitely in A-Fib again. I madly drove from one hospital to another seeking care only to meet with constant refusal, as they did not accept my California Kaiser Insurance. I actually beckoned to a policeman while stopped at a red light, begging for help to lead to yet another hospital. By the time I was finally seen by a doctor he pointed out the many black and blue spots covering my arms and chest, which he said was the incorrect amount of Warfarin medication which was causing internal bleeding right under my skin. Warfarin is a very powerful blood thinner used to prevent blood clots, which must be monitored closely to ensure taking the correct amount. At home in California, I kept a careful eye on the schedule of blood draws but must admit that with the insane schedule in Washington or while traveling, I was often sloppy about the monitoring of the drug. The doctor adjusted my dosage, then preceded with further testing and mentioned I must stay the night for observation. The timing could not have been worse, as I was expecting Norine and my granddaughter's visit for a week and they were to arrive at the airport within hours. So, the first chance I had alone, I quickly put on my clothes and quietly left the hospital. When I arrived at the airport almost near midnight, I saw the two lone figures standing outside of the baggage claim area, patiently waiting as I was very late. When we put the suitcases into the trunk of the car, Norine noticed a white streak and slight dent across the top of the car, and my hospital name band still on my arm. I ignored her questions as I smothered Dariella with kisses. Once she was tucked into bed and asleep, I told Norine of my day's adventures, thus explaining the arm band, and then confessed that as I approached the airport, I was so flustered and late, I had driven right through the white gate at the parking lot entrance before it was fully raised. The next day, thanks to the joy of the week ahead, I seemed fine and had carved out enough free time to show Dariella all the sights of Washington. She flew down the long empty hallway from California Representative Lois Capp's office doing her gymnastic flips and cartwheels, she steered the DuckMobile down the Potomac River, and our only

Granddaughter Dariella and I meeting "The Real Ben and Jerry" in Washington, D.C.

challenge was always finding veggie meals to feed my sweetie, who was a vegetarian 'from birth'. The Ben and Jerry Ice Cream Store saved the day many times and we even got to meet them in person on one visit.

I continued this intense labor of love until 2004 at which time we sold our beloved Hayward Hills home and moved to paradise in See Canyon a few miles outside of San Luis Obispo. We had visited our son Dave often as he studied there at Cal Poly University, and stayed after graduation, falling in love with the town and surrounding areas of The Central California Coast. Of course, nothing ever seemed to come easily and after spending a Christmas vacation in his home while they were off on their yearly jaunt to Baja California (their family tradition, which always saddened us without our grandchildren around for that major holiday, which was Norine's favorite) we had found the perfect house on Cuesta Drive. Norine, my financial negotiator, had made an accepted offer and we hoped to move in right after our January trip to Cuba, which was very urgent as we were now strapped with two mortgage payments. Our mid-January Cuba trip was incredibly exciting but trying at the same time, as we traveled to Santiago de Cuba with Victoria and Marti Romero on their second trip to travel the path that José Martí had followed at the beginning of the Cuban War of Independence from Spain in 1895. It was a historic event in all of our lives, reported in a book I wrote about our trips, under the title "A Human Legacy of José Martí."

When we returned to our Hayward home, we were rudely faced with an unbelievably awful mess that would prevent selling our house at that time. We found a major sewer project had been undertaken in the hills of our neighborhood and since our home was at the bottom of one major hill, a construction problem had completely flooded the lower level of our split-level home. The ugly markings eighteen inches up the walls and strong stench of sewer water greeted us upon our return. Instead of immediately putting the house on up for sale, we dealt with construction repairs, and fighting for insurance refunds over the next seven months. To make matters even worse, Norine had started sorting out financial papers for April tax time and sorted them in piles all over the floor in our back guest room. They were destroyed completely, so she had the daunting task of contacting many banks and fiscal providers to reconstruct our financial picture for the previous year. She was left alone to deal with all these problems, as I was off to Washington to deal with scheduled meetings and then an important Emigration Conference in Cuba in May. The house was ready in July, staged beautifully by an excellent real estate woman and sold above asking price in just a matter of days.

A NEW LIFE IN PARADISE BUT A-FIB PERSISTS

We had rented the new home on Cuesta that we had purchased in San Luis Obispo during that difficult time waiting to sell our Hayward home. The rental worked well, as it was just a block from the north entrance to Cal Poly University, and we realized we would always have renters from the student pool. On a whim we thought something just outside of town might be a bit cheaper and make Cuesta a permanent rental with a safe income flow. We spent just a few days madly looking at many wonderful places, only to fall totally in love with our future home in See Canyon. It was far from being less expensive, but Norine's mind was in overdrive as she schemed about turning an adorable cottage into a vacation rental and converting a two-story garage/storage area into two studio rentals. These structures were hidden from the main house by a magnificent stand of redwoods, so "we wouldn't even know the renters were there." It was a wonderful property with an eighty-tree orchard with five different kinds of apples (considered a small orchard in See Canyon, well known for its fine apples), many magnificent old oaks on each side of the home on the slopping hills creating our own little canyon, a creek with a rustic bridge to cross as you entered, and not a neighboring home in sight. Dan was with us on that first sighting and was as captivated as we were, so there was not a moment of hesitation, and we made an offer on the spot. We were already fantasizing of a family compound with David's architectural skills designing their homes and Dan's construction skills building them on a perfect spot of their choice with several acres to choose from, but best of all, the four grandchildren would be running around under foot.

Our Hayward home for over 36 years, when it was staged for sale in August 2004.

First impression of our See Canyon Property

The move was a major project having lived in our Bridle Drive home for over thirty-six years, having storage spaces filled to capacity with all those years of 'stuff.' It took a call for a smaller second moving van late in the afternoon, when the movers realized there was no way to fit it all in. Norine's organizational abilities had carefully marked every box with the contents and into which room in the new house the guys should unload them, but by the time they drove to San Luis Obispo after loading in Hayward, it was well after midnight. David was patiently waiting to direct them, but soon realized the movers were not about to unload in different rooms in different structures that were spread across the property in the middle of the night after a very long, very hard day. So, he gave into their idea of unloading on the spot and leaving everything in the lower garage where they had parked, even including the baby grand piano. When we arrived the next morning, we were faced with the daunting task of moving most boxes and the furniture about 500 feet up the hill to the main house. Both sons had pickup trucks and so with help and running on adrenaline and pure excitement we managed to move it all.

I had been filled with energy and even though I pretended to be superman, I knew the first order of business in this new town was to find a good cardiologist and present my medical history, so everything would be in order before leaving for my CAAEF activities, which had been put on hold during those fading summer months. I got several referrals and saw Dr. Robert Doria in the cardiology wing of French Hospital in our new town. He had a great reputation and his association with French Hospital was a plus with their outstanding heart wing. I knew my idyllic new home would be the perfect place to slow down, unwind, and take care of myself, although I never could figure out nor understood what brought on my bouts with A-Fib. Often, I had been in very tense, stressful situations – presenting at an important meeting or arguing with an opponent on a TV interview – or been in an insane physically demanding situation running from one gate in the airport to another or moving from a meeting in Los Angeles, to another the next day in Wisconsin, and then on to one all the way to Cuba -- yet, sometimes I would be at rest, as I was on New Year's eve sitting on my couch watching the ball drop in Time Square after two weeks of Christmas fun with my grandchildren. A-Fib seemed to hit me whenever, wherever, and however it wanted. The fact that the then President, George Bush's administration would no longer grant the two licenses necessary for our work: an export license from the U.S. Treasury Department along with a travel license detailing the places to visit and the donation items we were taking. Perhaps I had also seen the writing on the wall, when earlier that spring we had sold our condo in Washington D.C., which was used as the CAAEF office.

As we adjusted to life in See Canyon, I continued working with Luis Rumbaut in D.C. on publishing our La Alborada newsletter online, switching to a digital format to keep up with the times. Beyond that, I kept aware of everything going on in the news, but my daily activity did an about face. I was very busy fighting the gophers as they popped up until they grew weary and would just move to pop up somewhere else. Using our ride on mower was an enjoyable task to keep our huge lawn of 'country grass' as Norine call it, in check. It was mostly weeds, but if mowed regularly and watered now and then, it looked beautiful from our house with the yellow dandelions ever present, which I also obsessively tried to control. Walking down the hill to our mailbox often turned into a two-hour task, with so many little jobs to attract me along the way and having to walk back up that very slight hill was always a warning sign that A-Fib had arrived or was lurking around the corner. So, I soon learned to recognize that if I was so out of breath and had

to sit, by the time I got to our water tanks for the well, the halfway point on that very slight hill from the mailbox, I was in big trouble. Within days I would be at French Hospital for yet another Cardioversion and or adjustment to my medication.

The condition is best known for an irregular fast heartbeat or sometimes a fluttering that may be undetected and can possibly dislodge clots that would travel to the brain or lungs causing strokes. The two upper chambers of the heart beat out of sync with the lower chamber and additional symptoms are shortness of breath, feeling fatigued, weakness and dizziness. Once I cut my hand doing some pruning, which was gushing blood like crazy, and my regular doctor told me by phone to rush to emergency, as excessive bleeding could present real problems. Within three years of our move to San Luis Obispo, I had already had six more Cardioversions, making that a total of eleven, which seemed to shock and surprise everyone, even in the medical field. Unfortunately, several medications Dr. Doria tried always seemed to eventually lose their efficiency, and the hospital procedures too seemed less and less helpful, being effective for shorter periods each time.

FORGET CARDIOVERSION - LET'S TRY ABLATIONS

In early May of 2007, my seventh cardioversion was performed, but unlike the others, the irregular heartbeat symptoms reappeared within two days, this time accompanied by extreme fatigue, restless nights with severe headaches, urinary problems, and racing heart beats. A few days later my regular doctor sent me to the emergency room after I described symptoms which included a heart rate going from 44 to over 120 within minutes, without any physical exertion. Dr. Doria confirmed that this last cardioversion had failed and decided to make arrangements to have a procedure known as "cardiac ablation." This is a procedure where they scar tissue in your heart to block abnormal electrical signals. At that time there was no one in the central California coast area that preformed this delicate surgery. So, Dr. Doria called a colleague, Dr. Roger Winkle in Palo Alto, requesting that the ablation be done - just as soon as possible - as the symptoms were severe. The following day, the phone call came with instructions for a consultation, less than a week later on May 14 followed by doing the ablation the next day at Sequoia Hospital in the Bay Area – a familiar area where I had family and friends with whom I could stay if necessary, and being well acquainted with negotiating the freeways, since we had lived there for forty plus years.

The next day a call came informing me that Blue Cross HMO insurance would reject payment claims, so I immediately I contacted Dr. Doria to request an out of area authorization, which he sent off as a "rushed request" for authorization from Blue Cross. For more than a week we called daily, sometimes twice a day, as my condition was worsening, and I was feeling high levels of anxiety due to the unbearable waiting. Almost two weeks later I ask my doctor to intervene directly with the insurance, which he did to learn there were NO doctors in the Bay Area contracted with Blue Cross for the ablation and suggested that I travel to Los Angeles to see a recommended doctor. It had now been 14 days since Dr. Doria, my personal cardiologist urgently referred me to have the ablation done by Dr. Roger Winkle, a doctor with an excellent success record in performing this procedure and with whom Dr. Doria has worked closely on several occasions for the necessary follow-up. On the other hand, Dr. Doria had no knowledge of the recommend doctor in Los Angeles or of his record. and having to drive the Los Angeles freeways to find our way around was out of the question. I was completely frustrated, fearing for my life, and feeling exhausted from this whole ordeal. When told that there was only ONE doctor in the entire state of California that Blue Cross HMO recognized for this procedure, I felt absolutely helpless, as if someone was holding a gun over my head.

Almost another week later, I learned that Blue Cross had authorized the initial consultation only, and the Los Angeles doctor would have to request authorization for the procedure once he had seen me.

Again, Dr. Doria intervened and was making calls as well as Norine's daily attempts, only to be told that the only recourse was to file a complaint – after – we had received notification in writing, and that a decision "could be rendered within forty days." I was beyond desperate and ready to pack my bag to fly to Cuba, so I might have immediate free care, oh but NO! My government would not allow that.

For almost a month, absolutely nothing had been accomplished nor resolved. I related my problems to a friend who was able to put me in contact with John Metz, chairman of the board of the California Consumer Health Care Council, and executive director of Just Health, an advocacy group for justice and fair treatment of people in dire need of medical attention. Mr. Metz, immediately went to work on my behalf and within a couple of days was able to hold a phone conference with myself, as well as with an executive and a staff physician of Blue Cross. He was able to convince the executive and the physician (an OBGYN) of the need for proper care of my worsening health condition. A letter was received two days later from Blue Cross giving approval for Dr. Winkle in Palo Alto to proceed with a consultation of assessment followed immediately by the ablation procedure.

We drove to the Bay Area a few days later and after the initial consultation, Dr. Winkle informed me that my situation had worsened, and now I needed two different ablations, one for atrial fibrillation and another for atrial flutter. Instead of a one-hour procedure it would be a four-or five-hour event. We went to the Sequoia Hospital on August 13th for a general examination in preparation for the ablations scheduled for the next day, August 14, 2007 – three months and four days after being told of my "urgent condition." The procedure took much longer than I had anticipated, over six hours under anesthetics plus another six of laying perfectly flat and motionless on the recovery bed. Norine was alone at the motel and in the waiting room for those many hours and passed the time with a waiting room computer writing long, long letters to almost everybody we knew. Back home the recovery was slow but steady, when suddenly we rushed to emergency at French Hospital a week later with symptoms that included a fever, coughing, sore throat, bleeding from the incision, and terrible headaches -- worse than anything previously experienced, only to learn I had developed a bad case of sinusitis resulting from the lengthy procedure. The sore throat and coughing from the anesthetics continued for over two months, but my heartbeat was steady, thus giving me hope that a healthy and active life might still be possible, after all I was only sixty-seven and living in paradise. I was most grateful for Dr. Doria's persistence on my behalf, for the attentive care during and after by Dr. Winkle, but most of all grateful to John Metz for his dedication and selfless devotion for justice and fair treatment for those in need of medical attention. I learned that you must be your own strong and obnoxious advocate for your own good health, and finding a professional, who knows how and will fight for you can be even better, and certainly the next best thing.

NEW HOPE, BUT HOW LONG WOULD IT LAST?

The next four years were my best in a long time I continued with a morning routine of posting information on our digital web site of La Alborada and kept in close contact of Cuban happenings with Luis Rumbaut our dedicated colleague in D.C. who as part of the former CAAEF Board, continued contributing, working tirelessly on publishing the digital formatted newsletter for close to ten years, approximately 2005 to 2015. My appreciation for his and all board members dedication could never be fully expressed in words.

We had unforgettable family fun time together with every grandchild's birthday celebrated in grand style. Once for Isabella's eighth we brought a huge truck load of snow, so everyone could fly down a hill on a sled or snowboard. The "Toro" our work vehicle, was used to haul the birthday guests up the rough terrain

of our back yard canyon, as well as the vehicle where all four grandchildren learned how to drive, even if a block of wood was needed to reach the peddles. Sleeping overnight in the cottage, away from any adults, was a standard birthday treat, and any excuse to invite folks for a dinner or an overnight visit, brought many old friends. Norine always made sure the three rentals were free when folks wanted to visit.

◀ The Vacation Cottage

Upper& Lower Studios ▶

Welcoming for Family and Friends

Friends from our wedding: Karen Thursby, Sister-in-law
Clarice, Norine, Delvis, Walid Zeidan, and Jim Smith

Two memorable events must be mentioned when the entire family gathered to celebrate. Our 50th wedding anniversary in August of 2010 brought several from the original wedding party – Norine's sister Clarice from Arizona, my best man Jim Smith came from Maine, my dear old friend from Jordan, Frank (now in the Bay area) and Norine's friend from childhood and bridesmaid, Karen, came from Colorado with over a hundred others traveling from far and wide. Dave BBQ chicken and hamburgers while Dan cooked up Cuban favorites for everyone. The only tragedy was the wild wind and forgetting to buy white rice, so our Cuban American friend saved the day with Thai rice from his restaurant. which went surprising well with the black beans.

The following year the family gathered again for a Thanksgiving festival. Our immediate family, who all lived in San Luis Obispo and all of Clarice's family from Arizona and Los Angeles, gathered with twenty-two sitting at our turkey table in the living room. The following Friday, we dined on Mexican food made by MariTere, our daughter-in-law-and Fernando, the husband of Norine's niece, Dana. Then Saturday's dinner was Italian with Ben, the husband of niece Lisa, giving cooking lessons to the Mexican and Cuban chefs.

Just before that happy gathering, I had an episode of A-Fib in September, of 2011, which was corrected by my twelfth Cardioversion that only lasted two days. So, Dr. Doria had sent me off yet again to the Bay Area for a second Ablation with Dr. Winkle in October. This time fortunately without any problems from the insurance, but somewhat to everyone's surprise that the first was effective for just over four years. Norine was concerned that the planned Thanksgiving celebration would be too great a strain, but I was feeling fine and had certainly learned not to put things "on hold," but just plunge ahead and enjoy each day to its fullest, as long as you can. When I went into A-Fib again, just eleven months after that second Ablation, the feeling seemed slightly different and I do not recall, why or what was distinct that time, but Dr. Doria was pleased to tell me that I now had become a candidate for a pacemaker, which was placed at French Hospital in September of 2012.

This has been a long story, so now I want to give you the short of it which bring us to the present. The next years since receiving a Pacemaker, I have had several episodes of serious A-Fib, some of which were self-corrected by the Pacemaker, with four that required Cardioversions making a total of sixteen. The Pacemaker was replaced in August of 2019 by a newer and more sophisticated version referred to as a Generator. A small gismo with an eerie blue circular light gadget by my bed serving as a monitor that records every heartbeat while I am nearby in bed.

Perhaps the greatest challenge of those years has been the fight with depression, as this constant cloud hovers over my head. The bouts of despair would come and go, as the depth of that depression, but I often felt it was worse as a result of a lack of empathy from the medical community, from a lack of peer support, and an unawareness of the health problems around me. Luck and blessings came my way when my daughter-in-law, Mari-Tere, working now with a hospice and having become an expert on empathetic care, exposed me to the work of a national organization called Mended Hearts. There through compassion, understanding and people-to-people support in monthly meetings, I found an association offering hope to heart disease patients, their families, and their caregivers. I was so fascinated and filled with hope that my life took a turn with a renewal of daily activities in piano playing, writing, giving presentations, visiting patients in hospitals and care centers; without abandoning my passionate quest for normal relations between my two countries.

In summary:

- Mended Hearts is the largest peer-to-peer heart patient support network in the world.
- Mended Hearts has been offering hope and support for 65 years, visiting more than 200,000 patients every year.
- Mended Hearts provides education, support, and hope to all types of heart patients and their families.
- Mended Hearts and Mended Little Hearts has 300 chapters in North America, serving 460+ hospitals.

STATISTICS

- Cardiovascular disease, listed as the underlying cause of death, accounts for nearly 836,546 deaths in the US. Which is about 1 of every 3 deaths.
- Cardiovascular diseases claim more lives each year than all forms of cancer and Chronic Lower Respiratory Disease combined.
- About 92.1 million American adults are living with some form of cardiovascular disease or the after-effects of stroke.
- Cardiovascular disease is the leading global cause of death, accounting for more than 17.9 million deaths per year in 2015, a number that is expected to grow to more than 23.6 million by 2030.

Leaders of Mended Hearts Chapter 415 in San Luis Obispo, California: Richard Hatcher, Gary Lauterback, Delvis Fernández, Eileen Murta, Michael Mariscal, Jennifer Bailey, and Ron Manriquez

With my wife Norine at event in Paso Robles, spreading information about Mended Hearts in English and Spanish

I joined the San Luis Obispo chapter of Mended Hearts and soon became even more involved as a member of their board. With this group support, and friendship, I was filled with a new hope, and my life took a turn with a renewal of enjoyment and excitement for my daily activities in piano playing, writing, making artistic works with wood, giving presentations, visiting heart patients in hospitals and care centers, speaking with their families, and of course, without abandoning my passionate quest for normal relations between my two countries.

My labor of love, now as always is to bring hope for family reconciliation and promote peace and understanding between my two countries: my beloved homeland of Cuba, and the United States of America -- my *nueva* and dear *familia* homeland.

41

ART THROUGH NATURE

Living in our "paradise" of See Canyon lent itself to relaxation, which was exactly what I needed if I were to improve my heart problems. It did not come naturally, so I had to make an effort to learn how to relax. Walking down the winding canyon road with very little traffic was very pleasurable, and even walking down to our mailbox, which was a good hike to the main road could provide relaxation and exercise at the same time. I loved the beauty of nature that surrounded us and always brought home a small reminder of my walk, usually a flower or interesting piece of wood or stone that I found along the way. The flowers would grace our dining table for a day or two, but constantly needed replacement so always called me on another walk. Whereas the wooden pieces and sticks I gathered were growing to quite a pile in my workshop. I often "saw" something other than just a piece of wood, so I would embrace that imagination, by carefully working with the wood to bring out that image. It reminded me of the joy I had when young and working in a woodshop class that was a favorite and has resulted in many pleasant hours spent on my "wooden sculptures."

A few years later Norine needed the replacement of a very troublesome hip, and I realized that the many sticks I had collected would make wonderful walking canes. She always teased me about my obsession of picking up sticks as a childhood act, as our boys had always picked up any little sticks when we were camping or wandering down a path. Finally, I had a real purpose for my pile of sticks, and I started a new search for interesting things I could use for the handle - small pinecones were plentiful from our many pine trees and became a favorite.

Delvis turns over his beloved 1994 turquoise Nissan with far less than 100 thousand miles to Cian as he heads out into the world of university study in the Fall of 2017.

Now in our smaller home in San Luis Obispo, a few years later, we realized we had little use for two cars, since I could easily walk to many stores. Our grandson, Cian, needed a car as he prepared to leave for the University of Southern Oregon. I had bought that little two-door gem of a car during my first year in New Jersey when Frank helped me to set up an office for the Cuban American Alliance. We took it to Washington, D.C. on rare occasions, but it sat idle most days. I always marveled how it would start right up after being parked for weeks at a time in the cold and snow after coming back from California. It had exceptionally low milage for a car that old and only the rear bumper was badly dented and scratched from squeezing into many a tight parking spots in Washington, D.C. streets. Cian seemed to appreciate our little, old Nissan, and excitedly accepted the car-key when we offered it. That freed my garage and I soon converted half of it into a workshop as an office and art studio.

When we downsized from See Canyon, we had no idea what to do with our son David's model of Havana, which was about 4' x 5' and had been stored away in his garage. It was part of a thesis project for his architecture degree, which he had done around the area of the capitol building of Havana. When he threatened to get rid of it, I got his permission for jazzing it up with a bit of color and trees ready for hanging up in my new studio. Of course, it was all tan cardboard with white indicating his new plan, as such models always are. Over my desk we also hung posters from Cuba, and it became my phantasy Cuban corner. Folding tables provided the work surface for all my "arty projects" and the space provided enjoyment, relaxation, and best of all – great anticipation of more time and pleasure there, once I finish this book.

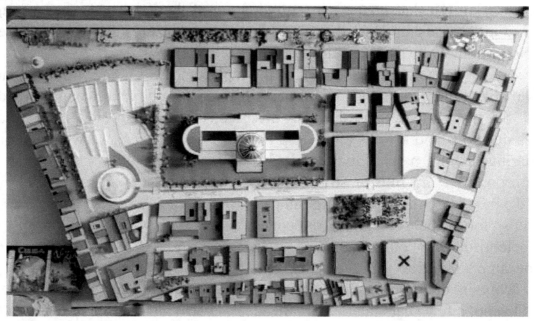

David's' model of proposal for Centro Habana, Cuba, which was part of his thesis for architecture. He allowed me to enhance it with some color, trees, and a few other ornaments.

The Cuba corner in my garage office, filled with posters, flags, book about Martí, the model, << canes in progress, and other memorabilia.

I have been making my "wood sculpture/projects" ever since I made my first fun one in See Canyon – a planter for succulents made from coconut shells - birdhouses and feeders were also a favorite. Here are a few samples of my work.

Capturing Nature on Film

Norine had always been the photographer, but as I took my daily walks, I discovered the pleasure of taking photos. She praised my artistic eye, which only encouraged my newfound hobby. Eventually I had taken enough pictures, that we decided a Christmas calendar would be a nice gift for family and friends. We have

2020 – JAN-Havana	FEB-Varadero, Cuba	MAR-Avila Beach	APR-Bob Jones Trail-SLO

done it for several years now, and always find it a wonderful way to share the beauty of the area we live in. Looking back on the Pandemic year of 2020, we remembered just sneaking in our Faces of Cuba trip with dear friend Rick Moniz the latter part of January and into February just before Covid-19 broke out all around the world and put a screeching halt to all travel. By March we were in full blown "lock down" and Avila Beach, less than 10 miles from home, became a favorite escape for getting away and watching the storm clouds roll over in March. By April the yellow mustard had taken over the walk along the Bob Jones Trail on the San Luis Obispo side, which was just a minute's walk from our home, and a safe isolated path with only the homeless to greet me. It was still a bit chilly, so I would wear my old brown hooded jacket, and looked just like one of them.

An earlier year, 2017, reflected a fun quick trip down to the quaint town of Ojai in May, where the road had washed out due to heavy rains, so (yes rain back in the day) we had to circle around to the south on a detour, almost to Los Angeles to reach our destination. Next came an overnighter along Highway 1 with a stay at romantic Ragged Point, but no further north, as once again, there had been a giant land slide covering the road to the beautiful Big Sur area. Then our big trip in July and August to Hayward for the Chicano 50th reunion at Chabot and a wonderful walk along our old path at Lake Chabot in Castro Valley, remembering the crazy walk the day I was released from ICU at Eden Hospital. Next on to visit our dear friends, Sheila and Erno Rosenthal, where I gave a piano recital at his nursing home in San Rafael. On to Muir Woods north of San Francisco with a quick lunch at a biker's stop I remembered from that treacherous bike ride with Stephen Maltz all the way up the coast to Oregon; reaching our destination that evening just in time for an incredible sunset at Gualala.

There in Gualala we spent many memorable weekends when my *mamí*, who was living with us in our Hayward home, would stay with her friend, Obdulia. The end point for this magnificent journey down memory lane was Mendocino for several days to enjoy all our old haunts. We returned through the gorgeous Anderson Valley for lunch but waited for wine tasting in the Napa Valley before heading on home.

2017–MAY in Ojai   **JUNE-Ragged Point**   **JULY-Lake Chabot in Castro Valley**

AUG - Gualala sunset   **with Mendocino vacation**   **SEPT – Napa Valley**

Just to finish off the months of the year I'll share my pictures from different years, showing: the Bob Jones Trail, but on the Avila side where we walk often and enjoy brunch at the Woodstone Deli;, the Johnson Trail where I had my first serious fall in 2021, that required 6 stitches; and my silhouette at Avila in 2017.

OCT – Bob Jones Trial, Avila   **NOV – Johnson Trail, San Luis Obispo**   **DEC – year's end sunset,**

Travel to my Homeland Has Two Sides

In addition to some of the overnight jaunts and short trips displayed in our photos for the calendars, we've had a few noteworthy trips to our homelands since moving to San Luis Obispo. I did have a couple of Cuba pictures and referred to our trip with Rick Moniz early in 2020. It was with a group of about twenty and while in Havana some chose to stay in *casas particulares,* private homes, but we stayed in the magnificent Hotel Nacional, which holds such fond memories for us. We did travel for a night in Cienfuegos and a first-time experience of staying in one of the exclusive hotels in Varadero. It was the feel of a true tourist and even though we enjoyed it immensely, we can now say 'been there, done that.' Rick's Faces-of-Cuba trips were always carefully planned, so interesting, and very entertaining, and this 2020 trip was no exception. Norine had not been to Cuba for quite a few years, so she really did enjoy it. I, on the other hand, had been with my son Dan, and grandson Daniel, just two years before in January of 2018.

The magnificent statue of José Martí on his horse that is in New York's Central Park, had been replicated exactly, and I was invited to be at its unveiling in front of the Presidential Palace in Havana. It was a meaningful ceremony early in the morning with a glorious sunrise on January 28th, - Martí's date of birth.

Delvis with grandson, Daniel after the formal dedication of the statue.

Our dear friends, Vicki and Marti, the great granddaughters of Martí were also present for the dedication, so we enjoyed several fun things with them: the March of the Torches – which we had participated in on our very first introductory trip with these two important women. On this 2018 trip it happened to fall on Daniel's 19th birthday, which was a thrilling way to celebrate kidding that the torches were his Birthday Candles. We saw many sights in Havana and rented a gorgeous "old" blue car, and with Dan at the wheel drove to a favorite eating place, *El Aljibe*.

After all the festivities in Havana, I headed east, with Dan and Daniel, to my hometown of Santa Clara. There we had the important mission of burying my mother's ashes with many of her dear relatives. We had a delicious dinner in the family home, and my sister, Puchi took us on an interesting walking tour with a few sights I had never seen. Our time was extremely limited, but I do believe Dan

enjoyed reminiscing, and Danielito was thrilled with his first visit to Cuba. On our return to Havana, we saw a few more touristy things, then moved on to a marvelous day in Pinar del Río including the caves, and of course. Las Terrazas. Unfortunately, our artist friend, Lester Campa, was away, but we enjoyed a few of his latest works with a visit to his studio.

Dan, Delvis, sister Puchi, and Daniel after presenting Sara's ashes at the family plot.

Cousin Salvador Levy with me in family home. He let Daniel take a spin on his motorcycle.

My sister, Puchi, takes Daniel and I to see a Monument to Ché Guevara, high on a hill, *La Loma del Capiro,* above Santa Clara

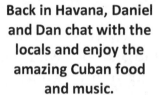

Back in Havana, Daniel and Dan chat with the locals and enjoy the amazing Cuban food and music.

The trip ends with the beauty of Pinar del Rio spread before us

42

ADVOCACY DAYS CONTINUE

JUSTICE FOR DREAMERS

During days of retirement, I felt a call to advocate for students affected by immigration policies that placed them at the risk of deportation, and separation from friends, and their familiar surroundings. So, once again I tried to sensitize political leaders about the hardships endured by some of the young men and women at California Polytechnic University, in San Luis Obispo, California, who bravely shared their testimonials.

In late 2017, I travelled to Washington, D.C. and walked the halls of the Senate and Congress, visiting as many offices as possible and met with political leaders and/or their aides. In conversations I included stories of my own life with a packet of testimonials brought from students at Cal Poly University.

On Monday, October 30, 2017. I dropped off a packet of 'TESTIMONIALS' from Cal Poly DREAMERS to each of many Congressional Offices in Washington, D.C. The reception, without exception, was very warm and positive. I also spoke at length with Max Hokit, alumnus of Cal Poly who was now an aide of Congressman Salud Carbajal. In addition, I met with representatives for The Rise Act, who were in the U.S. Congress that day, advocating for students with disabilities. It was a great learning experience for me since I was given information and a description of the work they do.

On that October day, I was close to 80 years of age and walking over 20 miles (according to my FitBit watch) in one day through Washington, D.C., was a great day of action advocating for justice, which gave me renewed hope that I could and must continue doing the work, and I hoped to inspire others to help our cause. Here are a few statistics from that period of time to help better understand the immenseness and importance of this work.

The following statistics are from the Fall Quarter of 2017, showing the number of   UNDOCUMENTED STUDENTS IN THE U.S:

800,000 DACA Recipients as of 2017

1,932,000 Immigrants in the U.S. who are eligible for DACA as of 2016

11,000,000 Total number of undocumented immigrants in the U.S. as of 2015

My visits were to inform Congress people and their aids about TPS – Temporary Protective Status – on behalf of the "Dreamers" from my hometown, hoping to gain their endorsements for TPS.

1. First, I met with leaders of the Latin America Working Group (LAWG), seeking advice for reaching out to members of Congress across the political spectrum who might sponsor legislation to bring peace, justice, and security to students in the U.S. referred to as DREAMERS.

2. I brought testimonials from 9 courageous students at California Polytechnic University who dared to openly share part of their life histories with US Government agents and members of Congress.

3. I met with assistants who gave signs of support for legislation that would bring an end to the fear of deportation that might extend into TPS legislation and approvals for immigrants from Haiti and Central America.

4. I also shared parts of my life coming to the US as a minor, not being able to embrace my sisters and visit most of my family for more than 20 years, working in farms in Idaho and as a dishwasher to pay for my education – becoming the first college graduate, reaching a PhD in Mathematics, and having the honor and distinction of being a faculty advisor to the Chicano movement from the mid 1960s in the San Francisco Bay Area.

5. Some senators and representatives were given copies of my recent book "The Chicano Movement," published through AMAZON.

6. The list of visits included the following House of Representative and Senate offices:

SENATORS:

Richard Durbin, Jeff Flake, Charles Schummer, Lisa Murkowski, John McCain, Diane Feinstein, Kamala Harris, Cory Gardner, Michael Bennet (Kate Henjum, Staff Assistant),

Catherine Cortez Masto (Joleen C. Rivera, Legislative Counsel).

REPRESENTATIVES:

Mark DeSaulnier (Evan C. Smith, Distinguish Educator Fellow, and Sarah L. Jackson, Legislative Director),

Zoe Lofgren, Ro Khana, Nancy Pelosi, DavidValadao, Jackie Speier (Michelle McGrain, Legislative Assistant), **Barbara Lee** (Klarissa Cagle Reynoso, Legislative Correspondent & Staff Assistant), **Eric Swalwell** (Andrew S. Ginsburg, Legislative Director), **Salud Carbajal** (Max Hokit, Staff Assistant and alumnus from Cal Poly).

My deep appreciation is conveyed to leaders at Cal Poly University for their valuable work in expanding access to education: **Patricia Ponce, Student Ombuds Services, José M.P. León, Lead Coordinator of the Cross-Cultural Center, and Katherine Zevallos Pastor, Dream Center Coordinator. Plus many thanks** for the work and assistance to students and faculty at CalPoly
¡Sí Se Puede! ¡Somos Mustang!

**The following are <u>excerpts</u> from Testimonials written
nine students from Cal Poly.**

NUMBER ONE
Major in Environmental Engineering

My family lived in Oaxaca, Mexico. Financial struggles for a better future led my parents to immigrate to the United States in 1999 when I was three. I was told we would be making a very important trip, a trip in which I would have to travel alone and hide my true identity. I was trained for several months to become someone else. I got a new haircut, new clothes, and new shoes. When the day arrived, I was separated from my parents and brought to the US. I stayed with my aunt and uncle for a week while my parents made the life-threatening journey across the Sonoran Desert.

Once here, my parents started working to provide for our needs. I was always informed of my immigration status in this country even as a child. Over the course of the years, I was gifted with 3 wonderful siblings that made me into the person I am today. I wanted to be the best I could for them and set the steppingstones as the eldest child. I may have been hopeless for myself when it came to obtaining a career, but I was confident in their future success.

On June 15, 2012, I was thrilled to find I was eligible for Barack Obama's executive order. I finally got a glimpse of hope but recognized the huge risk I would be taking by releasing my personal information to US Citizen and Immigration Services. I also knew it was not a road to citizenship and that it could get rescinded at any time, but I developed the mentality that something was better than nothing. When my Employment Authorization Document (EAD) arrived in the mail, I took back the identity that had been stripped away from me earlier in my childhood.

Throughout high school I participated in many organizations. I excelled academically and walked across the stage with a 4.52 GPA. I accepted a spot for Environmental Engineering at California Polytechnic State University SLO. I have gone through my own journey in an educational system not designed for me. Trump's administration has now terminated this program. I can only plan up to

January 2019 when my DACA expires. I am so close to finishing my educ education, but uncertainty lingers all Around unable to do anything frustrates me more than anything. I can't vote or have any political authority because I am a foreigner to this country.

NUMBER TWO
Major in Chemistry and Wine & Viticulture

My mom and I migrated to the United States, leaving everything behind. We left my mother's three younger brothers, her mother, her father and all the family we had ever known. With hope of finding a better life in the U.S., we packed up and moved to an entirely new country.

As I entered third grade, my life took a sudden turn. It was extremely challenging to understand the language and try to write it, but it was especially challenging to speak English. I remember going to school in the morning and feeling sick to my stomach. It was a major barrier because I felt embarrassed by not being able to fluently communicate. Moreover, I did not have the chance to play an instrument, take art, or use computers. I was instead slammed with English classes.

As an undocumented child, you have no sense of what being undocumented actually means. Most of us do not even know we are undocumented; all we know is we are different from the other kids. There were so many "doors" that were closed on me, and the only thing that I knew how to do was not letting my citizenship status create a wall in accomplishing my education. I began doing the best that I could to strive in my everyday life when I was informed of the Dream Act. The Dream Act helped me to continue (with my education.) There are many things I cannot do, but the few that I can, I will continue to do to the best of my ability.

I shook hands with Jerry Brown; and had the opportunity to sit and talk with the California State Assembly member, Bill Dodd on Senate Bill No. 4, discussing health coverage specifically for those with immigrant status. As I talked to him, I mentioned how important this was for my family. We also knocked on the door of other representatives to meet about AB 1561, to repeal the sales tax on tampons and other feminine hygiene products. In mid-August I received an email informing me that both bills had been approved. Even though I saw a major step being taken, I felt that I had more to contribute. So, I decided to take initiative, for my third consecutive year I will not only participate, but I will present along with three other

Latinas on Latinas Action Day, 2017. I have worked hard as a student to obtain the opportunity and become a political advocate."

NUMBER THREE
Rising Immigration Lawyer

"I arrived in the United States from Peru in 2003 with my father; my mother was already living in the U.S. She decided to leave her native country for better opportunities and was planning to be back in a year, but years passed, and she never returned. She left me in the care of my father when I was 4 years old, he was the one that raised me after my mother left. My father did everything that was possible for us to be with her, he applied for the U.S. green card lottery so many times, but we didn't have the luck to win, (and applied also for a VISA) but got denied 4 times due that a father (who) wanted to travel with a minor, a most important with a little girl.

I still remember and I will always do because it was hard coming to this country, even though I left my family, friends, school, my life – I can say It was worth it, I was barely 11 years old. I remember the moment I saw my mother for the first time, I used to talk to her over the phone and made video conferences, but that moment wasn't talking over the phone or seeing her over a camera – I was actually seeing her in real life, I was so happy, I couldn't believe it, I was feeling alive that I was with my mom and father now together.

We settled in Los Angeles, CA; the moment I arrived – my mother enlisted me in middle school, I started 6th grade. For my high school graduation, I was happy, excited that I made it and that I have finished high school, I remember my dad's face, he was really happy and proud to see his daughter finishing high school, now my next step was to graduate from college. I started college, the first semester I made it to the honors list since I had good grades and even though we moved to The Valley and my school was in Santa Monica, I remember it took me hours to get there, my father didn't want me to drive since I wasn't able to get a driver license so I continue taking the bus, I got to school tired but I knew that every sacrifice that I was doing, was going to be worth it.

Then 2012 came, I saw the news, the moment that President Obama policy was established named Deferred Action of Childhood Arrivals known as DACA, that open a lot of doors for me, the first thing my parents did was to call our family attorney to help me with the paperwork, then I will never forget the day that I received my paperwork that my DACA was approved, it was on my birthday, I was with my parents, I saw my father and I hugged him, I was happy, I cried of joy but also laugh because I couldn't believe it that I was able to not live in the shadows even though I knew it was temporary, I was able to obtain a work permit, I was able to obtain a social security, I was able to obtain a driver license, I was able to obtain an identification card. I was grateful to have that great opportunity, to drive without being afraid of being stopped by a police by not having a driver license.

Time passed and at the age of 24 I had a daughter but that didn't stop me, I was more eager and I had more desire to study and graduate from college, during my pregnancy I decided to continue school, then the great moment came, I graduated from college and obtained two diplomas one that I finished my college studies and the other my Political Science A.A, by that time my daughter was born.

I am currently in a 4 year university in my junior year, majoring in Political Science to obtain my B.A. and my goal is to become an immigration lawyer since that's what I love, to aware and help my community and I will do it for my daughter to give her a better future, a better education which is the most important, to give her the best I can and also for my father, to make him proud of his daughter and that his sacrifices were worthwhile. I want to continue and achieve my dreams. I want to give my father a better life, even though I don't have papers that identifies me as a U.S. citizen, I feel like one, even though I'm not able to vote, I can fight for my rights and make people aware of their rights and I would love to become one soon so I continue and teach people that they can't never stop dreaming, to never leave their goals, that everything is possible especially by being in this country, the country of great opportunities. The country that makes everything possible based on effort, discipline and perseverance. I'm planning to buy a house once I start working which I'm planning to do next year and so many things that I have on mind, this is not only my story but my father's and my daughter's story as well."

NUMBER FOUR

Future Product Designer

"I arrived in the US when I was three and a half years old. We immigrated to the US because my family and I lived in poverty. My parents wanted and sought a better life for (my) younger sister, (who was born in the U.S), and myself. A major barrier that I experienced throughout my academic career were trying to fit in and "Americanize" myself, so that I would fit in the legal group. Other barriers include asking for help and not receiving exactly what I needed.

I am experiencing something new, that neither of my parents ever experienced. I had to step out of my comfort zone and ask the questions about school. I never did because I felt like nobody would help me until a few years ago in my sophomore year of community college when I realized what I want to do in life. I will either become a Product Designer or go to space and possibly become an astronaut to be one of the first colonizers of Mars. Since both my parents never made it past the 6th grade and were forced to work to provide food for the family, I deal with a heavy pressure that I have to graduate college for them and not myself. I feel like giving up because I am no longer following my own dreams, but it's my parents' dreams (from my perspective). Some actions that I need to take are to stop fictitious support and have stubborn egos; we need to break stereotypes and not look bad from society's point of view. I feel suicidal at points in time and the only thing stopping me from taking the easy way out is that I want to look out for my nephew to make sure he has a very supportive person who will give him the best honest advice and direction in life. My parents were always scared of police especially when racism played a factor. I feel dumb for not trying hard enough in school, so I was not always the best at school. This work ethic began when I started getting bullied. This has caused me to feel hatred towards others and this has caused me to seclude myself from opening up about my problems.

My successes have been developing memorable experiences with friends and some family members as well as helping others in times of need. I have also developed skills that have helped me become a wiser, "well-rounded" person who can have intelligent conversations with other like-minded individuals. My nephew, new experiences with adventures, and my eagerness to learn about the Universe and its wonders are the only things that continue to motivate me. In the end, I know my words will not have a dramatic change on things, but I think it is important to stay aware of everything happening with social justice and understanding it."

[A Personal Note: I came to the United States in 1957 after departing from my beloved homeland and family back in 1957. I left every single family member and friend behind, and entered this strange land, with its unfamiliar culture and language. The struggles portrayed in these testimonials were similar to my own story. I identify and feel strongly empathetic with today's DREAMERS.]

NUMBER FIVE

My Journey – Industrial Engineering

"At the age of seventeen, my family was forced to bring me to the United States illegally due to killings and shooting in my hometown of Aguililla, Michoacán, Mexico. I was in the process of becoming a legal resident, but as a result of the war among cartels worsening, waiting for my paperwork to be fully processed was not an option. While in Mexico, my family hoped things would get better and that the government would do something to eliminate the cartels, but it never happened. I flew to Tijuana where my new journey began. I sometimes wish I had never come the way I did, but if I had stayed in Mexico, I would not have the opportunity to attend school and become an engineer, nor perhaps even survive.

When I was able to finally cross the border, I enrolled in an English as Second Language (ESL) program while simultaneously working 50 plus hours. I remember being so tired throughout the week and the only thing that kept me going was the excitement of learning a new language.

After graduating from the ESL program, I did not know what was left to do as I was told that undocumented students cannot go to universities. Regardless of what I was told, I began taking random classes and soon fell in love with science. I completed all the math, physics, and engineering courses but when I applied for colleges, I found out it would cost over $25,000 in tuition due to my immigration status. Fortunately, the year in which I transferred to Cal Poly I was granted a U Visa status that allowed me to receive financial aid and thus continue my career of engineering.

I always believed that being undocumented was just a way to differentiate between the person with documents and the person without. I truly never imagined what the word truly meant — not until I began facing serious personal emotions. The word undocumented meant not being able to be a free person who strives to be humble, help others and better the world. Being undocumented felt as if you are the enemy, an enemy that you know does not exist within yourself. I say that it is really hard to be undocumented and yet transfer to one of the best CSU's in California. Working a full-time job while in school delayed my graduation seven extra years. I spent a total of 11 years from the time I enrolled as ESL student to when I will be graduating from Cal Poly in engineering. I stay motivated by reminding myself where and how I got to where I am today and where I want to be in the next five years. I know that the struggle is not over. and the only thing that is ahead and waiting for me is success.

My goal after graduation is to go into Sales Engineering in the Bay Area. I also plan on giving back financially to the non-profit organizations that have supported and helped me so much."

～

NUMBER SIX
Major in Liberal Arts)

"I was born and raised in the small village of Tiradores, Michoacán in Mexico. During my first five years of life, my family moved around a lot to make ends meet. My dad, the sole provider of the family, struggled to find a job in construction. When he did find a job, often times, he wouldn't get paid which added stress to the family. Living paycheck to paycheck caused my parents to decide for all of us to move in with my aunt. By the age of six, I began elementary school in a new town called, Zinapécuaro, Michoacán. The reason for all my moving was because my family barely had enough to make ends meet, week after week.

With the constant moving, tensions increased around the house because my dad was struggling to support the family. My dad began contacting people in the U.S. to try immigrating in search of a better life. My dad was able to reach out to his friend, who lived in Santa Fe, New Mexico. (His friend) managed a construction company and was willing to help my dad immigrate to the U.S. if my dad agreed to work for him.

While my dad was working, he was able to save enough money to immigrate my brother, mom and myself to the U.S. My family and I grabbed our belongings and hopped a van that took us to a bus station, from there we took a bus to Durango, Mexico, and then another one to Nogales, Mexico. In Nogales, we had to stay the night in a motel with 20 people per room because too many border patrol vehicles had been spotted in the area. The next afternoon, we were taken to an abandoned home, where there were two trucks, an old ford pick-up and a newer ford pick-up. We were asked to choose which one we wanted to get into, and as a kid I wanted the new shiny one, but my mom chose the old pick-up truck. On both trucks there were at least 15 people. We managed to be inside the truck with the driver, with another 4 people.

After driving for a few hours, it was dark and we started hearing helicopters, and the driver got a call that immigration authorities were looking for a truck full of people. Our truck, the old beat-up F-150 was forced to get off the road and the driver turned off all lights. We drove through what seem to be corn fields but eventually made it to our destination, an old trailer home on the side of the U.S. At that home we found out the other, shiny newer truck had flipped over, and a few people had died. We drove to a safe house near the area till things cooled down.

We spent the night at the trailer home and then were split up into different groups of people based on what part of the United States we were going. Our group went to Phoenix, Arizona where we were taken to an apartment full of other immigrants. It seemed like every inch of the place was covered by an immigrant person sitting on the floor. We stayed there overnight and then the following day our smuggler transported us to Albuquerque, where we got picked up and then taken to Santa Fe, New Mexico. We met with my dad, and he was staying in (his friend's) a warehouse in the outskirts of town. Although it was an old warehouse that was full of junk, and had a rat infestation, I called it home. It was where my parents realized we had a chance at the American dream.

Being a first-generation immigrant, on top of being first generation high school student, college planning was extremely difficult for me. Having to be the first in my family to not only finish high school but be the first to even consider applying to a university meant that I had no reference in my family of someone that I can go to, to ask for help or even talk to about the stress associated with college. Having to seek out my own help and do everything on my own gave me a feeling of helplessness. At times I had people who would not want to help me or even want to talk about my imaginary dreams of going to college.

Planning for college was a barrier because when my family tried to make future plans, they would say *"Pos haber si no nos echan"* (hopefully we don't get deported). I took this phrase into consideration when applying to college because once my turn to apply came around, I realized everything could go down the drain, and all my efforts spent in academics, sports, clubs, and volunteer work would be meaningless if me or one of my family members were deported. The constant uncertainty of my future takes away from my focus of school, and it does not allow me to fully enjoy the successes I have achieved because those achievements would mean nothing if I got deported and had no use for them; all in a blink of an eye.

I have overcome these challenges by seeking resources. Being a part of the Educational Opportunity Program (EOP) on campus and utilizing the resources it offers to support low-income, first-generation college students has facilitated my transition into college. EOP has helped me access resources individualized advising and one on one tutoring. The Dream Center has showed me how to self-advocate for myself and other undocumented students. They have also given me the knowledge of different resources available to me such as financial assistance, legal assistance and just given us emotional support by creating a welcoming environment for undocumented students.

Being undocumented has deeply affected my family by creating uncertainty for all our futures. It has limited our ability to seek financial resources, such as financial aid, scholarships, and loans. I am one of the privileged few undocumented students that have received financial assistance at my school, but the amount of financial aid that I have received does not cover all tuition nor my housing expenses. Having to work over 20 hours while maintaining 16 units per quarter really puts a strain in my academics as well as my mental and physical health.

Being limited on financial resources for college not only puts a strain on myself, but also my family because they work tirelessly to provide me the few dollars they earn. Although these obstacles bring me down emotionally, I use that energy to motivate me because I can say I'm an immigrant who has earned everything with hard work despite the lack of help. My biggest success was being able to not only get into a good university like Cal Poly, but also being able to be more than just a statistic. There was a high probability that I would have dropped out of high school and ended up in jail rather than where I am today. It was important for me to be accepted into Cal Poly because it showed my parents that all their hard work in the sun - was worth it. My motivations are my parents and knowing that one day I will be able to make a difference in this world. I look at my parents as a source of inspiration because they have taught me the meaning of hard work, by taking me to work with them throughout my life, and by overcoming any obstacle despite everything that life has thrown at them. I persevere through challenge put in front of me and the success of overcoming such challenges is what keeps me going. Knowing that one day, I will be a lawyer and be able to help people with similar stories as mine inspires me to give it my all. After being a lawyer, I would like to pursue a career as a judge, because they have more authority to set precedents to help others from a legal standpoint. My ultimate goal in life is to become a Supreme Court Justice because I not only want to help people from my community, but from the country. If a low-income, first-generation immigrant can become a Supreme Court justice, then I will be able to inspire others—which is my motivation."

NUMBER SEVEN

"I was born in Nuevo Laredo Mexico I came to the United States when I was about 7 years old and entered as a visitor with a V1/V2 visa. My visa expired in 2011, but my family and I had no choice, but to remain in the United States. My father and I being immigrants made it difficult to look for a job so my father had to work in whatever job there was, so he could be able to feed us and support us. My mother worked and still works as a housekeeper. Both my parents have helped us to go to school because they want us to become successful in life.

My sister and I went to school, and I graduated high school. After graduating, I made the wrong decision of hanging out with the wrong group of friends. This led me to the wrong path; I do not mean using drugs or substance abuse, they were just bad influence. The trouble that I got into made me end up in jail, which caused me to be so afraid because I had no papers. When I was in jail, an ICE agent came to me and told me that after I finished my time in jail, I was going to go into custody in the detention center. I called my father, and I was so frightened that they started talking to my immigration lawyer to see what there was to do. Successfully she was able to remove the hold I had for my deportation, and I was able to get out of jail. Two months passed, and I was driving to pick up my cousins from school when I was pulled over by border patrol. They asked me for my papers, and I told them that I did not have anything that I was in the process of getting my DACA, but I did not have paperwork on me. I had to ride in the back of the truck with the border patrol agents, and they were making fun of me for being an undocumented immigrant. So once again, I had my dad call my lawyer because they were going to deport me overnight. I was able to get out from the border patrol detention-office. Being in that office is one the worst experience someone can ever have. Time passed by when I was in there and as a result, I became a better person. I no longer go out and I do not have that many friends anymore.

During 2014 my father got detained by the police for a traffic stop, and the police called border patrol on him. It was a long month without my father but as a 19-year-old, I was able to beat ICE and was able to get my father out. I was about to go crazy without him. At this moment we are just waiting for his immigration court and we're a happy family. Although as an undocumented immigrant I have not been able to work. I am saddened to see on the news how families are torn apart because of deportation.

I was able to get my DACA, even with my history of problems. I am working at a really good job and keeping my family together, which is one of the most important things for me."

NUMBER EIGHT

I am undocumented and unafraid. I moved to the US in February of 1994 at 18 months old. My mother dressed me in a fluffy yellow dress that was tossed outside of a Walmart on the outskirts of Phoenix because it was full of mud and dirt from crossing the border at 2am. The coyote left my parents, my 3-year-old brother, grandma and I stranded on the desert road that night. We walked aimlessly for over 2 hours until we saw signs of civilization. As my dad called our relative to pick us up, we walked inside the Walmart to change clothes and clean up from being full of dirt to not raise suspicion. I don't remember any of this, but it's the story my mom tells me, it's the story that's shaped my entire life. It's the story I cling onto that begins to tell the story of how I was given my identity. My undocumented identity.

My parents didn't hide the fact that I was different, on the contrary, they made it a point for me to be a "good" undocumented citizen. That if I kept my focus on education, life would be easier for me. I knew the language; culture and I could hide it. In our naïve minds we believed that I could work hard enough to convince a company to sponsor my citizenship one day. That was the dream. I was told I didn't have a social security number and if people asked, I should act dumb and say I didn't know it. The older I got the harder and more embarrassing it was to hide. I got my first slap in the face at the age of 11 when I couldn't officially join the girl scouts and I couldn't explain it to my friends.

When I was 16, I wanted to work, I wanted to contribute to save for college. At this point I had done research and realized I didn't qualify for FAFSA due to my status and knew it would be expensive. I pressured my mom to get me "fake papers" and walked into Chipotle feeling confident. I swayed the manager to hire me and when it came down to orientation and presenting my identification alongside with another new hire, I got the first taste of real rejection. My hands were sweating, and I could feel my heart pumping blood to every part of my body sitting in silent anxiety in those hard metal chairs. He kept flipping the green card front and back and I prayed he wouldn't know the difference. He looked up eventually and asked if he could talk to me on the side - leaving my would have been new coworker stunned and confused - he'd just met his first undocumented citizen. The manager gave me my identification back and said "You know I can't hire you. Please take this and leave." I walked to my car and blasted my music and sobbed as hard as I possibly could, my tears filled my eyes faster than I could blink that seeing the road was nearly impossible. I quickly learned the hardship that would follow.

My freshmen year of high school I met a man who saved me. Without Robert Barrientos and Latinos of Tomorrow I would not be who I am today. I was always heavily involved in my community and in school activities, especially those involving higher education. Being in the inner city, I wanted to get out and prove that "we" the undocumented were useful and capable and worth it. That fall, I attended Latino Youth Day at UMKC and that is where I met Robert. All my life I'd felt an outcast, someone living with a secret you couldn't tell anyone, unimportant and overlooked. I felt like I was fighting this fight alone and Robert changed it all for me that day. He was promoting a new community program for Latino youth wanting to pursue higher education, specifically undocumented youth. As he spoke passionately about kids like me, I fought the tears of joy and hope that someone recognized me, someone was pushing for me, someone out there supported me. After my first year of college, I fell into a very deep depression over my status. I was forced to watch as my friends attended career fairs and seek employment opportunities while I sat idle watching them from the stands. I could no longer afford student housing, so I sought out living on my own, and the roadblocks kept coming. I had to lie and bend truths to see if the applications required an SSN, ask a friend to put utilities in their name in order for me to have electricity and live off $100 a month because my parent couldn't afford my rent and school and that's all they could give me.

Everywhere you looked there was E-Verify - so working was out of the question for me. I wanted to give up on my dream, after all, what was I going to be able to do with a degree and no papers. I felt like I was trying to live in a fantasy. But throughout my college journey I discovered many allies who supported me, fed me when I had nothing, and comforted me when I wasn't' strong enough to stand on my own. I began therapy to deal with my depression over my legal status and was able to regain my identity and began using that hurt for something good. I became an underground spokesperson for the undocumented at KSU. I served on various organization executive committees and made my voice heard. My father died early into my junior year of college which added to the hurt. He was the one that always told me to work twice as hard as the white man because that's the only way I'd be recognized. That anything they could do, I could as well, regardless of my status.

Two weeks before DACA was announced I had been ridiculed by a classmate after disclosing I was undocumented in a "safe space." For the first time in all of my 20 years I felt validated as a human. For the first time I had hope that I had a fighting chance. Unfortunately, my father could not see me walk up that stage and be the first in my family in the US to receive a degree. He could not see me hustle and sell tamales to pay for tuition for the dream that led me to get internships with some of the largest companies in the food and beverage industry or see me get multiple offers from fortune 500 companies after graduation. DACA came at a time in my life when I needed it the most, at the time when I was about to throw in the towel and give up. Thanks to all the support from professors, mentors, family, and friends I have had the opportunity to live in more than 3 cities and travel all across the US for business and pleasure and feel "normal." I know that whatever direction my life may take post DACA, it will be a good one. I've had to fight the hardest of battles and climb the steepest hill of my life to a college education and career. Nothing after this will be nearly as hard mentally, emotionally, or psychologically. I wouldn't change who I am, as being undocumented has made me one of the strongest most resilient people I know."

NUMBER NINE
Major, Architecture

"I came here in 1995 at the age of 8 years with my mother, because my father was already here in the U.S in California. He came in 1992 with political asylum, I came with a visa tourist, I was given 1 year, although I didn't know anything about it because I was a kid, I thought I was just visiting my father, I missed him a lot, I came from Peru, a city called Miraflores, although I hardly remember much of it, I lived for 24 years here in California, now that I am 31 years old, my parents got divorced when I was 15, it was hard for me to accept it, but I did with time. My grandparents later passed away and I could not go back to see them, I was close to them when I was a kid, my father married a U.S citizen to become one and when he became a U.S citizen by 2009 he petitioned for me, and by 2016 my day finally came of my interview to become a U.S resident, my mother also remarried along the way to become a U.S resident.

By 2010 I already became a graduate with a bachelor's degree in Architecture. I paid for my books and my tuition, and with some help from my parents, but everything I have, I earned and bought myself. Nothing was given to me for free. In 2013 I applied for DACA and got my work permit; it was one of the happiest days of my life because at last I could work in my field of architecture as I did apply to a firm and got the job. During the years before I had a work permit thanks to DACA, I worked in my father's construction business where I learned so much about architecture too.

When the day came of my interview in 2016 December, the man who interviewed me saw all my files and he took his time as he walked outside and came back and started asking me the questions to become a U.S. resident. He mentioned that one form was missing and that was the i245, which I was not sure what it was, but it has something to do with a law that was passed back in 2001, that blocked me from been a U.S. resident. He told us that if there was some proof of my being here legally in U.S., before 2001, then my case could be saved. I could receive my residency, and then I was given 5 months to find something, which until now, has not been found. Back in the late 1990s my father did petition through work to get his U.S. residency and he had put my name on it as well, but because his boss died from old age, the case was closed, so who knows what could happen next?

Most of my life I was always looked down upon because of what I looked like even by other Hispanics too, just because I didn't have a green card, although I always did have a driver's license and social security number. My parents always feared that I would get into trouble, so I could never have a normal life like everyone else or travel much at all either unless it was with my parents. It has been 24 years since I saw Peru, as I never went back and I still wonder and hope that someday I can go back as a U.S resident, and as a professional with dignity and heart to see the rest of the family in Peru.

All those tears of pain and suffering - you would think that it would have made me bitter, but it did not. It made me stronger, because my parents were always hardworking, since the time I came, my father worked 3 jobs and my mother worked 2 jobs, although I saw my mother, I hardly saw my father, just for a few hours on every Sunday when I was a kid. I know of their sacrifice and their efforts to give me a better future than they ever had.

I am thankful that they brought me here and gave me an opportunity to a better future, they motivate me to work hard and fight for what I want and what I believe, all my life since I was a kid I always believed the U.S. was an amazing country because all these different types of cultures, religions and ethnicity could come together as one and work together to lead by example to the rest of the world. The dream is still there, still lives, and I am proud to say I am an American without forgetting where I came from, which is Peru. I pay my taxes, work hard to help my family, contribute to society, and I always paid for everything that I have. I earned my degrees, and I am proud to say I am American Peruvian."

I was very proud to present this packet of letters, as they told such important, heartfelt stories. The reception was very positive, and I truly believe the Congress people and their aides, that received the information, were genuinely interested and hopefully they will be able to help.

CONTINUED WORK for *LA CAUSA*

The San Luis Obispo Library invited me to give presentations on both the subject of Cuba as well as my work with the Chicanos back in the 1960s. My thanks to my son, David for helping to make the presentation more professional with a great computer slide show along with my comments.

On a daily basis, I have continued to post La Alborada on our web site. I constantly scour the web for interesting and informative articles that present an unbiased view of the happenings in Cuba. There are also many activities and events all across the island and the states that present Cuban culture, music, art and life, which I post on our web. La Alborada had begun as a hard print copy newsletter, which we mailed through the post office to thousands of supporters from CAAEF's beginning back in the 1990s. Once we had moved to San Luis Obispo and my health demanded calmer attention (and President Bush "forced my retirement" by no longer granting the licenses we needed for our humanitarian work), we had turned to the digital world and Luis Rumbaut continued the work of La Alborada by posting close to 1500 editions of our newsletter for several years. Since then, I have worked diligently to continue by posting almost every day of the week.

I also have continued to travel back to Washington D.C. and New York City for several important meetings. In D.C. I attended a major meeting at Howard University for the émigré community. It was a wonderful reunion with many of my old friends from the days of living and working from Washington. I was also honored to see several important friends from Cuba which are in photos below. Then in the fall of 2018 I attended the reception at the Cuban Embassy around the UN - meetings where Cuba's new president, Miguel Díaz-Canel Bermúdez, was introduced.

An important meeting and interview also took place with Eduardo Romero, Marti and Vicki's father, in 2014 when we took a trip to Hawaii with Rick Moniz and his wife Monique. Rick was filming the encounter for a video he planned to make. I was so pleased to meet Eduardo again and especially grateful to have time with him, as he passed away a few years later. Again, we enjoyed singing songs together, that were so meaningful, as I was always amazed at his knowledge of Spanish and Cuban culture when he had never even been to the Island. His memory was very sharp and words to old favorites were on the tip of his tongue. We spent time with Marti and Vicki again later in Havana in January of 2018 when we attended the dedication of the José Martí statue. My son and grandson also travelled with me to place my mother's ashes at the Santa Clara Cemetery.

In January of 2020 Norine and I took another trip with Rick Moniz and a group on his "Faces of Cuba" journey. We were thankful to have made it before the Pandemic of Covid-19 hit, weeks after our return. As always, the trip was absolutely

Left to Right: In Washington, D.C. at Howard University Delvis meets with historian Eusebio Leal, Diplomats Josefina Vidal and Bruno Rodríguez Parrilla, and in NY City with President Miguel Díaz-Canel Bermúdez.

marvelous and considering we have traveled to Cuba so many times, the new and exciting things we experienced just amazed us. Rick is in the process of writing a book regarding his many trips, and we are looking forward to that book. I also anticipate a documentary as he had a professional photographer from the media department at Chabot College filming, so I was talking on camera, sharing my life experiences.

Now I am staying closer to home trying to take care of myself, with music piano playing and daily walks in admiration of the beauty of nature around me.

43

The Ultimate Quest
Rekindling Passion for Music

Instilling 'music' in his grandchildren.

Isabella Guadalupe, Dariella Arianna, Daniel Alejandro, and Cian Delvis, viola playing, with Abuelo at the piano

MY LIFE'S DELIGHT

Music and dancing have been underlying passions in my life since childhood. When I came to Westminster College in Salt Lake City, Utah, all alone, as a minor, unable to speak English, I used body movements, winking, smiling, and dancing as a way to communicate and seek acceptance in my new cultural environment. At the first student gathering during orientation week, a day after arriving in Utah, I attended a party where all the students were dancing outdoor in a circle with lively music and following directions from a person in the center - this was my first exposure to "Square Dancing." Since I did not understand the words, or what steps to follow, I simply did my own thing, dancing as if this were a Cuban Conga for a carnival parade. People laughed and seemed to enjoy my weird approach to a traditional western dance style. From then on, I was a popular kid, not only as a math student ready to solve problems, but also as a crazy dancer that winked and smiled to all the passersby. The amazing joy inspired in others made me the selected Mardi Gras King during my first year in college.

During my second year in college, I was immersed in learning and labor as a dishwasher and maintenance worker to pay for tuition. But lo and behold! Thanks to good grades and school's generosity I managed to get a scholarship for books along with extra time to form part of the Westminster Choir. This was perhaps the best time for learning about cultures and civilization of Natives and Mexicans throughout the American Far West. At times I would combine learning classical choir music with my Cuban roots by showing friends the moves for Congas, Mambos, Boleros, or Cha-Cha-Chás.

Learning to play piano was always one of my strongest desires, so with Norine's mother who was a well-educated and trained pianist, I found a great attraction for expanding my family. My mother-in-law, Alice Dix Gunn, had studied at the Boston Conservatory and made a life as a professional teaching piano to students with her husband Ralph Gunn by her side as a financial dean in high schools and colleges. Prior to my coming to the U.S. I had learned a little about music theory, not from formal classes, but from the fact that my father assigned me the duty of watching over my sister Sarita while she took piano lessons from Rita Chapú, a well admired person who also had been my mother Sara's teacher.

Although I did not take piano classes until after receiving my PhD degree in mathematics, the magic sounds and desire to learn were present in my life. My first class for learning piano took place at Chabot College, where I was a mathematics teacher. Unfortunately, I do not recall the name of my first teacher, but she had a tremendous impact and connected me with Trula Whelan, a private teacher whose husband had been a professor at the Hayward California State University. The piano professor at Chabot made me part of a recital with another teacher, Janice Albert, a gifted piano player. There I was on stage with Janice, playing Sicilienne, a piano duet composition of Johann Sebastian Bach. Trula Whelan was my first rigorous teacher who also gave me valuable training in overcoming my fears of sharing music with people in general.

During years as an advocate for changes in U.S.-Cuba relations, the piano had to be placed away from my frontal desires, but I still managed to soothe the pain by getting a digital piano in my Washington, D.C. office and fiddled with old music pieces that I had struggled to learn, as a way to calm down before going to bed.

Around 2005 I moved to San Luis Obispo to be near my family, and lucky for me I also met a piano teacher, Eugenia German who exposed me to Tangos/Milongas of Argentinian composer Astor Piazzolla and to the soothing and vibrating Spanish classics of Enrique Granados. From there, past my age of 70-years, I decided to start a new chapter of life by registering as a student at Cal Poly University. Music surrounded me by going to concerts, as well as taking and auditing piano classes which involved sight reading, theory, and accompanying. It was of great inspiration to meet talented students playing music of Bach, Chopin, Debussy, and other European composers. Also, it was a great learning experience to enjoy music brought by a diversity of students from Asian and African American composers. On top of all this, I thoroughly enjoyed struggling with music near to my heart by Cuban composers and expand knowledge about music from Latin America by composers like: Argentinian Alberto Ginastera; Brazilian Heitor Villa-Lobos; Mexican Manuel Ponce; and Cubans Ernesto Lecuona, Ignacio Cervantes, and Leo Brower.

As a way to bring enjoyment to my mother when she was in a nursing home and transition to hospice care, I would play piano music for her in Santa María, California and then move on to giving concerts at various places in San Luis Obispo, Morro Bay, and San Rafael, California. Although I was not a professional, the smiles and strong handshakes from residents brought great satisfaction and truly a final call to dedicate the rest of my life to bringing the calming language of music to people near the last stages of life.

This new adventure in my life journey was possible with the teaching and support of faculty, students, and employees in the Music Department of California Polytechnic University. There I was able to listen and also play in the classroom for students. In one memorable occasion I accompanied Samantha Foulk, a talented soprano at the Performing Arts Center who sang "The Sun Whose Rays Are All Ablaze" from the Mikado Opera by Gilbert and Sullivan.

My last call to action came from Professor W. Terrence Spiller, the head of the Cal Poly Music Department. Thanks to his encouragement I was introduced to two talented music majors: Edmond McGinley and Gerardo "Tito" Hernández for rehearsals of diverse music styles to perform for residents at nursing homes and hospice centers. The opening of a new age in my life had to be placed on hold in 2020 until we could return to post pandemic times of normalcy. But we enjoyed bringing music to residents at various places like Las Brisas and the Alzheimer Care Center of Sydney Creek in San Luis Obispo. Music and piano playing brought peace a serenity during difficult times of required home confinement. Now the memories of my mother's last stages of life through nursing homes and hospice care reaffirmed my commitment to music as a way to communicate and bring eternal love and care to all of humanity.

Here is my last program with great assistance thanks to two wonderful students at Cal Poly University: *Tito Hernández and Edmond McGinley.*

Gerardo "Tito" Hernández, Delvis "Del" Fernández and Edmond McGinley

Edmond McGinley was a sophomore music major at Cal Poly who inspires to impact the world through his fresh music and collaborative spirit. He enjoys listening to music from the 60s-90s and hopes to keep the passion and thrill of music alive in today's society.

Gerardo "Tito" Hernández was a second-year student at Cal Poly San Luis Obispo who is a music major and aspires to become a Musical therapist who can one day help people out with his love and passion of music like it once did for him when he began his career in being a musician back in high school.

Delvis "Del" Fernández is a retired math professor who continues to be active in search of peace and serenity through the magic of music. He enjoys sharing the pleasure of harmonies through a world journey that provides a common bond for all of humanity.

A Musical Tour
"Bach" to San Francisco
At Sydney Creek in San Luis Obispo
Saturday, February 22, 2020

"Bach" to San Francisco

Invention No. 13 in A Minor
   Johann Sebastian Bach (Germany 1685-1750)
Ave María, Franz Schubert (Austria 1797 - 1828)
Träumerai (Dreaming), Robert Schumann, (Germany 1810–1856)
Preludes by Chopin, Frédéric Chopin (Poland & France 1810-1849)
   A Major,   (24 Preludes completed in Majorca, Spain)
   E Minor

Cuban Dances, Ignacio Cervantes Kawanaugh (Cuba, 1847-1905)
      Invitación
      Tres Golpes
      Adiós a Cuba
TÚ, Eduardo Sánchez de Fuentes (Cuba 1874-1944)
      Tango – Habanera
La Comparsa, Ernesto Lecuona (Cuba 1895-1963)
Milonga del Ángel, Ástor Piazzolla (Argentina 1921-1992)
Sabor a Mí, Álvaro Carrillo (Oaxaca, Mexico 1921-1969)
Estrellita (Silver Star),
      Manuel María Ponce Cuellar (Mexico 1882-1948)
Perfidia, Alberto Domínguez (Mexico 1911-1975)

Amazing Grace, Traditional US American
Charlie Brown, Linus & Lucy,
   Vince Guaraldi (US, San Francisco 1928-1976)
I Left My Heart in San Francisco
      Douglas Cross (US, NJ to Cal 1920-1975) &
      George Cory (US, NY to Cal 1920-1978)

EPILOGUE

Today, I come to you merely as one of the many thousands of people who despite years of separation from their beloved land and family - the nation, its people, and culture - continue to be an integral part of our very being and our soul.

WHO AM I?

- I am that old, tired woman, nearly blind who must hide like a delinquent and circumvent laws in order to nourish with love the daughters and grandchildren left behind.
- I am the rafter who risks life and limb in open seas to come to the "Promised Land" but once there they must break ties with loved ones back in his land of birth.
- I am the child trapped in my adult self, traumatized, and torn from a loving home by a cruel campaign against her family under the innocent name of "Peter Pan."
- I am the old man with callous hands who after years of daily toil for his United Fruit Company bosses dies without ever receiving a cent from the usurped retirement pension.
- I am the silent harassed minority who cries *"¡Basta!"* – enough! - to the mobs of hatred that defame and injure his loved ones.

Despite much analysis of U.S. exceptionalism with policies of interference in other nation's affairs, there is a lack of awareness about their profound impact on families and friends. The provisions in U.S. law that most directly affect us - Americans of Cuban descent - are those that include restrictions and conditions on visits to Cuba and assistance to our families. It is a sin under any religion to prevent contacts between mothers, fathers, and their children. No law should be in contraposition to our attempts to promote family values. We must not allow direct attacks on our most sacred unit of civilization - **The Family** - in order to promote a foreign policy. It is unacceptable by the world community at large, to cause pain and suffering on innocent people.

Speak loud and clear! *Awareness of Injustice makes Goodness Flow.*

GLOSSARY

Aguardiente	Strong alcoholic drink from fermented sugarcane.
Abuela, Abuelo	Grandmother, Grandfather
Ajiaco	A melting pot of races and ethnicities. In cooking anything involving various ingredients, often leftovers from previous meals.
Ahijado/a	Godchild
Alborada	Title for our publication "La Alborada" meaning "Dawn."- a word that implies the beginning of a new era.
Aldea	Village – a word used by folks in a town or city where people are friendly, and everyone knows each other.
Aljibe	A place to store water – cistern or tank. Name of a famous restaurant in Havana
Alliance Française	Educational place for the expansion of French culture.
Apóstol	Iconic figure or name for apostle.
Árabe	Used to identify a person of Arabic background – mostly Syrians and Lebanese.
Arroz con Frijoles Negros	White rice with black beans - one of the most popular dishes in Cuba.
Ay Dios Mío	Exclamation for "Oh my God!"
Aztlán	From Nahuatl, a mythical place of origin – ancestral home of the Aztecs.
Babalao	Spelled as Babalawo in English. A priest or spiritual leader of Afro Cuban Santeria religion
Bachiller	Bachelor education. Degree that may be obtained after five years of secondary education – High School degree with and extra fifth year.
Bar Mitzvah	Ceremonial blessings for a Jewish boy after reaching 13 years.
Barracón	Place for river side confinement for poor Afro Cubans working in American sugar mills.
Basta!	¡Basta Ya! A cry against injustice and oppression -- to indicate "STOP – Enough is enough!"
Batey	Used to indicate a town settlement around a sugar mill.
Beata	Applied to a person who is deeply religious and visits church on a daily basis.
Bloqueo	Blockade – term commonly applied to the U.S. embargo of Cuba.
Bohío	Thatched roof huts, common Cuban country dwellings with dirt floor, made mostly with royal palm remnants.
Bolita	Popular but illegal name based on Cuban lottery.
Botellas	Jobs where an "employee" may miss work but could transfer duties to a friend or receive a salary without accounting for anything accomplished.
Cacique	Chief of an indigenous group like the Taínos in the Caribbean.
Campesino	Peasant or country dweller.
Carne De Puerco	Pork Meat - traditional Cuban dish usually accompanied by rice and black beans.

CHACHAM	Also written as Hakham, a wise Torah, Jewish Scholar like a Rabbi. Pronounced similar to JAJAM in Spanish
Chavista	A supporter of Venezuelan leader Hugo Chávez.
Che	Used in Argentina for greetings like "Hey Fellow" or "Hi Friend." Now commonly used in Cuba and beyond as a name for Ernesto Guevara.
Chicana/o/x	Word that emerged from the Chicano Movement of the 1960s. Person of Mexican descent born or raised in the United States.
Chilango	Mexican accented Spanish or native of Mexico City.
China/o	Literally it means "Chinese" but Cubans may use it as a term of endearment": *Mi Chino* or *Mi China*.
Ciudad Natal	Native town, hometown of birth.
Comadrona	Midwife, health assistant to a woman for for childbirth.
Coño	WOW! Damn! Often unacceptable in public discourse.
Crème De Vie	Cuban Egg Nog mixed with Rhum, common during Christmas holidays and Nochebuena.
Cuban Music	Mambo, Bolero, Cha-Cha-Chá, Conga, Rumba, danzón, Multiple genres of Cuban music, particularly popular for fiestas and celebrations.
Cuñado, Cuñada	Brother-in-Law or Sister-in-Law.
Curandero/a	Healer or person who provides spiritual guidance and remedies.
Desdichado	Unfortunate – a nickname that may be given to a person projected to suffer difficult times in life.
Despertar	Awakening – a call to fight for major cause,
Despojo	Ritual by a *santera espiritista* (priestess) who prays while holding herbs and gently slapping them over a person in hopes to overcome a difficult life experience.
Doña	Title of respect given to a lady, equivalent to Madam.
Efemérides	Ephemerites –Historical data regarding to events.
El Norte	"The North" a word to identify the United States.
Escalafón	Priority spot on the list through exam results, but also, a place for hiring due to family *palancas or payment for* favors.
Espiritista	A person who works through religious rituals for healing purposes.
Familia	Family, sometimes used to identify a dear friend – "Oye Familia!"
Finca	Private farm or rural property.
Gachupín	Slang of Mexican origin to identify a person of light complexion or Spanish origin.
Gallego/a	From the Spanish region of Galicia, used in Cuba as a slang term to identify any Spaniard
Gringo	Someone from the U.S. – sometimes used as an offensive term.
Griot	Word of African origin to identify a person who transmits history and family stories accounts across generations.
Guagua	Term for omnibus or public bus.
Guajiro/a	Peasant or country dweller. At times used as a term to identify people from outside Havana.
Guanahatabeyes	Indigenous people of western Cuba.

GLOSSARY

Habana Vieja	Area of Havana noted by old colorful building in the center of the city.
Haggadah	Text used during Passover meals for blessings and guidance.
Hebreo	Means Hebrew but sometimes used as substitute for Jew.
Hogar	Home, place of birth.
Huelga	Labor strike, common during times of unrest and calls for justice.
Instituto de Bachillerato	Cuban High School with an extra year for entering a university.
Isleño	Islander, Cuban slang for a native of the Spanish Canary Islands.
Jiribilla	Magazine of Cuban Culture. Word with multiple meanings: "tingling, restless, fidgety
Judío/a	Jew, Jewish, at times used as a pejorative.
Turco (Turkish), or Polaco	Turkish) or Polish was often used as a substitute for "Judio."
Hebreo	Hebrew, also a word used as a substitute for "Judío."
La Carpa circus or	Tent that may be used as a sign of protest. A place for meetings, theatrical performances.
La Causa	"The Cause" used to mean " objective," or "reason for action."
Ladino	Language related to Spanish used by Sephardic Jews, infused with a mixture of Hebrew, Greek and Turkish.
Land of Zion	Interpreted as Utopia or a Land of Perfection.
Limpiabotas	Shoe shiners in Cuba that included populations of poor children.
Mamá-Vieja	Old-Mother but used as a term of endearment for grandmothers.
Mami	Means Mom but often used as a term of endearment like "babe."
Manigua	Cuban wild forest surrounded with royal palms, ceiba trees, sugar cane fields, expanses of tobacco, and arroyos.
Maqueta	Architecture scale model for a project or section of a city.
Mariquita	Offensive term meaning "gay, queer or sissy."
Merci Beaucoup	French expression meaning "Thank You Very Much."
Mi Gente	Term used to mean "my friends or people in my surroundings."
Milpas	Cornfields, from Mexican song "Las 4 Milpas" –The 4 Cornfields.
Mojo	A sauce using citrus, olive oil and garlic, common in Cuban cooking.
Moro, Mora	Identifies those expelled from Spain to northern Africa. In Cuba I was sometimes called "Morito" and my mother was "La Mora."
Mulato/a	Person of mixed ethnicity – Black, White and "other."
Nietas, Nietos	Granddaughters, Grandson, Grandchildren.
Nochebuena	Christmas Eve Fiesta in Cuba and Latin America.
Novelas	Spelled as "Novellas" in English. Source of entertainment for families via radio, TV dramas, tales and stories.
Novia / Novio	Steady Girlfriend / Boyfriend under cemented relationship.
Ombligo del Mundo	Belly Button of the World. Nickname applied to Cuba
Atrial fibrillation	Abnormal heart rhythm - arrhythmia
Orishas	Iconic figures or spirits that play a key role in Cuban Santería.
Paisajes	Landscapes, sometimes etched in our minds.
Paladar	A small family-owned restaurants.
Palanca	"Lever" is used as a slang term for support and carrying favors to family or friends outside government rules.

GLOSSARY

Palangana	Bowl for washing (see p. 97)
Papá Papá-Viejo	Old-Grandfather is used as a term of endearment for a grandpa.
Paradito	"Standing up," word used to identify a bar without sitting stools where one may eat, drink, or socialize.
Pasarela	Walkway for modeling.
Patacones	Word for fried plantains common in Caribbean cuisine. Also called tostones or tachinos in Cuba.
Patria Potestad	Legal Custody granted to parents.
Perviz	Persian name meaning "Fortunate" or "Victorious" that was misspelled as "Delvis," in my father's birth certificate.
Pésaj or Pesach	Words in Spanish for Passover, a Jewish holiday celebrated with a "seder meal" and a reading o the "Haggadah."
Picadillo	Popular ground beef at times cooked with olives and raisins served over white rice.
Pipo	Nickname given to a new acquaintance, similar to "Guy."
Plátanos	Plantains, common in Cuba cuisines from green to super ripe.
Polaco/a	Polish – from Poland, but used identify Jews from Europe.
Proyecto Pedro Pan	Plan from the early 1960s that brought over 14,000 unaccompanied minors from Cuba to the U.S.
Punto Guajiro	Genre of Cuban country music that mixes poetry and guitar playing.
Quisqueya	Taino for the island of Hispaniola – The Dominican Republic and Haiti.
Quincalla	Small store that sells basic school needs and magazines
Séder	Dinner for Passover blending rituals for blessings and storytelling.
Redes Sociales	Social networks, Face Book and other means of computer public contact.
Sambumbia	Watered down coffee, as substitute for strong Cuban expresso coffee.
Sephardic	Jewish person of Spanish or Portuguese descent. The word Sepharad (SEFARAD) from the Hebrew word for Spain.
Sí Se Puede!	Expression used during strikes or times of struggles: "YES WE CAN DO IT."
Siguaraya	Holy tree of Cuba.
Suegro	Father-in-law.
Tacita de Oro	Little Golden Cup. Nickname applied to Cuba.
Taíno	Most common indigenous people of the Caribbean: Cuba, Puerto Rico, Hispaniola, and the Antilles islands.
Terrateniente	Respectable landowner
Tibor	Metal bowl urinal for convenience placed under the bed
Tío, Tía	Uncle or Aunt.
Titán De Bronce	Bronze Titan, name that honors "El General Antonio Maceo y Grajales," the highly admired fighter for Cuba's independence from Spain during the late 1800s.
Torah	Instruction, teaching, 5 books of the Old Testament (Hebrew Bible).
Traga Nickel	Jukebox, Nickel slot machines common in the 1940s and 1950s for playing music in bars and areas of entertainment.
Trinar	Trill, vibration sound of guitar strings

Turco	Turkish (from Turkey) but used as a word to identify Sephardic Jews from Turkey or the Middle East and Africa.
U Visa	United States nonimmigrant visa for victims of crimes in the US
V1/V2	Nonimmigrant visa to allow a family to stay together while awaiting the processing of immigrant visas.
Yuca	Cassava roots – a staple of Cuban cuisine, often fried and served with a garlic sauce called "mojo criollo."
Yuma	Identifies the United States. Originates from the name of a town near in Arizona and the title of movie. "La Yuma."
Zafra	The 4 to 5 months' sugar harvest

ACRONYMS

ACLIFIM	Cuban Association of the Physical Motion Limited (*Asociación Cubana de Limitados Físico-Motores*)
ADHD	Attention Deficit Hyperactivity Disorder
A-Fib	Atrial fibrillation, abnormal heart rhythm (arrhythmia)
AFP	Association for Financial Professionals
AHTC	Americans for Humanitarian Trade with Cuba
AIN	Aviation International News
ANAP	National Association of Small Farmers
ANCI	The National Association for the Blind and Visually Impaired
ANSOC	The National Association for the Deaf
ARCA	Foundation dedicated to advancing equity, justice, and human rights
ATC	*Alianza de Trabajadores Cubanos* (Cuban Worker's Alliance)
BA	Bachelor of Arts
BBC of London	British Broadcasting Corporation
BWI	Baltimore/Washington International Airport
CAA	Cuban American Alliance
CAAEF	Cuban American Alliance Education Fund, Inc.
CAL POLY	California Polytechnic
CANA	Cuban American National Alliance
CBS	Columbia Broadcasting System
CDA	Cuban Democracy Act of 1992, also referred to as Torricelli's Law
CDH	*Comisión de Derechos Humanos*
CEAP	*Centro para el Estudio de Alternativas Políticas* Center for the Study of Political Alternatives
CELAC	*Comunidad de Estados Latinoamericanos y Caribeños*
CFO	Chief Financial Officer
CIA	Central Intelligence Agency
CIP	Center for International Policy
CNN	Cable News Network
CSU	California State University
DACCRE	*Dirección de Asuntos Consulares y de Cubanos Residentes En El Exterior* Bureau of Consular Affairs and Cuban Residents Abroad)
DACA	Deferred Action for Childhood Arrivals
DHS	Department of Homeland Security
DNA	Self-replicating material present in nearly all living organisms Main constituent of chromosomes - carrier of genetic information
EAD	Employment Authorization Document

ECDET	Emergency Coalition to Defend Education Travel
ELAM	Latin American School of Medicine – Escuela Latino Americana de Medicina
ENCASA	Emergency Network of Cuban American Scholars and Artists
EOP	Educational Opportunity Program
ESL	English as a Second Language
FAFSA	Free Application for Federal Student Aid
FBI	Federal Bureau of Investigation
GATT	General Agreement on Tariffs and Trade
GNP	Gross National Product
GPA	Grade Point Average
HIV	Human Immunodeficiency Viruses
HMO	Health Maintenance Organization *Organización para el Mantenimiento de la Salud*
HOCOFOCA	Howard County Friends of Central America and the Caribbean
ICAP	*Instituto Cubano de Amistad con los Pueblos*
ICU	Intensive Care Unit
INPUD	*Empresa Industrial Nacional Productora de Utensilios Domésticos*
INS	Immigration and Naturalization Service
JDC	The American Jewish Joint Distribution Committee
KBS	The Korean Broadcasting System
KFC	Kentucky Fried Chicken
LASA	Latin American Studies Association
LAWG	Latin American Working Group
LDS	Latter-Day Saints (Mormon Church)
LIBERTAD	Ministry of Public Health of Cuba *(Ministerio de Salud Pública)*
MECHA	*Movimiento Estudiantil Chicano de Aztlán*
MINAZ	*Ministerio de la Industria Azucarera*
MINREX	*Ministerio de Relaciones Exteriores* - Ministry of Foreign Affairs
MINSAP	Ministry of Public Health of Cuba / *Ministerio de Salud Pública*
NAFTA	North American Free Trade Agreement
NATO	The North Atlantic Treaty Organization
NNOC	National Network for Friendship with Cuba
OAS	Organization of American States
OBGYN	Obstetrician-gynecologist
OFAC	United States Office of Foreign Assets Control
OXFAM	Oxford Committee for Famine Relief
PAMLA	Pacific Ancient and Modern Language Association
PhD	Doctor of Philosophy
PL	*Prensa Latina*

PR Newswire	Press Release
QED	"Quod Erat Demonstrandum" "What Was to be Shown"
SLO	San Luis Obispo
SSN	Social Security Number
TA	Teaching Assistant
teleSUR	Latin American terrestrial and satellite television network
TPS	Temporary Protective Status
UCLA	The University of California, Los Angeles
UMKC	University of Missouri–Kansas City
UN	The United Nations
UNASUR	Union of South American Nations
UNESCO	The United Nations Educational, Scientific and Cultural Organization
UOP	University of the Pacific
USAID	United States Agency for International Development
USCSCA	U.S.-Cuba Sister City Association
USF	The University of South Florida
UTEHA	*Unión Tipográfica Editorial Hispano Americana*
V1/V2	Nonimmigrant visa to allow a family to stay together while awaiting the processing of immigrant visas.
VW	Volkswagen Car
WFP	United Nations World Food Program
WHO	World Health Organization
WOLA	Washington Office on Latin America
WTO	World Trade Organization

REFERENCES

"Collection of Nine Testimonials from Dreamers." Students at California Polytechnic University, San Luis Obispo, CA, 2010.

"Spring Festival - To Be Long Remembered." The Parson Newspaper of Westminster College, 1958.

"Tales of the Arabian Nights – *Las Mil y Una Noches.*" Text Revised and Edited by Henry William Dulcken, Ph.D., Castle Books, 1984.

"The Story of the St. Louis Passengers." United States Holocaust Museum Publication. A Diario de la Marina editorial, May 14, 1939.

DNA Estimates for Delvis Alejandro Fernández Levy based on Ancestry.com test procedures. c. 2000.

UTEHA Encyclopedia - Unión Tipográfica Editorial HispanoAmericana, 1953.

Yearbook "Etosian." Westminster College, Salt Lake City, Utah, 1958-1961.

Yearbook "IBIS." University of Miami, Coral Gables, Florida, 1963.

Aguirrechu, Iraida. "Only in Miami…," Editora Política, 2004.

Bernal Godoy, Ramón, "La "próspera" Cuba de 1959. MENTIRASENLAMIRA.WORDPRESS.COM, 19 February 2020.

Bravo, Estela. "Operation Peter Pan: Flying Back to Cuba," IMDbPro, June 24, 2011

Cullen, Arthur J. "Elbert Covell College: A New Kind of Spanish Language and Inter-American Area Center" (pp. 788-794). Source: Hispania, Vol. 47, No. 4 (Dec. 1964), Published by The American Association of Teachers of Spanish and Portuguese.

Fernández, David. "HAVANA IN TRANSITION. An Urban Redevelopment Proposal for Centro Habana." Architecture Dissertation, California Polytechnic University, 1995.

Fernández Levy, Gilda. "Resistencia de Materiales, Tomo I y II," Editorial Pueblo y Educación, 1983,

Galeano, Eduardo. Foreword by Isabel Allende. Translation by Cedric Belfrage,"Open Veins of Latin America." Monthly Review Press, New York, NY, 1973.

García Márquez, Gabriel. "Vivir para contarla," Alfred A, Knopf, New York 2002.

Hancock, Joel. Professor Emeritus of Latin American History. "My Blue-Colored World." Salt Lake City, Utah, Self-Published 2020.

Heredia, José María. "Ode to Niagara (*Oda al Niágara*)," www.ecured.cu, 1824.

Jones, Dr. Alberto N. "Mi Vida, mi verdad: Memorias de Alberto N. Jones," Amazon, June 2020.

"Life in a Cuba under U.S. Control," La Alborada Publications, v.1, number 8, Summer 1998.

Lamrani, Salim. "Cuba. Les médias face au défi de l'impartialité," with a prologue by Eduardo Galeano, Paris, Editions Estrella, 2013.

Lugovoy, Elaine and Julius. "PASSOVER SEDER 1996 – A HAGGADAH FOR THE 90s," March 30, 1996.

Masud-Piloto, Félix. "From Welcomed Exiles to Illegal Immigrants," The Cuban Migration to the U.S., 1959-1995, Amazon Publishing, 1995.

Maté, Gabor. "Beautiful dream of Israel has become a nightmare," The Toronto Star, July 22, 2014.

Milanich, Professor Jerald. "Indian-Country-Today Archives," April 2, 2017.

Murphy, Catherine. "Maestra," film about the 1961 Cuban Literacy Campaign. The Literacy Project in 2004 and *Tres Musas Producciones* in 2009.

Nehusi, Kimani. "Ah come back home: Perspectives on the Trinidad and Tobago Carnival" edited by Prof. Isidore Seers, Dudley, British economist noted for Developmental Economics, Amazon, January 1, 2000.

O'Reilly Herrera, Andrea. "ReMembering Cuba: Legacy of a diaspora," Section VIII: Maura Barrios: Memoirs of a Tampeña, University of Texas Press, January 2001.

Otto G. Richter Library Archives at the University of Miami

Pino Santos, Oscar. "Los Tiempos de Fidel, El Che y Mao," Editorial Nuestro Tiempo, S.A., 1997.

"Los Años 50," Instituto Cubano del Libro, Ciudad de La Habana, 2001.

REFERENCES

Rumbaut, Luis E., Esq. Publications of "La Alborada" covering topics about: (1) Developments in U.S. policy towards Cuba; (2) News capsules from the U.S., Cuba, and the world press media; (3) Reports on meetings and conferences; (4) Letters and opinion articles; (5) Cuba's accomplishments in education and health care; (6) *Efemérides* – List of Historical events; (7) Sports News and Cultural Events, Year 2005-2015.

Romero, Eduardo. Mensaje a los Cubanos del último hijo de María Mantilla. DVD CD self-published for the Centro de Estudios Martianos, c. 2010.

Russell, Bertrand. "History of Western Philosophy History." Simon & Schuster, Inc., 1972.

Santayana, George. "Reason in Common Sense," Dover Publication, February 1st, 1980

Skaine, Rosemarie. "The Cuban Family: Custom and Change in an Era of Hardship." McFarland & Company, Inc. Publishers 2004

Torres, María de los Angeles. "THE LOST APPLE: Operation Pedro Pan, Cuban Children in the U.S., and the Promise of a Better Future," Amazon, August 15, 2004.

Fernández Levy, Delvis.

    La Alborada Printed Publications (Spring 1996 – January 2003). News Capsules. Social Work Development and Practice in Cuba and in the U.S. At the Dawn - A New Era in U.S. Cuba Relations. Letters and opinion articles. Perspectives on U.S./Cuba Policy in the Year 2003.

    "Martí's Soul Testament: A Mi María." An English translation of José Martí's last letter to his beloved child María Mantilla, January 2004.

    "A Human Legacy of José Martí." Carmen Miyares: A Patriot in Silence." Published through Amazon, February 2018.

    "The Chicano Movement: Expanding Culture and Education," Amazon, June 24, 2017.

    "The Computer in Action. A Business Guide for the Diet Center. Self-Published copyright 1986.

    "Some velocity changes on ergodic flows and a skew product of a Poisson flow and a Bernoulli shift." University of California. Notices of The American Mathematical Society. October 1976.

    "Reflections from the Elbert Covell College (1963-1966).

    "Mi Mamá Sara – Sus Raíces Su Legado," Ancestry.mycanvas.com, Enero del 2014.

    "La Familia de Delvis y Norine. Nuestras Raíces – Nuestro Legado." Self Published 2010.

    "Moving Forward with Politics. Opinion about the emergent Peace Corps. Westminster College Newspaper the Parson, 1961.

    "Conversations with Marti Margaret and Victoria Romero and an interview by Norges Martínez Montero of *Juventud Rebelde*, Feb 4, 2003.

INDEX

624

CPSIA information can be obtained
at www.ICGtesting.com
Printed in the USA
BVHW051031251121
622517BV00015B/480